Francatelli's
THE MODERN COOK

A.Hervieu pinxt.   S.Freeman sculpt.

CHARLES ELMÉ FRANCATELLI.

LATE MAITRE D'HOTEL & CHIEF COOK

TO HER MAJESTY

Francatelli's

THE MODERN COOK

(1846)

1462 RECIPES BY
QUEEN VICTORIA'S CHEF

WITH A
NEW INTRODUCTION
BY
DANIEL V. THOMPSON

DOVER PUBLICATIONS, INC.
NEW YORK

International Standard Book Number: 0-486-21454-0
Library of Congress Catalog Card Number: 73-80347

Manufactured in the United States of America
Dover Publications, Inc.
180 Varick Street
New York, N. Y. 10014

INTRODUCTION

TO THE DOVER EDITION

FRANCATELLI'S *The Modern Cook* was an outstanding event in
the history of cookbooks, a practical working guide to cooking
of a high order, written in 1846 in English by an Englishman,
an Englishman whose qualifications as a French cook were im-
peccable. The book went through many editions and held its own
in the face of competition from the works of Francatelli's slightly
younger rival, Alexis Soyer, *The Gastronomic Regenerator* and
The Modern Housewife, and from the mighty 1859 *Household
Management* of Mrs. Isabella Mary Beeton. If copies of *The
Modern Cook* are rare, as indeed they are, it is no doubt because
the large numbers printed have been worn out in use.

When we try to determine Francatelli's qualifications, it is
hard to be precise; for his meteoric early career is wrapped in
mystery, and the scanty data available are strangely vague. He
seems to have been born like Pallas in full panoply and, profes-
sionally, to have begun at the top. But with some reasonable
speculation it is possible to reconstruct his course through life
fairly plausibly.

Of his origin and family nothing is known except that he was
born in London in 1805 and bore a name suggesting, at least
ultimately, an Italian heritage. We dare not assume that his
father was Italian born; for Italian names are not unusual in
France. In Francatelli's own words, he himself was

> happy in being an Englishman. He received his pro-
> fessional education in Paris, and acquired a knowledge

v

of his art in some of the most celebrated *cuisines* of
that capital, and was so fortunate as to become a pupil
of the renowned Carême. Qualified under such favorable auspices, he has subsequently served—he hopes with
satisfaction to his patrons—some of the most distinguished *bons vivants* among the English aristocracy and
gentry. He has had the good fortune to be *Chef-de-
cuisine* to the Earl of Chesterfield; Lord Kinnaird; and
to Sir W. Massey Stanley, Bart., and Rowland Errington, Esq., at Melton Mowbray; and he shall ever consider it the greatest honor to which he could aspire to
have served as Chief Cook and Maître-d'Hôtel to Her
Most Gracious Majesty the Queen.

To this imposing list of his employers (prior to February 21,
1846) the *Dictionary of National Biography* adds the names of
the Earl of Dudley, and of "Crockford's," the St. James's Club.

When Francatelli entered the Queen's service, presumably in
1841, though possibly late in 1840, he was not older than thirty-
six and had already held at least four important posts. The date
of his first employment is not known; but this would appear to
have been his position as *chef de cuisine* to the fourth Earl of
Chesterfield, a young man of Francatelli's own age. Colin Clair,
in *Kitchen and Table,* states that Francatelli was "for many
years chef at Chesterfield House."

If he was indeed chef also to the Viscount Ednam of Ednam
and Earl of Dudley of Dudley Castle, County Stafford, his term
must have begun before 1833; for in that year Dudley died and
the earldom remained extinct until 1860. In 1833, Francatelli was
twenty-eight years old, and any service under Lord Dudley
coupled with "many years at Chesterfield House" would argue,
perhaps justifiably, a phenomenal precocity on the young chef's
part.

Kinnaird was some two years younger than Francatelli himself. This ninth (Scottish) Baron Kinnaird was created Baron
Rossie in the peerage of the United Kingdom in 1831, and Baron
Kinnaird of Rossie in 1860. We may conjecture that his employment of Francatelli in the 1830's was in some degree a reaction

against his father's reputation for an "avaricious disposition."
The *Farington Diary* (April 9, 1807) preserves the scurrilous
lines:

> Here's a Park without a Deer
> A Cellar without Beer
> A Kitchen without Cheer—
> Lord Kinnaird lives here.

If the ninth Baron deserved the epithet of "distinguished *bon-
vivant*" it seems not unlikely that Charles Elmé Francatelli, his
senior by two years, may have been as much tutor as chef to him.

The periods of his employment by Sir W. Massey Stanley, Bart.,
and by Rowland Errington, Esq., may have followed his term at
Windsor, in the years between 1842 and 1846. His tenure as
chef at Crockford's Club was extremely brief, and seems to have
been followed immediately by his appointment as Chief Cook
and Maître-d'Hôtel to the young Queen, then newly married to
Prince Albert.

The (Scottish) Earl of Errol, to whom *The Modern Cook* is
dedicated, was born in 1801. He was created Baron Kilmarnock
of Kilmarnock by King William IV, and became the new Queen's
Lord Steward for the Household in 1839. It was clearly through
his influence that Francatelli was rescued from Crockford's and
inducted into the royal service. But in it he seems to have sur-
vived his patron; for Lord Errol's tenure ended in 1841 and
Francatelli's in 1842.

If the Earl of Errol wanted to choose for his royal mistress the
most eminent chef in the kingdom, the choice clearly lay between
the English-born Charles Elmé Francatelli, then chef of Crockford's and some thirty-six years old, and the French-born Alexis
Soyer, then chef of the Reform Club and thirty-two years old.
Francatelli's predecessor at Crockford's, Louis Eustache Ude,
though probably a greater cook than either of these young men,
was by then considered unemployable.

The 1830's had seen the construction in London of palatial
homes for men's clubs, notably the Athenaeum (literary) in
1830, the Carlton (political, Conservative) in 1831, and largest

of all, the Reform (political, Liberal) in 1834. Somewhat different was Crockford's, at No. 50, St. James's Street, which had
risen in 1827 "like a creation of Aladdin's Lamp," a gambling
club, built by a gambler for gamblers.

By 1840 Crockford's and the Reform Club had become the
centers of gastronomic excellence for Londoners. No two clubs
could have been more different. The Reform was the bulwark
of the Liberal Party, the most magnificent and spacious club in
London. Crockford's, furnished with unparalleled luxury, was
as notorious for the transactions which took place at its gaming
tables as for the splendor of its dining tables and cellars.

From the very beginning of William Crockford's fantastic
creation, supremely delicious food had been a cornerstone of his
plan. With luck comparable with the luck which put the vast
necessary capital within the reach of this Cockney fishmonger,
Crockford secured at the very start the services of Eustache Ude,
on whose unrivaled cooking and gracious and picturesque personality no small part of the fabulous renown of the establishment
was based. Some measure of his success may be gained from the
fact that, though no charge was made for foods and wines at
Crockford's, the disreputable old founder of that palace of pleas-
ure was willing to pay Ude a salary of 4,000 pounds—an income
which many a belted patron might have envied. In the end,
Ude's success became too much for him; he got "too big for his
boots," and Crockford was forced to dismiss him.

Francatelli was chosen as Ude's successor. The compliment
was enormous; but the consequences were not happy. Francatelli
lacked, and indeed any newcomer must have lacked, the ability
to win the confidence and enthusiasm of members whom Ude
had spoiled systematically for years. Thus Disraeli, whose ad-
mission to Crockford's as a member had presented considerable
difficulty, and who was slavishly devoted to Ude's genius, could
write to his sister of Francatelli: "Their new man is a failure."
A failure, we may be sure, Francatelli was not: but he was not
Ude. Crockford did not try again, but went into retirement, and
died not long after.

The distinction of having been chosen to succeed Ude was perhaps the springboard needed to land Francatelli in the halls and kitchens of Windsor Castle. It may well have been at Crockford's that the Earl of Errol became his admirer and supporter.

We do not know whom Francatelli succeeded as the Queen's Chief Cook, or even exactly when he rose to that eminence. The Registrar of the Royal Archives, Windsor Castle, writes me that

> Francatelli is listed in the Royal Kalendar for 1841 and 1842 as Chief Cook and Maître d'Hôtel to Queen Victoria; but this is all the information we have about him. A number of Queen Victoria's papers, including records of members of her household, were destroyed at the end of her reign, and no details about Francatelli's brief term of service have survived.

We do not know exactly when Francatelli's "brief term of service" at Windsor terminated. Nor do we know the reason for its termination. Of his employment during the remaining 1840's and the early 1850's we know only that for some years before 1854 he was the chef of the Coventry House Club in Piccadilly, the forerunner of the distinguished diplomatic and social St. James's Club of the present time. His service with Sir Massey Stanley and Mr. Rowland Errington, as we have said, may date from this period. But it is quite possible that for some time before 1846 he did not find, and perhaps did not even seek, any employment in his profession, but devoted himself to the writing of this book.

The year 1854 was to see his return to the London club world. In 1837 the Reform Club had appointed Alexis Soyer (born in Paris in 1809, he removed to London in 1831) as its first real chef. On the basis of his advice the enormous kitchens of the Reform Club had been made a model of efficiency for their time. But chefs' boots do tend to become tight, and after numerous crises and resignations and reinstatements Soyer was replaced by Guerrier in 1850. And in 1854 Francatelli became *chef de cuisine* of the Reform Club and held that eminent position for seven years.

Of Francatelli's retirement from this post and his subsequent management of the St. James's Hotel, Berkeley Street, and his final position as Manager of the Free Mason's Tavern, Great Queen Street, Lincoln's Inn Fields, we have no particulars.

On August 10, 1876, Francatelli died at his home at 1 Cavendish Place, Eastbourne, aged seventy-one, in the presence of his wife Elizabeth, who makes no other appearance in her distinguished husband's history.

We do not know his history in any great detail. We do not know just when and where he worked. We have no positive record of any periods of unemployment; yet his extensive writings, including *The Modern Cook*, must have been incompatible with unbroken full-time employment. (At Windsor, for example, the *chef de cuisine*, with two Yeomen of the Kitchen, directed the operation of a staff of twenty-four cooks in addition to cooking himself.) His *curriculum vitae* is veiled in a fog of imprecision out of which only the peaks of his employments appear. He himself makes no mention of his brief tenure with Crockford's.

It is perhaps of no great importance to his fame to trace his working career in detail. It does appear that in his youth and early manhood he moved somewhat rapidly from one important post to another, and only after his appointment to the Reform Club in 1854 did he remain long in that and in each subsequent position. We could wish to know how he achieved his start, beginning as he did, at the top of the heap. But it is perhaps enough to realize that French-trained chefs were rare in the London of the 1830's and that Francatelli was perhaps unique in being both French-trained and English-born.

Nothing in the mystery which surrounds him is more baffling than his brief, non-committal account of his Parisian education. Had he French relatives? The names "Charles Elmé" are certainly not Italian. He contrives to suggest, without quite asserting it, that he was trained under Carême in the sense of an apprenticeship such as Carême served under Bailly. He mentions no other master than Carême, yet gives no particulars whatever of their association. So we must review the possibilities.

Carême was born in 1784, in poverty. Under the mastership of Bailly and the inspiration of Avice, he rose to considerable eminence during the period of the First Consulate, and attracted the attention of Prince Talleyrand for whom, after a term of service with de Lavalette, he worked for twelve years. During that time Talleyrand more than once entertained the Czar Alexander I of Russia, and the imperial guest bore his host's outstanding chef in mind.

In 1815, on the heels of Waterloo and the Restoration under Louis XVIII, Carême served the Prince Regent of England to that self-indulgent master's profound satisfaction, though not his own, for two years. He left Brighton of his own volition, and though in 1821, a year after the death of George III, the former Regent, then George IV, begged Carême to return, he would not. Carême had no liking for the climate of England. Yet after his return to France he seems to have found the Paris of Louis XVIII little to his taste; for he soon left it for St. Petersburg and the service of the Czar Alexander I. Apparently still attached to the Russian Emperor, he went to the Congress of Vienna, and while there seems to have transferred his allegiance to "Lord Stewart," Charles Stuart de Rothesay, Ambassador and Plenipotentiary of England to Paris, first in 1815 and again in 1824.

Carême returned with Stuart to London, but stayed there only briefly. He was in great demand at the many political congresses convened in that era to remake Europe after the Napoleonic conquests, and Carême's magic in the kitchen was a useful instrument in the hands of whatever delegate he served. He attended the important meeting of the great powers, Britain, Austria, Prussia and Russia which began in October, 1818, at Aix-la-Chapelle, and also Congresses at Laybach and Verona. Details are obscure; but it is clear that Carême was fully occupied away from Paris throughout most of the reign of Louis XVIII. He is reported to have served at the British Embassy in Paris, and nothing is more likely than that his old friend Stuart de Rothesay recalled him at the beginning of his embassy to the Court of Charles X in 1824. That is perhaps the only moment at which the young Francatelli can realistically be supposed to have become Carême's pupil in Paris.

This association cannot have been of any very long duration; for Carême served also in the households of the Prince of

Württemberg and the Princess Bagration before, in 1827, or
certainly not later than 1828, he left Paris again, this time for
Ferrières and the supremely happy post of chef to the Baron de
Rothschild, a post he quitted only as his death (in 1833) drew
near and he wanted to complete his writings.

The dates of Carême's employment at the British Embassy in
Paris are known only vaguely; but his tenure there may well
have spanned the years 1824 and 1825 when Francatelli, then
about twenty, would presumably have been through his basic
training and ready for the inspiration of working under the
most renowned chef in Europe. That Francatelli may have gravi-
tated to his country's embassy is *prima facie* not improbable.
And if we allow full reign to our conjecture, we may even en-
visage the possibility that the Francatelli family, when Charles
Elmé was a boy of ten, may have been living at Eastbourne
(where he later died), while Carême was living in nearby
Brighton as chef to the Prince Regent, and that they may have
been acquainted there.

That Francatelli was a *student* of Carême goes without saying,
and the internal evidence of *The Modern Cook* supports this at
many points. A translation into English of Carême's *Le Pâtissier
Royal Parisien* appeared in London in 1834. But that Francatelli
should have been, as he proudly asserts, a *pupil* of Carême in
Paris seems explicable only on the basis of an association at
Stuart de Rothesay's Embassy as here suggested.

We do not know at what date Francatelli returned to England.
If he was employed at the Paris Embassy between 1824 and
1826, he might well have returned to England in 1826 and bene-
fited by associations formed during the period of that appointment. It is unlikely that he should have stayed in Paris after
the accession of Louis Philippe in 1830, when cooking at the
French Court fell to a dismal low ebb under the parsimony and
vulgarity of the Citizen King, and the gastronomic arts were left
to flourish privately or wither. Francatelli's own phrase, to
describe his professional experience in Paris, "some of the most
celebrated *cuisines*," would surely have been more particular if
he had followed his great master to the *cuisines* of prince, prin-

cess and the greatest of financiers. We shall probably not be far out if we put the date of his return to England somewhere between 1826 and 1830.

There is, in this attempt to outline the career of the great British-born pioneer exponent and expositor in England of the French *haute cuisine* of the early nineteenth century, necessarily a good deal of speculation. What of his personality?

Of his personal character, little evidence survives. That he was personable in appearance may be deduced from the portrait frontispiece, included here, engraved in 1846 by S. Freeman after a portrait by A. Hervieu. That he eventually married an "Elizabeth" we know from his death certificate. That his patrons were in his early days much of his age or younger, we may conclude. But it is mostly guesswork. It is not unreasonable to suppose that the Earl of Chesterfield may have visited the Embassy in Paris and heard of the prowess and promise of a young Englishman there, and employed him when he came to England. This is not history but reasonable fantasy, and unless the muniment rooms of the great houses in which Francatelli was employed someday yield more data than do the Archives of Windsor Castle, reasonable fantasy must be our guide.

The Gourmet's Book of Food and Drink attributes to Francatelli a droll remark on flavoring a salad: "After I have made all my preparations and the green food is mixed with the dressing, I chew a leetle clove of garlic between my teeth—so!—and then I breathe gently over the dish!" But there seem to be fewer legends about Francatelli as a person than usually surround great figures.

In his later years, Charles Elmé Francatelli made so much to-do about economy of food (which is certainly not a feature of *The Modern Cook*) that one wonders whether he did not perhaps feel himself on the defensive. A charge was brought against his style that he was overlavish in his use of truffles. Certainly he was not in general parsimonious of raw materials. It seems not altogether improbable that Prince Albert's efforts to reduce extravagance in the administration of Windsor may have had some connection with the brevity of Francatelli's employment there. It may be noted casually that though the Queen's name is attached by him to several delicate dishes, the name of Albert is applied to a sauce distinguished for its fiery ingredients, conspicuously horse-radish.

The epoch in which Francatelli lived, studied, worked and wrote did not by any means coincide with the summit of the *haute cuisine* of France; but on his return from Paris to London, Francatelli was undoubtedly faced with conflicting tastes: the conservative, massive, meaty menu of the old regime and the zest for novelty, delicacy, and charm which attached, in the more adventurous young minds, to the cooking of France.

The old *service* still dominated, though the classic third course of pastries, sweets, ices and confections had by his time become merged with the second, the course which followed the soups, the removes and the entrees (and hors d'oeuvres, hot or cold, if there were to be any), and began with the *rôts*. *Entremets* of vegetables gave way insensibly to *entremets de douceur*. The pattern of the meal was jeopardized; but the magnificence of the two courses was unimpaired. The table was set for each course, but the display of silver or gold, of glass, of flowers, of *pièces montées* and cold foodstuffs in a decorative role made necessary a veritable army of carvers, servers of wine, and footmen, and largely precluded any general conversation at table.

Francatelli's sideboards were a concession to the English taste. Old habits die hard, and though a household which boasted such a chef as Francatelli would certainly have guests eagerly appre-ciative of the still-novel elegance of French cookery, it would inevitably have other guests to whom beef, mutton and venison were the only dinner dishes acceptable to a proper Englishman. At Windsor or at the Reform Club, the chef had to provide for the dyed-in-the-wool conservative taste as well as to enchant the adventurer with ingenious novelties. His punch, cited by *The Gourmet's Book of Food and Drink*, would command respect in the backwoods or Park Avenue today:

Into a vessel holding 2 gallons put 1 quart of brandy, 1 quart of rum, ½ pint of old Arrack, ½ pint strong-

made green tea, juice of 12 lemons, thin rind of 4 lemons,
a nutmeg grated, stick of cinnamon (well bruised), 12
cloves (bruised), 30 coriander seeds (bruised), 2 lbs.
pine-apple sliced, 9 lbs. lump sugar, 2 quarts boiling
water; stir together; tie a bladder over top of pitcher;
let it steep undisturbed for two days. Boil 2 quarts of
pure milk; add this to the other ingredients; mix thoroughly; in an hour afterwards filter the punch through
a clean tammy bag; when filtered bottle off the punch,
and cork down tight; keep the bottles in a good cellar.
This is a truly excellent punch; but it should be iced for
use.

There is very little in *The Modern Cook* to suggest that the
disciple of Carême had absorbed the master's impassioned interest
in the design and execution of individual pieces. Carême, neo-
classic in his taste as became his time, devised and executed
socles of the utmost intricacy, beauty and perhaps unsuitability,
and at the same time created dishes of great refinement and
epicurean elegance. What Francatelli learned from Carême and
his writing seems to have been cookery, and not the art of
presentation which Carême developed to a point from which
progress could be made only in the direction of greater simplicity. If the plates which illustrate *The Modern Cook* are to
be believed, Francatelli's *presentation* inclined to be elaborate,
laborious, pretentious and uninspired. But we may find comfort
in the thought that it might have been worse still if Francatelli
had held his royal post long enough to come under the influence
of the Prince Consort's philosophy of design. Can we doubt that
if he had done so he would eventually have dressed a Scotch
salmon in a Hunting-Stuart tartan of *chaud-froid,* truffles and
colored jellies, plaited like a kilt?
    The present reprinting of *The Modern Cook* includes thirteen
menus for Her Majesty's Dinners, and very handsome dinners
they must have been. Remembering the young Queen's prompt-
ness to give hopes of a succession, we may imagine that so magnificent a display of luxurious foods, however admirable as fitting
and even necessary to her rank, may have seemed oppressive to

her person. At none of these dinners does a sturgeon appear, though any sturgeon taken in British waters is the Queen's prerogative and must by law be offered to her. Francatelli, perhaps taking this unique luxury for granted, mentions it only in connection with a sauce appropriate to it, from which we may conclude that sturgeon at the royal table was habitually braised.

The most sophisticated and fastidious of guests could not have failed to find in any of these royal menus a meal worthy of his palate; yet John Bull himself need never have lacked roast beef from the sideboard, nor any Forsyte his roast mutton. And venison, in at least one form, as indicative in those days of private parks as it is nowadays of a hunter in the family and a deep-freeze somewhere, appears magnificently at twelve of these thirteen dinners.

Noteworthy and puzzling is that at eleven of them *Riz au Consommé* figures among the furnishing of the buffet. No recipe for its preparation is given in *The Modern Cook,* and it is nowhere defined; though the name could reasonably be applied to the Pilaff, No. 383, or to the Cream of Rice à la Victoria, No. 318. Its presence on the sideboard is something of an oddity, not perhaps once by chance, but as a constant feature. May we imagine that this dish, whatever it was, was a favorite of Her youthful Majesty herself, to be always available whenever the normal menu of two, three or four soups, two, three or four dishes of fish, the two or more substantial "removes" and half-dozen or more entrees of the First Course, and the two or three roasts of poultry or feathered game, the two or three "removes," and the dozen or so of *entremets,* savory and sweet, of the Second Course might fail to tempt the little royal appetite?

DANIEL V. THOMPSON

Beverly Farms, Massachusetts
August, 1972

THE MODERN COOK;

A

PRACTICAL GUIDE TO THE CULINARY ART

IN

ALL ITS BRANCHES,

COMPRISING,

IN ADDITION TO ENGLISH COOKERY, THE MOST APPROVED AND RECHERCHÉ
SYSTEMS OF FRENCH, ITALIAN, AND GERMAN COOKERY;

ADAPTED AS WELL FOR THE LARGEST ESTABLISHMENTS AS
FOR THE USE OF PRIVATE FAMILIES.

By CHARLES ELMÉ FRANCATELLI,
PUPIL TO THE CELEBRATED CARÊME,
AND LATE MAÎTRE-D'HÔTEL AND CHIEF COOK TO HER MAJESTY THE QUEEN.

FROM THE
NINTH LONDON EDITION,
CAREFULLY REVISED AND CONSIDERABLY ENLARGED.

WITH SIXTY-TWO ILLUSTRATIONS.

Philadelphia:
T. B. PETERSON AND BROTHERS,
306 CHESTNUT STREET.

[*Title page of T. B. Peterson and Brothers Edition*]

PREFACE TO THE NINTH EDITION.

In introducing the present Edition of THE MODERN COOK to the public, I beg to return my thanks for the patronage that has been awarded to former Editions, by the public at large, as well as by the profession, of whose approbation I feel most proud. Indeed, I am so conscious of the value of the good opinion of these competent judges, that I do not hesitate to ascribe the steady demand with which the Work has hitherto been favored to their liberal support.

So gratifying an appreciation of my endeavors has naturally prompted me to render the present Edition in all respects worthy of a continuance of their patronage. I have in all cases most strictly studied economy,—by retrenching, as far as it appeared to me consistent with propriety, all unnecessary and too expensive accessories to the more costly kinds of dishes. The whole work has been entirely revised with scrupulous care and attention; and upwards of eighty entirely new dishes, principally belonging to the Second Course department, have been added. I have also enlarged the glossary of technical terms :—and, in order to render the Work of easier reference to the public, as well as to the practitioner, no trouble has been spared to improve the Index.

I have nearly doubled the original number of Bills of Fare; and have added many of dinners served to Her Majesty the Queen.

(21)

And now, generous and gentle patrons, I once more respect-
fully take my leave of you for a while; and to you, Gentlemen
of the Public Press, I beg to return my most sincere thanks for
the handsome and kindly manner in which you noticed my
earnest efforts to assist my English brethren to outrival their
hitherto successful foreign competitors for fame in the Culinary
Art.

But I should not do justice to my own feelings if I omitted
on this occasion to offer my special thanks to the Author of the
admirable little work, entitled "The Art of Dining, or Gastronomy and Gastronomers," for the very flattering terms in which
he has spoken of my professional labors.

C. E. FRANCATELLI.

WALTON VILLAS, BROMPTON,
    June 1st, 1853.

PREFACE TO THE FIRST EDITION.

In his present undertaking, the Author's object has been to produce a treatise which may be useful, not only to cooks themselves, but also to those who employ them. He has, accordingly, been as sparing as possible of the use of technical terms, and has endeavored, at the same time, to be concise as well as explicit in his directions.

Judicious economy being at all times a great desideratum, the Author has studied to apply its practice in the composition of every recipe contained in his book. Many dishes are obviously expensive, and can only be indulged in by the wealthy epicure ;—but even here, the cost may be reduced by avoiding waste, and by turning to account ingredients carefully reserved for the purpose by the aid of foresight and economical habits. In large establishments, when properly conducted, there is, indeed, less relative waste than in the kitchen of a small private family, under the management of an ordinary cook.

It is necessary to remark, that throughout this work, the Author has supposed the various dishes and preparations are required to be made for a large number of guests, with the usual resources at hand in a well-appointed kitchen ; perfection and economy can only be fully attained under such circumstances. The variety and quantity of the ingredients recommended to be used will probably often appear lavish, therefore, to those whose culinary practice is limited, and who are, nevertheless, desirous of combining comparative success with moderate means.

For persons so situated, when desirous of indulging occasionally in dishes of a sumptuous character, no written directions would probably suffice; the only sure method in such cases is to resort to professional aid. But, in the majority of instances, the Author's instructions will be found generally practicable; common sense, aided by some experience, will suggest the employment of available substitutes, when costly sauces and other *recherché* preparations are directed to be used.

Simplicity is as essential an element in cookery as it is in other arts: the Author, therefore, particularly cautions the inexperienced practitioner from attempting too much. Excess in the quantity and variety of spices and condiments—the bane of English cookery—is especially to be guarded against. Nothing vitiates the palate more than a superabundant use of such stimulants. In the preparation of soups and sauces, this rule must be constantly borne in mind.

In a treatise professing to treat of cookery as an art, by which refined taste is to be *gratified* rather than a coarse appetite *satisfied*, it would be out of place to attempt to translate its rules into the hackneyed terms employed in "Guides" and "Oracles" for economical makeshifts.

Such attempts, too frequently made by English writers on gastronomy, at once betray their origin. The greater part of these authorities are persons who, having neither studied the rudiments nor practised the art to any extent, take upon themselves to instruct the public, not from the fulness of their knowledge, but either as a pecuniary resource, or to gratify an idle whim. Need it be wondered at, while we possess in England a greater abundance of all kinds of food, generally of far better quality than is to be found elsewhere, that our cookery, in theory and practice, has become a by-word of ridicule, and that we should be compelled to have recourse to foreigners, ignorant for the most part of our tastes and habits, to prepare our feasts? "They manage these things better in France:" cookery is there considered as an important art, and its successful endeavors are regarded with a due appreciation. In Paris its great professors have achieved an almost historical celebrity, and their school of cookery has become pre-eminent. This can only be attributed to their assiduous study of its elementary principles, which, when properly understood, will be found to conjoin the highest enjoyment with due attention to the preservation of health.

The palate is as capable and nearly as worthy of education as the eye and ear.

A large proportion of the dishes contained in this work are quite new to the public, not merely as regards their names, but as respects their composition. This will be found to be the case, particularly with the soups, dressed Fish, Removes, Entrees, Hors-d'œuvres, and dressed Vegetables. The second course, moreover, is treated at greater length, and with more care than has hitherto been the case in English Cookery Books.

A copious and varied collection of Bills of Fare, adapted to every season of the year, has been added as an essential accompaniment to the work. In connection with this subject, the Author ventures to offer a few suggestions for the consideration of Epicures.

In the first place, the English custom of dividing a grand dinner into several courses is an error quite at variance with common sense and convenience. It is a needless complication that necessarily leads to useless profusion, and much additional trouble. Our neighbors across the Channel—the best authorities in all gastronomic questions —allow of *two* courses only in the largest dinners. With them, Fish and Hors-d'œuvres,—such as patties, croquettes, &c., form part of the First Course, and not a distinct course, as they are considered east of Temple Bar. The French, too, regard the dessert as a mere *delassement* after dinner, intended rather to propitiate than to thwart digestion.

The great and increasing intercourse between this country and the Continent, as well as the probable relaxation of the duty on foreign wines, will tend naturally to extend our use of many kinds especially appropriate to the dinner-table. On this head, the Author, without pretending to give any elaborate or detailed instructions respecting the service of wines at dinner, cannot refrain from alluding to an injudicious habit, frequently adopted at English tables—that of introducing *sweet* Champagne in the First Course. This wine, from its sweetness, naturally counteracts the flavor of savory dishes—there is a mutual repulsion between them. Madeira, Sherry, and Burgundy are better suited to the First Course; their stimulating and generous qualities tending considerably to assist digestion. In France, sweet Champagne is not introduced until the latter part of the Second Course: by that time, the palate has become more fit to appreciate the delicate *bouquet* of this delicious and exhilarating beverage.

The Author begs further to add, that the ordinary practice in London of serving Turtle and Venison indiscriminately, as mere accessories to *recherché* dinners, is, in his opinion, most injudicious. Turtle and Venison being generally reckoned by us as the best of good cheer, it follows that when they form part of a dinner, the Removes and Entrées are comparatively neglected. Very light Entrées should only be served with these; and on such occasions, indeed it would be preferable to arrange the dinner in the Russian fashion—placing the dessert upon the table at first, while the whole of the dinner is served from the side tables.' By this means, two advantages are gained : a less number of dishes are required—especially in the First Course ; and the dinner has a better chance of being served hot—an indispensable requisite to its due enjoyment. In pursuance of this recommendation, a series of Bills of Fare, after the Russian mode, has been included with the others.

A copious Index, together with a Glossary of French terms, will, it is hoped, augment the utility of the work.

The Author hopes he shall be excused for alluding to himself, and his pretensions for writing a book of this kind. Although bearing a foreign name, he is happy in being an Englishman. He received his professional education in Paris, and acquired a knowledge of his art in some of the most celebrated *cuisines* of that capital, and was so fortunate as to become a pupil of the renowned Carême. Qualified under such favorable auspices, he has subsequently served—he hopes with satisfaction to his patrons—some of the most distinguished *bons vivants* among the British aristocracy and gentry. He has had the good fortune to be *Chef-de-cuisine* to the Earl of Chesterfield ; Lord Kinnaird ; and to Sir W. Massey Stanley, Bart., and Rowland Errington, Esq., at Melton Mowbray ; and he shall ever consider it the greatest honor to which he could aspire, to have served as Chief Cook and Maître-d'Hôtel to Her Most Gracious Majesty the Queen.

LONDON:
21*st February* 1846.

CONTENTS.

GLOSSARY.

COMMON STOCK AND STOCK SAUCES.

GRAND SAUCES : Espagnole, Velouté, Béchamel, and Allemande.

SPECIAL SAUCES.

COLD SAUCES.

PUREES OF VEGETABLES for garnishing.

VEGETABLE GARNISHES.

ESSENCES, GRAVIES, AND PREPARED SAVORY BUTTERS for finishing Sauces.

RAGOUTS AND GARNISHES in general.

BROTHS AND CONSOMMES.

MEDICINAL DO.

BRAIZES, POELES, MIREPOIX, MARINADES, AND ROUX.

QUENELLE FORCEMEATS.

CLEAR CONSOMME SOUPS.

PUREES OF VEGETABLES for Soups.

SOUPS MADE WITH RICE OR PEARL-BARLEY.

BISQUES OF CRAYFISH, AND OTHER SHELLFISH SOUPS.

FISH SOUPS AND WATER-SOUCHETS.

ENGLISH SOUPS.

FOREIGN NATIONAL SOUPS.

ITALIAN SOUPS.

PANADAS AND LIGHT SOUPS for Infants, &c.

DRESSED FISH.

REMOVES—Beef. Veal. Lamb. Calves'-heads. Ox-cheek. Pork and Sucking pig. Braized Hams. Venison, Red-deer &c. Turkeys and Capons. Chickens, Goose and Cygnets. Pheasants. Partridges. Meat-pies. Meat-puddings. Black Game and Grouse.

ENTREES—Patés chauds, or raised Pies. Vol-au-vents and Tourtes. Timbales. Macaroni and Casseroles. Ornamental borders of Potato-paste. Chartreuses of Vegetables. Forcemeat Chartreuses. Ornamental croustades, Turbans and Mazarines. Beef. Ox-cheek dressed. Ox-palates. Ox-piths. Ox-tongues. Mutton. Mutton Cutlets. Scollops. Carbonades. Fillets. Sheep's Tongues. Sheep's Heads and Kidneys. Veal. Fricandeaux. Noix, &c. Heart and throat Sweetbreads. Calf's-ears, feet, liver, and brains. Lamb. Lamb's-head, ears, and feet. Pork. Venison, Roebuck, and Poultry. Quenelle forcemeat of Fowl.

(27)

Pigeons and Ducklings, Quails.   Larks.   Rabbits.   Hares.   Pheasants.
Partridges.   Boudins, Quenelles, and Soufflées of Partridges.   Wood-
cocks and Snipes.   Wild-fowl.   Ortolans and Wheatears.   Dressed fish.
SECOND COURSE ROASTS—Game, Poultry, Wild-fowl, &c.
VEGETABLES FOR ENTREMETS.
ENTREMETS OF EGGS, MACARONI, &c.
COLD ENTREES FOR BALL SUPPERS, &c.
COLD RAISED PIES AND PRESERVED GAME.
DIFFERENT KINDS OF PASTE.
VOL-AU-VENT AND TOURTE CASES.
CROUSTADE AND TIMBALE CASES.
CAKES IN GENERAL.
SMALL PASTRY.
FRITTERS.
ICED PUDDINGS AND ORNAMENTED ENTREMETS.
TIMBALES AND CAKES OF MACARONI, NOUILLES, &c.
SOUFFLES.
PUDDINGS.
JELLIES.
CREAMS.
MINCEMEATS.
BILLS OF FARE.
INDEX.

GLOSSARY.

ALLEMANDE. Reduced or concentrated white *velouté* Sauce, thickened with cream and yolks of eggs, and seasoned with nutmeg and lemon-juice.

ANGELICA is a plant, the tender tubular branches of which, after being preserved in syrup, are used for the purpose of decorating *entremêts*, &c.

BABA, a kind of very light plum-cake.

BECHAMEL is *velouté* Sauce boiled down with cream in equal parts. This Sauce takes its name from a celebrated cook.

BISQUE. A Soup generally made with shell-fish.

BLANCH. To parboil: to scald vegetables, &c., in order to remove their hulls or skins, such as almonds, &c.

BOUDIN. A delicate kind of *eutrée*, prepared with *quenelle* force-meat or mince.

BOUQUET (garnished), or faggot, consists of a handful of parsley, six green onions, a small bay-leaf, and a sprig of thyme, neatly tied together with twine.

BRAIZE, MIREPOIX, MARINADE, POELE, BLANC, are various kinds of compounds used for imparting flavor to braized meats; and also for keeping Calves'-Heads, Poultry, &c., white, while they are being braized.

BRAIZING signifies a slow process of simmering or stewing over a smothered charcoal-fire.

BRIOCHE. A species of light spongy cake, resembling Bath-buns.

CARAMEL. Burnt sugar, occasionally used as a make-shift for coloring.

CHARLOTTE consists generally of very thin slices of bread, steeped in clarified butter, and placed in symmetrical order in a plain mould garnished with fruit or preserve.

CHARTREUSE OF VEGETABLES. A mixed preparation, consisting of vegetables symmetrically and tastefully arranged in a plain mould, the interior of which is garnished with either game, quails, pigeons, larks, fillets, scollops, tendons, &c.

CHARTREUSE A LA PARISIENNE, &c. An ornamental *entrée* or side-dish, composed chiefly of *quenelle* force-meat; the interior being garnished with *ragouts*, scollops, &c.

COMPOTE generally means confectioned fruits, preserved in syrup, or apple and any other kind of fruit jelly; this word is also used to designate certain savory dishes, prepared with pigeons, quails, or larks, mixed with peas, or mushrooms, &c.

CONSOMME. Clear strong broth, much used in the preparation of Soups, Sauces, &c.

CONTISE. When small scollops of truffles, red tongue, &c., are inlaid, as ornaments, by incision in fillets of any kind, they are said to be *contisés*.

CROQUETTES AND RISSOLES. A preparation of mince, with a bread-crumbed coating. These words both signify something crisp.

CROQUANTES. A bright mixture of fruit and boiled sugar.

CROUSTADES, PATES-CHAUDS, TOURTES, TIMBALES, CASSEROLES OF RICE. Various ornamental pie-cases, made either of paste or prepared rice.

(29)

CROUTONS. Sippets of bread of various sizes and shapes, fried in clarified butter, and used to garnish *salmis, fricassées,* dressed vegetables, &c.; they are also served with certain Soups, chiefly with *purées.*

COLD *Entrées.* These consist of *fricassées, salmis,* cutlets, ham, tongue, fillets of game, poultry, and fish, *aspics,* salads of poultry, fish, or shell-fish; Boars'-heads, potted meats, &c. They are appropriate for ball suppers, public breakfasts, and upon all occasions where a cold collation is served.

ENTREES. A conventional term for Side-Dishes, comprising cutlets, *fricassées fricandeaux,* fillets, scollops, *salmis, boudins,* sweetbreads, *pâtés-chauds, chartreuses,* &c.

ENTREMETS, or second-course side-dishes, consist of four distinct sorts, namely, cold *entrées;* dressed vegetables; scolloped shell-fish and dressed eggs; and lastly of the infinitely varied class of sweets, consisting of puddings, *gateaux timbales,* sweet *croquettes, charlottes, croquantes,* pastries, jellies, creams, fritters, &c.

ESPAGNOLE AND VELOUTE. The two main Sauces from which all others are made; the first is brown and the other white.

FANCHONETTES AND FLORENTINES. Varieties of small pastry meringued over.

FARCE. Is a coarse kind of forcemeat used for raised pies and *gratins.*

FLANS, DARIOLES, AND MIRLITONS. Varieties of French cheese-cakes.

FRICANDEAU AND GRENADINS consist of the primest parts of veal, or fillets of poultry, &c., smoothly trimmed, larded, and brightly glazed with a concentration of their own liquor; they are served as side-dishes.

FRICASSEE consists of chickens cut in pieces, and prepared in a white sauce, with truffles, mushrooms, cocks'-combs, &c., as accessories

GAUFFRES. A light spungy sort of biscuit.

GLACE. Any thing iced. This word is also sometimes used figuratively, by French cooks, to signify a smooth glossy surface.

GRATINS. A term applied to consolidated soups and sauces; also to certain dishes of high character, consisting of game, poultry, fish, vegetables, or macaroni, &c., improved by great care and finish, through the use of concentrated sauces or gravies.

HORS-D'ŒUVRES (Hot). A species of very light *entrées,* such as patties of all kinds, *rissoles, croquettes,* scolloped fish, shell-fish, macaroni, poultry, game, sweetbreads, brains, ox-piths, *horlys* of fish, poultry, or game, &c.

HORS-D'ŒUVRES (Cold). These should be eaten immediately after the soup and fish; they are considered as appetisers, or whets to the appetite, and consist of sardines, anchovies, tunny, Dutch herrings, savory butters, oysters, oiled salads.

JARDINIERE. A mixed preparation of vegetables, stewed down in their own sauce.

LUTING. A paste made of flour and water, and used for fastening the lids on to fire-pans when preserving game, &c., in order to prevent evaporation.

MACEDOINE of vegetables is a jardinière, with the addition of some kind of white sauce.

MACEDOINE of fruit. A kind of jelly.

MADELINE. Resembling queen-cake.

MATELOTTE, a dish of mixed fresh-water fish, sometimes of one kind only, as Eels.

MERINGUES. A kind of light trifle.

MIGNIONNETTE PEPPER, A preparation from either white or black peppercorns; which, after being broken, chopped, or ground coarse, so as to resemble mignionnette seed, should be sifted in order to remove the dust.

NOUGAT. A mixture of almonds and sugar.

NOUILLES. A kind of vermicelli.

PANER, to bread crumb.

PANURE. Culets, scollops, *croquettes*, or any other *entrée* that is bread-crumbed.

PIPING. A kind of decoration made of icing used for ornamenting cakes, pastry stands, small pastry, &c. : it is thus effected :—Take a short funnel or conically-shaped instrument of tin, and insert the same within a larger-sized and similarly-shaped paper funnel or *cornet*, the pointed end of which must be cut off so as to allow the tin instrument to protrude : place the icing or glazing (a mixture of finely-pounded sugar and white of egg worked into a smooth and firm paste) in the *cornet* or forcer, the upper part of which must be completely closed ; the glazing is then forced out at the point by pressure of the thumb on the upper part of the *cornet*.

PLUCHE, or plushe, the leaves of parsley, chervil, tarragon, lettuce, or sorrel, snipped or cut small ; these are used mixed or separately, according to directions.

PROFITROLLES. A light kind of pastry, creamed inside.

PUREE. A kind of pulpy maceration of roasted meats, and of vegetables, or fruits, finished by being passed through a tammy or sieve.

QUENELLE. A delicate sort of forcemeat, used in the preparation of *entrées*, &c.

RAGOUT. A rich compound, consisting of *quenelles*, mushrooms, truffles, fat livers, &c., mixed in a rich sauce, and used for garnishing highly-finished removes and *entrées*.

RELEVES OR REMOVES. The top and bottom dishes (as they are designated in England), serve to replace the soup and fish on ordinary tables. These usually consist of roast joints, turkeys, capons, highly or plain dressed fillets, or rolls, &c., of beef, calves'-heads, &c.

ROUX. A mixture of fresh butter and flour, which, after being baked, is used for thickening sauces.

SALMIS. A highly-finished hash, made with game or wild-fowl, cut up and prepared in either a rich gravy or sauce.

SAUTE. Cutlets, scollops of game, poultry, or fish, &c., lightly fried in butter.

SOUFFLES. The word *soufflé* means strictly something puffed up, and is generally applied to a light kind of pudding, served as a remove to second-course roasts ; it is made with any kind of farinaceous substance, and may be flavored either with fruits, liqueurs, or essences.

TRIFLE. A second-course dish, composed of sponge-cake, macaroons, fruit-jams, custard, whipped cream, brandy, and other liqueurs.

TURBANS AND MAZARINES. Ornamental *entrées*, made of forcemeats, and fillets of either game, poultry, or fish.

VOL-AU-VENT. A figurative expression applied to puff-paste of the lightest kind.

FRANCATELLI'S MODERN COOK.

COMMON STOCK AND STOCK SAUCES.

1. COMMON STOCK, OR GRAND STOCK FOR GENERAL PURPOSES.

WHEN about to prepare for the reception of company, it is advisable to begin, if there be sufficient time, two days beforehand in summer, or three days in winter, by getting ready the grand stock—an article so essential to all the after preparations, that it may be looked upon as the basis of operations.

The meat required for this purpose should be sent in the over night if possible. The quantity to be ordered, must of course depend upon the extent of the dinner-party, and the number of *entrées*. For a dinner of twelve *entrées*, two legs of white veal (about forty pounds weight), the same quantity of gravy beef, and forty pounds of leg of beef and knuckles of veal, would be required.

First take the legs of veal in hand, and cut out the *noix* or *fricandeau* pieces, which is that part adhering to the udder; set these pieces apart to be used either for *fricandeaux, grenadins,* or *noix,* for removes or *entrées,* as the case may be. Cut all the meat away from the bones, keeping the veal separate from the beef. Break up the bones, and put them,—together with the inferior pieces of beef,—into a large stock-pot half full; fill this up with cold water, set it on the fire to boil; skim it well, garnish it with carrots, turnips, celery, and leeks; avoid the use of spices or herbs, and use salt sparingly. When the broth has boiled gently for seven hours, strain it through a broth napkin into large kitchen basins to cool, and place them in the larder for the next day's use.

In connection with this subject, I will now describe the preparation of the two grand stock sauces, *Espagnole* and *Velouté,* as these, being the basis of the various special sauces used in modern cookery, should, together with the grand stock, be first attended to.

2. STOCK SAUCES, BROWN AND WHITE.*

THE first thing to be attended to on the following morning is to " mark off," or prepare the stock sauces, viz. : the *Espagnole* or brown sauce, and the *Velouté* or white sauce, in the following manner:

Take two large stewpans, well tinned and thoroughly clean; spread

---

* Although great care and watchful attention are requisite in every branch of the culinary art, the exercise of these qualities is most essential in the preparation of the grand stock sauces. If the first process which these undergo be not successfully effected, no subsequent care will remedy the mischief.

the bottom of each with fresh butter, over which lay about one pound of lean ham cut in slices; then add the finest pieces of the veal in equal proportion to each stewpan. In that intended to be used for the brown sauce put two or three whole wild rabbits (or the mere carcasses may suffice); put into the stewpan marked for the white sauce, two old hens, or carcasses of fowls. Pour into each pan a sufficient quantity of grand stock to reach the upper surface of the veal; place the pans with their covers on, on brisk fires, and let them boil sharply till the broth is nearly reduced to a glaze; then take them off the fire immediately, and slacken the stoves, by putting on some charcoal ashes to decrease their heat; after which, replace the pans on the fire, adding to the brown sauce, one pound of glaze, to be reduced together with the stock, by which it will acquire a redder hue; it will also accelerate its progress,—a point of great importance; for if sauces or broths remain too long on the fire, the delicacy of their flavor is sure to be impaired.

As soon as the broth of the white sauce is reduced to the consistency of pale glaze,* fill it up with some grand stock; garnish it with a good-sized carrot, one onion, four cloves, a blade of mace, and a garnished fagot or bouquet, made of parsley, green onions, a bay-leaf, and thyme, tied together neatly. Set it on the stove to boil; skim it well, and then place it to simmer gently at the side of the stove. Pay strict attention to the brown sauce, in order to prevent the possibility of its being caught by the fire in the least degree. Such an accident always tends to lessen its unctuousness. Ascertain when the brown sauce is sufficiently glazed, by dipping the end of a knife into it, twirling the handle round in the hand, so as to take up a quantity of the glaze on the point of the blade; if you can then roll it into a ball without its sticking to the fingers, and it is of a beautiful brown-red color, you may proceed to fill it up in exactly the same manner as described for the white sauce.

About two hours after the above-mentioned operations have been attended to, pass the broths through napkins into large kitchen basins. Then pour the *roux* or thickening into the large stewpans to be used for mixing each of these sauces; take off all the fat, and pour the brown broth upon the brown *roux*, and the white broth upon the white *roux*. While the sauces are being mixed they should be well stirred. When thoroughly mixed, they must be kept sufficiently liquid to enable them (after boiling on the stove-fire, and while they are simmering on the side) to throw up the whole of the butter with which the *roux* was made, together with the skum, by which means they assume a velvety appearance, and from which the white sauce takes its name *Velouté*.

Finally, add a large ladleful of white chicken broth to the white sauce, and the same quantity of *consommé* to the brown sauce; let them clarify for about twenty minutes longer; and then, if sufficiently reduced, pass them through the tammy cloths into white basins, and put them away in the larder for future use.

---

* When time presses, or the veal used for this purpose is not white, the process of boiling down to a glaze recommended above, may be dispensed with; and, consequently, the white broth or water added at once.

SAUCES IN GENERAL.

GRAND SAUCES.

<small>COMPRISING</small>

*Espagnole,** or Brown Sauce.
*Velouté,** or White Sauce.
Béchamel Sauce.

Cream *Béchamel.*
Allemande Sauce.

3. ESPAGNOLE, OR BROWN SAUCE.

LET the stock *Espagnole* (No. 2) be turned out into a large stew-pan, adding thereto some essence of mushrooms, and sufficient *blond* of veal to enable the sauce to clarify itself; stir it over the fire till it boils, and then set it down by the side to continue boiling gently. When the sauce has thoroughly cleared itself, by gentle ebullition, and assumes a bright velvety smoothness, reduce it over a brisk fire, to the desired consistency, and then pass it through a tammy for use.

4. WHITE VELOUTE SAUCE.

To finish this sauce, proceed in every respect the same as for the *Espagnole*, substituting white *consommé* of veal or fowls, for the *blond* of veal, in order to clarify it; and the essence of mushrooms must be white, in order to prevent the sauce from taking a dark hue, contrary to its special character.

5. BECHAMEL SAUCE.

DIVIDE the *Velouté* sauce (according to the quantity required) into three parts; put one-third into a stewpan, and having reduced it, add thereto a quart (more or less) of boiling cream:—after allowing the sauce to boil a few minutes longer, stirring it the whole time, pass it through the tammy into a basin, or *bain-marie,*† for use.

6. CREAM BECHAMEL SAUCE.

PUT six ounces of fresh butter into a middle-sized stewpan; add four ounces of sifted flour, some nutmeg, a few peppercorns, and a little salt: knead the whole well together; then cut one carrot and one onion into very thin slices, throw them into the stewpan, and also a bouquet of parsley, thyme, and half a bay-leaf, tied together; next moisten these with a quart of white broth and a pint of cream; and having stirred the sauce over the stove-fire for about half an hour, pass it through the tammy into a basin for use.

This sauce is not expensive, neither does it require much time or trouble to make. It is very useful as a substitute for *Velouté*, or other white sauces, as also for many other purposes, as will be shown hereafter.

* These two grand sauces differ from the stock *Espagnole* and *Velouté*, in being worked or finished sauces.

† This is a French term for a distinct set of copper saucepans, tinned both inside and outside, and used only for the Special Sauces, when finished.

7. ALLEMANDE SAUCE.

REDUCE the quantity of white *Velouté* sauce intended for the *Allemande*, over a brisk stove-fire, adding a little essence of mushrooms or some mushroom trimmings; when the sauce is sufficiently reduced, take it off the stove, and incorporate with it a leason* of yelks of eggs (in the proportion of four yelks to a pint), a little nutmeg, cream, a pat of butter, and a little lemon-juice; set the leason in the sauce, by stirring it over the fire until it simmers; it must then be quickly stirred to keep the sauce from boiling, as, in that case, the yelks of eggs would be liable to curdle, which would considerably deteriorate from its quality. When the leason is set, pass the sauce through a tammy into a basin, or *bain-marie*, for use.

This sauce is in much request, as the foundation of many others, especially fish sauces.

SPECIAL SAUCES.

COMPRISING

Financière Sauce.
Turtle do.
Salmis do.
Do. *à l'ancienne*.
Brown Italian Sauce.
White Italian do.
Fine Herbs do.
Pascaline do.
D'Uxelles do.
Poor-man's do.
Piquante do.
Gherkin do.
White *Ravigotte* do.
Green   do.   do.
Tomata do.
Périgueux do.
Lyonnaise do.
Provençale do.
Venetian do.
Brêtonne do.
Bourguignotte do.
Poivrade do.
Génoise do.
Matelotte do.
Norman *matelotte* do.
Bigarrade do.
Aromatic do.
Russian do.
Atelets do.
Polish do.
Butter do.
Sauce for asparagus.
Anchovy Sauce.
Plain lobster do.
Shrimp do.
Suprême do.
Do. of Game.

Aurora Sauce.
Dutch   do.
Maître d'hôtel do.
Do. cold.
Princess Sauce.
Albert do.
Indian curry do.
Cardinal do.
Regency do.
White oyster do.
Brown oyster do.
Muscle do.
Shrimp do.
Crayfish do.
Lobster do.
Sturgeon do.
Bordelaise do.
Gasconne do.
Richelieu do.
Robert do.
Claremont do.
Portuguese do.
Sicilian do.
German sweet do.
Cherry do.
Napolitain do.
Cherry do., *à la Victoria*.
Red currant jelly Sauce for Venison.
Black currant jelly Sauce for Venison.
Fennel Sauce.
Parsley do.
Ravigotte do.
Plain Dutch do
Bread do.
Fried bread do.
Brown gravy Sauce for roast veal.
Cream Sauce for roast neck of do.

* From the French *liaison*, which here means a binding or thickening.

Parisian Sauce.	Caper Sauce for fish.
Mustard do.	Do. for boiled mutton.
Plain curry do.	Cream Sauce for salt fish.
Wastrefische do.	Orleans Sauce.
Flemish do.	Devil's do.
Egg do.	

8. FINANCIERE SAUCE.

PUT one glass of sherry or madeira into a stewpan with some essence of truffles and a little cayenne; reduce these to half their original quantity, then add a ladleful of finished *Espagnole* sauce; let it boil for five minutes longer, and pass the sauce through a tammy into a *bain-marie* for use.

9. TURTLE SAUCE FOR CALF'S HEAD.

PUT one glass of madeira into a stewpan with a spoonful of red tomata sauce, and a little cayenne; reduce these to half their quantity, then add a ladleful of *Espagnole* or brown sauce, and some essence of mushrooms; having stirred this over the fire until it boils, set it by the side to clarify; skim it thoroughly, and reduce it to a proper consistency; pass it through a tammy into a *bain-marie;* and just before using this sauce, mix in two anchovies (that have been pounded with a very small piece of fresh butter, and passed through a tammy) with a little lemon-juice.

10. SALMIS SAUCE.

PLACE the trimmings of the birds of which the *salmis* is to be made, in a stewpan with a tablespoonful of salad-oil, four shalots, one bay-leaf, and a sprig of thyme; pass these on the stove-fire for five minutes; add two glasses of any sort of good white wine; reduce this to half its quantity, add a ladleful of *Espagnole* and some mushroom trimmings or essence; set the sauce to boil, and then put it by the side of the stove to clarify. Having well skimmed it, pass the sauce through a tammy into a *bain-marie*, pouring a small portion of the sauce on the members of the birds to keep them moist, and to warm them in.

11. SALMIS SAUCE A L'ANCIENNE.

CHOP off the trimmings of the birds that have been roasted for an *entrée* (woodcocks or snipes are generally chosen for this purpose); place the trimmings in a stewpan, with six shalots, a little thyme, a bay-leaf, and half a bottle of red wine (claret is preferable); simmer these over the fire for ten minutes, add a ladleful of essence of game, and a gravy-spoonful of reduced *Espagnole* sauce; stir this on the fire until it boils, and then place it by the fire to clear itself; ten minutes after, skim it thoroughly, and having reduced it to the consistency of a thin glaze, pass it through a tammy on to the members of the birds. Just before dishing up, add a spoonful of chopped and blanched parsley.

12. BROWN ITALIAN SAUCE.

CHOP four shalots very fine, place them in a corner of a clean napkin, securing them tightly, and immerse them in cold water to extract their acrid taste; squeeze out the water and put them into a stewpan with a handful of white mushrooms chopped very fine, some thyme, a bay-leaf, and a tablespoonful of salad-oil; pass these on the fire for five minutes, add two glasses of white wine, and, when this is reduced to half its quantity, then add a small ladleful of finished *Espagnole* and a little *blond* of veal; set the sauce to boil; and having freed it from the oil, take out the thyme and bay-leaf; reduce it to the consistency of other sauces, and pour it into a *bain-marie*, to be kept for use.

13. WHITE ITALIAN SAUCE.

THE preparation of this sauce differs from the preceding only in substituting *Velouté* sauce for *Espagnole*.

14. FINE HERBS' SAUCE.

CHOP, separately, a large gravy-spoonful of prepared white mushrooms, three shalots, and a handful of parsley; place these in a stewpan with an ounce of fresh butter, a pinch of minionette pepper, a little grated nutmeg, and salt; pass the whole on the fire for five minutes, add a small ladleful of finished *Espagnole* or *Velouté* sauce (according to the color required); boil it quickly, finish with a little lemon-juice, and pour it into a *bain-marie* for use.

15. PISCALINE SAUCE.

CHOP a handful of white mushrooms very fine, and place them in a small stewpan with a small piece of butter; stir them on the fire for three minutes; add a glass of French white wine, and after allowing these to simmer on the fire a little while, add a small ladleful of white sauce and a little essence of fowl; reduce the sauce quickly, and then take it off the stove and mix in a leason of three yelks of eggs, and a small pat of butter; set the leason in the sauce over the fire, and then pour it into a *bain-marie* for use. Just before using the sauce, add to it a tablespoonful of chopped and blanched parsley, and the juice of half a lemon.

16. D'UXELLES SAUCES.

CHOP, separately, half a pottle of mushrooms, a handful of parsley, six shalots, and two ounces of truffles; place these in a stewpan with two ounces of fat bacon scraped into a kind of pulp, a pat of butter, some pepper, salt, and grated nutmeg; then stir the whole on the fire for five minutes; add two glasses of French white wine, reduced by boiling to half the quantity; and then a small ladleful of white sauce; reduce the whole quickly on the fire, and mix in a leason of six yelks of eggs; finish with the juice of a lemon. Set the leason in the sauce by stirring it again on the fire; place the sauce in a small basin, and keep it for the purpose of covering all those *entrées* denominated *à la D'Uxelles*, previously to bread-crumbing them.

17. POOR MAN'S SAUCE.

CHOP an onion very fine, put it into a stewpan with a small piece of butter, and gently fry the onion on the fire until it assumes a light-brown color; then add a tablespoonful of white wine vinegar, and a pinch of minionette pepper; allow these to simmer for three minutes, and then add a small ladleful of *blond* of veal or *consommé;* let the whole be reduced to half the original quantity; and just before using the sauce, throw in a spoonful of chopped and blanched parsley.

18. PIQUANTE SAUCE.

CHOP, separately, six shalots, as many green gherkins, and a tablespoonful of French capers; place these in a small stewpan with a gill of French vinegar, some thyme and a bay-leaf, and a good pinch of mignionette pepper; set the whole to boil on the fire till the vinegar is reduced to a third of its original quantity; then add a small ladleful of finished *Espagnole* sauce, and a little *blond* of veal; let the sauce boil gently on the side of the stove-fire to clear itself; skim it well, take out the thyme and bay-leaf, and pour it into a small *bain-marie* for use.

19. GHERKIN SAUCE.

TAKE six green gherkins; cut them into very thin slices; place them in a small stewpan with a little French vinegar and mignionette pepper; allow these to simmer quickly for a few minutes on the fire, then add a small ladleful of brown sauce and a little *blond* of veal; stir the sauce on the stove till it boils, then set it by the side to clear itself, skim it, and pour it into a *bain-marie* for use.

20. WHITE RAVIGOTTE SAUCE.

PUT into a small stewpan two tablespoonfuls of Chili vinegar, the same quantities of tarragon vinegar and of Harvey sauce; reduce these, by boiling, to half the quantity; then add a small ladleful of good *Béchamel* sauce, or, if not at hand, the same quantity of white sauce; finish by mixing in two pats of fresh butter, and just before using the sauce, throw in a tablespoonful of chopped and blanched parsley.

When white sauce is used instead of *Béchamel,* a little cream must be added.

21. GREEN RAVIGOTTE SAUCE.

WASH and blanch some chervil, parsley, tarragon, and chives (of each a small handful), and also a little burnet; cool these in fresh water as soon as they are blanched, and thoroughly extract the water by pressing them in a napkin; pound the herbs, thus prepared, in a mortar, with two pats of butter; after which rub them through a fine sieve with a wooden spoon, and place the residue in a small basin, to be kept on ice, or in a cool place.

About five minutes before requiring the sauce for use, put into a small stewpan a ladleful of *Allemande,* and, when thoroughly warmed, mix in with it the prepared *Ravigotte,* in sufficient quantity to give a bright green color to the sauce; add a tablespoonful of Tarragon vinegar, and the same quantities of Chili vinegar and of Harvey sauce, previously reduced, by boiling, to half the quantity.

This sauce is very generally used for fillets of fish.

22. TOMATA, OR LOVE-APPLE SAUCE.

PROCURE a dozen fine ripe tomatas, and, having first picked off the stalks, extract the seeds and watery parts, by squeezing them separately in the hand; then place them in a stewpan, containing four ounces of raw ham cut into dice, a few shalots, a bay-leaf, and thyme, fried in a little butter until they become brown; put the tomatas with these on the fire until they are melted; then, after having passed them through the tammy into a *purée*, mix the produce with a little *Velouté* sauce, a small piece of glaze, and a little *consommé*; stir the sauce on the fire till it boils, and then set it by the side of the stove to continue boiling gently, that it may clear itself; skim it thoroughly, and pour it into a *bain-marie* for use.

It is, perhaps, needless to observe, that, when the ready-prepared tomata sauce, as sold by oilmen, is used, as must be the case when tomatas are not in season, it will be necessary only to attend to the latter part of the foregoing directions.

23. PERIGUEUX SAUCE.

CHOP six or eight truffles exceedingly fine, put them into a stewpan with two glasses of white wine, a little lean ham, some thyme, and a bay-leaf; set these to boil gently on the stove-fire for a few minutes, then add a ladleful of brown sauce and a little *consommé;* stir the sauce on the fire till it boils, and then set it by the side to clear itself; skim it well, take out the ham, the bay-leaf, the thyme, and, after reducing it to a proper consistency, pour it into a *bain-marie* for use.

Just before dinner-time, add a small piece of butter, to soften the flavor.

24. LYONNAISE SAUCE.

PEEL four Portugal onions, cut them in halves, trim off the ends, so as to leave the onions an inch and a half thick; slice them across, that the pieces may separate at the junction of the several folds, or layers, of the onion; fry them in a deep sauta-pan, in half a pint of salad-oil; as soon as they assume a fine light color, drain them on a hair-sieve, and afterward lay them on a napkin, in order to extract all the oil; after which put them into a small stewpan, with a good pinch of minionette pepper, a very small ladleful of reduced brown sauce, and a piece of glaze; set the sauce to boil gently for a quarter of an hour, and finish by adding a little lemon-juice.

25. PROVENCALE SAUCE.

CUT two ounces of the lean part of a ham into very small dice, place them in a small stewpan, with two tablespoonsful of salad-oil, four cloves of garlic, some thyme, a bay-leaf, a spoonful of capers, the pulp of a lemon cut into slices, a good pinch of minionette pepper, and a few parsley stalks; stir these on the stove-fire for five minutes, then add a small ladleful of reduced brown sauce, and a piece of glaze. Boil the sauce on a quick fire for a few minutes longer, and then pass it through a tammy as you would a *purée;* remove it into a stewpan, add a little *consommé*, and set it to boil gently by the side of the stove for a few minutes, skim it, and pour it into a *bain-marie*, finish by adding a little anchovy butter.

26. VENETIAN SAUCE.

PREPARE a sufficient quantity of *Allemande* sauce for the purpose required, and, just before dinner-time, add a good spoonful of tarragon leaves, cut into diamond-shapes, and blanched green, a pat of butter, a little nutmeg, and a spoonful of tarragon vinegar.

27. BRETONNE SAUCE.

CUT two large onions into thin slices; fry them of a light brown color, in a little butter; then add sufficient brown sauce, according to the quantity required, a little *consommé*, and a pinch of pepper; boil the sauce gently for a quarter of an hour, and then pass it, as you would a *purée*, through the tammy, and put it into a *bain-marie* for use.

28. BOURGUIGNOTTE SAUCE.

PUT four shalots, two cloves, a blade of mace, thyme, and bay-leaf, together with three glasses of red wine and some mushroom-trimmings, into a stewpan, on the fire, there to boil for five minutes; add a small ladleful of brown sauce and a little *consommé*; stir the sauce on the fire till it boils, and then set it on the side to clear itself; skim it, reduce it to its proper consistency, and then pass it through the tammy into a *bain-marie*.

29. POIVRADE SAUCE.

TAKE a carrot, an onion, and a head of celery; cut them into very small dice, and place them in a stewpan, with two ounces of raw lean of ham cut similarly, some thyme, and a bay-leaf, a blade of mace, a few peppercorns, and some parsley; fry these with a little butter, of a light brown color; moisten with two glasses of sherry and one of French vinegar; reduce the above to one half its quantity, and then add a small ladleful of brown sauce and a little *consommé*; stir the sauce till it boils, and then set it by the side to clear itself; skim it, and pass it through a tammy into a *bain-marie* for use.

30. GENOISE SAUCE.

CUT some ham, carrot, celery, onion, parsley roots, and mushrooms, into very thin slices; place these in a stewpan with a little butter, some thyme, and a bay-leaf, a blade of mace, and two cloves, and fry them on the stove for a few minutes; moisten with half a bottle of red wine (claret suits best). Boil the whole for five minutes; add a small ladleful of brown sauce and a little *consommé*; stir the sauce on the fire till it boils, and then set it to clarify by the side of the stove-fire; skim it, and pass it through a tammy into a *bain-marie* for use. Just before dinner-time, add a piece of anchovy butter, a spoonful of chopped and blanched parsley, a little grated nutmeg, and lemon-juice.

31. MATELOTTE SAUCE.

TAKE the wine in which the fish has been stewed, and add to it a ladleful of brown sauce, and some trimmings or essence of mushrooms; stir this on the fire till it boils, and then set it by the side to clear itself; skim and reduce it, and then pass it into a *bain-marie*; finish by adding a little anchovy butter, grated nutmeg, and a pinch of sugar.

32. NORMAN MATELOTTE SAUCE.

REDUCE some white *Velouté* sauce with some essence of mush-rooms, three glasses of French white wine, and the liquor from the muscles and oysters used for the *matelotte :* add a leason of four yelks of eggs, a pat of butter, some nutmeg and lemon-juice ; and pass the sauce through a tammy into a *bain-marie.* Just before using the sauce, add a spoonful of chopped and blanched parsley.

33. BIGARRADE SAUCE.

WITH the carcasses of two or more roasted ducks, make an essence ; clarify it, and reduce it to half glaze. To this add a small *ragout-*spoonful of worked *Espagnole,* the juice of one orange, and the rind of two others entirely free from any portion of the white pith ; and having cut the rind into diamond shapes, blanch these pieces for three minutes in boiling water, and then put them into the sauce, which, after boiling for five minutes, pour into a *bain-marie* for use.

34. AROMATIC SAUCE.

PUT into a small stewpan a few sprigs of winter-savory, of sweet basil, and lemon thyme ; six leaves of sage, and two bay-leaves, two shalots, some nutmeg, and pepper, and a ladleful of good *consommé ;* boil this quickly on the fire for ten minutes ; pass it through a sieve into a stewpan, and reduce it with an equal proportion of white sauce ; add a leason of four yelks of eggs, and pass the sauce into a *bain-marie,* containing two dozen stewed morels. Just before using this sauce, add a pat of butter, some lemon-juice, and a spoonful of chopped and blanched tarragon and chervil.

35. RUSSIAN SAUCE.

HAVING chopped and blanched some tarragon, chervil, and parsley, in equal proportions, put these into some reduced *Velouté* sauce thickened with two yelks of eggs. Just before using the sauce, add a little grated horseradish, a pinch of sugar, some pepper, lemon-juice, and a little mustard.

This sauce is eaten with braized beef.

36. ATELETS SAUCE.

CUT two ounces of raw lean of ham into very small mince-meat ; put it into a small stewpan with half a bay-leaf, a sprig of thyme, one shalot chopped, a little nutmeg, and minionette pepper ; moisten with a few spoonsful of *consommé,* and set the whole to simmer on the fire for ten minutes ; after which, add a small ladleful of white sauce, and having reduced it to a proper consistency, mix in a leason of six yelks of eggs, and a pat of butter ; finish with a little lemon-juice, and pass the sauce through a tammy into a basin.

This sauce is used for covering all preparations for those *entrées* denominated *à la Villeroi,* or *à la Dauphine,* previously to their being dipped in the beaten egg for the purpose of being bread-crumbed.

37. POLISH SAUCE.

SCRAPE a stick of horseradish, and put it into some *Allemande* sauce with a dessert-spoonful of pounded sugar, the grated rind of one lemon, nutmeg, pepper, lemon-juice, a piece of glaze, and a little salt. Previously to using the sauce, add a spoonful of chopped and blanched parsley and fennel.

This sauce is eaten with roast veal.

38. SUPREME SAUCE.

THERE are two methods by which this sauce may be made with equal success : that most generally adopted is, to use reduced *Velouté* sauce which has been worked with some essence of mushrooms and white *consommé* of fowls, and finished by adding a little boiling cream at the last stage of reduction; the sauce should be then passed through a tammy into a *bain-marie*, and just before using it, a small piece of chicken glaze, a pat of fresh butter, and a little lemon-juice must be added.

The other method, and which I prefer to the former, is to put a sufficient quantity of *Allemande* sauce into a *bain-marie*, and finish it for the purpose, by mixing in a piece of chicken glaze, a pat of fresh butter, and a little lemon-juice ; care must be taken that the *Suprême* sauce be not thick.

39. SUPREME OF GAME.

THIS is made like the previous sauce, except that, according to the first method, some essence of game must be used instead of the chicken *consommé*, and in the second recipe, the *Allemande* sauce used for the purpose should be worked with an essence of game (pheasant or partridge), and also finished with a piece of game glaze.

40. PARISIAN SAUCE.

PUT some *Allemande* sauce into a *bain-marie*, add thereto a spoonful of essence of truffles, a piece of game or chicken glaze, according to the purpose for which the sauce may be required, whether for an *entrée* made of game or poultry ; add some crayfish butter in sufficient quantity to color it of a pinky tint, a little cayenne and lemon-juice ; when these ingredients are well mixed in the *Allemande*, add two dozen small truffles cut in the shape of small olives.

41. AURORA SAUCE.

PUT some *Béchamel* sauce into a *bain-marie*, and just before the sauce is required for use, mix in a small piece of lobster butter, a leason of three yelks of eggs, a tablespoonful of tarragon-vinegar, and a little cayenne.

42. DUTCH SAUCE.

PUT the yelks of six eggs, a small piece of glaze, six ounces of fresh butter, a spoonful of white sauce, some nutmeg, minionette pepper, and salt, into a small stewpan ; stir these quickly with a wooden spoon, over a slow fire, or else immerse the bottom of the stewpan into a deep sauta-pan half full of boiling water, which must be kept over a slow fire, while the sauce is worked : as soon as the sauce assumes a smooth compact body, take it away from the fire, work it smartly, and then pass it through a tammy into a *bain-marie* for use. If the sauce should appear to curdle or decompose, add a spoonful of any white sauce nearest at hand, which will set it right again.

Dutch sauce may be flavored with various sorts of vinegar, horse-radish, or lemon-juice, according to fancy, or as the case may require.

43. MAITRE D'HOTEL SAUCE.

PUT some *Béchamel* sauce into a stewpan, make it boil, and incor-porate with it six ounces of fresh butter, some chopped and blanched parsley, pepper, salt, and lemon-juice.

44. COLD MAITRE D'HOTEL SAUCE.

PUT about six ounces of fresh butter on a plate, knead it together with some chopped parsley, pepper, salt, and lemon-juice.

This butter is chiefly used for French beefsteaks, for broiled mack-erel, and other sorts of broiled fish, as will be shown hereafter.

45. PRINCESS SAUCE.

PUT into a small stewpan the rind of one lemon, and half a stick of horse-radish, both grated; a little nutmeg, pepper, and two table-spoonsful of French vinegar; simmer these on a slow fire for a few minutes, and then add a small ladleful of *Allemande* sauce; stir the whole on the fire till it boils, then pass it through a tammy into a *bain-marie*. Just before using the sauce, add a pat of fresh butter, and a tablespoonful of chopped and blanched parsley. This sauce will prove an excellent accessory, to be served with any *entrée* of poultry or game, when dressed *à la Dauphine,* or *à la Villeroi;* as also for fillets of dressed fish, bread-crumbed, and denominated *à la Princess;* in which case, a little anchovy butter may be added.

46. ALBERT SAUCE.

GRATE three large sticks of horse-radish, put them into a stewpan with a pint of good broth; let this simmer gently on a moderate fire for half an hour, then add a little white sauce and half a pint of cream; reduce the whole over a brisk fire, and pass the sauce through a tammy as you would a *purée,* and put it into a *bain-marie.* Just before using the sauce, make it hot, and mix in a little French vinegar, a dessert-spoonful of mixed mustard, some salt, a tablespoonful of chopped and blanched parsley, and two yelks of eggs.

This sauce is well adapted to be eaten with braized fillet of beef, garnished with potatoes cut into the shapes of olives, and fried in butter.

47. INDIAN CURRY SAUCE.

TAKE two large onions, one carrot, and one head of celery, and slice them very thin; place these with two ounces of fresh butter in a stewpan, and fry them over a slow fire till the onions are nearly melted, but without becoming brown; add three blades of mace, some thyme, and a bay-leaf, a bouquet of parsley, and two table-spoonsful of Cooks or Bruce's meat curry paste, a tablespoonful of curry powder, and as much *roux* or flour as may be required to thicken the quantity of sauce needed; moisten with some good broth or *consommé,* and stir the sauce on the fire till it boils; then set it by the side to clear itself of the butter, &c. Having skimmed and reduced the sauce to a proper consistency, pass it through a tammy (extracting the parsley), as for a *purée*, and take it up into a *bain-marie*, or add it to whatever kind of meat is prepared for the curry; observing that the broth thereof should be used for making the sauce.

48. CARDINAL SAUCE.

PUT some reduced *Velouté* sauce into a stewpan, add some essence of mushrooms, lobster butter, a little essence of anchovies, lemon-juice, and cayenne; work these well together, and pass the sauce through a tammy into a *bain-marie* for use.

Observe : that for whatever kind of meat or fish this sauce may be intended, the essence or liquor of the meat or fish should be first reduced to glaze, and then incorporated into the sauce, in order to give it a characteristic flavor.

49. REGENCY SAUCE.

CUT an eel of a pound weight into thin slices, and place them in a stewpan with six cloves, two blades of mace, some thyme, a bay-leaf, sweet basil, a carrot, mushrooms, an onion, and a little salt; moisten with three parts of a bottle of good claret, and put the whole to boil gently on the fire for half an hour; after which pass the essence thus obtained through the tammy with pressure, so as to extract every particle. Then mix the produce with a ladleful of reduced *Espagnole* sauce, and having boiled, skimmed, and reduced it, finish by working into it some essence of truffles, anchovy butter, nutmeg, lemon-juice, and a small pinch of sugar.

This sauce is peculiarly well adapted for every sort of colored fish, either fresh-water or salt.

50. WHITE OYSTER SAUCE.

PUT the oysters into a stewpan, and set them to boil for five minutes on the stove-fire, drain them on a sieve (saving their liquor in a basin), wash and beard them, taking care to cut off the tendons, as that part when eaten is troublesome to the teeth, and put them into a *bain-marie*—reserving only the fat part; then put four ounces of butter (more or less, according to the quantity of sauce) into a stewpan with two ounces of flour, cayenne pepper, and salt; knead these well together, and moisten with the oyster liquor, some cream, and a piece of glaze; stir the sauce on the fire, keeping it boiling for ten minutes; then pass it through a tammy upon the oysters. Just before sending to table, add a little lemon-juice.

51. BROWN OYSTER SAUCE.

PREPARE this precisely as the last sauce, but instead of the cream, use an equal quantity of brown gravy. Brown oyster sauce is a very desirable accessory to beefsteaks, beef pudding, beefsteak pie, broiled slices of codfish, and various other plain dressed dishes.

52. MUSCLE SAUCE.

CLEANSE, wash, beard, and blanch or parboil two quarts of muscles; take all the white fat muscles out of the shells, and place them in a *bain-marie*, reserving their liquor in a basin. Then knead four ounces of butter with two ounces of flour, some nutmeg, pepper, and salt;

add the liquor from the muscles, a piece of glaze, and half a pint of
cream ; stir the whole on the stove fire till it boils, and keep it boiling for ten minutes :—then add a leason of four yelks of eggs, and
pass it through a tammy on to the muscles. Just before sending the
sauce to table, throw in a tablespoonful of chopped and blanched
parsley, and a little lemon-juice.

This sauce is well adapted for broiled whiting, turbot, cod, haddock,
and gurnet.

53. SHRIMP SAUCE.

To about half a pint of melted butter, add a little lobster coral,
cayenne, some pickled shrimps, a little essence of anchovies, and
lemon-juice.

54. CRAYFISH SAUCE.

BOIL thirty crayfish in the usual manner, trim the tails, and with the
bodies and shells make some crayfish butter (No. 184), which incorporate into about half a pint of reduced *Velouté* sauce; add a little
essence of anchovies, cayenne, and lemon-juice, and pass this sauce
through a tammy on to the crayfish tails.

55. LOBSTER SAUCE.

CUT the fleshy part of a lobster into small square pieces; reserve
the spawn and coral, and pound it with two ounces of butter, and
pass it through a sieve. Then put about half a pint of melted butter,
or the same quantity of reduced *Velouté* sauce, into a stewpan, incorporate therewith the lobster butter, a small piece of glaze, cayenne,
and lemon-juice, add the pieces of lobster, and send to table.

56. STURGEON SAUCE.

TAKE some of the liquor in which the sturgeon has been braized,
and having reduced it to one third of its quantity, add half a bottle
of claret or port, a ladleful of worked *Espagnole* sauce, and some
essence or trimmings of mushrooms; allow the sauce to clear itself
by boiling gently on the side of the stove fire, skim it, reduce it, and
then pass it through a tammy into a *bain-marie.* Just before using
the sauce, mix in a pat of butter, some nutmeg, cayenne, essence of
anchovies, and lemon-juice.

57. BORDELAISE SAUCE.

MINCE two ounces of lean ham, and put it into a stewpan with two
cloves of garlic, a few peppercorns, a blade of mace, some thyme,
and a bay-leaf, some sprigs of tarragon, and half a pint of claret;
set these to simmer gently on a slow fire for twenty minutes, then
add a piece of glaze about the size of a walnut, a small gravy-spoonful of worked *Espagnole* sauce, and a little *blond* of veal; having
allowed the sauce to boil gently by the side of the stove-fire to clear
itself, pass it with pressure through a tammy into a *bain-marie* for
use. This sauce must be kept rather thin, and to be perfect, should
be bright and wholly free from grease; it is especially adapted, by
its flavor and character, for being served with broiled meats and fishes
generally. When this sauce is served with broiled fish, add to it, just
before sending to table, a little essence of anchovies, cayenne, and
lemon-juice.

58. CLAREMONT SAUCE.

CUT two or more large onions into halves, pare off the ends, cut them into thin slices, and fry them in a stewpan with some butter, of a fine yellow color; drain off the butter, add a pinch of minion-ette pepper, with a little brown sauce and *consommé;* set this to boil gently by the side of the stove fire, skim it, and then, when suffi-ciently reduced, pour it into a *bain-marie* for use. This sauce, as well as sauce *à la Brêtonne,* is well calculated for making an excellent hash, either with beef, veal, or mutton.

59. PORTUGUESE SAUCE.

GRATE the rind of a lemon, and put it into a small stewpan with a few bruised peppercorns, some mace, six cloves, thyme, and a bay-leaf, with half a pint of sherry; simmer the whole on a slow fire for ten minutes, then add a small ladleful of worked brown sauce, and a little *consommé;* set this to boil gently by the side of the stove-fire, skim it, reduce it, and pass it through a tammy into a *bain-marie* for use.

This sauce is used for a braized fillet of beef, or minced fillet of beef *au gratin à la Portuguaise.*

60. SICILIAN SAUCE.

CHOP two truffles, four shalots, a dozen mushrooms, and some parsley, separately; put them into a small stewpan with thyme, and a bay-leaf, one clove of garlic, and a little cayenne; moisten with two glasses of sherry, set the whole to simmer gently on a slow fire for ten minutes; add a sufficient quantity of *Allemande* sauce for the pur-pose required, reduce it to its proper consistency, and then put it into a *bain-marie* for use.

Just before using this sauce, add a spoonful of chopped and blanched parsley, the rind of two oranges—pared extremely thin, cut into fine shreds, and blanched—some lemon-juice, and a little pounded sugar.

61. GERMAN SWEET SAUCE.

STEW six ounces of dried cherries in two glasses of red wine, together with some bruised cinnamon, cloves, and lemon peel, for twenty minutes on a slow fire; pass the whole through a tammy into a *purée,* and put it into a stewpan with a little reduced brown sauce and six ounces of stewed prunes.

This sauce is in great request for German dishes; it improves the flavor of braized venison in its varied forms of preparation, and is preferred by many for that purpose to *Poivrade* or *Piquante* sauce.

62. CHERRY SAUCE.

PUT a pot of black currant jelly into a stewpan, together with six ounces of dried cherries, a small stick of cinnamon, and a dozen cloves tied up in a piece of muslin; moisten with half a pint of red wine, and set the whole to simmer gently on a slow fire for ten minutes; then take out the cinnamon and cloves, and send to table.

This kind of sauce is well adapted for roast hare or venison.

63. NEAPOLITAN SAUCE.

SCRAPE a stick of horse-radish quite clean, grate it, and place this in a small stewpan with two ounces of glaze, a small pot of currant-jelly, half a pint of red wine, and a spoonful of worked brown sauce; boil the whole gently on a stove-fire for twenty minutes, then pass the sauce through a tammy as you would a *purée*, and put it into a *bain-marie* for use.

This kind of sauce is generally used with larded fillets of beef. It may also be served with *entrées* of venison.

64. CHERRY SAUCE A LA VICTORIA.

PUT a small pot of red currant-jelly into a stewpan, together with a dozen cloves, a stick of cinnamon, the rind of two oranges, a piece of glaze, and a large gravy-spoonful of reduced brown sauce; moisten with half a pint of Burgundy wine, boil gently on the fire for twenty minutes; pass the sauce through a tammy into a *bain-marie*, add the juice of the two oranges, and just before sending to table boil the sauce.

This sauce is especially appropriate with red deer or roebuck, when prepared in a *marinade* and larded.

65. RED CURRANT-JELLY SAUCE FOR VENISON.

BRUISE one stick of cinnamon and twelve cloves, and. put them into a small stewpan with two ounces of sugar, and the peel of one lemon pared off very thin, and perfectly free from any portion of white pulp; moisten with three glasses of port wine, and set the whole to simmer gently on the fire for a quarter of an hour; then strain it through a sieve into a small stewpan containing a pot of red currant-jelly. Just before sending the sauce to table, set it on the fire to boil, in order to melt the currant-jelly, so that it may mix with the essence of spice, &c.

66. BLACK CURRANT-JELLY SAUCE FOR VENISON.

THIS sauce is made exactly in the same manner as the foregoing—substituting black currant-jelly for red; it is preferred by many to the other, as it possesses more flavor.

67. SAUCE A LA ROBERT.

PEEL two large onions and cut them in halves, pare off the ends, and cut them into very small dice in the following manner :—hold the half onion in the left hand, set it firmly on the table with the cut side downward, then with a knife held in the right hand horizontally, apply the edge of the point, and cut the onion into slices parallel with the surface of the table, without drawing the knife quite through; then turn the piece of onion half round and cut it nearly through in a vertical direction; this will form the whole into small dice like pieces. Next, put these into a small stewpan with about an ounce of fresh butter, and fry them of a light yellow color; then drain the butter, and add two tablespoonfuls of French vinegar: set this on the fire to simmer, and when the vinegar is nearly reduced, add a small ladleful of *Espagnole* sauce, and half that quantity of *consommé ;* stir this on the fire till it boils, then set it on the side to continue gently boiling that it may clear itself; skim it thoroughly, and having reduced it to a proper consistency, pour it into a *bain-marie*, and finish it by mixing in two teaspoonsful of French mustard and a little minionette pepper.

This sauce is peculiarly adapted, from its piquante, full, yet delicate flavor, for *entrées* of broiled pork.

68. SAUCE A LA GASCONNE.

TAKE a small spoonful of French capers, with about an ounce of truffles, and chop each separately, very fine; put these into a small stewpan, together with one clove of garlic, a tablespoonful of salad oil, some pepper, and nutmeg; fry them lightly on the stove-fire for two or three minutes; moisten with a glass of French white wine, set the whole to boil on the stove-fire for three minutes; then add a small ladleful of white *Velouté* sauce, a bay-leaf, and a sprig of thyme; stir the sauce on the fire till it boils, then set it by the side to continue boiling gently; skim it well, and after having added another glass of wine, reduce the sauce and thicken it with a leason of three yelks; pour the sauce into a *bain-marie*, and just before using it mix in a spoonful of chopped and blanched chives, parsley, and tarragon, a pat of anchovy butter, and some lemon-juice.

69. CHEVREUIL OR PIQUANTE SAUCE FOR ROEBUCK.

CHOP four ounces of lean ham, and put it into a stewpan, with a good pinch of minionette pepper, some thyme, and a bay-leaf, a few green onions, and some sprigs of parsley; moisten with a gill of French vinegar, boil the whole on the fire till reduced to half its original quantity, and then add a small ladleful of brown sauce, a small tumblerful of red wine, and a little *consommé;* stir this on the fire till it boils, and after having cleared and skimmed it in the usual manner, reduce it to a proper consistency, and finish by adding a spoonful of red currant-jelly and the juice of an orange.

70. BUTTER SAUCE.

BUTTER sauce, or, as it is more often absurdly called, *melted butter*, is the foundation of the whole of the following sauces, and requires very great care in its preparation. Though simple, it is nevertheless a very useful and agreeable sauce when properly made; so far from this being usually the case, it is too generally left to assistants to prepare as an insignificant matter; the result is therefore seldom satisfactory.

When a large quantity of butter sauce is required, put four ounces of fresh butter into a middle-sized stewpan, with some grated nutmeg and minionette pepper; to these add four ounces of sifted flour; knead the whole well together, and moisten with a pint of cold spring water; stir the sauce on the fire till it boils, and after having kept it gently boiling for twenty minutes (observing that it be not thicker than the consistence of common white sauce), proceed to mix in one pound and a half of sweet fresh butter, taking care to stir the sauce quickly the whole time of the operation. Should it appear to turn oily, add now and then a spoonful of cold spring water; finish with the juice of half a lemon, and salt to palate; then pass the sauce through a tammy into a large *bain-marie* for use.

Note.—This kind of sauce should not be made above twenty minutes before it is wanted, as, from its particular delicacy, when exposed much longer to heat of any kind, it is liable to be decomposed; should this occur, it may be remedied by simply adding a little cold spring water in winter, or a small piece of clean ice in summer; and then working the sauce briskly together with a spoon. This method is efficacious in restoring any sort of butter sauce, when turned or become oily, to its original smoothness.

71. BUTTER SAUCE FOR ASPARAGUS.

PREPARE some sauce as directed in the foregoing recipe, and add a little double cream, with a teaspoonful of French vinegar.

This sauce is also served with cauliflower, brocoli, seakale, salsifis, &c., &c.

72. ANCHOVY SAUCE.

PREPARE some butter sauce, add a sufficient quantity of essence of anchovies to give flavor, and a little lemon-juice.

73. PLAIN LOBSTER SAUCE.

CUT all the fleshy part of the lobster into small square dice, place them in a *bain-marie* with sufficient butter sauce (No. 70), a little cayenne, and lemon-juice, and also some lobster coral forced through a hair-sieve; stir the sauce with a spoon on the fire till it boils, and send to table. The coral may also be pounded with a little butter, and after being rubbed through a sieve or tammy, worked into the sauce. Either method may be adopted, but the latter is generally preferred.

74. PLAIN SHRIMP SAUCE.

TAKE half a pint of pickled shrimps, half a pint of butter sauce (No. 70), a little essence of anchovies, cayenne, and lemon-juice; stir these together in a small stewpan over the fire, and serve.

75. FENNEL SAUCE.

CHOP and blanch sufficient fennel to color the sauce of a bright green, and put it into a *bain-marie*, containing half a pint of butter sauce; add a little pepper, salt, and lemon-juice.

76. GOOSEBERRY SAUCE.

LET a pint of green young gooseberries be well picked, throw them into an untinned sugar-boiler, containing sufficient boiling water to blanch them in; boil them quickly on the stove-fire for ten minutes (more or less), but observe that the gooseberries be thoroughly done; drain them on a sieve, remove them into a small stewpan, and bruise them with a wooden spoon. The gooseberries after being boiled may be rubbed through a sieve or tammy into a *purée*, which has the effect of giving a smoother appearance to the sauce. This sauce is served with plain boiled mackerel.

77. PARSLEY SAUCE, USUALLY CALLED PARSLEY AND BUTTER.

PUT a tablespoonful of chopped and blanched parsley into half a pint of good butter sauce; and just before sending to table add a very little lemon-juice.

78. PLAIN RAVIGOTTE SAUCE.

TAKE one tablespoonful each of tarragon-vinegar, Chili ditto, and Harvey's sauce; put this into a small stewpan, and set it to boil down to half the quantity; then add about half a pint of good butter sauce (No. 70), and a tablespoonful of chopped and blanched tarragon, with chervil, chives, burnet, and parsley, in sufficient quantity to give a bright color to the sauce; stir the whole well together and serve.

This sauce is proper for boiled fowls or chickens, dressed fillets of various sorts of fish, when a plain dinner is served. If a small piece of glaze be added it will tend much to improve the quality of all plain sauces.

79. PLAIN DUTCH SAUCE.

POUR a large gravy-spoonful of melted butter into a small stewpan, add four raw yelks of eggs, a little grated nutmeg, some minionette pepper, two ounces of fresh butter, and a little salt; stir the sauce briskly on the fire in order to set the yelks in it, and then pass it through a tammy into a *bain-marie;* previously to using it add a little tarragon-vinegar or lemon-juice.

80. BREAD SAUCE.

PUT a gill of cream and a little milk into a small stewpan with a large gravy-spoonful of bread-crumbs, a small onion, some peppercorns, and a little salt; stir the sauce on the fire until it has boiled ten minutes, then take out the onion, work in a pat of fresh butter, and serve.

81. FRIED BREAD SAUCE.

MINCE a little lean ham and put it into a small stewpan with one chopped shalot, some grated nutmeg, minionette pepper, and half a pint of good gravy; simmer the whole on the stove-fire till reduced to half, then strain it with pressure through a tammy into another small stewpan, containing four tablespoonsful of fried bread-crumbs of a light-brown color, and some chopped parsley; and a little essence of chicken and the juice of half a lemon; stir the sauce till it boils, and serve.

This kind of sauce is appropriate for all small birds, such as wheatears, ortolans, ruffs and reeves, &c., &c.

82. BROWN GRAVY FOR ROAST VEAL.

PLACE four ounces of fresh butter in a stewpan and knead it with a good tablespoonful of flour; add a ladleful of good brown gravy, some essence of mushrooms or mushroom catsup, a little grated nutmeg, and minionette pepper; stir the sauce on the stove, and keep it gently boiling for ten minutes. If it becomes too thick add a little more gravy, so as to keep it of the same consistency as any other sauce; finish with a little lemon-juice.

If there is no gravy or essence of mushrooms at hand, use, in their stead, a ladleful of water, a piece of glaze, some mushroom catsup, and a little Indian soy; these will answer nearly the same purpose.

83. CREAM SAUCE FOR ROAST NECK OF VEAL.

KNEAD four ounces of fresh butter with two ounces of sifted flour; add half a pint of good cream and a small ladleful of white *consommé*, a little nutmeg and minionette pepper, some essence of mushrooms, and a garnished parsley-fagot; stir the sauce till it boils, and keep it gently boiling for twenty minutes; then extract the onion and fagot, and pass the sauce through a tammy into a *bain-marie* for use.

84. EGG SAUCE.

BOIL some eggs hard; when cold, break and pick off their shells, and then cut them up into square dicelike pieces, and put them into some good melted butter, with a little pepper and salt; stir gently on the fire till the sauce is hot, and then serve.

85. EGG SAUCE, ANOTHER METHOD.

BOIL four eggs hard, take the yelks out, and cut the whites into small shreds and put them into a stewpan; place a wire sieve over a clean plate, and rub the yelks through it on to the plate, keeping the vermicellilike substance which the operation will produce as whole as possible; pour some good butter sauce on to the shred whites of eggs, adding thereto a teaspoonful of English mustard, a little pepper and salt, and lemon-juice; just before serving, warm the sauce, and mix in lightly the vermicellied yelks of eggs, and serve.

86. SAUCE MOUTARDE, OR MUSTARD SAUCE.

INTO about half a pint of good butter sauce, mix two tablespoonsful of prepared English mustard and one of French ditto; make the sauce hot, and serve.

This sauce is seldom used for any other dish than broiled herrings.

87. PLAIN CURRY SAUCE.

PUT two ounces of fresh butter into a stewpan, together with rather more than an ounce of flour and a good tablespoonful of curry-paste or powder; knead these well together, then add a little shred carrot, celery, and onions; moisten with about a pint of good strong *consommé*; stir the sauce on the fire until it boils, and, after having kept it boiling for about twenty minutes, pass it through the tammy, as for a *purée*; then remove the sauce into a *bain-marie* or stewpan, to be used when required.

This economical method of making curry sauce should only be resorted to in cases of emergency or necessity, otherwise it is desirable to follow the directions contained in No. 47.

88. WASTREFISH SAUCE, FOR BOILED FRESH-WATER FISH.

CUT into small shreds the rind of an orange, the red part of a carrot, a handful of parsley-stalks, and an equal proportion of parsley-roots; blanch these, and, having drained them on a sieve or napkin, place them in a small stewpan, containing about half a pint of Dutch sauce, with the addition of two spoonsful of reduced essence of fish, a little cayenne, and lemon-juice; stir the sauce on the fire without allowing it to boil, and serve it with perch, or, indeed, with any other sort of plain boiled fresh-water fish, for which purpose the ingredients it contains render it peculiarly fitted.

89. FLEMISH SAUCE.

KNEAD two ounces of fresh butter with an equal quantity of flour, to which add an onion, some sprigs of parsley, a little shred carrot, and a sprig of thyme, a blade of mace, and a little minionette pepper; moisten with half a pint of cream and the same proportion of good *consommé*. Stir the sauce on the fire until it boils, and, after having kept it boiling for twenty minutes, pass it through the tammy into a *bain-marie*, containing the red part of a carrot, some parsley-stalks and roots, and some horse-radish, the whole of which should be previously cut into small diamonds and blanched; finish by mixing in a small spoonful of tarragon-vinegar and three or four green Indian gherkins cut into shreds; make the sauce hot, and serve.

90. CAPER SAUCE, FOR FISH.

KNEAD two ounces of fresh butter with one ounce of flour, a very little grated nutmeg, and minionette pepper; to these add a table-spoonful of capers, a piece of glaze, and a little essence of anchovies; moisten with about half a pint of good *consommé;* stir the sauce on the fire until it begins to simmer, then take it off; add a little lemon-juice, and serve.

This kind of sauce is peculiarly adapted for broiled salmon.

91. CAPER SAUCE, FOR BOILED MUTTON.

To about half a pint of good butter sauce, add a tablespoonful of capers, with a little pepper and salt.

92. CREAM SAUCE, OR BECHAMEL, FOR SALT-FISH.

PLACE four ounces of sifted flour in a stewpan, with an equal quan-tity of fresh butter; knead them together well with a wooden spoon; add an onion, a carrot, a head of celery—the whole cut up thin—some branches of parsley, a sprig of thyme, and half a bay-leaf, two cloves, a blade of mace, and a few peppercorns; moisten with about a pint of good white *consommé* and half a pint of cream, adding a little salt; stir the sauce on the fire until it boils; let it continue to boil for twenty minutes, stirring it the whole time; then pass it through a tammy into a *bain-marie*, to be kept for use.

93. BEURRE NOIR, OR BLACK BUTTER SHARP SAUCE.

PLACE about six ounces of good fresh butter in a small stewpan, put it on the fire to melt, and then allow it to fritter, so as to acquire a light brown color; then take it off the stove, skim it, and quickly pass it through a sieve, into a stewpan containing four tablespoonsful of French vinegar, a dessert-spoonful of chopped capers, ditto Har-vey's sauce, ditto mushroom catsup, and a piece of glaze the size of a walnut, and sufficient pepper and salt to season the sauce; boil the whole well together, and use it for boiled skate or broiled mackerel. With whatever kind of fish this sauce is served, fried parsley forms an indispensable adjunct.

93A. ORLEANS SAUCE.

TAKE the red part of a boiled carrot, the fillets of six washed anchovies, the white of two eggs boiled hard, and six green gherkins; cut these into small square dicelike shapes, and place them in a small *bain-marie*, add half a pint of *Poivrade* sauce, boil together gently for five minutes, and use this sauce for braized meats.

93B. DEVIL'S SAUCE.

CHOP three shalots fine, and place them in a small stewpan, with two tablespoonfuls of French vinegar, and a pinch of cayenne pepper; boil these together for three minutes; then add half a pint of thin strong *Espagnole* sauce, and a tablespoonful of tomata sauce; boil again, and finish by stirring in a small pat of anchovy butter (No. 179). This sauce is most appropriate for broiled meats.

COLD SAUCES.

COMPRISING

Cambridge Sauce.	*Mayonnaise* Sauce of savory jelly.
Remoulade do.	*Provençale* Sauce.
Tartar do.	Cold *Poivrade* do.
Mayonnaise do.	Wild Boar's Head do.
Green do. do.	Brawn do.
Red, or Coral do. do.	

94. CAMBRIDGE SAUCE.

TAKE the yelks of six eggs boiled hard, the fillets of four anchovies, cleaned, and put them into a mortar, with a tablespoonful of French capers, some tarragon, chervil, chives, and a little burnet, blanched; pound these well together with a teaspoonful of English mustard, the same quantity of French, and some pepper and salt; moisten with good salad-oil, and a little tarragon-vinegar, taking care that the sauce be kept rather thick. Having sufficiently moistened the sauce, take it out of the mortar into the tammy placed over a dish for that purpose, and proceed to rub the sauce through the tammy in the same manner as a *purée;* pass the back part of a knife along the under part of the tammy, in order to detach therefrom any adhesive particles; take the sauce up into a small basin, to be kept on the ice till wanted for use, and just before sending it to table add some chopped parsley. Observe that this sauce be kept about the same degree of thickness as reduced *Velouté* sauce; salt must be used in moderation, owing to the presence of anchovies in the composition.

95. REMOULADE SAUCE.

BLANCH some tarragon, chervil, chives, burnet, and parsley; extract the water and pound these herbs together, with four yelks of hard eggs; moisten with a gill of salad-oil, and a tablespoonful of tarragon-vinegar, and season with pepper and salt. Pass the sauce through a tammy as for a *purée*, and then take it up into a small basin; keep it on the ice till it is required for use.

96. TARTAR SAUCE.

PLACE a round-bottomed basin in a deep sauta-pan containing some pounded ice, put two raw yelks of eggs into the basin with a little pepper and salt, and with a wooden spoon proceed, with the back part of the bowl, to work the yelk of eggs, dropping in, at intervals, very small quantities of salad-oil, and a little tarragon-vinegar, until a sufficient quantity of sauce is produced; bearing in mind, that the relative quantity of oil to be used in proportion to the vinegar is as five to one. When the sauce is finished, add some chopped tarragon and chervil, and half a shalot.

In making this sauce, should it decompose through inattention, it may instantly be restored to its proper consistency by mixing in it a good spoonful of cold white sauce.

97. MAYONNAISE SAUCE.

PLACE two raw yelks of eggs in a round-bottomed basin, and set this in a deep sauta-pan containing some pounded ice; add a little pepper and salt to the yelks, and proceed to work them quickly with the back part of the bowl of a wooden spoon, moistening at intervals with salad-oil and French vinegar, which must, however, be sparingly used at first, and gradually increased as you proceed, until, by this means, the quantity of sauce desired is produced; add a little lemon-juice to make the sauce white. Previous to using the sauce, add a little aspic-jelly (No. 1218), which must be just barely melted before incorporating it with the *Mayonnaise*, as in the case of its being made warm it might have the effect of turning and decomposing the sauce.

98. GREEN MAYONNAISE SAUCE.

BLANCH some tarragon, chervil, a little burnet, and some parsley; extract the water therefrom; pass the *Ravigotte* thus produced through a sieve, and proceed to incorporate it with some *Mayonnaise*, prepared according to the foregoing instructions.

This sauce is usually colored with spinach-green (No. 286).

99. RED OR CORAL MAYONNAISE SAUCE.

POUND some lobster coral, pass it through a sieve, and mix it in with some *Mayonnaise* sauce; add a little cayenne pepper and a spoonful of mustard.

This sauce should be used exclusively for lobster and fish salads.

100. MAYONNAISE SAUCE OF SAVORY JELLY.

SET a round-bottomed basin in some pounded ice, place therein half a pint of light-colored aspic-jelly, a little pepper and salt, a gravy-spoonful of salad-oil, and a tablespoonful of tarragon-vinegar; whip this mixture quickly with a whisk, adding, from time to time, some oil and vinegar in the same proportions as heretofore directed; by whipping briskly, you will find the sauce assume a white, smooth appearance; add a little lemon-juice, to whiten it, and some chopped tarragon and chervil; or, if preferred, this sauce may be used without the latter. This kind of *Mayonnaise* sauce is considered as being the most delicate, and is particularly adapted for aspics of fillets of fowls, or any sort of white fish.

This sauce may also be colored, by using for that purpose either some pounded lobster coral, or extract of spinach (No. 286).

101. PROVENCALE SAUCE.

POUND four yelks of hard-boiled eggs, together with four anchovies, a spoonful of capers, some tarragon, chervil, burnet, parsley, a clove of garlic, pepper and salt, a gill of salad-oil, and a tablespoonful of tarragon-vinegar; rub the whole through a tammy with a wooden spoon as for a *purée:* add a little lemon-juice and serve.

This kind of sauce is well adapted to be served with broiled eels or fowls, and more especially with fish salads; in which case, a spoonful of chopped parsley should be added.

102. COLD POIVRADE SAUCE.

PUT a good spoonful of brown sauce into a round-bottomed basin, add thereto four tablespoonsful of salad-oil, one of Chili vinegar, a little tarragon-vinegar, pepper, and salt; work the whole well together with a whisk, then add a tablespoonful of chopped parsley and a little shalot.

This sauce is good with plain boiled artichokes, and also for brawn, by adding a little sugar for the brawn.

103. BOAR'S HEAD SAUCE.

GRATE a stick of horse-radish, and place it in a basin with four ounces of red currant-jelly, a spoonful of mixed mustard, the grated rind of an orange and lemon, together with the juice of both; two ounces of pounded sugar, a tablespoonful of French vinegar, and two tablespoonsful of salad-oil; mix these ingredients thoroughly together, and serve.

104. ANOTHER METHOD FOR MAKING BOAR'S HEAD SAUCE.

PARE the rind off two Seville oranges, free from any of the white pith, cut it into fine shreds, parboil this, and drain it on a sieve; then put it into a small stewpan containing the juice of the two oranges, together with one pound of red currant jelly, half a pint of port wine, and half a teaspoonful of cinnamon powder; simmer the whole together in a stewpan, and serve when cold.

105. BRAWN SAUCE.

MIX together one tablespoonful of moist sugar, two of French vinegar, three of salad-oil, a teaspoonful of mixed mustard, some pepper and salt, and serve.

PUREES OF VEGETABLES FOR GARNISHING,*

COMPRISING

Purée of Peas.	*Purée* of Artichokes.
„ Windsor Beans.	„ Asparagus.
„ Carrots.	„ Onions *a la Soubise.*
„ Turnips.	„ Tomatas.
„ Celery.	„ Truffles.
„ Cauliflowers.	„ Mushrooms.
„ Spinach.	„ Brussels Sprouts.
„ Sorrel.	„ Cucumbers.
„ Endive.	„ French Beans.
„ Chestnuts.	„ Jerusalem Artichokes.
„ Potatoes.	„ Seakale.

106. PUREE OF PEAS.

BOIL a quart of marrowfat, or Prussian-blue peas, in the usual manner, with some mint, a few green onions, and a handful of parsley; strain off the water, and pound the whole thoroughly in a mortar; then take this up into a stewpan, and after adding a little sugar, a gravy-spoonful of good white sauce, make it hot, and pass it through a tammy as usual; put the *purée* into a small stewpan, in which it must be warmed before using it: mix in a small piece of glaze, and a pat of fresh butter.

107. PUREE OF WINDSOR BEANS.

PROCURE a quart of young Windsor beans, and boil them with a handful of parsley, a few green onions, and a little winter savory; drain them and pound the whole together in a mortar: take them up into a stewpan, add a gravy-spoonful of good white sauce, and make the *purée* warm. Rub it through the tammy with a wooden spoon; then take it up into a stewpan, and just before using it make it sufficiently hot; mix in a small piece of glaze, a pat of butter, a little sugar, and some spinach-green (No. 285).

108. PUREE OF YOUNG CARROTS.

CLEAN a bunch of young carrots, slice them up thin, wash and drain them in a sieve; then place them in a stewpan, with two ounces of fresh butter, a little salt, grated nutmeg, and sugar; sweat them on a slow fire, turning them over now and then. When the carrots begin to get colored, moisten with a ladleful of good broth, and set them on the fire; allow them to boil down gently to a glaze, then pound them in the mortar, and rub them through the tammy into a *purée*; put this *purée* into a small stewpan, and when required for use, add a spoonful of thick *Allemande* sauce, a pat of fresh butter, and a pinch of sugar.

109. PUREE OF TURNIPS A LA CREME.

PEEL and wash a dozen good turnips, cut them into small square

* All the *purées* here described being intended for *entrées*, should be kept firm, that they may stand up well when placed in the centre of an *entrée*.

pieces, or slices; first blanch, and then drain them on a napkin, and afterward place them in a stewpan with two ounces of fresh butter, a little sugar and salt; let them stew gently on a slow fire to extract the moisture, turning them occasionally, and taking care that they do not become at all colored. When the turnips are nearly melted, add a small ladleful of *Velouté* or *Béchamel* sauce; stir the *purée* with a wooden spoon on the fire, in order to reduce it to the consistency of a soft paste; then add half a pint of double cream; reduce the *purée* still further, then rub it through a tammy, next remove it into a small stewpan, and previously to using it, make it sufficiently hot, mixing in a pat of fresh butter, and serve.

110. PUREE OF CELERY.

CUT the white part of six or eight heads of celery into half-inch lengths, boil these in water for five minutes, plunge them in fresh water, and drain the celery in a napkin; then place them in a stew-pan with two ounces of butter, some white broth, a little sugar, and grated nutmeg; cover the celery thus prepared with a round of buttered paper, place the lid on the stewpan, and set it on a slow fire to extract the moisture and melt the celery, taking care that in the course of process it does not color: when the celery is melted or softened, moisten with a ladleful of white sauce, and half a pint of cream; reduce quickly on the fire, stirring the *purée* the whole time with a wooden spoon. As soon as the *purée* is reduced to its proper consistency, proceed immediately to rub it through the tammy, after which take it up into a small stewpan; previously to using it, make the *purée* hot, and mix with it a little double cream and a pinch of pounded sugar.

111. PUREE OF CAULIFLOWERS.

CUT two or more heads of white fresh cauliflowers into small pieces, and after trimming these, boil them in some boiling water with a little salt, minionette pepper, and a pat of butter; when done drain them on a sieve, and afterward place them in a deep sauta-pan, with a large gravy-spoonful of reduced *Allemande*, or white sauce; stir the *purée* on the fire with a wooden spoon, and keep it boiling until reduced to the consistency of a soft paste. Then instantly rub it through a tammy, remove the *purée* into a small stewpan, and previously to using it make it hot, and mix in a little grated nutmeg, a pinch of sugar, and a little double cream to whiten it and make it more delicate.

112. PUREE OF SPINACH.

PICK, wash, and boil a small dish of spinach, refresh it in cold water, squeeze it thoroughly free from water, examine it carefully by separating it with the point of a knife on the chopping-board, so as to remove any straws, &c., left in it; next pound it well in the mortar, and then take it up in a deep sauta-pan, add a small ladleful of good white sauce, a little grated nutmeg, salt, and a pinch of sugar; reduce the *purée* over a brisk fire to preserve its color; rub it through a tammy, and remove it into a small stewpan; just before using it make it warm, and add two pats of fresh butter and a small piece of glaze.

113. PUREE OF SORREL.

PICK, and well wash the sorrel in several waters; drain off the water, and place the sorrel in a large stewpan on the fire, stirring it the whole time with a wooden spoon; as soon as the sorrel is melted, and has boiled a few minutes, turn it out on to a large hair-sieve, there to remain until the water has run off. Next, cut two large onions into thin slices, place these in a stewpan, with two ounces of fresh butter, and put them to fry of a light color on the stove-fire; after which, add a good tablespoonful of flour, some grated nutmeg, a tea-spoonful of sugar, some minionette pepper, and salt; moisten with a gravy-spoonful of sauce, either white or brown, then add the sorrel, prepared as above directed, and reduce the *purée* over a brisk fire, stirring it the whole time with a wooden spoon; when the sorrel is sufficiently reduced, rub it instantly through a tammy, and place it in a small stewpan. Previously to using the *purée*, make it hot; add a pat of butter and a piece of glaze.

114. PUREE OF ENDIVE.

TRIM off all the outside leaves of a dozen full white-heart endives; wash them thoroughly, and carefully remove all insects, &c.; throw the endives into a stewpan of boiling water, and, after allowing them to remain boiling for the space of twenty minutes, immerse them in cold water. When thus cool, squeeze each endive separately, entirely extracting the water; then cut off the root end from each endive, and after first chopping the leafy portion, place them in a stewpan with two ounces of fresh butter, nutmeg, sugar, and salt; stir the whole over a stove-fire with a wooden spoon for five minutes, moisten with a ladleful of white broth, then cover with a round of buttered paper, place the lid on the stewpan, and set it on a slow fire to continue very gently simmering for half an hour; next add a small ladleful of white sauce and half a pint of cream, and reduce the *purée* quickly on a brisk fire; as soon as it is reduced to its proper consistency, instantly remove it into a small stewpan for use.

This kind of *purée* is usually rubbed through a coarse hair-sieve in preference to a tammy.

115. PUREE OF CHESTNUTS.

SLIT the husks of fifty chestnuts, and place them in a stewpan with a piece of butter; put the lid on the stewpan, and set it on a slow fire, taking care, now and then, to toss up the chestnuts, so that they may get an equal degree of heat; in about twenty minutes the husks will easily peel off, and should then be removed. Put the chestnuts into a clean stewpan with a ladleful of good *consommè*, and place the lid thereon; set them to simmer gently on the corner of the stove; when they are done, pound them in a mortar, take them up into a deep sauta-pan, and a little sugar, nutmeg, and half a pint of cream; reduce the *purée*, and rub it through a tammy on to a dish; remove it into a small stewpan; and just before using it, make it hot, mix in a small pat of butter and a piece of glaze.

116. PUREE OF POTATOES.

PEEL and wash eight potatoes, cut them into slices, and place them in a stewpan with two ounces of butter, some minionette pepper,

salt, and a little nutmeg; moisten with a pint of white broth, put
the lid on the stewpan, and set it to boil on the fire.   By the time
the broth is reduced, the potatoes will be done; then add half a pint
of cream, and with a wooden spoon reduce the *purée* on the fire to
the usual consistency of mashed potatoes; rub the *purée* through the
tammy on to a dish, and then remove it into a small stewpan; previously to using it, add a pat of butter.

117. PUREE OF ARTICHOKES.

FIRST, pick off the outer leaves of six young full-grown artichokes;
then turn, or pare off with a knife, the whole of the outer green part
of the bottom of the artichokes, so as to leave it white; when this is
finished, rub each artichoke thus turned with a piece of lemon, and
put them directly into a pan of water with a little vinegar in it.
Then place the artichokes in a stewpan with boiling water, a little
butter, lemon-juice, salt, and minionette pepper; after three-quarters
of an hour's gentle boiling, take the artichokes up, extract the fibrous
interior from each, and place them in a deep sauta-pan with a ladleful
of white sauce, half a pint of cream, nutmeg, a little salt, and a tea-
spoonful of sugar; reduce the *purée* quickly over a brisk fire, stirring
it the whole time with a wooden spoon, and then rub it through a
tammy; after which remove it into a small stewpan; finish with a
pat of butter, and a small piece of glaze.

118. PUREE OF ASPARAGUS.

BREAK off the tender portions of a bundle of sprue asparagus, wash
them in a large pan, with a good handful of green onions and double
that quantity of picked parsley; set these on the fire to boil in an
untinned pan half full of boiling water, and throw in a spoonful of
salt; as soon as the asparagus are done, drain them in a sieve, and
remove all the water.   Put the asparagus, parsley, and green onions,
altogether into a deep sauta-pan, with a small ladleful of white sauce,
the crumb of a French roll (that has previously been soaked in
water, and afterward pressed in a napkin to remove the moisture),
some grated nutmeg, a little salt, and a teaspoonful of sugar; ·reduce
the *purée* quickly on the fire, rub it through a tammy on to a dish, and
from thence remove it into a small stewpan, and keep it in the cool
until wanted for use.   Finish by adding a pat of fresh butter, a piece
of glaze, and some spinach-green, if required, to give it a bright-
green color.

119. PUREE OF ONIONS A LA SOUBISE.

PEEL and cut into slices eight large onions, parboil them in water
for five minutes, drain them on a sieve, immerse them in cold water,
and press them in a napkin to extract the water; place them in a
stewpan with two ounces of butter, nutmeg, minionette pepper, a
little salt, and a spoonful of white broth; put a round of buttered
paper on them, and cover the stewpan with its lid; and set it on a
very slow fire to simmer gently for half an hour.   Then turn the
onions out into a deep sauta-pan, moisten with a small ladleful of
good white sauce, and half a pint of cream, reduce the *purée* quickly
on a sharp fire, rub it through a tammy on to a dish, and take it up
into a small stewpan.   Just before using it, add a pinch of sugar.

When this *purée* is required to be made very firm and thick, it is necessary to increase the quantity of onions used for the purpose, and to add a couple of hot mealy potatoes.

120. PUREE OF TOMATAS.

CUT four ounces of raw ham into small pieces, and place them in a stewpan with two shalots, a bay-leaf, a sprig of thyme, two cloves, a blade of mace, and a few peppercorns; add a small piece of butter, and fry these ingredients on the fire of a light color; to this add either a dozen squeezed ripe tomatas, or a sufficient quantity of preserve of tomatas, and a small ladleful of *Velouté* sauce; reduce the *purée* thus prepared on a quick fire; then rub it through a tammy, and place it in a small stewpan for use. Finish by adding a little glaze and a small piece of fresh butter, just before sending to table.

121. PUREE OF TRUFFLES.

FIRST peel and then pound ten ounces of truffles; put them into a stewpan with a pat of butter, half a bay-leaf, a sprig of thyme, some grated nutmeg, and a very small clove of garlic; set these on the stove to simmer for a few minutes, then add a small ladleful of brown sauce and a small piece of glaze; reduce the *purée* quickly, and rub it through the tammy on to a dish; remove it from thence into a small *bain-marie* for use.

Omit the garlic, should its flavor be objectionable.

122. PUREE OF MUSHROOMS.

CLEAN a pottle of white button mushrooms, chop them up, adding meanwhile the juice of half a lemon to prevent them from turning black; when chopped fine, place them in a deep sauta-pan with a pat of butter, and with a wooden spoon stir them on the fire for five minutes; moisten with a ladleful of good white sauce, reduce the *puree* quickly, and then add half a pint of double cream; stir the *purée* on the fire for five minutes longer, rub it through a tammy on to a dish, and from thence remove it into a small stewpan for use.

123. PUREE OF BRUSSELS SPROUTS.

BOIL a good plateful of Brussels sprouts, place them in a deep sauta-pan with a ladleful of good white sauce, nutmeg, minionette pepper, a little salt, and a pinch of sugar; reduce the whole on a brisk fire, stirring all the time with a wooden spoon; rub the *purée* through a tammy in the usual manner, and afterward put it into a small stewpan; previously to using the *purée*, add a little spinach-green, a pat of butter, and a piece of glaze.

124. PUREE OF CUCUMBERS.

MINCE two ounces of lean ham, place it in a small stewpan with a pat of butter, a little nutmeg, and a few peppercorns; to these add four cucumbers, trimmed and cut up for the purpose; set the stewpan on a slow fire, there to simmer for twenty minutes, at the expiration of which time add a small ladleful of white sauce; reduce the *purée* quickly on a brisk stove, and when it assumes the appearance of a soft paste, pour in half a pint of good sweet double cream and a teaspoonful of sugar; reduce the *purée* for five minutes longer on the fire, and then rub it through the tammy in the usual manner, and take it up into a small stewpan for use.

125. PUREE OF FRENCH BEANS.

SHRED a good plateful of French beans, boil them quickly of a green color, taking care to boil with them a handful of picked parsley and a few green onions; when they are done, drain the whole on a sieve, and afterward place them in a deep santa-pan with a gravy-spoonful of good white sauce, a piece of glaze, and a little sugar; reduce the *purée* on the fire, and then rub it through a tammy, take it up into a small stewpan, and just before using it mix in a small pat of butter and a little spinach-green.

126. PUREE OF JERUSALEM ARTICHOKES.

THIS *purée* is made exactly in the same manner as the *purée* of potatoes, merely substituting Jerusalem artichokes for potatoes.

127. PUREE OF SEAKALE.

BOIL a punnet of good white seakale, and drain it on a napkin; cut it into half-inch lengths, and place it in a stewpan with two ounces of fresh butter, some minionette pepper, nutmeg, salt, a little sugar, and some white broth; place thereon a round of buttered paper, and cover the stewpan with its lid; set it on a moderate fire to simmer for twenty minutes, then add a small ladleful of good white sauce; reduce the *purée* quickly to the condition of a soft paste, and then add half a pint of cream; after reducing it five minutes longer, rub the *purée* through the tammy, and take it up into a small stewpan for use.

VEGETABLES FOR GARNISHING,

COMPRISING

Garnish of Truffles in Glaze.	Garnish of Asparagus-heads.
„ *à la Parisienne.*	„ Asparagus Peas.
„ in *Suprême.*	„ Button Onions, for *matelotte.*
„ of whole Truffles.	„ White Button Onions.
„ Mushrooms *à l'Allemande.*	„ Windsor Beans.
„ do. in *Espagnole.*	„ French Beans.
„ of young Carrots.	„ Artichoke Bottoms.
„ Carrots cut in fancy shapes.	„ Glazed Onions.
„ Turnips.	„ Brocoli, or Cauliflower.
„ Carrots and Turnips *à la Ni-vernaise.*	„ Brussels Sprouts.
„ Cucumbers in scollops.	„ Chestnuts for roast Turkey.
„ Cucumbers *farcis.*	„ Jerusalem Artichokes.
„ Celery *à la crème.*	„ Cloves of Garlic.
„ Celery *à l'Espagnole.*	„ White Haricot-Beans.
„ Young Carrots *à la Flamande.*	„ Red Haricot-Beans.
„ White *Macédoine* of vegetables.	„ Braized Cabbage Lettuces.
„ Brown do.	„ Braized Cabbages.
„ Green Peas.	„ Stewed Red Cabbages.
„ Stewed Peas.	„ Sauërkraut.
	„ Sauërkraut *à la Française.*

128. GARNISH OF TRUFFLES IN GLAZE.

CUT about one pound of truffles in various fancy shapes, such as small round balls, olives, or like quarters of orange, small pillars, and circular scollops; place them in a small stewpan, with a little fresh butter, a pinch of salt, and a piece of glaze; put on the lid of the stewpan, and set it on a slow fire to simmer for five or ten minutes; toss the truffles thus prepared in their glaze, and use them to garnish the centre of an *entrée*, or for any other appropriate purpose.

129. GARNISH OF TRUFFLES A LA PARISIENNE.

PREPARE the truffles as directed in the foregoing case, and, having boiled them down in their glaze, add a good ragout-spoonful of Parisian sauce (No. 40).

130. GARNISH OF TRUFFLES WITH SUPREME SAUCE.

PREPARE the truffles in fancy shapes, simmer them with a small quantity of butter and glaze, and boil them down in their glaze; then add a spoonful of *Suprême* sauce. This garnish may be served with all *entrées*, fillets of poultry, or game.

131. GARNISH OF WHOLE TRUFFLES.

BRUSH and clean any quantity required of fine fresh truffles, boil them in a wine *mirepoix* (for making which see No. 236)—one hour's gentle boiling will suffice; just before using them, take the truffles out of the *mirepoix*, glaze them, and dispose them round or about the *entrée* or remove in a circle or in groups.

132. GARNISH OF MUSHROOMS IN ALLEMANDE SAUCE.

CLEAN and turn a pottle of mushrooms, put them into a small stewpan with an ounce of butter, a little salt, the juice of a lemon, and about two tablespoonsful of water; boil them quickly on the fire for five minutes, drain the mushrooms, and put them into a *bain-marie* containing a large ragout-spoonful of *Allemande* sauce; reduce the liquor the mushrooms were boiled in, and add it to the mushrooms. This garnish is proper for all white *entrées*, and especially for *entrées* of game or fowl *à la Dauphine* or *à la Villeroi*.

133. GARNISH OF MUSHROOMS IN ESPAGNOLE SAUCE.

PREPARE the mushrooms as directed in the foregoing recipe, drain them on a napkin, and place them in a stewpan or *bain-marie*, with sufficient finished *Espagnole* sauce, according to the quantity required, adding the essence of the mushrooms, cleared from the butter, and reduced. This sauce is appropriate for every kind of brown *entrée*.

134. GARNISH OF YOUNG CARROTS.

TURN a bunch of young carrots, keeping them in their own shape, as far as may be consistent with uniformity of size; boil them in water for three minutes, drain them on a sieve, place them in a stewpan with an ounce of sugar, a pat of butter and a little salt; moisten

---

* This is the foundation of all garnishes of truffles and mushrooms; an infinite variety may be made by adding to the truffles prepared as above some special sauce, the addition of which will then give its name to the garnish.

with a pint of broth or *consommé*, and set them to boil on the stove-fire; when they are done, boil them down quickly to a glaze, roll the carrots in this glaze, and use them to garnish the intended dish.

135. GARNISH OF CARROTS IN OLIVES, ETC.

SCRAPE and wash four good carrots, cut the red part, either with a small root-knife, vegetable scoop, or cutter, into various fancy shapes, as olives, small round balls, pillars, half-moons, diamonds, or fluted shapes; parboil, drain, and prepare them as directed above; finish them in the same manner, and, having run them down in ther own glaze, either use them as they are, or else add a ragout-spoonful of *Allemande, Béchamel, Suprême,* or, indeed, any other kind of sauce that may be appropriate for the dish they are meant to garnish.

136. GARNISH OF TURNIPS.

PEEL four turnips, cut or turn them into fancy shapes, as directed in the preceding article, boil them for three minutes, drain them on a napkin, place them in a stewpan, with a little sugar, salt, and a small pat of butter; moisten with some white broth, put them on the stove, and, when they are nearly done, boil them down quickly in their glaze, without allowing them to acquire much color. These turnips may be used for a garnish, merely rolled in their own glaze, or a spoonful of either *Allemande, Béchamel, Suprême,* or finished *Espagnole* sauce may be added.

137. GARNISH OF CARROTS AND TURNIPS A LA NIVERNAISE.

CUT or turn the red part of three carrots into the shape of small olives or round balls, place these in a small sauta-pan, with a little clarified butter and a teaspoonful of pounded sugar; fry them on the stove-fire, so as to give them a light color, then place them on a sieve to drain off the butter, and put them into a small stewpan, with a piece of fresh butter, a little sugar, and salt; moisten them with some *consommé,* and set them to boil gradually until nearly done, when they must boil rapidly to glaze. Having thus disposed of the carrots, prepare an equal quantity of turnips, cut in a similar shape, and boil them down to a glaze, similarly to the carrots, and when both are done, mix them together, and use them for *entrées* of braized mutton, beef, or any sort of cutlets.

138. GARNISH OF CUCUMBERS IN SCOLLOPS.

CUT three cucumbers into inch lengths; divide each piece, length-wise, into two or more pieces, according to the size of the cucumber, so that, when trimmed, they should be rather larger in size than a shilling; in trimming them, first scoop out the seedy part with a small root-knife, then peel off the green rind and pare away the angles slightly, so as to give them a somewhat rounded appearance. Next, place them in a basin, with two spoonsful of French vinegar and one of salt, and allow them to remain in this pickle, or *marinade,* for about a couple of hours, then drain them on a sieve, and place them in a stewpan, with a pat of butter, a lump of sugar, and a ragout-spoonful of white *consommé ;* set them on a slow fire to sim-mer gently for half an hour, when they will be nearly done; boil them down quickly to a glaze, and keep them separately until they are wanted for immediate use; then set them on the fire to boil, in order to absorb any moisture they may have thrown out, previously to adding a ragout-spoonful of *Allemande, Béchamel, Suprême,* or brown sauce, as the case may require.

139. GARNISH OF CUCUMBERS FARCIS.

CUT three or more cucumbers into two-inch lengths, with a vegetable cutter, scoop out the seeds and peel off the green rind, pare away the sharp angles at the ends, and then parboil them in water for three minutes, plunge them in cold water, and put them to drain on a napkin; then fill up the cavities with some *quenelle* force-meat of fowls. Next garnish the bottom of a deep sauta-pan with some thin layers of fat bacon; place therein the cucumbers thus prepared, and in the centre put a fagot of parsley and green onions; cover the whole with layers of fat bacon, and moisten with some white *consommé* of chicken. Let them simmer very gently on a slow fire for about an hour, and just before the cucumbers are wanted for use, drain them on a napkin, and then put them into another sauta-pan with their own liquor, freed from all grease, and afterward reduced to a demi-glaze; just roll the cucumbers lightly in this glaze over a sharp fire, so as to cause the glaze to adhere to them, and thus give them a bright appearance.

This kind of garnish of cucumbers is frequently used for whole *entrées* and removes, such as larded *entrées* of sweetbreads,*fricandeaux*, fillet of beef, *carbonades*, fowls, &c., &c.

140. GARNISH OF CELERY A LA CRÈME.

TRIM and well wash six heads of full-sized white celery, cut them into half-inch lengths, boil these in water for five minutes, drain them on a sieve, and immerse them in cold water; then place them on a napkin. Next, put the celery in a stewpan with a lump of sugar, a pat of butter, a little salt, and grated nutmeg; moisten with a ladleful of white *consommé*, and set it to boil gently on a stove-fire for about an hour; as soon as the celery is well done, boil it down in its glaze, and then add a spoonful of good reduced *Béchamel* sauce.

When this garnish is required as a sauce for fowls, &c., it will be necessary to increase the quantity of *Béchamel* sauce, and also to add a little cream.

141. GARNISH OF CELERY A L'ESPAGNOLE.

PREPARE the celery as directed in the foregoing article, and when it is thoroughly done, add a ragout-spoonful of finished *Espagnole* sauce and a small piece of glaze.

142. GARNISH OF YOUNG CARROTS A LA FLAMANDE.

TURN a bunch of young carrots into the shape of small pears, boil them in water for three minutes, drain them on a napkin, and then place them in a stewpan with a pat of butter, one ounce of sugar, a little salt, and grated nutmeg; moisten with a ladleful of *consommé*, and set them to boil gently on a stove-fire for half an hour; as soon as they are done, boil them down to a glaze, and then add a ragout-spoonful of good *Allemande* sauce, and a spoonful of blanched parsley leaves. This kind of garnish is very appropriate for braized beef, lamb, and hams.

143. WHITE MACEDOINE OF VEGETABLES.

PREPARE some carrots and turnips in fancy shapes of small size, let each sort be separately boiled down to a glaze in a little broth, with the addition of a little sugar and salt, and a very small piece of butter; when done, put the whole together in a small sauta-pan; to these add a cucumber cut up and prepared for the purpose in scollops, a spoonful of boiled green peas, a spoonful of French beans cut in the shape of diamonds, a spoonful of asparagus heads boiled green, and also some very small flowrets of boiled cauliflower; add a gravy-spoonful of *Allemande*, *Béchamel*, or *Suprême* sauce, a little nutmeg and sugar; shake the whole lightly together over the stove-fire, and use this garnish for the *entrée* intended.

144. GARNISH OF BROWN MACEDOINE.

PREPARE the vegetables for the *Macédoine* according to the directions given in the preceding recipe; when nearly ready, use some finished *Espagnole* sauce, instead of the other sauces there mentioned.

145. GARNISH OF GREEN PEAS.

BOIL about a pint of young peas, drain them, and place them in a sauta-pan, then add a spoonful of *Béchamel* sauce, a pinch of sugar, a little chopped and blanched mint, some nutmeg, a pat of butter, and a piece of glaze; shake the whole up well together over the fire, and serve them in the centre of an *entrée*.

146. GARNISH OF STEWED PEAS.

PUT a quart of young peas into a stewpan with four ounces of fresh butter, on these pour a quart of cold spring water, and commence kneading the peas and butter together, with the hand, in the water; as soon as all the butter adheres to the peas, pour the water off, and then add a dessert-spoonful of sugar, a little salt, an onion, and a fagot of parsley, and green onions; set the peas to stew on a moderate fire; when they are done, set them on a brisk fire to boil quickly, in order that they may, by this means, absorb all their moisture; then add a spoonful of *Béchamel* sauce, with a pat of butter, and dish them up in the centre of an *entrée*.

147. GARNISH OF ASPARAGUS HEADS.

TRIM and cut the heads of as many asparagus as may be required, boil them green, and drain them on a napkin, then place them in a sauta-pan with a spoonful of *Allemande* sauce, a little sugar, nutmeg, and a piece of glaze; toss them gently over the fire, and serve.

148. GARNISH OF ASPARAGUS PEAS.

CUT a bundle of sprue asparagus into peas, boil them green, and follow the directions contained in the foregoing article.

149. GARNISH OF BUTTON ONIONS FOR MATELOTTE.

PEEL a pint of small button onions, boil them in water for five minutes, drain them on a napkin, and afterward place them in a small stewpan with some clarified butter and a little pounded sugar; then place the stewpan on a slow fire, and fry the onions of a light-brown color, taking care to toss them up now and then that they may be equally colored; when sufficiently colored they will be nearly done. Then place them on a sieve to allow the butter to drain, and put them in a small stewpan with a lump of sugar and a little *consommé;* lastly, set them on the fire and boil them down to a glaze.

150. GARNISH OF WHITE BUTTON ONIONS.

PEEL and blanch a pint of small button onions, put them into a stewpan with a pat of butter, a lump of sugar, a little salt, and a ladleful of white broth; set them on the fire to boil gently for half an hour, then boil them down quickly to a glaze, and finish by adding a spoonful of *Allemande* sauce.

151. GARNISH OF WINDSOR BEANS.

BOIL a quart of young Windsor beans, peel off their husks, and place them in a sauta-pan with a little pepper, salt, and nutmeg, a pat of butter, and a spoonful of *Béchamel* sauce; throw in a spoonful of chopped and blanched parsley, and a little winter savory; shake the whole well together over the fire, and place them in the centre of an *entrée.*

152. GARNISH OF FRENCH BEANS.

CUT a plateful of French beans into the shape of diamonds, boil them green, drain them on a napkin, and then put them into a sauta-pan with a pat of butter, a little pepper and salt, a spoonful of white sauce, and a little lemon-juice; toss them well together on the fire, and serve.

153. GARNISH OF ARTICHOKE BOTTOMS.

REMOVE the outer leaves from four artichokes, pare off with a knife the green surface from the bottom of the artichokes, so as to render them smooth and white; rub over each artichoke as it is finished with lemon-juice, and instantly throw it into a basin of water in which a little vinegar has been mixed; then boil them in a stewpan containing hot water, a piece of butter, minionette pepper, salt, and a little lemon-juice. When they are done, take them out, and after allowing them to cool, extract the hay or inside fibres; trim them, and divide each artichoke into six pieces. Then place them in a sauta-pan with a spoonful of *Suprême* sauce, a pat of butter, a little cream glaze, nutmeg, and sugar; toss them gently on the fire, and when the whole is well mixed, serve.

154. GARNISH OF GLAZED ONIONS.

PEEL eighteen onions, of a similar size, with a small vegetable cutter, scoop out the heads of their roots—perforating the onions through—and extracting the centre from each; boil them from three to five minutes in water, drain them on a napkin, and then place them in a sauta-pan well buttered, add a little sugar, and sufficient broth to cover the onions; set them on the stove to boil, and afterward remove them to a slow fire, or place them in the oven, to simmer gently down to a glaze. Take care to turn the onions over in their glaze occasionally, so that they may become equally colored.

155. GARNISH OF BROCOLI OF CAULIFLOWERS.

CUT one or more heads of cauliflower or brocoli into small buds, trim these and boil them in a stewpan with some butter, salt, and a little minionette pepper, in the water; when they are done, drain them on a sieve, put them into a stewpan with a little *Allemande* or *Béchamel* sauce and serve.

156. GARNISH OF BRUSSELS SPROUTS.

BOIL a plateful of Brussels sprouts, drain them well, and put them into a stewpan with a spoonful of white sauce, two pats of butter, salt, nutmeg, minionette pepper, and lemon-juice; toss the whole well together over the fire, and serve.

157. GARNISH OF CHESTNUTS FOR ROAST TURKEY.

SLIT the husks of fifty chestnuts, and put them into a stewpan with a little clarified butter, fry them on a slow fire until the husks easily peel off from the chestnuts; clean them thoroughly, and place them in a stewpan with two lumps of sugar, a little salt, a pat of butter, and a ladleful of good *consommé;* set them to boil, and then place them by the side of the fire to continue boiling gently until they are nearly done; then boil them down to a glaze; occasionally tossing them over, so as to cover them with their own glaze, and give them a bright shiny appearance.

158. GARNISH OF JERUSALEM ARTICHOKES.

PEEL a dozen Jerusalem artichokes, and then turn or cut them into the shape of olives, small pillars, cloves of garlic, half moons, round balls, quarters of orange, or diamonds; first wash them, place them in a stewpan with a little sugar, salt, a pat of butter, and a ladleful of white broth; set them to boil on the fire for about twenty minutes; when they are nearly done, boil them down in their glaze, add a little *Allemande* or *Béchamel* sauce, toss them together over the fire, and serve.

159. GARNISH OF CLOVES OF GARLIC.

PEEL as many heads of garlic as will produce a pint of cloves,* boil these for ten minutes in plenty of water, drain them on to a sieve, and then place them in a stewpan with a pat of butter, some minionette pepper, a little salt, and a ladleful of *consommé;* boil them gently until they are nearly done, then let them boil down quickly to a glaze; add a spoonful of *Allemande* or *Espagnole* sauce (according to the color of the *entrée*), and a little lemon-juice; toss them up over a stove-fire, and serve.

160. GARNISH OF WHITE HARICOT BEANS.

FRESH white *haricôt* beans, in their proper season, form a very excellent change among the more ordinary vegetables. Its cultivation is, however, much neglected by gardeners in England.

When fresh *haricôt* beans are not procurable, get a pint of dried *haricôt* beans, and steep them in cold water for twelve hours; let them be washed and placed in a stewpan with a pat of butter, min-

---

* A head of garlic contains within its outer husk, or skin, a number of triangular seeds, usually called cloves of garlic.

ionette pepper, salt, and two quarts of cold water; set them to boil gently by the side of a stove for about an hour; when done, drain them on to a sieve, place them in a clean stewpan with a pat of butter, a gravy-spoonful of white sauce, a little pepper and salt, lemon-juice, and a spoonful of chopped and blanched parsley; shake them well together over the fire, and serve.

161. GARNISH OF RED HARICOT BEANS.

These should be prepared exactly in the same manner as the white beans. There is, also, a species of small brown peas, called lentils—to be had of all oilmen, which may be prepared after the same method as the *haricôt* beans. They are useful in the winter season, when there is a scarcity of fresh vegetables.

162. GARNISH OF BRAIZED CABBAGES.

Trim, wash, and thoroughly cleanse four good Savoy cabbages, cut them in halves, and boil them in water for a quarter of an hour; refresh them in cold water, drain them, and place them on a napkin; cut the stalks away, season them with salt and minionette pepper, tie them up with a string—joining two halves together; cover the bottom of a stewpan with thin layers of fat bacon, place the cabbages in it; add a carrot, an onion stuck with three cloves, and a fagot of parsley, thyme, and bay-leaf; moisten with sufficient broth to cover the cabbages, and spread a buttered round of paper over the whole; then set them on the fire to boil, place the lid on the stewpan and allow it to remain gently boiling on a very slow fire for about an hour, when they will be done. Then drain the cabbage on to a sieve, remove the strings, press it in a napkin so as to be able, afterward, to cut it into square, oblong, round, or oval shapes, according to taste; and therewith garnish the *entrée* or remove it is intended for.

163. GARNISH OF STEWED RED CABBAGES.

Trim, wash, and quarter a couple of red cabbages, shred them as you would if about to make pickled cabbage; then put about four ounces of butter at the bottom of a stewpan, and place the shred cabbages in it; season with minionette pepper and salt, and half a gill of French vinegar, cover the stewpan with its lid, and set it on a moderate fire to stew gently; take care to stir it occasionally with a wooden spoon. When the cabbage has, by melting, been reduced to half its original quantity, moisten with a large-sized ladleful of topping from the boiling stockpot, to nourish the cabbage; allow it to simmer gently on a slow fire for an hour longer; then drain the cabbage on a sieve, afterward press it in a napkin to extract the butter, &c., and use it for the purpose of garnishing the *entrée* or remove for which it has been prepared.

164. GARNISH OF BRAIZED CABBAGE LETTUCES.

Trim, wash, and blanch a dozen full white-heart cabbage lettuces; drain them on a napkin, cut and spread them open, season with pepper and salt, tie them up with a string, and place them in a stewpan on thin layers of fat bacon; add a carrot, a fagot of parsley and green onions, and an onion stuck with two cloves; cover with a buttered round of paper, and moisten with the toppings of white stock. Allow them to boil gently by the side of the fire for an hour, drain them on a sieve, remove the strings, press them neatly in a napkin, and open each lettuce with a knife; then smooth the inner part, and with the knife turn the ends of the leaves under so as to give to the lettuce a smooth rounded end; cut off the stalk neatly, and place each lettuce successively in a clean sauta-pan; next pass their liquor through a sieve into a stewpan, remove every particle of grease, and boil it down to the consistency of half-glaze; add it to the lettuces, cover them with a buttered paper, and a quarter of an hour previously to their being required for use, set them in the oven to get warm.

165. SAUERKRAUT.

PROCURE two pounds of fresh imported sauerkraut, wash it thoroughly in several waters, and then drain it in a colander. Next, put it into a stewpan with one pound of parboiled streaky bacon, one pound of German sausage, two carrots, two onions stuck with two cloves each, and a garnished fagot of parsley; cover with a round of buttered paper, and moisten with a quart of stockpot toppings. Braize the sauerkraut for about three hours over a slow fire; and when done, drain it in a colander, remove the bacon and German sausage, throw away the carrot, onion, and fagot; then put the sauerkraut into a stewpan with a gravy-spoonful of *Poivrade* sauce, toss it over the fire, and use it to garnish the intended dish.

166. FRENCH SAUERKRAUT.

SPLIT four white-heart cabbages into quarters, remove the cores, and shred them up fine; wash them thoroughly in several waters, then drain them in a colander. Next, place the shred cabbages in a large earthen pan, throw in a good handful of salt and one pint of vinegar; toss the cabbage in this, and allow it to steep for three hours; then wash and drain it, and put it into a large stewpan, season with half a pound of butter, some minionette pepper, a little salt, and a gill of French vinegar; place on the top one pound of streaky bacon, and one pound of German sausage, moisten with a quart of good stock, cover the whole with buttered paper, and then set the sauerkraut to braize very gently over a slow fire for two hours; and when it is done, proceed in the same manner as directed in the previous article.

ESSENCES, GRAVIES, AND PREPARED SAVORY BUTTERS FOR FINISHING SAUCES, &c.,

COMPRISING

Essence of Shalots.
  „   Truffles.
  „   Mushrooms.
  „   Fine Herbs for broiled meats.
  „   Orange for wild fowl.
  „   Aspic-jelly.
  „   Woodcocks.
  „   Game for broiled partridges, &c.
  „   Garlic for broiled fowls, &c.
  „   Anchovies for broiled steaks, &c.

Essence of Sage and Onions for geese and ducks.
  „   Onions for broiled pork.
  „   Anchovy butter.
Ravigotte butter.
Provençale do.
Lobster do.
Montpellier do.
Crayfish do.
Green *ravigotte* do.
Epicurean do.

167. ESSENCE OF SHALOTS.

PEEL a dozen shalots, cut them into thin slices, and place them in a small stewpan with two tablespoonsful of French vinegar; set them to simmer gently on the fire until the vinegar is nearly boiled down; then moisten with a pint of *consommé*, set the essence on the fire to boil, and when it is reduced to half its original quantity, strain it with pressure through a napkin into a *bain-marie*, and keep it hot till wanted.

168. ESSENCE OF TRUFFLES.

CHOP or pound four ounces of truffles—or if you have any trimmings, use them instead; place them in a small stewpan with half a bay-leaf, a sprig of thyme, and a very small quantity of bruised garlic; moisten with a glass of French white wine, and allow the whole to simmer on the fire till the wine is nearly boiled down; add half a pint of good *consommé;* set the essence to boil gently on the side of the fire for ten minutes, and then pass it with pressure through a napkin or tammy into a small basin or stewpan.

This essence will be found extremely useful for flavoring sauces and *ragouts*, in which the flavor of truffles should predominate.

169. ESSENCE OF MUSHROOMS.

CHOP any quantity of mushrooms, place these in a stewpan with a little lemon-juice and a small piece of butter, simmer them on the fire for two or three minutes, and then moisten with a ladleful of white broth; set the essence to boil gently on the stove for ten minutes, and then pass it with pressure through a sieve into a basin for use.

This essence is useful for flavoring sauces.

170. ESSENCE OF FINE HERBS FOR BROILED MEATS, ETC.

CHOP six shalots, a handful of mushrooms, and the same quantity of parsley, each separately; place these in a small stewpan with a sprig of thyme, half a bay-leaf, and a small piece of butter; put the whole on the fire to simmer gently for two or three minutes, stirring the ingredients with a wooden spoon; moisten with the juice of half a lemon and a ladleful of strong *consommé;* add a little minionette pepper, and then set the essence to boil gently on the side of the fire till it is reduced to half its original quantity ; then pass it with pressure through a sieve, and use it as a gravy for plain broiled bread-crumbed *entrées.*

171. ESSENCE OF ORANGE FOR WILD FOWL.

Chop two shalots and put them into a small stewpan with the rind of an orange, quite free from the white or pith, and a little chopped lean of raw ham and cayenne pepper ; moisten with two glasses of port wine and a little strong gravy; set the essence to simmer gently on the fire for about ten minutes, then add the juice of the orange with a little lemon-juice, and pass it through a silk sieve.

172. ESSENCE OF ASPIC-JELLY.

Put the following ingredients into a small stewpan : a few branches of green tarragon, a little chervil, a handful of chives, a bay-leaf, and sprig of thyme, mignionette pepper, a blade of mace, and a little chopped raw lean of ham ; moisten with a large ladleful of good *consommé;* set the essence to boil gently by the side of the fire for about ten minutes. Next, take it off the stove, proceed to clarify by mixing with it half the white of an egg whipped up with a spoonful of water ; add a spoonful of tarragon-vinegar, and place it on the fire to boil, whipping it with a wire whisk the while ; as soon as it boils up, remove it on the side, to continue boiling gently in order to set the egg ; then strain it through a napkin, and use it for braized fowls or chickens *à l'Estragon* or *à l'Ivoire.*

173. ESSENCE OF WOODCOCKS.

Chop up any carcasses of woodcocks or snipes that may be left from the previous day's dinner, place them in a small stewpan with four shalots, a bay-leaf, and a sprig of thyme, mignionette pepper, a little mace, and a small piece of butter ; fry the whole on the stove-fire till the ingredients become lightly colored ; moisten with a small glass of white wine; and after allowing it to boil down to a glaze, add a ladleful of good *consommé,* and set the essence to boil gently on the side of the fire for half an hour ; skim and strain it through a silk sieve, and finish by adding a little lemon-juice.

This essence or gravy should be sent to table with roasted woodcocks or snipes ; it will also be found useful for making a light hash of remnants of woodcocks or snipes, for breakfast.

174. ESSENCE OF GAME FOR BROILED PARTRIDGES, ETC.

This essence is prepared in the same manner as the preceding, substituting the remnants or carcasses of pheasants or partridges, for woodcocks.

175. ESSENCE OF GARLIC FOR BROILED FOWL.

Chop a little raw lean of ham, some parsley, thyme, and a bay-leaf ; place these in a small stewpan with a blade of mace, two pounded anchovies, and six cloves of garlic ; moisten with two tea-spoonsful of French vinegar, and set the whole on the fire to simmer gently for five minutes ; add a small piece of glaze and a ladleful of good *blond* of veal, and allow the essence to boil gently by the side of the fire for a quarter of an hour ; reduce it to half its original quantity, and then strain it through a tammy into a small stewpan ; finish by adding a little lemon-juice and cayenne pepper.

176. ESSENCE OF ANCHOVIES FOR STEAKS, ETC.

WASH and clean six anchovies, pound them in a mortar, with a tablespoonful of capers and two shalots ; place these in a small stewpan with thyme and a bay-leaf, mace, minionette pepper, and two tablespoonsful of mushroom catsup ; set these ingredients on the fire to simmer gently for five minutes, and then moisten with a ladleful of good *consommé ;* boil the whole till reduced to half its original quantity, then strain it with pressure through a tammy into a small stewpan ; finish by adding a small piece of glaze and a little lemon-juice.

177. ESSENCE OF SAGE AND ONIONS FOR GEESE AND DUCKS.

CHOP two large onions and a dozen sage-leaves separately, put them into a small stewpan with a pat of butter, some pepper and salt, and fry them on a slow fire ; as soon as the onion begins to get lightly colored, moisten with a ladleful of *blond* of veal, and allow the essence to boil on the fire till reduced to half the quantity ; strain it through a tammy into a small stepwan for use.

This gravy may also be used for bread-crumbled *entrées* of broiled pork.

178. ESSENCE OF ONIONS FOR BROILED PORK.

CUT three onions into slices, and fry them in a small stewpan with a little butter, pepper, and salt ; when they are of a light color, moisten with a ladleful* of *blond* of veal ; reduce the essence by boiling to half its quantity, and strain it into a *bain-marie* for use.

179. ANCHOVY BUTTER.

WASH and wipe dry six anchovies, separate the fillets from the bones, and pound them in a mortar, with two pats of butter and a little cayenne pepper ; rub this mixture through a hair-sieve, gather this up and keep it in a small basin for use, in a cool place.

180. RAVIGOTTE BUTTER.

WASH and wipe four anchovies, blanch a good handful of green tarragon, chervil, burnet, chives, and parsley ; press these in a napkin to expunge the water ; and put the anchovies, herbs, two pats of butter, a spoonful of capers, a little cayenne pepper, and a pinch of salt, into a mortar, and pound them well together ; then rub the mixture through a hair-sieve, gather it up, and keep in a small basin on the ice for use.

181. PROVENCALE BUTTER.

THIS is prepared in the same manner as the preceding, adding, however, four cloves of garlic to the other ingredients.

---

* Whenever the term ladleful occurs in the course of this work it refers to a bowl-shaped spoon, capable of holding about a pint.

182. LOBSTER BUTTER.

PROCURE some lobster spawn or coral, and pound it with twice as much butter, one anchovy, and a little cayenne pepper; rub it through a hair-sieve, collect it into a small basin, and keep it in a cool place till wanted for use.

183. MONTPELLIER BUTTER.

BLANCH some tarragon, chervil, burnet, chives, and parsley, a hand-ful of each; expunge the water, and pound them with the yelks of six boiled eggs, six cleaned anchovies, two tablespoonsful of French capers, and half a dozen green gherkins; when these ingredients are thoroughly pounded together, mix in six ounces of fresh butter, then add, by degrees, two tablespoonsful of Tarragon-vinegar, and six of salad-oil; season with pepper and salt; rub the butter thus prepared through a sieve or tammy, color it with some spinach-green, and keep it in a basin on the ice till wanted for use.

184. CRAYFISH BUTTER.

REMOVE the shells from three or four dozen crayfish, place them on a baking-sheet in the oven to dry; let the shells cool, and then pound them in a mortar, with a little lobster coral and four ounces of fresh butter; thoroughly bruise the whole well together, so as to form them into a kind of paste, put this into a stewpan, and then set it on the stove-fire to simmer for about five minutes; then rub it through a tammy with considerable pressure into a basin containing some cold water, with a piece of ice in it; as soon as the colored crayfish butter is become set, through the coldness of the water, take it out, and put it into a small basin in a cool place till wanted for use.

185. GREEN RAVIGOTTE BUTTER.

BLANCH a handful of tarragon, chervil, burnet, chives, and parsley; press them in a napkin, and pound them with four ounces of fresh butter, cayenne pepper and salt; rub the butter through a hair-sieve, and keep it on the ice in a small basin for use.

186. EPICUREAN BUTTER FOR THE TABLE.

POUND four cleaned anchovies, a few chives, a good teaspoonful of green tarragon-leaves, four green West India gherkins, two boiled yelks of eggs, three ounces of butter, and a good teaspoonful of French mustard; mix thoroughly, season with little salt, and rub the butter through a hair-sieve; gather it up into a small basin, make it sufficiently firm by keeping it on the ice, and mould it into pats for the purpose of being sent to table to be served with the cheese.

RAGOUTS AND GARNISHES IN GENERAL,

COMPRISING

Toulouse ragout.	*Ragout* of soft roes of mackerel.
Financière do.	Cardinal *ragout.*
Calf's head do. *à la Tortue.*	*Ragout* of scollops of soles.
Chipolata do.	Do. of salmon or trout.
Strasbourg do. of fat livers.	Parisian *ragout.*
Périgueux do.	*Ragout* of scollops of game, &c.
Matelotte do.	Do. of larks.
Do. *Normande* do.	Do. of cock's kernels, *à la Soubise.*
Bourguignotte do.	*Richelieu ragout.*
Crayfish do.	*Ragout* of chicken's wings.
Rouénaise do.	Do. of ox palates.
Ragout of scollops of sweetbreads.	Do. of sheep's tongues, *à l'écarlate.*

Regent's *ragout.*

187. TOULOUSE RAGOUT.

PREPARE some fine large white cocks' combs and kernels, button mushrooms, small scollops of sweetbread, and a proportionate quantity of truffles turned in the shape of scollops or olives; place these in a small stewpan, and add thereto a small ladleful of *Allemande* or *Suprême* sauce; toss the whole together over the fire a few minutes, it will then be ready for use.

188. FINANCIERE RAGOUT.

PLACE in a stewpan a similar *ragout* to the foregoing, with an equal portion of small *quenelles,* and add a small ladleful of well-finished *Financière* sauce; allow the whole to boil slightly on the fire. Use this *ragout* for garnishing the remove or *entrée,* as the case may be.

189. CALF'S HEAD RAGOUT A LA TORTUE.

PUT a large gravy-spoonful of fine white cocks' combs into a *bain-marie* or stewpan, a similar quantity of cocks' kernels, small truffles, button mushrooms, *quenelles,* and green gherkins, cut into the shape of olives; to these add a sufficient quantity of Turtle sauce (No. 9) for the purpose, and set the whole on the fire to boil for a minute or two, and serve.

190. CHIPOLATA RAGOUT.

TWIST one pound of pork sausages into small round balls, separate these, fry them, and when they are cold, trim and put them into a *bain-marie* containing a proportionate quantity of cocks' combs and kernels, button mushrooms, truffles, *quenelles,* carrots, and turnips, turned in the shape of olives, and boiled down in their own glaze, also some round balls of braized streaky bacon, and an equal proportion of chestnuts, pealed and boiled in *consommé;* add a ladleful of *Financière* sauce (No. 8), a little essence of truffles and mushrooms; then set the ragout on the fire to boil for two minutes, and serve.

Note.—The above is the simplest mode for preparing this *ragout;* it is far better, however, that the whole of the ingredients of which this very rich and popular *ragout* is composed should be kept sepa-

rately in small stewpans, and be placed alternately in groups about
the dish they are meant to garnish and ornament; then the boiling
sauce should be poured over the turkey, capon, or poulards, when
ready to serve.

191. STRASBOURG RAGOUT OF FAT LIVERS.

BRAIZE a fat liver in some *mirepoix* (No. 236), take it out to cool,
cut it into scollops, and trim them neatly; put them into a small
stewpan with some of the *mirepoix* freed from every particle of fat,
add a proportionate quantity of scolloped truffles, and just before
using these, set them on the stove and boil them down to a glaze;
add a sufficient quantity of *Financière* sauce, and serve.

192. PERIGUEUX RAGOUT.

PREPARE some scollops of fat livers and truffles, as for the foregoing *ragout;* to these add some small *quenelles,* cocks' combs and
kernels, and some button mushrooms; then add a ladleful of
Perigueux sauce (No. 23), and boil the whole together for two or
three minutes.

193. MATELOTTE RAGOUT.

PEEL and blanch half a pint of button onions, fry them of a light-
brown color over a slow fire; when done, drain them on to a sieve,
in order to free them from the butter, and place them in a *bain-marie*
with an equal quantity of white button mushrooms, crayfish tails, and
small *quenelles* of whiting; to these add a ladleful of *Matelotte* sauce
(No. 31), and after allowing the *ragout* to boil for two or three minutes,
use it for garnishing the *Matelotte,* or any other dressed colored fish
it is intended for.

194. MATELOTTE NORMANDE RAGOUT.

PREPARE thirty crayfish tails, and place them in a stewpan with
about half a pint of muscles, three dozen of parboiled oysters, and
an equal proportion of white button mushrooms; to these add a
ladleful of *Matelotte Normande* sauce (No. 32), allow the whole to boil
up a minute or two on the stove, and use the *ragout* to garnish soles
or other fish for which it is prepared.

195. BOURGUIGNOTTE RAGOUT.

PEEL and blanch half a pint of small button onions, put them
into a stewpan with a lump of sugar, a little grated nutmeg, and a
pat of butter, moisten with half a pint of good broth, and set the
onions to stew gently on a moderate fire; when nearly done, boil
them down to a glaze, and add them to an equal quantity of white
button mushrooms and very small *quenelles;* to these put sufficient
Bourguignotte sauce (No. 28) for the purpose required; allow the *ragout* to boil up on the stove-fire for a minute or two, and use it to
garnish the *entrée* it may be intended for.

196. CRAYFISH RAGOUT.

TAKE out and trim the tails of thirty crayfish; with the bodies
and shells make some crayfish butter (No. 184), to be used in coloring some *quenelles* of whitings, afterward moulded with teaspoons,
poached, and placed with the crayfish; to these add some *Allemande*

or *Suprême* sauce, with which mix in a little of the butter made with the shells of the crayfish, and serve the *ragout* with the dish it is meant for.

197. ROUENAISE RAGOUT.

PREPARE an equal proportion of the following shell-fish—oysters, muscles, and shrimps; to these add some button mushrooms and *quenelles* of lobster, and moisten the *ragout* with a sauce made in the following manner : reduce some of the liquor of the muscles, oysters, and mushrooms, with two glasses of French white wine, and the addition of a small ladleful of *Velouté* sauce; finish by mixing in four yelks of eggs, a pat of butter, and a little cream : stir the sauce on the stove-fire till it boils, and then pass it through a tammy on to the *ragout*. Before sending it to table, add a spoonful of chopped and blanched parsley, and the juice of half a lemon.

About a dozen smelts, trussed in the same manner as whiting for frying, and boiled in a little salt and water, and afterward skinned and glazed, should be prepared to garnish round the fish with which the *Rouénaise ragout* is served.

198. RAGOUT OF SCOLLOPS OF SWEETBREADS.

FIRST blanch, and then braize, a little white broth, three or more throat sweetbreads, for about twenty minutes; then take them up on a plate, and allow them to cool; cut them into neat scollops and place them in a small stewpan with a small ladleful of any sort of sauce appropriate to the *entrée* which this *ragout* is intended to garnish.

A similar kind of *ragout* may be prepared with lambs' sweetbreads, calf's, sheep's, or lamb's brains.

199. RAGOUT OF SOFT ROES OF MACKEREL, OR OTHER FISH.

PARBOIL the soft roes of six mackerel or carp, in a little boiling water mixed with two spoonsful of French vinegar and a little salt; drain them on a napkin, and put them into a sauta-pan containing some *Allemande* or *Suprême* sauce; add some chopped and blanched parsley, and a little nutmeg and lemon-juice; toss the whole gently together over the fire, taking care not to break or bruise the roes, and place them in the centre of the fillets of fish prepared to receive them.

200. CARDINAL RAGOUT.

PREPARE two dozen small *quenelles* of lobster, which place in a stewpan, with thirty picked and trimmed prawns' tails, two dozen button mushrooms, and a similar quantity of small round truffles; to these add a sufficient quantity of cardinal sauce for the remove or *entrée ;* then boil the *ragout* for three minutes on the fire, when it will be ready for use.

201. RAGOUT OF SCOLLOPS OF SOLES, ETC.

FILLET two pairs of soles, or a proportionate quantity of any other sort of fish, place them in a sauta-pan with some clarified butter, pepper, salt, and lemon-juice; cover them with a round of buttered paper, and set them in the oven for about ten minutes; when they are done, drain them on a napkin, and afterward place them on a dish to put them in the larder to cool; next cut them into neatly-trimmed scollops, and put these into a stewpan; add either some *Allemande, Béchamel, Suprême,* or Dutch sauce, whichever is most suitable for the kind of fish these scollops are intended to garnish.

202. RAGOUT OF SCOLLOPS OF SALMON OR TROUT.

THESE scollops should be prepared in every respect in the same manner as the foregoing, except that, previously to adding the sauce a little lobster butter, cayenne, and lemon-juice should be mixed in.

203. PARISIAN RAGOUT.

AN equal quantity of trimmed crayfish tails, button mushrooms, small round truffles, and cocks' kernels should be put into a stewpan containing some Parisian sauce (No. 40); make the *ragout* hot previously to using it.

204. RAGOUT OF SCOLLOPS OF POULTRY OR GAME.

FILLET one or more heads of poultry or game, according to the quantity of *ragout* required; trim, and place them in a sauta-pan with a little clarified fresh butter, season with a little salt, cover them with a buttered paper, and set them over a moderate fire to simmer; as soon as they become firm and white on the under side, turn them over that they may be effectually done through, taking care that they do not become brown; then drain them on a napkin, and cut them on the slant into scollops, trim them neatly, and put them into a stewpan with some *Allemande, Béchamel,* or *Suprême* sauce, previously reduced with either an essence of fowl or game, as the case may be, according to the nature of the scollops, whether of poultry or game.

205. RAGOUT OF SCOLLOPS OF LARKS.

CUT out, trim, and slightly simmer, in a little butter, the fillets of two dozen larks; drain them on a napkin, and place them in a small stewpan, with a sauce made as follows: Fry the carcasses of the larks in a stewpan, with a pat of butter, one shalot, half a bay-leaf, and a sprig of thyme, a little salt and grated nutmeg; when they are of a light-brown color, moisten with three glasses of French white wine; allow the carcasses to stew gently on a moderate fire for half an hour; pound the whole thoroughly, and rub it through a tammy into a *purée;* take this up into a small stewpan, add a little reduced brown sauce, and pour it on to the scollops; warm them with care, for if they be allowed to boil, it will spoil the look of the *purée,* and render it rough.

206. RAGOUT OF COCKS' KERNELS A LA SOUBISE.

PUT about half a pound of cock's kernels, with cold water, into a stewpan, let it stand by the side of a slow fire to remove the little blood they contain, taking care that the water does not become too warm; as soon as they whiten, drain them on a sieve, and put them into a small stewpan, with a pat of butter, the juice of a lemon, and a little salt, toss them over the fire for two or three minutes, moisten with a little white chicken broth, and set them to simmer gently on a slow fire for about ten minutes longer; they will be then done. Drain them on a napkin, put them into a small stewpan, with a ragout-spoonful of *Soubise* sauce and a little *Allemande* sauce, toss them gently over the fire till they are hot, and place them in the centre of an *entrée* of fillets of fowl *à la Marechale, à la D'Uxelles.*

207. RICHELIEU RAGOUT.

PREPARE some *quenelle* force-meat of chicken, and before moulding the *quenelles*, incorporate with it two spoonsful of brown *purée* of onions (of which there must be prepared a sufficient quantity for the sauce of the *ragout*); mould two dozen small *quenelles*, poach them, and, after draining them on a napkin, put them into a small stewpan, with a dozen white cocks' combs and a few scollops of fat livers; to these add the remainder of the brown *purée* of onions, which must be no thicker than sauce.

This *ragout* may be used for garnishing *boudins à la Richelieu*, or any *entrées* of poultry or game that are bread-crumbed and broiled.

208. RAGOUT OF CHICKENS' WINGS.

THIS *ragout* is only to be recommended when it happens that a number of fowls or chickens have to be cut up for other purposes; in such case, save the wings, which cut off close to the breast, bone them neatly, without tearing or cutting the skin, and fill up the cavity occasioned by taking the bone out with some *quenelle* force-meat of fowl; shape them neatly and parboil them, immerse them in cold water, then drain and trim them. Line a stewpan with thin layers of fat bacon, place the wings therein with a fagot of parsley, thyme, a bay-leaf, and an onion; moisten with white broth, cover them with a round of buttered paper, and set them to boil gently by the side of the stove for about twenty minutes, when, if the fowls are young, the wings will be done. Then drain the wings on a napkin, and, when trimmed, put them into a small stewpan with some *Allemande* sauce.

This *ragout* is more generally made use of for filling *vol-au-vents*, *casseroles* of rice, and *chartreuses;* it is also useful, as an accessory, for garnishing large removes.

209. RAGOUT OF OX-PALATES.

STEEP six ox-palates in water for several hours, keeping the vessel that contains them near the stove-fire, so that the water may become gradually tepid, which materially helps to cleanse them; then scald and scrape them clean, trim, wash, and set them to braize in some *blanc* or *poële* (No. 230); about four hours will suffice. When the palates are done, drain and put them in press between two dishes; when cold, shape them out with a round cutter an inch in diameter, and place them in a stewpan with a sufficient quantity of either of the following sauces : *Allemande, Béchamel, Suprême, Italienne, Financière, Poivrade,* or Tomata. This *ragout* is strictly appropriate only for garnishing *patés-chauds* and *vol-au-vents,* but it may, in cases of emergency, be served as an *entrée* garnished round with *croquettes,* of potatoes or *fleurons* of pastry.

210. RAGOUT OF SHEEP'S TONGUES A L'ECARLATE.

BOIL and press eight sheeps' tongues that have been cured with saltpetre; trim and cut them into round scollops, and then put these scollops into a small stewpan, with any kind of sauce that may be suitable for the *entrée* they are meant to garnish.

211. REGENT'S RAGOUT.

FILLET an eel, cut it into scollops, and simmer these in a stewpan with a little butter, chopped parsley, lemon-juice, pepper, and salt; when done, drain the scollops on a napkin, and then put them into a stewpan containing an equal proportion of white button mushrooms, cocks' combs, small round truffles, and small *quenelles* of whiting colored with lobster coral; to these add a small ladleful of Regency sauce (No. 49), then allow the *ragout* to boil up on the stove-fire, and use it for garnishing the dressed fish it is intended for.

BROTHS AND *CONSOMMES* IN GENERAL, FOR SOUPS, &c.,

COMPRISING

Nutritive Soup.
Empotage or *Consommé* for soups in general.
Brown *Consommé* of fowls.
    „   „   pheasants or partridges.
    „   „   rabbits.

White *Consommé* of fowls.
    „   „   pheasants or partridges.
Brown extract of larks, &c.
    „   „   hare or rabbit.
Common gravy.
Blond of veal, or veal gravy.

212. NUTRITIVE SOUP.

INTO a three-gallon stockpot, put a knuckle of veal, six pounds of the shoulder part of beef (commonly called the gravy piece), and a bone of roast beef or mutton. Fill the stockpot with cold water to within two inches of the brim, and set it upon a stove-fire to boil, taking care not to hurry its ebullition, but allow it to take place gently, so that it may have time to throw up its skum; this should be removed, as it rises to the surface, and a little cold water should be thrown in occasionally to effect that purpose.

When the stock has thrown off all its skum, which will easily be perceived by the water becoming clear again, lift it off the stove, and put it by the side. Then proceed to garnish it with four leeks and two heads of celery, trimmed and tied together, two good-sized carrots, two turnips, and two onions, into each of which two cloves have been inserted; add one good tablespoonful of salt, and let the whole boil gently for about three-quarters of an hour. During this time, an old hen and a partridge should be partially roasted, and then put into the stock; this should continue to boil during five hours unremittingly: care being taken that the stockpot be kept full.

Previously to the soup being served, take off every particle of fat that appears on the surface, with a ladle; take out the vegetables—carefully placing them on a napkin, then remove the fowl and the partridge from the stock: these operations should be so managed as not to disturb the brightness of the broth. Cut the fillets of the fowl and the partridge into slices, and place them in the soup-tureen, and upon these put some of the vegetables (which have been drained on the napkin) neatly cut with a vegetable cutter a quarter of an inch in diameter ; then pour in the broth, to which add a little brown *consommé* of veal to give it color. Let it be sufficiently seasoned with salt and a few grains of minionette pepper, then serve.

213. EMPOTAGE, OR CONSOMME FOR SOUPS IN GENERAL.

WHEN preparing for company, take about thirty pounds of gravy beef, and a similar quantity of knuckles of veal, together with four wild rabbits, and put the whole into a large stockpot which has been previously spread with butter, add common broth in sufficient quantity so as nearly to cover the meat. Put the stockpot on the stove-fire to boil until the broth is reduced to a light-colored glaze ; then fill it up with the remainder of the grand stock, and after it has boiled and been skimmed, garnish it with carrots, turnips, leeks, onions, and celery ; add also two blades of mace and six cloves. In all cases be sparing of salt, especially in the first stages of preparation. Allow the broth to boil gently on the side of the stove for six hours, and then pass it into kitchen pans for further use.

In connection with this subject, I may here point out that, if it be contemplated to have as one of the removes a piece of beef braized, a saving provision may be effected by using, in the first instance, instead of about thirty pounds of stock beef, only ten pounds of that quality in preparing the grand stock ; the deficiency being made up by twenty pounds of sirloin. This latter must be boned, and the fillet taken out, either to be used to ornament the remove, or for an *entrée*, as occasion may require ; the meat must then be rolled up tightly and strung round in the manner of Hambro' beef. This will thus answer the double purpose of giving strength to the *consommé*, and of serving afterward as a remove.

When the beef thus prepared has boiled gently in the stockpot for about five hours, take it out and put it in press between two dishes till wanted ; it must be then trimmed, and placed in a long braizing-pan with a little good stock to warm it in ; glaze it nicely, and having dished it up, garnish the remove with such vegetables as have been prepared for the purpose.

214. CONSOMME OF FOWLS FOR SOUPS.

TAKE two or more fowls, according to the quality of broth required ; roast them before a brisk fire until half done ; and then put them into a small, well-tinned stockpot, nearly filled up with water, and place this on the fire to boil ; skim the *consommé*, and then add one good-sized carrot, two turnips, one onion, one head of celery, two cloves, a small piece of mace, and a little salt. Set the stock on the side of the stove to boil gently for about two hours, and then strain it off for use.

This kind of *consommé* is admirably adapted for persons of delicate health as a restorative. It is also very serviceable in imparting delicacy of flavor to all clear soups.

215. BROWN CONSOMME OF PHEASANTS OR PARTRIDGES.

ROAST off two pheasants, after having taken out the fillets for the purpose of making them into an *entrée*, or four partridges may be

used, (removing the fillets in the same way) ; put them into a stockpot
with a small knuckle of veal, and about one pound of lean of ham ; fill
up with water, then set it on to boil on the stove-fire. Meanwhile slice
up a carrot, an onion, two turnips, a head of celery, and a leek : fry
these roots in a stewpan, with a small piece of butter, till they become
slightly browned, then throw them into the *consommé*, after having
previously well skimmed it. Add three cloves, a piece of mace, and
a little salt; let it boil gently about three hours, and then strain it
off for use.

This preparation will serve for all kinds of clear *consommé* soups,
such as *au Chasseur*, or *à la Désclignac*, &c.

216. BROWN CONSOMME OF RABBITS.

TAKE three or four wild rabbits, cut them up in pieces, and put
them into a small stockpot with five pounds of knuckle of veal which
has been roasted enough to color it; fill up with light broth or
water, then set it on the stove to boil, skim it well, and garnish with
carrot, onion, and celery, two cloves, a piece of mace, and a little
salt. Let this boil gently for three hours, and then strain it off for
use.

This *consommé* is very essential in clarifying *Espagnole* or brown
sauce, and is also serviceable for all soups in which *quenelles* of game
are served.

217. WHITE CONSOMME OF FOWLS.

TAKE two or more old hens or fowls, or, in their stead, the carcasses
of fowls, or any other sort of poultry you may have. Let them steep
in cold water to cleanse them from any blood they may contain ;
then drain and put them into an appropriate-sized stockpot or stewpan, and fill it up with common broth or water ; garnish with celery,
onions, tnrnips, carrots, and leeks. Set it to boil gently by the fire
for two hours, if made with carcasses, but if old hens are used, it
will require at least an hour longer. When done, skim off the fat
and pass the *consommé* through a napkin into a basin for use.

This *consommé* may be considered as the proper basis of all white
soups, and is most useful in clarifying and flavoring all white
sauces.

218. WHITE CONSOMME OF PHEASANTS OR PARTRIDGES.

THE same process is to be followed in making this *consommé*, as
the foregoing, substituting, of course, game for poultry.

This *consommé*, after being partially reduced to glaze, is used for
the purpose of imparting the flavor of game to any white sauce,
such as *Suprême, Allemande, Béchamel,** *Velouté*, or white Italian
sauce. It is also useful for mixing white *purées* of game.

219. BROWN EXTRACT OF LARKS OR QUAILS.

AFTER having filleted the larks or quails, and removed the gizzards
from the trail of the larks, put a stewpan on the fire with an ounce of
fresh butter in it; when the butter begins to fritter, put the bones or
carcasses of larks or quails into the stewpan and fry them brown.
Then add half a bay-leaf, a sprig of thyme, two shalots, and two

* So called after the celebrated cook Béchamel, who lived in the reign of Louis XIV.

glasses of sherry or Madeira. Let these simmer gently for five minutes, after which add one quart of common broth. Allow the extract to boil slowly by the side of the fire for three quarters of an hour, pass it through a lawn sieve into a basin, and reserve it for working the sauces intended for *gratins* of quails or larks, and also for *fumet* sauces for *pâtés-chauds* of either of the forementioned small birds.

Extract of woodcocks or snipes is obtained in a similar manner.

220. EXTRACT OF HARE OR RABBIT.

THIS is made by putting the bones or carcasses of either into a stew-pan with two or three glasses of any sort of white wine, a bay-leaf, a sprig of thyme, and two shalots; and then submitting it to the action of a rather slow fire, until the liquid becomes reduced to a glaze, when a quart to three pints of common broth should be added. Put it on a brisk fire to boil, skim it well, and then put it by the side of the stove to simmer gently for an hour and a half; after which time pass it through a napkin into a basin, and keep it for use as occasion may require.

221. COMMON GRAVY.

SPREAD the bottom of a middle-sized stewpan with butter, and cover it with thin slices of beef suet; place some slices of onions over this, and then add six pounds of gravy-beef cut into thick slices, and any trimmings of meat there may be to spare; moisten with a quart of common broth, and set the stewpan over a brisk stove-fire to boil. When the broth is reduced to glaze, slacken the heat of the stove, by partially smothering it with ashes, and allow the gravy to acquire a deep red brown color; then, fill the stewpan up with common broth or water, garnish with two carrots, two heads of celery, six cloves, two blades of mace, and a few peppercorns, and, if the gravy has been filled up with water, add a spoonful of salt. Put the gravy to boil on the stove-fire, skim it thoroughly, then remove it to the side to continue gently boiling for about three hours; next, strain it through a broth-cloth into another stewpan, and proceed immediately to clarify it, in the following manner: whisk up three whites of eggs with a little spring water, and, after having removed all the grease from the surface of the gravy, incorporate the whites of eggs in with it; whisk it over the stove-fire until it is nearly boiling, and then set it to simmer by the side for a quarter of an hour, and strain it through a broth-cloth into a basin for use.

222. BLOND DE VEAU, OR VEAL GRAVY.

HAVING first well buttered a large stewpan, lay therein one pound of the lean of a York ham cut in slices, a knuckle of veal, and the under part of a leg of veal; to these add an old hen and a couple of wild rabbits. Pour three pints of common broth over the meat, &c., and after putting the cover on the stewpan, place it on the stove-fire to boil down to a glaze; then slacken the heat so that it may gradually become browned. When the glaze darkens to a deep red tinge, fill it up with common broth or water, and set it on the stove; as soon as it boils, skim it thoroughly, garnish with carrots, turnips, onions, celery, three cloves, and a blade of mace; and after it has boiled gently by the side of the stove-fire for three hours, strain it through a napkin into basins for use.

This *consommé* is used for clearing and working the grand *Espagnole* sauce, for coloring clear soups, and also for finishing some of the special sauces.

MEDICINAL BROTHS AND CONSOMMES FOR INVALIDS,

COMPRISING

Plain chicken broth.	Crayfish broth.
Pectoral do. do.	Decoction of snails.
Mutton do.	Mucilaginous chicken broth.
Beef tea.	

223. PLAIN CHICKEN BROTH.

CUT a young fowl or chicken into four parts, wash these well in cold water, and put the pieces into a stewpan with one quart of spring water, and a very little salt; set it to boil on the stove-fire, skim it well, and then add the heart of a white cabbage lettuce, and a handful of chervil; boil the broth for about an hour, and then strain it through a napkin into a basin.

224. PECTORAL CHICKEN BROTH.

CUT up a young fowl into several pieces, put them into a stewpan with three pints of spring water; set it on the stove-fire to boil; skim it well, and add a little salt. Take two tablespoonsful of pearl barley, wash it in several waters, and add it to the broth—together with one ounce of marsh-mallow roots cut into shreds, for the purpose of better extracting its healing properties. The broth should then boil one hour, and be passed through a napkin into a basin, to be kept ready for use.

225. MUTTON BROTH.

TAKE three pounds of the scrag-end of a neck of very fresh mutton, cut it into several pieces, wash them in cold water, and put them into a stewpan with two quarts of cold spring-water; place the stewpan on the fire to boil, skim it well, and then add a couple of turnips cut into slices, a few branches of parsley, a sprig of green thyme, and a little salt. When it has boiled gently by the side of the stove for an hour and a half, skim off the fat from the surface, and then let it be strained through a lawn sieve into a basin, and kept for use.

226. BEEF TEA.

TAKE two pounds of the lean part of the gravy piece of beef, and carefully pare away every portion of fat, skin, or sinew; cut this into small square pieces the size of a nut; put the beef into a stewpan capable of containing two quarts, and pour three pints of boiling water upon it; add a little salt, put it on the stove-fire, and as soon as it boils skim it, and then remove it to the side of the stove, to continue boiling gently for an hour, after which the beef tea should be strained through a napkin for use.

227. CRAYFISH BROTH, FOR PURIFYING THE BLOOD.

TAKE two pounds of the lean part of very white veal, cut it into small pieces, and pound it well in a mortar; to this add three dozen crayfish and a handful of green chervil, and pound these together so as to thoroughly bruise the crayfish. Then remove the whole into a stewpan, and pour upon it three pints of cold spring water; add a little salt, and place the stewpan on the stove to boil; after which set it by the side of the stove-fire, and keep it gently simmering for three quarters of an hour; it may then be strained through a napkin for use.

This kind of broth, in order to promote the desired effect, should be taken by the convalescent upon an empty stomach.

228. ·DECOCTION OF SNAILS FOR INVETERATE COUGHS.

TAKE two dozen garden snails, add to these the hind quarters only of two dozen stream frogs, previously skinned; bruise them together in a mortar, after which put them into a stewpan with a couple of turnips chapped small, a little salt, a quarter of an ounce of hay saffron, and three pints of spring water. Stir these on the fire until the broth begins to boil, then skim it well, and set it by the side of the fire to simmer for half an hour: after which it should be strained by pressure through a tammy-cloth into a basin for use.

This broth, from its soothing qualities, often counteracts, successfully, the straining effects of a severe cough, and alleviates, more than any other culinary preparation, the sufferings of the consumptive.

229. MUCILAGINOUS BROTH FOR PERSONS IN DELICATE HEALTH.

TAKE a young fowl, cut it into several parts, and wash them thoroughly; put these into a stewpan capable of containing three quarts of water, add thereto three pounds of the lean of very white veal, a couple of turnips, one carrot, and one head of celery—the whole to be cut into small pieces; fill up the stewpan with spring water, and put it on the stove to boil, taking care to remove the scum as it rises to the surface. After the broth has thrown off the albumen of the meat in the shape of scum, add to it two ounces of Previté's preparation of Ceylon moss, taking special care to well mix the preparation with the broth. Keep the pan gently boiling by the side of the stove-fire for one hour and a quarter; then pass the broth through a napkin into an earthen vessel, and put it by for use.

This broth is nutritious and cooling, and its use in cases of sore throats will often prove beneficial.

BRAIZES, POELES, MIREPOIX, ETC.,

COMPRISING

Braize for general purposes.
White *poële* for poultry.
Frying batter for fillets of fish, &c.
Do. for fruit fritters.
Boiled *Marinade*, or pickle.
Cold *Marinade*.

Blanc or White Braize for dressing calves,
　heads.
Mirepoix, or Braize for truffles,
White *roux* for thickening sauces.
Brown *roux* for do.

230. BRAIZE FOR GENERAL PURPOSES.

TAKE two pounds of fillet of veal, one pound of fat Yorkshire ham, two heads of celery, and the same number of onions and carrots; cut all these into small square pieces, add a bay-leaf, thyme, parsley, one clove of garlic, two blades of mace, and a dozen cloves; throw these ingredients into a middle-sized stewpan in which has been melted down a pound of fresh butter; put the stewpan on the stove-fire, stirring its contents frequently with a wooden spoon, while the vegetables, &c., are frying. When this mixture becomes slightly browned, pour into the pan half a pint of Cognac brandy, allow it to simmer for five minutes, and then add three quarts of common broth. Keep the braize gently boiling for an hour and a half, then strain it off through a tammy cloth (using considerable pressure) into a kitchen-pan, and put it away in the larder, to be used for purposes that will be hereafter explained.

231. WHITE POELE FOR POULTRY.

CUT into dice-shaped pieces two pounds of beef suet, an equal quantity of veal, and the same kind of vegetables, &c., as described in the above-mentioned braize; to these add the pulp of two lemons, removing the pips; put these ingredients into a middle-sized stewpan with half a pound of butter, and stir them on a slow fire until the suet is quite melted; then add three quarts of common broth, and keep the *poële* gently boiling for an hour; it should then be passed through a sieve into an earthen pan, and reserved for the purpose of braizing poultry in.

Note.—The two foregoing preparations, although very desirable in imparting a rich succulent flavor to poultry, game, &c., are nevertheless to be regarded rather as luxurious than essential. Good white or brown stock, as the case may require, can be used as economical substitutes.

232. FRYING BATTER FOR FILLETS OF FISH, POULTRY, GAME, ETC., A LA HORLY, OR A LA ROYALE.

PUT into a two-quart basin three-quarters of a pound of sifted flour, a little salt, two yelks of eggs, and two ounces of fresh butter previously melted in a small stewpan; to these add gradually about half a pint of tepid water, and stir the whole together with a wooden spoon until the butter has acquired the consistency and appearance of rich-looking double cream; it may then be put aside in the larder until within half an hour of its being wanted, when the whites of two eggs, well whisked into a snowlike froth, should be incorporated with it.

233. FRYING BATTER FOR ALL SORTS OF FRUIT FRITTERS.

PUT into a basin three-quarters of a pound of sifted flour, three ounces of fresh butter (melted), one wine-glassful of Curaçoa, and a very little salt; mix these gently together with a wooden spoon, gradually pouring into the basin about half a pint of bitter ale. When the batter becomes mixed to the thickness of double cream, set it aside while you whisk the whites of three eggs into a substantial froth, and instantly incorporate this with it.

Many prefer such fritters as pineapple, peach, apricot or plum, fried with a plainer kind of batter, in making which, water is substituted for ale.

234. BOILED MARINADE.

CUT into slices, and put into a stewpan, four carrots, the same number of onions, and two heads of celery, to which add parsley, four bay-leaves, thyme and sweet basil, a dozen cloves, a few blades of mace, two cloves of garlic, and one pound of raw ham (cut into small square pieces), a tablespoonful of peppercorns, and half a pound of butter. Stir these ingredients together over the fire until they become lightly browned; then pour over them a quart of French white wine vinegar, and let the *marinade* boil quickly for five minutes, then add two quarts of common stock; allow the whole to boil gently for one hour; strain it off through a tammy-cloth (using considerable pressure), into a kitchen pan, and reserve it for use.

This *marinade* is used for the purpose of preserving larded beef, mutton, venison, or roebuck, as well as to braize either of these in, when it is wished to dress them *à la Chêvreuil* or roebuck fashion.

235. COLD MARINADE OR PICKLE.

TAKE a large earthen vessel capable of containing whatever joint is intended to be *marinaded* or pickled; then cut into very thin slices or shreds, four carrots and as many onions; add to these, cloves, mace, peppercorns, thyme, bay-leaves and basil, and a handful of salt; after having mixed all these together, pour in, according to the quantity of *marinade* that may be required, cold spring water and vinegar in the proportion of two-thirds of the former to one-third of the latter; keep the pan (containing the *marinade*) covered with its lid in a cool place, for the purpose of pickling therein, joints of red deer, roebuck, mountain hares, fillets of mutton or beef, &c.

In Scotland, this sort of *marinade* will prove very serviceable, especially if cooking for a shooting-party, and when the larders are well supplied with moor and Highland game.

236. BLANC OR WHITE BRAIZE FOR CALVES' HEADS OR EARS, AND ALSO LAMBS' FEET OR EARS.

CHOP one pound (more or less, as occasion may require) of beef suet, and the same quantity of fat bacon; put these into a stewpan together with a garnished* fagot of parsley, a couple of carrots and

---

* A garnished fagot of parsley, consists of a handful of parsley, half a dozen green onions, and a bay-leaf and sprig of thyme tied together neatly with twine.

onions, inserting four cloves into one of the latter; add the pulp of two lemons, a teaspoonful of whole pepper, and a little salt, place the stewpan on the stove-fire for about ten minutes, carefully stirring the ingredients the whole time, in order to prevent them from acquiring a brown color; then pour in a sufficient proportion of water to produce the quantity of *blanc* required. Allow the *blanc* to boil one hour, then strain it through a hair-sieve, and use it for the purpose intended.

237. MIREPOIX FOR BRAIZING LARDED FILLETS OF ROEBUCK, ETC.

TAKE two pounds of veal, one pound of fat bacon, and one pound of lean ham, four carrots, four onions, a pottle of mushrooms, six shalots, a clove of garlic, two bay-leaves, some sprigs of thyme, six cloves, two blades of mace, and a teaspoonful of peppercorns; cut these ingredients up into small square pieces, and put them into a stewpan with half a pound of butter, and fry them brown; then add a bottle of Madeira or sherry, and a quart of good broth; boil the *mirepoix* by the side of a stove-fire for about an hour and a half, and then strain it through a tammy (with considerable pressure, to extract all the goodness) into a basin, to be kept for such purposes as will be hereafter directed.

238. WHITE ROUX OR THICKENING FOR SAUCES.

TAKE some fresh butter—say one pound, put it into a stewpan on a moderate fire to clarify; skim it, and then pour it off into a thick-bottomed stewpan, care being taken that none of the milk be allowed to mix with the butter. Fill the butter up with sifted flour in sufficient quantity to form a paste requiring some strength to work it with a wooden spoon; the *roux* should then be placed on a moderate fire, and continually stirred with the spoon until it becomes somewhat softer; then take the spoon out, wipe the sides of the stewpan, put the lid on it, and place it in a moderately-heated oven, and there let it remain for about three-quarters of an hour—taking care to stir it every ten minutes, and to watch it closely, in order to prevent the possibility of its getting burnt or colored, an accident which would render it use-less for white sauce. At the expiration of the time above-named, or before, if the *roux* be sufficiently done, (which may easily be ascertained by its becoming thinner), it should be taken out of the oven, and put aside until wanted for use.

This *roux* is used for thickening *Velouté* or white sauce.

239. BROWN ROUX, OR THICKENING FOR BROWN SAUCE.

THIS is made exactly in the same way as the white *roux* with the exception that it should remain longer in the oven, to allow it to acquire a fawn or buff color, before it is taken out. When the *roux* is considered to be done, three or four shalots should be thrown in, in order to diminish the action of the heat of the copper stewpan on its contents, and for the purpose of imparting flavor to it.

This *roux* is used to thicken *Espagnole* or brown sauce.

QUENELLE FORCE-MEATS IN GENERAL, AND FORCE-MEATS FOR GRATINS,

COMPRISING

Bread Panada for *quenelles*.
Pâte à choux Panada.
Preparation of Calf's Udder.
Quenelle of Chicken or Fowl.
Do. of Pheasant or Partridge.

Quenelle of Hare.
Do. of Rabbit.
Do. of small Birds.
Do. of Fish or Lobsters.

240. BREAD PANADA FOR QUENELLES.

TAKE the crumb of two new French rolls, and steep it in tepid water for ten minutes, then put it into a napkin and wring it tightly, in order to remove the water from the bread. Put the crumb into a stewpan with two ounces of fresh butter, a little salt, and two spoonsful of white broth. Put these on the stove-fire, continuing to stir the panada the whole time with a wooden spoon, until it assumes the appearance of paste, and no longer adheres to the bottom of the stewpan, then add three yelks of eggs, and turn it out on a plate, smooth it over the surface with the blade of a knife, and having covered it with a round piece of buttered paper, place it in the larder until required for use.

241. PATE A CHOUX PANADA.*

To half a pint of white chicken broth add four ounces of fresh butter and a little salt; put the stewpan containing these on the fire; as soon as it begins to simmer, mix in with the fore-mentioned ingredients five ounces of sifted flour, and by continuing to stir this batter on the fire for five minutes, it will become a delicately firm paste, which must be worked over the fire until it freely leaves the sides of the pan. Then take three yelks of eggs and quickly mix them in the batter; put it on a plate, cover it with a buttered paper, and keep it in the cool till wanted for use.

This kind of panada is preferred by some cooks to bread panada; being considered by them more delicate and less liable to produce fermentation in warm weather; however, bread panada has the advantage of not collapsing, as is the case with the *pâte à choux* panada, if prepared some time before the *quenelle* in which it is used be eaten.

242. PREPARATION OF CALF'S UDDER.

THE udder is an elongated piece of fat-looking substance attached to the inner part of a leg of veal. It is easily separated from the meat by a knife, and should then be bound round with twine in the shape of a sausage, so as to prevent it from falling to pieces on taking it out of the stockpot; the udder so tied up is then put into the stockpot to boil. Having allowed the dressed udder time to cool and get firm, either on the ice or otherwise, pare off the outside with a knife, cut it into small pieces, and pound it in a

* Anglicé, " pretty shoes."

mortar; then rub it through a wire sieve with a wooden spoon, and put it on a plate upon the ice to cool, in order that it may be quite firm when required for use.

Note.—The two foregoing preparations being the basis of a great variety of force-meats, it is essential that they should be well understood before attempting the following more complicated amalgamations.

It should also be observed that all meat and fish intended for *quenelles* must be forced through a wire-sieve by rubbing it vigorously with the back of a wooden spoon, and then be kept on ice till used.

243. QUENELLE OF FOWL.

TAKE of panada and prepared udder, or fresh butter, half a pound of each, to these add ten ounces of prepared fillets of chicken, as directed above, and pound all three together in a mortar; when they are well mixed, add salt, and as much grated nutmeg as will cover a sixpence, a little pepper, and one egg; pound the whole together till thoroughly mixed, then add another whole egg and two yelks, and a tablespoonful of *Béchamel* or *Suprême* sauce. Pound the whole thoroughly and quickly, and after having taken the force-meat out of the mortar and put it into a kitchen basin; keep it in a cool place until wanted for use.

Previously to taking the *quenelle* up out of the mortar, its consistency should be thus ascertained. Take a piece of the force-meat the size of a large nut, roll it with a little flour into the form of a round ball, put it into a small stewpan half full of boiling water; place it by the side of the fire to simmer for three minutes, after which take it out and cut it in halves; taste it in order to ascertain if it be correctly seasoned, and see, that when cut asunder, the inner part presents a smooth, light, compact surface.

244. QUENELLE OF FILLETS OF GROUSE, PHEASANT, OR PARTRIDGE; QUENELLE OF RABBIT, OR HARE.

THE process for making these is precisely similar to the foregoing, substituting, of course, the respective sort of game required, for fowl. It requires, however, the addition of a tablespoonful of strong essence of game and mushrooms, and a little *Allemande* sauce; which not only imparts a richer flavor to the *quenelle*, but also renders it smoother.

245. QUENELLE OF FILLETS OF SMALL BIRDS.

TAKE the fillets of such a number of small birds (as quails, snipes, larks, plovers, and dottrel) as are likely to weigh about three-quarters of a pound. Prepare them just as directed in the process for making *quenelle* of fowl—adding a little glaze made from their carcasses, and reduced with a small quantity of *Allemande* sauce.

246. QUENELLE OF WHITINGS.

FILLET four large whitings, after having previously skinned them; pound them in a mortar, and force the produce through a wire-sieve with a wooden spoon. To this substance add equal proportions of bread panada and fresh butter; pound these effectually, so as to mix them well together; add two whole eggs, and the yelks of two others gradually; season with pepper, salt, and grated nutmeg. Mix well by pounding the *quenelle* vigorously, and then take it up into a basin for use as required.

Quenelle of every sort of delicate fish is prepared in a similar manner to the above.

247. QUENELLES OF LOBSTERS.

TAKE the meat of two or more hen lobsters, cut this into thin slices, and pound it thoroughly with two ounces of fresh butter; force it through a wire sieve with a wooden spoon, and add two-thirds of its quantity of panada, and a similar proportion of fresh butter. Pound these well together, adding, by intervals, three whole eggs and a spoonful of *Allemande* sauce, a little cayenne pepper, salt, and grated nutmeg; mix well together by pounding, and then take the *quenelle* up into a basin for use.

248. FORCE-MEAT OF LIVER AND HAM, FOR RAISED PIES.

TAKE the whole or part of a light-colored calf's liver, or several fat livers of any kind of poultry, if to be obtained. If calf's liver be used, cut it into rather small square pieces, and, if time permit, steep them in cold spring water, in order to extract the blood, so that the force-meat may be whiter. Take the pieces of liver out of the water, and place them upon a clean rubber to drain the water from them. Meanwhile cut some fat ham or bacon (in equal proportion to the liver) into square pieces, put them into a sauta-pan on a brisk fire to fry, after which add the pieces of liver, and fry the whole of a light brown color; season with cayenne pepper and salt, and a little prepared aromatic spice (No. 1250), some chopped mushrooms, parsley, and three shalots. After this, take the pieces of liver and ham out of the pan, lay them on a chopping-board, and chop them fine; then put them into a mortar with the remaining contents of the pan; pound the whole thoroughly, and rub it through a wire sieve on to an earthen dish.

This kind of force-meat, or *farce*, is an excellent ingredient in making raised pies.

249. FORCE-MEAT, OR FARCE, FOR PRESERVING GAME IN.

To six pounds of boned game, of the kind intended to be preserved, add four pounds of fat bacon or ham, and two pounds of fat livers (or, failing these, calf's liver); cut the whole into small square pieces, and proceed as follows: First fry the pieces of bacon in a large sauta-pan, and when they become slightly browned, throw in the game and livers; season with pepper and salt, aromatic spices, chopped mushrooms, and three or four shalots; fry the whole till the game is thoroughly done; then chop and pound all these ingredients together; and afterward rub them through a wire sieve; after which put the *farce* into a clean pan, and keep it covered over with buttered paper. It should be used the same day that it is made, for the sooner preserves are out of hand the better.

The use of this *farce* will be shown in its proper place.

Note.—When about to preserve game in earthen pans for the spring or summer season, great care should be taken in selecting fresh game for that purpose, as when preserves are made with stale game, the preparation will most likely not bear keeping so as to be eatable when opened for use.

250. FARCE OF FAT LIVERS FOR GRATINS.

IF the *farce* be required for turbans or fillets of fowls or rabbits, or *pâtés-chauds* of game or small birds, it should be made of fat livers or leg of veal, and prepared in exactly the same manner as directed for making *farce* of livers for game pies, excepting that, to finish it for use, it is necessary to add one-third the quantity of well-made bread panada, and an equal proprotion of raw eggs to bind it, and give it body.

In order to ascertain whether this farce is perfect, roll a small quantity in a little flour on a plate, then put it on a small baking sheet in the oven for five minutes ; when done through, cut it asunder, and if it preserves its shape and remains firm to the touch, it may be used with safety ; but if it appears to shrink or melt in the oven, then a little more panada and another egg must be added, which will render it more compact.

251. GODIVEAUX IN GENERAL.

To one pound of either veal, fillets of fowls, pheasants, partridges, &c., chopped exceedingly fine and smooth to the touch, add one pound of beef suet, two whole eggs, the crumb of one French roll soaked in water and well wrung in a napkin, grated nutmeg, pepper, and salt. Chop these ingredients until thoroughly mixed, then pound them in a mortar until the whole presents the appearance of a compact body. Then place the substance upon a plate, cover it with buttered paper, and set it upon ice to cool for a couple of hours.

After the *godiveau* has been cooled, put it in the mortar again and pound it with considerable force, taking care to mix in with it, by degrees, about three-quarters of a pound of clean washed rough ice. This last process will cause it to resemble somewhat the *quenelle* of fowl. Put it away in a basin in a cool place till wanted for use.

Godiveau of any kind, when well made, is very delicious eating, and is not so expensive to make as *quenelle*. It is used for garnishing *vol-au-vents, pâtés-chauds, tourtes á la ciboulette,* and also for stuffing calfs' heads, as a substitute for *quenelle* force-meats.

CLEAR CONSOMME SOUPS IN GENERAL,

COMPRISING

Spring Soup.
Do. *à la Vertpré.*
Juliénne Soup.
Jardinière do.
Chiffonade do.
Nivernaise do.
Xavier do.
Dauphine do.
Barley do. *à la Princesse.*
Quenelles of fowl in *consommé.*
Vermicelli clear Soup.
Macaroni do. do.
Indian Paste Soup.
Lasagnes do.
Clear rice do.
Do. with asparagus points.
Chicken and rice Soup.
Cocky Leeky Broth.

Scotch Broth.
Hodge-podge.
Knuckle of veal and rice Soup.
Brunoise do.
Lettuce and whole pea do.
Flemish do.
Sportsman's do. clear.
Soup *à la Désclignac.*
Partridge Soup *à la Chasseur.*
Paysanne Soup.
Tendons of veal *à la Jardinière.*
Do with peas and lettuces
Ox-tail Soup.
Soup of gratinated crusts *à la D'Orléans.*
Do. *à la Princesse.*
Do with lettuces.
Do *à la Régence.*
Do *à la Paysanne.*

252. SPRING SOUP.

TAKE four carrots and as many turnips scraped and washed, scoop them into the form of small olives or peas, with a vegetable scoop of either shape; add the white part of two heads of celery, twenty-four small onions (without the green stalk), and one head of firm white cauliflower cut into small flowerets. Blanch or parboil the foregoing in boiling water for three minutes, strain them on a sieve, and then throw them into three quarts of bright *consommé* of fowl; let the whole boil gently for half an hour by the side of the stove-fire; then add the white leaves of two cabbage-lettuces (previously stamped out with a round cutter the size of a shilling), a handful of sorrel-leaves, snipped or cut like the lettuces, a few leaves of tarragon and chervil, and a small piece of sugar; let these continue to boil gently until done. When about to send the soup to table, put into the tureen half a pint of young green peas, an equal quantity of asparagus-heads boiled green, and a handful of small *croùtons à la duchesse,* prepared in the following manner :—Cut the crust off a rasped French roll into strips; stamp or cut out these with a round tin or steel cutter, into small pellets about the size of a shilling, and dry them in the oven to be ready for use.

Before sending the soup to table, taste it to ascertain whether it be sufficiently seasoned.

253. SPRING SOUP A LA VERTPRE.

THIS is prepared in the same manner as the foregoing—except that the *croùtons à la duchesse* are omitted, and in their stead a *purée* of green spinach, in sufficient quantity to thicken and color the soup, should be added.

254. JARDINIERE SOUP.

PREPARE the same vegetables as for spring soup, boil them in a strong *consommé*, and just before sending the soup to table add to it a pint of *purée* of green peas.

255. JULIENNE SOUP.

TAKE three red carrots of a large size, as many sound turnips, and the white parts of the same number of leeks, heads of celery and onions. Cut all these vegetables into fine shreds an inch long. Put them into a convenient-sized stewpan with two ounces of fresh butter, a little salt, and a teaspoonful of pounded sugar. Simmer these vegetables on a slow stove-fire, taking care they do not burn; when they become slightly brown, add three quarts of *blond de veau* or light-colored *consommé;* let the soup boil, skim all the butter off as it rises to the surface, and when the vegetables are done, throw in the leaves of two cabbage-lettuces and a handful of sorrel, shred like the carrots, &c., add a few leaves of tarragon and chervil; boil the whole for ten minutes longer, taste the soup in order to ascertain whether the seasoning is correct, and serve.

256. CHIFFONADE SOUP.

TRUSS two spring chickens, and boil them in some good white *consommé*. When done and cooled, cut them into small members, paring off the skin; put these into a well-tinned stewpan, together with the stock they were boiled in, which should be clarified, if it be not sufficiently bright. Set the stewpan on the stove-fire to boil, and then add the white leaves of four cabbage-lettuces, a small handful of sorrel, a little tarragon and chervil, and one head of celery shred fine. See that the soup be perfectly seasoned and of delicate flavor, and send to table.

257. NIVERNAISE SOUP.

TAKE four turnips, cut them into the form of small cloves of garlic, fry them in a little butter and sugar in a stewpan over the fire to give them a light brown color, then drain them upon a sieve and put them into a soup-pot. Scoop out the red part of two large-sized red carrots, blanch or parboil these for ten minutes, and, when strained, add them to the turnips; then pour upon the vegetables three quarts of strong bright *consommé*, and set the soup to boil gently by the side of the stove-fire until the vegetables are thoroughly done, taking care to skim off the butter as it rises to the surface. Ten minutes before dinner-time, throw into the soup, while boiling, some very small Brussels sprouts that have been previously parboiled : and just before sending this soup to table, add to it about two or three dozen very small *quenelles* of pheasant.

258. XAVIER SOUP.

MIX with six ounces of sifted flour, half a pint of double cream, four ounces of fresh butter, and two ounces of grated Parmesan cheese, a little minionette pepper, salt, and grated nutmeg. When these ingredients have been thoroughly mixed together with a wooden spoon, put the stewpan containing them on the fire—stirring it quickly and continually, until it begins to thicken, when it should be well worked with the spoon for about five minutes. By this time the batter will have assumed the appearance of a firm, compact paste; two whole eggs and two yelks should then be worked into it; then add a tablespoonful of chopped and blanched parsley.

When this paste is so far ready, make up two half-sheets of paper in the shape of a funnel, with a hole at the point, a quarter of an inch in diameter, and fasten them with a pin. Into each of these papers or *forcers*, put as much of the paste as will nearly fill it; close the large ends in the same way as you would a paper of brown sugar; and with gentle pressure force the paste out at the pointed extremity on to a large stewpan cover (previously buttered) in the shape of large peas; this is done with a sudden jerk of the wrist. When the stewpan lid is covered with these fragments of paste—which, however, must not be close enough to touch each other—prepare some boiling *consommé* in a stewpan over the fire, and shake off the peas into it (which will be easily effected by just passing the lid containing the fragments of paste over the fire), in order to detach them, and thus facilitate their slipping into the broth. Let these boil very gently for five minutes; strain them on a sieve, and then throw them into three quarts of strong bright *consommé* of fowl or game prepared for the purpose; allow them to boil again gently for five minutes; add a *pluche* of tarragon and chervil, and let these boil a short time previously to serving up the soup.

Send some grated Parmesan cheese on a plate, to be handed round simultaneously with this soup.

259. DAUPHINE SOUP.

TAKE half a pint of strong *consommé* of fowl, and pour it gradually into a stewpan containing eight yelks of eggs beaten up with a little salt, nutmeg, and pepper; when the egg is well mixed with the *consommé*, strain it through a sieve into a round plain mould, which should be previously buttered carefully for that purpose. Put the mould holding the preparation into a large stewpan containing water, to the depth of about an inch, and cover the stewpan with the lid; let the water in it simmer—or gently boil—on the corner of the stove-fire, so as to produce sufficient steam to set the custard. When this is done, take it out of the water; and after having allowed it time to cool, cut it into shapes resembling thick wafers, which put into two quarts of strong *consommé* of fowl, together with a pint of green asparagus heads, previously boiled for that purpose, a small piece of sugar, and a few tarragon-leaves. Allow the soup to boil very gently by the side of the stove-fire for about three minutes, and then send to table.

260. BARLEY SOUP A LA PRINCESSE.

TAKE half a pound of Frankfort pearl barley, wash and blanch it, and put it to boil in one quart of bright *consommé* of fowl. When the barley is sufficiently done, put it into the soup tureen with the members of two spring chickens (previously roasted and cut up for the purpose); to these add a sufficient quantity of *consommé* of fowl; and after having tested the seasoning of the soup, send to table.

261. QUENELLES OF FOWL IN CONSOMME.

Mould three or four dozen of very small *quenelles* of fowl in the following manner:—Take up a spoonful of chicken force-meat, smooth it over with the blade of a small knife, which must be occasionally dipped in hot water, in order to prevent the *quenelle* from sticking to it; and with another teaspoon, dipped in hot water, scoop out the *quenelle* from the filled teaspoon, and drop it gently on the bottom of a buttered sauta-pan. When this part of the operation is completed, a stewpan cover is held with the left hand in a slanting direction toward the inner part of the edge of the sauta-pan; with the other hand sufficient boiling water should be poured in to poach the *quenelles:* then set the sauta-pan by the side of the fire to simmer for about ten minutes, when the *quenelles* will be done. Take them out and lay them upon a clean cloth to drain; after which place them in the soup tureen, and having poured thereon two quarts of bright *consommé* of fowl, send to table.

262. CLEAR VERMICELLI SOUP.

Take half a pound of vermicelli, break it small and blanch it—by allowing it to boil three minutes in water—drain it on a sieve, and then put it into a stewpan with two quarts of strong bright *consommé* of fowl or game, or *blond* of veal, according to taste or circumstances. After allowing the soup thus prepared to boil up on the stove-fire, skim the froth from the surface, and set it to continue boiling gently on the corner of the stove till the vermicelli be sufficiently done. Then pour the soup into the tureen, and send to table with some grated Parmesan cheese on a plate, separately, to be handed round to the guests simultaneously with the soup. This should be observed as a general rule, in serving up all soups containing Italian pastes in any form.

263. MACARONI CLEAR SOUP.

Boil one pound of Naples macaroni in two quarts of water, an ounce of fresh butter, a little salt, and minionette pepper. When the macaroni is done, which will take about half an hour, drain it on a sieve, wash it in clear water, and then drain it upon a napkin, that it may be cut into pieces an inch long. Then put it into a soup-pot with two quarts of *blond* of veal, or *consommé* of fowl or of game, according to circumstances; let it boil ten minutes longer and serve.

264. ITALIAN PASTE SOUP.

Take half a pound of Italian paste, blanch or parboil it first, and afterward boil it in two quarts of bright strong *consommé*, as directed for vermicelli soup, and send to table.

265. LASAGNES SOUP.

Lasagnes are a kind of Italian paste resembling ribbons, and must be treated in exactly the same way as when using macaroni for soup, excepting that they do not require so much boiling.

266. CLEAR CONSOMME WITH RICE.

Take half a pound of Carolina rice well picked and washed, blanch or parboil it for ten minutes, drain the water off; and after adding two quarts of good clear *consommé*, boil it gently by the side of the stove-fire till the grains of the rice begin to feather or separate, when it will be ready to send to table.

Observe, that broths and *consommés* should be always stronger when used for soups containing Italian pastes of any kind, rice, or barley: as these farinaceous substances decrease the flavor and apparent strength of soups, and render them less acceptable to the palate of the epicure—unless counteracted by increasing the strength of the *consommé*.

267. CLEAR RICE SOUP WITH ASPARAGUS POINTS.

THIS soup is prepared in the same way as the foregoing—with the addition of one pint of asparagus points boiled green and thrown into the soup just before sending to table.

268. CHICKEN AND RICE SOUP.

TRUSS, boil, and cut into small members, two spring chickens; the skin should be removed, and the pieces neatly trimmed and placed in the soup tureen, together with two quarts of clear rice soup, which should be made with chicken broth or *consommé*, of a light color. The seasoning of this soup must be light.

269. COCKY-LEEKY SOUP.

TAKE two fowls, which truss, boil, and cut up as for the foregoing soup. To the broth they have been boiled in add two quarts of *blond* of veal, and in this boil (after having first parboiled them in water) the white part of a dozen leeks cut into lengths of about an inch, and these again cut lengthways into four. When the leeks have been boiled thoroughly soft in the broth, add the pieces of fowl; and after allowing the whole to boil ten minutes longer, send to table.

Note.—This kind of soup is objected to by many who dislike the odor of leeks; it is considered, however, to be a fine restorative, and is especially recommended to the notice of sportsmen, after a hard day's riding with the hounds, or fagging over the moors.

270. SCOTCH BROTH.

TAKE a neck of fresh mutton, trim it the same as for cutlets; take the scrag and trimmings, with two carrots, three turnips, two heads of -celery, two onions, a bunch of parsley, and a sprig of thyme, and with these make some mutton broth—filling up with either broth from the common stockpot, or with water. While the mutton broth is boiling, cut up the neck of mutton, previously trimmed for the purpose, into chops, which should have the superfluous skin and fat pared away, and place them in a three-quart stewpan, together with the red or outer part of two carrots, three turnips, two leeks, one onion, and two heads of celery—the whole of these to be cut in the form of very small dice; add six ounces of Scotch barley previously washed and parboiled, and then pour on to the whole the broth made from the scrag, &c., when strained and the fat removed. Allow the soup thus far prepared to boil gently until the chops and the vegetables be thoroughly done. Five minutes before sending the soup to table throw into it a tablespoonful of chopped and blanched parsley.

Be sparing in the use of salt, so as not to overpower the simple but sweet flavor which characterizes this broth.

271. HODGE-PODGE.*

MAKE the mutton broth as shown in the preceding directions, and in addition to its contents add a pint and a half of green peas (either marrow-fats or Prussian-blues). Allow the soup to boil gently until the ingredients be thoroughly done, then mix in with them one pint of *purée* of green spinach and parsley : taste to ascertain that the seasoning be correct, and serve.

272. KNUCKLE OF VEAL AND RICE SOUP.

TAKE a good-sized knuckle of fresh veal, cut it into four pieces— sawing the bones through. Place the pieces in a small stockpot with two calf's-feet, a partridge (an old one will do) that has been roasted for a quarter of an hour ; to these add three quarts of common broth or water. Put the soup on the stove-fire to boil, skim it well, garnish it with one carrot, one turnip, an onion in which has been inserted four cloves, and one head of celery ; also a little salt and a few peppercorns. Having allowed the soup to boil gently by the side of the stove-fire for about three hours, proceed with care to take up the partridge, the calf's-feet, and also the glutinous pieces of veal, which place on a dish to cool in the larder. Then pass the broth through a napkin into a stewpan, and after having taken off every particle of fat, add to it half a pound of Carolina rice, which must be blanched or parboiled for the purpose. Allow the rice to boil gently in the broth till it is nearly done, then cut the fillet of partridges into pieces about an inch in length and a quarter of an inch wide, take the glutinous pieces of the veal and the inner tendons of the calf's feet, and cut these also in pieces in a similar manner to the partridge ; put the whole into the broth with the rice, and after boiling them together for five minutes send to table.

This kind of soup may be also finished with the addition of a pint of green peas, which must be boiled a few minutes before serving up the soup, and placed in the tureen previously to pouring in the soup.

Asparagus points may be used for the same purpose.

273. BRUNOISE SOUP.

TAKE carrots, turnips, heads of celery, leeks, and onions, of each a couple ; cut them into small dice and fry them in a stewpan, over a slow fire, with an ounce of fresh butter, a little pounded sugar, and a sprinkling of salt. When the vegetables have acquired a light brown color, pour into them three quarts of good strong bright *consommé* or *blond* of veal, and put the soup on the stove to boil ; skim it well, and then remove it to the side, there to continue gently boiling until the vegetables are thoroughly done. Add half a pint of green-peas, a handful of French beans (cut into the form of diamonds), and half a pint of asparagus points (the whole having been previously boiled green for the purpose), also a few duchess' crusts ; and having tested the flavor and seasoning of the soup, send to table.

* From the French, *Hoche-pot.*

274. LETTUCE AND WHOLE-PEA SOUP.

Pick, wash, and blanch, a dozen white-heart cabbage-lettuces ; cut them open, and spread them on a clean napkin ; season them with minionette pepper, and salt ; then put two together, face to face, and proceed to tie them up with twine. Cover the bottom of a stewpan with thin layers of fat bacon, and place the lettuce thereon ; pour upon them some broth from the boiling stockpot, over which lay a round of buttered paper ; place the lid on the stewpan, start them to boil on the fire, and then place them on a slackened stove, to simmer gently for about an hour ; after which, drain the lettuces on a clean napkin, untie them, and after having cut them into inch lengths, lay them in the soup-tureen, together with a pint of young green peas boiled for the purpose, and a small pinch of minionette pepper. Take every particle of fat off the broth in which the lettuces have been braized, and add it to the lettuces and peas already in the tureen, over which pour two quarts of bright strong *consommé* of fowl ; ascertain that the soup be palatable, and having thrown in a handful of duchess' crusts, send to table.

275. FLEMISH SOUP.

Take carrots, turnips, and cucumbers, of each two, and with a vegetable scoop cut them out into the shape of olives or pears. To the foregoing add the white parts of two heads of celery, and three leeks, which must be cut into thick shreds half an inch long ; blanch or parboil these for five minutes ; drain them on a sieve, and afterward place them in a small soup-pot capable of containing three quarts ; add rather better than two quarts of good *consommé*, and set the soup on the stove-fire to boil, skim it, and place it by the side to boil gently until the vegetables are sufficiently done. While the soup is boiling, blanch the following vegetables, which, when done, put into the soup with the others : a handful of Brussels sprouts, half a pint of young peas, a few French beans cut small, and a handful of asparagus heads. Add a pinch of minionette pepper ; allow the soup to boil three minutes longer, and having placed some duchess' crusts in the tureen, pour the soup upon them, and serve.

276. SPORTSMAN'S CLEAR SOUP.

With two teaspoons mould about four dozen very small *quenelles* of any sort of game ; poach these in broth, and then drain them on a clean napkin, and afterward put them into a stewpan containing two quarts of strong bright *consommé* of game ; place the soup on the fire, and allow it to boil very gently by the side for a few minutes ; ascertain that the seasoning is correct, and send to table.

This soup takes its special title from the species of game of which it may chance to be made ; as, for instance, Sportsman's Clear Soup of *Pheasant*, of *Partridge*, of *Hare*, &c. &c.

277. DESCLIGNAC, OR IMPERIAL SOUP.

Put eight yelks of eggs into a basin, with a little grated nutmeg and salt ; beat them together, mixing therewith half a pint of strong *consommé* of fowl or game : strain this preparation through a hair sieve into a plain mould, which has been buttered for the purpose.

Steam this in the same way as you would any other custard ; and, when done, put it to cool in the larder. Cut the custard, thus prepared, into fanciful shapes, and having placed them in the tureen, pour on gently two quarts of boiling, strong, bright *consommé*, of the same kind that is used to mix the custard with.

278. PAYSANNE SOUP.

THIS is to be prepared in exactly the same manner as the Flemish soup, except that, instead of the Brussels sprouts, the following must be used : the leaves of two summer cabbages cut into pieces the size and shape of a shilling, the hearts of four lettuces slit into thick shreds, a few leaves of sorrel, tarragon, and chervil. After these have been boiled with the other vegetables ten minutes, add to them two dozen scollops of braized beef; season with a little minionette pepper, and serve.

279. SOUP OF GRATINATED CRUSTS A LA JARDINIERE.

FOR a dinner of sixteen covers, order a dozen small rolls to be made of the size and shape of an egg ; rasp them, and take the crumb out carefully without disturbing the shape of the rolls. When the crumb is taken out, put the rolls or hollow crusts on a baking sheet in the oven, for the purpose of making them crisp, as well as to give them a light brown color.

An hour before dinner, put the crusts, thus prepared, into a deep silver dish, and pour over them a sufficient quantity of *consommé* of fowl to cover them. Place the dish, containing the crusts, on a trevet over a stove-fire of moderate heat, and there allow the crusts to become *gratinated*, that is to say, to acquire, by means of boiling down, a concentration of flavor, and that appearance of crispness, which is as alluring to the eye as it is savory to the palate. When the *consommé* is perfectly absorbed by the crusts, put them in the oven, in order to increase their crispness ; but be extremely careful that they do not burn. Just before sending to table, pour on to the crusts, thus prepared, a *jardinière*, composed of small pipelike pieces of carrots, turnips, celery, leeks, a few small button onions, green peas, French beans, asparagus-heads, and also a few flowerets of white cauliflower. Only a small quantity of *consommé* should be put with the crusts and *Jardinière*,* as it is usual to serve up a tureen of clear *consommé* separately, from which the guests are served ; a small ladleful of the gratinated crusts, &c., should be first put into the soup-plate, and some of the *consommé* added afterward.

280. SOUP OF GRATINATED CRUSTS A LA PRINCESSE.

PREPARE the same number of rolls, according to the preceding instructions.

A few minutes before dinner, add to the crusts three dozen small *quenelles* of chicken rolled into the shape of pieces of macaroni, an inch long, half a pint of asparagus-heads, and a little boiling *consommé*. Send up two quarts of *consommé* in a soup-tureen, and serve as described in the last-mentioned soup.

281. SOUP OF GRATINATED CRUSTS A LA ROYALE.

PREPARE the crusts as before stated, adding four ounces of grated

* This observation is applicable to all gratinated soups.

Parmesan cheese and a little minionette. Just before dinner-time, lay upon the crusts (gratinated in the usual way) some shapes of chicken custard, described in the preparation of *Désclignac* soup; and serve up according to the preceding detail.

282. SOUP OF GRATINATED CRUSTS A LA FERNEUSE.

PREPARE the crusts as before described, cut three large sound turnips into small fancy shapes, fry them in a stewpan, with two ounces of butter, a teaspoonful of pounded sugar, and a little salt, over a slow fire, until they have gradually acquired a light brown color; then add a pint of *consommé*, and let them simmer gently by the side of the stove-fire until thoroughly done. When about to send the soup to table, pour the turnips thus prepared on to the gratinated crusts, and to them add a pint of young peas boiled green, and a few white button onions boiled in broth. Serve as before stated.

283. SOUP OF GRATINATED CRUSTS A LA BEAUJON.

PREPARE the crusts as before, and when they are gratinated, add a pint of reduced *purée* of young carrots, put these into the oven for ten minutes, and just before sending to table, pour over the crusts thus prepared half a pint of large heads of asparagus and some shreds of celery kept ready boiled in broth for the purpose, and serve with the *consommé* in a tureen separately.

PUREES OF VEGETABLES IN GENERAL FOR SOUPS,

COMPRISING

Purée of Peas *à l'Anglaise.*
Do. of Green Split Peas.
Do. of Red *Haricôt* beans *à la Condé.*
Do. of White *Haricôt* Beans.
Do. of Lentils *à la Reine.*
Do. of Lentils *à la Soubise.*
Do. of Lentils *à la Brûnoise.*
Do. of Green Peas.
Do. of Roots *à la Croissy.*
Do. of Carrots *à la Crécy.*
Brown *purée* of Turnips.
White do. of Turnips.
Palestine Soup.
Purée of Artichokes.
Do. of Endive.
Brown *purée* of Chestnuts.
White do. of Chestnuts.

Purée of Spinach *à la Beauvaux.*
Do. of Peas *à la Faubonne.*
Do. *à la Ferney.*
Do. *à la Fabert.*
Do. of Spring Herbs.
Do. *à la Victoria.*
Do. *à la Princesse.*
Do. of Young Carrots *à la Stanley.*
Crécy Soup with whole Rice.
Do. of Potatoes *à la crême.*
Do. of Potatoes *à la Victoria.*
Quenelles of Potatoes.
Do. of Asparagus *à la Condé.*
Do. *à la St. George.*
Bonne Femme Soup.
Soup *à la Hollandaise.*

284. PUREE OF PEAS A L'ANGLAISE.

TAKE a quart of yellow split-peas, wash them several times in water, drain them, and put them into a small stockpot with half a pound of raw ham, two heads of celery, one carrot, and an onion with four cloves stuck in it, add three quarts of common broth, let the soup boil, skim it well, and then set it by the side of the stove-fire to boil gently for about three hours. The peas having then become entirely dissolved, pass them through a tammy-cloth with the aid of two wooden spoons, to be used in the following manner: spread the tammy-cloth over a large dish, pour the *purée*, or part thereof, into the hollow thus formed; then let two persons take hold firmly of each end of the tammy-cloth with the left hand, so as carefully to secure the *purée* against flowing over; then, with the right hand, they should work the edge of the spoon, the bowls being back to back, in the cloth, in regular time and with some force, until the whole of the *purée* is rubbed through: it will be, however, necessary to scrape off with the back of a large knife any portion that may adhere to the cloth. When this is done, hasten to remove the *purée* from the dish into a soup-pot of adequate size; add a large ladleful of *consommé*, carefully stirring the *purée* on the stove-fire until it begins to boil, then remove it to the side of the stove, to continue gently boiling until it has clarified itself by throwing up all the froth, which should be removed as it rises to the surface. Ascertain whether the seasoning be palatable, and send to table with some dried and sifted mint in a plate; and in another plate serve some *Condé* crusts, prepared as follows:

Take a piece of stale bread, pare away the crust, and then cut the crumb into very small square dice, fry these in fresh butter till they become slightly browned, then drain them on a sieve, and afterward place them on a sheet of paper, moving them about for a short time that the butter may be absorbed. Keep these *croûtons* in a dry place until wanted. Just before dinner-time, they should be put inside the oven for a few minutes.

285. PUREE OF GREEN SPLIT-PEAS.

FOLLOW the foregoing instructions, taking care, however, to substitute green split-peas for yellow. When the *purée* is ready, in order to give it as much as possible the appearance of having been made with green peas, mix in with it some extract of spinach,* adding two small pats of butter and a little sugar. Serve separately some mint in powder, and *Condé* crusts on plates.

286. PUREE OF RED HARICOT BEANS.

TAKE one quart of red *haricôt* beans, and having put them to soak the overnight, drain off the water on the following morning; put the beans into a small stockpot, with carrots, celery, an onion stuck with three cloves, and a knuckle of raw ham; add three quarts of good stock, and set the whole on the stove-fire to simmer gently for about four hours. Then remove the carrot, celery, onion, and the ham; drain off the broth from the beans, and pound them in a

---

* Extract of spinach is thus prepared: Wash and pound in a mortar a sufficient quantity of spinach for a small dish, until it assumes a pulpy appearance; turn it out upon a strong kitchen rubber, the opposite ends of which are to be gathered up and held in the left hand by two persons, who must take care to fold the extremity of the cloth firmly round the handle of a wooden spoon, which will give them a strong purchase, acting as a windlass, and will enable them to wring the cloth so tightly as to express all the moisture of the spinach. To receive this extract, a stewpan should be placed ready; it should be held over the fire until it becomes coagulated, and must be put upon a hair sieve to drain off any remaining watery particles. Work the spinach-green through the sieve with a spoon, and this will form the extract.

mortar, after which place them in a stewpan, add the broth, and then pass the *purée* through the tammy-cloth in the usual manner; it should then be poured into a soup-pot, and if too thick to clarify, a little broth should be added; stir it over the stove-fire until it boils, and then remove it to the side of the stove, to continue gently boiling until it becomes bright: of course all the scum must be carefully removed while boiling. Finish the soup by adding two small pats of fresh butter and a little pounded sugar. *Condé* crusts should be handed round with this soup.

287. PUREE OF WHITE HARICOT BEANS.

Is made like the preceding, except that white *haricôt* beans must be substituted for red; moreover, in finishing this *purée*, in addition to the butter and sugar, half a pint of boiling cream should be poured in Serve with *Condé* crusts on a plate.

288. PUREE OF LENTILS A LA REINE.

TAKE one quart of reddish-brown lentils, prepare them exactly as described for the treatment of red *haricôt* beans in making that *purée;* finish also in a similar manner, and serve with *Condé* crusts.

289. PUREE OF LENTILS A LA SOUBISE.

THIS is made like the foregoing, but there must be added a *purée* of four large onions, prepared in the following manner :—slice up the onions, fry them brown in a little butter, adding to them a little broth; having allowed them to simmer gently on the fire until done, pass them in the usual way through a tammy, and mix the *purée* thus obtained with the soup; and when it has cleared itself by boiling, taste it to ascertain its seasoning, and send to table with *Condé* crusts separately.

290. PUREE OF LENTILS A LA BRUNOISE.

THIS soup is recommended to be served when there happens to be in the larder any remaining stock of *purée* of lentils, or *brûnoise* soup, which can be mixed for this purpose. The *Condé* crusts should be omitted.

291. GREEN-PEAS SOUP.

TAKE two quarts of green-peas, a double-handful of parsley, four stalks of green mint, and a good handful of green onions. Having put two quarts of common broth on the stove-fire, throw in the above ingredients as soon as it begins to boil; when the peas are thoroughly done, drain them and the other vegetables in a colander, then pound them well together; the *purée* thus far prepared should be put into a stewpan together with its own liquor, warm it until it becomes sufficiently dissolved, and then rub it through a tammy-cloth in the usual manner. Just before sending to table, warm the soup on a brisk stove-fire, adding two pats of fresh butter and a little pounded sugar.

Send *Condé* crusts on a plate.*

* In order to avoid unnecessary repetition, it should be observed, that *Condé* crusts must be served with the succeeding *purées* of vegetables, except when otherwise directed.

292. PUREE OF ROOTS A LA CROISSY.

CUT into thin shavings six large carrots, and slice very small the same number of turnips, three onions, and three heads of celery; add a handful of sorrel, and a little chervil and tarragon; put these into a stewpan with a quarter of a pound of fresh butter on a slow fire, and let it remain there until the vegetables are steamed sufficiently to reduce their quantity to one-half; then add two quarts of broth, and put the pan on the fire to boil; skim it, and remove it to the side to boil gently for about an hour and a half; after which, proceed to drain the roots from the broth in a colander, pound them in a mortar, and having mixed them with the liquor, warm the *purée* thus obtained, and rub it through the tammy-cloth in the usual way. Then put the *purée* into a soup-pot (with more broth if needed), and allow it to boil on the stove-fire; after this, place it by the side to clarify itself by gentle ebullition; and when it ceases to throw up any froth or scum, finish the soup by adding one pat of fresh butter and a little pounded sugar, and send to table.

293. PUREE OF CARROTS A LA CRECY.

SHAVE off the red part of about twelve large carrots, add one head of celery and one onion; blanch these in boiling water on the fire for ten minutes; drain them in a colander, and afterward put them into a small stockpot with two ounces of fresh butter, an ounce of lump sugar, and a little salt. Set the carrots thus prepared on a slow fire to steam, and when they have become considerably reduced in quantity (without burning or acquiring any color) add to them two quarts of good broth, and let the carrots boil gently for an hour; then drain them—pound and rub them through a tammy in the usual way, and clarify the *purée* in the same manner as directed in the preceding article. Finish this soup by incorporating with it one pat of fresh butter and a little pounded sugar.

294. BROWN PUREE OF TURNIPS.

SLICE up about eight large sound turnips, put them into a stewpan, into which a quarter of a pound of fresh butter has been previously melted, and add a tablespoonful of pounded sugar. Fry the turnips thus prepared over a rather brisk fire, in order to give them a light brown color; when this is effected, add two quarts of good stock, allow the soup to boil gently by the side of the stove-fire for about three-quarters of an hour; then drain, pass, and proceed to clarify the *purée* in the usual manner.

Observe, that this kind of *purée* should not be thick.

295. WHITE PUREE OF TURNIPS.

SLICE up a dozen large sound turnips, put them into a stewpan with a quarter of a pound of fresh butter, a tablespoonful of pounded sugar, and a little grated nutmeg. Put these to simmer on a slow fire, without allowing them to acquire any color. When the turnips begin to melt, add two quarts of white *consommé* of fowl; and having set the whole to boil gently on the corner of the stove for about three-quarters of an hour, proceed to drain, pass, and pound the turnips—reserving the broth they have been boiled in to clarify the *purée* with ; after it has boiled, skim off all the froth, and finish the soup by adding (just before sending to table) a pint of boiling cream and a pat of fresh butter, which must be thoroughly incorporated with the soup.

296. PALESTINE SOUP.

CLEANSE, peel, wash, and, slice up half a peck of Jerusalem artichokes ; put them into a stewpan with four ounces of fresh butter, and allow them to simmer gently on a slow fire, until they are reduced in quantity and partially melted—taking care that they do not get colored in the process. Then add two quarts of strong white *consommé* of fowl, and after allowing it to boil gently for three-quarters of an hour, proceed to rub the whole through a tammy-cloth in the usual way, and clarify the *purée*. Just before sending to table, add a pint of boiling cream, a small piece of glaze, and a little pounded sugar.

297. PUREE OF ARTICHOKES.

TURN or peel the bottoms of a dozen fine artichokes, and, after taking out the fibrous part inside, cut each into four pieces ; put them into a large stewpan previously well buttered, and strewn with a little pounded sugar,—placing the pieces of artichokes closely beside each other, and then set them on a slow fire to stew very gently, that they may acquire a light brown color. Then proceed in every respect to finish this soup in the same manner as directed for Palestine soup.

298. PUREE OF ENDIVE.

THIS soup should be made only when endives are plentiful and of good quality, as in the autumn season, when they are full and white. Having trimmed away all the green and outer leaves of about three dozen endives, which should be thoroughly washed and examined in order to pick out any insects, blanch them in boiling water and a little salt for ten minutes ; then take them out and throw them into cold water ; drain them in a colander, and with both hands press all the water from them. Having so far prepared the endives, cut off the roots and put them into a stewpan with four ounces of fresh butter, a little grated nutmeg, salt, and a little sugar. With a wooden spoon, stir the endives over a slow fire for about ten minutes ; then add a ladleful of good white *consommé* of fowl ; allow this to continue gently simmering on a very slow fire, or in the oven, for an hour : and then pass the endives through a tammy as usual. To the *purée* thus obtained, add one quart of white *consommé* of fowl ; clarify it according to custom, and just before sending the soup to table, mix with it a pint of boiling cream and a pat of fresh butter, and serve.

This soup is recommended for its lightness and cooling effect.

299. BROWN PUREE OF CHESTNUTS.

TAKE a hundred chestnuts (Spanish or Lyons chestnuts are the best), cut off the points or slit them across to prevent them from bursting and flying about ; put them in a stewpan with two ounces of fresh butter, and fry them on a moderate fire until they shed their husks readily ; then peal them clean, and put them into a stewpan

with a quart of veal gravy, and set them by the side of the stove to
boil gently until they become quite soft to the touch; drain them
from the liquor, and, after having first pounded, and afterward
rubbed them through the tammy (pouring in the liquor reserved for
the purpose to enable the *purée* to pass quicker), add another quart of
veal gravy to clarify the *purée*,—this, after being set to boil on the
stove, must be then removed to the side, there to continue gently
boiling that it may throw up the butter to the surface, which must
be removed with a spoon as it rises. Finish by mixing in with the
purée a small pat of butter, a little sugar, and a small piece of glaze,
and serve up.

300. WHITE PUREE OF CHESTNUTS.

PREPARE a hundred large chestnuts as for the preceding soup,
except that white *consommè* of fowls or rabbits must be used to boil
them in, as well as to finish the *purée* with. When the *purée* has
been clarified as directed above, just before serving it up add a pint
of boiling cream, a pat of fresh butter, and a little pounded sugar.

301. PUREE OF SPINACH A LA BEAUVAUX.

PICK, wash, and boil a large dish of spinach; chop it well and
pound it into a soft paste, and then put it into a stewpan with four
ounces of fresh butter, a little grated nutmeg, and salt; stir it on a
stove-fire for about ten minutes; then add a large soup-ladleful of
Velouté sauce and about a quart of white *consommé* of fowl, or any
other strong white broth at hand; warm the *purée* on the stove-fire,
and rub it through the tammy.

Observe, that this *purée* must not be clarified, it should be kept in
the coolest part of the larder until twenty minutes before sending it to
table; it must then be made hot by stirring it on the stove-fire, and
when just on the point of boiling, mix with it a pat of butter, a small
piece of glaze, and a little pounded sugar.

302. SOUP A LA FAUBONNE.

THIS soup consists of a *purée* of green peas, made in the usual way,
in which must be mixed, previously to serving it up, a pint of young
peas boiled green, six cabbage-lettuces braized, and cut into pieces an
inch long, and two cucumbers cut up into scollops, and afterward
boiled in *consommé*.

There need not be any crusts sent to table with this soup, nor indeed is it customary to serve *croutons* or crusts of any sort for *purées*
that contain a garnish of any kind.

303. SOUP A LA FERNEY.

THIS excellent soup is thus made: prepare twelve very small custards (made with *consommé*) in *dariole* moulds; cut three turnips into
very small fancy shapes, and fry them in a little fresh butter and sugar
until they become of a light brown color; a little *consommé* should
then be added, and they must be allowed to finish simmering on a very
slow fire, and when done, must be set to drain upon a clean napkin,
and afterward put into a soup tureen with the small custards; to these
add two cucumbers—cut into scollops and boiled in *consommé* for the
purpose; and lastly, pour some boiling *purée* of green peas on the
above, and serve.

The *purée* in this and similar cases, should be kept rather thinner than when intended to be served without a garnish.

304. SOUP A LA FABERT.

TAKE six quails, draw, singe, and cut them into quarters, making two fillets with the pinion left on as for a *fricassée*, and bone the legs, leaving only sufficient length of the thigh-bone to give it the shape of a cutlet, rolling the skin round so as to give it a cushionlike appearance. Place these in a stewpan, the bottom of which has been covered with thin layers of fat bacon; take care to preserve the shape of the members, and braize them in a light wine *mirepoix* (No. 236).

Having thus prepared the quails, when done, drain and trim them, and afterward place them in the soup-tureen, together with their own stock, which when freed from every particle of fat, must then be clarified, and also a proportionate quantity of *Juliènne* vegetables— prepared as for the soup bearing that name; and then, over these, pour a *purée* of green-peas nearly boiling, and send to table.

305. PUREE OF SPRING HERBS.

TAKE a double-handful of sorrel, three cabbage-lettuces, a handful of chervil, the same proportion of dandelion, and a little balm and burrage. Wash these thoroughly and place them in a stewpan with two ounces of fresh butter, and set the whole on the stove-fire to simmer, quickly stirring them the whole time; then add three pints of good *consommé* of veal or fowl; allow the soup to boil gently by the side of the fire for half an hour; and just before sending to table, finish the soup by mixing in it gradually, a leason* of six yelks of eggs and half a pint of cream, a pat of butter, a little grated nutmeg, and pounded sugar. Put some duchess' crusts in the soup-tureen, pour the soup thereon, and serve up.

Be careful that the soup be not allowed to boil, as, in that case, the eggs would curdle, and thereby render the soup unsightly, if not unpalatable.

306. PUREE OF GREEN-PEAS A LA VICTORIA.

JUST before dinner-time, roast off two plump spring chickens; as soon as they are taken off the spit, cut the breasts and legs into small members, put them into the soup-tureen with two dozen small *quenelles* of fowl, and then pour on the whole a *purée* of green-peas nearly boiling and prepared in the usual manner, and send to table.

307. PUREE OF GREEN-PEAS A LA PRINCESSE.

PREPARE a steamed custard in the manner following:—Take one pint of cream of rice (No. 317), mix gradually therewith eight yelks of eggs; pass this preparation through a tammy into a plain round mould—previously buttered for the purpose—and after having steamed it in the same way as you would any other custard, allow it to get cold, turn it out of the mould, and then cut it into small pillar-like shapes an inch long: put these into the soup-tureen with a little *consommé*, to prevent them from being clogged together, pour a boiling *pureé* of green-peas on them, and send to table.

---

* From the French *liaison*, a connection or binding.

308. PUREE OF CARROTS A LA STANLEY.

HAVING prepared about two quarts of *purée* of young carrots, when ready to serve up, pour it boiling into the soup-tureen containing a pint of young peas boiled green, and three dozen very small *quenelles* of fowl.

309. CRECY SOUP WITH WHOLE RICE.

WASH, blanch, and boil in *consommé*, half a pound of Carolina rice ; add this to a sufficient quantity of Crécy or carrot soup, either prepared for the occasion, or reserved from the previous day's dinner. Mix these together gently, and take care not to break the grains of rice, nor to serve it too thick.

Note.—This may be varied by substituting macaroni, vermicelli, or any other kind of Italian paste for the rice. This rule is applicable to *purées* of vegetables in general.

310. POTATO SOUP A LA CREME.

CLEANSE, peel, wash, and slice up about twenty large-sized, good potatoes. Put them into a stewpan with one large onion, and one head of celery—also sliced up ; add four ounces of fresh butter, a little pepper, salt, and grated nutmeg ; set them to simmer on a slow fire, stirring them occasionally, until they are nearly dissolved into a kind of *purée*. Then add to them three pints of good white *consommé*, and after having allowed the potatoes to boil gently by the side of a moderate fire for half an hour, pass them through the tammy, and having removed the *purée* into a soup-pot, add, if requisite, a little more *consommé*, and set the *purée* on the fire to boil gently by the side of the stove, in order to clarify it in the usual manner required for other *purées* of vegetables. Just before sending to table, add a pint of boiling cream, a pat of fresh butter, and a little pounded sugar.

Serve the fried crusts with this soup.

311. POTATO SOUP A LA VICTORIA.

PREPARE a *purée* of potatoes as directed above, and finish it in the same manner. When about to send to table, place three dozen of small *quenelles* of potatoes (No. 312) in the soup-tureen, with half a pint of large heads of asparagus boiled green, and the same proportion of French beans cut into diamond shapes and boiled, and then pour the boiling *purée* thereon, and serve.

312. QUENELLES FOR POTATOES.

BAKE six large potatoes, cut them into halves, scoop them out on to a wire sieve, and rub them through it, on to a dish, with a wooden spoon ; then put the potato thus obtained into a stewpan, with four ounces of fresh butter, half a pint of double-cream, a little grated nutmeg, pepper, and salt. Stir this on a rather brisk fire until the paste ceases to adhere to the spoon ; then remove the potatoes from off the fire, and mix in with them the yelks of three eggs and also two whites of egg which have been whipped to a froth observing that this preparation must be kept of the same consistency as any other *quenelles*. Then mould the *quenelles* according to the size and shape required, and poach them in boiling water with a little salt in it.

313. PUREE OF ASPARAGUS A LA CONDE.

ORDER two quarts of very young and green asparagus peas, or two large bundles of good sprue asparagus; break off the heads so far down to the foot of the stalks that they will readily snap off without resistance, which will prove them to be young and tender; throw these into a large pan of cold water, together with a handful of spinach, the same quantity of parsley and of green onions. Having got these ready, set a large stewpan on the fire half filled with boiling water, with a handful of salt in it. First drain the asparagus, &c., into a colander, and then put the whole into the stewpan on the fire to boil fast; when they are done, drain them again in a colander, let some cold water run over them for the purpose of retaining their greenness; and being well drained of the water, put them into a middle-sized stewpan, with a quart of good *Velouté* sauce (No. 4), a tablespoonful of pounded sugar, and a little grated nutmeg and salt. Stir the whole on a brisk fire until it has boiled about three minutes, when it must be passed through a tammy-cloth or sieve on to a large dish, and after being removed into a soup-pot, should be placed on the ice in the larder to keep cool, in order that it may the better retain its green color and delicate flavor. Ten minutes before serving up the soup to table, stir it on a brisk fire until it is nearly boiling, remove it from the stove, and, having mixed in with it a pat of butter and a small piece of light-colored glaze, send to table with a plate of *croûtons*.

314. PUREE OF ASPARAGUS A LA ST. GEORGE.

PREPARE a *purée* similar to the foregoing, place in the soup-tureen about three dozen very small *quenelles* of fowl, and about half a pint of small fillets or shreds of red tongue, cut in the same lengths and thickness as vegetables for *Julienne* soup; then, with a silver spoon, stir the above about gently in the tureen, so as to mix the ingredients with the *purée* (which must be poured on to them quite hot), and send to table.

315. BONNE FEMME SOUP.

TRIM and wash six cabbage lettuces; and having also well washed a double-handful of sorrel, shred these as you would do if they were intended for *Julienne* soup. Put two ounces of butter into a stewpan, and having melted it on the fire, add the lettuces and sorrel, and with a wooden spoon stir them over the stove until they are stewed, which will require about ten minutes; then add two quarts of good strong chicken *consommé*, and having allowed the soup to boil gently by the side of the stove-fire for about half an hour, take it off, in order that it may cool a little, and mix in with it a leason or binding of eight yelks of eggs, half a pint of cream, a small pat of butter, and a little pounded sugar to rectify the acidity of the sorrel. Stir the soup quickly on the fire, in order to set the leason in it, taking care that it does not curdle; add a small piece of glaze, pour the soup into the tureen upon some duchess' crusts, and serve.

316. SOUP A LA HOLLANDAISE.

PEEL three carrots, and an equal number of turnips and cucumbers; scoop these out into the shape of small olives, and, after blanching them, boil them in two quarts of good strong *blond* of veal; when the vegetables are done, remove the soup from the fire, and mix in with it a leason of eight yelks of eggs, half a pint of cream, a pat of butter, and a little sugar; set the leason by stirring the soup over the fire, and then pour it into the soup-tureen, containing about half a pint of young peas boiled green, and an equal proportion of French beans cut into diamonds, and serve.

SOUPS MADE WITH RICE OR PEARL-BARLEY,

COMPRISING

Cream of Rice *à la Royale.*
Do. *à la Victoria.*
Do. *à la Cardinal.*
Do. *à la Juvenal.*
Do. *à la Chasseur.*
Cream of Pearl-barley *à la Victoria.*

Cream of Pearl-barley *à la Reine.*
Do. *à la Printanière.*
Do. *à la Royale.*
Do. *à la Princesse Alexandrina.*
Do. *à la Duchesse.*

317. CREAM OF RICE A LA ROYALE.

WASH and blanch one pound of Carolina rice, drain it from the water, and put it into a stewpan with about three quarts of white *consommé* of fowls; set it to boil on the stove, and skim it well, after which remove it to the side of the fire to boil gently until the grains of rice are thoroughly done; then rub the whole through a tammy, moistening with more broth, if necessary. When this is done, put the *purée* into a small soup-pot, to be clarified by ebullition, in the same manner as a sauce; and just on the point of sending it to table, add half a pint of boiling cream, and then pour the soup into the tureen containing a dozen small custards of chicken, made thus :—

Roast a young fowl, from which take the whole of the breast and all the white part of the legs; chop and pound them with a large spoonful of white sauce, then pass this through a tammy with the wooden spoons; put the *purée* thus obtained into a quart basin, together with eight raw yelks of eggs, a little grated nutmeg, and salt; having well stirred these together, mix with them half a pint of *consommé* of fowls, and then pour this preparation into twelve small *dariole* moulds, previously buttered for the purpose; set them carefully in a fricandeau pan, containing sufficient boiling water to reach half way up the moulds, put the lid on the pan, and place it either on a very moderate fire, or in the oven—observing, that in the former case some live embers of charcoal must be put on the lid. About ten minutes will suffice to poach the custards, when they must be turned out of the moulds on to a napkin, and afterward placed in the soup-tureen, previously to pouring the *purée* upon them.

318. CREAM OF RICE A LA VICTORIA.

PREPARE the cream of rice as above directed, and twenty minutes before sending to table add to it about a quarter of a pound of whole rice, well boiled in white *consommé* of fowls : this rice must be boiled in the *purée* for twenty minutes ; and just before serving the soup, mix in with it a pint of boiling cream and a pat of fresh butter.

319. CREAM OF RICE A LA CARDINAL.

PREPARE a cream of rice in the usual way, and pour it into a soup-tureen containing thirty tails of crayfish and three dozen very small *quenelles* of fowls. A good tablespoonful of crayfish or lobster butter, and the juice of half a lemon, should be mixed in with the soup previously to pouring it upon the crayfish tails, &c.

320. CREAM OF RICE A LA JUVENAL.

To a cream of rice prepared according to the instructions for making the cream of rice *à la Royale*, there must be added, with a leason of six yelks of eggs, half a pint of cream, and two ounces of grated Parmesan cheese ; having thoroughly incorporated these, while stirring the soup over the fire (taking care that it does not boil), pour the soup into a tureen containing three dozen very small *quenelles* of fowls, colored with a little spinach-green (No. 285).

321. PUREE OF RICE A LA CHASSEUR.

WASH and blanch half a pound of Carolina rice, and after draining all the water from it, put it on to boil with a quart of *consommé* of pheasant or partridge. When the rice is sufficiently done, rub it through the tammy, and having clarified it in the usual way, by adding some of the same sort of *consommé* the rice is boiled in, about five minutes before sending the soup to table, mix in with the cream of rice the *purée* of one pheasant or two partridges (as the case may be).

Be careful not to allow the soup to get too hot after adding the *purée* of game to it, as it would be sure to decompose, and become rough and unsightly. Should this accident, however, occur, it may be remedied by taking the soup away from the fire, putting a little *consommé* to it, and quickly rubbing it through the tammy again ; by these means it will resume its proper smoothness.

This remedy will be found effectual for rectifying similar accidents, should they occur, with meat *purées* in general.

322. CREAM OF PEARL-BARLEY A LA VICTORIA.

WASH a pound of pearl-barley in several waters, blanch, and drain it upon a sieve, and having allowed some cold water to run over it for a few minutes, put it into a stewpan with two quarts of white *consommé* of fowls, and set it to boil by the side of a slow fire for four hours. When the barley is sufficiently done to admit of its being bruised easily, set one-third of it apart in a small soup-pot, and immediately proceed to rub the remainder through a tammy ; then mix the cream of barley thus obtained with the whole barley which has been set aside. Ten minutes before serving up this soup, add to it half a pint of boiling cream.

323. CREAM OF PEARL-BARLEY A LA REINE.

THE process for making this soup is exactly the same as that used for making the cream of rice *à la Chasseur*, barley being substituted for rice, and poultry for game: see No. 321.

324. CREAM OF PEARL-BARLEY A LA PRINTANIERE.

HAVING prepared a cream of pearl-barley as above directed, just before sending to table, pour it into a soup-tureen containing three dozen small *quenelles* of fowl, and half a pint of large heads of asparagus boiled green, and serve.

325. CREAM OF PEARL-BARLEY A LA ROYALE.

THE *purée* of barley being prepared as described in the foregoing directions, and finished in the same manner, pour it into a soup-tureen containing two spring chickens, roasted for this purpose just before dinner-time, and cut into small members neatly trimmed.

326. CREAM OF BARLEY A LA PRINCESSE ALEXANDRIA.

To make this soup, white *consommé* of game should be used to prepare the cream of barley, the *purée* being finished according to the method observed in former cases; when about to send the soup to table, pour it into a tureen containing scollops of the fillets of three young red-legged partridges, roasted a few minutes previously for the purpose.

327. CREAM OF BARLEY A LA DUCHESSE.

HAVING prepared a steamed custard of fowl, as directed in the preparation for making Desclignac soup (No. 258), cut the custard thus made (allowing it time to become cold and firm) into small pillars an inch long, then place them carefully in the soup-tureen with a little *consommé;* proceed to pour on them a cream of barley prepared and finished in the usual way, and to which has been added a tablespoonful of lobster butter and a little cayenne pepper.

BISQUES OF CRAYFISH AND SHELLFISH SOUPS IN GENERAL,

COMPRISING.

Bisque of Quails *à la Prince Albert*.	Bisque of Crayfish *à la Malmesbury*.
„ Rabbits *au Velouté*.	„ Crab *à la Fitzhardinge*.
„ Snipes *à la Bonne bouche*.	„ Lobsters *à la Stanley*.
„ Crayfish *à l'Ancièune*.	„ Prawns *à la Cerito*.

328. BISQUE OF QUAILS A LA PRINCE ALBERT.

FILLET six quails, half of which must be made into force-meat *quenelle*, and kept in a cool place until wanted for use; reserve the remainder of the fillets to be lightly simmered in fresh butter, seasoned with a little salt, and eventually cut into scollops.

Take the larger bones out of the carcasses of the quails, and having roughly chopped the latter, put them into a stewpan with two ounces of fresh butter, a small bay-leaf, a sprig of thyme, three shalots, a little grated nutmeg, and a pinch of minionette pepper; set these on a brisk fire, and pass or fry them brown, then add half a bottle of chopped mushrooms and a bottle of Sauterne wine. Allow this to boil quickly for ten minutes, and then add about half a pound of rice, which has been partly boiled in broth, and a quart of *blond* of veal; after the fore-mentioned ingredients have been gently boiling for about an hour, drain them into a sieve, and pound the whole thoroughly in a mortar; then replace them in the stewpan, add the broth they were boiled in, stir the *purée* on the fire to warm it a little, and rub it through the tammy in the usual way. When this is done, place the *purée* in a well-tinned soup-pot, in a cool place. Just before dinner-time, warm the *purée* of quails, carefully observing that it does not get too hot; finish seasoning it by mixing in a little crayfish butter, a table-spoonful of partridge glaze, and a little salt if needed; pour the soup into a soup-tureen containing the fillets of quails cut into neatly-trimmed scollops, as well as three dozen very small *quenelles* made with the fillets kept in reserve for the purpose, and send to table.

329. BISQUE OR RABBITS AU VELOUTE.

FILLET two young rabbits, make half the fillets into force-meat for *quenelles;* pare off all the meat from the rabbits, and with the carcasses prepare a brown *consommé* in the usual manner. Put the remainder of the fillets and all the meat that has been cut from the rabbits into a stewpan, with two ounces of fresh butter, three shalots, bay-leaf, thyme, parsley, nutmeg, minionette pepper, and salt, and fry them brown. Then add two glasses of sherry; and after allowing the whole to boil briskly for about three minutes, pour in the *consommé* made from the carcasses. Let the stock thus far prepared boil gently by the side of a stove-fire for about an hour, then drain the contents of the stewpan into a sieve, pound them thoroughly, and after having mixed the produce with their own stock, rub the *purée* thus obtained through a tammy, together with a large ladleful of good *Velouté* sauce. The *purée* should then be put into a soup-pot, and kept in a cool place until within ten minutes of dinner-time, when it must be stirred over the fire to make it sufficiently hot; and after ascertaining that its seasoning is correct, pour the *bisque* into a soup-tureen containing three dozen small *quenelles* of rabbit, made with the fillets which have been reserved for that purpose, and serve.

330. BISQUE OR SNIPES A LA BONNE BOUCHE.

PROCURE six fat snipes, perfectly fresh and not fishy; fillet them, and follow the instructions given for making the *bisque* of quails *à la Prince Albert* (No. 328), but omitting the crayfish butter. Warm the *purée* of snipes just before it is wanted for table, pour it into a soup-tureen containing the scollops made from half the fillets, and three dozen small *quenelles* made from the remainder.

Send up with this soup, to be handed round, some *crôutons* of fried bread cut in small circular pieces about the eighth of an inch thick ; a circular incision having been made on one side of the bread before it is fried, the inner part is afterward easily taken out, and in its place should be put a *farce*, made with the trail of half the snipes (the remainder should be used in the *purée*). This *farce* is to be prepared thus :—

Put the trail into a small stewpan with a little fresh butter, pepper, and salt, and after frying it lightly on the fire for a minute or two, add a tablespoonful of good brown sauce, and then rub it through a hair-sieve with a wooden spoon. Fill the *croûtons* with this *farce*, smoothing the surface with a small knife ; and previously to serving them, put them on a sauta-pan in the oven for five minutes to warm them ; serve them on a plate, to be handed round with the soup.

Take care not to throw the *croûtons* into the soup, as that would destroy their crispness.

331. BISQUE OF CRAYFISH A L'ANCIENNE.

To make soup enough for sixteen persons, procure sixty crayfish, from which remove the gut containing the gall, in the following manner :—Take a firm hold of the crayfish with the left hand, so as to avoid being pinched by its claws ; with the thumb and fore-finger of the right hand pinch the extreme end of the central fin of its tail, and, with a sudden jerk, the gut will be withdrawn. Then mince or cut into small dice, a carrot, an onion, one head of celery, and a few parsley roots ; to these add a bay-leaf, a sprig of thyme, a little minionette pepper, and two ounces of butter. Put these ingredients into a stewpan, and fry them on the fire for ten minutes ; then throw in the crayfish, and pour on them a bottle of French white wine. Allow this to boil, and then add a quart of strong *consommé*, and let them continue gently boiling for half an' hour. Then pick out the crayfish, and strain the broth through a napkin by pressure into a basin, in order to extract all the essence from the vegetables. Pick the shell off fifty of the crayfish tails, trim them neatly, and set them aside until wanted. Reserve some of the spawn, and also half the body shells, with which to make the crayfish butter (No. 184) to finish the soup. Take all that remains, and add thereto six anchovies washed for the purpose, and also a plate of crusts of French rolls fried of a light brown color in butter. Pound all these thoroughly, and then put them into a stewpan with the broth that has been reserved in a basin, and having warmed the *bisque* thus prepared, rub it through a tammy into a *purée*. Then take the *purée* up into a soup-pot ; finish by incorporating therewith the crayfish butter, season with a little cayenne pepper and the juice of half a lemon. Pour the *bisque* quite hot into the soup-tureen containing the crayfish tails, and send to table.

332. BISQUE OF CRAYFISH A LA MALMESBURY.

CLEANSE thoroughly two quarts of muscles, steam them in a well-covered stewpan, and then pick out all the white muscles from the shells, and put them into a stewpan with some of their own liquor. To these add forty tails of crayfish, and three dozen very small *quenelles* of whiting which have been mixed with sufficient chopped and blanched parsley to give them a green color. Just before dinner-time, warm the muscles, &c., in a little *consommé*, put them into the soup-tureen, and then pour the *bisque* of crayfish quite hot on to them. Let the *bisque* be prepared in the same way as described in the *bisque* of crayfish *à l'ancienne*. When there is not sufficient time for thickening the *purée* by the addition of the fried crusts of the Frence rolls, a little well-boiled rice, some reduced *Velouté* sauce, or even the crumb of two French rolls soaked in hot broth and pounded with the crayfish, may be used, but the fried crusts are to be preferred.

333. BISQUE OF CRAB A LA FITZHARDINGE.

PROCURE one large boiled crab, pick the white meat from the claws into shreds, and put it away between two plates in a cool place until wanted. Scoop out all the pulpy part of the crab, as well as all the white meat to be found in the shell, and pound these well, with about half the quantity of rice boiled in broth; dilute the whole with a quart of good *consommé*, and then rub it through a tammy into a *purée*, put it into a soup-pot, and keep it in a cool place.

Just before sending to table, stir the *purée* over the fire with a wooden spoon, taking care that it does not get too hot, as that would cause the soup to curdle. Finish seasoning the soup by mixing with the *purée* a pint of boiling cream and a little cayenne pepper; then pour the soup into a tureen containing the shredded meat taken out of the claws, previously made warm in a small quantity of *consommé*, and send to table.

334. BISQUE OF LOBSTERS A LA STANLEY.

TAKE all the meat out of two hen-lobsters, reserving the pith, coral, and spawn, separately. Cut the meat of the lobster into small pieces, and put them into a stewpan with two ounces of fresh butter, one head of celery, and a carrot, cut into small shreds, a small piece of mace, thyme, pepper, and a little salt; fry these over the fire for five minutes, and then, having moistened them with about a pint of Rhenish white wine, allow the whole to boil smartly on the fire for about twenty minutes. Drain the lobster, &c., into a sieve, then pound this thoroughly in a mortar, and put it again into the stewpan with the pith or inside part reserved for the purpose, and also the broth, adding thereto about a quart of clarified and reduced *Velouté* sauce, and a pint of strong *consommé*, then rub the *purée* through the tammy; and after having taken it up into a soup-pot, place it in the cool until wanted.

Ten minutes before dinner-time, put the *bisque* to warm, stirring it the whole of the time, taking care to prevent its curdling. Finish seasoning it with some lobster butter, a little soluble cayenne pepper, the juice of half a lemon, and a piece of light-colored glaze, the size of a walnut. Pour the soup into the tureen containing fifty tails of prawns, with three dozen small *quenelles* of whiting, and serve.

335. BISQUE OF PRAWNS A LA CERITO.

PROCURE two pounds of fresh prawns, pick and trim fifty of the largest of them, which, when done, put into a small stewpan, to remain in the larder until wanted. Then cut into small shreds or dice six young carrots, a little celery, and a few parsley roots ; and having put these into a stewpan with two ounces of butter, a sprig of thyme, some minionette pepper, and a little salt, set the whole on the fire to be fried of a light color. Next, throw in the remainder of the prawns, as well as the bodies of those from which the tails have been taken ; and then add a pint of Sauterne wine ; allow these ingredients to boil for ten minutes, and then add a quarter of a pound of rice previously boiled in broth, and also a quart of strong white *consommé* of veal. Having allowed this to boil gently by the side of the stove-fire for half an hour, strain the whole into a sieve—reserving the broth in a basin. Then pound the prawns, rice, and vegetables all together in a mortar, dilute with the broth which has been reserved, and rub the whole through a tammy in the usual manner ; put the *purée* into a soup-pot, and keep it in a cool place until dinner-time, when, having made it sufficiently hot without allowing it to boil, finish it by mixing in with it some lobster coral butter, a little soluble cayenne pepper, and the juice of half a lemon. Pour the soup into the tureen containing the fifty prawns' tails, with three dozen small *quenelles* of trout, and serve.

FISH SOUPS AND WATER SOUCHETS IN GENERAL,

COMPRISING

Oyster Soup *à la Plessy.*
Soup of fillets of Soles *à la Bagration.*
Potage of Eels *à la Richmond.*
Do. of fillets of Flounders *à l'Anglaise.*
Sturgeon Soup *à l'Américaine.*
Do. *à l'Anglaise.*

Sturgeon Soup *à la Chinoise*
Do. *à l'Indiènne.*
Water-souchet of Crimped Salmon.
Do. of Plain Salmon.
Do. of fillets of Perch.
Do. of fillets of Soles.

336. OYSTER SOUP A LA PLESSY.

Four dozen of oysters will suffice for eight persons. Blanch or scald these by boiling them for a few minutes on the fire, drain them and save the liquor ; wash the oysters, and pull off the beards and tendons, leaving only the delicate fat part of the oysters, which put into a basin with their liquor. Next, prepare some *quenelles* from the fillets of three whitings ; put their bones and trimmings into a small stewpan with six flounders, an eel cut into pieces, some parsley roots, a carrot, one head of celery, a sprig of thyme, two blades of mace, and a few peppercorns. To these add a pint of French white wine and the liquor of the oysters ; set the whole to boil briskly for ten minutes, then add six whole anchovies (washed for the purpose) and three pints of white *consommé.* Allow the stock thus prepared to boil gently for three quarters of an hour ; then strain it off through a sieve into a stewpan, and thicken it with some white *roux*, and as soon as it has boiled, set it by the side of the stove to clarify itself in the usual way. When the body of the soup thus far prepared has been rubbed through a tammy, finish it for table, just before dinner-time, by mixing in with it a leason of six yelks of eggs, a gill of cream, a little soluble cayenne pepper, and the juice of half a lemon; then pour the soup into the tureen containing the oysters reserved for that purpose, with about three dozen *quenelles* of whiting, and serve.

337. SOUP OF FILLETS OF SOLES A LA BAGRATION.

FILLET three large soles, and place the fillets lengthwise in a sauta-pan with about two ounces of clarified butter, season with a little pepper and salt, and some lemon-juice, cover them with a round of buttered paper, and set them in the oven, or on a stove-fire, for ten minutes, when they will be done. Take the fillets up, and set them in press between two dishes, and when cold, with a round tin cutter, stamp them out into small scollops, and place them in a small stewpan in the larder until wanted. Make some *quenelle* of the fillets of one large sole, color it with some lobster coral, and mould it with two teaspoons into very small *quenelles*, which, when poached, place with the scollops of soles; to these add about three dozen blanched muscles. Mix with these ingredients about two quarts of the same kind of soup-sauce as used for the preceding soup, and when about serving it up for table, place the scollops of soles, the muscles, and the red *quenelles* (first warmed in a small quantity of the soup) into the tureen, and then mix in with the soup a table-spoonful of chopped and blanched parsley, pour it on to the scollops, &c., and serve.

338. EEL SOUP A LA RICHMOND.

FILLET three Thames eels, and cut the fillets into small scollops; place these, in circular order, in a large sauta-pan containing about four ounces of clarified butter; season with cayenne pepper, salt, lemon-juice, and chopped parsley; set the covered sauta-pan on the stove-fire to simmer gently for about twenty minutes, then add two glasses of sherry, after which let it boil sharply for a few minutes longer. Put the scollops of eels thus prepared into the soup-tureen, with three dozen tails of crayfish, and instantly pour over these a soup sauce, previously prepared according to the following directions:

Cut into shreds or dice, carrot, celery, parsley-roots, one shalot, and half a pottle of mushrooms. Put these into a stewpan with a sprig of thyme, a small bay-leaf, a little sweet basil, a few peppercorns, and one blade of mace. Fry these ingredients with four ounces of butter until they begin to be of a light brown color; then throw in the bones and trimmings of the eels, three dozen bruised crayfish, and a pint of Chablis wine. Allow this to boil briskly on the fire for five minutes, then add three pints of *blond* of veal, and after it has boiled gently by the side of the stove-fire for three-quarters of an hour, strain the stock through a tammy-cloth with considerable pressure, in order to extract all the goodness from the vegetables, &c.

Put the broth thus prepared into a stewpan, and having thickened it with some white *roux* to the consistency of a thin sauce, work it according to the method observed for all sauces. *Observe*, that as this sauce is for soup, it should be lighter in substance. Finish with a leason of eight yelks of egg and season accordingly, and mix in with it a spoonful of chopped and blanched parsley.

339. SOUP OF FILLETS OF THAMES FLOUNDERS A L ANGLAISE.

FILLET ten Thames flounders, simmer the fillets in a little fresh butter, seasoned with pepper, salt, and lemon-juice. When done, place them in the soup-tureen with three dozen *quenelles* of Spey trout, and pour on them a soup made according to the following directions :

Put the bones and the trimmings of the flounders and the trout, from which the small *quenelles* are to be made, into a stewpan with carrot, celery, parsley-roots, a sprig of thyme, and a few peppercorns. To these add three pints of common broth from the boiling stockpot (if possible) and a couple of glasses of Sauterne. When it has boiled for three-quarters of an hour, strain off the broth into a small soup-pot, and make it into a smooth white *Velouté* sauce ; just before pouring it into the soup-tureen (containing the fillets of flounders and the small *quenelles* of trout already mentioned) finish it by mixing in with it a leason of six yelks of egg, a gill of cream, and a dessert-spoonful of chopped and blanched parsley, a little lemon-juice, and cayenne pepper.

340. STURGEON SOUP A L'AMERICAINE.

PROCURE six pounds of fresh sturgeon, one-third of which must be trimmed and tied so as to preserve it from falling to pieces while being braized, then put it in a stewpan, and cover it with some *mirepoix* (No. 236) or wine braize prepared as directed. Let it boil, and then set it in the oven for about an hour and a half, more or less, according to the size of the fish. When this portion of the sturgeon is done, let it be put away in the larder to get cold, in order that it may be afterward cut into scollops to be put into the soup.

While the above is in course of preparation, make a brown sauce with the remainder of the sturgeon, as follows :

Butter a large stewpan, then cut two onions in slices and strew them over the bottom ; on these place the sturgeon cut in thick slices, also two old hens partly roasted, and well colored, a carrot, one head of celery, some parsley-roots, thyme, bay-leaf, six cloves, two blades of mace, and a dozen peppercorns ; then add a large ladleful of good stock, and put the whole to boil briskly on the fire until the broth is nearly reduced ; slacken the stove to prevent the glaze thus obtained from being burnt, by which the unctuousness would be lost. Then proceed with this sauce exactly as shown for the treatment of brown sauce or *Espagnole*. Having thus produced a bright, thin, brown sauce, finish the soup by mixing in a ragout-spoonful of *purée* of turtle herbs, a piece of anchovy butter, a little grated nutmeg, cayenne pepper, lemon-juice, and a glass of Madeira. Let the scollops boil a few minutes in the soup previously to adding the butter, &c. When about to serve up the soup, pour it into a tureen containing three dozen small *quenelles* of lobster, and send to table.

341. STURGEON SOUP A L'ANGLAISE.

PREPARE the sturgeon for this soup in the same way as for the preceding, with the exception that the sauce must be white. Having made a thin white *Velouté* sauce, in sufficient quantity for the purpose, and seasoned it with the same ingredients as before-named, add a ragout-spoonful of essence of turtle herbs, two glasses of sherry, a leason or binding of six yelks of eggs, a gill of cream, a little cayenne pepper and lemon-juice. When about to send the soup to table, pour it into the tureen containing the scollops of sturgeon cut into square pieces, three dozen small round pellets of yelks of eggs (prepared as for mock-turtle), and all the cartilaginous parts of the sturgeon cut into scollops also.

The pellets of yelks of eggs here alluded to are thus prepared :—

Take the yelks of six eggs boiled hard, pound them in the mortar with a pat of fresh butter, a piece of bread-crumb twice the size of an egg, soaked in milk, and afterward squeezed in a napkin to extract all the moisture from it; to these add a little nutmeg, pepper, and salt, and one whole egg. Mix the whole well together by pounding, and then proceed to mould this paste into small round balls or pellets, the size of a nut, and poach them as you would any other *quenelles*.

341A. STURGEON SOUP A LA CHINOISE.

PROCURE the head of a large sturgeon, saw it in▪ halves from the back of the head down to the snout; then saw the halves into pieces of the size of your fist, and place them in a large-sized pan with cold water to soak for several hours; taking care to wash them and change the water frequently. Next, put the pieces of sturgeon into a large stewpan in plenty of cold water, and set them on the fire to boil gently until the husk or shell is easily detached from the pieces of cartilage or gristle; place the latter, when thoroughly freed from the meaty and fatty substances, in a large stewpan; moisten with good veal stock in sufficient quantity to make soup enough for the number of guests. Garnish with carrots, onions, celery, a fagot of parsley, green onions, marjoram, thyme, and sweet basil, three blades of mace, twelve cloves, and twenty peppercorns; boil gently for about two hours. As soon as you find that the pieces of cartilage are become transparent and rather soft to the touch, they must be immediately drained upon a sieve, and the liquor placed in a clean stewpan and set beside a stove-fire, adding half a bottle of good sherry and a small pinch of cayenne. Allow the soup to boil gently by the side of the stove for about half an hour, taking care to remove all the scum and grease that rises to the surface; after which add the pieces of cartilage and the juice of a lemon, and serve. This soup is very strengthening; the wine, lemon-juice, and cayenne may be dispensed with for invalids. The head of the sturgeon forms an excellent substitute for turtle, and may be dressed after the same manner.

342. STURGEON SOUP A L'INDIENNE.

PREPARE the sturgeon *consommé* as for the preceding soups, bearing in mind that it should have no more color than it acquires from the roasted hens. Having strained the stock when done into a large basin, and preserved all the cartilaginous parts of the sturgeon, get a carrot, one head of celery, and two onions, cut these into thin slices, and put them into a stewpan with a quarter of a pound of butter, and half a pound of raw ham cut into small square pieces; fry the whole of a light brown color over a slow fire. When this is done, add to the fore-named ingredients some sifted flour, in suffi-

cient quantity to thicken the soup, and stir it on the fire a few minutes longer; then take the stewpan off the stove and mix the sturgeon
broth in carefully, so as to keep the sauce smooth. Add two tablespoonsful of *Cook's* or *Bruce's Indian Curry Paste*, and after allowing it to boil, lift it off the fire and set it by the side of the stove, there
to throw up all the butter it contains, and to clarify itself in the usual
way. When this is effected, rub the soup-sauce, including the vegetables, &c., through a tammy into a *purée*, which put into a soup-pot
with the scollops and the cartilaginous parts of the sturgeon; after
boiling the whole together for a quarter of an hour, skim the surface,
and finish by adding a teaspoonful of essence of anchovies and the juice
of a lemon. Send to table with a plate of plain boiled Patna rice, to
be handed round with the soup.

343. WATER SOUCHET OF CRIMPED SALMON.

PERFECTION in the preparation of this dish can only be attained by
using the fish a few hours after it is caught. Moreover, those engaged
in catching the fish should be instructed to cut it into slices half an
inch thick, and to keep it in cold spring water for a couple of hours or
so; when, as is well known, the salmon will acquire that degree of
firmness peculiar to all crimped fish.

Place the slices of salmon in a stewpan with some shred parsley
roots previously boiled for the purpose, and also the water they have
been boiled in, some picked parsley leaves, minionette pepper, and
sufficient salt to season it; moisten with some essence of fish, which
should be made either from the inferior pieces of the salmon, or else
with half a dozen flounders or slips. Let the water souchet thus far
prepared boil briskly until the salmon be done, which will require about
six minutes. It should be served quickly, but just before sending to
table you may add a little bright *consommé*. Many, however, prefer
the latter omitted, considering that it diminishes the sweetness of the
crisp creamy salmon.

With all water souchets send plates of brown bread and butter.

344. WATER SOUCHET OF PLAIN SALMON.

TRIM and fillet the required quantity of plain salmon; place the
fillets neatly side by side in a stewpan, and put them by till dinner-
time.

Meanwhile prepare the water souchet broth as follows:—Put the
trimmings of the salmon into a stewpan, with carrot, celery, and
parsley roots, the whole sliced up. Add a little minionette pepper
and salt, and about two glasses of French white wine; fill up with
water or weak broth, allow it to boil, and then set it by the side of the
stove to continue gently boiling for half an hour; then strain the
souchet off through a napkin on to the fillets of salmon, set them to
boil briskly on the fire for about five minutes, add the shred parsley
roots and picked parsley leaves; and when the whole has boiled
together for three minutes, serve the water souchet in a deep silver
dish or small soup-tureen.

345. WATER SOUCHET OF FILLETS OF PERCH.

PROCURE four good-sized perch, clean and fillet them. Place the
fillets neatly in a deep sauta-pan, and put them in the larder until

wanted. Meanwhile, with the bones and trimmings prepare the souchet broth according to the directions given for making the preceding souchet, and finishing in precisely the same manner.

346. WATER SOUCHET OF FILLETS OF SOLES.

HAVING filleted the soles and trimmed the fillets, take hold of each and fold one end over the other; batter the ends together with the handle of a knife, pare off any rough fragments that may remain about them, and place them in circular order in a stewpan; then pour over them the souchet prepared in the usual manner with the bones and trimmings, &c. Let the fillets thus arranged boil for five or six minutes; ascertain that they are done, and serve them in a water-souchet dish, with parsley roots and leaves, previously prepared for that purpose.

Water-souchets of fillets of trout, char, and indeed of almost every species of the more delicate kinds of fresh-water fish, are made according to the foregoing directions.

ENGLISH SOUPS,

COMPRISING

Turtle Soup.	Calves'-feet Soup à la Windsor.
Do. clear.	Hare Soup à l'Anglaise.
Mock-Turtle Soup.	Do. à la St. George.
Do. clear.	Leveret Soup à la Rossie.
Mulligatawney do.	Ox-cheek Soup.
Giblet Soup à l'Anglaise.	Deer's-head do.
Do. à l'Irlandaise.	Grouse do. à la Montagnarde.
Ox-tail Soup.	

347. TURTLE SOUP.

PROCURE a fine lively fat turtle, weighing about 120 lbs.: fish of this weight being considered the best, as their fat is not liable to be impregnated with that disagreeable strong savor objected to in fish of larger size. On the other hand, turtle of very small size seldom possess sufficient fat or substance to make them worth dressing.

When time permits, kill the turtle overnight that it may be left to bleed in a cool place till the next morning, when, at an early hour, it should be cut up for scalding—that being the first part of the operation. If, however, the turtle is required for immediate use, to save time, the fish may be scalded as soon as it is killed.

The turtle being ready for cutting up, lay it on its back, and with a large kitchen-knife separate the fat or belly-shell from the back, by making an incision all round the inner edge of the shell; when all the fleshy parts adhering to the shell have been carefully cut away, it may be set aside. Then detach the intestines by running the sharp edge of a knife closely along the spine of the fish, and remove them instantly in a pail, to be thrown away. Cut off the fins and separate the fleshy parts, which place on a dish by themselves till wanted. Take particular care of every particle of the green fat, which lies chiefly at the sockets of the fore-fins, and more or less all around the interior of the fish, if in good condition. Let this fat, which, when in a healthy state, is elastic and of a bluish color while raw, be steeped for several hours in cold spring water, in order that it may be thoroughly cleansed of all impurities.

Then, with a meat saw, divide the upper and under shells into pieces of convenient size to handle; and, having put them with the fins and head into a large vessel containing boiling water, proceed quickly to scald them; by this means they will be separated from the horny substance which covers them, which will then be easily removed. They must then be put into a larger stockpot nearly filled with fresh hot water, and left to continue boiling by the side of the stove-fire until the glutinous substance separates easily from the bones. Place the pieces of turtle carefully upon clean dishes, and put them in the larder to get cold; they should then be cut up into pieces about an inch and a half square, which pieces are to be finally put into the soup when it is nearly finished. Put the bones back into the broth to boil an hour longer, for the double purpose of extracting all their savor and to effect the reduction of the turtle broth, which is to be used for filling up the turtle stockpot hereafter.

In order to save time, while the above is in operation, the turtle stock or *consommé*, should be prepared as follows:

With four ounces of fresh butter, spread the bottom of an eighteen-gallon stockpot; then place in it three pounds of raw ham cut in slices,—over these put forty pounds of leg of beef and knuckles of veal, four old hens (after having removed their fillets, which are to be kept for making the *quenelles* for the soup); to these add all the fleshy pieces of the turtle (excepting those pieces intended for *entrées*), and then place on the top the head and fins of the turtle; moisten the whole with a bottle of Madeira and four quarts of good stock; add a pottle of mushrooms, twelve cloves, four blades of mace, a handful of parsley roots; and a good sized *bouquet* of parsley tied up with two bay-leaves, thyme, green onions, and shalots. Set the *consommé* thus prepared on a brisk stove-fire to boil sharply, and when the liquid has become reduced to a glaze, fill the stockpot up instantly, and as soon as it boils, skim it thoroughly, garnish with the usual complement of vegetables, and remove it to the side of the stove to boil gently for six hours. Remember to probe the head and fins after they have been boiled two hours, and as soon as they are done drain them on a dish, cover them with a wet napkin well saturated with water to prevent it from sticking to them, and put them away in a cool place with the remainder of the glutinous parts of the turtle, already spoken of. The stockpot should now be filled up with the turtle broth reserved for that purpose, as directed above. When the turtle stock is done, strain it off into an appropriate-sized stockpot, remove every particle of fat from the surface, and then proceed to thicken it with a proportionate quantity of white *roux* to the consistency of thin sauce. Work this exactly in the same manner as practiced for *Espagnole* or brown sauce, in order to extract all the butter and scum, so as to give it a brilliant appearance.

One bottle of old Madeira must now be added, together with a *purée* of herbs of the following kinds, to be made as here directed:

Sweet basil must form one-third proportion of the whole quantity of herbs intended to be used; winter savory, marjoram, and lemon-thyme, in equal quantities, making up the other two-thirds: add to these a double-handful of parsley, half a bunch of green onions, a handful of green shalots, and some trimmings of mushrooms; moisten with a quart of broth, and having stewed these herbs for about an hour, rub the whole through the tammy into a *purée*. This *purée* being added to the soup, a little crystallized soluble cayenne pepper should then be introduced. The pieces of turtle, as well as the fins, which have been also cut into small pieces, and the larger bones taken out, should now be allowed to boil in the soup for a quarter of an hour, after which carefully remove the whole of the scum as it rises to the surface. The degree of seasoning must be ascertained that it may be corrected if faulty.

To excel in dressing turtle, it is necessary to be very accurate in the proportions of the numerous ingredients used for seasoning this soup. Nothing should predominate, but the whole shold be harmoniously blended.

Put the turtle away in four-quart sized basins, dividing the fat (after it has been scalded and boiled in some of the sauce) in equal quantities into each basin; as also some small *quenelles*, which are to be made with the fillets of hens reserved for that purpose, and in which, in addition to the usual ingredients in ordinary cases, put six yelks of eggs boiled hard. Mould these *quenelles* into small round balls to imitate turtle's eggs, roll them with the hand on a marble slab or table, with the aid of a little flour, and poach them in the usual way.

When the turtle soup is wanted for use, warm it, and just before sending it to table, add a small glass of Sherry or Madeira, and the juice of one lemon to every four quarts of turtle.

The second stock of the turtle *consommé* should be strained off after it has boiled for two hours, and immediately boiled down into a glaze very quickly, and mixed in with the turtle soup previously to putting it away in the basins; or else it should be kept in reserve for the purpose of adding proportionate quantities in each tureen of turtle as it is served.

348. CLEAR TURTLE SOUP.

PROCEED in the preparation of the turtle stock, in every respect, according to the preceding instructions.

The glutinous parts of the turtle having been cut into squares, select the dark-colored pieces proceeding from the back shell, and keep them for the clear turtle. When the turtle stock has boiled six hours, strain it off and divide it into two equal parts; the one to be finished in the usual manner, the other to be first freed from every particle of grease, and afterward clarified in the usual manner, with two whites of eggs whipped up with a little spring water, and the addition of a glass of French white wine, or the juice of a lemon; add a proportionate quantity of turtle herbs, to give the requisite flavor, and set it to boil on the stove-fire, whisking it the whole time. As soon as the egg begins to separate in the stock, remove it to the side of the stove, pour in half a bottle of Madeira, and allow the whole to simmer gently until the egg be thoroughly set. Then proceed to strain it through a napkin into a large stewpan, in which afterward put the pieces of turtle selected for the purpose; boil them in it until they are sufficiently done, and then add a little crystallized soluble cayenne pepper, and serve.

If considered desirable, a little lemon-juice and a few *quenelles* of fowl may be added, as also some of the finest pieces of the green fat.

Clear turtle soup is preferred by some epicures to that which is dressed in the usual way, from its bing free from the additional compounds used in the full-dressed turtle. It is, in consequence, much lighter, more delicate and pure, and is unquestionably easier of digestion.

349. MOCK-TURTLE SOUP.

PROCURE a scalded calf's head, or, as it is sometimes called, a turtle-head; bone it in the following manner:—Place the calf's head on the table with the front part of the head facing you; draw the sharp point of a knife from the back part of the head right down to the nose, making an incision down to the bone of the skull; then with the knife clear the scalp and cheeks from the bones right and left, always keeping the point of the knife close to the bone. Having boned the head, put it into a large stewpan of cold water on the fire; as soon as it boils, skim it well, and let it continue to boil for ten minutes; take the calf's head out and put it into a pan full of cold water. Then get a proper sized stockpot, and after having buttered the bottom thereof, place in it four slices of raw ham, two large knuckles of veal, and an old hen partially roasted, moisten with two quarts of broth, and put the stockpot on the stove-fire to boil until the broth is reduced to a glaze, when instantly slacken the heat by covering the fire with ashes, and then leave the soup to color itself gradually. Allow the glaze at the bottom of the stewpan to be reduced to the same consistency as for brown sauce, and fill up the stockpot with water, leaving room for the calf's head, which separate into two halves, and pare off all the rough cuticle about the inner parts of the mouth, then place it in the stock, and after setting it to boil, and thoroughly skimming it, garnish with the usual complement of vegetables, six cloves, two blades of mace, half a pottle of mushrooms, four shalots, and a good bunch of parsley, green onions, thyme, and bay-leaf tied together, and a little salt. Set it by the fire to boil gently till the calf's head is done; then take the pieces of head out, and place them on a dish to cool, afterward to be cut into squares, and put into a basin till required for adding them to the soup. Strain the stock through a broth cloth, and thicken it with some light-colored *roux*, to the consistency of thin brown sauce; let it boil, and allow it to throw up all the butter, and clarify itself thoroughly; then add half a bottle of Sherry, about half a pint of *purée* of turtle herbs (No. 347) in which six anchovies have been mixed, a little crystallized soluble cayenne pepper, and the calf's head cut into squares, as also the tongue braized with it. Let these boil together for about ten minutes, then add three or four dozen small round *quenelles* and a little lemon-juice, and send to table.

350. CLEAR MOCK-TURTLE SOUP.

To make this soup, follow the instructions laid down for making clear turtle, merely substituting calf's head for turtle.

351. MULLIGATAWNEY SOUP.

CUT up two or more chickens as for *fricassée*, place them neatly in a stewpan, in which previously put carrot, onion, celery, parsley, thyme, bay-leaf, cloves, and mace; fill up with good veal broth, and when the members of chicken are nearly done, strain them off into a sieve, saving their broth in a basin. Cool the pieces of chicken in spring water, and then take them up on a clean napkin, trim them neatly, and place them in a soup-pot, to be put into the soup afterward. Then cut four large onions in halves, taking out the head or root part, and again cut these into slices; place them in a stewpan with four ounces of butter, a carrot, and two heads of celery cut small, and fry these over a slow fire until the onion is nearly melted, and become of a fine light brown color; then throw in as much flower as will suffice to thicken the quantity of soup you wish to make; stir this on the fire two or three minutes, and after adding a good tablespoonful of curry powder, and the same quantity of curry paste, proceed gradually to mix in with these, first the broth the chickens were boiled in, and afterward as much more *consommé* of veal as may be found requisite to produce the quantity of soup desired. Place this on the stove-fire, stirring it the whole time, and as soon as it boils, put it by the side of the stove to clarify itself in the usual way; then rub it through the tammy into a *purée*, and pour it upon the pieces of chicken. Half an hour before dinner-time, place the soup on the stove-fire, stir it till it boils, place it by the side to continue boiling gently for ten minutes, by which time the chickens will be done; skim the soup, ascertain that the seasoning be correct, and send to table with two plates of plain boiled Patna rice, to be handed round with the soup.

352. GIBLET SOUP A L'ANGLAISE.

TAKE four sets of giblets properly cleaned and trimmed, put them into a stewpan full of boiling water, to scald for five minutes; drain them in a colander, immerse them in cold water, and then place them on a napkin to drain. Singe the necks and wings over the flame of a charcoal fire, and carefully pick out all the stubble feathers, cut the giblets up into inch and a half lengths, place these in a stewpan with two heads of celery, carrots, onions, turnips, in equal proportions; also, four cloves, two blades of mace, and a bunch of parsley, with a moderate quantity of basil, winter savory, lemon-thyme, and green onions, a sprig of common thyme, and one bay-leaf. Fill the stewpan with four quarts of *blond* of veal, and after allowing these to boil gently by the side of the stove-fire till they are done (which will be seen when the pieces of gizzard are become tender), immediately drain them in a large sieve, pouring their broth into a basin. Immerse the giblets in cold water, then pick them out free from any particles of herbs or vegetables that may adhere to them; place them on a napkin, and when neatly trimmed, put them by in the soup-pot. Next, pour the giblet broth into an adequate-sized stewpan, and having thickened it in the usual manner with a sufficient quantity of *roux* to the consistency of thin sauce, set it to boil on the stove-fire, and afterward place it by the side to clarify itself. When the sauce has been cleared of the butter, &c., add half a bottle of Sherry and a little cayenne, and then pass the sauce on to the giblets, and put the soup in the larder till dinner time; when, having allowed the giblets to boil in the sauce a few minutes, add a little lemon-juice, and send to table.

353. CLEAR GIBLET SOUP A L'IRLANDAISE.

PREPARE the giblet broth in every respect as directed for making the foregoing soup, trim and put the giblets away in a soup-pot, skim off every particle of fat from the surface of the broth, and clarify it by incorporating therewith the whites of three eggs whipped up with a little cold water; set the *consommé*, thus prepared, on the stove to boil, then add to it half a bottle of Sherry; and as soon as it boils up again, place it by the side of the stove, there gently to simmer for twenty minutes, in order to set the eggs. Then strain the *consommé* through a napkin on to the giblets, reserving one quart of it in a stewpan, in which boil the white parts of three heads of celery, and four large leeks, cut into inch lengths, and shred as for *Juliènne* soup, adding this to the giblets; ascertain that the seasoning be palatable, and send up to table.

354. OX-TAIL SOUP.

PROCURE two fresh ox-tails, cut each joint, after dividing them, into inch lengths with a small meat saw, steep them in water for two hours, and then place them in a stewpan with three carrots, three turnips, three onions, and two heads of celery, four cloves, and a blade of mace. Fill up the stewpan with broth from the boiling stock-pot; boil this by the side of the stove-fire till done, drain the pieces of ox-tail on a large sieve, allow them to cool, trim them neatly, and place them in a soup-pot. Clarify the broth the ox-tails were boiled in, strain it through a napkin into a basin, and then pour it into the soup-pot containing the trimmed pieces of ox-tails, and also some small olive-shaped pieces of carrot and turnip that have been boiled in a little of the broth, and a small lump of sugar; add a pinch of minionette pepper, and previously to sending the soup to table, let it boil gently by the side of the stove-fire for a few minutes.

This soup may be served, also, in various other ways, by adding thereto a *purée* of any sort of vegetables; such, for instance, as a *purée* of peas, carrots, turnips, celery, or lentils.

355. CALF'S FEET SOUP A LA WINDSOR.

PLACE in a two-gallon stockpot a knuckle of veal, a pound of raw lean ham, two calf's feet, and an old hen minus the fillets, which reserve for making *quenelles* with, for further use. To these add two carrots, two onions stuck with four cloves, celery, a bouquet of parsley, green onions, sweet basil, and lemon-thyme, tied neatly together; moisten with half a bottle of light French white wine, and put the stockpot on a moderate fire to boil for ten minutes or so; then fill it up from the common stock, or any white broth you may have ready, set it to boil on the stove, skim it well, and after four hours' gentle ebullition, take the calf's feet out, and put them in water to clean them; then take all the bones out, and lay them on a dish to cool, to be trimmed afterward, so as to leave the inner part of the feet only, all the outer skin being thinly pared off, that the feet may have a more transparent appearance; cut them into inch lengths, by half an inch in width, and put them by in a small soup-pot till required. Strain the *consommé* through a napkin, thicken it moderately with a little white *roux* (going through the regular process for making white *Velouté*), then add thereto a little essence of mushrooms, and finish by incorporating with the sauce thus prepared a leason of six yelks of eggs mixed with a little grated Parmesan and half a pint of cream; squeeze the juice of half a lemon into it, and season with a little crystallized soluble cayenne. Pour the soup into the tureen containing two dozen very small *quenelles* (made with the fillets of the old hen), some boiled macaroni cut into inch lengths, and the tendons of the calf's feet, previously warmed in a little *consommé*, with the addition of half a glass of white wine. Stir the soup gently in the tureen to mix these ingredients together, and send to table.

356. HARE SOUP A L'ANGLAISE.

SKIN and paunch a hare, and cut it up as follows:—first take off the legs close to the loins, and divide them into three pieces, slip the shoulders off and cut them into two parts, cut the back into six pieces, and divide the head in halves. Next place a stewpan on the stove-fire, containing four ounces of butter, a carrot, two onions, a head of celery cut into small slices, and fry these of a light color; then add the pieces of hare, over which, when also fried brown, shake a good handful of flour, and moisten with half a bottle of Port wine, at the same time adding a garnished bouquet, three cloves, a blade of mace, and two quarts of *blond* of veal; stir the whole on the fire until it boils, then take it off and set it by the side to boil gently for an hour and a quarter, taking care in the meantime to skim off the butter, &c., as it rises to the surface. Take out the pieces of hare when done, from the sauce, and place them on a dish; select the finest pieces of meat, remove the bones, and set these pieces aside in a soup-pot; clear the remainder of the meat from the bones, and pound it thoroughly, with the vegetables, from the sauce; when these are pounded, mix them again with the sauce, and pass the whole through a tammy into a *purée*, and pour it on to the pieces of hare reserved in the soup-pot.

Observe, that this soup must not be thick, consequently it may be necessary after passing it through the tammy to add a little *blond* of veal to thin it.

Just before sending it to table, make the soup hot, but be careful that it does not boil; ascertain that its seasoning be palatable, and serve.

357. HARE SOUP A LA ST. GEORGE.

GET two good-sized leverets and fillet them. Place the fillets in a small sauta-pan with a little fresh butter, pepper, and salt; cover them with a round of buttered paper, and put them in the larder till dinner-time. Reserve a sufficient quantity of the meat from the leveret's hind-quarters, in order to make some *quenelles;* cut the remainder into small pieces, and fry them exactly in the same manner as directed in the preceding soup; shake into them a sufficient quantity of flour to thicken the sauce of the soup, moisten with a bottle of Claret, and two quarts of *blond* of veal; add a garnished bouquet made with basil, marjoram, parsley, bay-leaf, and thyme, four cloves, mace, and four shalots. Let the sauce boil, skim it well, and when the hare is thoroughly done, pass the sauce through a tammy into a soup-pot ; put this on the fire to throw off any remaining roughness, and that it may be reduced if necessary ; and then pour it into the soup-tureen, which should contain three dozen small *quenelles* made with the meat reserved for that purpose, as before mentioned ; also the scollops of hare prepared by lightly frying the fillets in the sauta-pan, and which must be afterward scolloped. Ascertain that the seasoning be correct, and send to table.

358. LEVERET SOUP A LA ROSSIE.

GET a good-sized leveret, cut it into pieces, and fry these in a stew-pan with two ounces of butter ; as soon as they are colored, moisten with half a bottle of Sherry, allow the wine to boil, then add two quarts of *consommé* or *blond* of veal, garnish with carot, onion, and celery, mace, cloves, and peppercorns, a bouquet of bay-leaf, thyme, basil, marjoram, and winter savory ; let these herbs be used in small quantities, in order that they may give flavor, without predominating. When the soup has boiled three-quarters of an hour, let the pieces of hare be drained on a sieve, and at the same time pass the broth into a basin ; afterward place the pieces of hare on a napkin, and when neatly trimmed, put them into a soup-pot.

Next, clarify the *consommé* in the usual manner, and strain it through a napkin on to the pieces of leveret ; and, just before sending to table, add to the soup three dozen very small *quenelles* of leveret, and some white celery cut into shreds and boiled in a small quantity of the soup.

359. OX-CHEEK SOUP.

PROCURE a fresh ox-cheek, and put it to braize in a small stockpot with a knuckle of veal and some roast-beef bones, fill the pot up from the boiling stockpot, or with water ; garnish with the same complement of stock vegetables used for ox-tail soup (No. 354), adding six cloves, a blade of mace, and a few peppercorns. As soon as the ox-cheek is done, take the meat off the cheek-bone, and put it in press between two dishes. Strain off the broth, adding to it a ladleful of gravy to color it, and proceed to clarify it with a couple of whites of eggs. While the *consommé* is clarifying, trim the ox-cheek and cut it into neat scollops an inch square and half an inch thick ; put these into a small soup-pot and add to them some small carrots and turnips cut in fancy shapes and boiled in a little broth, a lump of sugar, and also a dozen and a half very small white button onions. Strain the clarified *consommé* thus prepared into the soup-pot, and having allowed the soup to boil a few minutes by the side of the stove-fire, just before serving, add two dozen blanched Brussels sprouts, and a pinch of minionette pepper, and send to table.

360. DEER'S-HEAD SOUP A LA CHASSEUR.*

PROCURE a young deer's head, perfectly fresh, scald it and cleanse it thoroughly ; proceed then to prepare the soup in exactly the same

---

* This will be found a very useful soup in those parts of the country where deer abound.

manner as for mock-turtle ; just before sending to table, add two dozen small *quenelles* made with deer's flesh, together with some small scollops of deer simmered in a little fresh butter and fine herbs.

Take care that the soup does not boil after the scollops are added to it.

361. GROUSE SOUP A LA MONTAGNARDE.

Roast off three brace of young grouse, take the whole of the meat from the bones, carefully cutting out the lower part of their backs, which being bitter, must be rejected. Set aside four of the fillets, cut them into scollops, to be put in the soup afterward. Put the carcasses and bones of the grouse into a stewpan with half a bottle of Sherry, a carrot, onion, celery, a few cloves, a couple of shalots, and a blade of mace ; set these to simmer gently on the fire for ten minutes, after which add two quarts of good stock, and having allowed it to boil an hour and a half, strain it off into a basin. Pound the whole of the meat yielded by the grouse, excepting the four fillets before named, mixing with it a little rice boiled in broth ; moisten with the grouse essence, and pass it through the tammy into a *purée*, and put it into a small soup-pot. Just before dinner-time, warm the *purée*, taking the usual precaution to prevent it from curdling, pour it into the soup-tureen containing the scollops of the fillets of grouse, and three dozen very small *quenelles* of the same.

PUREES OF POULTRY AND GAME,

COMPRISING

Purée of Fowl *à la Reine.*	*Purée* of Pheasants *à la Dauphine.*
„ „ *à la Printanière.*	„ „ *à l'Anglaise.*
„ „ *à la Princesse.*	„ Partridges *à la Beaufort.*
„ „ *à la Celestine.*	„ „ *à la Balzac.*
„ Red-legged Partridges *à la Conti.*	„ Hare *à la Conti.*
„ Pheasants *à la Royale.*	„ Rabbits *à la Maître d'hôtel.*
	„ " *à la Chantilly.*

362. PUREE OF FOWL A LA REINE.

Roast off two good-sized young fowls, clear all the meat from the bones, chop and pound it thoroughly with half a pound of boiled rice ; dilute it with three pints of chicken broth, made with the skins and carcasses of the two fowls used for the *purée*, and rub it through a tammy with the aid of two wooden spoons, into a large dish. Take the *purée* up into a soup-pot, and put it away in the larder till dinner-time ; then warm it, with the usual precaution to prevent its curdling ; mix with it a pint of boiling cream, and having ascertained that the seasoning be correct, send to table,

363. PUREE OF FOWL A LA PRINTANIERE.

Prepare the *purée* of fowls as for the preceding soup ; just before sending it to table, add the boiling cream, and then pour the *purée* into the soup-tureen containing a pint of asparagus-heads boiled green.

Send a plate of fried *croutons* to be handed round to the guests.

364. PUREE OF FOWL A LA PRINCESSE.

PREPARE the *purée* of fowl in the usual manner, and having mixed the boiling cream in it, pour it into the tureen containing three dozen very small *quenelles* of fowl, and four ounces of Frankfort pearl-barley, well blanched and boiled for two hours in some white chicken broth. Ascertain that the seasoning be delicate, and send to table.

365. PUREE OF FOWL A LA CELESTINE.

ROAST off two fowls; as soon as they are cold, pound the meat thereof in a mortar, together with six ounces of bleached Jordan almonds, and eight yelks of eggs, beginning with the almonds, then adding the yelks of eggs, and lastly, the fowl. Dilute with the chicken broth made with the carcasses of the fowl; rub the *purée* through the tammy, and put it into a soup-pot, to be kept in the cool till dinner-time; when, after having warmed it, add a pint of boiling cream, and send to table.

A plate of duchess' crusts should be sent to table with this soup, to be handed round.

366. PUREE OF RED-LEGGED PARTRIDGES A LA CONTI.

ROAST off two brace of red-legged partridges; take the meat from them, make a *consommé* with their carcasses, pound the meat thoroughly, mixing therewith half a pound of barley boiled for the purpose; dilute with the *consommé*, rub it through the tammy, and having made the *purée* sufficiently hot (taking care that it be not too thick), send to table with a plate of *Condé croutons*, to be handed round.

367. PUREE OF PHEASANTS A LA ROYALE.

ROAST off a brace of pheasants, take out the fillets and white part of the legs; make a *consommé* with the remainder. Pound the fillets, &c., with a proportionate quantity of boiled rice, dilute with the *consommé*, and rub the *purée* through the tammy; finish with a small piece of game glaze or essence, and serve.

The *croutons* to be sent in a plate as usual.

368. PUREE OF PHEASANTS A LA DAUPHINE.

PREPARE a *purée* of pheasants as in the preceding case; when about to send the soup to table, pour it into a tureen containing four dozen small potato *quenelles*, and serve.

The potato *quenelles* should be prepared as follows :—Bake four. large York potatoes, and rub the pulp through a wire-sieve; put this into a stewpan with two ounces of butter, half a pint of cream, pepper, salt, and nutmeg. Stir these on the fire until the mixture forms a compact paste; then take the stewpan off the stove, and proceed to incorporate with the paste three yelks and one white of egg; and then mould the small *quenelles* with teaspoons, and poach them as you would any others, in water or broth.

369. PUREE OF PHEASANTS A L'ANGLAISE.

PREPARE a *purée* of pheasant in the usual manner, and having finished it as in the foregoing article, pour it into a tureen containing the fillets of one pheasant cut into scollops, and serve.

370. PUREE OF PARTRIDGES A LA BEAUFORT.

PREPARE a *purée* of partridges in the manner described for making the *purée* of red-legged partridges ; warm and finish the *purée* in the same manner, and just before sending to table, pour into the tureen containing three dozen small *quenelles* of partridges, the tails of three dozen crayfish, and half a pound of cocks kernels (previously simmered in a little white broth, with butter, lemon-juice, and salt), and serve.

371. PUREE OF PARTRIDGES A LA BALZAC.

PREPARE a *purée* of partridges in the usual manner, and finish by incorporating with it two ounces of crayfish butter and a piece of game glaze ; then pour the hot *purée* into a tureen containing three dozen crayfish tails, and three dozen *quenelles* of partridges—in the preparation of which two tablespoonsful of chopped truffles have been mixed, previously to moulding the *quenelles ;* and send to table.

372. PUREE OF HARE A LA CONTI.

SKIN, paunch, and cut up a hare into pieces. Put two ounces of butter into a stewpan with two shalots, a blade of mace, a sprig of thyme, and half a bay-leaf. When the butter has been made hot on the stove-fire, put the pieces of hare into the stewpan, and having fried these of a brown color, moisten them with a bottle of Sauterne wine ; when the wine has boiled ten minutes, add three pints of good *consommé ;* and then, after allowing the hare to boil gently on the side of the stove-fire for about an hour and a quarter, strain the pieces of hare into a sieve, reserving the broth in a basin ; and after having separated the meat from the bones, &c., pound it thoroughly with a little boiled rice ; dilute it with the stock it was boiled in, and pass it through the tammy into a *purée.* Just before sending to table, make the *purée* sufficiently hot, and having tested its degree of seasoning, serve with a plate of fried *croutons*, to be handed round to the guests.

373. PUREE OF RABBITS A LA MAITRE D'HOTEL.

ROAST off three good-sized young rabbits ; and, while they are before the fire, season them with a little nutmeg, pepper, and salt, and baste with half a pint of cream mixed with two ounces of fresh butter and two ounces of flour. This batter should not be used until the rabbits have been roasted ten minutes, and care should be taken to make it adhere to the rabbits while they continue roasting ; when they are done, clear off all the meat, and pound it in a mortar with four ounces of barley, previously boiled for the purpose ; dilute with the *consommé* made from the carcasses, rub the whole through the tammy, and put this *purée* into a small soup-pot. Just before dinner-time make it hot, and incorporate therewith half a pint of cream and a pat of fresh butter ; then pour it into a tureen containing three dozen small *quenelles* of rabbit, in preparing which a little grated Parmesan cheese, minionette pepper, and a spoonful of chopped and blanched parsley must be added.

374. PUREE OF RABBITS A LA CHANTILLY.

PREPARE a *purée* of rabbits as for the preceding soup, finish it by adding a pint of cream and a piece of glaze; then pour the hot soup into a tureen containing twelve small custards previously prepared for the purpose, in manner following: Pass eight yelks of eggs through a tammy into a stewpan, to these add a tablespoonful of spinach-green (*No.* 285), a little grated Parmesan cheese, nutmeg, pepper, and salt, some essence of game, and half a pint of cream; beat the whole well together, and pass this mixture through a tammy into a basin, and then pour it into twelve small *dariole* moulds (previously buttered), place them in a stewpan containing hot water to the depth of an inch, and set them to steam by the side of the stove-fire, taking care that the stewpan has the lid on, and some live embers of burning charcoal placed upon it. A quarter of an hour will suffice to steam these custards; when done, turn them out of the moulds with care, and place them instantly in the soup-tureen as directed.

NATIONAL SOUPS,

COMPRISING

Raviolis *à la Napolitaine.*
Rice *à la Florentine.*
Soup *à la Piémontaise.*
Do. *à la Béarnaise.*
Bouillabaisse *à la Provençale.*

Borsch, or Polish Soup.
Ouka, or *Russian* do.
Tschi, or Cabbage do., *à la Russe.*
Olla Podrida, or Spanish national do.
Turkish *Pilaff,* or *Pilau.*

375. RAVIOLIS A LA NAPOLITAINE.

PREPARE a *consommé* gravy soup, in the following manner: Butter the bottom of a small stockpot, and place in it some slices of raw ham, three pounds of gravy beef, a small knuckle of veal, and either one old hen or two partridges. To these add two heads of celery, the same number of leeks and carrots, sprigs of thyme and winter savory, tied into a fagot with some parsley, cloves, mace, and pepper-corns; moisten with a large ladleful of broth, and put the gravy, thus marked, on a stove-fire to boil down to a glaze, taking the usual precautionary measures to prevent it from burning. As soon as the glaze is sufficiently colored, fill the stockpot up with good broth; when it boils, skim it, and set it down by the side of the stove-fire to boil gently for three hours; then strain off the *consommé,* clarify it with a couple of whites of eggs, and pass it through a napkin into a soup-pot, to be used as follows:

RAVIOLIS.

Mix half a pound of sifted flour with four yelks of eggs, a little salt, and half a pat of butter; let these ingredients be placed on a paste slab, putting the yelks of eggs, &c., in the centre of the flour; then knead them into a firm, smooth, compact paste; and after allowing it to rest in a damp cloth for half an hour, spread it out with the rolling-pin until it becomes nearly as thin as a sheet of paper. Place the paste, thus rolled out, lengthwise on the slab, then, with the paste-brush dipped in water, moisten its whole surface, and lay thereon, about two inches apart from each other, some small round balls of *raviolis farce* of the size of a cob-nut, in rows. This farce is prepared as follows:—Put the white parts of a boiled or roasted fowl, pheasant, or partridge, into a mortar; pound the meat thoroughly, and add thereto about four ounces of fresh-made curd, two ounces of grated Parmesan cheese, two spoonsful of blanched spinach, pepper, salt, and nutmeg; moisten with four yelks of raw eggs, and mix the whole well together into a smooth compact body, ready for use.

Wrap the outer part of the paste, when the *raviolis farce* has been laid on it, over the outer row of balls, cover them as if for making puffs, finish them by fastening down the paste with the thumb, and then cut them out with a small round fluted cutter into half-moons; and as they are cut out, place them on a large dish, there to be left for some time, in order to dry the surface, so that it may more resemble Italian paste. Having repeated this operation until you have made five or six dozen *raviolis*, after they have been dried in the larder, proceed to blanch them; this is done by throwing them into a large stewpan containing some boiling broth, and allowing them to continue boiling therein for a quarter of an hour; then drain the *raviolis* on to a napkin.

Next take the lining of a soup-tureen, butter it, place therein a layer of *raviolis* and a layer of grated fresh Parmesan cheese, and so on alternately, until the silver tureen-lining be filled; shake some grated cheese on the top, and moisten with two glasses of old Madeira, and a ladleful of the gravy made for the purpose, and then put the lining into the oven, or on a slow stove-fire, there to reduce the gravy to a *gratinate*. Brown the top over with the heated salamander, and send to table with the remainder of the clear *consommé* in the soup-tureen.

This soup should be thus served: With a gravy-spoon help a part of the *gratinated raviolis*, in a soup-plate, and add to these a ladleful of the *consommé*.

376. RICE A LA FLORENTINE.

PREPARE a thin *purée* of rice, and moisten it with *consommé* of fowls; finish by adding two ounces of grated Parmesan cheese, a leason of six yelks of eggs, half a pint of cream, a pat of butter, and a little minionette pepper; then pour the soup thus prepared into the soup-tureen, and send to table with two plates of very small *croquettes* of rice, which are to be handed round with the soup.

The *croquettes* of rice here alluded to, are thus made:—

Wash and blanch half a pound of Carolina rice, and boil it in a little broth with two ounces of fresh butter, and a pinch of minionette pepper, and a little salt; when done, add two ounces of grated Parmesan cheese, and four yelks of eggs; work the whole on the stove-fire for five minutes, spread it on a plate, and when this paste is sufficiently cold, mould it into very small round balls. Just before dinner-time, dip these in some beaten egg, and roll them in flour; then put them into a large-sized parsley frier, and immerse them in a quantity of hot clean lard; fry them of a fine deep yellow color, and send to table in two hot plates, on napkins, to be handed round with the soup as before stated.

377. SOUP A LA PIEMONTAISE.

PREPARE a brown *purée* of turnips (No. 294), in which mix a large gravy-spoonful of tomatas; just before sending to table, incorporate with the soup a paste composed of four anchovies washed, filleted, and pounded, with a clove of garlic and a pat of butter, all passed through a fine hair-sieve; and pour the soup into a tureen containing four dozen very small *quenelles* of potatoes (No. 310), and a *pluche* of chervil and tarragon (that is to say, the leaves of chervil and tarragon picked and parboiled green), and send to table with some grated Parmesan cheese on a plate, to be handed round with the soup.

378. SOUP A LA BEARNAISE.

LET a quart of *garbanças*, or large yellow Spanish peas, be put in soak the overnight, place them in a small stockpot with a piece of raw ham, and having filled up with common broth, set the stockpot on the stove-fire to boil; skim it well, and put it by the side to boil gently for four hours.   Meanwhile, cut three large onions, one carrot, and two heads of celery, into small dice, put these into a stewpan with two ounces of fresh butter and two cloves of garlic; fry them of a very light brown color, and after adding half a dozen fresh tomatas, mix the whole in with the *garbanças*.   As soon as the *garbanças* are done, pound and rub them through the tammy, diluting with good *consommé;* take the *purée* up into a small soup-pot, and clarify it in the usual manner, by allowing it to throw up its roughness while boiling gently by the side of the stove-fire: remember that this *purée* must be kept rather thin.   During this process, cut a white-heart cabbage into quarters, removing the core, shred them as fine as possible, place them in a stewpan with two ounces of butter on a moderate stove-fire, and fry them as you would vegetables for *Juliènne* soup.   When they are considerably reduced in quantity, and become of a yellowish color, moisten them with a little broth; keep them gently simmering until they are thoroughly done; add them to the *purée*, together with a pinch of minionette pepper, and about half a pint of whole *gar-banças* reserved for this purpose, and from which take off the hulls previously to putting them into the soup.   When the cabbage has boiled a few minutes in the *purée*, pour the soup into the tureen, and send to table with an accompanying plate of grated Parmesan cheese, to be handed round with the soup.

379. BOUILLABAISSE OR PROVENCALE SOUP.

CUT four large Portugal onions into slices, and fry them in a gill of Lucca oil; when they begin to assume a light brown color, add thereto a sprig of thyme and two cloves of garlic, and shake in a good handful of flour, stir this on the stove-fire for a few minutes, moisten with half a ottle of Sauterne wine, and add three pints of good *consommé;* stir this sauce on the fire till it boils, then set it by the side to continue gently simmering for half an hour, and rub it through the tammy like any other *purée;* then take it up and pour it into a small soup-pot.   Just before dinner-time, make the soup hot, and finish by incorporating with it a leason of six yelks of eggs, a little cayenne, the juice of a lemon, and two ounces of grated Parmesan cheese; pour the soup into the tureen containing a plateful of scollops of any sort of fish (crimped cod or whiting is the best for the purpose) prepared as follows : cut two slices of crimped cod into small scollops, and put them into a deep sauta-pan with a little Lucca oil, minionette pepper, and a little salt, some chopped tarragon and chervil, and the juice of half a lemon ; fry these on the fire, put them into the soup-tureen, and when the soup is poured on them, throw in a small plateful of duchess' crusts fried in Lucca oil, and send to table.

380. BORSCH, OR POLISH SOUP.

PLACE in a good-sized stockpot a large knuckle of veal, an old hen, partially roasted and colored, a couple of marrow-bones, one pound of streaky lean bacon (trimmed and parboiled for the purpose), two carrots, two heads of celery, and two onions stuck with six cloves ; also a large fagot of parsley and green onions tied together with a little thyme, sweet basil, bay-leaf, and mace ; then add a teaspoonful of white peppercorns. Fill the stockpot up with prepared juice of beet-root,* set it upon the stove-fire to boil, and after being skimmed, let it boil gently by the side of the fire for an hour ; then add a fowl, a duck, a partridge (trussed for boiling), and six pork sausages. Observe, that the foregoing articles be not overdone, and be careful to take them up directly they are sufficiently braized ; then place them on a dish, and set them in the larder to get cold.

While the stock is in preparation, peel two raw beet-roots, and shred them, also two onions, and an equal quantity of the white part of two heads of celery, as if for *Juliènne* soup ; fry these vegetables in a little butter, of a light color, moisten with a quart of broth from the boiling stock, and having gently boiled them down to the consistency of a demi-glaze, set them by in a soup-pot in the larder. Then chop four ounces of fillet of beef with the same quantity of beef suet, add a little pepper, salt, and nutmeg, and two yelks of eggs ; pound this force-meat thoroughly, and use half of it to make thirty small round *quenelles,* by rolling them with a little flour on the table ; poach these in a little broth, and having drained them upon a napkin, add them to the shred vegetables put by in the soup-pot. With the remainder of the force-meat make the same number of very small oval *quenelles,* which, after being rolled with flour, set in a small sauta-pan to be fried of a light color, just before dinner-time. Boil four eggs hard, cut them in halves lengthwise ; take the yelks out and pound them with two raw yelks of eggs, a little grated horse-radish, chopped parsley, nutmeg, pepper, and salt ; fill the eggs again with this *farce,* and having replaced the halves together, dip them in a beaten egg, and then roll them in bread-crumb, and set them aside to be fried at the same time as the small *quenelles* before mentioned. After five hours' boiling, strain off the stock-pot ; when every particle of fat is removed, clarify it in the usual way, and then keep the *consommé* boiling, in order to reduce it to the quantity required for the soup.

---

* The beet-root to be used in the *borsch* is thus made:—Procure two dozen fine beet-roots, scraped and washed, bruise them in a mortar, and place them in a large-sized earthen pan, into which throw in a pailful of water, and two pounds of bread-crumb. Cover the pan with the lid, carefully cementing it down with a paste of flour and water, in order to exclude the air; and set the pan in a moderately warm place, so as to accelerate the fermentation. Ten days will suffice to produce the desired result; on uncovering the pan, it will be found to contain a bright red, acidulated liquor.

In the meantime, trim the meat off the fowl, duck, and pheasant, into neat scollops ; cut the bacon and sausages into small round balls, and carefully place all these ingredients in the silver lining of a soup-tureen, keeping the shreded vegetables and braized beef *quenelles* on the top ; put them in the hot closet until dinner-time. Then grate or pound a couple of beet-roots, place this in a stewpan on the fire, and boil it up for a few minutes, extract the juice by strong pressure through the tammy-cloth, and use it to color the *consommé*, so as to give it the appearance of claret. Just before sending to table, pour the boiling *consommé* to the ingredients contained in the soup-tureen, adding a pinch of minionette pepper ; send up the fried eggs cut in halves, and also the fried *quenelles*, in a plate, to be handed round with the *borsch*.

381. OUKA, OR RUSSIAN SOUP.

PLACE in a stockpot a large knuckle of veal, about a pound of raw ham, and two old hens, roasted for the purpose ; fill up with common broth, set it to boil, and having skimmed it, garnish it with the usual vegetables, adding thereto either a handful of parsley-roots or a couple of parsnips. After five hours' boiling, strain off the *consommé*, and clarify it in the usual manner ; strain it again through a napkin into a soup-pot, to be set aside until wanted to finish the soup. While the stock is boiling, take two pounds of crimped salmon, two large live perch, a Thames eel, and two fine mullets ; fillet and cut these into scollops, placing them neatly in a deep sauta-pan ; season with a *plûche* of picked parsley, chervil, and tarragon leaves (the latter in a small proportion), some boiled shred parsley-roots, minionette pepper, grated nutmeg, salt, and the fourth part of a bottle of Chablis or Sauterne ; having first allowed these scollops to boil on the stove for five minutes, moisten with a quart of essence of fish (made with the carcasses and trimmings of the fish used for the scollops), let them boil quickly for ten minutes longer, and then pour the *consommé* to them ; after they have boiled together two or three minutes, pour the soup into the tureen containing three dozen small *quenelles* of whiting, in which some lobster coral and *purée* of mushrooms have been mixed. Ascertain that the seasoning is appropriate, and send to table.

This soup is a species of souchet, and may be varied by using different kinds of fish. It is much esteemed by those who are fond of fish.

381A. TSCHI, OR CABBAGE SOUP A LA RUSSE.

FIRST, cut four onions into small dice, and fry them with a little butter in a stewpan over a slow fire, and when they assume a light yellow-brown color, add to these a white-heart cabbage which has been previously shred fine for the purpose, and, after having continued to fry this also with the onions for about ten minutes, two tablespoonsful of flour should be added ; stir the whole well together, moistening with three pints of good *consommé*, season with a little nutmeg and minionette pepper, and when, after the soup has boiled gently by the side of the stove for about an hour, in order to clarify it, let it be well skimmed ; and previously to sending the soup to table, add a *plûche* of tarragon leaves and some lemon-juice. Previously to pouring the Tschi into the soup-tureen, place therein

about three dozen small sausages made in manner following, viz. :—
To four ounces of lean fillet of beef, add an equal quantity of beef suet ;
first chop, and then pound these well together in a mortar, season with
grated nutmeg, pepper, and salt, and some chopped parsley ; add
three yelks of eggs, mix well together by pounding the whole ten
minutes longer, after which proceed to roll the sausage meat into small
round or oval shapes the size of a cob-nut ; and, after frying these of a
light color in a little clarified butter use them as directed above.

382. OLLA PODRIDA, OR SPANISH NATIONAL SOUP.

PLACE some slices of raw ham at the bottom of the stockpot, add
five pounds of gravy beef cut in slices, and a roasted old hen ; garnish
with the usual vegetables, two cloves, and mace ; moisten with a quart
of broth, set the stockpot on the fire, and let the broth be reduced to a
glaze ; fill it up with water as soon as it boils, skim it, and then set
the stock to boil gently by the side of the stove. When the *consommé*
has boiled two hours, throw in a large fowl and two partridges trussed
for boiling, six pork sausages, and two Spanish savaloys (which are to
be had at all the first-rate Italian warehouses), watch the braizing of
these, to prevent their being overdone ; take them out when they are
sufficiently braized, place them upon a dish to get cool, then divide the
fowl and partridges into small members, trimming them neatly, and
cut the sausages and savaloys also into small round balls, and place
all these in a soup-pot, together with three carrots and as many turnips
cut into the form of rather large-sized olives, and some shred celery
and leeks, previously boiled in *consommé* with a small lump of sugar ;
to these must also be added some boiled yellow Spanish peas (*garbanças*) free from their hulls. After four hours' boiling, strain the
stock off, clarify it, and strain it again through a napkin ; add it to the
fore-named ingredients with a pinch of minionette pepper ; boil the
whole for ten minutes, and send to table.

383. TURKISH PILAFF, OR PILAU.

PLACE a knuckle of veal on some slices of raw ham in a stockpot,
also a roasted shoulder of lamb and a large fowl trussed for boiling ;
fill up with common broth or water, and having skimmed the broth,
garnish with the usual vegetables. As soon as the fowl and lamb are
done, take them up, and when cold cut the meat off the shoulder of
lamb into small cutletlike pieces, and the fowl into neatly-trimmed
members. Place these in a small soup-pot with half a pound of
Carolina rice, boiled in some of the *consommé*, after it has been clarified and seasoned with an infusion of rather less than a quarter of an
ounce of hay saffron, and cayenne ; and then having reduced the *consommé* to two-thirds of its original quantity, pour it upon the foregoing
ingredients, adding six ounces of dried cherries or Sultana raisins ; boil
these together for a quarter of an hour, and send to table.

This kind of soup is very nutritious, and, from the cayenne and
saffron contained in it, is calculated to give tone to the stomach.

ITALIAN SOUPS,

COMPRISING

Macaroni Soup *à la Royale.* Semolina Soup *à la Palermo.*
  „   „   *à la Medicos.*   „   „   *à la Vénitienne.*
  „   „   *à la St. Pierre.*   „   „   *à la Pisane.*

384. MACARONI SOUP A LA ROYALE.

BOIL ten ounces of Naples macaroni in two quarts of boiling water, with two ounces of fresh butter, a little minionette pepper, and salt. When the macaroni has boiled half an hour, drain it off upon a sieve, cut it into half-inch lengths, and boil it in two quarts of good chicken or game *consommé* for ten minutes; take it off the stove and mix with it a leason of six yelks of eggs, half a pint of cream, two ounces of grated Parmesan cheese, and a little minionette pepper; set the leason in the soup by stirring it on the stove-fire for three minutes, and send to table.

Vermicelli or any other Italian paste may be substituted for the macaroni. This soup is sometimes designated *"à l'Italienne."*

385. MACARONI SOUP A LA MEDICIS.

BOIL ten ounces of Naples macaroni, and cut it into inch lengths; at the same time trim the tails of thirty crayfish, and the same number of *quenelles* of fowl, colored with crayfish butter; place these in the silver lining of a soup-tureen according to the following directions:—

Butter the bottom of the lining and spread thereon a layer of macaroni, then a layer of grated Parmesan cheese, after which place a layer of crayfish tails; repeat the layer of grated cheese, and place on that a layer of small *quenelles:* and thus proceed until the several articles prepared for the purpose are disposed of. Then add a pint of strong *consommé*, and cover the top with grated cheese; melt a small pat of fresh butter over the fire, and sprinkle it on the top of the whole preparation; then set the tureen lining thus filled to *gratinate* in the oven, which will require about half an hour. Lastly, place the lining on a dish to be served from the side-table, while the bright clear *consommé* is to be sent up in another tureen.

In helping the soup at table, first put a small ladleful of the preparation of macaroni, &c., on a soup plate, and add to it a ladleful of the *consommé*.

386. MACARONI SOUP A LA ST. PIERRE.

CUT some macaroni that has been boiled, into inch lengths, place them in a stewpan with four ounces of lobster-coral butter and a little cayenne, simmer it gently on the fire for ten minutes, and then place a fourth part in a silver soup lining; on this sprinkle some grated Parmesan cheese, then put a layer of blanched soft roses of mackerel, over which place some grated cheese, again cover this with some prepared scollops of salmon; and thus repeat the foregoing instructions until the ingredients are all used up, finishing this part of the operation by sprinkling over the whole some grated cheese, and adding a pint of good *consommé;* lastly, place the lining in the oven to *gratinate,* which must be carefully attended to. Send the soup to table with another tureen of clear bright *consommé,* to be served to the guests in the same manner as described in the preceding article.

387. SEMOLINA SOUP A LA PALERMO.

MIX four ounces of wheaten flour with the same quantity of Turkish wheat flour, place these on the paste-board or slab, and having made a hollow in the centre, place in it four yelks of eggs, a little cream, pepper, salt, and nutmeg; proceed to work these into a firmly-kneaded paste. Spread this out very thin with the aid of a rolling-pin, and having cut it into bands an inch wide, shred these so as to resemble vermicelli. Strew these shreds on a large baking sheet covered with paper, and put them to dry for four hours in the hot closet. A quarter of an hour before dinner-time, throw the shreds thus prepared into two quarts of boiling game *consommé;* skim this, and place the stepwan containing the soup by the side of the stove-fire, to continue gently boiling until the time for serving; then, after adding a pinch of minionette pepper, send to table with some grated Parmesan cheese on a plate, to be handed round with the soup.

388. SEMOLINA SOUP A LA VENITIENNE.

THROW six ounces of semolina into two quarts of boiling *consommé* of game; after boiling gently by the side of the stove-fire for a quarter of an hour, add a glass of Madeira, two ounces of grated Parmesan cheese, half a pint of cream mixed with four yelks of eggs, a little crystallized soluble cayenne, and the juice of half a lemon. Set this preparation on the stove-fire, taking care not to let it curdle, then pour the soup into a tureen containing the fillets of two dozen larks which have been simmered with fine herbs. Stir the soup gently into the tureen, in order to mix the scollops with the semolina. In Italy, the fillets of a small delicious bird, called Beccaficas, are used instead of larks.

389. SEMOLINA SOUP A LA PISANE.

BONE and braize two calf's feet, and having pressed them between two dishes, cut them out into round pieces the size of a shilling, with a tin cutter; place these in a stewpan together with three dozen very small *quenelles à la Xavier* (No. 257) and a glass of Madeira; allow them to simmer on the fire for five minutes, and add them to a similar quantity and description of soup as directed in the preceding article, but omitting the fillets of larks, and send to table.

Note.—The foregoing soups may be prepared, with equal success, by using any of the numerous sorts of Italian pastes, instead of keeping to those described for the purpose. The soups may also be infinitely varied by changing their garnishes.

PANADAS AND LIGHT SOUPS FOR INFANTS AND INVALIDS,

COMPRISING

Chicken *Panada.*
Pheasant or Partridge *Panada.*
Chicken or game custards
Venison *Panada.*

Nutritious liquid custards of chicken.
      „   „   game.
Ceylon moss gelatinous chicken broth.

390. CHICKEN PANADA.

ROAST off a young fowl, take all the white parts and pound them with the crumb of a French roll soaked in broth; dilute these with a little chicken broth (made from the remains of the roasted fowl) to the consistency of a soft batter or creamy substance; pass it through a tammy as in preparing any other *purée.* Previous to serving this *panada,* it should be moderately warmed, and put into custard cups. In the composition of every sort of dietetic preparation for the use of infants and invalids, it is strictly necessary to avoid the use of herbs, vegetables, and spices; even salt should be used sparingly.

391. PHEASANT OR PARTRIDGE PANADA.

PHEASANT or partridge *panada* is prepared in the same manner as described for making the chicken panada; game being substituted for poultry.

392. CHICKEN OR GAME CUSTARDS.

CUT a young fowl into quarters, take the lungs away from the backbone, wash the fowl, and then place it in a stewpan with a little parsley, chervil, half a head of celery, and a turnip. Fill the stewpan with three pints of cold water, place it on the fire, and as soon as it boils, skim it thoroughly, and set it by the side of the fire to remain boiling for an hour; after which strain the broth into a basin through a napkin, and use it in the following manner :—

According to the number of custard-cups required to be filled, place so many yelks of eggs in a basin; to these add the same number of custard-cupsful of prepared chicken broth, and with a spoon or fork, beat these together, in order to mix them thoroughly; then pass them, by pressure, through the tammy, fill the custard-cups, steam them in the usual manner, and send them up quickly.

These custards should be eaten very soon after being made, as they become heavy when warmed a second time.

393. VENISON PANADA.

TAKE a pound (more or less) of the lean part of either a roasted haunch or neck of venison, mince it, and then pound it with the crumb of a French roll which has been soaked in good broth; dilute with a little *consommé,* and pass the panada through a tammy as usual. Just before sending this panada up, warm it carefully, so as not to allow it to get too hot, as it would then be liable to become somewhat decomposed and rough, and rather indigestible for a delicate stomach.

394. NUTRITIOUS LIQUID CUSTARD OF CHICKEN.

PREPARE the chicken broth as directed for making chicken custards, take half a pint of this, and mix it thoroughly with two yelks of new-laid eggs; stir it over the stove-fire, or, if practicable, over the heat of steam, until the mixture becomes somewhat thickened, assuming a soft creamy appearance; pour it into a broth basin or caudle-cup, and let it be instantly served.

395. NUTRITIOUS LIQUID CUSTARD OF GAME.

THIS sort of custard is prepared similarly to the foregoing, substituting pheasant or partridge for poultry.

396. CEYLON MOSS GELATINOUS CHICKEN BROTH.

CUT a fowl into four parts, take out the lungs, and wash it thoroughly, place it in a stewpan with four ounces of prepared Ceylon moss, adding three pints of water and a little salt; having boiled the broth for three-quarters of an hour by the side of a stove-fire, pass it through a napkin, and serve it in a caudle-cup to the invalid.

DRESSED FISH IN GENERAL.

TURBOT AND BRILL,

COMPRISING

Turbot, plain boiled.	Turbot, *à la Maréchale.*
„ *à la Parisiènne.*	Fillets of Turbot, *à l'Indiènne.*
„ broiled *à la Provençale.*	„ „ *à la Ravigotte.*
„ *à la Carême.*	„ „ *à la Vertpré,* or green.
„ *à la Vatel.*	„ „ *Ravigotte.*
„ *à la crême au gratin.*	„ „ *à l'Italiènne.*
„ *in Matelotte Normande.*	„ „ *à la Cardinal.*
„ *à la Béchamel.*	Brill,—John Dory.

397. PLAIN BOILED TURBOT OR A L'ANGLAISE.

PROCURE if possible a turbot conveyed by land-carriage, of moderate size : the larger fish are never delicate ; choose it thick and plump, open it to ascertain that the back-bone is free from color, as when it has a reddish appearance, although perfectly fresh, it is sure to boil of a bad color. Wash the turbot, wipe it dry, and rub it over with the juice of a lemon and a little salt; put it into a fit-sized turbot-kettle, add a sufficient quantity of spring-water to cover the fish, then throw in a good handful of salt, and set the turbot on the stove to boil; as soon as the water begins to simmer, skim it thoroughly, and lift the kettle from the fire down by the side, there to remain gently boiling for half an hour, more or less, according to the size of the fish. When the turbot is done, lift it out of the water with the drainer; slip it carefully on to a dish prepared to receive it, and send it to table with two sauce-boats filled with lobster and Dutch sauces (Nos. 42 and 55).

398. TURBOT A LA PARISIENNE.

CHOOSE a turbot weighing about 4 lbs., trim the fins off close, make an incision in the back from head to tail, and, inserting the knife on either side, detach the fish from the bone right up to the fins ; then cut the back bone through, close to the head and tail, and carefully separate the under part of the fish from the bone, so as not to run the knife through ; bone the turbot in this manner, wipe it with a clean cloth, season it inside with a little pepper and salt, and spread a layer of *quenelle* force-meat of whitings, mixed with a spoonful of chopped fine herbs, inside. Then butter a large baking-sheet, and place the turbot upon it, with the white side uppermost; moisten with a bottle of French white wine, some essence of mushrooms, and oyster liquor; season with a little pepper and salt, place a buttered paper over the whole, and set the fish to boil on the stove : next put it in the oven to simmer gently for about three-quarters of an hour, taking care to baste the turbot with its liquor every five minutes, so that it may thus be made to absorb the greater portion while stewing. When the turbot is done, drain it from its liquor on to a large earthen dish, and put it to cool in the larder, reserving the liquor in which it has been stewed to be reduced and mixed with a sufficient quantity of Parisian sauce (No. 40), to be used for garnishing the turbot when dished up. When the turbot is cold, place it on a buttered baking-sheet, and spread it over with a thin layer of reduced *Allemande* sauce, over which shake some very finely-sifted bread-crumbs, fried of a light color; moisten the fish with a little *consommé* and wine, and put it in the oven about twenty minutes before sending it to table, that it may get thoroughly warm through; when about to dish it up, slide it gently off the baking-sheet on to a dish, and sauce it round with part of the Parisian sauce prepared for the purpose; garnish it round with groups of crayfish tails, muscles, oysters, button-mushrooms, and small round truffles, tossed in a little glaze to give them a bright appearance. Send up the remainder of the sauce in a boat.

399. BOILED TURBOT A LA PROVENCALE.

PROCURE a small plump turbot, make an incision in the back, and, with a strong knife, cut away an inch of the spine, trim the fins close, score it rather deep on the back, and then place it on an earthen dish to steep for four hours in a *marinade* made of the following ingredients: sliced carrot, onions, sprigs of parsley, bay-leaf and thyme, three cloves of garlic, pepper and salt, the juice of a lemon, and a gill of salad-oil. Let the turbot be frequently rubbed and turned in this *marinade*, that it may be thoroughly impregnated with its flavor. About three-quarters of an hour before dinner, remove every particle of vegetable from the turbot, place it, with the white side under, on a gridiron (previously rubbed with chalk of whiting), and set it to broil on a clear fire, of moderate heat: twenty minutes will suffice to broil it on one side; it must then be carefully removed on to a deep baking-sheet, upon its back, first placing the whole of the *marinade* in the baking-sheet or dish; moisten with half a bottle of light white wine, and then put the turbot in the oven to bake; observing that it must be basted every five minutes with its liquor. When the turbot is done, lift it carefully on to its dish, put the whole of the *marinade* in which it has been baked into a stewpan with the remaining half bottle of wine; boil the whole together for five minutes, strain it with pressure through a tammy into a stewpan, and reduce it with some *Allemande* sauce: add a pint of anchovy butter, some chopped and blanched parsley, a spoonful of capers, and a little cayenne; garnish the turbot round with this sauce, adding groups of muscles fried in batter, and some lobster cut into neat scollops, and tossed in lobster-coral to give them a scarlet hue. Send some of the sauce to table in a boat.

400. TURBOT A LA CAREME.

PREPARE a turbot according to the foregoing directions, omitting the garlic; when it is done, reduce the liquor, and incorporate it it in a sufficient quantity of Dutch sauce, having *Suprême* sauce for its foundation; add some lobster butter, cayenne, and lemon-juice; work the sauce well together over the fire, and pour it round the turbot; glaze the fish lightly, garnish it with groups of fine large cray-fish and *quenelles* of whiting colored with some green *Ravigotte* (No. 185). Serve the remainder of the sauce in a boat.

400A. TURBOT A LA VATEL.

PREPARE and dress a turbot according to the directions given for turbot *à la Parisiènne* (No. 398); when done, drain and place it on a dish, reduce the liquor in which it has been baked, and incorporate it with some *Suprême* sauce, finished with green *Ravigotte* butter (No. 185); add two dozen oysters, some button mushrooms, and thirty crayfish tails, lemon-juice, and cayenne. Cover the turbot with this sauce, and garnish it round with fried smelts, trussed with their tails in their mouths, (and previously boned and stuffed), with an inner row of small fillets of soles, which have been *contisés*, one-half with truffles, and the other with thin scollops of the red part of the tail of a lobster turned round, and simmered in a little butter in a sauta-pan. Serve as usual some of the sauce in a boat.

401. TURBOT A LA CREME AU GRATIN.

BOIL a turbot, drain it on a dish, and while it cools, prepare some cream *Béchamel* sauce (No. 5); reduce it, and add the yelks of four eggs, four ounces of grated fresh Parmesan cheese, a little minionette pepper, grated nutmeg, and lemon-juice. With a spoon cut the turbot into flakes, and put them in the sauce, taking care to waste none of the delicate meaty part of the fins, the cheeks, and the glutinous mem-branes of the fish. Stir the whole lightly together, and pile it neatly in the shape of a dome on the dish; cover it thoroughly and smoothly with some finely-sifted bread-crumbs fried and mixed with a fourth part of grated Parmesan cheese; garnish round with fried *croquettes* of potatoes; and twenty minutes before sending to table, put the turbot thus prepared into the oven to *gratinate;* pass the redhot salamander over it to melt the cheese, and pour round the inner circle of the *croquettes* some *Béchamel* sauce made with good rich cream. Send up some of the sauce in a boat.

401A. TURBOT A LA CREME AU GRATIN, ANOTHER WAY.

THIS, as well as the foregoing, may be prepared from the remnants of a previously-dressed fish, as follows:

Place the flakes of turbot in a stewpan with a sufficient quantity of cream *Béchamel* sauce (No. 6), pile it up in the centre of the dish, shake some grated Parmesan cheese on the surface, pour some double cream over this, and having placed the dish over a moderate stove-fire in order to *gratinate* the fish slightly, at the same time hold a red-hot salamander over it to give the surface a very light brown color; which, when satisfactorily terminated, some potato *croquettes*, or pas-try *fleurons*, should be neatly placed round the edge of the dish and immediately served.

402. TURBOT AS MATELOTTE NORMANDE.

PREPARE a small plump turbot in every respect according to the directions given for dressing a turbot *à la Parisiènne* (No. 398);

when done, drain and place it on a dish ; reduce the liquor, add to it some *Allemande* sauce, in which mix two pats of butter, some chopped and blanched parsley, the juice of a lemon, and a little cayenne ; work the sauce well together on the fire, and then add two dozen button-mushrooms, the same quantity of blanched oysters or muscles, and an equal proportion of very small *quenelles* of whiting ; cover the turbot with the sauce, and garnish it round with some trimmed large crayfish and glazed *croûtons* of fried bread.

403. TURBOT A LA BECHAMEL.

PREPARE some good rich cream *Béchamel* sauce (No. 6), put the flakes of some boiled turbot in it, toss them lightly together on the fire, serve the turbot piled up on the dish in the form of a dome, and garnish it round with potato *croquettes*, *fleurons* of puff paste, or *croûtons* of bread.

This method of dressing turbot, as well as turbot *à la crème au gratin*, is generally had recourse to for the purpose of turning the previous day's fish to a good account ; nevertheless the sauces, in both cases, really deserve that the turbot should be boiled for the express purpose.

Turbot dressed as above may also be served in a *vol-au-vent*.

404. TURBOT A LA MARECHALE.

PREPARE a turbot as for *Matelotte Normande* (No. 402), drain it, and set it on a dish to cool ; then spread it over on both sides with some reduced *Allemande* sauce ; shake some fine bread-crumbs over this, and after dipping it in some eggs seasoned with a little salt, and whipped up in a dish for the purpose, bread-crumb it over again thoroughly. About twenty minutes before dinner, place the turbot on a wire receiver, and fry it in a convenient-sized pan, containing some clean hog's lard, heated to a proper degree. As soon as the coating on the turbot is colored of a very light brown color, take the fish out of the fat on to a cloth, press it lightly with a clean napkin, in order to absorb any grease there may be on it, and placing it on a baking-sheet, keep it in the hot closet till required to be dished up, put the turbot then on a dish, and pour round the following sauce :—

Reduce the liquor in which the turbot has been baked, and add to it some *Allemande* sauce, and mix in a pat of anchovy butter, some green *Ravigotte*, lemon-juice, and cayenne. Next, garnish round with *quenelles* of whiting shaped with two dessert-spoons, one-half of which must be colored with lobster-coral, and the other with some black truffles chopped very fine, and mixed in the *quenelle* force-meat previously to their being shaped. Send to table some of the sauce as usual in a boat.

405. FILLETS OF TURBOT A L'INDIENNE.

CUT a small turbot into neatly-trimmed fillets or scollops, set them carefully in a deep sauta-pan with a little fresh butter, and two spoonsful of Cook's excellent fish curry paste ; put the lid on the sauta-pan, and place it on a slow fire, or in the oven, to simmer gently for twenty minutes ; then take it out, and add thereto some *Velouté* sauce (No. 2), and set the whole to boil together a few minutes on the stove; then dish up the fillets, one overlaying the other—in a circle; pass the sauce through a tammy, make it hot, and mix in a pat of butter; mask the fillets with the sauce, and serve.

406. FILLETS OF TURBOT A LA RAVIGOTTE.

PREPARE the fillets of turbot as directed in No. 405, place them in a sauta-pan with some fresh butter, season with pepper and salt, and lemon-juice; ten minutes before dinner set them on a moderate fire, and when sufficiently simmered on one side, turn them carefully on the other, so as not to break them; when done, drain the fillets on a napkin, and dish them up, overlaying each other—so as to form a close circle; sauce them with some white *Ravigotte* sauce (No. 20), and send to table.

407. FILLETS OF TURBOT A LA VERTRE.

PREPARE the fillets as for the previous *entrée*, and dish them up in a similar manner; fill the centre with thirty crayfish tails; pour some sauce *à la Ravigotte* (No. 21), over the fillets, and serve.

408. FILLETS OF TURBOT A L'ITALIENNE.

PREPARE, dress, and fish up the fillets of turbot as in the previous case, and sauce the *entrée* with some brown Italian sauce (No. 12), in which incorporate a pat of anchovy butter and a teaspoonful of chopped capers.

409. FILLETS OF TURBOT A LA CARDINAL.

CUT, dress, and dish up the fillets of turbot as directed in former cases; sauce them with some *Cardinal* sauce (No. 48), and garnish the centre of the *entrée* with prawns or crayfish tails, small *quenelles* of whiting or lobster, and a few small button-mushrooms.

Fillets of turbot may be dressed in a variety of ways, according to the sauce or garnish used, from which accordingly the fillets derive their denomination: as, for instance, *à la Maître d'Hotel, à la sauce Homard,* or Lobster sauce, *à la sauce aux Huitres,* or Oyster sauce, &c., &c., &c.

410. BRILL.

THIS species of fish, bearing a great resemblance to turbot, may be dressed in every variety of form in which turbot is capable of being sent to table; it may also be served plain, boiled with either Lobster, Shrimp, Crayfish, Anchovy, Caper, Dutch, Oyster, Muscle, or *Ravigotte* sauce.

411. JOHN DORY.

THIS kind of fish, although a great favorite with many, is very seldom sent to table in any other shape than as a plain boiled fish, either with Lobster or Dutch sauce; it may, however, be broiled with Champagne sauce, for which see turbot dressed in that manner (No. 398).

SALMON,

COMPRISING

Salmon *à la Chambord*.
   „ *à la Régence*.
   „ *à la Gênoise*.
   „ *à la Cardinal*.
   „ *à la Victoria*.

Salmon *à la Maréchale*.
   „ *à l'Anglaise*.
   „ *à l'Ecossaise*.
Slices of Salmon *à la Tartare*.
Matelotte of Salmon.
   „   „ *à la Vénitiènne*.

412. SALMON A LA CHAMBORD.

TAKE a whole salmon, and when properly cleansed, truss it in the shape of the letter S, which is effected in the following manner:— Thread a trussing needle with some twine, pass this through the eyes of the fish, and fasten the jowl by tying the string under the jaw; then pass the needle through the centre part of the body of the salmon, draw the string tight, and fasten it round the extremity of the tail; the fish will then assume the desired form.

Boil the salmon in salt and water; when done, drain it on a dish, and immediately take off the whole of the skin, and put the fish to cool in the larder. In the meantime, prepare some *quenelle* force-meat of whitings, part of which should be colored with some pounded lobster coral, and as soon as the salmon is cold, spread a layer of this over the whole surface of the fish, taking care to smooth it with the blade of a large knife dipped in hot water; this part of the process being completed, ornament the salmon by laying some fillets of soles which have been *contisés* with truffles in a slanting position across the back, fastening the ends under the belly of the salmon by means of the force-meat; mark out the head and eyes of the fish with fillets of black truffles. Then place the salmon on a buttered drainer of a fish-kettle, and cover the fish with thin layers of fat bacon; moisten with a bottle of dry Champagne, garnish with a fagot of parsley, thyme and bay-leaf, sliced carrot, and onion; place a buttered paper over the whole, and put the lid on. Next, make it boil on the stove-fire, and then put it in the oven or on a slow fire to simmer gently for three-quarters of an hour; drain the salmon and place it on a dish, and put it in the hot closet till wanted for table.

Meanwhile, strain the liquor in which the salmon has been braized, reduce it to a glaze, add some finished *Espagnole* or brown sauce, essence of mushrooms, a little grated nutmeg, a pat of anchovy butter, and lemon-juice; and pass the sauce through a tammy into a *bain-marie*.

Just before sending to table, remove the layers of bacon, and arrange groups of *quenelles* of whiting, mushrooms, truffles, large crayfish, and soft roes of mackerel, round the salmon, sauce the fish round in the inner circle with the hot sauce, and serve. Let there be some of the sauce, with truffles, mushrooms, and small *quenelles* of whiting in it, sent to table in a boat.

413. SALMON A LA REGENCE.

BOIL a whole salmon, remove the skin, and mask it over with strong glaze, mixed with some pounded lobster coral; place the salmon on an oval *crôustade* of fried bread, about three inches high, on the dish; pour round it some Regent's sauce, finished with some anchovy butter and lemon-juice; and garnish it with alternate groups of *quenelles* of salmon (mixed with some finely-chopped truffles), some large crayfish, button-mushrooms, and small fillets of soles decorated with green gherkins, rolled in a spiral shape, and simmered in a little butter and lemon-juice. Form a decoration on the back and head of the fish, with some ornamented fillets of soles; send up some of the sauce in a boat.

414. SALMON A LA GENOISE.

BOIL a salmon, skin it, and place it on a dish; mask it with *Génoise* sauce (No. 30), and garnish it round with lobster *quenelles*, button-mushrooms, some glazed tails of very small lobsters, *quenelles* of whiting, half of which must be colored with extract of spinach or *Ravigotte* herbs, and the remainder with chopped truffles. All these garnishes are appropriate in ornamenting this dish, but it is desirable not to use too many sorts of garnishes in the preparation of one dish, so as not to produce an unseemly species of medley. Send up some *Génoise* sauce in a boat.

415. SALMON A LA CARDINAL.

BOIL and skin a salmon that has been previously trussed, as directed in the first article of this chapter; cover it with a thin smooth coating of lobster *quenelles;* ornament it with a representation of the scales of the fish, by placing alternate rows of half-moons of truffles on its surface, marking out the eyes and gills, also with fillets of truffles. Cover the salmon with very thin layers of fat bacon, moisten with half a bottle of white wine, and a ladleful of good broth; cover with a buttered paper, place the lid on the fish-kettle containing the salmon, and set it to simmer on a moderate fire for three-quarters of an hour. Then drain the salmon, place it in a dish, on a *croûstade*, and keep it in the hot closet till wanted. Meanwhile, reduce the liquor in which the salmon has been braized with the remaining half-bottle of wine, and mix with it some *Cardinal* sauce (No. 48); remove the layers of bacon, glaze the fish lightly and sauce it. Garnish it round with groups of truffles, mushrooms, crayfish tails, and *quenelles* of lobster.

As usual, send up some of the sauce in a boat.

416. SALMON A LA VICTORIA.

BRAIZE a salmon in a *mirepoix* (No. 237) made with claret; when the fish is done, skin it, and place it on a low *croûstade*, on a dish. Then, after divesting the *mirepoix* in which the fish has been done, of all grease, put one-third of it into a stewpan, boil it down to a demiglaze, and work it in with some brown sauce; add a pat of anchovy butter, and a good piece of lobster butter, cayenne, and lemon-juice; mix the whole well together, and pour the sauce over the salmon. Garnish it round with groups of crayfish tails, fried fillets of smelts, and small *quenelles* of whiting.

Send some of the sauce up to table in a boat, and put some thin scollops of lobster in it.

417. SALMON A LA MARECHALE.

TRUSS a salmon in the shape of the letter S, boil it in salt and water, skin and cover it with a coating of reduced *Allemande* sauce, and set it to cool in the larder; then shake some very fine bread-crumbs over it, and after fixing them on the sauce by gentle pressure with the blade of a knife, egg the salmon over with a paste-brush dipped in three whole eggs beaten up with a little nutmeg, pepper, and salt; again shake some bread-crumbs over it, smoothing them on the salmon with the blade of a knife; place the fish on a deep baking-dish, previously buttered for the purpose, moisten with a little white wine and *consommé*, or some *mirepoix*. About three-quarters of an hour before dinner-time, put the salmon in the oven, and bake it of a deep yellow or very light brown color; then place the salmon carefully on a dish, sauce it round with Crayfish or *Suprême* Dutch sauce, in which has been added an infusion of horse-radish, and garnish round with a border of *quenelles* of gurnets, and fried smelts trussed as whitings are for frying.

418. SALMON A L'ANGLAISE.

BOIL the salmon, either whole or in slices, in salt and water; when done, dish it up on a silver drainer, without a napkin. Plain boiled fish should never be sent to table on napkins, nor garnished round with cold wet parsley, neither is it advisable to garnish with fried small fish, the latter thereby generally becoming soddened and spoilt; the mixed vapor arising from both kinds of fish, when thus covered up, is detrimental to the flavor of each.

Dish up the salmon, and send it to table with either of the following sauces: Lobster, Shrimp, Crayfish, Dutch, Parsley and butter, or Muscle sauce.

419. SALMON A L'ECOSSAISE.

To dress salmon or trout in perfection in this style, it is quite neces
sary that the fish be dressed a short time after being caught: sportsmen
well know that it is only while this kind of fish is yet almost alive, that
it retains that white creamy substance which appears between the
flakes of the boiled fish, and which makes it so truly delicious : this is
little known to the London epicure. If it be practicable to procure
what is termed a *live salmon*, take out the gills, draw it, wash the fish,
and crimp it on either side, by making deep incisions with a sharp
knife, and then throw it into a large vessel, containing clean, cold,
spring water, fresh from the pump—to remain there about two hours.
In crimping any sort of fish, the colder the water is the better ; the
coldness of the water, petrifying the fish to a certain degree, gives it
the firmness so much desired. As soon as the salmon or trout is
crimped, put it into the fish-kettle containing boiling water in sufficient
quantity to cover the fish, at the same time throwing in a good handful
of salt ; let the fish boil on the side of the fire, remembering that
crimped fish require considerably less time in boiling than when plain.
As soon as the fish is done, take it out of the water immediately :
leaving fish of any kind in the water after it is done, detracts from its
flavor and firmness. When the salmon is dished up, send it to table
with Lobster sauce, Parsley and butter, or the following sauce :—Put
half a pound of fresh-churned butter into a clean stewpan, add a
spoonful of chopped and blanched parsley, a little grated nutmeg, a
pinch of minionette pepper, some salt and juice of lemon ; set the
stewpan in a bath of hot water, and keep stirring the butter quickly as
it melts, with a wooden spoon ; when the whole of the butter is melted,
work the sauce well together, and send to table. With crimped salmon
or trout, this kind of melted butter will be found to surpass all other
sauces.

420. SLICES OF SALMON A LA TARTARE.

Steep some slices of salmon in a dish with a little salad-oil, pepper
and salt, and a few sprigs of parsley ; about half an hour before dinner,
place the slices of salmon on a clear gridiron rubbed over with whiting,
and broil them on a clear fire ; when done on one side, turn them on
the other : both sides should be of a fine light brown ; dish them up,
and send to table with either some *Tartare*, Cambridge, or *Rémoulade*
sauce in a boat (Nos. 94, 95, 96).

421. MATELOTTE OF SALMON.

Boil and take the skin off one or more slices of salmon, mask them
with some glaze mixed with pounded lobster-coral ; place them on a
dish and garnish with a rich *Matelotte ragout* (No. 193).

422. SLICES OF SALMON A LA VENITIENNE.

Boil, trim, and glaze the slices of salmon, as in the foregoing case,
and sauce them round with a sauce *à la Vénitiènne* (No. 26). Garnish
with a border of *croquettes* of fillets of soles.

TROUT,

COMPRISING

Trout *à l'Italiènne*.	Trout *à l'Aurore*.
„ *à la Gasconne*.	„ *à la Périgueux*.
„ *à la Chevalière*.	„ in paper cases, with fine herbs.
„ *à la Vertpré*.	„ *à la Royale*.
„ *au gratin*.	„ broiled, with Dutch sauce.

423. TROUT A L'ITALIENNE.

BOIL the trout in salt and water, divest it of the skin, glace and place it on a dish; then mask it with some Italian sauce in which has been mixed a pat of anchovy butter, a very little nutmeg, and lemon-juice. Garnish with crayfish and *quenelles* of whiting.

424. TROUT A LA GASCONNE.

BOIL and dish up the trout as directed in the foregoing instance, and pour round it some of the sauce denominated *à la Gasconné* (No. 68). Garnish with fillets of soles prepared as *paupiettes* (for which see No. 1131), and between each *paupiètte* place a group of crayfish tails that have been tossed in a little glaze, and some pounded lobster-coral.

425. TROUT A LA CHEVALIERE.

BOIL, skin, and trim one or more trout, and cover them all over with some *D'Uxelles* or *Papillotte* sauce: when the sauce, by getting cold, has become set on the trout, roll them in very fine bread-crumbs, and afterward egg them over and roll them again in the bread-crumbs, in which Parmesan cheese has been mixed in the proportion of one-third; place the trout on a buttered baking-sheet, and about half an hour before dinner, first sprinkle them over with a little melted fresh butter, and then put them in the oven to be baked of a fine light brown color. Dish them up and sauce round with the following *ragout*:—Reduce half a bottle of dry Champagne or Sauterne, with some essence of mushrooms, down to one-fourth part, then add a ladleful of *Allemande* sauce, incorporate with it a pat of anchovy butter, a little lobster-coral, nutmeg, cayenne, and lemon-juice; sauce the trout round, and garnish with a border of small fillets of soles that have been *contisés*, one half with truffles, and the remainder with tongue, and then turned round in the shape of half-moons, and simmered in a little butter, salt, and lemon-juice. In the inner circle, place small groups of prawns' tails tossed in lobster-coral and glaze, soft roes of mackerel tossed in a spoonful of sauce, colored with some green *Ravigotte*, and between the trout a row of large crayfish trimmed and glazed. Send up some of the sauce in a boat.

426. TROUT AU GRATIN.

PARBOIL the trout sufficiently to remove the skin, and, when trimmed, place them on a buttered sauta-pan; season with pepper and salt, sprinkle over them a good spoonful of chopped parsley, three times that quantity of chopped mushrooms, and two chopped shalots; add a small ladleful of finished brown sauce, and two or

three glasses of Sherry. Half an hour more or less before sending to
table, according to the size of the fish, put the trout thus prepared
into the oven to bake, taking care to baste it every five minutes ; when
done, put the trout out on a dish, reduce the sauce, if necessary, incorporate in it a pat of anchovy butter, add the juice of half a lemon, and
pour the sauce over the trout ; then shake some baked bread-crumbs
bruised fine, over the whole, replace the fish in the oven for five
minutes, and then send them to table after placing round them a
border of lobster *croquelles*.

427. TROUT L'AURORE.

BOIL and trim one or more trout, mask them over with some
reduced *Allemande* sauce, put them on a silver dish, and then place a
wire sieve over the trout ; rub the yelks of six or more eggs boiled
hard through the sieve with a wooden spoon, on the fish, taking care
that the curling shreds which fall through the sieve cover the surface
of the trout equally. About half an hour before dinner, put the trout
in the oven to get colored of a fine amber hue ; pour round them some
Aurora sauce (No. 41), and garnish them with a border of muscles
fried in batter.

428. TROUT IN CASES, WITH FINE HERBS.

PROCURE as many small trout as may suffice for a dish, clean, parboil, trim, and place them each in a separate paper case previously
oiled, and then baked for five minutes, for the purpose of hardening
the paper to enable it to contain the sauce ; add to each trout a
moderate quantity of fine herbs' sauce (No. 14) ; put them in the oven
twenty minutes before dinner-time to bake, and when done, dish them
up, and send to table with some of the sauce in a boat.

429. TROUT A LA ROYALE.

CLEAN and draw a fine trout, stuff it with some *quenelle* force-
meat of whitings, stew it with a bottle of Chablis wine, a few mushrooms, parsley, green onions, thyme, and a bay-leaf, pepper-corns,
and a blade of mace : when done, remove the skin, glaze, and put it
on its dish in the hot closet till required for dishing up. Then
strain the liquor in which the trout has been stewed, reduce it to
half glaze, add to it some *Suprême* sauce, work in a pat of anchovy
butter, a little cayenne pepper, and lemon-juice, and then pour the
sauce into a stewpan containing some small *quenelles* of whiting,
button-mushrooms, and prawns' tails. Allow the whole to boil together for a few minutes, sauce the trout, and garnish them round
with a border of *croûstades* of *quenelle* of whiting, poached, bread-
crumbed, and fried ; the interior should be removed and filled with
soft roes of mackerel tossed in a little of the sauce

430. BROILED TROUT, WITH DUTCH SAUCE.

SPLIT a trout at the back, oil it over, season with pepper and salt ;
just before dinner-time, broil it, and send it to table with some Dutch
sauce in a boat separately.
In addition to the different methods given here for dressing trout,
this kind of fish may be prepared in every variety of form and style in
which salmon is sent to table.

STURGEON,

COMPRISING

Sturgeon à la Beaufort.
    ,,   à la Cardinal.
    ,,   à la Gènoise.
    ,,   à la Dauphine.
    ,,   à la Périgord.

Sturgeon à la Bourguignotte.
    ,,   à l'Indiènne.
    ,,   au gratin with fine herbs.
    ,,   à la Russe.
    ,,   à l'Anglaise.

431. STURGEON A LA BEAUFORT.

CHOOSE a small sturgeon, draw, skin, and truss it in the shape of the leter S; braize it in a *mirepoix* moistened with sherry, or with common broth, and a little brandy. When the fish is done, drain it and put it in the larder to cool; then mask it all over with a coating of *quenelle* force-meat of whitings; observing that the form of the head should be restored by covering that part of the sturgeon with some of the force-meat mixed with some lobster-coral. Form the eyes, mouth, and gills, with some black truffles cut into shapes for the purpose. Place some fillets of soles previously *contisés* with truffles, crosswise along the back of the sturgeon, allowing the space of an inch to intervene between each fillet of sole, which spaces are to be filled up by the insertion of crayfish tails, trimmed and secured by being stuck into the force-meat in close rows; then cover the fish with very thin layers of fat bacon, place it on a drainer, and put it in the braizer with a little of the *mirepoix* in which it has been braized. About an hour before dinner-time, put it in the oven or on a slow fire, with live embers upon the lid, and after the fish has simmered gently, without boiling, during the time allotted, take it out of the braize upon the drainer, and after divesting it of the layers of bacon, slide it off the drainer on to its dish; sauce it round with a rich *Matelotte* sauce made with Sauterne wine, add also some of the liquor in which the sturgeon has been braized; garnish round with alternate groups of the soft roes of mackerel (cut in halves, blanched, and fried in batter) and some dessert-spoon *quenelles* of lobster.

432. STURGEON A LA CARDINAL.

PROCURE a prime cut of sturgeon weighing about 12 lbs.; remove its skin in the following manner:—Place the piece of sturgeon on the kitchen table, lengthwise before you, so as to have a command on either side; then take a long thin-bladed knife, insert its point immediately between the flesh and skin, run the knife right up, keeping close to the back fin, and minding that the edge of the knife be kept to the left; press, with the palm of the left hand, on the skin of the fish, drawing the knife to and fro, so as to sever the skin from the flesh; and after effecting this on one side, repeat it on the other. Replace the skin over the sturgeon, and fasten it on with a string, in order to preserve the color of the fish; at the same time taking care to give shape and appearance to the sturgeon. Then put it into a fish-kettle or braizing-pan on the drainer belonging to it, moisten with a good wine *mirepoix*, and set it to braize with fire under and over. If the quality of the sturgeon be good, about four hours' gentle

boiling will suffice to braize it; the fish must be well basted with
its liquor every now and then. When the sturgeon is done, take it up,
remove the skin, drain, and afterward mask it with some stiff glaze,
in which has been mixed some pounded lobster-coral in sufficient
quantity to give the sturgeon a bright scarlet color; form on its
centre a palm or star, with some *contisés* fillets of soles. The ornamental skewers that appear in the woodcut, must, if used—which is
not strictly essential—all be garnished with a large truffle, crayfish,
mushroom, *quenelle*, and truffle. Pour some *Cardinal* sauce (No. 48)
round it, garnish with a border of tails of very small lobsters, and
alternate groups of small *quenelles* of whiting, button-mushrooms, and
truffles.

433. STURGEON A LA GENOISE.

PREPARE the sturgeon as in either of the foregoing instances, and
after having glazed and dished it up, pour some *Genoise* sauce No.
30) round it; garnish with a border of large crayfish, and serve.

434. STURGEON A LA DAUPHINE.

PARE off the whole of the skin of a prime cut of sturgeon, weighing about 8 lbs.; garnish the inside to its full extent with some
quenelle force-meat of whiting, mixed with some, chopped and simmered fine herbs; wrap the sturgeon in thin layers of bacon—
secured on with string; set the sturgeon to braize in some wine
mirepoix; when done, drain it and put it to cool in the larder, after
which cover it well over—first divesting it of the bacon, &c.,—with a
coating of stiffly-reduced *Allemande* sauce, and when the sauce has
cooled upon the fish, bread-crumb it in the usual manner, drop a
little clarified butter over it through a straining-spoon, put it on a
drainer into a deep baking-dish, and set it in the oven to be baked
of a light color. Then place it on a dish, sauce with Sturgeon
sauce (No. 56), garnish with an outer row of *quenelles* of gurnets,

mixed with some chopped and blanched parsley, and garnish the inner circle with alternate groups of thin scollops of lobster (tossed in a little lobster-coral butter, to render them of a bright scarlet color), and some button mushrooms and scollops of gurnets tossed in a spoonful of *Béchamel* sauce. Stick on four ornamental *Atelets*, or silver skewers, garnished each with a large truffle, *quenelle*, crayfish, and mushroom.

435. STURGEON A LA PERIGORD.

Prepare the sturgeon as in the preceding case, but instead of bread-crumbing it, glaze and dish it up ; sauce it with a good *Périgueux* sauce (No. 23), in which has been mixed some of its own liquor boiled down to glaze, a pat of anchovy butter, and a little lemon-juice ; garnish with a border of truffle *croustades* made as follows :—

Choose a dozen or eighteen large truffles of equal size, boil them in some wine *mirepoix*, cut a piece from the top, of the thickness of a penny piece, scoop out the inside of the truffles, and cut the produce into thin scollops, which after mixing with a little of the sauce, replace in the truffles ; cover them with some small fillets of soles *contisés* with some red tongue, and turned round in the shapes and size of half-a-crown piece, and simmered in a little butter. Send up some of the sauce to table in a boat.

436. STURGEON A LA BOURGUIGNOTTE.

Stuff and braize the sturgeon according to the foregoing directions, trim, glaze, and dish it up ; then pour some *Bourguignotte* sauce (No. 28) round it, garnish with groups of mushrooms, glazed button-onions, small *quenelles*, and crayfish tails.

Send some of the sauce to table in a boat.

437. STURGEON A L'INDIENNE.

Braize the sturgeon in some wine *mirepoix*, take about a pint of the liquor, reduce and mix it in some Indian curry sauce (No. 47) prepared for the purpose, add a pat of anchovy butter, and some lemon-juice, sauce the sturgeon, and garnish it round with a border of rice *croustades*, filled with curried prawns or shrimps ; ornament it with four *Atelets*—each garnished with a large crayfish, a *contisé* fillet of sole, and a fine smelt, fried : the smelt here alluded to must be trussed previously to its being fried, and the point of a skewer run through its tail and eyes, and again through the centre of the body, also through the fillet of sole, and the large crayfish. Send up, as usual in such cases, some of the sauce in a boat.

438. STURGEON AU GRATIN, WITH FINE HERBS.

This method of dressing sturgeon should be resorted to only when it happens that a sufficient remnant is left from the previous day's dinner. In such a case, cut the sturgeon into neatly-trimmed scollops, and toss these in some reduced *Allemande* sauce, incorporated with some of the essence of the sturgeon—previously boiled down to glaze; add some fine herbs, lemon-juice, a little grated nutmeg, and half a pat of anchovy butter ; mix the whole well together ; put the scollops on a silver dish, piled up in the form of a dome ; cover them with some fried bread-crumbs, mixed with one-third part of grated fresh Parmesan cheese. About twenty minutes before dinner-time, place the dish in the oven to gratinate the scollops : pass the red-hot salamander over them, to melt the cheese ; pour round some of the sauce reserved for the purpose ; garnish with some *croquettes* of sturgeon, lobster, or potatoes, and send to table.

439. STURGEON A LA RUSSE.

BRAIZE the sturgeon as usual, either in some wine *mirepoix,* or merely in vinegar and water, when economy is an object. When the sturgeon is done, take off the skin, trim, and mask it with some stiff glaze mixed with some pounded lobster-coral ; ornament it on the centre with some small fillets of gurnets *contisés* with green gherkins,—previously placed in a buttered sauta-pan, in the shape of half-moons, and simmered in a little butter ; at each end place a row of turned olives ; pour round it some rich *Génoise* sauce (No. 30)—finished with a good piece of lobster butter, cayenne, and lemon-juice, a spoonful of chopped and blanched parsley, two spoonsful of capers, some turned olives, two dozen crayfish tails, and about the same quantity of small *quenelles* of anchovies. Garnish round the inner edge of the dish with some smelts trussed in the same way as whitings, and fried.

440. STURGEON A L'ANGLAISE

TRIM and skin a fine piece of sturgeon—or a small whole fish ; line the inside with some well-seasoned ordinary veal-stuffing ; re-place the skin, and secure it with string ; put the sturgeon on a drainer in the fish-kettle ; garnish with carrot, onion, parsley, thyme, and bay-leaf, mace, peppercorns, and six cloves, a handful of trim-mings of mushrooms, and a little salt ; moisten with a bottle of port wine ; cover with a well-buttered paper, and set it on the fire to boil ; then place it on a slow fire to stew gently till it is done. Next drain, trim, and glaze it ; place it on a dish, and put it in the hot closet until dinner-time. Meanwhile, take some of the liquor in which the sturgeon has been stewed, with three glasses of good Port wine, and boil the whole down to half-glaze, and add it to some finished *Espagnole,* or brown sauce ; work in a pat of anchovy butter, and two pats of fresh butter, a little cayenne, grated nutmeg, and lemon-juice ; pour the sauce into a stewpan containing some button-mushrooms, scollops of lobster, and small *quenelle* of whiting, colored with some very fine chopped and blanched parsley ; allow the whole to boil up for a minute on the stove ; sauce the sturgeon over with this *ragout ;* garnish it round with a border of large crayfish, and serve.

Sturgeon, in addition to the preceding modes of preparation, may be dressed similarly to salmon, in all its varieties.

COD FISH,

COMPRISING

Cod, and Oyster Sauce.
Do. stuffed and baked.
Do. *à la crême au gratin.*
Crimped slices of Cod, and Oyster Sauce.
    „   „   „   *à la Séville.*
Fillets of Cod *à l'Indiènne.*

Crimped slices of Cod *à la Hollandaise.*
    „   „   „   *à la Colbert.*
    „   „   „   in   *Matelotte Nor-
                   mande.*
Scollops of Cod *à la Béchamel.*
Slices of crimped Cod *à la Maître d'Hôtel.*
Baked Cod's head.

441. COD, AND OYSTER SAUCE.

BOIL the cod, whether it be crimped or plain, in boiling spring water, into which throw a handful of salt; as soon as the fish is done, drain it instantly, and place it on a dish, with a clean wet napkin over it, to keep it moist: just before dinner, take off the napkin, and send the cod to table with a sauce-boat full of white Oyster sauce (No. 50).

Cod-fish is rarely dressed whole, as, in addition to its unwieldy size, the length of time required to boil so large a fish deprives it materially of its peculiar attraction, which is never so effectually obtained as when the fish is crimped, and cut into slices, previously to its being boiled.

442. COD STUFFED AND BAKED.

CLEAN, trim, and stuff a cod with some well-seasoned veal-stuffing; secure this by sewing up the belly; then truss the fish in the shape of the letter S; make several deep incisions on either side, and place it in a deep baking dish previously well spread with fresh butter; season with chopped parsley and mushrooms, pepper and salt; moisten with half a bottle of Sherry, and the liquor of two dozen oysters; then set the fish in the oven to bake; and every ten minutes, or oftener, baste it with its own liquor; when it is nearly done, sprinkle it over with some fine raspings of bread, and again put it in the oven for ten minutes longer. When the cod is baked, draw the strings out of it; place it on its dish, then pour two glasses of Sherry into the dish in which the cod has been baked, and also a little *consommé*—to detach the glaze from round the pan; pass the whole through a tammy into a stewpan; add some brown sauce; reduce the whole to a proper consistency; work in a pat of anchovy butter, a little cayenne, and lemon-juice, beard the oysters, and add them to the sauce; pour it round the cod, and send to table.

443. COD A LA CREME AU GRATIN.

Is prepared in a similar manner to tubot *à la crême au gratin* (for which see No. 401).

444. CRIMPED SLICES OF COD AND OYSTER SAUCE.

PUT crimped slices of cod in boiling spring water containing a handful of salt, as before directed; as soon as it boils up again, set the fish-kettle by the side of the stove to continue boiling for about a quarter of an hour; when done, drain and dish up the fish with some pieces of liver and *charlton**,—which should be boiled apart from the fish, so that the oil contained in the liver may not spoil the color or flavor of the cod. Send up to table with a boat of Oyster sauce (No. 50).

445. SLICES OF COD A LA SEVILLE.

Wash and dry half a pound of Carolina rice; fry it in salad-oil, drain it on a sieve, and afterward put it into a large *fricandeau* pan; then cut some pieces of crimped cod, about four inches square, and fry them of a fine color in some salad-oil, after which drain and place them on the rice. Next cut a Spanish onion into very thin slices, and fry these in some of the oil used for the fish; drain off the oil and add six large ripe tomatas, from which the seeds have been squeezed; simmer the tomatas and the onions together on the fire for five minutes, and pour the whole on the fish and rice; season with a little cayenne, salt, and lemon-juice; moisten with a pint of good broth; place a buttered paper on the top, cover with the lid of the pan, and put the whole to bake in the oven. In about half an hour, the fish and rice will be done, when take the pieces of cod out of the rice, place them on an earthen dish, and with a wooden spoon stir the rice over the fire, in order to mix it with the seasoning; after which put the rice on a silver dish, and place the pieces of cod-fish on it; sauce it round with some Muscle sauce (No. 52), and send to table. This is a favorite dish in Spain.

446. COD A L'INDIENNE.

Trim some pieces of cod in the shape of fillets; keep them rather thick; place them neatly in a deep sauta-pan, previously buttered; then moisten them with some Indian Curry sauce (No. 47) prepared for the purpose; cover with a stewpan-lid, and set the fillets on a sharp fire to simmer; about twenty minutes will suffice to stew them; then dish up the fillets—the one overlaying the other—in the form of a circle; pass the sauce through a tammy, pour it over them, and send to table.

447. CRIMPED SLICES OF COD A LA HOLLANDAISE.

In order to produce this fish in perfection, it is advisable to bespeak some very thin slices of crimped cod, not more than half an inch thick, of the fishmonger, a day or two beforehand. About an hour or two before dinner, sprinkle the slices of cod with salt; and ten minutes before sending to table, boil them quickly; as soon as done, dish them up, and send them to be eaten immediately, with some delicately-prepared Dutch sauce (No. 42).

This method of preparing crimped fish is a favorite one in Holland; where, however, plain butter is taken with it, prepared as follows:—

Put the butter in a small stewpan, with a little salt, pepper, nutmeg, and lemon-juice; then keep stirring it by a slow fire till the butter is sufficiently melted, taking care that it does not become oily.

448. CRIMPED SLICES OF COD A LA COLBERT.

Procure some very thin slices of crimped cod; bread-crumb and

---

* A soft whitish substance in curling folds found inside cod-fish.

fry them; dish them up with some cold *Maître d'Hôtel* butter (No. 44) under them; then sauce them round with an essence prepared for the purpose, as follows:

Put the trimmings of the fish with a sole, or two or three flounders, cut into pieces, into a small stewpan, with carrot, parsley roots, thyme, mace, and peppercorns; moisten with two glasses of white wine, and allow the whole to boil down to half; add a small ladleful of good *consommé;* set the essence to boil gently for half an hour; strain and reduce it down one-third, to which add a spoonful of *Béchamel* or *Allemande* sauce, and use it as directed above.

449. CRIMPED SLICES OF COD, IN MATELOTTE NORMANDE.

PLACE some thin slices of cod on a silver dish, previously spread with butter; season them with a little pepper and salt, and sprinkle some chopped parsley over them; moisten with two glasses of French white wine and some oyster liquor; cover with a buttered paper, and half an hour before dinner put them in the oven to bake, taking care to baste them occasionally. When the fish is done, pour the liquor there may be in the dish into a *ragout* prepared for the purpose, in the usual manner (No. 194), and wipe the edges of the dish with a wet napkin; sauce the slices of cod over with the *ragout*, and garnish round with a border of fried smelts and large crayfish; place some glazed oval *croutons* round the inner circle, and send to table.

450. SCOLLOPS OF COD A LA BECHAMEL.

CUT and trim some crimped cod into neat scollops; simmer them in a sauta-pan with a little fresh butter and salt; when done, drain them on a napkin, and afterward toss them gently in a stewpan, with some good cream *Béchamel* sauce (No. 6); dish them up, pyramidally, in the *entrée* dish, and garnish round with a border of potato *croquettes*.

To save time, or indeed as a variety, these scollops may also be prepared in the following manner:

Boil the slices, or piece of cod, drain it, and then break it gently into large flakes, which toss in some *Béchamel* sauce; dish up and garnish as directed above.

451. SLICES OF CRIMPED COD A LA MAITRE D'HOTEL.

STEEP some thin slices of crimped cod in a little oil, pepper, and salt; broil them on a gridiron rubbed with whiting, and when done, glaze them over very lightly; dish them up, and sauce them under and round with a well-seasoned *Maître d'Hôtel* sauce (No. 43), and send to table.

452. COD'S HEAD BAKED.

FILL the hollow of the gills with some veal stuffing; put the head into a deep baking dish—season with pepper and salt, a little chopped shalot, and a spoonful of chopped parsley; moisten with two glasses of Sherry and a little mushroom catsup; put two pats of butter on the fish, and place it in the oven to bake, remembering that it must be frequently basted with its liquor, adding, if necessary, a little *consommé* for the purpose. After the cod's head has been in the oven ten minutes, sprinkle it over with some bruised raspings of bread, and when its baking is completed, place it on its dish; then add a spoonful of brown sauce and half a glass of wine to the liquor in which the head has been baked, and allow the whole to boil down to the consistency of sauce; add a pat of butter, a little essence of anchovies, and lemon-juice; work the whole together, pour the sauce round the cod's head, and send to table

---

HADDOCKS AND COD'S SOUNDS,

COMPRISING

Haddocks *à la Royale.*
  „   stuffed and baked.
  „   *à la Belle-vue.*
  „   broiled, with Dutch sauce.
  „   broiled, with Egg sauce.
Fillets of Haddocks *à la Royale.*

Fillets of Haddocks *à la Maréchale.*
  „   „   *à l'Italiènne.*
Cod's sounds and Egg sauce.
  „   „   *à la Ravigotte.*
  „   „   *à la Gasconne.*
  „   „   *à la Royale.*

453. HADDOCKS A LA ROYALE.

Bone and stuff two haddocks with some *quenelle* force-meat of whiting; place them head to tail on a baking-sheet; then season them with a little pepper and salt, and bake them. After allowing the haddocks to cool, cover them with a thin layer of *quenelle* force-meat of whitings, and place thereon some *contisés* fillets of soles, in a slanting direction; mask the heads with a little of the force-meat, mixed with some pounded lobster-coral, and form the eyes and mouth with truffles; cover the haddocks with very thin layers of bacon, placing over all a buttered paper. About three-quarters of an hour before dinner, put the haddocks in the oven to finish baking. Just before serving, take off the paper, and remove the layers of bacon, and with a clean napkin absorb all the grease and moisture there may be upon them; then carefully remove the haddocks on to their dish, sauce them round with some Parisian sauce (No. 40), and garnish them with some *quenelles* of lobster, with a large scollop of truffle intervening between each *quenelle*, and send to table.

454. HADDOCKS, STUFFED AND BAKED,

Are prepared in the same manner as cods' heads baked, previously described.

Haddocks, after being baked, may also be served with *Poivrade, Piquante,* Tomata, *Italian,* Oyster, Muscle, or caper sauces.

455. HADDOCKS A LA BELLE-VUE.

Skin two haddocks; truss them as you would whitings for frying, and put them into a baking dish; cover them with a layer of *quenelle* force-meat of whitings, covered with lobster-coral; then place across their backs some fillets of soles *contisés* with green gherkins, taking care to leave the space of an inch between each fillet, so as to insert some small truffles cut in the shape of olives; cover them with thin layers of fat bacon, and over all place a buttered paper; moisten with three glasses of white wine, and put the haddocks in the oven to bake for about half an hour. Then remove the paper and bacon, and slip them, with great care, on to their dish; sauce them round with *Ravigotte* sauce (No. 20) and garnish with a border of *quenelles* of whiting in which has been mixed a sufficient quantity of very fine chopped parsley, to color them, and send to table.

456. HADDOCKS BROILED, WITH DUTCH SAUCE.

To broil haddocks in perfection, it is necessary, first, to wipe them well over, and then to score them with a sharp knife; next to steep them in a little salad oil, pepper, and salt. About half an hour before dinner, place the haddocks on a gridiron which has been rubbed with whitening, and broil them; when done on both sides, dish them up on a napkin, and send some Dutch sauce (No. 42) to table in a boat.

457. HADDOCKS BOILED, WITH EGG SAUCE.

BOIL the haddocks in salt and water; when done, drain and dish them up, and send them to table with egg sauce (No. 84) in a boat.

This fish, when plain boiled, may be sent to table with almost every kind of fish sauce.

458. FILLETS OF HADDOCKS, A LA ROYALE.

FILLET one or more haddocks; remove the skin by passing the knife under the fillet, so as to detach the tail end of the skin from the fish, then take a firm hold of the piece of detached skin, and inserting the knife, with the edge of the blade turned from you, draw the skin toward you, and keep moving the knife to and fro, at the same time pressing the blade firmly on the skin. Having thus removed the skin, cut each fillet into two or more smaller fillets, trim them neatly, by paring off the rough edges; place them in a basin with two sliced shalots, some sprigs of parsley, oil, and lemon-juice, and season with pepper and salt. About ten minutes before dinner, drain the fillets on a napkin, and afterward dip each fillet separately in some light batter, and fry them of a fine color in some hog's-lard, heated for the purpose; when done, drain them on a napkin to absorb the greese; dish the fillets in the form of a wreath, lying shoulder to shoulder, pour in the centre some white *Ravigotte* sauce (No. 20), and send to table.

459. FILLETS OF HADDOCKS, A LA MARECHALE.

PREPARE these in the same manner as fillets of turbot *à la Marèchalé* (see No. 404).

460. FILLETS OF HADDOCK, A L'ITALIENNE

FILLET one or more haddocks, remove the skins, cut and trim them into smaller fillets; place these neatly in a sauta-pan with some clarified butter; season with pepper and salt, squeeze a little lemon-juice over them, sprinkle some chopped parsley; over all place a round of buttered paper, and put them in the oven, or on a moderate fire, to simmer for about ten minutes; then drain the fillets on a napkin, and afterward dish them up in the form of a wreath, one fillet resting on the other, and pour some Italian sauce, mixed with a pat of butter, a little anchovy and lemon-juice over them, and send to table.

By varying the sauce, fillets of haddocks prepared in the above manner, are named according to the sauce employed : as for instance, *à la Ravigotte, à la Maître d'Hôtel, à la Hollandaise*, &c.

461. COD'S SOUNDS, AND EGG SAUCE.

PREPARATORY to boiling cod's sounds, it is quite necessary that they should be soaked in milk and water for at least six hours, and then washed and put to boil in a stewpan containing fresh milk and water, then continue gently boiling till they are done ; about an hour will suffice for this. When done, drain them on a napkin, cut them into pieces about an inch and a half square, and put them into a stewpan with a sufficient quantity of egg sauce (No. 84) ; toss the whole together over the fire, pile them upon a dish in a pyramidal form, garnish them round with neatly-cut boiled parsnips, and send to table.

462. COD'S SOUNDS, A LA RAVIGOTTE.

PREPARE and cut the sounds into pieces, as directed in the preceding article ; toss them in some *Ravigotte* sauce (No. 20), dish them up, garnish round with a border of potato *croquettes*, and send to table.

463. COD'S SOUNDS, A LA GASCONNE.

PREPARE the sounds as usual, step them in oil, vinegar, shalot, and parsley, season with a little minionette pepper ; just before dinner, fry the sounds in butter, dish them up in the form of a wreath, pour under them some *Gasconne* sauce (No. 68), and send to table.

464. COD'S SOUNDS, A LA ROYALE.

THE sounds should be prepared and fried as in the preceding case ; and afterward dished up similarly, with white *Ravigotte* sauce (No. 29) poured under them, and sent to table.

Cod's sounds may also be dressed *à la Poulette, à l'Indiènne, à la Béchamel, à la Maître d'Hôtel*, in the same manner, of course substituting any of the above sauces for the *Ravigotte*.

DRESSED SOLES, GURNETS, AND MACKEREL,

COMPRISING

Soles fried, with Shrimp sauce.
  „ boiled.
  „ *à la Colbert.*
  „ *au gratin.*
  „ with fine herbs.
  „ *à la Parisènne.*
  „ *à la Maréchale.*
  „ in *Matelotte Normande.*
  „ *à la Plessy.*

Gurnets stuffed and baked.
  „ *à la Dauphine.*
  „ *à la Génoise.*
Mackerel boiled.
  „ broiled, *à la Maître d'Hôtel.*
  „ broiled with nut-brown butter.
Fillets of Mackerel, *à la Maître d'Hôtel.*

465. FRIED SOLES WITH SHRIMP SAUCE.

MODERATE-SIZED soles are preferable for frying, as when large, from their size and thickness, they must necessarily remain a considerable time in the frying-fat, and will thereby contract a strong flavor, as well as imbibe a greater portion of the fat; they are also less likely to appear crisp, so essential a requisite in all fried fish. Clean the soles thoroughly, pull off the brown skin, cut off the head transversely, and with a pair of large scissors trim away the fins close up to the fillets; then wash and wipe the soles dry, and roll them in a little flour; dip them first into some beaten egg, and then in fine bread-crumbs, and place the fish on a dish in a cool place until within twenty minutes of dinner-time; then fry them in some hot lard; when done, drain them on a napkin, and dish them up with some fried parsley, and serve with a sauce-boat full of shrimp, anchovy, Dutch, or lobster sauce.

466. BOILED SOLES.

FOR boiling, crimped soils are preferable; but when these are not to be obtained, choose large and thick fish—such, for instance, as Torbay soles. Trim the soles, and rub them over with lemon-juice; sprinkle over some salt, and put them on in boiling water; when done, dish them up, and send to table with a sauce-boat filled with Dutch, Lobster, Shrimp, Anchovy, or French Caper sauce.

467. SOLES, A LA COLBERT.

CLEAN and trim the soles, wash and wipe them dry with a clean cloth; then flour them over and fry them, after which cut them open at the back, and carefully take out the backbone; fill the inside with some cold *Maître d'Hôtel* butter (No. 44); turn the soles on their backs in a dish, pour round them an essence of fish, or of anchovies (No. 176), and serve them quite hot.

468. SOLES, AU GRATIN.

SPREAD some fresh butter on a silver dish, and place the soles, head and tail, on it; season with pepper and salt, sprinkle some chopped parsley over them, and moisten with two glasses of white wine; half an hour before dinner, put them in the oven to bake; when they have been in twenty minutes take them out; and, after saucing them all over with some brown Italian sauce (No. 12), shake some fine raspings of bread over the whole, and put the soles back in the oven to *gratinate* for a few minutes; just before sending to table pass the red-hot salamander over them, and serve.

469. SOLES WITH FINE-HERBS.

TRIM the soles close up to the fillets; put them on a buttered sauta-pan; sprinkle over them some chopped mushrooms, parsley, and one shalot; season with pepper and salt, and a little nutmeg, and moisten with two glasses of white wine; cover them with a buttered paper, and set them in the oven to bake. When done, drain their liquor into a small stewpan containing some *Allemande* sauce; add a spoon-ful of chopped and blanched parsley, a pat of fresh butter, and lemon-juice; work the whole well together on the fire; wipe the edges of the dish with a clean napkin dipped in hot water, and sauce the soles over; place round them a border of glazed thin *croûtons*, and send them to table.

470. SOLES, A LA PARISIENNE.

TRIM a pair of fine large soles, slit them down the back, and take the bone out ; line the soles with some *quenelle* force-meat of whitings mixed with some chopped fine-herbs ; put them on a buttered sauta-pan, season with pepper and salt, moisten with two glasses of white wine, cover with a buttered paper, and put them in the oven to bake. When done, put them in press between two earthen dishes, and set them in the larder to cool. In the mean time, prepare some stiffly-reduced *Allemande* sauce, with which, after neatly trimming the soles, cover them all over ; and when the sauce, by getting cold, has set firmly upon them, cover them with egg and bread-crumbs ; fry them of a fine light color, dish them up, and garnish with a Parisian *ragout* (No. 203), place round them a border of large crayfish and glazed *croûtons*, and send to table.

471. SOLES, A LA MARECHALE.

BONE a pair of soles, line them with *quenelle* force-meat of whiting, bread-crumb, with *Allemande* sauce, and then fry the fish ; drain them on a napkin, dish them up, and sauce them round with some Venetian sauce (No. 26), and serve.

472. MATELOTTE NORMANDE OF SOLES.

BONE two fine soles ; line them with *quenelle* force-meat of whitings mixed with some chopped fine-herbs ; place them on a buttered sauta-pan, season with pepper and salt, moisten with half a bottle of French white wine, some oyster liquor, and white essence of mushrooms ; put them in the oven to bake, and when done, remove the soles carefully on to their dish. Reduce the liquor, incorporate it in a rich *Matelotte Normande ragout* (No. 194), with which sauce the soles all over, and garnish round with a border of crayfish, and some oval *croûtons*, made with the crusts of French rolls fried in butter, and glazed, then serve.

473. MATELOTTE OF SOLES, A LA PLESSY.

BONE, stuff, and bake a pair of large soles, as described in the pre-ceding directions, and when done, put them in press between two earthenware dishes ; as soon as they have cooled, mask them over with some fish *quenelle* force-meat, colored with lobster coral ; smooth them over with the blade of a large knife, dipped in hot water ; then place the soles carefully on a silver dish buttered for the purpose, and after ornamenting the centre of each sole with a bold decoration,—composed of truffles,—cover them with some very thin layers of fat bacon : moisten with a glass of French white wine, and put them in the oven for about a quarter of an hour, in which time they will be done. Re-move the bacon, glaze them slightly, and garnish them round with a Parisian sauce (No. 40), with the addition of some fine white muscles ; place round the *Matelotte* a border of fried smelts, previously boned and stuffed with force-meat, and serve.

474. GURNETS STUFFED AND BAKED.

CUT off the fins and head from two or more gurnets, stuff them with veal stuffing, sew them up, and score them with a sharp knife on both sides ; then place the gurnets in a buttered baking-dish, season them with pepper and salt, some chopped parsley, and two pats

of butter; moisten with two glasses of Sherry, some essence of mushrooms, and a little *consommé*, and put them in the oven to bake,—
taking care to baste them every five minutes until they are done.
Then remove the gurnets on to their dish, and detach the glaze from
the bottom and sides of the dish in which they have been baked, with
a glass of Sherry; reduce the essence to a demi-glaze, and incorporate it into one of the following sauces, with a pat of butter and a
little essence of anchovies; pour the sauce over the gurnets and send
to table. Either *Piquante, Italiènne, Gasconne, Provençale, Poivrade, Génoise,* or Tomata sauce, will suit this fish, when prepared in
the above manner.

475. GURNETS, A LA DAUPHINE.

CUT off the heads and fins from two gurnets, boil them in water with
a little salt and vinegar; when done, drain and skin them, then cover
them with some stiffly-reduced *Allemande* sauce (No. 7), and when this
has cooled upon them, egg them over and cover with bread-crumbs, and
place them on a buttered baking-sheet; half an hour before dinner put
them in the oven to bake, and as soon as they have acquired a fine
color, dish them up, and garnish round with some *Ravigotte* sauce,
containing some crayfish tails, and send to table.

476. GURNETS, A LA GENOISE.

BOIL or bake one or more gurnets in some *mirepoix* (No. 236);
drain, skim, glaze, and place them on their dish, and sauce them with
Génoise sauce (No. 30); garnish round with large crayfish, or *quenelles* of whiting or gurnet.

Gurnets, either boiled or baked, may be sent to table with any kind
of fish sauce; but as they do not possess any decided flavor of their
own, sharp or *Piquante* sauce should be used in preference.

Note.—Fillets of gurnets may be dressed in every variety of form,
and served with any kind of sauce, similar to soles.

477. BOILED MACKEREL.

BOIL the mackerel in salt and water, dish it up, and send to table,
either with fennel, parsley, or gooseberry sauce.

478. BROILED MACKEREL, A LA MAITRE D'HOTEL.

SPLIT the mackerel down the back, season with pepper and salt, and
oil it over; then place it on a gridiron, over a moderate fire; when the
mackerel is done on one side, turn it over on the other; and as soon
as it is done through, take it up on a dish and put some cold *Maître
d'Hôtel* butter (No. 44) inside it, and pour a well-finished *Maître d'Hotel*
sauce (No. 43) round it, and send to table.

479. BROILED MACKEREL, WITH NUT-BROWN BUTTER.

BROIL the mackerel as directed in the last article, dish it up, garnish
it round with fried parsley, and pour over it some nut-brown butter
(No. 93).

480. FILLETS OF MACKEREL, A LA MAITRE D'HOTEL.

FILLET the mackerel thus:
Place the fish on the table with its back toward you, then run the
knife in just below the gills, turn the edge of the blade under, press

with the fingers of the left hand full on the upper end of the fillet, and bearing with the blade of the knife upon the side of the backbone, draw the knife gently down to the tail, and turn the mackerel over and take the fillet off the other side : when this is done, cut each fillet into two, trim the ends neatly, and place them side by side on a buttered sauta-pan, season with pepper and salt and chopped parsley, squeeze the juice of half a lemon over them, and then pour a little oiled butter upon each, and cover with a round of buttered paper. About twenty minutes before dinner, either put them in the oven or on a stove-fire to simmer, and when done, drain the fillets on a napkin, dish them up in the form of a wreath, the fillets resting upon each other; sauce them over with some *Maître d'Hôtel* sauce (No. 43), and send to table.

The soft roes, if any, in the mackerel, should be parboiled in boiling water containing a little vinegar and salt ; then drain them on a napkin, and place them in the centre of the fillets when dished up.

Fillets of mackerel, prepared as described in the first part of the above directions, may be sent to table with either of the following sauces : *Vertpré, Ravigotte, Italiènne,* or *Génoise.*

DRESSED MULLETS, &c.,

COMPRISING

Mullets in cases, with fine-herbs.	Fillets of Whiting, *à la Maître d'Hôtel.*
„ *à l'Italiènne.*	„ „ *à la Horly.*
„ *à la Génoise.*	„ „ *à la Maréchale.*
„ *au ragout Cardinal.*	„ „ *à la Royale.*
„ *à la Chesterfield.*	Whitings boiled.
Gray Mullets, Graylings, &c.	fried.
	broiled, &c.

481. MULLETS IN CASES, WITH FINE-HERBS.

SCALE and trim the mullets, place them in a sauta-pan spread with fresh butter for the purpose; season with a little pepper and salt, cover them with some fine-herbs sauce (No. 14), moisten with two glasses of Sherry or white wine. About half an hour before dinner (the exact time depending on the size of the fish), put the mullets in the oven to bake; occasionally basting them with their own liquor. When done, put each of them, separately, in an oblong paper case saturated with oil, and then lightly colored in the oven ; add a glass of wine to the sauce remaining in the sauta-pan, shake it about to detach the glaze from the sides, and then mix the whole with the remainder of the fine-herbs sauce reserved for the purpose ; reduce the whole, mix in a little essence of anchovy, and the juice of half a lemon ; add a spoonful of chopped and blanched parsley, sauce the mullets over in their cases, dish them up, and send to table.

Mullets may be dressed with fine-herbs, also, in the following manner : Trim and place the mullets on a buttered sauta-pan, season with pepper and salt, strew over them chopped mushrooms, shalot, and parsley ; moisten with two glasses of Sherry and a large spoonful of brown sauce; bake and finish them exactly in the same manner as previously directed.

482. MULLETS A L'ITALIENNE.

WHEN the mullets are trimmed, put them in a buttered sauta-pan, season with pepper and salt, and moisten with three glasses of French white wine, and some essence of mushrooms; bake the fish, taking care to baste them frequently while in the oven; when done, dish them up, and mask them over with some glaze mixed with some finely-bruised lobster-coral; sauce them round with some Italian sauce (No. 12), incorporated with the liquor in which the mullets have been baked, after it has been reduced, also a little essence of anchovy, butter and lemon-juice, and send to table.

483. MULLETS, A LA GENOISE.

PREPARE the mullets in a sauta-pan, as before-mentioned, moisten with two glasses of claret, and some essence of mushrooms; when the mullets are baked, glaze them with some lobster-colored glaze, and dish them up. Then reduce the liquor in which the mullets were baked, and incorporate it with some *Génoise* sauce (No. 30), together with a pat of anchovy butter, and some lemon-juice; sauce the mullets round, garnish with a border of large crayfish and *quenelles* of whiting, and send to table.

484. MULLETS, AU RAGOUT CARDINAL.

PREPARE the mullets as *à l'Italiènne*, dish them up after being glazed of a fine scarlet hue; garnish them round with a rich *cardinal ragout* (No. 200); finish by placing a border of large crayfish and decorated *quenelles* of whiting round them, and send to table.

485. MULLETS, A LA CHESTERFIELD.

WHEN the mullets are trimmed, put them into a buttered sauta-pan with half a bottle of dry Champagne, some essence of mushrooms and a little pepper and salt; bake them in the oven, taking care to baste them frequently; when done, glaze and dish them up, reduce their liquor, and add to it some *bisque* of crayfish sauce, previously prepared as follows:—

Thoroughly wash and draw the gall from two dozen crayfish, put them into a stewpan with a small quantity of carrot and celery cut fine, one shalot, half a bay-leaf, a sprig of thyme, and some parsley; moisten with the remaining half-bottle of Champagne; boil the crayfish, and when done, remove the shells from the claws and tails, reserving the shells for the purpose of making crayfish butter afterward (No. 184). Next, pound the bodies, tails, and claws in the mortar, take the produce up into a stewpan, moisten with a large *ragout* spoonful of good *Allemande* sauce, and after warming the *purée* over the fire, rub it through a tammy in the usual manner; remembering that it must be kept sufficiently thick to be able to mask the fish with it. Then reduce the liquor in which the mullets and crayfish have been dressed to half a glaze, and incorporate a sufficient quantity of it with the *bisque*, to give it flavor; add a pat of lobster or crayfish butter, made with the shells reserved for this purpose, a little essence of anchovies and lemon-juice; pour the sauce over the mullets, and garnish them round with a border of *quenelles* of whiting, colored with chopped and blanched parsley, and some small fillets of soles *contisés* with truffles : place them alternately overlapping each other. The fillets of soles after being *contisés* with truffles, should be turned round and placed in a sauta-pan with some fresh butter, previously to being simmered.

Note.—Mullets should never be drawn ; it is sufficient to take out the gills only, as the liver and trail are considered the best parts of this fish. According to Yarrell's History of British Fishes, there are two distinct species of red mullets : the one is called the striped red, the other the plain red mullet, the former being the sort generally exposed for sale by the London fishmongers. Mr. Yarrell also informs us, that the generic term *mullus*, from which their name is derived, is said to have reference to the scarlet color of the sandal or shoe worn by the Roman Consuls, and in later times by the Emperors—which was called *mullus*. It would seem that in those days, the almost incredible price of £240 was given for three mullets of large size.

Gray Mullets should be dressed in the same manner as red mullets ; they are sometimes plain boiled or broiled, and sent to table with any of the various fish sauces in use : but this fish, from its want of flavor, especially requires the assistance of the most skillful cookery.

The Grayling is seldom seen in the London market, although, from its claims to the notice of epicures, it certainly deserves to be better known ; when dressed in the manner described for the preparation of mullets or whitings, it will be found deserving a higher estimation than has hitherto been accorded to it. This fish is in season in the months of October and November.

Whiting Poult, which in shape somewhat resembles perch, and in color is like the whiting, having when fresh much of its silvery hue, is found to be in best condition during the months of November and December, although they are sometimes taken in the spring of the year. Partaking in a great measure of the same character as the grayling, it should, like that fish, be prepared for table in a similar manner to red mullets. The same method is also to be used in dressing gwynniad, a species of lake fish, commonly found in Wales, Cumberland, and some parts of Ireland and Scotland.

486. FILLETS OF WHITINGS, A LA MAITRE D'HOTEL.

Fillet the number of whitings required, cut each fillet in two, trim the ends neatly round, and place the fillets side by side in a buttered sauta-pan ; season with pepper and salt, strew over them some chopped parsley, cover the fillets with a little melted fresh butter, and squeeze the juice of half a lemon over them ; cover with a buttered round of paper, and set them in the oven, or on the stove-fire—from five to seven minutes will suffice to do them ; then, take the fillets up carefully on to a napkin to drain, and afterward dish them up in the form of a close circle, pour some *Maître d'Hôtel* sauce (No. 43) over them, and serve.

Note.—Fillets of whitings thus prepared may be sent to table with any of the following sauces :—Italian, *Ravigotte*, shrimp, fine herbs, crayfish, Dutch sauce, *Suprême*, with scollops of lobster, or oyster sauces : the dish is named according to the sauce used for the fillets.

487. FILLETS OF WHITINGS, A LA HORLY.

FILLET the whitings, and remove the skin from each, by first placing the fillet on the table, with the skin downward, then inserting the point of the knife between the skin and the flesh, bearing lightly with the left hand on the fillet, gradually draw the knife under, so as to separate the skin from the fish without wasting its flesh : having thus trimmed the fillets, next put them into a basin with pepper and salt, thyme and bay-leaf, three chalots cut into slices, and some sprigs of parsley ; add two tablespoonsful of oil and one of French vinegar, and after the fillets have been steeped for about a couple of hours, drain them on a napkin, dip them thoroughly in flour, and fry them of a fine light color ; dish them up in a pyramidal form, with some parsley fried of a green color, and serve up with the fish a sauce-boat of either of the following sauces :—white or brown Italian, Tomata, *Poivrade*, Dutch, *Ravigolle*, or *Gasconne*.

488. FILLETS OF WHITINGS, A LA MARECHALE.

TRIM the fillets of any number of whitings as in the previous instance ; cut each in two, trim the pieces neatly, and place them separately on a large earthen dish. Then mask each fillet with a thin coating of reduced *Allemande* sauce, first seasoning the fillets with pepper and salt ; when the sauce has stiffened on them, dip each fillet in some very fine bread-crumbs, afterward in beaten eggs, and then in bread-crumbs again ; smooth and shape the fillets with the blade of a knife, and as each is finished off, place it with care in a sauta-pan containing some clarified butter. Twenty minutes before dinner, set the fillets on a brisk stove-fire to fry ; as soon as they have acquired a light color on the under side, turn them carefully over with a knife, and when the fillets are nicely colored on both sides, remove them on to a napkin, in order to absorb the butter that may remain about them ; then dish them up in the form of a wreath, and sauce them in the centre with some Dutch sauce—with the addition of an infusion of horseradish in French vinegar—some shrimps, oysters, muscles, prawns, crayfish, or merely some chopped and blanched parsley, according to taste or convenience.

489. FILLETS OF WHITINGS, A LA ROYALE.

TRIM and *marinade* the fillets of whitings in the manner directed for preparing whitings *à la Horly* (No. 487). About twenty minutes before dinner, drain the fillets on a napkin, and then dip each fillet separately in some light-made frying batter, and then throw them one after another in some frying fat heated for the purpose ; as soon as they are done, and have acquired a light-brown color, take the fillets out of the fat on to a cloth, with the corners of which touch them lightly in order to absorb any grease they may retain ; then dish the fillets up either in a pyramidal form, or else in a circle, and pour some white *Ravigotte*, white Italian, Venetian, or Dutch sauce, under and round them, and send to table.

490. WHITINGS, BOILED.

WHEN the whitings are trimmed, boil them in spring water with a little salt—about seven minutes will suffice to do them ; take the fish out of the water as soon as done, dish them up on a fish-plate covered

with a napkin, and send to table with a boatful of either of the following sauces :—Anchovy, Shrimp, Plain butter, or Dutch.

491. WHITINGS, FRIED.

To prepare whitings for frying, it is necessary first to skin them as
follows :—

With a cloth in the left hand, take a firm hold of the whiting at the
back part of the head, just below the gills, then loosen the skin on each
side of the fish, just at the commencement of the upper dorsal fin, by
inserting the point of a small knife, and with the right hand pull the
skin off sharply, first on one side and then on the other.   When the
fish is skinned and trimmed, turn the tail round into its mouth, and
fasten the ends together with a short peg of wood; dip each fish into
some beaten eggs, and cover it with fine bread-crumbs.   A quarter of
an hour before dinner, fry them of a fine color in some fat heated for
the purpose, dish them on a napkin with fried parsley, and send to
table with a boatful of either of the following sauces :—Anchovy,
Dutch, Shrimp, or Plain butter.

492. WHITINGS, BROILED.

TRIM and score the whitings on both sides, rub them over with oil,
and broil them on a gridiron, previously rubbed with whitening ; when
broiled on one side, turn them over on the other, taking care to keep
them of a fine color; when done, dish them on a napkin, and send to
table with a boatful of either of the following sauces : Dutch, white
Ravigotte, Venetian, brown oyster sauce, or *Maître d'Hôtel*.

Note.—Whitings in cases with fine herbs, stuffed and baked *à la
Vileroi, à la Cardinal*, &c., are dressed in the same manner as mullets.

FRESH-WATER FISH,

SECTION I.

COMPRISING

Char, *à la Génoise.*	Lamprey, *à la Beauchamp.*
„ in *Matelotte.*	Smelts fried.
„ *à la Hollandaise.*	„ in *Matelotte.*
„ *à la Beaufort.*	„ in cases, with fine-herbs.
Lamprey in *Matelotte.*	„ *à la Royale.*
„ *à la Foley.*	

Char is in season from July till October, and forms a most delicious
variety for the table in the summer season.   When perfectly fresh, it
makes perhaps the best water *souchet* of any fish.*

493. CHAR, A LA GENOISE.

BOIL the fish in salt and water, and when done, skin and glaze
them ; dish them up, sauce with some *Génoise* sauce (No. 30), garnish with a border of small *quenelles* of whiting, and crayfish tails, and
send to table.

* Water Souchet of Char is described among the Water *Souchets.*

494. CHAR, IN MATELOTTE.

TRIM the char intended to be dressed, place them in an oval stewpan with an onion and carrot cut in thin slices, also a bay-leaf and a sprig of thyme, a *bouquet* of parsley and green onions, a blade of mace, a few pepper-corns, some parings of mushrooms, and a little salt; moisten with a bottle of Claret, and set the whole to stew gently on a stove-fire for about twenty minutes or half an hour, according to the size of the fish. As soon as the fish are done, drain them on a wet napkin; remove their skin with a knife, and place them neatly on the dish. Then, reduce the liquor in which the char have been stewed (after first being strained and skimmed), with a sufficient quantity of brown sauce for the purpose; when the sauce is reduced, add a little nutmeg, a pat of butter, and some lemon-juice, and pass it through a tammy into a stewpan containing some prepared button-mushrooms, button-onions, and very small *quenelles* of whiting; warm the *ragout*, pour it over and about the char, garnish the *matelotte* with a border of large crayfish, and some *croûtons*, and serve.

495. CHAR, A LA HOLLANDAISE.

BOIL the char in salt and water, dish them up on a napkin, and send to table with a boatful of Dutch sauce.

Char, thus plain boiled, may also be sent to table with parsley and butter, green *Ravigotte*, or Crayfish sauce.

496. CHAR, A LA BEAUFORT.

PLACE the char when trimmed in an oval stewpan, with sliced carrot and onion, a fagot of parsley and green onions, mace, mushrooms, pepper-corns, thyme, bay-leaf, and salt; moisten with French white wine, and set the fish to stew gently on the stove fire. When done, drain them on to a napkin, skin and mask them with some glaze mixed with some bruised coral of lobster, place them on their dish, and sauce them round with a Parisian *ragout* (No. 203) mixed with the liquor in which the char has been stewed, after this liquor has been reduced to glaze; garnish round with a border of lobster *croquettes*.

497. LAMPREY MATELOTTE.

To cleanse lampreys,* it is necessary to put them into a large earthen vessel with plenty of salt, with which they should be well scoured, and afterward thoroughly washed in several waters: by this means they are freed from the slimy mucus which adheres to this kind of fish. The lamprey should then be trimmed and cut into pieces about three inches long, or it may be left whole, according to taste; it should be placed in a stewpan with sliced carrot and onion, mace, pepper-corns, thyme, and bay-leaf, parsley, mushrooms, and salt;

---

* Of this kind of fish there are two different sorts in general use for the table; one being the sea or marine lamprey, which is abundant at Gloucester and Worcester, where it is dressed and preserved for the purpose of being given as presents. The other sort, the lampern, is much smaller; this is to be found in the Thames, and may easily be obtained at any of the London fishmongers from the month of October till March, at which period they are in season. The lamprey is considered to be in best condition during the months of April and May, when it ascends the Severn from the sea, for the purpose of depositing its spawn.

moisten it with Port wine, and set the whole to stew gently on the stove-fire. When done, take half the liquor in which the lampreys have been stewed, and reduce it with some brown sauce; add a glass of Port wine, and as soon as the sauce is reduced to a proper consistency, incorporate with it a pat of butter, a little essence of anchovies, and lemon-juice, and pass it through a tammy into a *bain-marie*, containing some button-mushrooms, stewed small button-onions, and some small *quenelles* of perch. Drain the lampreys, place them on a dish, sauce them over with the *ragout*, garnish round with crayfish, and send to table.

498. LAMPREY, A LA FOLEY.

Take two fine lampreys, thoroughly cleansed, form each into a circular shape, and fasten them with string : then stew them in Claret, with the addition of vegetables, &c., as in the foregoing cases; as soon as the lampreys are done, reduce two-thirds of their liquor with an equal proportion of brown sauce, and some essence of mushrooms—when sufficiently reduced, incorporate with this some crayfish butter, and a little essence of anchovies, a very little nutmeg, lemon-juice, and cayenne, and pass the sauce through a tammy into a *bain-marie* containing three dozen crayfish tails, and as many button-mushrooms—previously prepared for the purpose. Then drain the lampreys on a napkin, and afterward place them, one resting on the other, in the dish, sauce them over with prepared *ragout ;* garnish round with a border of glazed *crôutons* and fried small fillets of perch.

499. LAMPREYS, A LA BEAUCHAMP.

Truss the lampreys as directed in the previous article, stew them in old Madeira, cider, and the requisite vegetables, &c. ; add two-thirds of their liquor to an equal quantity of good brown sauce, work the whole by boiling on the fire, skim and reduce it to its proper consistency, add some lobster-butter, cayenne, and lemon-juice, and pass the sauce through a tammy into a *bain-marie* containing some small round truffles, lobster *quenelles*, and tails of crayfish. Dish up the lampreys as in the last case, and sauce them over with the prepared *ragout ;* garnish round with some glazed pastry *fleurons*, and send to table.

Lamperns are treated in the same manner as lampreys, being similar in flavor.

500. SMELTS, FRIED, ETC.

When preparing smelts* for frying, take the gills out carefully, trim the fins, wipe the fish with a clean cloth, dip them first in flour, and afterward in beaten egg, and then in fine bread crumbs ; fry them in some heated hogs' lard, of a fine color; dish them up on a napkin, and garnish them with fried parsley, and send to table with a boatful of either Anchovy, Dutch, Shrimp, Crayfish, or Lobster sauce.

Smelts may also be dressed with advantage in *Normande matelotte*, in cases, with fine-herbs, *à l'Italiènne, à la Royale*, &c.; by observing the directions given for dressing mullets or whitings in a similar manner.

---

* This kind of fish, which is in general estimation, is in season from August till March, when after depositing their spawn in fresh water, they return to the sea.

FRESH-WATER FISH.

SECTION II.

COMPRISING

Eels, spitchcocked.	Carp, *à la Chanbord.*
„ plain broiled.	„ *à la Royale.*
., stewed, *à l'Anglaise.*	„ *à la Bourguignotte.*
Matelotte of Eels, *à la Bordelaise.*	„ *à la Périgueux.*
„ „ *à la Parisiènne.*	„ *à la Provençale.*
„ „ *à la Génoise.*	„ *à l'Allemande.*
Eels, *à la Dauphinoise.*	„ *à la Vénitiènne.*
„ *à la Vénitiènne.*	Stewed Carp, a *l'Anglaise.*
„ *à la Tartare.*	Small Carp fried.
„ *à la Poulette.*	Tench.
„ *à l'Indiènne.*	

501. EELS, SPITCHCOCKED.

As eels,* when brought into the kitchen, are frequently alive, it is first necessary to kill them; this, from their tenacity of life, is found by many not easy to accomplish; it is, however, merely necessary to insert the point of any sharp instrument into the spine, at the back of the head, to the depth of an inch, and the eel will become perfectly motionless. Then take a firm hold of the eel with a cloth in the left hand, and with the right hand proceed to detach the skin just below the gills, with the point of a small knife; when there is a sufficient quantity of skin loosened, so as to gain a purchase, hold the head firmly with the left hand, and with a cloth in the right, force the skin to slide off the fish. Then cut off the head, make an incision about two inches in length at the vent, and the same at the neck, draw the gut, &c., trim away the fins, wash and thoroughly cleanse each fish; wipe them with a cloth, and then, after sprinkling them with salt, let them lie on a dish for an hour or so, previously to dressing them. After having trimmed the eels, lay each on its back in a straight line on the table, and with a knife, open it from one extremity to the other; detach the back-bone, and take it out; then cut the eel into several pieces about three inches long, season them with pepper and salt, and sprinkle them over with chopped parsley and shalot; dip each piece of eel separately in some beaten egg, and afterward in some fine bread-crumbs. Place the eels thus prepared on a dish in the larder, until within twenty minutes of dinner-time; then proceed to fry them of a fine color, and dish them up with fried parsley round them, and send to table. Either of the following may be served in a sauce-boat with spitchcocked eels :—Dutch, *Italiènne, Venitiènne, Poivrade, Piquante, Tartare,* Tomata, or *Gasconne* sauce.

---

* There are four distinct sorts of eels: the snig, the broad-nosed, the grig, and the sharp-nosed; the latter is the kind generally known. The London markets are supplied principally from Holland: Thames eels are, however, in high repute; being caught in a running stream, their skin is brighter and more silvery; they are preferable, too, from their greater sweetness, to the Dutch eels.

502. EELS, PLAIN BROILED.

BONE and cut the eels into three-inch lengths, put them on a dish, season with pepper and salt, lemon juice, and two spoonsful of oil; twenty minutes before dinner, broil them of a light color, dish them up on a napkin with fried parsley, and send to table with either of the sauces named in the foregoing article, in a sauce-boat, separately.

503. EELS, STEWED A L'ANGLAISE.

THE eels being skinned, trimmed, and cut into pieces about two inches long, place them in a stewpan, with some sliced carrot, onion, parsley, bay-leaf, and thyme, a handful of mushroom trimmings, a few pepper-corns, four cloves, a blade of mace, and a little salt; moisten with half a bottle of Port wine, cover with a round of buttered paper, replace the lid on the stewpan, and set the eels on the stove-fire to stew. When they have boiled gently on the corner of the stove for about twenty minutes, they will be done; then drain and trim them, keeping their liquor to make the sauce; place the pieces of eel in a clean stewpan, and then proceed to make a sauce for them in the following manner:—Put about two ounces of fresh butter into a stewpan on the fire, and as soon as it is melted, add two tablespoons-ful of flour; with a wooden spoon stir them both together over the fire, until the *roux*, or thickening, becomes slightly colored; then throw in a couple of shalots, and moisten gradually with the liquor in which the eels have been stewed, adding thereto a small ladleful of good stock, and a couple of glasses of Port wine. Stir the sauce over the fire till it boils, and set it on the corner of the stove, to continue gently throwing up the scum, which, having entirely removed, reduce the sauce, if necessary, to its proper consistency; and then pass it through a tammy into the stewpan containing the pieces of eel already mentioned. Just before sending to table, add a few prepared button-mushrooms, a pat of fresh butter, some chopped and blanched parsley, lemon-juice, and a very small quantity of essence of anchovy; toss the whole well together over the fire until well mixed; then dish the eels up in a pyramidal form on their dish, pour the sauce over them, garnish round with a dozen *croûtons* of fried bread, and send to table.

504. MATELOTTE OF EELS, A LA BORDELAISE.

CUT some eels into three-inch lengths, place them in a stewpan with sliced carrot, onion, parsley-roots, mushrooms, thyme, and bay-leaf, mace, four cloves, and a few pepper-corns; season with a little salt, and moisten with a bottle of claret. Set the eels to stew on the fire, and when done, drain, trim, and place them in a clean stew-pan with a little of their liquor to moisten them. Then put the remainder of the liquor into a stewpan with a ladleful of brown sauce, some essence of mushrooms, and two glasses of claret; let this boil, then set it by the side of the stove to continue gently boiling, that it may throw up the scum, and become bright; when this is effected, reduce it to its proper consistency, by boiling it down quickly, stirring the sauce the whole time with a wooden spoon to prevent its sticking to the bottom of the stewpan and burning. Then pass the sauce through a tammy into a *bain-marie*, and just before

using it, make it hot, and incorporate with it the following preparations :—mix a pint of butter with three anchovies, a tea-spoonful of
capers, a clove of garlic, and a little nutmeg, pound the whole together
and pass them through a sieve : having well worked this into the sauce,
pour it over the matelotte, and dish up the latter as follows :—place
the pieces of eel on the dish, in circular order—each piece resting on
the other, with a glazed *crôuton* of bread between—fill the centre
with *quenelles* of perch, place a trimmed and glazed crayfish across
each *crôuton*, and garnish round the inner edge of the dish with
alternate groups of white muscles, button-mushrooms, and stewed
button-onions.

505. MATELOTTE OF EELS, A LA PARISIENNE.

CUT the eels into four-inch lengths, put them into a stewpan with
sliced carrot, &c. ; moisten with a bottle of French white wine, some
essence of mushrooms, and the liquor produced by three dozen
blanched oysters ; stew the eels thus prepared ; drain, trim, and put
the pieces of eels into a clean stewpan, with a little of their own
liquor to keep them moist and to warm them in. Put the remainder
of the liquor into a stewpan with a large ladleful of white *velouté*
sauce, and two glasses of white wine ; reduce the whole quickly on
the fire, incorporate therein a leason of four yelks of eggs, a large pat
of crayfish butter, some lemon-juice, and a little nutmeg ; pass the
sauce into a *bain-marie* containing the three dozen oysters before
alluded to, some button-mushrooms, and crayfish tails. When about
to dish up, first place upon the dish an oval piece of bread, about
three inches high, cut in flutes all round and fried of a light color ;
then set the pieces of eels in a perpendicular position up against the
fried bread, garnish the *crôustade* with a group of small *quenelles* of
whitings, sauce with the *ragout* prepared for the purpose, garnish
round with large crayfish, and small fluted bread *crôustades* filled with
soft roes of mackerel or carp, and send to table.

506. MATELOTTE OF EELS, A LA GENOISE.

EITHER cut the eels into three or four-inch lengths, or truss them
into an oval or round shape ; prepare them for stewing with the usual
vegetables, &c., moisten with Claret or Burgundy wine, and set the
eels on the fire to stew. When done, drain, trim, and glaze them
with some lobster coral in the glaze ; pile the eels up in a pyramidal
group on a dish, sauce with some good *Génoise* sauce (No. 30), made
with the liquor in which the eels have been stewed ; garnish round
with alternate groups of button-mushrooms, small *quenelles* of carp,
and crayfish tails, and send to table.

507. EELS, A LA DAUPHINOISE.

BONE two large eels, fill them with force-meat of whitings mixed
with some simmered fine-herbs ; then sew the eels up with a large
worsted needle and some coarse thread ; truss them in a circular
form, place them in an oval stewpan with some *mirepoix* (No. 236),
and set them to stew on the fire, or in the oven, basting them
frequently with their own liquor, and taking care that they are not
allowed to boil fast, as that would cause them to break, and otherwise
disfigure them. When the eels are done, glaze and dish them up,

one resting on the other in the dish; in the centre of one, place a group of *quenelles* of whitings mixed with some chopped truffles, and in the centre of the other, place another group of *quenelles* of whitings colored with lobster coral; sauce them with some *Périgueux* sauce (No. 23), in which has been mixed half the *mirepoix* the eels have been stewed in, and finish with a pat of anchovy butter and lemon-juice. Garnish round with large crayfish, placing a group of half-a-dozen of the finest of these in the centre of the dish.

508. EELS, A LA VENITIENNE.

CUT the eels into pieces four inches long, stew them in some *mirepoix* of French white wine; when done, drain, trim, and glaze them with some lobster coral-colored glaze, and dish them up in two parallel conical groups; pour round them some Venetian sauce, (No. 26), which has been finished with the addition of half the *mirepoix*, in which the eels have been stewed, a pat of anchovy butter and the juice of half a lemon; pass this through a tammy into a stewpan containing a pottle of prepared button-mushrooms; some blanched chopped parsley must be added the last thing. Garnish round with groups of muscles fried in batter, and serve.

509. EELS, A LA TARTARE

EITHER cut the eels into three-inch lengths, or truss them whole, in a circular form; place them in a stewpan with sliced carot and onion, parsley, bay-leaf and thyme, a few peppercorns and salt; moisten with a gill of vinegar and some water; then put them on the fire to boil, and as soon as they are done, set them to cool partially in their liquor :—after which drain, trim, and bread-crumb them with egg, fry them of a fine color, dish them up with fried parsley, and send to table with some *Tartare* sauce (No. 96), in a sauce-boat.

Eels *à la Tartare* may also be bread-crumbed as follows. Mix the yelks of six eggs and three ounces of fresh butter melted over the fire, with pepper, salt, and nutmeg; with this preparation cover the eels, and afterward bread-crumb them—causing plenty of bread-crumbs to adhere; put the eels on a buttered baking-sheet, drop some butter through a spoon with holes in it over them, and about half an hour before diner, place them in the oven to be baked of a fine color, dish them up as in the foregoing case, and send to table with the *Tartare* sauce, separately in a sauce-boat.

510. EELS, A LA POULETTE.

STEW the eels in the usual manner with white wine, or merely as directed for *à la Tartare*, then drain, trim, and place them in a clean stewpan, with some of their liquor to keep them moist. Just before dinner, dish the eels up in a group, in the centre of the dish, sauce them with some good sauce *à la Poulette* mixed with a pat of anchovy butter (and if the eels have been stewed in white wine, half their liquor, reduced to a glaze, should also be added to the sauce); place round them alternate groups of crayfish tails tossed in lobster butter to give them a brighter color, and some scollops of perch tossed in some green *Ravigotte* sauce; place in the centre of the eels, just at the top of the group, six large crayfish, eight glazed *croûtons* of fried bread round the base, and serve.

511. EELS, A L'INDIENNE.

STEW the eels as directed in the foregoing cases, dish them up in the form of a circle, garnish the centre with plain boiled rice, sauce the eels with a good curry (No. 74), and garnish round with some rice *croquettes*, to be made as follows :—

To four gravy-spoonsful of boiled rice, add one of good *Allemande* sauce, some nutmeg, and a little grated Parmesan cheese ; stir the whole on the fire till it has boiled two or three minutes, and set it on a plate to cool ; then mould the *croquettes* in the form of corks, pears, or round balls, bread-crumb them with egg in the usual way, fry them of a fine color, and use them as directed.

Eels stewed and glazed according to the different modes above described, as well as when bread-crumbed and fried, or baked, may also be sent to table with the following sauces :—*Bourguignotte*, Tomata, Italian (white or brown), *Cardinal, Matelotte, Normande, Ravigotte, Provençale, Poivrade, Piquante*, Aurora, or Crayfish sauce.

512. CARP, A LA CHAMBORD.

CHOOSE, if possible, a carp* weighing about six pounds, and after scalding, drawing, and thoroughly cleansing the fish, stuff it with some *quenelle* force-meat of whitings. Then lay the carp on a buttered sheet of paper, placed upon the drainer of an oval fish-kettle, cover the entire fish with a coating of force-meat of whitings about half an inch thick, keeping the head clear, and with some " *contises*" fillets of soles, form thereon a decoration resembling scales, but larger ; in the angles of these, place the tail of a crayfish, trimmed for the purpose ; cover the whole with thin layers of fat bacon, moisten with a white wine *mirepoix*, and set it to braize gently on a moderate fire, carefully preventing it from boiling fast, as that would tend to displace the fillets, &c. with which the carp has been decorated. If the fish is of large size, it will require about an hour to braize it ; when done, drain it from its braize, remove the layers of fat bacon, &c., and place it on a large silver dish ; garnish round the extremity of the inner edge of the dish with alternate groups of small *quenelles* of whitings *à la Perigueux*, button-mushrooms, white muscles, and crayfish tails ; sauce round the carp, without covering any part of it, with some *Allemande* incorporated with part of the liquor in which the fish has been braized, a pat of anchovy butter, and some lemon-juice ; glaze the head of the carp, and after ornamenting each end of the dish with a group of large crayfish, send to table.

513. CARP, A LA ROYALE.

CLEANSE a carp of large size, wipe it with a clean cloth, and lay it on a buttered paper, place it upon a drainer of an oval fish-kettle, and cover it entirely with *quenelle* force-meat of whitings colored with

---

* This fish is held in high estimation on the Continent, especially those caught in the Rhine and Moselle. In England they are seldom found good, and this is the case also with tench ; both these fish being found when cooked to taste muddy : this is chiefly owing to their being taken from stagnant ponds. Those only can be expected to be free from this disagreeable peculiarity that are caught in running streams.

When about to clean carp for dressing, it is quite necessary to extract an angular substance, called the gall-stone, which is to be found at the back of the head ; if not removed, this is sure to impart a bitter taste, and render the best fish unfit for table.

lobster-coral ; smooth the surface of the force-meat with the blade of a knife dipped in whipped white of egg ; place some fillets of soles *con-tisés* with green gherkins crosswise upon the carp, leaving the space of an inch between each fillet—these spaces are to be filled up by inserting in the force-meat some pieces of truffle, cut in the shape of small olives ; cover the whole with thin layers of fat bacon, and braize the carp as in the former case, in a white wine *mirepoix ;* when done, place it on a large oval dish, remove the layers of bacon, &c., sauce it round with a *Génoise* sauce (No. 30), and garnish it with a border of large *quenelles* of soles, half of which must be colored with lobster-coral, and the re-mainder with chopped and blanched parsley ; within the inner circle of the *quenelles,* place alternate groups of prepared oysters and the tails of prawns ; at the extremities, and on the flanks of the dish, place groups of crayfish, and send to table.

514. CARP, A LA BOURGUINOTTE.

Stew the carp whole in red wine, when done, drain, and place it on an oval dish ; sauce it with a rich *Bourguignotte* sauce (No. 28), gar-nish with soft roes and crayfish, and send to table.

515. CARP, A LA PERIGUEX.

Stew the carp in wine, drain it, and dish it up ; sauce it with *Peri-gueux* sauce incorporated with a pat of anchovy butter and some lemon-juice ; garnish with a border of lobster *quenelles,* and serve.

516. CARP, A LA PROVENCALE.

Stew the carp in a *mirepoix* of white wine, when done, drain and dish it up ; pour some *Provençale* sauce over it, garnish it with groups of muscles fried in batter, and scollops of perch tossed in green *Ravigotte* sauce ; place a border of crayfish round the dish, and send to table.

517. CARP, A L'ALLEMANDE.

Clean one or more carp, cut the fish into slices about two inches thick ; place the slices in a basin, and season them with a gill of oil, a little tarragon-vinegar, minionette-pepper, and salt, bay-leaf, thyme, and shalot ; let the carp steep in this *marinade* till within about half an hour of dinner-time ; then drain them on a napkin, and dip each piece separately in flour, bread-crumb them in the usual way with egg and bread-crumbs mixed with one-fifth of Parmesan cheese ; fry the pieces of carp of a fine color, and dish them up on a napkin, placing the pieces so as to make the fish look whole ; surround the carp with a border of fried parsley, and slices of lemon, and send to table with two sauce-boats containing some butter sauce (see No. 70), and some *Génoise* sauce (No. 30).

518. CARP, FRIED A LA VENITIENNE.

Stew one or more carp in a white wine *mirepoix* (No. 236) ; drain them on an earthen dish, and after removing the skin, proceed to mask them with a coating of stiffly-reduced *Allemande* sauce (No. 7) ; in which has been added some of the liquor the fish have been stewed in. When the sauce has cooled upon the carp, first strew over some bread-crumbs, then egg them over with a paste-brush, and cover them entirely with bread-crumbs mixed with one-third of grated Parmesan cheese : then place the carp in a buttered baking-dish or sheet, and half an hour before dinner put them in the oven to bake : they should be of a light-brown color : set the fish on an oval dish, sauce them round with some good Venetian sauce (No. 26), garnish with *quenelles* of carp mixed with some *purée* of mushrooms, and send to table.

519. CARP, STEWED A L'ANGLAISE.

FOR dressing carp in this way, see the directions for stewing eels *à l'Anglaise* (No. 503).

520. SMALL CARP, FRIED.

CLEANSE and scale the carp, split them down the back, open them flat, season with pepper and salt, dip them in flour, and immediately fry them of a fine color; dish them on a napkin, garnish round with fried parsley, and send to table with either Italian, anchovy, or Dutch sauce, separately in a sauce-boat.

If preferred, the carp may be bread-crumbed for frying in the usual way.

TENCH being somewhat similar to carp, may be dressed in the various ways in which that fish is prepared for the table, with equal success ; both these kinds of fish make excellent *Matelottes*, and, indeed, it is not unusual to prepare *Matelottes* of carp, tench, and eels all in the same dish. Tench may be sent to table either fried or boiled, with Dutch sauce.

FRESH-WATER FISH.

SECTION III.

COMPRISING

Pike, or Jack, stuffed and baked.	Perch, *à la Stanley.*
„ *à la Chambord, &c.*	„ *à la Wastrefische.*
„ fried in slices, *à la Hollandaise.*	„ *à la Venitiènne.*
„ crimped in slices, *à la Hollandaise.*	Fillets of Perch, *à l'Italiènne, &c.*
Fillets of Pike.	

521. PIKE, OR JACK, STUFFED AND BAKED.

SCALE, draw the gills, and thoroughly cleanse and wipe the pike with a clean cloth; fill the paunch with well-seasoned veal stuffing; sew it up with a trussing-needle and fine string, and either turn the tail round into the mouth, securing them together by means of string, or truss the pike into the shape of the letter S ; make several deep incisions in a slanting direction on both sides of the fish, and place it in a baking-dish; season with pepper and salt, chopped parsley, and mushrooms, and a little shalot, and from six to eight ounces of fresh butter :—moisten with half a bottle of Sherry, and a little good stock, or essence of mushrooms ; cover with a well-buttered paper, and put the pike thus prepared in the oven to bake—observing, that it should be frequently basted with its liquor. When done, dish it up ; then with two glasses of Sherry—detach all the glaze and herbs from the bottom and sides of the dish in which the pike has been baked, add to this a ladleful of good brown sauce, reduce the whole to a proper consistency, and mix in two ounces of fresh butter, a little essence of anchovies, lemon-juice, and a trifle of cayenne; with this sauce mask the pike and send to table.

522. PIKE, A LA CHAMBORD.

This dish is prepared in a similar manner to carp *à la Chambord* (see No. 512).

This is also the case with pike *à la Cardinal*, ditto *à la Royale*, and ditto fried *à l'Allemande;* in fact, pike may be dressed in all respects the same as carp.

523. PIKE, FRIED A LA HOLLANDAISE.

WHEN the pike is cleaned, cut it into slices an inch thick, and place them in an earthen vessel; season with pepper and salt, oil, lemon-juice, chopped parsley, and a little grated nutmeg; turn the slices of pike over in the seasoning occasionally, in order that they may be well saturated with it, and half an hour before dinner-time, drain them on a napkin, dip each separately in flour, and immediately fry them in hogs' lard, made sufficiently hot for the purpose; dish them on a napkin, place round them a border of fried parsley, and send to table with a boat of well-seasoned Dutch sauce (No. 42).

524. CRIMPED SLICES OF PIKE, A LA HOLLANDAISE.

To produce this dish in perfection, the following instructions must be closely attended to in every particular :—

Scale* and clean the pike, immediately on its being taken from the water; cut the fish into slices nearly an inch thick, and put them into a panful of spring water—fresh from the pump—which, from its coldness, has the power of crimping the comparatively live fish thrown into it. About twenty minutes before dinner, boil the slices in hot water with a little salt; as soon as they are done, drain and dish them up on a napkin, and send to table with either of the following, in a sauce-boat :—Parsley and butter, Dutch sauce, *Maître d'Hôtel*, or Crayfish sauce.

525. FILLETS OF PIKE.

MAY be dressed in every variety in which salmon, turbot, or soles are capable of being sent to table; and the directions given under those heads will suffice. It is necessary, however, to describe here the operation of filleting pike.

The smaller-sized of this fish are best suited for this purpose; these should be filleted as follows :—

First lay the fish on the table, with its back placed toward you, insert the knife just below the gill, press with the left hand slightly on the upper part of the fillet, and then draw the knife down—close to the back-bone; when one fillet is removed, repeat the same operation on the other side. Then lay the fillets alternately on the table,

---

* The easiest way is to place the pike in a sink, and then to pour some boiling water over it, by which means the scales are effectually removed by scraping them off with a knife.

with the skin downward, insert the edge of the knife close to the skin, at the extreme end, and by drawing the knife to and fro, keeping the blade clossly pressed to the skin, it will come away from the fillet. Then cut these fillets into smaller ones, according to taste or convenience, or into scollops, as the case may require.

526. PERCH, A LA STANLEY.

THOROUGHLY cleanse two or three fine bright perch, which should weigh not less than one pound and a half each; stew them in Rhenish wine, and when done, drain them on a napkin, dish them up, and garnish with a Parisian *ragout* (No. 203), omitting the truffles, but containing the liquor the perch have been stewed in. Garnish round with a border of large crayfish, and send to table.

527. PERCH, A LA WASTREFISCHE.

BOIL the perch in French white wine, and when done, after removing the skin, dish it up, and stick the red fins straight up in a row, down the centre of the fish; on each side of the fins thus placed, decorate the perch by laying on its uppermost fillets streaks of carrot and parsley-roots, shred exceedingly fine, and boiled; also in alternate rows with these, some blanched leaves of green parsley. Pour round the perch the following sauce:

Reduce the liquor in which the perch have been stewed with a proportionate quantity of white *Velouté* sauce; add a pat of fresh butter, some white essence of mushrooms, a little nutmeg, and lemon-juice; mix the whole well together, and serve.

528. PERCH, A LA VENITIENNE.

BOIL the perch, skim and dish them up, placing the red fins in a row down the centre; moisten them over with some sauce *à la Vénitiènne* (No. 26), and send to table.

In addition to the foregoing methods for preparing perch for the table, this fish may also be dressed in the same way as pike, carp, and tench, in *Matelotte*, *à la Dauphine*, Water Souchet, *à l'Allemande*, *à la Génoise*, *à la Hollandaise*, *à la Maître d'Hôtel*, and also with Shrimp, Parsley and butter, and plain Butter sauce.

Note.—Perch should be served in fillets only, when it happens that they are small, or that they are plentiful; otherwise it is usual to dress this kind of fish whole.

529. FILLETS OF PERCH, A L'ITALIENNE.

FOLLOW the directions given for filleting pike, divesting the fillets of the skin in like manner; trim them neatly, by rounding them at one end, and bring the other end to a point. Then lay the fillets in a circle in a sauta-pan, with some clarified fresh butter; season with a little salt, pepper, and lemon-juice. Twenty minutes before dinner-time, set the fillets on the stove-fire, or in the oven, for about ten minutes to simmer; and when they are thoroughly done, drain them on a napkin, and dish them up in the form of a close circle; sauce them with a white or brown Italian sauce, and send to table.

Fillets of perch thus prepared, may also be sent to table with either of the following sauces, from which the dish will take its name: *à la Ravigotte*, *à la Maître d'Hôtel*, *à la Cardinal*, *à la Vertpré*, *à la Hollandaise*.

SKATE, WHITEBAIT, AND SCOLLOPED SHELL-FISH,

COMPRISING

Crimped Skate, boiled.	Crimped Skate, à la *Pascaline.*
„ „ fried.	„ „ à la *Royale.*
„ „ with nut-brown butter.	White Bait.
„ „ à *l'Italiènne.*	Scolloped Oysters.
„ „ with fine-herbs *au gratin.*	Muscles, Lobsters, Cockles, &c.

THERE are many varieties of skate, amongst these that generally called the blue or gray skate is deemed best for the table. Although not held in much repute, it nevertheless is not unworthy the notice of the epicure, when properly dressed. In order to clean this fish, skin it on both sides, draw and wash it thoroughly; then lay the skate flat on the table, and cut it up in the following manner: First, with a sharp knife separate, on both sides, the fleshy parts of the fish from the back-bone, drawing the knife in a curving direction; afterward, cut these winglike pieces into long strips, by cutting right through the cartilaginous or finny parts; then, place these strips in a pan filled with fresh water from the pump, in order to crimp them. In like manner cut the fleshy parts remaining, and also the back-bone itself, into three-inch lengths, and place them also in the cold water to be crimped. Reserve the liver of the fish to be dressed with it. The water in which the fish is placed should be changed often, until the crimping be effected.

530. CRIMPED SKATE, BOILED.

TURN the fin-pieces of skate round and fasten them with string; boil the fish in hot water with a handful of salt in it; when done, drain and dish it up on a napkin, placing the pieces of liver in the centre; garnish round with a row of green parsley, and send to table with either of the following, in a sauce-boat: Lobster, Crayfish, Shrimp, Anchovy, Dutch, Muscle, or Oyster sauce.

531. CRIMPED SKATE, FRIED.

WITH a clean napkin, absorb all the moisture from the pieces of skate intended to be fried; after which dip each piece into flour preparatory to its being again dipped in beaten egg, and then rolled in very fine bread-crumbs; turn the pieces of skate round into shape again, and fry them of a fine bright color, and dish them up on a napkin with a border of fried parsley, and send to table with either of the sauces recommended for boiled skate.

532. CRIMPED SKATE, WITH NUT-BROWN BUTTER.

BOIL the skate, drain and place it on a silver dish, surround it with a border of fried parsley, and pour over it some well-seasoned nut-brown butter (No. 93).

533. SKATE, FRIED A L'ITALIENNE.

BREAD-CRUMB and fry the fish as directed for fried skate; when done, place it on a dish, pour under it a good brown Italian sauce (No. 12), and serve.

534. SKATE, WITH FINE-HERBS, AU GRATIN.

BUTTER a baking-dish or sauta-pan, and after first turning the pieces of skate round, lay them neatly in the dish, strew over them some chopped mushrooms, parsley, and a very little shalot; season with pepper and salt, and moisten with two glasses of Sherry and a spoonful of *consommé;* then shake some fine browned bread-crumbs or raspings over the whole, and set it in the oven to bake; when done, place the pieces of skate on the dish, in the same position which they occupied on the baking-dish; reduce the liquor they have been baked in, and add to it some *Espagnole* or brown Italian sauce, mix therewith a small piece of butter, a little essence of anchovies, and lemon-juice; pour the sauce round the fish; shake some fresh raspings over the whole, and then set the dish (if it be silver) on the stove to *gratinate* or consolidate the sauce and fish, for a minute or two; pass the red-hot salamander over it, and send to table.

535. CRIMPED SKATE, A LA PASCALINE.

TURN the pieces of skate round in the usual manner, boil, drain, and dish them up; then pour over the fish a well-seasoned sauce *à la Pascaline* (No. 15) made rather *piquante;* garnish round with glazed *croutons* of fried bread, on which should be placed a neatly-trimmed piece of the liver, and send to table.

536. SKATE, A LA ROYALE.

BOIL the skate till it is half done, drain it, and after allowing it to cool, cut it into pieces about two inches long, place these in a basin and *marinade* them in oil, vinegar, pepper, and salt. Twenty minutes before dinner, drain the pieces of skate on a napkin, and then having first dipped each piece separately in some frying batter prepared for the purpose, fry them of a fine color in plenty of hogs'-lard, heated for the purpose; dish the skate up in a pyramidal form, sauce round with *Ravigotte* or *Poivrade* sauce, garnish the dish with alternate groups of fried parsley and pieces of the liver, and serve.

537. WHITEBAIT.

THIS very delicious fish is in season during the months of June, July, and August: it is then eaten in the greatest perfection at Greenwich and Blackwall. Owing to the extreme delicacy of this fish, and its very fragile nature, it cannot be conveyed any distance during the season, without injuring its quality, neither can it be kept many hours after it has been taken.

The following is the best method of preparing whitebait for the table.

Drain the fish on a clean napkin, thoroughly absorbing all the water; then roll them in flour, and afterward drop them into some heated frying fat: as soon as they become crisp, drain them on a sieve, and after drying them for a minute or two before the fire, sprinkle on them a little salt, dish them on a napkin, and send to table accompanied by plates of white and brown bread and butter, and quarters of lemon,—to be handed round, with cayenne pepper.

538. SCOLLOPED OYSTERS.

OPEN a sufficient quantity of oysters for the purpose, and put them in a stewpan on the fire to blanch or parboil; after boiling for a few minutes, drain them on a sieve, reserving their liquor to make the sauce with; immerse the oysters in cold water so as to wash off any scum or surf that may adhere to them; take away the beard and gristly substance, and place the oysters thus prepared on a plate, while the sauce is being made in manner following: Into a small stewpan put two ounces of fresh butter, one tablespoonful of flour, a very little pepper, and salt; with a wooden spoon mix the whole thoroughly, moisten with the oyster liquor and half a pint of cream, add a small piece of glaze, and then stir the sauce on the fire till it boils; keep stirring this for about ten minutes, by which time it will be sufficiently reduced to admit of the oysters being added to it; then squeeze in the juice of half a lemon, mix the whole well together, and after putting the oysters in the silver scollop-shells, (or, clean scoured oyster-shells will do,) cover them with fried bread-crumbs. About ten minutes before serving, place them in the oven till they are sufficiently hot to send to table, dish them on a napkin, and serve.

538a. SCOLLOPED OYSTERS ANOTHER WAY.

THE oysters being prepared as set forth in the foregoing recipe, first boil down their liquor to a fourth part of its original quantity, add thereto half a pint of white sauce, the yelks of two eggs, a little grated nutmeg, cayenne pepper, and the juice of half a lemon, a tea-spoonful of essence of anchovies and a similar quantity of Harvey sauce; and, after stirring the whole over the fire for five minutes, the oysters should be mixed in, and then, after being placed neatly in the shells,—finished as directed in the preceding article.

Scolloped muscles, cockles, shrimps, lobsters, or crayfish, may be prepared in like manner; a little essence of anchovies should however be added to the sauce for all these—except muscles and cockles; and for lobsters, the coral should be added also.

REMOVES OF BEEF,

COMPRISING

Braized Roll of Beef, à la Flamande.	Braized Roll of Beef, à la d'Orléans.	
" " à la Printanière.	" " à la Milanaise.	
" " à la Polonaise.	" " à la Richelieu.	
" " à l'Allemande.	" " à la Dauphinoise.	
" " à la Royale.	" " garnished with glazed	
" " à la Windsor.	roots.	
" " à la Claremont.	Braized rump of Beef.	

539. BRAIZED ROLL OF BEEF, A LA FLAMANDE.

TAKE a piece of sirloin of beef, well covered with fat, weighing about twenty pounds; bone it, leaving the fillet adhering to the upper part; *daube* or interlard the fillet in a slanting position, by inserting with a large *daubing* needle some pieces of ham or bacon about a quarter of an inch square and four inches long; then roll the beef up close, and fasten it round with a string so as to secure its shape. Break up the bones and place them with the trimmings at the bottom of a braizing pan ; then place the roll of beef on the bones, and garnish with four carrots, four onions, with a clove stuck in each, four heads of celery, and a fagot of parsley with thyme and a bay-leaf, and two blades of mace ; moisten with half a bottle of Sherry and two glasses of brandy ; set the whole on the stove to simmer for about ten minutes, then add a sufficient quantity of good stock or *consommé*, nearly to cover the beef; place thereon a well-buttered paper, and, after having caused it to boil, set the braizing pan to continue gently boiling on a smothered stove for about five or six hours : the time for this must be regulated by the degree of tenderness of the meat. When the beef is done, drain, trim, and put it into a convenient-sized pan, containing a little of the liquor in which it has been braized ; and with a portion of the remaining part, work some brown sauce for the remove ; boil the rest down, and with this glaze the beef. Place it on a dish, garnish round with alternate groups of turned and glazed carrots and turnips, glazed onions, and Brussels-sprouts ; pour the sauce above alluded to round the dish, glaze the beef, and send to table.

540. BRAIZED BEEF, A LA PRINTANIERE.

PREPARE and braize a piece of sirloin of beef, according to the foregoing directions ; dish it up, and place round it groups of young carrots (turned in their own shape and glazed in the usual manner), asparagus-heads, small buds of cauliflowers, and French-beans, cut in the shape of diamonds, and boiled green ; round the dish place a border of turnips cut in the form of deep saucers, and filled with green peas ; pour some bright *Espagnole* sauce (No. 3) round the remove, glaze the beef, and stick on it five or seven ornamental silver skewers, all of them garnished with carrots, turnips, &c., similar to the centre-skewer in the above wood-cut, and send to table.

541. BRAIZED ROLL OF BEEF, A LA POLONAISE.

BRAIZE the roll of beef as in the previous cases, mask it with some glaze in which beet-root juice has been mixed ; dish the beef up on a bed of braized red cabbage (No. 163), garnish round with alternate groups of glazed small onions, and thoroughly well-boiled beet-root cut into the shape of small pears or half-moons, and glazed ; pour some *Poivrade* sauce (No. 29) round the remove, and serve.

542. BRAIZED ROLL OF BEEF, A L'ALLEMANDE.

BRAIZE the beef in the usual manner, garnish it round with stewed *sauër-kraut* (No. 165), round which place a border of potatoes cut in the shape of large olives, and fried of a fine light color in butter ; sauce round with *Poivrade* or brown sauce, and send to table.

543. BRAIZED ROLL OF BEEF, A LA ROYALE.

PREPARE and braize the roll of beef, as directed for dressing the beef *à la Flamande ;* after trimming and glazing the roll, place it on a dish, and sauce it round with a rich ragout *à la Financière* (No.188) ; garnish round with a border of larded lambs' sweet-breads and whole truffles, placed alternately round the dish, and ornament the roll of beef by inserting six silver *attelets* or skewers garnished as follows :— First run the point of a skewer through a large double cock's-comb, then a large mushroom, a fine truffle, and lastly, a fine crayfish ; use them as directed to ornament the roll of beef, and send to table.

544. BRAIZED ROLL OF BEEF, A LA WINDSOR.

BRAIZE the roll of beef perfectly tender, trim, glaze, and place it on a dish ; garnish round with alternate groups of stewed peas, and potatoes—turned in the shape of large olives, and fried of a fine light color in butter. Clarify and reduce the braize in which the beef has been done, and with it sauce the beef round, reserving part to be sent to table in a sauce-boat, to be handed round with the beef.

545. BRAIZED ROLL OF BEEF, A LA CLAREMONT.

PROCURE about eighteen pounds of sirloin of beef, cut square from the centre ; bone and trim it, and then proceed to *daube** the fillet and upper part of the beef with tongue and the fillets of a pheasant, cut into lengths of about four inches, and a quarter of an inch square in thickness ; roll the beef and secure its shape with string, place it in a braizing-pan with the bones broken small, and the trimmings, three carrots, four onions, celery, a garnished fagot of parsley and green onions, four cloves, and two blades of mace ; moisten with half a bottle of Sherry, and two glasses of brandy, and set the whole to simmer on the stove-fire for about ten minutes ; then add sufficient broth from the stock-pot to nearly cover the beef, place a well-buttered paper on it, cover the pan with its lid, and set the beef to boil gently on a slow fire for about five hours—taking care that, when the liquor has become somewhat reduced in quantity by boiling, the beef should be frequently moistened on the exposed surface, by being basted with the braize. When the beef is done, drain, trim, glaze, and place it on a dish ; pour round it a ragout *à la Claremont,* consisting of a brown sauce, mixed with one-fourth part of brown *purée* of onions and some thin scollops of truffles, mushrooms, and red

---

* To *daube,* is to lard or garnish the inner part of fowls, or any joints of meat, by inserting long strips of ham, bacon, &c., with the aid of a larding-pin.

tongue, the whole to be cut out with a round cutter, about the size of half-a-crown piece; ornament the centre of the surface of the beef with fillets of rabbits *contisés* with tongue and truffle, turned round into the shape of palm leaves, and simmered in a little fresh butter for the purpose;. at each corner insert a silver skewer garnished with a large cock's-comb, a decorated *quenelle,* and a thick scollop of red tongue; place a border of decorated *quenelles* and large crayfish round the edge of the dish, and send to table.

546. BRAIZED ROLL OF BEEF, A LA D'ORLEANS.

PREPARE, braize, and trim the beef as in the foregoing case; thoroughly absorb the oily matter from the surface of the fat, and cover it all over with the following preparation :—

Take two dozen very green pickled gherkins, chop them very fine and put them into a small stewpan; stir them over a quick fire till their moisture be entirely absorbed by the heat, then take the stewpan off the fire, and after allowing the contents to cool, add the yelks of three eggs, pepper, salt, and nutmeg; mix well together, and use as paste, as directed, for the purpose of covering the entire surface of the beef with a coating about a quarter of an inch thick; smooth it over with the blade of a knife dipped in hot water; decorate the centre and ends of the roll of beef with carrots and turnips, French-beans and asparagus-heads, cut and prepared for the purpose, in fancy designs, by placing, for instance, young carrots and turnips cut in the shape of a crescent, alternately side by side so as to form a circle, and in its centre a group of heads of asparagus boiled green, and again round this a border of large marrow-fat peas boiled green; at each end place a row of small carrots and turnips in the shape of small olives, while round the roll of beef thus decorated pour a well-made *Poivrade* sauce (No. 29), garnish round with a border of potato *croquettes* fried of a light color (made in the form of pears, with a stalk of parsley stuck in the point, to resemble the stalk of a pear); glaze the decoration of vegetables slightly with a paste-brush dipped in some thin glaze, so as not to disturb the order of their arrangement, and send to table.

547. BRAIZED ROLL OF BEEF, A LA MILANAISE.

BONE and trim about twenty pounds of the prime cut from the centre of a well-covered sirloin of beef; *daube* the under and upper fillets with ham, season with a little chopped green thyme and winter-savory, minionette, pepper and salt; roll the beef up tight, and secure its shape with string, place it with the trimmings and usual accessories recommended in the foregoing cases, in a braizing pan; moisten with a bottle of red wine and two glasses of brandy, and set the whole to simmer very gently on a slow fire for about twenty minutes; then add a sufficient quantity of good stock, to reach rather better than half way up the beef; place thereon a well-buttered paper, cover with the lid of the pan, and set the whole to braize gently for about five hours— taking care frequently to baste the beef with its liquor. When the beef is done, drain, trim, and glaze it—first straining off the braize, and divesting it of every particle of grease; then clarify, and afterward reduce it to the consistency of thin glaze, to which add half a pot of red-currant jelly, a glass or two of Malaga or fine old Madeira. Dish up the roll of beef, pour this sauce over it, at each end garnish with macaroni dressed with Parmesan cheese, and at the flanks of the dish place groups of *Raviolis* (No. 375) prepared for the purpose, and send to table.

548. BRAIZED ROLL OF BEEF, A LA RICHELIEU.

BRAIZE the roll of beef in exactly the same manner as directed for beef *à la Flamande* (No. 539); when done, drain, trim, glaze, and dish it up; garnish it round with glazed onions, and round the outer circle of the well of the dish, place a border of *quenelles* of pheasant (previously mixed with a little *Soubise* sauce), which, after being first poached in the usual manner, are to be bread-crumbed and fried of a light color; then sauce lightly with the essence in which the beef has been braized (clarified and boiled down to the consistency of half glaze for the purpose). Send some of the essence separately in a sauce-boat, and serve.

549. BRAIZED ROLL OF BEEF, A LA DAUPHINOISE.

FOR this purpose, the roll of beef should be braized sufficiently tender to enable it to be cut with a spoon; it should be allowed to cool in its own liquor, and when nearly cold, drained out carefully on to a dish, trimmed and placed on a deep baking-dish, and then covered over entirely with a coating of thick *Soubise* sauce, thickened with four yelks of eggs : when the sauce has become firmly set on the beef by getting cold, egg it over, and bread-crumb it twice; sprinkle a little clarified butter over the surface of the beef; and about half an hour before serving the dinner, set the beef thus prepared in a very hot oven, that it may be baked of a fine light color; place it on its dish, sauce it round with a brown Italian sauce (No. 12), and garnish it with a border of tomatas prepared *au gratin* (No. 1160), and send to table.

550. BRAIZED ROLL OF BEEF, GARNISHED WITH GLAZED ROOTS.

BRAIZE, trim, glaze, and dish the roll of beef up as directed for Beef *à la Flamande;* garnish it round with young carrots, turnips, and onions, turned and stewed in the usual manner, and placed in alternate groups; sauce the beef with some *Espagnole* or *Poivrade* sauce, and send to table.

551. BRAIZED RUMP OF BEEF.

THIS piece of beef is considered to be the best for braizing, and should be chosen of fine quality for this purpose : rich grained, of a deep bright-red color, and well covered with a thick coating of delicate-looking fat. Bone the beef, and, after having trimmed it, secure its shape with a string, and braize it as directed for braized rolls of beef, following those instructions, according to the manner in which the rump of beef is intended to be dressed; as, for instance, *à la Flamande, à la Printanière, &c., &c., &c.*

BRAIZED AND ROAST FILLETS OF BEEF,

COMPRISING

Fillet of beef, *à la Napolitaine.*
    „   *à la Macédoïne.*
    „   *à la Jardinière.*
    „   with *Chêvreuil* sauce.
    „   *à l'Allemande.*
    „   *au Madère.*

Fillet of Beef, *à la Milanaise.*
    „   *à l'Anglaise.*
    „   *à la Nivernaise.*
    „   *à la Royale.*
    „   *à la Parisiènne.*
    „   *à la Provençale.*

552. FILLET OF BEEF, A LA NAPOLITAINE.

PROCURE a whole fillet of beef, and, with a thin-bladed knife, pare off the sinewy skin which covers it, lard it closely in the usual manner, and prepare it for braizing, as follows :—First, place the trimmings in a narrow oblong braizing-pan on the drainer, then put in the fillet and garnish it round with carrot, celery, a couple of onions with two cloves stuck in each, a fagot of parsley and green onions garnished with thyme and bay-leaf, and two blades of mace ; moisten with a bottle of light white wine, cover the whole with a well-buttered paper, put the lid on the pan, and set the fillet to boil gently on a slow fire, with live embers on the lid, basting the fillet frequently with its own liquor while braizing, which will require about two hours. Toward the latter part of the time, glaze the larding with some thin, light-colored glaze, and set the fillet in the oven to dry the larding, taking care that it does not burn, or get too much colored. In the mean time, strain off the braize, divest it of every particle of grease, and clarify it ; reduce it to one-third of its original quantity, and then add a spoonful of good *Espagnole* sauce (No. 3), two chopped shalots, half a pot of red-currant jelly, and a spoonful of grated horse-radish ; set the whole to boil on the stove-fire for five minutes, after which pass the sauce through a tammy into a *bain-marie*. When about to serve the dinner, place the fillet on a dish, and surround it with groups of macaroni dressed with cheese, in the usual manner, some *raviolis* (No. 375), tossed in a little glaze, and some sultana raisins stewed for ten minutes in a little white wine; glaze the beef over, pour the sauce round the fillet, on which, at each end, and at the centre, with an ornamental skewer, fix a turnip, cut in the shape of a cup, (par-boiled in salt and water colored with cochineal), and filled with grated horse-radish, and send to table; observing that some of the sauce should be sent in a sauce-boat separately.

553. FILLET OF BEEF, A LA MACEDOINE.

TRIM, lard, and prepare a fillet of beef according to the first part of the preceding instructions; moisten it with two ladlefuls of good stock, and proceed to braize the fillet in exactly the same manner; when done, glaze and dish it up. Garnish it round with groups of carrots, turnips, French-beans, asparagus-heads, and buds of cauliflower—the carrots and turnips to be turned or cut into the shape of small olives, or cloves of garlic, the French-beans in the shape of diamonds; and observe that each kind of vegetable should be separately prepared and tossed in a little *Béchamel* or *Allemande* sauce, previously to being placed round the fillet of beef. Sauce round the fillet with the clari-fied and reduced braize in which it has been done, glaze the fillet, and send to table.

554. BRAIZED FILLET OF BEEF, A LA JARDINIERE.

BRAIZE a larded fillet of beef according to the foregoing instructions, and when done, glaze and place it on its dish; garnish it round with alternate groups of turned carrots and turnips, to which give the shape of olives, round balls, diamonds, small half-moons, or any other suitable fancy shape—all which must be previously boiled in broth, with a grain of salt, a little sugar, and a small piece of butter. Intermixed with these, place also some groups of green-peas, French-beans cut in dia-monds, asparagus-heads, and buds of cauliflower. Sauce the fillet of beef round with bright *Espagnole* sauce, mixed with some of the essence in which the fillet has been braized (previously clarified and reduced for this purpose), glaze the fillet and send to table.

555. BRAIZED FILLET OF BEEF, DRESSED AS CHEVREUIL. (ROEBUCK.)

PROCURE part or a whole fillet of beef, as occasion may require, remove the sinewy skin which covers the fat side, trim it neatly, and lard it closely; then lay the fillet for a day or so to steep or pickle in a pan containing a sufficient quantity of cold *marinade* (No. 234), pre-pared for the purpose. Next, when the fillet has become saturated with the *marinade*, drain it, and prepare it for braizing exactly in the same manner as in any one of the preceding cases; moisten with a bottle of Sherry, and braize the fillet of beef in the usual way; when it is done, glaze it well, and place it on its dish. Garnish it round with potatoes turned in the shape of large olives, and fried of a fine light color in clarified butter; sauce the fillet round with a well-made *Chevreuil* sauce (No. 69), with the addition of half the essence in which the beef has been braized, and which, as usual, has been previously clarified and reduced to half glaze for the purpose ; glaze the larding and send to table. If preferred, the fillet may be roasted instead of braized.

556. BRAIZED FILLET OF BEEF, A L'ALLEMANDE.

PREPARE a fillet of beef in every respect according to the foregoing directions, when done, glaze and dish it up ; garnish it round with stewed *sauër-kraut* (No. 165), sauce it with *Poivrade* or *Espagnole* sauce, and send to table.

The fillet of beef *à l'Allemande* may also be garnished with stewed prunes, *quenelles* of potatoes (No. 312), and sauced round with German sweet sauce (No. 61).

557. BRAIZED FILLET OF BEEF, WITH MADEIRA SAUCE.

LARD a fillet of beef, prepare it for braizing in the usual manner, moisten it with a bottle of good Madeira, and then set the fillet to braize gently on a slow fire ; keep basting it frequently with its own liquor, and when done, glaze it and place it on its dish. Garnish it round with a *Jardinière* (No. 143), a *Macédoine* (No. 144), or some nicely-fried potatoes ; clarify the whole of the liquor in which the fillet has been braized, reduce it to the consistency of half glaze, and use it for the purpose of saucing the fillet, and send to table.

558. BRAIZED FILLET OF BEEF, A LA MILANAISE.

BRAIZE a larded fillet of beef in an oval braizing-pan garnished with the usual quantity of vegetables, &c. ; moisten with a bottle of Sherry or Malaga ; when the beef is done, glaze and dish it up, and garnish it round with macaroni prepared as follows :—Boil three-quarters of a pound of macaroni, cut it into two-inch lengths, and put it into a stew-pan containing some scollops of mushrooms, truffles, tongue, and the fillets of one fowl ; to these add a ragout-spoonful of *Béchamel* sauce (No. 5), four ounces of grated Parmesan cheese, and a pat of butter ; season with a little grated nutmeg and minionette pepper, toss the whole well together over the fire until well mixed, and use it as directed. Sauce the fillet round with the essence (clarified in the usual manner), and send the remainder to table in a sauce-boat, to be handed round with the fillet of beef.

559. ROASTED FILLET OF BEEF, A L'ANGLAISE.

PROCURE a good thick fillet of beef, trim and lard it in the usual manner, place it in a large earthen dish, strew over it carrot and onion cut into thin slices, thyme, bay-leaf, and branches of parsley, some thin slices of the pulp of a lemon, and a little minionette pepper ; pour about a gill of salad-oil over the whole, and allow the fillet of beef to steep in this *marinade* for several hours—taking care to turn it over occasionally, so that it may absorb a portion of the oil impregnated with the flavor of the various ingredients contained in this kind of *marinade*.

About an hour and a half before dinner, remove every particle of vegetable from the fillet of beef, run a strong-made iron skewer through it lengthwise, fasten it on the spit by tying it with string at each end, and then put it down to the fire to roast—basting it frequently ; take care that the fire is not too fierce, as in that case the larding will be

scorched, which would spoil not only its appearance, but also injure
the flavor. Toward the last five minutes of the fillet's roasting, and
before it is taken up from the fire, glaze over the larding with some thin
light-colored glaze, twice or thrice, take it off the spit, and dish it up;
garnish it round with small turned potatoes, fried in clarified butter,
placing at each end a *bouquet* of scraped horse-radish; pour a bright
Financière sauce round it (No. 8), glaze the fillet over afresh and send
to table.

560. BRAIZED FILLET OF BEEF, A LA NIVERNAISE.

BRAIZE a larded fillet of beef according to the instructions given for
the fillet of beef *à la Macèdoine* (No. 553); when done, glaze it
brightly, dish it up and garnish it round with a *Nivernaise* (No. 137),
and send to table.

561. BRAIZED FILLET OF BEEF, A LA ROYALE.

CLOSELY lard a thick fillet of beef, *daube* or interlard it with small
square fillets of lean ham, fat bacon, and truffles; prepare it for braizing
with the trimmings and the usual quantity of vegetables, &c., one or
two carcasses of game, and moisten with a bottle of Madeira. Set the
fillet to simmer gently on a slow fire in the usual way, carefully basting
it occasionally with its liquor; when done, glaze it brightly, and afterward dish it up; strain off the braize, clarify and reduce it, then add it
to a *Financière ragout* (No. 188), with which garnish the fillet of beef;
place round it a border of large crayfish, whole truffles, and cock's-
combs, and send to table.

562. ROASTED FILLET OF BEEF, A LA PARISIENNE.

ROAST a larded fillet of beef according to directions given for the
fillet of beef *à l'Anglaise* (No. 559); when done, dish it up, and surround it with alternate groups of green peas, and crayfish tails (tossed
in a little glaze and lobster coral butter, to make them of a bright
scarlet); sauce the fillet round with a rich *Financière* sauce (No. 8),
finished with some cravfish butter, and a little lemon-juice, and send to
table.

563. ROASTED FILLET OF BEEF, A LA PROVENCALE.

STEEP a larded fillet of beef in the *marinade* as directed for the fillet
of beef *à l'Anglaise*, adding to the ingredients therein mentioned, four
cloves of garlic and the pulp of an extra lemon; allow the fillet sufficient time to become thoroughly saturated with the *marinade;* roast
it off, as before directed, glaze and dish it up, garnish it round with
tomatas *au gratin* (No. 1160), and pour round it some sauce *à la Provençale* (No. 25), for making which, use the *marinade* in which the
fillet of beef has been pickled.

Note.—Fillets of beef may also be dressed plain, that is, without
being larded, as some dislike the mixture of fat bacon with beef. In
all other particulars, the directions for dressing braized rumps, rolls
or larded fillets of beef, are to be followed when dressing fillets plain.
For purposes of economy, the fillet of beef should be thus prepared for
braizing : trim the fillet as if intended to be larded, and then cover
the upper or smooth part with layers of beef-suet prepared for the

purpose, by taking some large pieces of suet and placing them between a wet cloth, and with the cutlet-bat flatten them until they do not exceed half an inch in thickness; fasten the layers on the fillet with string, and for braizing the fillet, follow the directions given in the foregoing dishes.

BOILED AND STEWED BRISKETS, EDGEBONES, ROUNDS, AND RIBS OF BEEF,

COMPRISING

Boiled Brisket of Beef, *à l'Anglaise.*	Ribs of Beef, *à la Chasseur.*
” ” *à l'Ecarlate.*	” *à la Piemontaise.*
Stewed Brisket of Beef, *à la Flamande.*	” *à la Mode.*
Edgebone of Beef, *à l'Anglaise.*	” *à la Bourgeoise.*
Round of Beef, *à l'Anglaise.*	” *au Madière.*
” *à la Chasseur.*	” *à la Baden.*

564. BOILED BRISKET OF BEEF, A L'ANGLAISE.

PROCURE a piece of brisket of beef, well covered with fat, and which has been in salt about a week or ten days; wash the beef in cold water, and then place it on a drainer in a large oval braizing-pan; garnish with three carrots, two large onions with two cloves stuck in each, and two heads of celery; pour in sufficient cold water to fill the pan nearly, and set it to boil on the fire. As the scum rises to the surface, take it off with a spoon, and when the beef has been thoroughly skimmed, set the pan down by the side of the stove, to continue gently boiling for about four or five hours—according to the size and weight of the brisket; when the beef is done, take it up on to an earthenware dish, trim, glaze, and then dish it up; garnish it round with plain boiled turnips and carrots, that have been neatly cut into the shape of pears, eggs, or small fluted leaflike shapes; at each end place a group of small suet dumplings, pour some gravy under the beef, and send to table. Some *Piquante* sauce (No. 18), lightly seasoned, should be served in a sauce-boat, to be handed round with the beef.

565. BOILED BRISKET OF BEEF, A L'ECARLATE.

THE brisket of beef, *à l'Ecarlate*, should be prepared according to the foregoing instructions, in every respect—except the salting or curing operation, which must be thus effected:

To six pounds of common salt, add four onces of saltpetre, half a pound of moist sugar, some bruised bay-leaves, thyme, winter-savory, and sweet-marjoram, a dozen cloves, and a few blades of mace: with this mixture rub the piece of brisket of beef for a few minutes every day—for four or five days running; after which, merely turn it over in the brine once a day, for the succeeding five days—altogether making up ten days for salting the beef. The brisket of beef is then ready for use—provided it is to be eaten while hot; but if intended to be eaten cold, the beef should remain in the brine at least a fortnight, by which time only it can be expected to have sufficiently absorbed the flavor of the herbs and spices.

The foregoing instructions apply equally to every kind of salted meat.

566. STEWED BRISKET OF BEEF, A LA FLAMANDE.

PARE off the breast-bone and rough parts adhering to a well-covered piece of fresh brisket of beef; place it on the drainer of a large braizing-pan, garnish with carrots, onions, celery, fagot of parsley, green onions, thyme, and bay-leaf, six cloves, and two blades of mace; moisten with sufficient good broth (from the boiling stock) to cover the beef. Set the pan to boil gently for about five hours; when done, drain the brisket on a dish, trim and place it on a baking-sheet, pour a little broth under it, glaze it well and put it in the oven to dry, and glaze it again; then place the brisket of beef on its dish, garnish it round with alternate groups of turned carrots and turnips (boiled down with *consommé* and a little sugar), Brussels-sprouts, and glazed onions; sauce the beef round with a well-finished *Espagnole* or *Poivrade* sauce, and send to table.

Briskets of beef prepared in the foregoing manner, may also be sent to table in every variety of method described for the preparation of rolls of beef, as wells as rumps and fillets—in their various forms.

567. EDGEBONE OF BEEF, A L'ANGLAISE.

PROCURE a fine edgebone of beef well-covered with rich and delicate-looking fat; take out the kernels, and salt it in the usual manner, by merely rubbing the salt well into the meat; repeat this operation every morning during four days, and then be careful that the beef is turned over in its brine every morning for seven successive days: by this time the edgebone of beef will be ready for use. Next, put it on in cold water, with a couple of carrots and turnips in the pot, and set it to boil gently for about four hours: when done, drain it, trim off the soiled parts of the fat, dish it up, and surround it with alternate groups of well-turned carrots, turnips, summer cabbages, and small suet dumplings; pour gravy under the beef, and send to table.

568. BOILED ROUND OF BEEF, A L'ANGLAISE.

FOLLOW the foregoing directions in every particular—(observing that a round of beef should remain ten days in the brine, and that the time it will require for boiling must necessarily vary, according to the weight of meat); in fact, dress the round of beef according to the old English manner, garnishing it with the same sort of vegetables as directed to be used for the edgebone, and send it to table with some lightly-seasoned *Piquante* sauce, separately in a sauce-boat.

569. BOILED ROUND OF BEEF, A LA CHASSEUR, OR "HUNTING BEEF."*

CURE a round of beef according to the directions given for salt-

---

* The apparently large quantity of ale required to dress a round of beef in this fashion seems at first sight preposterously extravagant; but it should be borne in mind that this, like others of the more expensive kind of dishes which are supposed to be indulged in only by the wealthy, is in point of fact not so extravagant as it appears; inasmuch as that the liquor in which the spiced beef has been boiled, serves to ameliorate the soup which is now so bountifully supplied twice a week to the poor of the adjacent parishes, by the generous owners of the noble mansions throughout the land.

ing a brisket à *l'Ecarlate* ; it will require a fortnight or three weeks thoroughly to impregnate the beef with the flavor of the herbs, spices, &c. When the round of beef is sufficiently salted, put it on to boil in home-brewed ale; as soon as it is done, dish it up with carrots, turnips, baked Spanish onions, summer-cabbages, or Brussels-sprouts, and small suet dumplings—the whole of these to be placed in groups round the beef; pour some gravy under it, and send to table. Rounds of beef prepared in the foregoing manner are more frequently sent to table cold,—for breakfast and luncheon; especially at Christmas time, when they are considered a desirable feature on the sideboard.

570. STEWED RIBS OF BEEF, A LA CHASSEUR.

PROCURE three or four small ribs of beef well covered with fat, saw off the spine-bone close up to the rib-bones, and with the saw shorten the rib-bones to about ten inches; then *daube* or interlard the lean right through with fillets of fat bacon or ham, a quarter of an inch square—seasoned with prepared herb-seasoning (No. 1250). Next, cure the ribs of beef, as described for the preparation of the hunting-beef, and when it is ready, wash the brine off in cold water, place the ribs of beef in a braizing-pan on a drainer, garnish with the bruised carcasses of any sort of game, four carrots, four onions, three heads of celery, and a well-garnished fagot, moisten with half a bottle of Sherry, and sufficient broth to cover the beef. Set the pan on the fire to continue gently boiling for about four hours : when the beef is done, drain, trim, and glaze it, put it in the oven to dry the surface, and glaze it again ; then dish it up, garnish it round with glazed Spanish onions, and carrots—turned in the shape of pears ; sauce the ribs of beef round with a well-finished Madeira sauce (No. 8), and send to table.

It is usual to dress ribs of beef in this manner to be eaten cold ;— for this purpose it is necessary to allow them to cool in their own braize, by which means they are materially benefitted, as they absorb a considerable proportion of the essence—thereby acquiring both flavor and delicacy. When the ribs of beef are cold, take them out of their braize, trim, glaze, and dish them up ; surround them with a border of bright aspic-jelly (to be made from the liquor in which the meat has been braized), and send to table.

571. BRAIZED RIBS OF BEEF, A LA PIEMONTAISE.

TRIM and *daube* with ham and truffles three small ribs of fresh beef; prepare them for braizing with the trimmings, three carrots, three onions, two heads of celery, a garnished fagot of parsley, six cloves, two blades of mace, and two cloves of garlic ; moisten with a bottle of Sherry and a ladleful of broth ; set the beef to boil very gently on a slow fire—with live embers on the lid of the pan—for about four hours, taking care to baste it frequently with its own liquor ; when the beef is done, drain, trim, and glaze, and keep it in the hot closet for a few minutes ; during this time, strain off the liquor in which the beef has been braized, divest it of every particle of fat, clarify it, and then add one-half to a pound of Naples macaroni, previously boiled in water with a little salt and butter, for about ten minutes, and then drained on a sieve, cut into three-inch lengths, and put into a stewpan with a pinch of minionette-pepper; then stew the macaroni for a quarter of an hour longer, by which time it will be done; add a table-spoonful of tomata-paste, two pats of fresh butter, and six ounces of fresh-grated Parmesan cheese; toss the whole well together over the fire, and place the ribs of beef on their dish; surround them with the macaroni thus prepared, glaze the beef afresh, pour into a sauce-boat the remaining half of the clarified braize reduced nearly to the consistency of half glaze, and send to table.

572. SMALL RIBS OF BEEF, A LA MODE.

PREPARE the ribs of beef for braizing according to the foregoing instruction, moisten with half a bottle of Sherry or Madeira and two wine-glassesful of brandy; then set the pan containing the ribs of beef on the stove-fire to simmer for about a quarter of an hour; after which add two ladlefuls of good *consommé*, cover the whole with a buttered paper and the lid, and set the pan again on the fire to continue gently simmering for three or four hours—according to the weight or size of the piece of beef. When done, drain and trim it, place it in a sauta-pan with a little of its own liquor, put it in the oven to dry for a minute or two—previously to glazing it; unless, indeed, it has been already glazed during the latter part of the braizing, which is the better method—frequent basting with its own liquor imparting additional flavor; when glazed, dish the ribs of beef up, and garnish them round with groups of glazed carrots, turnips, and onions; sauce round with the essence in which the beef has been braized, clarified and boiled down to the consistency of half-glaze for the purpose, and send to table.

573. SMALL RIBS OF BEEF, A LA BOURGEOISE.

TRIM three small ribs of beef, *daube* and prepare them for braizing, with their trimmings and the usual complement of vegetables, &c.; moisten with two large ladlefuls of good broth; set the beef to boil very gently on a slow fire till done, which will require about four hours and a half, if the piece of beef be small; taking care to turn it over in its braize occasionally; when the ribs are done, drain, trim, and glaze them; dish them up with a border of glazed carrots, onions, turnips, Brussels-sprouts or stewed cabbages, round them; pour the essence on them, and serve.

574. BRAIZED RIBS OF BEEF, WITH MADEIRA SAUCE.

PREPARE the ribs of beef for braizing in the usual manner, moisten with half a bottle of Madeira and a ladleful of good *consommé*; braize the beef gently for about four or five hours; when done, trim, glaze, and dish it up with alternate groups of fried potatoes in the shape of large olives, and any green vegetables the time of year may afford; use the clarified braize, reduced to an essence, as sauce, and send to table.

575. BRAIZED RIBS OF BEEF, A LA BADEN.

TRIM and *daube* three small ribs of beef with some fillets of lean ham and fat bacon; place them in an oval braizing-pan, garnish with six shalots, a grated stick of horseradish, and a garnished fagot of parsley and green onions; moisten with a bottle of Rhenish wine

FILLETS OF VEAL.197

and a single ladleful of good strong broth, braize the beef gently on a
slow fire, with live embers on the lid of the pan, taking care to baste
the beef frequently with its own liquor; when done, glaze and dish it
up; strain the braize through a silk sieve into a stewpan, take off all
the fat, add a small pot of red-currant jelly, the grated rind of two
oranges, and the juice of four; reduce the whole to the consistency of
sauce, pour it round the beef, garnish with a border of *quenelles* of
pototoes (No. 312), glaze the beef afresh, and send to table.

Braized ribs of beef may also be sent to table in a variety of other
forms; as, for instance, *à l'Anglaise, à la Milanaise, à la Macédoine,
à la Royale*, &c., for which see Braized Rolls of Beef.

REMOVES OF VEAL,

COMPRISING

Roast Fillet of Veal, *à l'Anglaise.*
    „   „   *à la Macédoine.*
    „   „   *à la Jardinière.*
Roast Neck of Veal, *à la Crême.*
    „   „   *à la Montmorency.*
    „   „   *à la Dreux.*
    „   „   *à la D'Uxelles.*
    „   „   *à l'Ecarlate.*
    „   „   *à la Royale.*
Cushion of Veal, *à la St. George.*
    „   „   *à la Financière.*
    „   „   *à la Macédoine.*

Cushion of Veal, *à la Jardinière.*
Roast Loin of Veal, *à la Monglas.*
    „   „   *à la Dauphine.*
    „   „   *à la Royale.*
    „   „   *à la Financière.*
    „   „   *à la Crême.*
Breast of Veal, *à l'Anglaise.*
    „   *à la Bourgeoise.*
    „   *à la Windsor.*
    „   *à la Financière.*
    „   *à la Romaine.*
    „   *à la Royale.*

576. ROAST FILLET OF VEAL, A L'ANGLAISE.

VEAL, to be in perfection, should, if possible, be procured fresh
killed, as it does not improve either in flavor or color by being kept.
Take out the bone from a good fat fillet of veal, and with the cutlet-
bat, flatten the udder so as to lengthen it out; make a deep incision
between the udder and the fillet with a knife, and fill it with about
1 lb. of well-seasoned stuffing (No. 662); sew it up with small twine,
wrap the udder tightly round the fillet, and secure its shape with
skewers and twine; spit the fillet in the usual manner, cover it well
with buttered thick white paper, roast it about two hours and a half;
just before it is done, take off the paper, and, after first shaking some
flour over it from a dredger, baste the veal with a little fresh butter,
and froth it; then dish it up, pour round it some light-brown sauce
incorporated with 4 oz. of fresh butter, some essence of mushrooms,
and a little lemon-juice, or else use No. 82: garnish round with potato
croquettes, and send to table.

577. ROAST FILLET OF VEAL, A LA MACEDOINE.

ROAST a fillet of veal according to the foregoing directions, glaze
and dish it up, garnish it round with a *Macédoine* of such vegetables
the season of the year may afford; sauce round with *Suprême* or
Béchamel, and send to table.

578. ROAST FILLET OF VEAL, A LA JARDINIERE.

PREPARE the fillet of veal as before described, dish it up, and garnish it round with groups of turned carrots and turnips, small heads of cauliflower, French-beans, cut into diamonds, green-peas, and asparagus-heads ; sauce with half glaze, or a well-finished *Espagnole* sauce, and send to table.

579. ROAST NECK OF VEAL, A LA CREME.

PROCURE a neck of white fat veal, saw off the scrag and spine-bones, shorten the ribs to four inches in length, run a stout iron skewer through the neck of veal, lengthwise, and then secure it on the spit by tying it with string at each end ; about an hour and a quarter before dinner, put it down to roast, baste it frequently, and about twenty minutes before taking the veal off the spit, baste it with some good *Béchamel* sauce, made with plenty of cream. As in course of roasting the sauce dries on the veal, keep adding a fresh coating, until a light-colored, delicate crust is produced all over the meat ; then take it off the spit with great care, in order that the crust may not be disturbed ; dish it up, pour a good cream *Béchamel* sauce (No. 6) under it, garnish it round with groups of French-beans cut in diamonds and buds of cauliflower, and send to table.

580. BRAIZED NECK OF VEAL, A LA MONTMORENCY.

TRIM a neck of white veal, according to the directions given in the preceding article ; then, with a thin long-bladed knife, pare off the skin and sinew which cover the fillet part of the neck, leaving the ribs well covered ; lard the part which has been trimmed as closely and neatly as possible, and prepare it for braizing as follows :

Strew the bottom of the drainer of an oval braizing-pan with three carrots, three onions, two heads of celery, and a garnished fagot ; cover the vegetables with thin layers of fat bacon, and then put in the neck of veal ; lay the trimmings round it, and moisten with two ladlesful of good veal stock ; put a buttered paper on the top, cover with the lid, upon which place live embers of charcoal, and set it to braize gently on a slow fire, taking care to baste it frequently with its own liquor. When it is done, which will require about three hours, glaze it brightly, and dish it up ; garnish with a white *ragout* of small *quenelles*, truffles, mushrooms, and cocks'-combs ; then place round the *ragout* a border of lambs' sweetbreads, larded, and large *quenelles* of fowl, decorated with tongue, and send to table.

581. NECK OF VEAL, A LA DREUX.

TRIM a neck of vea... *daube* or interlard it through the fillet with some truffles, tongue, and fat bacon ; first cut these into three-inch lengths, by a quarter f an inch square, and then introduce them into the fillet part of the neck of veal, without showing through the skin which covers it ; it should then be braized according to the directions in the foregoing article, and when done, glazed, and dished up. Garnish with a white *ragout* of scollops of tongue and mushrooms, and round this place a border of large crayfish, and glazed whole truffles ; glaze the neck of veal, and send to table.

582. NECK OF VEAL, A LA D'UXELLES.

PREPARE a neck of veal in every particular the same as described in the foregoing article, braize it, and allow it partly to cool in its own stock ; drain, trim, and spread a coating of thickly-reduced *d'Uxelles* sauce (No. 16) over it; when the sauce has become set, proceed to bread-crumb the neck of veal in the usual manner with beaten egg and bread-crumbs, observing that one-fourth part of grated Parmesan cheese should be introduced into the bread-crumbs used for the purpose. Place the neck of veal on a buttered baking-sheet, and three-quarters of an hour before dinner-time, put it in the oven, and bake it of a fine bright light-brown color : during this part of the process, be careful to sprinkle a little clarified fresh butter over the bread-crumbed surface of the veal, in order to prevent it from drying or burning. When the neck of veal is done, place it on a dish, garnish round with a *Toulouse ragout* (No. 187), and send to table.

583. NECK OF VEAL, A L'ECARLATE.

TRIM and lard a neck of veal in the usual manner, mark it for braizing according to the instructions set forth for the preparation of neck of veal *à la Montmorency*, and braize it in a similar manner; dish it up, garnish it round with a border of circular scollops of tongue that have been glazed ; sauce round with either *Suprême*, *Allemande*, or *Béchamel* sauce, and send to table.

584. NECK OF VEAL, A LA ROYALE.

TRIM and braize a neck of veal, and afterward let it get partially cool in its own braize ; drain it on an earthen dish, and mask it entirely with a coating of thick and well-seasoned *Allemande* sauce ; as soon as the sauce has become set upon the neck of veal, bread-crumb it with egg and bread-crumbs, in which introduce a fourth part of grated Parmesan cheese ; place it on a buttered baking-dish, three-quarters of an hour before dinner, and put it in the oven to bake. When done, dish it up, garnish round with a *Toulouse ragout*, surround the whole with a border of *quenelles*, decorated with truffles, and large crayfish ; place a heart sweet-bread (decorated with pieces of the tip of a tongue, cut into the shape of large hob-nails, and inserted in circular rows in the sweet-breads, previously to their being simmered in a little white braize) at each end of the dish, glaze the crayfish lightly, and send to table.

Note.—Necks of veal, either braized or roasted plain, or larded and braized, may, in addition to the foregoing, be sent to table garnished with a *Macédoine* of vegetables, a *Jardinière*, potato *croquettes*, mushrooms, or tomatas *au gratin* (in the last two cases, the neck of veal must be sauced with *Espagnole*, *Poivrade*, or brown Italian sauce), *à la Milanaise*, *à la Financière*, &c., &c.

585. NOIX OR CUSHION OF VEAL, A LA ST. GEORGE.

THE *noix*, or cushion, is that part of a leg of veal to which the udder adheres. In order to separate it from the round, or fillet, the leg should be placed on the table, with the knuckle from you, then with the left hand, take hold of the upper part of the fillet of veal, and with the right insert the point of a knife into the separation which divides the *noix*, or cushion, from the under part of the fillet; cut the *noix* away, following the separation right through, round to the knuckle, terminating at the left, under the udder, which must be left adhering to the *noix*.

Pare off the sinewy parts from the *noix,* trim the udder without reducing its size, and then, with a sharp pointed-knife, make a very slight incision in a circular direction on the surface of the *noix*, round the inner edge of the udder; next remove the outer part with a knife, trimming it smooth and neatly; lard the trimmed part closely with fat bacon, in the usual manner, and prepare the *noix* for braizing as follows :—First place at the bottom of a large *fricandeau* or oval stew-pan, on the drainer thereof, some sliced carrots, a head of celery, two onions, with a clove stuck in each, and a garnished fagot; cover the whole with thin layers of fat bacon, and then put in the *noix* of veal; surround it with the trimmings, and moisten with half a bottle of Sherry or Madeira, and a sufficient quantity of good stock, barely to reach the surface of the veal; cover with a well-buttered white paper, and set it to boil on the stove; place the lid on the pan, and put it on a slow fire, or in the oven, to braize gently for about four hours (with live embers on the lid), remembering to baste the larding frequently with the liquor, in order to moisten the veal and glaze it of a bright color; the udder should be covered with thin layers of fat bacon, to preserve its whiteness during the braizing. When the *noix* is done, drain and glaze it, remove the layers of bacon, and dish it up; garnish it round with groups of button-mushrooms, small *quenelles* of fowl (colored with crayfish butter), cocks'-combs and kernels, and turned truffles tossed in glaze; surround these with a border of lambs' sweet-breads, one-half of which should be larded, and the others, *contisés* with tongue, placed alternately; stick four silver skewers, each garnished with a large double cocks'-comb, a large truffle, mushroom and crayfish, into the *noix*, sauce with a rich Madeira sauce (No. 8), and send to table.

586. NOIX OF VEAL, A LA FINANCIERE.

PREPARE and braize a *noix* or cushion of veal in every respect the same as the foregoing; the wine may, however, if thought proper, be omitted ; when the *noix* is done, glaze and drain it, dish it up, pour a rich *Financière ragout* (No. 188) under it, garnish round with a border of *quenelles* and crayfish, and send to table.

587. NOIX OF VEAL, A LA MACEDOINE.

PREPARE the *noix* of veal as in the foregoing cases, dish it up, garnish it with a *Macédoine* of carrots, turnips, green-peas, asparagus-heads and cauliflower-buds, tossed in some good *Allemande* sauce, with a pinch of sugar, and the glaze produced from the small carrots and turnips, place round these a border of small artichoke-bottoms, filled alternately with green-peas, small carrots, and turnips; glaze the larded part of the *noix*, and send to table.

588. NOIX OF VEAL, A LA JARDINIERE.

THE *noix*, or cushion of veal, must be first trimmed, larded, and braized, according to the directions given for the *noix à la Financière ;* when done, dish it up, and garnish it round with a *Jardinière*, or garnish of small roots and vegetables, composed as follows :—Turn some carrots and turnips in the shape of either small olives, diamonds, corks, or cloves of garlic, &c., and boil them separately in *consommé* with a very small piece of fresh butter, a pinch of sugar, and a grain of salt, observing that the turnips must be kept white, and that the carrots should be boiled down and rolled in their glaze : prepare also some small heads of cauliflower, green peas, French-beans cut into diamonds, asparagus-heads, and small new potatoes ; place these vegetables round the *noix*, in alternate groups, sauce with an *Espagnole* sauce, or else with the essence in which the *noix* has been braized,—first clarified, then reduced to half glaze, and added to a well-finished *Espagnole* sauce ; glaze the larded part of the *noix*, and send to table.

In addition to the foregoing methods of dressing *noix*, or cushions of veal, for the table, they may, after being first prepared and braized (either larded or stuck with circular rows of truffles, cut in the shape of large hob-nails, and inserted in the semicircular lean part of the *noix*), be served with a *Napolitain, Milanese*, or *Chipolata ragout*, with tomatas *au gratin*, potato *croquettes*, and sauced with *Béchamel* sauce, with stewed peas, or asparagus-peas, tossed in a little *Allemande* sauce, with a pat of butter, a pinch of sugar, and a little nutmeg.

589. ROAST LOIN OF VEAL, A L'ANGLAISE.

ORDER a loin of veal to be cut without the chump end, and with the skirt left on ; trim it square, and placing the veal stuffing (No. 662) in an incision made in the flap part for that purpose, wrap the flap, or skirt-piece, round tight, so as to secure the kidney-fat ; fasten it with skewers and string, cover it with two sheets of buttered paper, to be tied on with string, and place the loin of veal in a cradle-spit to roast ; or a common spit may be used. If the loin of veal be of the usual size, weighing about 10 lbs., it will require about two hours and a half to roast it ; when nearly done, take off the paper, shake some flour over it with a dredger-box, and afterward froth it over with 4 oz. of fresh butter, previously put to melt in a spoon, in the dripping-pan, before the fire ; as soon as the veal has acquired a fine light color, and the butter and flour have frothed up, take it off the spit, and dish it up : pour some brown melted butter under it (No. 32), and send to table

590. ROAST LOIN OF VEAL, A LA MONGLAS.

ROAST off a loin of veal, according to the foregoing directions : next, with a sharp knife, make an incision two inches deep along the sides and ends of the loin, and endeavor to cut out the square piece without tearing the meat, the joint resembling an oblong case. The fillet thus taken out, should be cut into thin round scollops, and put into a stewpan with an equal quantity of scollops of tongue and mushrooms : to these add a *ragout* spoonful of good *Béchamel* sauce, and with this mixture fill the loin of veal, previously put on a buttered baking-sheet ; smooth the top over with the blade of a knife, and cover the whole with very fine bread-crumbs, fried with butter, of a light color, and mixed with a third part of Parmesan cheese ; sprinkle a little melted fresh butter over it, and set it in the oven to get hot, salamander it over and dish it up ; garnish with a white *Toulouse ragout* (No. 187), and place round a border of *croquettes* of veal, or sweetbread : at each corner of the loin stick an ornamental silver skewer garnished with a large cock's-comb, mushroom, decorated *quenelle*, crayfish, and truffle; glaze the sides of the loin of veal, and send to table.

591. LOIN OF VEAL, A LA DAUPHINE.

PROCURE a loin of very white veal, cut square, with the whole of the flap, or skirt, left on; bone it entirely, taking care, at the same time, to divest it of every portion of sinew; *daube* or interlard the lean part of the fillet with small fillets of tongue, or ham: the veal must then be laid square on the table, and with some *quenelle* force-meat of chickens (mixed with chopped parsley and mushrooms), spread the whole of the inner part about an inch thick; the kidney and fat should then be replaced in the centre, the loin rolled up tight, and its pillowlike shape be secured with small iron skewers, and fastened with string. Then put it in a large oval braizing-pan, on the drainer; garnish with the trimmings, a couple of carrots, onions, celery, and garnished fagot of parsley and green onions, two blades of mace, and four cloves; moisten with two large ladlesful of good *consommé*, cover with an oval of double paper, well-buttered, put the lid on, and then set the pan to boil on the stove-fire; after which, put it to braize in the oven, or on a slow fire, with live embers on the lid; baste the veal frequently with its own liquor, and when it is done, drain, trim, and mask it all over with a coating of the following mixture :—To six yelks of eggs, add 2 oz. of fresh butter, melted, and two tablespoonsful of *Béchamel* sauce, season with nutmeg, pepper, and salt, mix this well together, and use it as directed above. Cover the whole with very fine bread-crumbs, mixed with a third proportion of grated Parmesan cheese, sprinkle some drops of melted, or oiled butter, over it, and placing the loin of veal on a buttered baking-sheet, put it in the oven to bake of a light-brown color; when done, dish it up, pour round it a Parisian *ragout* (No. 203), and garnish with a border of *quenelles* of veal, or fowl, decorated with truffles, and send to table.

592. LOIN OF VEAL, A LA ROYALE.

PREPARE and braize a loin of veal, as directed in the preceding article; when done, allow it partially to cool in its own braize, then strain it on the drainer of the braizing-pan, and absorb any grease there may be on it with a clean napkin; cover it all over with a *quenelle* farce of veal, mixed with a little lobster coral; decorate the ends and centre with a bold design, using for the purpose some black truffles, in order that the decoration may show well on the scarlet surface. Next, place the loin of veal in a large oval braizing-pan with just sufficient *consommé* to bathe it, to the depth of an inch, cover the loin with very thin layers of fat bacon, or, in lieu thereof, a well-buttered oval covering of paper; set it in the oven, or on a moderate stove-fire, with live embers on the lid, to boil or simmer gently for about three-quarters of an hour, when it will be done. Then drain the veal, and divest it of the bacon or paper used to cover it; pour round it a *ragout* of button-mushrooms, small *quenelles* of fowl, cock's-combs and kernels; garnish with a border of large truffles and crayfish, glaze the loin of veal with thin, light-colored glaze, and send to table.

Note.—This remove may also be decorated with ornamental skewers garnished with a piece of red tongue, cut in the shape of a cock's-comb, a large double white cock's-comb, a mushroom, and a red *quenelle*, ornamented with truffle.

593. ROAST LOIN OF VEAL, A LA FINANCIERE.

PROCURE a loin of veal, cut square without the chump, and with the flap, or skirt, left on ; bone it carefully, truss it tightly in the shape of a pillow, and after first laying the fillet bare, by paring off the whole of the skin and sinew which covers it, lard it closely, as you would a *fricandeau*. When the loin is so far prepared, get it ready for braizing in a large oval braizing-pan, with carrot, onion, celery, garnished fagot, two blades of mace, and four cloves; moisten with two ladlesful of good stock, cover with an oval of paper, well-buttered, place the lid on the pan with live embers on it, and then set the veal to braize gently on the fire, taking care to baste it frequently with its own liquor. When done, drain, glaze, and dish it up ; pour round it a rich brown *Financière ragout* (No. 188), garnish with a border of plain *quenelles*, and crayfish, and send to table.

594. ROAST LOIN OF VEAL, A LA CREME.

To prepare this, follow the directions given for dressing neck of veal *à la Crème* (No. 579) ; garnish in the same manner, and send to table.

595. ROAST BREAST OF VEAL, A L'ANGLAISE.

FIRST take the tendons out of the breast of veal intended to be dressed, and reserve them for an *entrée* ; then bone it completely, cut the ends square, and trim it ; place about 1 lb. of well-seasoned veal-stuffing (No. 662) along the centre of the inner part, roll the veal up tight, so as to secure the stuffing in the middle; fasten it with string and small skewers. About an hour and a half before dinner-time, spit the breast of veal, cover it with buttered paper, and put it down to roast ; when done, dish it up, pour round it either some brown melted butter (No. 82), light *Espagnole* sauce, or *Béchamel*, and send to table.

596. BREAST OF VEAL, A LA BOURGEOISE.

BONE, trim, and roll a breast of veal, according to the preceding instructions ; prepare it an oval stewpan, with 4 oz. of fresh butter, and set it to simmer on a moderate fire, until it becomes colored all over ; then add a garnished fagot of parsley and green onions, moisten with a large ladleful of good stock, and put it to braize gently on the stove-fire, or in the oven ; half an hour after, add two dozen small carrots, nicely turned, and in another half hour, add as many heads of middle-sized onions, a pinch of sugar, and a little salt. When the veal is done, take it up, and after taking away the strings and skewers, put it on a baking-sheet in the oven and glaze it ; dish it up, garnish round with the glazed carrots and onions, and after removing all the fat from the surface of the stock, or essence of the veal, and reducing it down to the consistency of half-glaze, use it to sauce the breast of veal, and send to table.

597. BREAST OF VEAL, A LA WINDSOR.

BONE and trim a breast of veal, lay it on the table, and after spreading the inner part with *quenelle* force-meat of veal or rabbits, at least an inch thick, place some square fillets of boiled tongue lengthwise, and between the fillets of tongue put some pieces of black truffles, cut square to match the size of the pieces of tongue; then roll up the breast of veal carefully, secure its shape with the aid of small iron skewers and string, and to prevent the force-meat from escaping, cover the ends with layers of fat bacon. Put the veal thus prepared into an oval braizing-pan, with the trimmings and the usual complement of roots, &c., moisten with two ladlesful of good stock, and set it to braize gently on a slow fire ; when done, drain, glaze, and dish it up, garnish round with French-beans cut in diamonds—which, after being boiled green, must be dressed with a spoonful of *Béchamel* sauce, a little minionette-pepper, nutmeg, salt, fresh butter, and lemon-juice ; round these place a border of young carrots nicely glazed, and send to table.

The braize in which the breast of veal is done should be divested of grease and clarified, and after being reduced to half glaze served separately in a sauce-boat.

598. ROAST BREAST OF VEAL, A LA FINANCIERE.

TRIM, stuff, and truss a breast of veal as directed for the preparation of a breast of veal *à l'Anglaise,* roast it off in the same manner, dish it up, and surround it with a rich *Financière ragout* (No. 188), and send to table.

599. ROLLED BREAST OF VEAL, A LA ROMAINE.

PREPARE a breast of veal as for *à la Windsor*, and braize it accordingly ; when done, glaze and dish it up, garnish it with *lasagnes* (No. 265) prepared as macaroni, surround the whole with a border of rice *croquettes*, made with rice boiled in *consommé*, and to which should be added a little *Allemande* sauce, grated Parmesan cheese, nutmeg, and minionette pepper ; and when the preparation is cold, mould the *croquettes* according to taste, bread-crumb and fry them of a light color, and use them as directed. Send the remove to table, accompanied with a sauce-boat containing Sicilian sauce (No. 60).

600. ROLLED BREAST OF VEAL, A LA ROYALE.

FOR this preparation, follow the directions given for loin of veal *à la Royale.*

Note.—In addition to the foregoing methods of preparing breasts of veal for the table, they may, after being either roasted or braized, also be garnished with a *Jardinière* or *Macédoine* of vegetables, with stewed peas, or with a *ragout à la* Claremont, *à la* Toulouse, *à la Chipolata*, &c. &c., as convenience or fancy may suggest.

REMOVES OF LEGS, LOINS, AND NECKS OF MUTTON,

COMPRISING

Boiled Leg of Mutton, à l'Anglaise.	Necks of Mutton, à l'Anglaise.
Braized „ with roots.	„ à l'Irlandaise.
„ „ à la Provençale.	„ à la Jardinière.
„ „ à la Soubise.	„ larded with Poivrade
„ „ à la Bretonne.	sauce.
„ „ à la Jardinière.	„ à l'Allemande.
Braized Saddle of Mutton, à la Macédoine.	„ à la Soubise.

601. BOILED LEG OF MUTTON, A L'ANGLAISE.

SELECT a leg of Southdown mutton, rather fat, and not kept above three or four days; trim it, and put it on to boil in a stock-pot or braizing-pan, filled up with cold water; when it boils, remove the scum, and put it on the side of the stove to continue gently boiling for about two hours and a half: a handful of salt and a couple of turnips and carrots should be put into the pot to boil with the leg. When the mutton is done, drain and dish it up, garnish it round with mashed turnips, dressed with a little sweet cream, a pat of butter, pepper and salt: mould the mashed turnips in the shape of large eggs—with a table-spoon, and place these closely round the leg of mutton, introducing between each spoonful of mashed turnips, a carrot nicely turned, that has been boiled, either with the mutton, or in some broth separately: pour some gravy under it, put a paper ruffle on the bone, and send it to table, accompanied with a sauce-boat full of caper-sauce (No. 91).

602. BRAIZED LEG OF MUTTON, GARNISHED WITH ROOTS.

TRIM a leg of Southdown or Scotch mutton, interlard it with fillets of ham or bacon cut a quarter of an inch square and about six inches long, seasoned with pepper and salt, a little grated nutmeg and some chopped parsley; pare off the ends of ham, &c., and place the leg of mutton in an oval braizing-pan with two carrots, a head of celery, a couple of onions, four cloves, and two blades of mace; moisten with a glass of brandy, and two large ladlefuls of fresh stock, cover with an oval buttered paper and put on the lid; then set the braizing-pan on the fire to boil gently for about four hours, from time to time moistening the mutton with its liquor, and keeping a continual supply of live embers on the lid of the pan. When done, take it up on to a deep baking-sheet, with a little of its own liquor, and put in the hot closet till wanted. In the mean time, strain off the braize, divest it of all the fat, clarify it in the usual manner, and when strained, reduce it to the consistency of half glaze, and set it aside in a small bain-marie. Then glaze the leg of mutton nicely, and place it on its dish; garnish it round with alternate groups of young carrots and turnips turned and boiled in broth as usual, for the purpose, and afterward boiled down in their own glaze, also some glazed young onions; pour the clarified essence under the leg of mutton, put the ruffle on the bone, and send to table.

603. BRAIZED LEG OF MUTTON, A LA PROVENCALE.

BONE a leg of four-year old mutton, commencing at the thigh bone, by detaching the meat from round it with a knife, and throwing it back right up to the joint of the leg-bone; then cut the sinewy ligatures, and remove the thigh-bone entirely; saw off the shank and scrape the end of the bone remaining in the leg as in preparing a cutlet. Then interlard the interior with seasoned *lardoons* or fillets of ham or fat bacon, introduce the *Provençale* stuffing (described below), and sew the hollow opening whence the bone has been extracted, with small twine; place the leg of mutton in a braizing-pan with carrots, turnips, celery, six cloves, two blades of mace, two garnished fagots, and six cloves of garlic; moisten with half a bottle of Sherry, and two large ladlefuls of good fresh stock, cover with an oval of buttered paper and the lid; set the pan on the stove to boil, and then put it on a small stove-fire, with live embers on the lid, and allow it to continue gently simmering for about four hours; taking care to moisten it frequently with its own liquor. When it is done, take it up on to a baking-sheet with some of its own liquor, and set it in the hot closet for a few minutes. Strain the remainder of the liquor through a sieve, and remove all the fat, clarify it, strain the essence through a napkin, and reduce it to half glaze, and add it to some *Gasconne* sauce (No. 68). Then dish up the mutton, garnish it round with tomatas or mushrooms dressed *au gratin* (No. 1160), pour the *Gasconne* sauce under the remove, and send to table.—The *Provençale* stuffing for the leg of mutton is to be made as follows:

Chop half a pottle of mushrooms very fine, and put them into a small stewpan; to these add some chopped parsley and shalot, with an equal quantity of grated lean and fat ham, and a little grated lemon-peel: season with pepper, salt, and nutmeg; set the whole on the fire and stir it with a wooden spoon for five minutes, that the watery parts of the mushrooms may evaporate; add the yelks of four eggs, and after setting the yelks of eggs in the fine-herbs, by stirring the whole on the fire, add them to some *quenelle* force-meat made with the fillets of a partridge, mix these well together, and use the stuffing as directed above.

604. BRAIZED LEG OF MUTTON, A LA SOUBISE.

BONE a leg of mutton, and lard it as in the foregoing case, stuff it with some *quenelle* force-meat, made with game, and secure the stuffing with twine. Then prepare the leg of mutton for braizing with a couple of carrots and onions, a head of celery, and garnished fagot, four cloves, and two blades of mace; moisten with two large ladlesful of common stock, cover these with buttered paper, then put on the lid, and set it on a moderate fire to braize gently for about four hours: taking care to moisten it frequently with its liquor. When the mutton is braized perfectly tender, take it up on to a baking-sheet with some of the liquor in which it has been braized, and put it in the oven to finish glazing. In the mean time strain off and clarify the remainder of the liquor, and keep it in a small *bain-marie;* and after having glazed the mutton brightly, dish it up on a bed of well-made *Soubise purée* of onion (No. 119), garnish round with potato *croquettes*, and send to table.

The clarified essence, after being reduced to half glaze, should be sent to table in a sauce-boat to be served with the mutton when carved; if poured round the mutton, it would mix with the *Soubise* sauce.

605. BRAIZED LEG OF MUTTON, A LA BRETONNE.

PREPARE and braize a leg of mutton as directed in the foregoing case; when done, glaze and dish it up on a bed of white *haricòt*-beans dressed *à la Brétonne* (No. 1186); garnish it round with a border of potatoes cut in the shape of large olives, and fried in butter, of a light color; ornament the bone with a paper ruffle, and send to table.

606. BRAIZED LEG OF MUTTON, A LA JARDINIERE.

BONE and braize a leg of mutton according to the preceding directions; and when done, glaze and dish it up; garnish it round with alternate groups of prepared small carrots, turnips, cauliflowers, French beans cut in diamonds, small new potatoes, cucumbers, asparagus-heads, and green peas—the whole, or any part of these, according to the season. Pour round the mutton some *Espagnole* sauce in which has been incorporated, after reduction, the clarified essence in which the mutton has been braized; put on a ruffle, and send to table.

Note.—In addition to the foregoing garnishes for braized legs of mutton, they may also be appropriately served with new potatoes *à la Maître d'Hôtel*, fresh *haricòt*-beans, stewed peas, and a border of young carrots glazed, artichoke bottoms cut in quarters, and tossed in *Allemande* sauce, or with a *Macédoine* of vegetables (No. 143).

607. BRAIZED SADDLE OF MUTTON, A LA MACEDOINE.

PROCURE a well-covered saddle of mutton, and extract the spine-bone with the knife, without injuring the fillets, or perforating any part of the fat which covers them; trim the tail end quite round, cut the flaps square, season the inner part of the saddle with pepper and salt, and having rolled up each flap or skirt piece, so as to give it a tight and neat appearance, secure its shape by passing some string round it several times. After this, the mutton should be prepared for braizing with carrots, onions, celery, garnished fagots, cloves, and mace; moisten with a sufficient quantity of good stock, to merely cover the mutton; place a buttered paper and the lid over all, set the braizing-pan on a moderate fire, and after it has boiled, let it continue gently braizing for about four hours—carefully basting it frequently with its own liquor. When it is done, take it up on to a baking-sheet, and put it in the oven to dry the moisture from the surface, preparatory to its being glazed; then dish it up, and garnish it round with prepared small vegetables, such as carrots, turnips, cauliflowers, French-beans, cucumbers, asparagus-heads, small new potatoes, and green-peas: each separately tossed in a little *Allemande* sauce (after being first prepared in the usual manner, and the carrots and turnips boiled down in their glaze, as also the cucumbers), pour some *Allemande* sauce round the saddle of mutton, and send to table.

Note.—Instead of saucing this remove with *Allemande, Espagnole*

may be used, if preferred, or even the clarified and reduced essence in
which the mutton has been braized ; but it is essential that the vegetables intended to be used for garnishing should be dressed with *Allemande* or *Béchamel* sauce.

Saddles of mutton prepared and braized according to the foregoing
instructions may also be sent to table in all the varieties described for
braized legs of mutton.

608. BOILED NECKS OF MUTTON, A L'ANGLAISE.

SAW off the scrag of two necks of mutton, and shorten the rib-bones
to four inches in length ; next, detach the spine-bone from the fleshy
part of the neck, and afterward saw off the whole of the spine adhering
to the base of the ribs ; pare the fat smooth, and about two hours
before dinner-time, put them on to boil in a stewpan with water, a
little salt, and two or three carrots and turnips.   When they are done,
dish them up so as that the uncovered ends of the rib-bones may fall
in between each other—representing a *chevaux-de-frize.*   Garnish
round with mashed turnips, and with turned carrots, between each
spoonful of the mashed turnips, or else placed round in a row.

Send two sauce-boats filled with gravy and caper-sauce (No. 91).

609. BRAIZED NECK OF MUTTON, A L'IRLANDAISE.

TRIM two necks of mutton as directed in the previous article, put
them to braize in an oval stewpan with carrot, onion, celery, and garnished fagot ; moisten with common stock, and put them to boil on the
stove ; after which set them by the side of a moderate fire, and while
the necks of mutton are being braized, turn two or three dozen potatoes in the shape of small eggs, and place them in a stewpan with half
a dozen small onions ; season with pepper and salt, moisten with a
ladleful of broth, and put them on a moderate fire to boil gently :
taking care that the potatoes are kept as whole as possible, although
they must be thoroughly boiled.   When the necks of mutton are done,
take them up, trim them, if necessary, and dish them up as directed
in the foregoing article ; strain the broth in which the mutton has
been boiled, remove all the grease from its surface, and reduce it to
half glaze : add part of it to the potatoes, and with these garnish the
necks of mutton round neatly, pour the essence under, glaze them, and
send to table.

610. BRAIZED NECK OF MUTTON, A LA JARDINIERE.

TRIM two necks of mutton, and prepare them for braizing with carrot, onion, celery, fagot, four cloves, and two blades of mace ; moisten
with two ladlesful of stock, cover with an oval piece of buttered paper,
and the lid ; put them to braize gently on a moderate fire for about
two hours and a half : when done, glaze and dish them up, giving them
an appearance of *chevaux-de-frize;* garnish them round with a well-
prepared *Jardinière* of every variety of small vegetables in season,
sauce them with *Espagnole* sauce, and send to table.

611. BRAIZED NECKS OF MUTTON LARDED—AS ROEBUCK, WITH POIVRADE SAUCE.

FOR the preparation of this remove, it is necessary that the necks
of mutton be trimmed as directed for braizing, and afterward that

the upper part of the fillet be laid bare without loosening it from the bones; they must then be larded closely as a *fricandeau*, and put to steep in a cold *marinade* (No. 234), for at least twenty-four hours. It will be readily understood that this must be attended to a day before the necks of mutton are required to be used. Trim, lard, and *marinade* the necks of mutton as directed; and then prepare them for braizing in the following manner:—Place the necks of mutton in an oval braizing-pan on the drainer, garnish with carrot, onion, celery, garnished fagot of parsley, &c., four cloves and two blades of mace; moisten with some light wine *mirepoix* (No. 236), or in lieu thereof, use half a pint of Sherry or Madeira, and a large ladleful of stock; cover the necks of mutton with an oval piece of buttered paper, and set them to boil on the stove-fire; after which put the lid on the pan, and set the braizing-pan on a moderate fire with live embers on the lid, to continue gently boiling for about two hours; taking care to baste the larded necks frequently with their own liquor. When done, take them up on to a small baking-dish with a little of their own broth, and put them in the oven that the larding may dry for a minute or two, then glaze and dish them up; garnish them round with a border of potatoes turned in the shape of large olives, corks, or balls, and fried in clarified butter; pour some *Poivrade* sauce (No. 29), under them, and send to table.

612. NECKS OF MUTTON, LARDED AND BRAIZED, A L'ALLEMANDE.

TRIM, lard, and prepare for braizing, two necks of mutton, as directed in the preceding article; and about two hours before dinner-time, set them on the fire to braize in the usual manner. When done, glaze and dish them up, surround them with alternate groups of *quenelles* of potatoes, and prunes stewed in red wine; pour some German sweet sauce (No. 61) under them, and send to table.

613. NECKS OF MUTTON LARDED, A LA SOUBISE.

TRIM and lard two necks of mutton, prepare them for braizing with carrot, onion, celery, garnished fagot of parsley, three cloves, and two blades of mace; moisten with a large ladleful of good stock, cover them with an oval piece of buttered paper as well as the lid of the brazier: set them on a moderate fire to braize gently for about an hour and a half; when done, glaze, and dish them up (having previously poured in the dish a rich *purée* of onions *à la Soubise* No. 119), place a border of potato *croquettes* round them, and send to table.

Note.—Larding may be dispensed with, when considered objectionable, without deteriorating much from the excellence of any of the foregoing methods of dressing necks of mutton. It is, however, generally regarded as a proper characteristic of these dishes. In addition to the above methods for garnishing braized necks of mutton, they may also be finished by placing round them a garnish of stewed peas, asparagus, glazed young carrots and turnips, *sauer-kraut,* baked tomatas, or *Lyonnaise* tomatas, or *Piquante* sauce.

REMOVES OF LAMB,

COMPRISING

Baron of Lamb, *à la Montmorency.*   Saddle of Lamb, *à la Godard.*
    „   *à la Printanière.*   „   *à la Financière.*
    „   *à la Jardinière.*   „   *à la Royale.*
    „   *à la Maître d'Hôtel.*   „   *à la Macédoine.*
Hind-Quarters of Lamb.   „   *à la Milanaise.*
Saddle of Lamb, *à la Dauphine.*

614. BARON OF LAMB, A LA MONTMORENCY.

PROCURE the hind quarters of a fine fat lamb, take off the transparent skin which covers the fat of the saddle, and with the point of a small knife, make a slight incision, in an oval form, all over the surface of the upper part of the legs; and afterward with a sharp thin-bladed knife, pare off the skin, so as to leave the place bare; this will give to the surface of each leg, the appearance of *fricandeaux* prepared for larding. Then saw off the shank bones, as well as the projecting part of the spine bone; cut off the tail, and truss the skirts neatly up with small skewers. Next, place the baron on the spit for roasting, and be careful to cover it with buttered white paper. Two hours and a half before dinner, put the lamb down to the fire to roast, and about ten minutes before it is done, take off the paper; and after allowing the larding to get lightly colored, glaze it well over, then take it off the spit, and dish it up; garnish it round with groups of button mushrooms, truffles, fine white cocks'-combs, and scollops of red tongue; round the whole place a border of spoon-*quenelles* decorated with truffles, and a lamb's sweetbread larded between each *quenelle;* sauce with good *Allemande* sauce; glaze the lamb brightly, and send to table.

615. BARON OF LAMB LARDED, A LA PRINTANIERE.

TRIM, lard, and roast a baron of lamb according to the directions contained in the foregoing article; dish it up, pour round it some *Printanière* sauce (No. 21), garnish it with groups of small new potatoes first partly boiled, and afterward fried of a light color in clarified butter, glaze the lamb all over, and send to table.

616. BARON OF LAMB, A LA JARDINIERE.

PREPARE and roast the baron of lamb according to the preceding directions; and when dished up, garnish it round with a rich and varied *Jardinière* of such vegetables as are in season; sauce the lamb round with *Espagnole* sauce, and send to table.

617. BARON OF LAMB, A LA MAITRE D'HOTEL.

PREPARE the baron of lamb as previously directed, dish it up and pour round it a rich *Maître d'Hôtel* sauce (No. 43); garnish it round with alternate groups of small buds of cauliflowers, and fried olive-shaped potatoes; glaze the lamb well, and send to table.

Note.—Hind-quarters of lamb should be dressed in the same manner as barons of lamb), and may therefore be garnished with every sort of sauce and garnish used for the latter.

When the larding is dispensed with, the whole of the fat as a matter of course should be retained on the surface of the lamb, to protect the meat from losing its juices, and consequently render it unfit for table.

618. SADDLE OF LAMB, A LA DAUPHINE.

Select a moderate-sized saddle of lamb, bone it, and having laid it on the table, season the inside with pepper and salt, and line it with some *quenelle* force-meat of veal or fowl, about an inch in thickness, placing on the force-meat some fillets of tongue and truffles, after which, fold the skirts of the saddle over—so as to encase the force-meat, &c., thereby giving it a plump appearance; and in order to secure its shape, bind it in a napkin on which butter has been spread : when the saddle of mutton is rolled up tightly in it, tie the ends with twine. Then place the saddle so prepared on the drainer of an oval braizing-pan, cover it with the bones and trimmings; garnish with carrot, onion, celery, garnished fagot of parsley, four cloves, and two blades of mace ; moisten with sufficient good stock to cover the lamb, and set it to braize gently on a moderate fire for about two hours and a half. When the lamb is done, place it on an earthen dish, untie the ends of the napkin, and fold the saddle up tightly, and smooth it in again; fasten the ends as before, and put it in press between two dishes until it is nearly cold. Then take the lamb out of the napkin, trim it neatly, and cover it over with a coating of well-seasoned reduced *Allemande* sauce, which must be allowed to set, afterward being egged over, and then be covered with very fine bread-crumbs mixed with one-fourth part of grated Parmesan cheese ; sprinkle some drops of melted fresh butter with a paste-brush over the whole, and put it on a baking-sheet in the oven to acquire a light-brown or fawn color. The saddle of lamb being ready, dish it up, garnish it round with some *bouchées* of wild rabbits *à la Pompadour* (No. 1010); sauce round and under the lamb with some white Italian sauce (No. 13), and send to table.

619. SADDLE OF LAMB, A LA GODARD.

Bone, stuff, and braize a saddle of lamb according to the preceding directions ; when done, put it in press between two dishes till cold. It should then be taken out of the napkin, trimmed neatly without removing any of the fat, or diminishing its size, and put into a deep baking sheet with the broth in which it has been braized—previously clarified, and afterward reduced to half glaze for the purpose ; put a buttered oval piece of white paper on the top, and half an hour before dinner put it in the oven to be warmed and glazed of a fine light color. Then dish it up, and pour round it a rich *ragôut à la Godard*—composed of cock's-combs and kernels, button-mushrooms, small sweetbreads cut into scollops, and truffles—the whole to be tossed in some good *Allemande* sauce. Put a border of large *quenelles* decorated with truffles, and some larded lamb's-heart sweetbreads—placed alternately round the remove, and send to table.

620. SADDLE OF LAMB, A LA FINANCIERE.

PREPARE a saddle of lamb exactly as the foregoing, and when dished up, garnish it with a rich *Financière ragout* (No. 188); glaze the remove, and send to table.

621. SADDLE OF LAMB, A LA ROYALE.

For the preparation of this remove, follow the directions for loin of veal *à la Royale* (No. 592).

622. SADDLE OF LAMB, A LA MACEDOINE.

BONE, stuff, and braize a saddle of lamb as for *à la Godard* (No. 619), warm and glaze it, also, in the same manner; dish it up, garnish it round with a rich and well-prepared *Macédoine* of vegetables tossed in some *Allemande* sauce : surround the remove with a border of artichoke bottoms, or small turnips cut in the shape of cups, boiled in white broth with a lump of sugar and a little salt, and filled—half with green peas, and the remainder with very small turned or scooped carrots, nicely glazed ; glaze the remove, and send to table.

623. SADDLE OF LAMB, A LA MILANAISE.

PREPARE and braize a saddle of lamb as previously directed; when glazed, dish it up, and garnish it round with macaroni prepared as follows :—

Boil one pound of Naples macaroni in two quarts of boiling water, a pat of butter, a little salt and minionette pepper; when done, drain it on a sieve, and afterward on a clean napkin, cut it into pieces two inches long, and put this into a stewpan with two pats of butter, six ounces of grated Parmesan cheese, a small piece of glaze, a *ragout*-spoonful of good white sauce, minionette pepper, and a little salt : toss the whole well together over a stove-fire until quite hot, and then use it to place round the remove, as also some truffles, and tongue cut into small circular scollops; these are to be warmed in a tablespoonful of half glaze, and placed round the remove in alternate groups with the macaroni; glaze the saddle of lamb before serving, and send to table with it a sauce-boat containing some of the clarified and reduced broth, in which the lamb has been braized, to be handed round with the remove.

CALVES'-HEADS AND OX-CHEEKS,

COMPRISING

Calf's-head, *à l'Anglaise.*		Ox-cheek, braized, *à la Flamande.*	
„	plain, with *Piquante* sauce.	„	*à la Polonaise.*
„	*à la Financière.*	„	*à l'Allemande.*
„	*à la Beauvaux.*	„	*à la Portuguaise.*
„	*à la Tortue.*	„	*à la Pompadour.*
„	*à la Marigny.*		

624. CALF'S-HEAD, A L'ANGLAISE.

PROCURE a fine, fat, white, scalded calf's-head, bone it in the manner described for preparing mock-turtle soup (No. 349) ; then put it into a large panful of cold water, in order that it may be thoroughly cleansed, after which, put it on the fire in a large stewpan with cold water, and as soon as it boils, skim it well, and allow it to boil for five minutes; then take it up and put it into cold water to cool. Next, drain it on a napkin, cut the ears out, leaving a sufficient base round them to allow them to stand up; cut the cheeks, &c., into pieces two inches square, round the angles, and pare off any rough cuticle there may be about them; this done, proceed to rub each piece of calf's-head with lemon-juice, then place the whole, including the tongue, in a large stewpan, with carrot, onion, celery, parsley roots, sweet-basil, a garnished fagot of parsley, &c., four cloves, and two blades of mace; moisten with half a bottle of Sherry or Madeira, and two ladlesful of good white stock, and set the whole to braize gently on a moderate fire, for about two hours. When the pieces of calf's-head are done, drain them upon a napkin, and dish them up in a close circle round the tongue, (previously trimmed, glazed, and placed in the centre of the dish); then cut the brains into scollops, and place them in the flanks, and at each end place the ears, previously trimmed and curled; pour some parsley and butter (No. 77) over the remove, and send to table.

The calf's ears should be trimmed as follows :—First drain them upon a napkin, then scrape off all the glutinous surface from the thin part with the edge of a spoon, leaving the white gristly membrane quite clear; wash them in warm water, put them back upon the napkin, and then slit them into narrow stripes, taking care not to run the knife through the ends, but merely from the inner part to within half an inch of the point, so as that, when the ear is turned down, it may present the appearance of a looped frill.

It is customary to send a piece of boiled streaky bacon on the side-table, when calf's-head is intended to be eaten plain. A boatful of sauce *à la Diable* (No. 17) as an accessory to plain calf's-head, is generally preferred to parsley and butter, the latter being considered too insipid.

625. CALF'S-HEAD, PLAIN WITH PIQUANTE SAUCE.

PREPARE the calf's-head as directed in the preceding article; then put about one pound of chopped beef-suet into a large stewpan, with carrot, onion, celery, garnished fagot of parsley, four cloves, and two blades of mace. Stir the whole with a wooden spoon over the fire until the suet is melted, then add the pulp of two lemons and a small handful of flour; moisten with common white broth, or water, add a little salt and a few pepper-corns, and then set the calf's-head to boil gently for about two hours. When it is done, drain the pieces upon a napkin, and dish them up neatly round the tongue, trimmed and glazed, and placed in the centre of the dish; place the ears, after trimming them, at each end, and on either side of the tongue place half the brains (which should be boiled in vinegar and water, with a little salt, and some fat from the stock-pot); make an incision lengthwise in each half portion of the brains, then pour a well-made *Piquante* sauce (No. 18) over the whole : garnish round with eight fried eggs, and some *croutons*, and send to table.

Calf's-head, prepared according to the foregoing directions, may also be served with either Italian, *Ravigotte*, Tomata, *Poivrade*, or Poor-man's sauce.

626. CALF'S-HEAD, A LA FINANCIERE.

BONE a calf's-head, blanch it in boiling water for about ten minutes on the fire, then put it into cold water for ten minutes ; drain it upon a napkin, trim off all the rough parts, and cut it into large scollops, leaving the tongue and ears whole, as usual; the brain should be carefully taken out of the head, and boiled separately, as directed in previous cases.

The pieces of calf's-head after being first rubbed over with lemon-juice, should be placed in a braizing-pan with half a bottle of Sherry or Madeira, two ladlesful of good stock, carrot, onion, celery, garnished fagot of parsley, &c. ; four cloves, two blades of mace and a few peppercorns ; cover with a thickly buttered oval piece of strong white paper, and put on the lid ; then set it to braize gently for about two hours, with live embers on the lid. Twenty minutes before dinner time, drain the pieces of calf's head on to a napkin, dish them up in the form of a wreath, round the base of a fried *cròustade* (previously stuck on the centre of the dish with a little flour and white of egg mixed together), at each end place the ears, on the *cròustade* place the tongue (separated down the centre, and rather spread out), and the brains laid thereon ; around these should be stuck in the *cròustade* six or eight ornamental skewers, each furnished with a double cock's-comb, a large mushroom, a truffle, and a crayfish ; pour round the whole a rich *Financière ragout* (No. 188), and send to table.

627. CALF'S-HEAD, A LA BEAUVAUX.

SELECT a small, well-shaped white calf's-head, bone it carefully, as before directed, keeping the skin as whole as possible. When the head has been boned, wash it thoroughly, wipe it with a clean cloth, season inside with pepper and salt, and then fill up the entire vacant space, occasioned by the extraction of the skull and jaws, with a well-seasoned *quenelle* force-meat made of veal mixed with some chopped parsley and mushrooms; when the calf's-head is thus again plumped up to its original size, by means of the force-meat, it must be secured, by sewing up all the apertures with twine and a trussing needle of proper size. When this part of the process is completed, roll the calf's-head up tightly in a well-buttered napkin saturated with lemon-juice (to keep the head white) ; then place the calf's-head in a braizing-pan with one pound of chopped suet, carrot, onion, celery garnished fagot cloves, mace, peppercorns, and a spoonful of salt; moisten with good common white stock, cover with the lid, and set it to boil gently for about two hours.

About half an hour before dinner-time, take the calf's head up on a dish, remove the napkin, trim the ears, slit them and turn them down, that they may appear frilled ; then place the calf's-head, perfectly drained from any moisture, on the centre of the dish, and remove all the twine with which it has been sewn up, and mask it all over, excepting the ears, with a preparation of four yelks of eggs, mixed with a pat of melted butter, and seasoned with pepper and salt, and a little nutmeg; then cover the whole with fine bread-crumbs, fried in a sauta-pan, with a little butter of a fine bright color, and place the head in the oven for five minutes, that the bread-crumbs may dry on, taking care to cover the ears with wet paper to keep them white, and prevent them from cocking up and spoiling their effect. As soon as the bread-crumbs have dried on, remove the paper from the ears, sauce round with a *ragout*, composed of the tongue cut into scollops, as also the brains, some button mushrooms, and green gherkins, cut into the shape of olives ; allow these to boil up for two or three minutes in a well-made *Poivrade* sauce (No. 29) ; garnish round with some *quenelles* of veal or chicken, colored with *Ravigotte*, or spinach-green (No. 285) ; stick in four silver ornamental skewers, garnished with a crest of red tongue, a large truffle, and a decorated *quenelle*, and send to table.

628. CALF'S-HEAD, A LA TORTUE.

BONE, blanch and trim a calf's-head, cut it up into large scollops, keep the ears whole, neatly trim the pieces, and toss them in the juice of a lemon ; put them into a stewpan, with carrot, onion, celery, garnished-fagot, cloves, mace, and a few peppercorns ; moisten with half a bottle of Madeira or Sherry, and two large ladlesful of good stock ; cover with a well-buttered stiff paper, and put on the lid ; set the whole to braize on the stove for about two hours. When the pieces of calf's-head are done, drain them on a napkin, and afterward dish them up in the form of a close wreath, round the base of a fried bread *croustade ;* place the ears at the ends and on the flanks : if the party be large, two extra ears should be procured, as the four make the dish look much handsomer : next, place the tongue, cut down its centre, and spread out on the top of the *croustade ;* on this put the brains, which must be kept whole and white, and round these, on the *croustade*, should be stuck six ornamental silver skewers, garnished with a double cocks-comb, a large mushroom, a *quenelle*, a truffle, and a large crayfish : sauce round with a well-made sauce *à la Tortuë* (No. 9) ; garnish the dish round between the spaces of the ears, with four larded and glazed sweetbreads, and eight decorated *quenelles*, and send to table.

629. CALF'S-HEAD, A LA MARIGNY.

PREPARE and braize a calf's-head as directed for dressing a calf's-head *à la Beauvaux*. When done, take it out of the napkin, and drain all the moisture from it, place the head on a dish, remove the twine used to secure its shape, trim the ears, and then sauce it all over (the ears excepted) with a well-seasoned *Ravigotte* sauce ; garnish round with a border of crayfish, and green gherkins, and send to table.

Note.—It is not necessary, in all cases, to garnish each remove as richly as heretofore set forth : many of the accessories, on every-day occasions, might be regarded as extravagant. What to omit in such cases, must be left to the judgment of the experienced cook, acquainted with the means and taste of his master.

630. OX-CHEEK BRAIZED, A LA FLAMANDE.

PROCURE two fresh ox-cheeks, bone and trim them, and then place them in a large oval braizing-pan on the drainer, garnish with the usual complement of vegetables, &c., add the trimmings, moisten with sufficient broth from the stockpot to cover the whole, and set them to boil very gently by the side of the stove-fire for about five hours. When the ox-cheeks are thoroughly braized, and are become quite tender, take them up carefully, and put them in press between two dishes, until cold ; then trim them neatly, giving them an oval or oblong shape, and put them into a deep *fricandeau* pan, with the broth in which they have been braized (clarified and reduced to half its original quantity), and set them by in the larder, till about three-quarters of an hour before dishing up ; then put the ox-cheeks in the oven or on a slow fire, to get gradually warm, and to glaze them brightly, with their own stock. Next place them on their dish, the one resting on the other, garnish them round with a border of Brussels-sprouts boiled green, and tossed over the fire in a stew-pan, with two pats of butter, grated nutmeg, pepper and salt ; or when these fail, in their stead use braized cabbages ; then add a border of alternate groups of well-prepared, and nicely glazed carrots and turnips, cut into fancy shapes, and also some small-sized glazed onions. Sauce with an *Espagnole* or *Poivrade* sauce, and send to table.

631. OX-CHEEK, A LA POLONAISE.

BONE and trim two ox-cheeks ; prepare them for braizing as directed in the foregoing case ; moisten with half a bottle of Sherry, and allow them to simmer on the stove-fire for about ten minutes, add sufficient stock to cover them, and again set them on the stove to boil ; skim and put them by the side of the fire, to continue gently boiling for five hours. When the ox-cheeks are sufficiently braized, and are become quite tender, put them in press between two dishes ; when cold, trim, and afterward cut them across the grain into very thin slices. Then stick a number of triangular *croûtons* of fried bread in an oval form on the dish, within two inches of the edge, and within this coronet place a layer of the thin slices of the ox-cheeks, over which spread some sauce made in the following manner :—

Shred the rind of two oranges very thin, and perfectly free from pith, boil it in water for five minutes, drain and refresh it in cold water, and then add to it a small ladleful of good *Espagnole* sauce, half a pound of red-currant jelly, four chopped shalots, a little grated nutmeg, and the juice of one lemon ; boil the whole together, stirring it the while with a wooden spoon, and use this preparation as directed above. Having thus continued alternately adding layers of ox-cheek and sauce, until the whole forms a dome ; mask it over with the remainder of the sauce, and after smoothing the surface with the blade of a knife, cover it with some light-colored raspings of roll, bruised and sifted for the purpose. About three quarters of an hour before dinner, put the dish in the oven, when moderately hot to allow the preparation to get thoroughly warm ; garnish with a border of fried eggs and glazed onions, pour some of the same sauce round it—

this, however, must be thinner than that directed to be used for mixing with the ox-cheeks—and serve.

632. OX-CHEEKS, A L'ALLEMANDE.

BRAIZE the ox-cheeks as directed in the foregoing case; when done, put them in press, and after being trimmed, place them on a buttered baking-sheet, and mask them all over with the following preparation :—Bake some pieces of crumb of bread of a light color, pound and sift them; use this powder to mix into a paste with Port wine, a table-spoonful of cinnamon-powder, and 2 oz. of pounded sugar; mix the whole well together, and spread it all over the ox-cheeks. Three quarters of an hour before dinner-time, put the ox-cheeks in the oven, when moderately hot, to get warmed through; then place them on their dish, garnish round with groups of small *quenelles* of potatoes (No. 312) and stewed prunes, sauce them round with German sweet sauce (No. 61), and send to table.

633. OX-CHEEKS, A LA PORTUGUAISE.

BRAIZE the ox-cheeks; when done, put them in press, trim and place them in a *fricandeau* pan, with the clarified and reduced broth in which they have been braized; and having warmed them in this, and glazed them with it, dish them up; garnish round with a border of eggs, *farcis*, or stuffed and fried (No. 380), pour some Portuguese sweet sauce (No. 59) round the ox-cheeks, and send to table.

634. OX-CHEEKS, A LA POMPADOUR.

BRAIZE the ox-cheeks very tender, and after having put them in press, and then trimmed them, mask them over with a coating of reduced *Atelet* sauce (No. 36); when the sauce has become set by cooling on the ox-cheeks, egg them over and bread-crumb them with very fine bread-crumbs mixed with one fourth of grated Parmesan cheese; sprinkle over a little butter, place them on a well-buttered baking-sheet, and an hour before dinner put them in the oven to bake of a fine bright color; dish them up, garnish round with a *ragout* of ox-palates in a brown Italian sauce (No. 209), finish with a border of *croquettes* of ox-palates, and send to table.

Note.—Besides the foregoing methods of dressing ox-cheeks, they may also be served with a *Jardinière, Macédoine,* tomatas *farcis* (No. 1160), braized red cabbage, *Soubise,* or *Brétonne purées,* stewed peas, or asparagus peas.

Although in the preceding cases it is directed that two ox-cheeks should be used for a remove, it does not follow that in all cases two are requisite; more frequently one will prove to be quite sufficient for the purpose.

REMOVES OF PORK AND ROASTED SUCKING PIGS,

COMPRISING

Boiled Leg of Pork, *à l'Anglaise.*	Roast Sucking Pig, *à l'Anglaise.*
,, ,, *à l'Allemande.*	,, ,, *à la Périgord.*
Roast Leg of Pork.	,, ,, *à la Chipolata.*
Roast Loin of do.	,. ,, *à la Provençale.*
Roast Neck of do.	,, ,, *à la Napolitaine.*
Roast Griskin of do.	

635. BOILED LEG OF PORK A L'ANGLAISE.

SAW off the shank bone of a salted leg of dairy-fed pork, then put it into a large braizing-pan or stock-pot : fill this nearly full with cold water, and add six carrots, as many turnips, one head of celery, and an onion stuck with three cloves. Set the pork to boil gently by the side of the stove-fire for about three hours—the exact time depending on its size. While the pork is boiling, trim a dozen and a half of small turnips and as many young carrots, boil these separately, and reserve them for garnishing the remove. When the pork is done, drain, trim, and dish it up ; place the carrots and turnips alternately round the remove, pour some plain gravy under it, put a ruffle on the bone, and send to table.

A peas-pudding is usually served from the side-board, made as follows : soak a pint of yellow split peas in cold water for about six hours ; drain and tie them rather loosely in a napkin or pudding-cloth, and boil them with the pork—about three hours will suffice. Take them up, pound them in a mortar with two pats of fresh butter, and rub them through a fine wire-sieve : then put this *purée* into a stew-pan, add the yelks of four eggs, pepper, salt, and nutmeg ; mix the whole well together with a wooden spoon, and after having spread a napkin with fresh butter, place the *purée* in the centre, draw the corners up on the left hand, and with the right tie up the pudding with string ; then place it to boil for an hour, after which turn it out carefully on to a vegetable dish, and serve.

636. BOILED LEG OF PORK A L'ALLEMANDE.

PICKLE a leg of pork with four ounces of saltpetre, ditto of moist sugar, half a pint of vinegar, cloves, mace, sweet basil, and marjoram, thyme, and bay-leaf, and the usual quantity of common salt ; boil it as directed in the foregoing article. When done, dish it up, and after garnishing it with *sauër kraut* (No. 165), surround it with a border of glazed carrots, turnips, and onions ; pour some *Poivrade* sauce (No. 29) over it, and send to table.

637. ROAST LEG OF PORK, A L'ANGLAISE.

PROCURE a leg of fresh dairy-fed pork ; make a large incision just below the knuckle, between the skin and meat, for the purpose of introducing the stuffing of sage and onion, which must be secured by sewing it up with small twine ; then with a sharp-pointed knife score it all over in the following manner : with the left hand hold the pork firmly, and with a very sharp knife score the skin across in parallel lines a quarter of an inch apart; then spit the joint, and roast it for about two hours and a half; when done, dish it up, pour a rich brown gravy under it, and send to table with apple sauce.

The stuffing for the pork should be thus prepared: chop a dozen sage leaves and six large onions, boil these in water for three minutes, and after having drained them on a sieve, put them into a stewpan with pepper and salt, and a pat of butter; set the stuffing to simmer gently over a very slow fire for ten minutes, and then use it as directed above.

638. ROAST LOIN OF PORK.

TRIM, score, and separate the bones of the loin of pork with a small chopper or meat saw; make an incision in the upper part of the loin for placing the stuffing, sew it up with small twine, and having passed a strong iron skewer through it lengthwise, tie it firmly on to a spit at both ends. About an hour and a quarter before dinner-time, put the pork down to the fire to roast, and when done dish it up; pour some brown gravy under it, garnish it round with a border of small potatoes fried of a light color, and send to table with apple sauce.

639. ROAST NECK OF PORK.

SAW the chine bone neatly off, stuff the neck of pork with sage and onion, spit, roast, and dish it up as directed for the loin, and serve.

640. ROAST GRISKIN OF PORK.

THE piece called griskin is that part of the pig which is cut from the side of a bacon-hog, being the lean from the neck and loin: this should be lightly sprinkled with salt the day before dressing it for table; it must then have a long iron skewer passed through it lengthwise, and tied on to a spit. About an hour and a quarter before dinner put it to roast, and when the griskin has been down an hour, shake some flour over it with a dredger, and afterward sprinkle some chopped sage and onions upon it. When the pork is done, dish it up, pour some brown gravy under it, and send to table with two sauce-boats containing apple and sage and onion sauce, the latter to be prepared as follows: chop a dozen sage-leaves and four onions, and after having boiled them two minutes in water, drain, and put them in a stewpan with a pat of butter, pepper and salt; set these to simmer on a very slow fire for ten minutes, and then add half-a-pint of good brown gravy, boil the whole together for five minutes, and serve.

641. ROAST SUCKING-PIG, A L'ANGLAISE.

IN selecting a sucking-pig for the table, those of about three weeks old are generally preferred, their meat being more delicate than when allowed to grow larger. Let the pig be prepared for dressing in the usual way, that is, scalded, drawn, &c., pettitoes cut off, and the paunch filled with stuffing previously prepared for the purpose as follows: chop two large onions and a dozen sage-leaves, boil them in water for two minutes, and after having drained the sage and onion on to a sieve, place it in a stewpan with a pat of butter, pepper and salt, and set the whole to simmer gently for ten minutes on a very slow fire; then add a double handful of bread-crumbs, two pats of butter, and the yelks of two eggs; stir the whole over the fire for five minutes, and then use the stuffing as before directed. When the sucking-pig is stuffed, sew the paunch up with twine, spit the pig for roasting, carefully fastening it on the spit at each end with small iron skewers, which should be run through the shoulders and hips to secure it tightly, so that it may on no account slip round when down to roast. The pig will require about two hours to roast thoroughly, and should be frequently basted with a paste-brush dipped in salad oil. (Oil is better adapted for this purpose than either dripping or butter, giving more crispness to the skin; when basted with oil, the pig will, while roasting, acquire a more even, and a finer color.) When done, take it up from the fire *on* the spit, and immediately cut the head off with a sharp knife, and lay it on a plate in the hot closet. Next, cut the pig in two, by dividing it first with a sharp knife straight down the back to the spine, finishing with a meat-saw; a large dish should be held under the pig while it is thus being divided, into which it may fall when completely cut through; place the two sides back to back on the dish, without disturbing the stuffing, split the head in two, put the brains in a small stewpan, trim off the snout and jaws, leaving only the cheeks and ears, place these one at each end of the dish, surround the remove with a border of small potatoes fried of a light color, in a little clarified butter; pour under some rich brown gravy, and send to table with the following sauce: to the brains, put into a small stewpan as before directed, add a spoonful of blanched chopped parsley, pepper, and salt, a piece of glaze the size of a large walnut, some well-made butter sauce, and the juice of a lemon: stir the whole well together over the fire, and when quite hot, send it to table separately in a boat, to be handed round with the sucking-pig.

642. ROAST SUCKING-PIG, A LA PERIGORD.

PROCURE a plump fresh killed sucking-pig, and fill the paunch with the following preparation. Wash and thoroughly clean two pounds of fresh truffles, pare them and afterward cut them into pieces resembling small walnuts, but without trimming them much; pound the parings and trimmings in a mortar with about two ounces of butter; then put them into a stewpan with the truffles, and add thereto about one pound of scraped fat bacon, a bay-leaf, and a few sprigs of thyme and sweet-basil chopped fine, some grated nutmeg, pepper and salt, a small clove of garlic, and half-a-pound of fat livers of fowls pounded for the purpose. Set the whole over a moderate fire, stirring it the while with a wooden spoon: when the truffles have simmered on the stove for about ten minutes, take them off and allow them to cool, fill the paunch of the sucking-pig with the above, sew it up with twine, spit and roast it as directed in the preceding article; when done, dish up in the same manner, taking care to send with it all the truffles; pour some *Périgueux* sauce (No. 23) under it, and send to table.

643. ROAST SUCKING-PIG, A LA CHIPOLATA.

ROAST sixty chestnuts, peel and then boil them with a quart of *consommé* for twenty minutes: reserve half in a small stewpan, and mix the remainder with one pound of pork sausage-meat, and use this kind of stuffing to fill the paunch of a sucking-pig; sew it up with a trussing-needle and string, spit, and roast it in the usual manner: and when done, dish it up as directed in the foregoing cases; observing, that the stuffing should be kept as whole as possible in the separated sides. Garnish with a richly varied *Chipolata* ragout (No. 190), and again, round this, place eight decorated *quenelles;* a dozen large cray-fish should also be placed up the centre, one overlaying another: glaze the pig and serve.

644. ROAST SUCKING-PIG, A LA PROVENCALE.

ROAST sixty large chestnuts, remove their husks while yet hot, and after pounding them in a mortar with four ounces of butter, rub the produce through a wire sieve, and put the *purée* into a stewpan; add thereto a few chives, sweet-basil, parsley, thyme, and one bay-leaf well chopped, a little grated nutmeg, pepper and salt, and the yelks of three eggs; mix well together, and use this preparation to fill the paunch of a plump sucking-pig, and roast it in the manner already directed. Then, cut it up and place it upon the dish, garnish the remove with a border of tomatas *au gratin* (No. 1160), pour some *Gasconne* or *Provençale* sauce under it, and send to table.

645. ROAST SUCKING-PIG, A LA NAPOLITAINE.

TAKE half a pound of polenta,* mix it in a stewpan with a quart of good *consommé*, four ounces of grated Parmesan cheese, and the same quantity of butter; season with nutmeg, pepper and salt; stir the whole on the fire quickly till it boils, and then continue stirring it on the fire until it assumes the appearance of a soft paste, when add four ounces of picked Sultana raisins and a small pot of orange marmalade; mix the whole lightly together, and with it fill the paunch of the sucking-pig: roast it in the usual way, divide and dish it up, garnish with a border of *polpéttes* (No. 1062), pour a well-made Napolitaine sauce (No. 63) under the pig, glaze the remove, and send to table.

Note.—In addition to the foregoing different methods for dressing sucking-pigs, they may also be served *à la Financière*, with *Poivrade*, Tomata, *Maître d'Hôtel*, *Piquante*, *Robert*, or *Brètonne* sauce.

BRAIZED HAMS,

COMPRISING

Braized Ham, with Spinach, &c.	Westphalia Ham, roasted, *à la St. James*
Westphalia Ham, *à l'Essence.*	„ *à la Parisiènne.*
„ baked.	Granada and Bayonne Hams.

646. BRAIZED HAM, WITH SPINACH, ETC.

WHEN about to dress a ham, care must be taken after it has been trimmed, and the thigh-bone removed, that it be put to soak in a large

---

* A kind of farina much used in Italy, obtained from Indian corn.

pan filled with cold water; the length of time it should remain in soak, depending partly upon its degree of moisture, partly whether the ham be new or seasoned. If the ham readily yields to the pressure of the hand, it is no doubt new, and this is the case with most of those sold in London in the spring season; for such as these, a few hours' soaking will suffice; but when hams are properly seasoned, they should be soaked for twenty-four hours. Foreign hams, however, require to be soaked much longer, varying in time from two to four days and nights. The water in which they are soaked should be changed once every twelve hours in winter, and twice during that time in summer: it is necessary to be particular also in scraping off the slimy surface from the hams, previously to replacing them in the water to finish soaking.

When the ham has been trimmed and soaked, let it be boiled in water for an hour, and then scraped and washed in cold water; place it in a braizing-pan with two carrots, as many onions, a head of celery, garnished fagot, two blades of mace, and four cloves; moisten with sufficient common broth to float the ham, and then set it on the stove to braize very gently for about four hours. To obtain tenderness and mellowness, so essential in a well-dressed ham, it must never be allowed to boil, but merely to simmer very gently by a slow fire. This rule applies also to the braizing of all salted or cured meats.

When the ham is done, draw the pan in which it has braized away from the fire, and set it to cool in the open air, allowing the ham to remain in the braize—by this means it will retain all its moisture— for when the ham is taken out of the braize as soon as done, and put on a dish to get cold, all its richness exudes from it. The ham having partially cooled in its braize, should be taken out and trimmed, and afterward placed in a braizing-pan with some of its own stock; and about three-quarters of an hour before dinner, put either in the oven or on a slow fire. When warmed through, place the ham on a baking-dish in the oven to dry the surface, then glaze it; replace it in the oven again for about three minutes to dry it, and glaze it again; by that time the ham, if properly attended to, will present a bright appearance. Put it now on its dish, and garnish it with well-dressed spinach (No. 1155), placed round the ham in table-spoonsful, shaped like so many eggs; pour some bright *Espagnole* sauce round the base, put a ruffle on the bone, and serve.

Note.—Any of our home-cured hams, dressed according to the fore-going directions, may also be served with a garnish of asparagus-peas, young carrots, a *Jardinière*, *Macédoine*, green-peas, broad-beans, French-beans, or Brussels-sprouts.

647. WESTPHALIA HAM, A L'ESSENCE.

TRIM and remove the thigh-bone from a Westphalia ham, and let it soak in cold water for two or three days, according to the probable length of time it may have been cured; then boil it in water for an hour, and after having washed it in cold water, put it into a large braizing-pan, with two carrots, as many onions, a head of celery, a fagot of parsley and green onions, thyme, sweet-basil, and bay-leaf, four cloves, and two blades of mace; moisten with two glasses of brandy, half a bottle of Sherry, and sufficient broth to float the ham.

Then set the ham to boil, or rather to simmer, very gently on a slow fire, from five to six hours : taking care, during the process of braizing, to probe it occasionally after the first four hours, in order thereby to ascertain how much longer it may be necessary for it to remain on the fire to effect the desired purpose.

When the ham is braized sufficiently tender, and after it has been allowed to remain in its own liquor for an hour or so, drain it on to a dish, divest it of the rind to within four inches of the knuckle-bone : this portion of the rind must be cut with a small sharp knife, so as to form a neat design in the shape of leaves, palms, or scollops, disposed in a fanlike form. Trim the fat of the ham smooth, without removing any more of it than is really necessary to give it a neat appearance. Put the ham in the oven on a baking-sheet for ten minutes, first absorbing every particle of grease from the surface with a clean cloth ; then glaze it, replace it in the oven again for five minutes ; glaze it once more, and place it on its dish ; garnish it round with any of the dressed vegetables indicated for Braized Ham, with spinach, &c., (No. 646), sauce with bright *Espagnole* sauce, mixed before reduction with a glass of Sherry, and about a pint of the liquor in which the ham has been braized ; place a ruffle on the bone, and send to table.

648. WESTPHALIA HAM, BAKED.

TRIM, and partially bone, a Westphalia ham, by removing the thigh-bone ; soak it, as usual, in cold water, for forty-eight hours, at least, and afterward boil it in water for half an hour ; this part of the operation should be executed in time to allow the ham to soak a day and night, previously to its being dressed in some wine *mirepoix* (No. 236) in a deep baking-dish. Cover the ham with two sheets of oiled paper, and over the whole lay a covering of paste, such as is used to cover venison with, and applied similarly to a pie-crust, taking care to secure it thoroughly all round, so as to prevent the escape of the volatile properties of the essence of the ham, &c., which by condensation, and subsequent absorption, impart to the ham that peculiarly fine flavor which renders this method of dressing hams so much esteemed by *gastronomes*. Having prepared the ham in every particular according to the above directions, about five hours before dinner-time, let it be put in the oven to bake slowly, observing that the heat of the oven should be moderate, in order that the moisture be not reduced, so as to render the ham dry, which would spoil it entirely. When the ham has been in the oven about four hours, take it out of its braize, trim it, and then place it on a baking-sheet in the oven, to dry the surface ; glaze it in the usual manner, and after having clarified the *mirepoix* in which the ham has been baked, add as much thereof as will suffice to give flavor to some *Espagnole* sauce, reduce it to a proper consistency, and use it to pour round the ham when sent to table. Hams dressed according to the foregoing method, may be garnished as follows :—*à la Financière, à la Périgueux, à la Parisiènne, à la Macédoine, à la Jardinière, à la Flamande ;* with stewed peas, asparagus-peas, young carrots, spinach, broad-beans, &c.

Note.—If the ham, dressed as above, be intended to be eaten cold, it should be allowed to remain in its braize, until it becomes set in a jelly, it must be then taken out, trimmed, glazed, and dished up, with some aspic-jelly, made with the addition of the essence of ham.

649. WESTPHALIA HAM, ROASTED A LA ST. JAMES.

PREPARE a Westphalia ham in every respect according to the first part of the previous directions, and having allowed it to steep in the *mirepoix* the allotted time, run a large iron skewer through it, and fasten it at each end on to the spit with string ; next reduce the *mirepoix*, vegetables, &c., of which it is composed, and cover the under part of the ham therewith ; then wrap the whole of the ham up with large sheets of cartridge-paper, previously well oiled for the purpose ; over the paper put a covering of venison paste, as is usual when about to prepare venison for roasting. Cover the said coating of flour and water paste, with greased paper, and tie on this with string. About five hours before the ham is required for table, put it down to roast before a moderate fire ; when it has been down about three hours and a half, take it up, make a hole in the paste, and, with a funnel, infuse half a pint of brandy, or, in preference to this, if you have it, as much Malaga wine ; stop the hole up with paste, and put the ham down to the fire to roast for twenty minutes longer ; then take it up, and remove it carefully from the spit, so as not to lose any portion of the essence contained within the coating of crust that surrounds the ham. Trim the ham, and set it to dry on a baking-sheet in the oven, glaze it and dish it up, using the essence reserved for the purpose, in order to give flavor to the sauce intended to be served with it.

Westphalia hams, thus dressed, may be served with any of the garnishes described as appropriate for baked hams.

650. BRAIZED HAM, A LA PARISIENNE

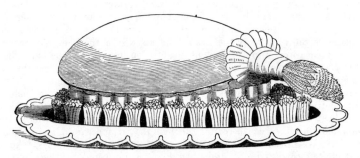

TRIM, soak, and boil a ham, either Westphalia or home-cured, as the case may be ; when it has boiled in water about an hour, take it up and put it into cold water, and after having scraped the rind clean, place it in an oval braizing-pan, with two carrots, as many onions, a head of celery, and garnished fagot of parsley, six cloves, and two blades of mace ; moisten with a glass of brandy and half a bottle of Sherry, and sufficient broth to cover the surface of the ham ; put the lid on, and as soon as it has boiled, set the pan on a slow fire, to continue gently braizing for about five hours and a half. When the ham is done, take it up and trim it, leaving, as usual, enough of the rind adhering to the knuckle part, and on this cut out (with the point of a sharp knife) an ornament resembling leaves, or scollops, spread out in a fan-like form; glaze the ham, and put it on its dish, raised on an oval *cròustade*, two inches and a half high, formed to the shape of the ham, cut round in flutes, and fried of a light color; round the base place a dozen or fifteen small fluted *cròustades* of fried bread, filled with green peas, asparagus-heads, carrots and turnips, scooped out in the form of very small olives, and nicely glazed. Glaze the ham, put the paper ruffle on the bone, and serve.

Send some bright *Espagnole* sauce, mixed with some of the essence of ham, previous to reduction of the same, in a sauce-boat, to be served with the ham from the sideboard, when it is carved.

Note.—Granada, Bayonne, and foreign hams in general, are prepared for the table according to the directions given for dressing Westphalia hams.

REMOVES OF VENISON, RED DEER, AND ROEBUCK,

COMPRISING

Haunch of Venison, *à l'Anglaise.*	Haunch of Red Deer, *à la Kinnaird.*
„ *à l'Allemande.*	Necks of Red Deer, *à la Marie Stuart.*
„ *à la St. George.*	„ *à la St. Andrew.*
Haunch of Red Deer roasted, *à l'Écossaise.*	Fillets of Red Deer, *à la Royale.*
„ *à la Glengarry.*	

651. HAUNCH OF VENISON ROASTED, A L'ANGLAISE.

SAW off the shank-bone, remove the sinew, pare away the dark, dry skin from the skirt, and also the dried surface of the under part. Then cover the haunch with a large sheet of buttered paper, and over that place a covering of flour and water paste, about half an inch in thickness; envelop the whole with two large sheets of cartridge-paper, and having fastened these on with string, place the venison on a cradle-spit, or, if that be wanting, the haunch of venison should be first put on the common spit, preparatory to its being covered as aforesaid. If the haunch be a fine one, it should be allowed from four hours to four and a half to roast, and about twenty minutes before it is done the paste and paper should be removed, and a little salt sprinkled over it. Then with a dredger-box shake over some flour to froth and color it; baste it with four ounces of fresh butter, and about five minutes after take the haunch up from the fire, place it on its dish, pour a rich brown gravy under it, put a paper ruffle on the bone and send to table, with a sauce-boat filled with sweet sauce (No. 65).

652. HAUNCH OF VENISON, A L'ALLEMANDE.

TRIM and remove the spine-bone from a small haunch of venison, place it in an oval braizing-pan with four carrots, four onions, two heads of celery, a garnished fagot of parsley, six cloves, and two blades of mace; moisten with a bottle of red wine, and sufficient broth to cover the surface of the venison; lay on it a buttered paper, and put on the lid, and after having allowed it to boil on a brisk stove-fire, place it in the oven or on a moderate fire to continue braizing very gently for about from five to six hours—taking care to moisten the surface frequently with its own braize. When the venison is done, take it up on a deep baking-dish, put about a pint of its own broth under it, trim it neatly and mask it all over with a thick coating of the following preparation : bake some slices of bread of a light-brown color, and afterward pound and sift them, put one pound of this into a basin, and add thereto half an ounce of powdered cinnamon, four ounces of fine sugar, and as much Port wine as will suffice to moisten the whole into a thick paste; use this to cover the haunch of venison, smooth it over with the blade of a knife, and put it in the hot closet to dry the surface of the crust. When about to send to table, place the venison on a dish, pour some Victoria cherry sauce (No. 64) round it, garnish with alternate groups of prunes stewed in wine, and potato *quenelles,* put a ruffle on the bone and serve.

653. HAUNCH OF VENISON, A LA ST. GEORGE.

TRIM a haunch of venison in the usual manner, and with the point of a small knife make a circular incision about eight inches in diameter, just below the knuckle, on the upper part of the haunch, and with a large knife remove the surface of the part so marked out, in order to leave the place bare, preparatory to its being thickly and neatly larded as for a *fricandeau.* Then prepare the venison for braizing—in every respect following the directions given for that part of the process in the preceding article. Having carefully and frequently moistened the surface of the venison during the time it is braizing, and kept a supply of live embers of charcoal on the lid of the braizing-pan, the venison, when done, will present, if properly attended to, a bright appearance. It should then be taken up to drain on to a common dish, and after being glazed and dished up with a rich *Financière ragout* (No. 188), in a *Poivrade* sauce made with Port wine, garnish the haunch with eight ornamental silver skewers, each furnished with a large double white cock's-comb, a large black truffle, a crayfish, and a decorated *quenelle ;* put a handsome ruffle on the bone, and send to table.

654. HAUNCH OF RED DEER ROASTED, A L'ECOSSAISE.

PREPARE and roast this kind of venison as described for dressing a haunch of venison à *l'Anglaise ;* observing that it is necessary to allow it to hang longer than any other sort before dressing it, as it will be found to eat tough if due attention be not paid to the time of keeping it.

655. HAUNCH OF RED DEER, A LA GLENGARRY.

TRIM and remove the whole of the chine-bone of a haunch of red deer, saw off the shank, and scrape the leg-bone so as to show about an inch. Then pare off the whole of the surface (excepting the fat part) in an oval form, and lard it closely like a *fricandeau ;* place the haunch in a large earthen pan with sliced carrot and onion, parsley, bay-leaves and thyme, cloves, mace, and bruised peppercorns, adding to these a gallon of common vinegar, a handful of salt, and half a gallon of water; let the haunch steep in this pickle for about ten days, taking care to turn it over twice a-day, and at the expiration of that time, the venison will be fit for dressing.

After the venison has been *marinaded,* place it in a large oval braizing-pan, and garnish with four carrots, four onions, four heads of celery, two garnished fagots of parsley, &c., eight cloves, and four blades of mace; moisten with a bottle of Madeira, and three large ladlesful of good broth : cover with a sheet of thick brown paper well buttered, let it boil, and then place the lid on with live embers of charcoal upon it, and put the pan on a moderate stove-fire to braize gently for seven hours—moistening the larding of the venison frequently with its own liquor, by which means, when the venison is done, it will be nicely glazed. It should now be taken up on to a baking sheet, and placed in the oven for a few minutes to dry the larding : then glaze and dish it up. Pour a well-made *Poivrade* sauce (No. 29) under it, garnish it round with *quenelles* of grouse, bread-crumbed and fried, and at each end place groups of venison fry ; put a ruffle on the leg-bone, and send to table with sweet sauce, separately in a boat.

656. HAUNCH OF RED DEER, A LA KINNAIRD.

PREPARE and dress a haunch of red deer exactly as the foregoing ; when done, glazed and dished up, garnish it round with alternate groups of fried potatoes (cut in the shape of large olives, and fried in clarified butter) and round potato *croquettes ;* pour a well-made sweet sauce (No. 66) under it, and send to table.

657. NECKS OF RED DEER, A LA MARIE STUART.

To make a handsome remove, two necks are required ; from these, saw off the chine-bones and shorten the ribs to about five inches in length ; then remove the whole of the sinewy covering from the meaty part of the necks, leaving a perfectly even surface, which must be larded closely in the usual manner—observing that when about trimming the necks of deer, care must be taken to leave the whole of the fat that covers the ribs. When the necks have been larded, *marinade* them in the pickle prescribed for the haunch ; and allow them to steep in this about six days and nights, when they will be ready for dressing. Take them out and prepare them for braizing in like manner to the haunch, proceeding in all respects the same way. When done, take them up on to a baking-sheet, and put them in the oven to dry the larding for a few minutes, glaze them, and place them on their dish in the form of a *Chevaux-de-frise :* this is effected by placing the necks on their base, and allowing the rib-bones to fall over, or between each other, showing the larded parts outside. Garnish them with a Parisian *ragout* (No. 203), and a border of *quenelles* of pheasant *à la Richelieu* (No. 1004), at each end : and along the ridge occasioned by the meeting of the rib-bones, place a line of trimmed crayfish ; glaze the larding of the venison, and serve.

658. NECKS OF RED DEER, A LA ST. ANDREW.

PREPARE and braize two necks of red deer in the manner last mentioned ; when done, glaze and dish them up after the same directions ; garnish with a rich *Financière ragout* (No. 188), with *Poivrade* sauce : surround them with a border of *quenelles* of grouse, decorated with truffles ; at each end place a *crôustade* of bread cut in the shape of a vase, and fried of a light color, and fill it with a group of four large truffles ; and on the flanks of the dish, put a group of large crayfish : glaze the larding, and send to table.

659. FILLETS OF RED DEER, A LA ROYALE.

TAKE out the fillets of two necks of red deer, which must be cut with part of the loin adhering to them ; trim and lard them all over the upper surface, after which steep them in a *marinade* (No. 233) for six days.   Then proceed to dress them in the same manner as directed for the haunch *à la Glengarry.*   When the fillets are done, take them out of their braize on to a baking-sheet, and put them in the oven for a few minutes to dry the larding ; then glaze them nicely, and afterward dish them up, side-by-side, on an oval *crôustade* of fried bread, about two inches high, and cut round in flutes ; garnish with a *ragout* composed as follows : braize six pork sausages, and after they have been allowed to cool, cut them up and throw the pieces into a large *bain-marie ;* to these add an equal quantity of round balls of streaky bacon (previously braized), some button mushrooms and green gherkins.   A rich *Poivrade* sauce must be poured on the ingredients ; let the whole boil on the stove-fire for two minutes, pour the *ragout* round the fillets, and place a border of *quenelles* of potatoes (No. 312) (rolled in fried bread-crumbs) round the edge of the dish, and serve.

REMOVES OF TURKEY AND CAPONS,

COMPRISING

Roast Turkey, *à la Périgord.*	Capon, *à la Macédoine.*
„ *à la Chipolata.*	„ *à la Printanière.*
„ *à l'Anglaise.*	„ *à l'Ivoire.*
„ *à la Financière.*	„ *au gros sel.*
Boiled Turkey, with Celery sauce.	„ *à l'Estragon.*
„ with Oyster sauce.	„ *à la Périgord.*
Capon stuffed with Truffles, *à la Périgord.*	„ and Rice.
„ *à la Godard.*	„ *à la Milanaise.*
„ *à la Chipolata.*	„ with *Macaroni.*
„ *à l'Anglaise.*	„ with *Nouilles.*
„ *à la Jardinière.*	

660. ROAST TURKEY, A LA PERIGORD.

FOR this purpose, choose a fine young hen turkey, make an incision at the back of the neck, and through it draw out the entrails, &c. ; with a knife cut away the vent and close the opening thus made, by sewing it up with twine, then singe off the hairs, and by scalding the legs, divest them of their black skin.   The neck should then be cut off close into the back, and the crop left entire ; clip the talons and claws, wipe the turkey clean, and lay it upon a napkin.   With a strong kitchen knife break the breast-bone, and after detaching the angular part, remove it with the fingers.   Previous to this operation, some truffles should be prepared as follows, to be used in stuffing the turkey :—
Have about four pounds of truffles thoroughly washed ; peel and

cut them into pieces the size of a small walnut; place these in a stew-pan, and after pounding the parings with about two pounds of fat ham or bacon, add them to the truffles. Season with minionette pepper and salt, grated nutmeg and chopped bay-leaf and thyme, and one clove of garlic; a few fat livers of poultry may also be added, after being pounded separately. Set the stewpan containing the foregoing ingredients on a slow fire, and allow them to simmer very gently for about half an hour, stirring them occasionally with a wooden spoon. They should be removed from the stove, and after allowing this preparation time to get partially set by cooling, proceed to stuff the turkey with it; keep the crop full, and with a small trussing-needle and twine draw the crop up in a purselike form, and fasten the ends of the twine to the back of the turkey so as effectually to close up the paunch. The turkey must then be placed upon an earthen dish, and put away in the larder till the next day, (time permitting,) when it should be trussed in the usual manner for roasting.

The turkey when placed on a spit for roasting should have the breast covered with thin layers of fat bacon, and the entire of the turkey should be carefully wrapped round with thick paper well buttered, and securely fastened on to the spit at each end with string. It should then be roasted, and care should be taken when about to remove it from the spit, that the crop is not torn. Dish up, and glaze it, pour under it a rich *Périgueux* sauce (No. 23), garnish with large *quenelles* of fowl, and truffles, and serve. The *quenelles* and truffles are, however, not indispensable to the completion of this remove.

661. ROAST TURKEY, A LA CHIPOLATA.

DRAW and prepare a turkey for stuffing, fill it with well-seasoned veal stuffing and chestnuts, or, if preferred, pork sausage-meat may be substituted for the veal stuffing.

The chestnuts are prepared as follows :—Take about sixty chestnuts, and after splitting them across the outer skin, fry them with a little butter in a frying-pan until they shed their husks easily; when peeled, boil them in a little good *consommé* till done; half should then be reserved to be put in the sauce, and the remainder used as directed above.

The turkey being thus prepared, truss and cover with thin layers of fat bacon as directed in the foregoing case, and having roasted it of a light color, dish it up and garnish with alternate groups of the ingredients composing the *Chipolata ragout* (No. 190), pour some of the sauce round the remove, and send to table.

662. ROAST TURKEY, A L'ANGLAISE.

STUFF a turkey with some well-seasoned veal stuffing, let it be trussed in the usual manner, and previously to putting it down to roast, cover it with thin layers of fat bacon, which should be secured on with buttered paper tied round the turkey, so as entirely to envelop it on the spit; then roast it, and when done, dish it up, garnish with stewed chestnuts, and small pork sausages, nicely fried; pour a rich *Poivrade* sauce (No. 29) round it, glaze the turkey, and send to table.

663. ROAST TURKEY, A LA FINANCIERE.

THE turkey may be stuffed either with veal stuffing or *quenelle* of fowl; it should be roasted in the usual manner, and when done, dished up and garnished with a rich *Financiére ragout* (No. 188); at each end place a larded sweetbread, and at the sides, a sweetbread decorated with scollops of truffles inserted in the form of a' rose ; between these should be placed groups of large truffles and *quenelles* of fowl; glaze the turkey and send to table.

As this is rather a sumptuous kind of garnish, suitable for great occasions only, the sweetbreads, large truffles, &c., may be dispensed with, and the *Financiére ragout* only retained.

664. BOILED TURKEY, WITH CELERY SAUCE.

DRAW a fine young hen turkey, and remove the angular part of the breast-bone, stuff it with veal stuffing, and truss it for boiling ; wrap some buttered paper round it, and place it in an oval braizing-pan with carrot, onion, one head of celery, and a garnished faggot of parsley ; add as much white *poële* (No. 230), or white stock, as will suffice to cover the turkey, then set it on a stove to boil ; it should after that be removed to the side, or placed on a slackened stove to continue gently boiling till done ; then take it up out of the braize, remove all the string, &c., and set it to drain upon a napkin ; dish it up, pour over it a well-made *purée* of celery (No. 110), place round it some stewed heads of celery, and send to table.

665. BOILED TURKEY, WITH OYSTER SAUCE.

THE turkey should be boiled as directed in the last article ; when done, dish it up, and previously to sending it to table, pour over it some well-made oyster-sauce (No. 50), and serve.

666. CAPON STUFFED WITH TRUFFLES, A LA PERIGORD.

THIS should be prepared according to the directions given for dressing a turkey after the same fashion (No. 660).

667. CAPON, A LA GODARD.

THE capon being drawn and singed, trim the feet and wings ; then remove the angular part of the breast-bone by inserting a strong-bladed knife, taking care not to tear the breast nor cut the fillets. Next, cut the under part of the thighs close up to the bend of the joint, and by introducing the finger through the vent, loosen the skin all round the thighs in order to facilitate the slipping of the legs inside, so as to show the feet only. Then lay the capon flat on its breast, and having turned the skin of the breast upon the back, and twisted the pinions round to make them lie even with the back, run a trussing-needle and string through the pinion on the left, pass again through the lower joint of the pinion, and from thence through the upper joints of the thighs ; the needle must afterward be brought round and inserted through the other wing in the same manner ; the strings should then be drawn tight, and fastened. The legs must now be secured by running the needle through the upper part, leaving the *drum-sticks* under, and then again the needle should be drawn through the back, and the strings tightened to secure their position ; the tail-end must be pushed into the vent, and the string passed through it twice (up and down), and tied : all this giving to the capon an appearance of plumpness. It should then be rubbed with half a lemon, and wrapped in a sheet of buttered paper (to keep it white), and

placed in a stew-pan with some white *poële* or stock, to braize; for which purpose it must be first put on the stove-fire, and after it has boiled, placed by the side to continue gently simmering for about an hour and a quarter. Just before dinner-time, take the capon out of the braize, and drain it on to a napkin; remove the strings, ornament the breast with some *contisès* fillets of fowls, dish it up and garnish it with a richly-composed *ragout à la Godard* (No. 187), and serve.

When this remove is intended for a large party, it will be necessary to serve two capons; in which case, an ornamental *cròustade* of bread should be put in the centre of the dish, and the capons at each end, placing at either end of the dish, a fine, larded heart-sweetbread; two nicely-trimmed calf's ears with a black truffle on each, should also be placed on the flanks. Fill up the intervening spaces with groups of *quenelles* of fowl, large truffles, cocks'-combs and mushrooms; in the centre of the *cròustade* put either a larded sweetbread, or a group of truffles—or these may be replaced by inserting six ornamental skewers garnished each with a large double cock's-comb, a mushroom, a truffle, a *quenelle*, and a large cray-fish. Sauce the remove with *Allemande* or *Béchamel*, and serve.

668. CAPONS, A LA CHIPOLATA.

THESE are dressed in the same way as turkeys *à la Chipolata* (No. 66).

669. CAPONS, A L'ANGLAISE.

TRUSS and boil two plump capons, and when they are done, dish them up, placing a neatly-trimmed tongue between them; garnish round with boiled heads of broccoli or cauliflower, sauce the capons with a rich *Béchamel* sauce (No. 5), glaze the tongue and serve.

670. CAPONS, A LA JARDINIERE.

THESE should be boiled and dished up as in the foregoing case. Garnish them with alternate groups of prepared vegetables, such as small carrots, turnips, flowerets of cauliflower, green peas, asparagus heads, and French-beans cut in the form of diamonds. Sauce the capons with *Béchamel* sauce, glaze the tongue and serve. In some cases the tongue may be replaced by an ornamental *croûstade* of bread, fried of a light color, and filled with mashed potatoes, in which should be inserted some young carrots, and French-beans (cut in the form of pointed olives), and placed in alternate rows.

671. CAPONS, A LA MACEDOINE.

THIS method is very similar to the foregoing, with this exception, that the capons, when dished up, should be garnished with a well-prepared *Macédoine* (No. 143) ; a border of very small heads of cauliflowers and bundles of sprue asparagus about two inches long, should also be placed alternately round the edges of the dish ; sauce with *Allemande* and serve.

672. CAPONS, A LA PRINTANIERE.

TRUSS and boil two fat capons, and when they are done, dish them up with a nicely trimmed and glazed tongue, in the centre ; sauce them with a *Printanière* sauce (No. 21) ; garnish them round with a border of small deep cups, cut out of young turnips ; these when boiled in white broth with a little butter, sugar, and salt, should be drained on a napkin, and filled with carrots scooped out in the form of very small peas or olives, and also with young green-peas : these cups when disposed alternately round the dish, will be found to produce a very pretty effect.

673. CAPONS, A L'IVOIRE.

THESE must be trussed and braized in the usual manner, and when done, the broth in which they have been braized should be strained through a sieve, then divested of every particle of grease, and clarified with a little white of egg. After this has been strained, it should be boiled down to the consistency of half-glaze, and when the capons are dished up, should be poured over them, and sent to table. It is also customary in serving this remove to use a rich *Suprême* sauce (No. 38), with small *quenelles* of fowl for garnish.

674. CAPON, AU GROS SEL.

THIS is dressed in the manner described in the first part of the foregoing article ; a little rock salt should, however, be placed upon the breast, just before sending it to table.

675. CAPON, A L'ESTRAGON.

BRAIZE the capon in the usual way ; when done, the broth in which it has been braized must be clarified, and a few sprigs of green tarragon thrown into it while boiling ; the *consommé* should then be strained through a napkin, and boiled down nearly to the consistency of half-glaze, to be poured over the capon when served. Some leaves of green tarragon must be boiled for a minute or two in water, and used to ornament the breast of the capon.

676. CAPON AND RICE.

AFTER the capon has been drawn, wash the inside thoroughly clean, and absorb all the moisture with a napkin. Then nearly fill the capon with rice, boiled quite soft in white broth, and mixed with a spoonful of white sauce; it should afterward be trussed for boiling, and placed in an oval stewpan, with an onion stuck with two cloves, and a carrot. Add as much white broth as will cover the breast of the fowl, over which lay an oval piece of buttered paper; place the lid on the stewpan, and about an hour before it is wanted set it to boil gently on a slow fire. When done, drain the fowl, and having removed the strings, place it upon its dish, garnish it round neatly with rice, previously boiled in white broth, to which has been added a large spoonful of white sauce, two yelks of eggs, a little mignionette pepper, grated nutmeg, and a small pat of fresh butter. Work the rice over a brisk stovefire for five minutes, and then, with two table-spoons, mould it into the form of large eggs, and place these round the capon in a close border: sauce the capon with *Suprême* or *Béchamel* sauce, and serve.

If the capon is intended to be served plain, the sauce, &c., must be omitted, and instead of masking it with sauce, pour some essence of fowl under it; this may be obtained by clarifying some of the broth in which it has boiled, and afterward boiling it down to the consistency of half-glaze.

677. CAPON A LA MILANAISE.

Truss and boil a capon in the usual way, and when done, dish it up, and garnish it with a *ragout* of macaroni dressed with truffles, red tongue, and mushrooms; place a border of *rissoles* (No. 1020) round the dish, and serve.

678. CAPON WITH MACARONI.

Boil the capon as directed for the capons *à la Godard;* dish it up, and garnish it with macaroni, prepared as follows :—Boil half a pound of Naples macaroni in two quarts of water, with a small pat of butter, a little salt and mignionette pepper; when it is done, drain it in a colander, cut the pipes into pieces, two inches long, and put them into a stewpan, with 6 oz. of grated Parmesan cheese, two pats of butter, a little mignionette pepper, and a large spoonful of white sauce; stir the macaroni, or rather toss it, over a brisk fire, and when the cheese is incorporated with the sauce, &c., use it as directed; mask the breast of the capon with *Béchamel*, and serve.

679. CAPON WITH NOUILLES.*

Braize the capon as directed in the foregoing article, and when done, dish it up, and garnish round with the *nouilles*, previously prepared for the purpose, in the following manner :—Parboil the *nouilles* in water for five minutes, throw them on to a sieve to drain the water from them, and afterward replace them in the stewpan; season with mignionette pepper, a little grated nutmeg, and a pat of butter; moisten with about a quart of good broth, cover with a round of buttered paper, place the lid on the stewpan, and set the *nouilles* to simmer gently on

---

* *Nouilles* are a kind of vermicelli prepared in the following manner: Place six ounces of sifted flour upon a marble slab or paste-board; make a well in the centre by spreading the flour out in the form of a ring with the back of the hand; then place therein a little salt, and add a tea-spoonful of water to melt it; after which, add the yelks of five eggs, and knead the whole well together into a firm, smooth, compact paste; and after allowing it to rest for ten minutes, roll it out as thin as paper, and then divide it into bands three inches wide, cut these into very fine shreds, and spread them upon a large sieve to dry.

a slow fire for about an hour; then remove the paper, and add a *ragout-spoonful* of *Allemande* sauce and two ounces of grated Parmesan cheese; toss the whole together over the fire until well mixed, and then use them as before directed; sauce the poulard, or capon, with *Suprême* or *Allemande* sauce, and serve.

In addition to the foregoing methods of dressing capons, they may also be served with celery-sauce, oyster, green *Ravigotte* sauce, or with cray-fish, or *Financière ragouts*.

Poulards are dressed in the same manner as capons.

CHICKENS FOR REMOVES OR FLANKS,

COMPRISING

Chickens, *à la Reine.*	Chickens, *à la Florentine.*
„ *à l'Italiènne.*	„ *à la Cardinal.*
„ *à la Sauce Tomate.*	„ *à l'Allemande.*
„ *à la Vénitiènne.*	„ *à l'Indiènne.*
„ *à la Dauphine.*	„ *à l'Africaine.*
„ *à la Montmorency.*	„ *à la Turque.*
„ *à la Milanaise.*	„ *à l'Espagnole.*
„ *à la Chivry.*	

680. CHICKENS, A LA REINE.

TRUSS two small spring chickens for boiling, rub them over with lemon-juice, and wrap them up separately in a sheet of thickly-buttered paper; then place the chickens in a stewpan, with a garnished faggot of parsley, a carrot, and an onion stuck with two cloves; moisten with some of the surface of the boiling stockpot, in sufficient quantity to nearly cover the chickens; set them to boil gently for about forty minutes, when they will be done. When about to send to table, drain the chickens upon a napkin, and after having removed the paper and string, dish them up side by side, and cover them with *Suprême* sauce, garnish the dish with four groups of very small *quenelles* of fowl, and serve.

681. CHICKENS, A L'ITALIENNE.

TRUSS and boil two small chickens according to the foregoing directions; when done, divest them of the paper, and dish them up; sauce with a rich brown Italian sauce (No. 12), garnish with a border of mushrooms *farcis* (No. 1161), and serve.

682. CHICKENS WITH TOMATA SAUCE.

THESE are prepared in the same manner as the foregoing, with this exception, that, when dished up, they must be sauced with a well-finished tomata sauce (No. 22), and a border of tomatas *au gratin* (No. 1160) should be placed round them.

683. CHICKENS, A LA VENITIENNE.

THE chickens, when boiled and dished up, must be sauced with a *Vénitiènne* (No. 26), and garnished with a border of *raviolis* (No. 375).

684. CHICKENS, A LA DAUPHINE.

DRAW two spring chickens, proceed to bone them as for *"galantines,"* excepting that the legs and wings must be left entire. The void must be then filled with *quenelle* of fowl, in which has been mixed some chopped mushrooms and parsley ; the chickens should afterward be trussed, taking care to give them the same shape as they would have were the bones not removed, and after rubbing them over with lemon-juice, cover the breasts with thin layers of fat bacon, and secure their shape by wrapping them in sheets of buttered paper ; then place them in a stewpan, with carrot, onion, and a garnished faggot ; moisten with some light *mirepoix* (No. 236), and set the chickens to simmer very gently by the side of a slow fire for about three-quarters of an hour ; when done, drain them upon a napkin, remove the string, &c., and dish them up ; sauce them with the clarified essence in which they have been braized, and serve.

It is also customary to serve chickens, fowls, capons, or *poulards,* when prepared in this fashion, with *ragouts, à la Financière, à la Parisiènne,* with *Macèdoine,* or *Jardinières* of vegetables, Italian, *Poivrade,* Tomata, or *Suprême* sauces.

685. CHICKENS, A LA MONTMORENCY.

TRUSS two or more chickens (as may be required), and let their breasts be entirely covered with close larding ; next place them in a stewpan containing a wine *mirepoix* (No. 236), covering the unlarded parts with thin layers of fat bacon ; add as much good *cônsommé* as will suffice to reach up to the larding, cover the chickens with a round of buttered paper, and set them to braize gently on a slow fire, taking care that the lid of the stewpan be covered with live embers of charcoal, to effect the glazing of the larding. When the chickens are done, dish them up, garnish them with a white *ragout à la Financière* (No. 187), or a *ragout à la Parisiénne* (No. 203), and serve.

Chickens, à la *Montmorency*, may also be dished up with an ornamental *croûstade* in the centre, in which should be fixed five *atelets*, garnished as shown in the wood-cut, p. 235.

686. CHICKENS, A LA MILANAISE.

THESE should be trussed and boiled, and when done, dished up with a *ragout à la Milanaise*, see Capon *à la Milanaise* (No. 677); they may also be garnished with a border of *rissoles* (No. 1020).

687. CHICKENS, A LA CHIVRY.

TRUSS the chickens so as to look very plump, boil or braize them in some white *poële* (No. 231) or broth; and when done, dish them up in the following manner :—Some small rings of onions about the size of a shilling should be first boiled in white broth, then filled with blanched *ravigotte* of chives, tarragon, and chervil, and afterward used to ornament the breasts of the chickens. Place these in their dish, pour under them a *Chivry* or *Ravigotte* sauce (No. 20), and send to table.

688. CHICKENS, A LA FLORENTINE.

TRUSS two chickens, and lard the breasts very closely with black truffles cut into strips, which must be used instead of bacon for this purpose; the chickens should be covered with thin layers of fat bacon, (to prevent the truffles from drying and breaking off), then braized in white broth, and when done, dished up with an ornamental *croûstade* of bread fried of a light-brown color, and placed in the centre of the dish, garnish with alternate groups of small *quenelles* of fowl colored with lobster spawn, truffles cut in the form of olives, mushrooms, large double cocks'-combs, and small *croquettes* of rice mixed with a little grated Parmesan cheese; sauce the chickens, without masking the breasts, with some *Allemande* sauce, in which have been added two table-spoonsful of tomata sauce, and a little Chili vinegar. Fill the *croûstade* with trimmed crayfish tails tossed in a little of the sauce, and serve. If this dish be intended for a grand dinner, four ornamental silver skewers, garnished with a double cocks'-comb, truffles, decorated *quenelle*, and a cray-fish, may be inserted in the *croûstade*.

689. CHICKENS, A LA CARDINAL.

DRAW two chickens, taking care to leave the crop entire, cut off the feet two inches from the joint of the leg, and make an incision just under the thigh; insert the legs inside, and then put the chickens in a basin of cold water to soak for a quarter of an hour; after which, with the aid of the forefinger, detach the skin as much as possible from the breasts and legs of the chickens without tearing it; they must then be placed upon a napkin, and all the water absorbed from them; after which the interstices between the skin and fillets, &c., should be covered with some *quenelle* of fowl colored of a deep red with lobster spawn. The chickens are then to be trussed for boiling in the usual manner, being covered with thin layers of fat bacon, to protect the skin while braizing; place them in a stewpan with the customary vegetables, &c., moisten with white broth, and set them to braize very gently on a slow fire; care must be taken to prevent their boiling

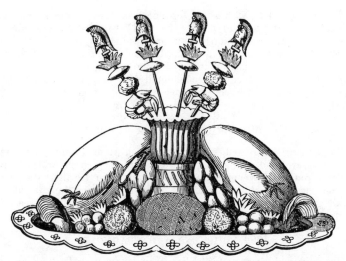

fast, as in that case the *quenelle* would burst the skins.   When done, dish them up with an ornamental fried bread *crôustade* in the centre of the dish ; garnish with small groups of glazed truffles, cocks'-combs, large *quenelles* of fowl decorated with truffles, button-mushrooms and cray-fish tails, and at each end place a larded sweetbread ; sauce with some *Cardinal* sauce (No. 48), insert four garnished ornamental silver skewers into the *crôustade*, and serve.

690. CHICKENS, A L'ALLEMANDE.

THESE must be trussed and boiled as usual, and when done, dished up with a border of *quenelles* of potatoes (No. 312), first poached, then covered with fried bread-crumbs, and placed round the chickens ; sauce them with a rich *Allemande* sauce (No. 7), and send to table.

691. CHICKENS, A L'INDIENNE.

TRUSS two chickens for boiling, lard the breasts closely, and place them in a conveniently-sized stewpan with a carrot, an onion stuck with two cloves, and a garnished faggot of parsley, &c.; add some good stock in sufficient quantity to reach up to the larding, place a buttered paper over the chickens, and having put the lid on the stewpan, set them to braîze gently, with some live embers of charcoal upon the lid of the pan : about forty minutes will suffice to do them.   Then remove the paper, and after drying the larding in the oven for a minute or two, glaze the chickens nicely, dish them up, garnish them round with a border of rice *croquettes* formed in the shape of an egg, and between each *croquette* place a minion fillet of fowl decorated with tongue, sauce them round with some *Financière* sauce (No. 8), in which have been added two mangoes sliced small, and serve.

692. CHICKENS, A L'AFRICAINE.

PREPARE the chickens in the same way as for *à la Cardinal*, and detach the skins in the same manner, fill up the interstices between the skin and fillets, with some forcemeat of fowl in which has been mixed sufficient *purée* of truffles (No. 121) to color it ; the chickens must then be trussed as for boiling, and after being covered with thin layers of fat bacon, should be braized, and when done, dished up side by side. Garnish them round with alternate groups of very small *quenelles*, half of which must be colored with chopped truffles and the remainder with lobster coral ; sauce with a *Financière ragout* (No. 188), in a *Poivrade* sauce (No. 29), and serve.

693. CHICKENS, A LA TURQUE.

THESE must be trussed, boiled, and dished up as usual ; they should then be garnished with a close border of rice boiled in broth, with a little saffron and Cayenne pepper ; place round the rice alternate groups of Smyrna raisins stewed in a little Malaga wine, and tongue cut into small pipelike forms about half an inch long ; pour a lightly-seasoned curry sauce (No. 47) over the chickens, and serve.

694. CHICKENS A L'ESPAGNOLE.

TRUSS two chickens as for boiling, then take a deep *fricandeau* pan, spread it thickly with butter, and lay therein, in circular order, a dozen pieces of raw ham cut in the shape and about twice the thickness of a crown-piece ; upon these place the chickens, and garnish with carrot, onion, faggot of parsley, a clove of garlic, a little grated nutmeg, pepper and salt ; cover with a buttered paper and the lid, and then set them upon a moderate fire (with some live embers of charcoal upon the lid), to simmer for about forty minutes : taking care to turn the chickens occasionally, in order that they may be equally colored of a light brown all over. This being done, the butter should be drained off from the chickens, and the vegetables removed ; then add a glass of Sherry or Madeira, two spoonfuls of Tomata sauce (No. 22), and the same quantity of Brown sauce, a small piece of glaze, lemon-juice, and a little Cayenne pepper. Let the whole simmer together on the fire for five minutes, then draw the strings from the chickens, and dish them up ; garnish them round with the pieces of ham placed alternately with a *crôuton* of the same shape ; round these place four groups of Spanish-peas (*garbanças*) boiled and divested of the hulls, and some dressed tomatas *au gratin* (No. 1161) ; pour the sauce over the chickens and serve.

In addition to the foregoing methods of dressing chickens for small Removes, Flanks, or *Entrées*, they may also be served with rice, macaroni, *nouilles*, oyster sauce, *à l'Anglaise, à l'Ivoire, à l'Estragon*, &c., and indeed in every variety of form described for dressing capons.

REMOVES OF GOOSE,

COMPRISING

Goose, *à l'Anglaise.*
 „   *à l'Estouffade.*
 „   *à la Flamande.*
 „   *à l'Allemande.*
 „   *à la Dauphinoise.*

Goose, *à la Normande.*
Wild Goose, *à l'Aberdeen.*
 „   *à l'Allemande.*
Cygnets.
 „   *à la Norwich.*

695. GOOSE, A L'ANGLAISE.

DRAW a fine fat goose, and stuff it with the following seasoning :—
Chop six large onions and about one third of the quantity of green-sage-leaves ; parboil these in water for three minutes, then drain them upon a sieve, and afterward put them into a small stewpan with two ounces of butter, pepper and salt, and allow the whole to simmer gently over a slow fire for a few minutes, stirring the seasoning the whole of the time with a wooden spoon. When the goose is stuffed, truss it for roasting, run the spit through it, then fasten it on by the means of a strong iron skewer laid upon the back of the goose, and secured at each end with string. The goose should now be put down to the fire to roast, which will require about an hour and a half, according to its size—taking particular care to baste it frequently ; when done, take it off the spit, dish it up with a rich brown gravy under it, and send to table with a boat of apple-sauce.

696. GOOSE, A L'ESTOUFFADE.

DRAW a fine fat young goose, and stuff it in the following manner :—
Parboil two large onions and chop them fine ; to these add six sage-leaves, and a proportionate quantity of green thyme and mugwort : these also must first be parboiled and then chopped. Put the onions and the herbs into a small stewpan with two ounces of butter, a little grated nutmeg, pepper and salt ; and set the whole to stew gently on a very slow fire for about ten minutes. Then put the stuffing into the goose, and truss it in the usual way ; place it in an oval stewpan with half-a-pound of butter, a garnished faggot of parsley, an onion stuck with four cloves, one head of celery, and a carrot cut into slices, and moisten with two glasses of Sherry. Put the lid on the stewpan, place it on a slow fire, with some live embers of charcoal and ashes on the lid, and allow the goose to simmer gently for about an hour and a half, taking particular care to turn it, so as to give it an equal color all over. When done, pour off all the fat, and a ragout-spoonful of reduced brown sauce, and a little *consommé* to detach the glaze from the sides of the stewpan ; and having allowed it to boil quickly, in order to reduce the sauce to its usual consistency, the goose should be dished up, and garnished round with a border of glazed turnips ; then pour the sauce over it, and serve.
This dish may also be garnished with macaroni, with glazed carrots, or onions.

697. GOOSE, A LA FLAMANDE.

TRUSS and braize a goose; when done, dish it up and garnish it round with alternate groups of glazed carrots, turnips, Brussels-sprouts, and indeed almost every variety of vegetables in season, previously prepared for the purpose; glaze the goose, and pour some bright brown sauce (with the addition of some of the braize in which it has been done, reduced to a glaze for that purpose) round the vegetables, and send to table.

698. GOOSE, A L'ALLEMANDE.

PROCURE a double-handful of mugwort, rub off all the buds, and blanch them in boiling water for two minutes; then drain and put them into a small stewpan, with a large onion chopped fine, a little grated nutmeg, pepper and salt, and four ounces of butter; set these to simmer gently on the fire, for ten minutes, and having put this stuffing in the goose, truss and place it in an oval stewpan with four ounces of butter, and set it on a moderate fire, with some live embers on the lid. Care should be taken to turn the goose every now and then, so as to give it an equal color all over. When it is done, pour off all the grease, add the juice of one lemon and one orange, together with the peel of an orange cut into very thin shreds previously parboiled in water; add also a spoonful of brown sauce and a little *consommé*. Allow these to boil together for two or three minutes, dish up the goose, garnish it round with groups of potatoes—cut into the shape of large olives and fried in butter—pour the sauce over the goose, and send to table.

699. GOOSE, A LA DAUPHINOISE.

STUFF a goose with chestnuts prepared as follows :—Slit, scald, and peel about sixty large chestnuts; put them into a stewpan with two ounces of butter, a little salt, and a quart of good broth, one shalot, chopped fine, and a garnished faggot of parsley; set the chestnuts to stew upon a slow fire, and when they are done, put them in the goose and truss it. Then place the goose in a deep earthen dish, moisten with a wine *mirepoix* (No. 236), and cover the dish effectually with some stiff-made flour-and-water paste, so as entirely to prevent the aroma of the several ingredients from escaping. Set it in the oven to bake for about two hours, and when it is done, remove the crust, dish up the goose, strain the gravy through a sieve into a stewpan, skim off every particle of grease, and then boil it down to the bare quantity required for saucing; to this add the juice of two oranges and one lemon, half a pound of currant jelly, and some orange peel shred fine; boil the whole together for two minutes, then pour the sauce over the goose, and send to table.

700. GOOSE, A LA NORMANDE.

CHOP one large onion fine, blanch, and afterward drain it upon a sieve; then fry it with a little butter of a light brown color, and mix it with mashed potatoes, in sufficient quantity to stuff the goose; this being done, truss it and roast it in the usual manner, and when removed from the spit, dish it up; garnish it round with a border of small round apples neatly turned, and stewed with a little broth, a small piece of butter, and two ounces of sugar ; when nearly done, the apples should be boiled down quickly, in order to glaze them of a bright light brown color : be careful that they remain whole. Pour a rich gravy round the goose, and send to table.

701. WILD GOOSE, A L'ABERDEEN.

WHEN the goose is drawn, scald the feet and remove the rough cuticle that covers them ; then singe it over the flame of a charcoal-fire, wipe it with a clean cloth, and pick out all the stubble, and stuff the goose with the following preparation :—

To one pound of chopped beef-suet, add the same quantity of bread-crumbs, half a pound of butter, two whole eggs, a little chopped thyme, sweet-basil, and marjoram, two shalots, and a handful of parsley ; season with grated nutmeg, pepper and salt ; knead the whole well together, and stuff the goose with it.

Then truss the goose, and put it on the spit in the same fashion as directed for a haunch of venison. It will require about three hours to roast ; when done, dish it up with a border of glazed Portugal onions (No. 1164), pour some *Poivrade* sauce (No. 29), under it, and send to table. The goose should be frothed with flour and butter in the same manner as venison, after the crust has been removed.

702. WILD GOOSE, L'ALLEMANDE.

PREPARE the goose at first as directed in No. 698, then place it in a deep earthen dish, and strew upon it the following vegetables cut into thin slices : two carrots, two onions, one head of celery, a handful of parsley, four bay-leaves, thyme, marjoram, and sweet-basil in small quantities ; also four blades of mace, a dozen cloves, and a spoonful of Jamaica pepper-corns, two lemons peeled and cut into slices, a pint of salad oil, and half a pint of French vinegar. Allow the goose to remain in this *marinade* or pickle for a couple of days, taking care to turn it frequently. When about to dress the goose, put it on the spit, cover with a stout paper well buttered, lay the whole of the vegetables, &c., on the breast, cover these with two sheets of buttered paper, and fasten them on securely with string. Put the goose thus prepared down to the fire to roast for about two hours, taking care to baste it frequently ; when done, take it from the spit, glaze and dish it up, garnish with a border of *quenelles* of potatoes rolled in fried bread-crumbs, and pour under it a sauce, made as follows :—

Grate a large stick of horseradish ; peel and slice up two lemons, removing the pips, and put these in a stewpan with four shalots, six cloves, two blades of mace, and a tea-spoonful of pepper-corns, two bay-leaves, a large sprig of thyme, and half a pint of French vinegar ; set these to boil on the fire until reduced to half the quantity, then add a large spoonful of rich gravy, one pound of currant jelly, and the juice of two Seville oranges ; allow the whole to boil together for five minutes, and then strain the sauce through a tammy with considerable pressure into a small stewpan, and make it hot for use.

703. CYGNET A LA NORWICH.

PROCURE a Norwich-fed cygnet (these birds are in best condition in September), stuff it with the following preparation :—

Three pounds of rumpsteaks chopped fine, seasoned with three shalots, grated nutmeg, pepper and salt. Truss the cygnet in the usual manner, spit it, then envelope it with well-buttered paper, and encase it with flour-and-water-paste in a similar way to that practised for haunches of venison ; after which let the whole be again secured with stout paper well greased and fastened on with twine. About four hours will suffice to roast the cygnet, during which it should be frequently basted. When done, remove the coating, froth it with flour and butter in the usual manner, and dish it up with a rich brown gravy under it ; and send a boatful of Port-wine sauce to be handed round with it.

Note.—Cygnets may be prepared for the table, according to the directions for dressing wild geese.

REMOVES OF DUCKS,

COMPRISING

Ducks, à la Macédoine.	Braized Ducks, with stewed Peas.
Braized Ducks, with Turnips.	„ à la Provençale.

703. DUCKS, A LA MACEDOINE.

Truss two ducks for boiling, and put them into an oval stewpan with a carrot, an onion, two cloves and a garnished faggot of parsley ; moisten with a quart of white broth, cover with an oval piece of well-buttered paper, place the lid on the stewpan, and set it on the stove to boil ; then put some live embers on the lid, and remove the ducks to the side of the stove to braize gently for about an hour. When about to send them to table, drain them upon a napkin, remove the string, and dish them up with alternate groups of a copious and varied *Macédoine* of vegetables (No. 143)—such as carrots and turnips, cut in fancy shapes and nicely glazed, after being previously boiled in broth, asparagus heads, French-beans, green-peas, cauliflower, &c., as they may happen to be in season. Sauce the ducks with some *Allemande,* and serve.

704. BRAIZED DUCKS, WITH TURNIPS.

These should be trussed in the usual way, and placed in an oval stewpan with a carrot, an onion stuck with two cloves, and a garnished faggot of parsley ; moisten with sufficient white stock to cover the ducks, put a buttered paper over them and set them to boil gently on a slow fire for about an hour. While they are being braized, cut some turnips into fancy shapes, such as large olives, half-moons, &c., fry them in two ounces of butter and a little sugar ; when they are all equally browned, throw them into a stewpan, containing about a pint of *Espagnole* sauce, with the addition of some of the broth the ducks are braized in. Allow the turnips to boil very gently by the side of the fire until done ; they must then be drained upon a sieve, their sauce clarified, skimmed, reduced to its proper consistency, and passed through a tammy into a small stewpan containing the turnips. Dish the ducks up, place the turnips neatly round, pour the sauce over them, and send to table.

705. BRAIZED DUCKS, WITH STEWED PEAS.

BRAIZE the ducks as directed in the foregoing case, and when done, dish them up with stewed peas round them ; sauce with a brown sauce in which some of the broth from the ducks has been reduced. They may also be prepared as follows :—

Put two ounces of butter in a stewpan on the fire : when melted, add two table-spoonfuls of flour, and stir this over the fire until the *roux* becomes of a fawn-color; then add a quart of good broth or gravy, carefully working the whole while mixing. Stir this sauce on the fire, and when it boils, put the ducks trussed for boiling into it, and also a quart of young peas, and a faggot of parsley and green onions. Allow these to stew very gently by the side of the stove for about an hour ; when the ducks are done, take them out of the sauce, skim off all the grease, remove the faggot of parsley ; and if there is too much sauce, boil it down to its proper consistency, pour the peas and sauce over the ducks, previously dished up, and serve.

706. BRAIZED DUCKS A LA PROVENCALE.

THESE should be braized as in the former cases, and when dished up, garnished with the following preparation :

Cut six large onions into halves, remove the ends of these, and slice them up. Meanwhile, heat half a pint of salad oil in a deep sautapan over the fire ; fry the onions in it of a light-brown color, carefully stirring them with the end of an iron skewer to avoid breaking the pieces. When the onions are done, drain them upon a sieve, and afterward put them into a small stewpan with the juice of a lemon, a little mignionette pepper and a piece of glaze about the size of a walnut, and set them on a slow fire to simmer gently for a quarter of an hour ; add some finished *Espagnole* sauce in sufficient quantity for the purpose, boil the whole together, pour it round the ducks and serve.

This dish is sometimes designated *à la Lyonnaise.*

In addition to the foregoing methods for serving braized ducks, they may also be garnished with a *Jardinière*, stewed olives, a *Nivernaise*, or with *saüer-kraut* (No. 165) ; for preparing which, see Vegetable Garnishes.

REMOVES OF PHEASANTS,

COMPRISING

Pheasants, *à la Périgueux.*	Pheasants, *à la Dauphinoise.*
„ *à la Chipolata.*	„ with braized cabbage.
„ *à l'Italienne.*	„ *à la Flamande.*
„ *à la Beauveaux.*	„ *à l'Allemande.*
„ *à la Financière.*	„ *à la Régence.*
„ with *purèe* of celery.	„ *à l'Espagnole.*
„ *à la Soubise.*	„ *à l'Aspic.*
„ *à la Dauphine.*	„ *à la Monglas.*
„ *à la Paysanne.*	

707. PHEASANTS, A LA PERIGUEUX.

FOLLOW in every respect the directions for dressing turkeys *à la Périgueux* (No. 660).

708. PHEASANTS, A LA CHIPOLATA.

THESE are to be trussed and nicely roasted, and when taken from the spit, should be dished up and neatly garnished with a *Chipolata ragout* (No. 190).

709. PHEASANTS, A L'ITALIENNE.

TRUSS two pheasants as for boiling, and place them on the spit in the usual way, then cover the breasts with a reduced wine *mirepoix*, retaining the vegetables in it; wrap them in two large sheets of well-buttered paper, securely fastened at each end with a string; place a long stout-made iron skewer at the backs of the pheasants, which must be likewise tightly secured with string to prevent them from slipping round. Roast the pheasants for an hour, take them up, place them on their dish, garnish with a border of *raviolis* (No. 375), pour an Italian sauce (No. 12) over them, and serve.

710. PHEASANTS, A LA BEAUVEAUX.

THE pheasants must be boned, except the legs and wings, which should be left entire : stuff them with a *farce* made with fat livers of fowls or game (No. 249) : then truss them so as to give them the appearance of being whole ; run a strong iron skewer through them, fasten this upon a spit with string at each end of the skewer; cover the breasts with some reduced *mirepoix* (No. 236), and wrap them up in two sheets of buttered paper, which must also be securely fastened with string. Roast the pheasants an hour and a quarter, and when done, dish them up with a *ragout* of scollops of fat livers and truffles (No. 191) in a *Financière* sauce, and serve.

711. PHEASANTS, A LA FINANCIERE.

TRUSS and roast the pheasants, and when done, dish them up with a rich *Financière ragout* (No. 188).

712. PHEASANTS, WITH PUREE OF CELERY.

TRUSS the pheasants for boiling, braize them in some good stock, garnished with a carrot, an onion stuck with two cloves, and a garnished faggot of parsley ; when done drain them upon a napkin, dish them up, and pour over them a white *purée* of celery (No. 110) ; garnish round with a border of potato *croquettes*, and serve.

713. PHEASANTS, A LA SOUBISE.

THESE should be larded through the breasts, lengthwise, with strips of fat bacon about four inches long and a quarter of an inch square, seasoned with pepper and salt and chopped parsley ; they must be afterward trussed for boiling, then braized as in the foregoing case ; when done, dish them up with a *purée* of onions *à la Soubise* (No. 119) poured over them, and send to table.

714. PHEASANTS, A LA DAUPHINE.

SEE *Poulards à la Dauphine.* (No. 684.)

715. PHEASANTS, A LA PAYSANNE.

TRUSS the pheasants as for boiling with the legs tucked inside; then put them into an oval stewpan with four ounces of butter, and a piece of glaze the size of an egg, and set them to simmer very gently over a slow fire. They must be frequently turned, and care should be taken to prevent the glaze and butter from burning. When the pheasants are done, let the butter and grease be poured off; add a glass of white wine and some good stock in sufficient quantity to serve for the gravy, the juice of half a lemon and a little pepper and salt; boil these together to detach the glaze from the sides of the stewpan, and when the pheasants are dished up, pour this gravy over them, garnish them round with groups of potatoes cut into the shape of large olives and fried in butter, and serve.

716. PHEASANTS, A LA DAUPHINOISE.

TRUSS the pheasants as for boiling, braize them in a wine *mirepoix* (No. 236), and when done, take them up, draw the strings, and allow them to get partially cold; then cover them entirely with some reduced *Allemande* sauce in which has been mixed half the *mirepoix* the pheasants have been braized in, (this previously to its being boiled down for the purpose of adding it to the sauce, must be freed of all the grease, &c.) This coating of sauce should be allowed to cool, and then must be bread-crumbed over with grated Parmesan cheese mixed with the bread-crumbs in equal proportions. The pheasants must now be placed in a deep sauta-pan or pie-dish, previously well-buttered, and the remaining half of the braize added to moisten the bottom of the pan.— Three-quarters of an hour before dinner-time, sprinkle the pheasants with a little clarified butter, and set them in the oven to be baked of a very light fawn color, frequently basting them with clarified butter while baking. When done, dish them up side by side, garnish round with a border of *quenelles* of polenta, pour a brown Italian sauce (No. 12) under them, and serve.

The *quenelles* of polenta above alluded to should be thus made:—

Put into a small stewpan six ounces of butter, half a pint of water, a little mignionette pepper, and salt; set these on the fire to boil, and then mix in with them six ounces of polenta (a preparation of Indian corn); stir this again over the fire until it becomes a a smooth compact paste, and then work in with it two whole eggs and two yelks, and two ounces of grated Parmesan cheese. Shape this composition into *quenelles* with two table-spoons in the usual manner, and poach them in hot water.

717. PHEASANTS, WITH STEWED CABBAGES.

THESE must be trussed as for boiling, and placed in a rather large oval stewpan with three white-heart or Savoy cabbages previously cut into halves, the cores taken out, and blanched or parboiled; afterward the two halves of each cabbage, previously seasoned with mignionette pepper, and salt, must be tied up with string; add two carrots, one head of celery, two onions, each stuck with two cloves, one pound of streaky bacon from which all the rust has been pared off, and which must also be parboiled like the cabbages, one pound of German sausage, and a garnished faggot of parsley; moisten with good stock in sufficient quantity to cover the pheasants, cover with a piece of buttered paper, put the lid on the stewpan, and then set the whole on a moderate fire to stew very gently for about two hours. Just before sending to table, take out the pheasants, drain them upon a napkin, remove the strings, and dish them up with an ornamental *crôustade* of fried bread in the centre; then put the bacon and German sausage upon a plate, and after having drained the cabbages in a colander, roll them in a clean napkin in the form of a rolling-pin; cut this into two-inch lengths, and place them round the pheasants, trim the bacon, cut it into strips, and lay them on the top of the circle of the pieces of cabbages in alternate layers with slices of the sausage; about the upper part of this dish, place well-formed groups of nicely-shaped glazed carrots, turnips, and onions, prepared for the purpose; pour an *Espagnole* sauce over the whole, glaze the pheasants and the roots, and serve.

718. PHEASANTS, A LA FLAMANDE.

TRUSS and braize the pheasants in common stock, garnished with carrot, onion stuck with two cloves, and a faggot of parsley; when done, dish them up side by side, garnish round with alternate groups of carrots and turnips, cut into fancy shapes, and nicely glazed, and some dressed Brussels sprouts and glazed onions; pour an *Espagnole* sauce round them, glaze the pheasants, and serve.

719. PHEASANTS, A L'ALLEMANDE.

SEE chickens *à l'Allemande* (No. 690.)

720. PHEASANTS, A LA REGENCE.

TRUSS the pheasants with plump breasts as for roasting, lard them closely, and about an hour before dinner-time, put them on the spit before the fire to roast for about forty minutes, taking particular care to baste them frequently, and glaze them well just before taking them off the spit. When done, dish them up, garnish round with groups of white cocks'-combs, button-mushrooms, small *quenelles* and truffles;

in each flank of the dish place a large decorated *quenelle*, and at the ends put a larded sweetbread; sauce the remove neatly round with some *Allemande* sauce, so as not to touch the pheasants, glaze the larding, and serve.

721. PHEASANTS, WITH RICE, A L'ESPAGNOLE.

THESE must be trussed as for boiling, and then placed in an oval stewpan, with carrot, celery, two onions stuck with three cloves each, a garnished faggot of parsley and a couple of red Spanish sausages; moisten with some red wine *mirepoix*, cover them up, and set them to stew very gently for about two hours on a slow fire.

While the pheasants are stewing, prepare some rice in the following manner :

Thoroughly wash ten ounces of Carolina rice, and afterward boil it for three minutes in water, and drain it on a sieve until all the moisture is absorbed; then put a gill of salad-oil into a large santa-pan over a brisk fire, and, as soon as the oil is quite hot, throw the rice in and fry it until it becomes slightly browned, stirring it with a spoon the whole of the time it remains on the fire. Then put the rice into a stewpan, moisten it with a pint and a half of good *consommé*, season with a little Cayenne pepper and a pinch of saffron powder; set it to simmer very gently on the fire for half an hour, and when the pheasants are dished up, work the rice with a teaspoonful of tomata sauce and a little glaze, then mould it in the shape of ordinary *quenelles* with a table-spoon, and place these closely round the pheasants after they are dished up; sauce them over with *Poivrade* sauce in which part of their broth has been mixed after being first boiled down to glaze, and serve.

722. PHEASANTS, A L'ASPIC.

BONE the pheasants, and take care to leave the legs and wings entire; then season the inside with pepper and salt, and fill them out with some forcemeat of pheasant (No. 243) previously mixed with some chopped parsley and mushrooms; truss them so as to give them their original shape and size, cover them with thin layers of fat bacon and wrap them securely in napkins spread with butter, fastened at each end with string. When the pheasants are thus far prepared, place them in an oval stewpan with a carrot, an onion stuck with three cloves, and a garnished faggot of parsley; moisten with good white stock in sufficient quantity to cover them, and then set them to braize very gently on a slow fire for an hour and a half. When the pheasants are done, take them up, remove the napkins and strings, drain all the moisture from them upon a clean napkin, and dish them up; pour under them some bright essence of game, made from the carcasses of the pheasants, which, previously to its being used, must be clarified and reduced to half-glaze.

723. PHEASANTS, A LA MONCLAS.

ROAST two pheasants, and as soon as they come off the spit, cut the meat from the breasts by making an incision in the shape of a heart; this meat must then be cut into very small dice and mixed with two gravy-spoonfuls of reduced *Béchamel* sauce or *Allemande*, and two dozen mushrooms, a couple of black truffles and a small piece of red tongue should be also cut into dice and mixed with the pheasant. With this preparation fill up the breasts of the pheasants, smooth them over with the blade of a knife, and then cover them with bread-crumbs fried of a light-brown color; set the pheasants in the oven or hot closet to keep warm, and when about to send them to table place them in their dish side by side, pour under them a white *ragout* of cock's-combs, mushrooms, and truffles, and serve.

Note.—This dish is generally served when there happens to be some ready-dressed game left from the previous day's dinner.

REMOVES OF PARTRIDGES,

COMPRISING

Partridges, *à la Séville.*	Partridges, *à la Ravigotte.*
Red-legged Partridges, *à la Plessy.*	„ *à la Soubise.*
„ „ *à la Cerito.*	„ *à l'Ellsler.*

724. PARTRIDGES, A LA SEVILLE.

TRUSS four or six partridges as for boiling, fry them of a light-brown color in four ounces of fresh butter, and then set them aside upon a plate; cut about one pound of raw ham (that has been previously soaked and parboiled) into small pieces in the form of olives, and two dozen small pieces of the red part of a carrot cut with a round scoop, with the same number of small button-onions; fry these also of a light-brown color, withdraw them from the fire, and then put them with the partridges back into the stewpan; add a faggot of parsley garnished with thyme, bay-leaf, sweet basil, and one clove of garlic; season with a little salt and Cayenne pepper, moisten with two glasses of Madeira or Malaga, and a table-spoonful of tomatas; then set the stewpan (covered with the lid containing live embers) on a slow fire, to simmer gently for three-quarters of an hour. Observe that the moistening of the partridges should be reduced to one half of its original quantity while braizing. When done, dish them up in a triangular form, skim off the grease from the carrots, &c., add a gravy-spoonful of finished *Espagnole* and the juice of half a lemon; boil the whole together for two minutes, place the ham, carrots, and onions in separate groups round the partridges, pass the sauce through a tammy, pour it over the partridges, and serve.

In the centre of the partridges place some *garbanças*, or yellow Spanish peas, prepared as follows:—

Soak a pint of *garbanças* in tepid water for twelve hours; then drain, and put them into a stewpan with half a pound of ham, a carrot, an onion, a garnished faggot of parsley, and a little mignionette-pepper; moisten with three pints of broth, and set them to boil gently for three hours.

725. RED-LEGGED PARTRIDGES, A LA PLESSY.

THESE are to be trussed as for boiling, braized in a white *poële* (No. 230), and when done to be dished up in a triangular form, and garnished with neat groups of small *quenelles* of partridge and white button mushrooms; pour round a *Suprême* sauce (No. 38), finish with an essence of game over the partridges, and serve.

726. PARTRIDGES, A LA CERITO.

BONE three red-legged partridges and fill them out with some *quenelle* force-meat made with the fillets of two partridges, and with which should be mixed previously to using it, two black truffles and a small piece of red tongue cut into small dice : when the partridges are filled with this preparation, truss them so as to give them their original shape ; scald the red legs and insert them on each side of the birds, at the same time pushing the ends of the skin of the leg neatly in with each foot. Then, wrap each bird in a separate small napkin spread with butter, and fasten the ends with string ; braize them for about an hour in some white *poële* (No. 230), over a slow fire, and take particular care that they do not boil fast. When done, take them out of the napkins, remove the strings, drain all the unnecessary moisture from them, and dish them up : garnish them with a border of *raviolis* (No. 375), pour a *Provençale* sauce (No. 25) over them, and serve.

727. PARTRIDGES, A LA RAVIGOTTE.

THESE should be trussed as for boiling, and must be roasted just before they are wanted ; when dished up, pour a *Ravigotte* or *Provençale* sauce under them, glaze and send to table.

728. PARTRIDGES, A LA SOUBISE.

TRUSS the partridges for boiling, braize them, and when done, dish them up, pour an onion sauce *à la soubise*, finished with a gill of cream (No. 119) over them, and send to table.

729. PARTRIDGES, A L'ELLSLER.

TRUSS four red-legged partridges as for boiling, lard the breasts closely, braize them in wine *mirepoix* (No. 236) ; when done, glaze them nicely and dish them up in a row ; garnish with a group of small truffles, cock's-combs and mushrooms at each end place a heart sweet-bread *contisé* with black truffles, and on the sides a border of dessert-spoon *quenelles*, made with game force-meat, in which has been mixed some lobster-coral; pour a Parisian sauce (No. 40) round the partridges, and serve.

Note.—In addition to the foregoing methods for dressing red-legged and common partridges, they may also be treated according to the various directions given for dressing pheasants.

MEAT PIES FOR REMOVES,

COMPRISING

Chicken Pie, *à la Reine.*   Veal and Ham Pie.
Pigeon Pie, *à l'Anglaise.*   Mutton Pie, *à l'Anglaise.*
Grouse Pie, *d l'Ecossaise.*   Pie of Woodcocks or Snipes, *à l'Irlandaise.*
Partridge Pie, *à la Chasseur.*   Fieldfare, or Blackbird Pie.
Gibblet Pie, with fine-herbs.   Lark Pie, *à la Melton Mowbray.*
Beefsteak and Oyster Pie.

730. CHICKEN PIE, A LA REINE.

CUT two chickens into small members as for fricassee; cover the bottom of the pie-dish with layers of scollops of veal and ham placed alternately; season with chopped mushrooms and parsley, pepper and salt, then add a little white sauce; next place in the dish the pieces of chicken in neat order, and round these put a plover's egg in each cavity; repeat the seasoning and the sauce, lay a few thin slices of dressed ham neatly trimmed on the top; cover the pie with puff-paste, ornament this with pieces of the same cut into the form of leaves, &c., egg the pie over with a paste-brush, and bake it for one hour and a half. A very good chicken pie may be made by omitting the plover's eggs, mushrooms, ham, and the sauce—substituting for these, the yelks of eggs boiled hard, chopped parsley, bacon, and a little mushroom-catsup, some common gravy, or even water.

731. PIGEON PIE, A L'ANGLAISE.

DRAW, truss, and singe, six young pigeons; then, stuff them with the chopped livers, mixed with some parsley, a small piece of butter, pepper and salt. Next, cover the bottom of the dish with rather large scollops of beef, taken either from the fillet or rump; season with chopped parsley and mushrooms, pepper and salt; over these place the pigeons, and between each pigeon put the yelk of an egg boiled hard, placing two or three in the centre also; add some white or brown sauce, whichever may be at hand, in sufficient quantity to produce sauce enough for the dish, or if neither of these be ready, then substitute some gravy or common broth; repeat the seasoning, cover the pie with puff-paste, bake it for an hour and a half, and send to table.

732. GROUSE PIE, A L'ECOSSAISE.

WHEN the grouse are picked, cut off the legs and wings, and tuck the thighs inside; then cut away the lower parts of the backs, which, if permitted to remain, would, from their bitter taste, spoil the pie. Cover the bottom of the dish with large scollops of beef, seasoned with chopped mushrooms, parsley, and shalots, pepper and salt : over these place the grouse, and between each bird put the yolk of an egg boiled hard ; lay some small thin slices of streaky bacon or ham upon the top, and then mix a pint of good gravy with two table-spoonfuls of " Hickson's Mogul Sauce," and the same proportion of genuine Harvey sauce : pour this preparation into the pie, sprinkle some chopped parsley and mushrooms on the surface, cover with puff-paste, bake the pie for an hour and a half, and serve.

733. PARTRIDGE PIE, A LA CHASSEUR.

Cut the partridges into small members, in the same manner as directed for cutting up fowls for a fricassee, and set them apart on a plate. Then, cover the bottom of the pie-dish with neatly-trimmed scollops of veal, and thin slices of streaky bacon, first partially boiled to extract the salt; cover these with six spoonfuls of the following preparation :—Make about half a pint of *Soubise* sauce (No. 119), to this add half that quantity of white sauce, a pottle of button-mushrooms, some chopped parsley, and a littly thyme ; season with cayenne pepper, and salt. When the veal, &c., is covered with the foregoing, place the members of the partridges, in neat order, upon the whole ; pour the remainder of the sauce on these, and smooth over the surface with a knife ; place on the top some yolks of eggs boiled hárd and cut into halves, and between each yolk put a small piece of streaky bacon ; cover the pie with puff-paste, bake it for one hour and a half, and serve.

734. GIBLET PIE, WITH FINE-HERBS.

Procure two sets of goose giblets (cleaned), scald them, afterward immerse them in cold water, and drain them upon a napkin. Then, cut the giblets into pieces about two inches long, trim them neatly and place them in a stewpan with a carrot, an onion stuck with four cloves, a garnished faggot of parsley, and season with pepper and a little salt; moisten with a quart of good broth and a glass of Sherry and set them to stew gently on a slow fire. When done, remove the carrot, onion, and faggot of parsley ; drain the giblets into a sieve, skim off all the grease from the broth, and after having put it back into a small stewpan, thicken it with a little *roux*, and boil the sauce over a brisk fire for a quarter of an hour, stirring it the whole time with a wooden spoon. Reduce the sauce by boiling to about a pint, and then remove it from the fire. Next, cover the bottom of the dish with scollops of fillet of beef, season with fine-herbs, consisting of mushrooms, parsley, a very little sweet-basil, and two shalots, adding cayenne pepper, and salt ; over these pour half the sauce, then fill the dish up with the giblets, which place in neat order ; sprinkle some fine-herbs upon them, and pour the remainder of the sauce over the whole. Cover the pie with puff-paste, bake it for an hour and a quarter, and send to table.

735. BEEFSTEAK AND OYSTER PIE.

Cut three pounds of fillet of beef or rump-steaks into large scollops, fry them quickly over a very brisk fire, so as to brown them before they are half done; then, place them on the bottom of the dish, leaving the centre open, in two successive layers; fill the cente with four dozen oysters, previously parboiled and bearded, season with pepper and salt, and pour the following preparation over the whole. When the scollops of beef have been fried in a sauta or frying-pan, pour nearly all the grease out, and shake a table-spoonful of flour into it; stir this over the fire for one minute, and then add a pint of good gravy or broth, two tablespoonsful of mushroom-catsup, and an equal quantity of Harvey sauce and the liquor from the oysters; stir the whole over the fire, and keep it boiling for a quarter of an hour. Half an hour after this sauce has been poured into the pie, cover it with puff-paste in the usual way, bake it for an hour aud a half, and serve.

736. VEAL AND HAM PIE.

TRIM the veal and ham into scollops, and season with pepper and salt in moderation. Next chop a handful of mushrooms and some parsley very fine, and put them in a small stewpan with a small pat of butter, and one shalot also chopped fine; fry these lightly over the fire, then add nearly a pint of *Velouté* sauce or good stock; boil the whole for five minutes, and pour it into the pie; place six yolks of eggs boiled hard in the cavities, cover with puff-paste, bake the pie for an hour and a half, and serve.

737. MUTTON PIE, A L'ANGLAISE.

PROCURE a neck of mutton, remove the scrag and the spine-bone, shorten the ribs to about three inches, and use these trimmings to make some stock or gravy for the pie. Next cut the mutton into neat chops, pare off the superfluous fat, season them with pepper and salt, and place them in the dish in circular order, one resting upon another in the same way as cutlets are dished up; fill the centre with small new potatoes, or old ones turned into round balls; boil the mutton stock down to the quantity required to nearly fill up the dish, season with pepper and salt, cover with puff-paste, bake the pie an hour and a half, and send to table.

738. PIE OF WOODCOCKS OR SNIPES, A L'IRLANDAISE.

PICK the birds clean, cut off the legs and wings, singe them, and then cut each woodcock or snipe into halves: remove the gizzards, leaving the trail, and set them aside on a plate. Then, cover the sides and bottom of a white glazed earthen oval pan (used for preserving game) with very thin layers of fat bacon, place the woodcocks or snipes in the pan in close layers, each well-seasoned with ground black pepper and salt, and a small proportion of prepared aromatic spices (No. 1250). When this is done, fill up the pan with a sufficient quantity of clarified fresh butter to cover the birds, place some layers of fat bacon on the top, cover the pan hermetically with a firm flour-and-water paste: bake the pie in a moderately-heated oven for about two hours; when it has become cold, remove the crusts, wash the edges and sides of the pan, and run a little fresh clarified butter on the top; when cold, ornament with a neat border of picked double parsley, set the pie on a folded napkin laid on its dish, and serve.

This is perhaps the best method for making pies of woodcocks or snipes, as from the simplicity of the ingredients used, the birds retain their flavor : an important consideration with amateurs of this kind of game.

739. FIELDFARE OR BLACKBIRD PIE.

THESE birds are only fit for table during the months of November, December, and January, and are in the greatest perfection during severe frosty weather. Procure a dozen fieldfares or blackbirds—which should be fat and fresh killed ; pick them very clean, draw and singe them : next cut the legs and wings off, and tuck the thigh bones inside the birds, and stuff them with the following preparation :

Soak the crumb of two French-rolls in a little milk, put them in a stewpan with two ounces of fresh butter, a little grated lemon-peel, a small shalot chopped fine, and a handful of parsley also chopped ; season with pepper and salt, a little grated nutmeg, and a pinch of aromatic spices (No. 1250); stir this over the fire until the whole forms a compact paste ; then add the yolks of two eggs, and use this stuffing as above directed. Cover the bottom of a pie-dish with scollops of beef previously fried brown, place the birds in close circular order upon these ; between each bird put a slice of streaky bacon, and fill up the centre with stewed mushrooms prepared as follows. Clean a plateful of mushrooms, cut them up and put them in a stewpan with a small pat of butter, half a pint of rich gravy or brown sauce, two table-spoonfuls of Harvey sauce, a little Cayenne pepper and salt; stew these over a quick fire for ten minutes, and then, if gravy be used for the purpose instead of sauce, thicken it by mixing in a small pat of butter kneaded with a table-spoonful of flour. The pie must be afterward covered with puff-paste, baked for one hour and a half, and then sent to table.

740. LARK PIE, A LA MELTON MOWBRAY.

PICK clean four dozen Dunstable larks, singe them over the flame of a charcoal fire, cut off the wings and legs, and with the point of a small knife remove the gizzards, and then set the larks aside on a dish. Next cut two pounds of veal cutlets and a pound of ham into scollops ; fry these in a sauta-pan with a little fresh butter, a pottle of button mushrooms, some parsley and two shalots, half a bay-leaf, and a sprig of thyme chopped fine ; season with cayenne and salt, and the juice of a lemon. To these add half a pint of *Velouté* or *Espagnole* sauce, and the same quantity of rich gravy ; boil the whole together for three minutes, then place the veal and ham scollops one upon the other in the bottom of the dish ; put the larks neatly and close to each other upon these, pour the sauce over them, and place the mushrooms in the centre ; cover with puff-paste, bake the pie for one hour and a quarter, and serve.

MEAT PUDDINGS,

COMPRISING

Beefsteak and Oyster Pudding.
Mutton Pudding.
Kidney Pudding.

Pudding of small Birds, à la Chipolata.
Snipe Pudding, à la D'Orsay.
Sausage Pudding.

741. BEEFSTEAK AND OYSTER PUDDING.

LINE a two-quart pudding basin with some beef-suet paste; fill this lining with a preparation similar to that described for making beef-steak and oyster pie, except that the sauce must be more reduced. When the pudding is filled, wet the edges of the paste round the top of the basin with a paste-brush dipped in water, cover it with a piece of suet-paste rolled out to the size of the basin, fasten it down by bearing all round the edge with the thumb; and then with the thumb and fore-finger, twist the edges of the paste over and over so as to give it a corded appearance. This pudding must be either steamed or boiled three hours; when done, turn it out of the basin carefully, pour some rich brown-gravy under it, and serve.

742. MUTTON PUDDING.

LINE a basin as in the above case, fill the lining with thick mutton cutlets, slightly trimmed, or, if preferred, with steaks cut from the leg; season with pepper and salt, some parsley, a little thyme, and one small shalot chopped fine, and between each layer of meat, put some slices of potatoes. Cover the pudding as in the foregoing article, steam or boil it for three hours, and serve some rich gravy under it when sent to table.

743. KIDNEY PUDDING.

CUT two pounds of sheep's or lamb's kidneys into scollops, put them into a basin with some chopped parsley, shalot, and a little thyme, and season with pepper and salt; then add a large gravy-spoonful of good sauce, and the juice of half a lemon: mix these ingredients well together. Line a basin with suet-paste, and fill the pudding with the foregoing preparation; cover it in the usual way, steam or boil it for two hours and a half, and when sent to table, pour under it some rich brown gravy to which has been added a little Indian soy, and serve.

744. PUDDING OF SMALL BIRDS, A LA CHIPOLATA.

MOST kinds of small birds may be used for this purpose, such as larks, sparrows, fieldfares, and wheatears, &c.

Take two pounds of small birds which have been picked clean, remove the gizzards, and fry them over a brisk fire until they are browned; add chopped mushrooms, parsley, and shalot, season with a little grated nutmeg, lemon-juice, pepper and salt, and a large gravy spoonful of brown sauce, also two dozen roasted chestnuts previously peeled, and a like number of small pieces of parboiled streaky bacon:

boil these ingredients for three minutes, then fill the pudding with them, and cover it with paste, as usual. This pudding must be steamed on account of its richness. When done, turn it out of the basin with care, in order not to break it; pour a rich brown sauce under, and serve.

This pudding may be made in a plainer manner, by omitting the mushrooms, lemon-juice, sauce, and chestnuts—following in all other respects the same process.

745. SNIPE PUDDING, A LA D'ORSAY.

PICK eight fine fat fresh snipes, singe them over a charcoal flame, and divide them into halves, remove the gizzards and reserve the trail for further use; season the snipes with a little Cayenne pepper, salt, and lemon-juice, and set them aside on a dish till wanted. Then peel a Portugal onion, cut it into thin slices and fry these in a stewpan with a small piece of butter; when they are slightly browned, throw in a tablespoonful of flour, and stir them together on the fire for three minutes; then add a handful of chopped mushrooms and parsley, a small bay-leaf, a sprig of thyme, a small blade of mace and a clove of garlic; moisten with a pint of Claret; stir the whole upon the fire, and when these have boiled ten minutes, add the trail and a piece of good glaze. Set the sauce to boil for three minutes longer, and then rub it through a tammy into a *purée* upon the snipes. Next, line a pudding basin with suet-paste, fill it up with the foregoing preparation, and when covered with a piece of paste and properly fastened round the edges so as to prevent the escape of the volatile properties of the sauce, steam it in a covered stewpan for two hours and a half. When the pudding is done, turn it out of the basin with care, pour a rich brown game gravy under it, and serve.

746. SAUSAGE PUDDING.

PROCURE two pounds of Cambridge sausages, and twist each into three round balls; put these into boiling water, on the stove, merely to parboil them for a minute or so, then throw them into cold water and afterward remove the skins. Line the pudding basin with suet paste, fill it with the sausages, and pour the following preparation upon them : chop one onion and three sage leaves, boil these in water for two minutes, drain them upon a sieve, and then fry them in small stewpan with a piece of butter; as soon as they become of a light-brown color, add a table-spoonful of flour and a tea-spoonful of curry paste, season with pepper and salt, and moisten with half a pint of good broth; stir the sauce upon the fire, and when it has boiled a quarter of an hour, rub it through a sieve or tammy, and use it as above directed. Cover the pudding with paste, steam or bake it for two hours, and when turned out of the basin, send to table with plain gravy under it.

REMOVES OF BLACK GAME AND GROUSE,

Black Game, à la Montagnarde. Black Game, à la Paysanne.
" à l'Italiènne. " à la Norwegiènne, &c.
" à la Suédoise.

747. BLACK GAME, A LA MONTAGNARDE.

CUT off the legs and wings, tuck the thighs inside the birds, and split them down the back; season well with pepper and salt, rub them over with a paste-brush dipped in clarified butter, and then broil them carefully on a gridiron, over a clear fire perfectly free from smoke: or place the birds in a baking-dish or sauta-pan with a piece of butter; set them to bake in the oven, and baste them frequently. When done, glaze them nicely, and dish them up with a border of potato *croquettes*, and then pour under them some *Poivrade* sauce (No. 29), finished with a piece of anchovy-butter and some lemon-juice.

748. BLACK GAME, A L'ITALIENNE.

TRUSS the birds as for boiling, put them into an oval stewpan with garnished faggot of parsley, two carrots, two heads of celery, two onions, each stuck with three cloves, a blade of mace, twenty pepper-corns and two cloves of garlic; moisten them with a gill of brandy and a large ladleful of good stock; place a buttered paper on the top, put the lid on, and set them to braize on a very slow fire, with some live embers on the lid. If the birds are young, one hour and a quarter will suffice to braize them; but if old they will require longer time. When the birds are done, drain, glaze, and dish them up, garnish with macaroni finished with the liquor from the birds, freed from every particle of grease, and boiled down with the macaroni; to this add six ounces of grated Parmesan cheese, a spoonful of tomata sauce (No. 22), and four ounces of fresh butter; pour some brown Italian sauce (No. 12) over the birds and round their base, and serve.

749. BLACK GAME, A LA SUEDOISE.

THESE must be trussed as for boiling, and then placed in an oval stewpan with one pound of streaky bacon, and one pound of German sausage, a good-sized carrot, two heads of celery, two onions stuck with four cloves each, a garnished faggot of parsley, and a tea-spoonful of black peppercorns; moisten with three pints of fermented juice of beetroot (No. 380) and two glasses of brandy, cover with buttered paper and the lid containing live embers, and set them to braize slowly on a stove-fire partially smothered with ashes. When the birds are done, take them up on a dish and keep them covered up in the hot closet until they are dished up. Next, strain the liquor through a napkin, skim off all the grease, boil it down nearly to half-glaze, then add to it a small ladleful of finished *Espagnole* sauce (No. 3), together with a glass of red wine; allow this sauce to boil by the side of the stove-fire for five minutes; skim it and pass it through a tammy into a small stewpan, and keep it hot. Then place the black game on their dish side by side, garnish them round with carrots prepared in the Swedish fashion, and round this place another border composed of neatly-cut scollops of the streaky bacon and German sausage; pour the sauce over the remove, and serve.

The carrots above alluded to should be thus prepared: slit the outside or red part of a dozen large carrots into thin stripes, cut these again into thin shreds of about two inches long. Next, place them in a stewpan with four ounces of butter and half a pint of vinegar; season with four ounces of sugar, a little grated nutmeg and a little salt; set them to stew very gently upon a partially-smothered charcoal fire, taking care to turn them over now and then with a spoon: about an hour will suffice to do them: when, if any moisture remains, it must be boiled down, and they will be ready for use.

750. BLACK GAME, A LA PAYSANNE.

SEE pheasants *à la Paysanne*. (No. 715.)

751. BLACK GAME, A LA NORWEGIENNE.

TRUSS these as for roasting, lard the breasts closely with well furnished rows of larding; set them to braize in an oval stewpan, moistened with a *mirepoix* (No. 236) made with two parts of good stock and one third of French vinegar; baste the birds frequently while they are being braized, when done, set them upon a baking-sheet in the oven for two minutes to dry the larding, then glaze and dish them up; garnish with a border of stewed red cabbage dressed in the same way as French *sauer-kraut* (No. 165), and round this place a border of small sausages prepared as follows:

Chop one pound of calf's liver with ten ounces of fat bacon and six ounces of brown bread-crumbs, season with black pepper, salt, grated nutmeg, and lemon-peel, some parsley, thyme, one bay-leaf, and some sweet-basil, all chopped fine; add the yolks of three eggs, mix the whole thoroughly, and then form this preparation into small flat, round, or oval sausages, which must be wrapped up in pig's caul; fry these of a brown color, and use them as directed above.

Sauce the remove with a *Poivrade* (No. 29), mixed with half the liquor in which the birds have been braized, previously cleared of all grease and boiled down to half-glaze; glaze the larding, and serve.

In addition to the foregoing methods of dressing black game, they may also be served *à la Soubise, à la Périgueux, à la Financière,* with a *purée* of celery, *Richelieu* sauce, braized cabbages, and *à la Dauphinoise;* for the preparation of which, see those articles.

Note.—Grouse should be dressed in the same way as black game.

PATE-CHAUDS, OR RAISED PIES FOR ENTREES,

COMPRISING

Pâté-Chaud of Young Rabbits with fine-herbs.
     "   *à la Sauce Poivrade.*
     "   of Leverets with Truffles, *à la Périgueux.*
     "   of ditto *à la Financière.*
     "   of *Godiveau à la Ciboulette.*

Pâté-Chaud of Young Partridges, *à la Chasseur.*
     "   of Ox Palates, *à l'Italiènne.*
     "   of Quails, *à la Financière.*
     "   of Larks boned, *à l'Essence.*
     "   of Snipes, *à la Bordelaise.*

Pâté-Chaud Cases.

752. PATE-CHAUD* OF YOUNG RABBITS, WITH FINE-HERBS.

CUT up two young rabbits into small members, place these in a deep sautapan with two ounces of butter, a handful of chopped mushrooms, some parsley and two shalots chopped also; season with pepper and salt, a little grated nutmeg and a garnished faggot. Then set the rabbits on a brisk fire, and fry them of a light-brown color; add a glass of French white wine, cover the sautapan with its lid containing some live embers of charcoal, and again set them on the fire to stew very gently for twenty minutes, when they will be done. Next, add a gravy-spoonful of brown sauce, a small piece of glaze, and the juice of half a lemon; toss the whole together over the fire, and allow it to boil sharply for two minutes; then dish up the pieces of rabbit neatly in the pie, pour the sauce over them, and serve.

753. PATE-CHAUD OF YOUNG RABBITS, A LA SAUCE POIVRADE.

CUT the rabbits into small members, and place them in a sautapan with about two ounces of clarified butter, season with pepper and salt,

---

* General directions for making a *Pâté-Chaud*, or raised pie, will be found in that part of the work which treats of *Entrées* of Pasty.

and then set them over a brisk fire to be fried brown; next, add a glass of Madeira, and a piece of glaze the size of a walnut; cover the sautapan with its lid containing some live embers of charcoal, and again place it upon a moderate fire, that the rabbits may stew very gently for twenty minutes longer; then add some *Poivrade* sauce (No. 29) in sufficient quantity for the *entrée*, allow the whole to boil together for three minutes, garnish the *pâté-chaud* as in the former case, and send to table.

754. PATE-CHAUD OF LEVERETS, WITH TRUFFLES, A LA PERIGUEUX.

THE leverets must be cut into small members or joints as follows :—
First, take off the hind legs and make two pieces of these; detach the shoulders, and cut the loins transversely into pieces about two inches long; split the head into halves, trim the whole neatly without waste, and place these members in a sautapan with three ounces of clarified butter: season with pepper and salt, and set them on a brisk fire to be fried brown. Next, add four ounces of truffles cut into thick scollops, and a small piece of glaze, cover with the lid containing live embers of charcoal, and replace the sautapan on a slow fire, to simmer for twenty minutes longer. Then add the *Périgueux* sauce (No. 23), allow the whole to boil together for three minutes, garnish the *pâté-chaud*, and serve.

755. PATE-CHAUD OF LEVERETS, A LA FINANCIERE.

PREPARE these in the manner directed in the foregoing article, and when the members of the leverets are ready to receive the sauce, add a rich *Financière ragout* (No. 188); after the whole has boiled together for three minutes, garnish the pie, and serve.
A border of large white cocks'-combs may be placed round the edge of the pie, and a larded sweetbread or a large truffle in the centre.

756. PATE-CHAUD OF GODIVEAU, A LA CIBOULETTE.

To one pound and a half of sifted flour, add three-quarters of a pound of butter, the yolks of two eggs, a tea-spoonful of salt, and about a gill and a half of cold water, then knead the whole into a fine smooth paste. Take rather more than two-thirds of this, mould it into a round ball with the palm of the hand, and afterward roll it out to the size of a common dinner-plate; then with the fingers of both hands, take up the edges of the paste to the depth of two inches, and gather it into the shape of a round or oval purse (according to the shape of the dish): and having previously buttered a raised pie-mould for the purpose, line it with the paste, by first rolling it out and then pushing the paste into the mouldings of the case with another piece of paste, used as a cushion for the purpose. When the mould is thus lined, fill it with some *godiveau* (No. 251), previously mixed with some chopped chives or green onions, parsley, and mushrooms; smooth the top over with a blade of a knife dipped in water, cover the pie with the remainder of the paste, and after it has been neatly fastened and trimmed round the edge, nip it round with the pastry-pincers; place upon the top a circular piece of puff-paste, egg this over with the paste-brush, and score it with the point of a small knife, forming some device or ornament. Make a small hole in the centre for the steam to escape, bake the pie for one hour and a quarter, and when it is done, remove the top carefully with a knife; score the *godiveau* to the bottom, in the shape of squares or diamonds; pour some *Poivrade*, Italian, or *Espagnole* sauce over it, and after replacing the cover, send to table.

757. PATE-CHAUD OF YOUNG PARTRIDGES, A LA CHASSEUR.

When the partridges have been drawn and singed, cut them into small joints as follows:—First, remove the legs and wings; then cut the fillets with the pinion-bone adhering to them, leaving the breast-piece entire, as also the back, after having detached the thighs. Let all these be neatly trimmed without waste, and observe that the skin of the thighs must be rolled under to give them an appearance of plumpness. Next, place them in neat order in a deep sautapan with three ounces of clarified butter, and season with pepper and salt, and a little grated nutmeg; fry them brown over a brisk fire, after which add a glass of Madeira or Sherry, a piece of glaze the size of a walnut, four ounces of truffles cut into thick scollops, and two dozen button-mushrooms. Cover this with the lid containing some live embers of charcoal, and set the sautapan again on a moderate fire to simmer gently for a quarter of an hour: then remove the lid, add some brown Italian sauce in sufficient quantity for the *entrée*, allow the whole to boil together for three minutes longer, add the juice of half a lemon, and a teaspoonful of chopped and blanched parsley; toss these in with the partridges, &c., garnish the pie, keeping back the truffles and mushrooms to place on the top, lastly pour the sauce, and serve.

758. PATE-CHAUD OF OX-PALATES, A L'ITALIENNE.

Procure six fresh ox-palates, steep them in tepid water for six hours, then throw them into a large stewpan of boiling water and scald them for about five minutes; after which immerse the palates in cold water, and scrape off all the white cuticle from the surface; next, wash them in plenty of cold water, and drain them on a napkin. Then place them in an oval stewpan, moisten with some *blanc* (No. 235), covered with buttered paper, and put on the lid, and set them to braize very gently over a slow fire for about four hours. As soon as the palates are done, put them in press between two baking-sheets or earthen dishes, and when they are cold, take a circular tin-cutter an inch in diameter, and cut them into scollops without wasting any part. Put these into a stewpan with about two dozen large button-mushrooms cut into scollops, also two dozen *raviolis* (No. 375), and enough brown Italian sauce for the *entrée ;* boil the whole together for two minutes, garnish the pie, and serve.

759. PATE-CHAUD OF QUAILS, A LA FINANCIERE.

For a small *entrée*, eight fine fat quails will suffice; bone these by making an incision in that part of the back nearest the crop, through which all the bones, &c., must be drawn out, so as to give them as much as possible the appearance of being whole. Next, fill each quail with some *farce* of fat livers (No. 249), and truss them with their legs turned back: be careful that the crop is securely fastened in order to prevent the stuffing from escaping—a large worsted needle and very fine twine must be used for the purpose. Then, place the quails in a small *fricandeau* pan which has been previously lined with thin layers of fat bacon; in the centre place a garnished faggot of parsley; cover the whole with more layers of fat bacon, moisten with a wine *mirepoix* (No. 236), and having put a buttered paper over all, set the lid on the pan and place it on a stove-fire, or in the oven, to braize very gently for about three quarters of an hour. As soon as the quails are done, drain them on a dish, set them to cool, and trim them neatly. Next line the inside of the pie with some of the remainder of the *farce* of fat livers, to within an inch of the top, place the quails in it in circular order, with the breasts uppermost, and a thin layer of the force-meat between each; cover the whole with thin layers of fat bacon, place a double round of paper well-buttered on the top, and then set the pie in the oven to bake: this will take about an hour. When done, remove the bacon, drain off all the grease carefully, place a decorated small fillet of fowl in between each quail, and on the breast of each, a large white button-mushroom, round the edge a border of large white cocks'-combs, and in the centre a larded heart sweetbread; sauce sparingly with a bright *Financière* (No. 8) mixed with some reduced extract of quails made from the bones.

Note.—Observe, that the raised pie for this purpose must be only half baked previously to filling it with the quails; as it has to undergo another baking. This remark refers also to the two succeeding cases.

760. PATE-CHAUD OF LARKS BONED, A L'ESSENCE.

FOLLOW the preceding directions, but substituting larks for quails.

761. PATE-CHAUD OF SNIPES, A LA BORDELAISE.

BONE eight snipes, and with the trail and one pound of fat livers, make some force-meat for *gratin* (No. 249), and with part of this fill the snipes; truss them in the same way as directed for the quails, and braize them accordingly, after which follow in all respects the second part of the directions. When the pie is baked, drain off carefully all the grease; between each snipe place a large white cock's-comb, on the breast of each put a small fillet of fowl, decorated with red tongue, and afterward turned round in a circle, with a round ball of black truffle in the centre: these fillets must be placed in a small sauta-pan between thin layers of fat bacon, and set in the oven for about three minutes; garnish the edge of the pie with a close border of scollops of red tongue cut in the form of large cocks'-combs, in the centre put a large truffle, bearing a double comb, and a border of these round its base; sauce the pie carefully with a rich *Bordelaise* (No. 57), mixed with some reduced extract of snipes, made from the bones, and serve.

VOL'AU'VENTS AND TOURTES,

COMPRISING

Vol'au'vent, à la Nêsle.
„ à la Financière.
„ of Turbot, à la Béchamel.
„ of Salmon, à la Ravigotte.
„ of Cod, à la Crême.

Vol'au'vent of Salt Fish, à l'Anglaise.
Tourte of Whitings, à la Dauphine.
„ of Godiveau au Madère.
„ of Ox Palates, à la Française.
„ of Lobsters, à la Cardinal.

762. VOL'AU'VENTS, A LA NESLE.*

CLEANSE one set of calf's-brains, and boil them in a stewpan with water, a small carrot and an onion both sliced very thin, two cloves, a little mace, twelve peppercorns, and a little salt, for a quarter of an hour; when done, remove them from the fire to get cold. Prepare also a throat sweetbread, which must be steeped in tepid water for two hours or more, then scalded, cooled in water, and gently simmered on the stove in some toppings of white *consommé* for a quarter of an hour; when done, put the sweetbread on a plate to get cold. Prepare also twelve *quenelles* of fowl, moulded in dessert-spoons, and poached, a like quantity of large button-mushrooms, and the same proportion of double cocks'-combs, and round balls of black truffles. Put these into a middle-sized stewpan, add to them the calf's-brains and sweetbread, previously cut into neat scollops, and just before dinner-time, pour over the whole sufficient *Allemande* sauce (No. 7) for the *entrée* (previously mixed with a small piece of good glaze, and two tea-spoonfuls of Chili vinegar.) Toss the whole lightly together over the fire, and with this *ragout* garnish a handsome *vol'au'vent*, cut either square, oval, or round, so as to suit the shape of the dish.

The top of this *entrée* may be ornamented with very small fillets of fowls, decorated with red tongue or black truffle: or a border of small *quenelles*, decorated similarly, may also be placed round the edge of the *vol'au'vent*, and a small larded sweetbread in the centre of these.

763. VOL'AU'VENT, A LA FINANCIERE.

SEE the directions for a *pâté-chaud, à la Financière* (No. 759); substituting a *vol'au'vent* for the shell or crust.

764. VOL'AU'VENT OF TURBOT, A LA BECHAMEL.

THIS *entrée* is generally served when there happens to be any turbot reserved from a previous day's dinner; in which case, the fish must be pulled, or cut into scollops, warmed in a rich *Béchamel* sauce (No. 5), made with a full proportion of cream; let the *vol'au'vent* be filled with this, and sent to table.

765. VOL'AU'VENT OF SALMON A LA RAVIGOTTE.

PROCURE 2 lbs. of fresh salmon, cut it into rather thick round scollops about two inches in diameter; place these in a sauta-pan, with

---

* Instructions for making a *vol'au'vent* case will be found in that part of the work treating of Puff-paste.

3 oz. of clarified butter, season with pepper and salt, and squeeze the juice of a lemon over them. When about to send to table, set the sauta-pan containing the scollops in the oven, or on a stove-fire, for about five minutes, then turn them over in the pan with a fork, taking care not to break them; allow them to remain on the fire five minutes longer, and drain them upon a clean napkin. Next, put the scollops into a stewpan, with sufficient *Allemande* sauce (No. 7) for the *entrée*, add two tea-spoonsful of tarragon-vinegar, the like quantity of Harvey sauce, a tea-spoonful of chopped and blanched parsley, and a little cayenne; toss the whole together lightly over the fire, and with this garnish a handsome *vol'au'vent*, and serve.

766. VOL'AU'VENT OF COD, A LA CREME.

CRIMPED cod is best for this purpose, although plain cod may be used, but, in either case, the fish must be dressed in boiling water, with plenty of salt thrown in at the same time. A few minutes, in most instances, will suffice to boil this kind of fish, especially if it be crimped. If allowed to remain in the water after it is done, it becomes soft and tasteless. When the cod is boiled, drain it upon a napkin, and as soon as all the water has been absorbed, put the flakes and the sounds carefully, without breaking them up, into a stewpan, containing enough rich cream *Béchamel* (No. 6) for the *entrée*, to this add 2 oz. of grated fresh Parmesan cheese and the juice of a lemon; toss the whole together over the fire with care, so as to avoid breaking the pieces; when it is quite hot, garnish the *vol'au'vent*, and serve.

767. VOL'AU'VENT OF SALT FISH, A L'ANGLAISE.

THE whitest and thickest fish are the best for this purpose. About 2 lbs. will suffice; cut from the middle of the fish, and soak it in cold water for forty-eight hours previously to its being dressed, the water being changed every six hours. Set the fish on in cold water, and when it boils remove the scum, and set it by the side of the stove to finish boiling. As soon as it is done, drain it on a sieve or a napkin, and when all the water is absorbed from it, remove it in large flakes into a stewpan containing some scollops of dressed parsnips, in the proportion of one-third to the quantity of fish, and a like quantity of slices of eggs, boiled hard; to these add enough cream *Béchamel* sauce (No. 6) for the *entrée*; toss the whole gently over a stove-fire until quite hot, then garnish a large *vol'au'vent* with this *ragout*, and serve.

768. TOURTE* OF WHITINGS, A LA DAUPHINE.

PROCURE four large fresh whitings, fillet them, and set one-half aside on a plate in a cool place; with the remainder prepare some *quenelle* force-meat (No. 245), which, when finished, gather up in a basin, and mould with dessert-spoons into *quenelles*. Trim the four remaining fillets, cut each in two transversely, and after paring off the angles, decorate or *contisés* them in manner following: Place the fillet lengthwise upon the edge of the kitchen table, then make incisions across with a knife, cutting down in a slanting direction, and in these open-

* Directions for making this kind of *Tourte* will be found in that part of the work which treats of Puff-pastry.

ings insert small, round, thin scollops of red tongue, black truffle or green gherkins. Next, place these in a santa-pan with 4 oz. of clarified butter, season with a little salt, and squeeze the juice of a lemon over them; cover with thin layers of fat bacon, or a round of paper buttered, and set them aside in the larder till wanted. While this is going on, make an extract or essence with the bones and trimmings of the whitings, as follows :—Put the bones, &c., into a stewpan, with two shalots, one bay-leaf, and a sprig of thyme, eight pepper-corns, a blade of mace, and a handful of parsley; moisten with two glasses of white wine (French is preferable), and a pint of white broth. Set this to boil gently on the stove-fire for half an hour, then strain it through a sieve; boil it down nearly to a glaze, and mix it with enough *Allemande* sauce, or *Béchamel,* for the *entrée,* and pass it through a tammy into a stewpan containing the *quenelles* of whiting before alluded to, with the addition of a dozen button-mushrooms, double that quantity of crayfish-tails and claws, trimmed, and 3 oz. of truffles, cut into thick slices; toss the whole together gently over the fire until quite hot, then garnish the *tourte* with this *ragout,* and with the fillets before mentioned (previously set in the oven for ten minutes to simmer, and afterward drained on a napkin) make a border round the inner edge of the *Vol'au'vent,* or tourte; place a group of crayfish-tails, previously warmed in a small stewpan with a bit of glaze, and a morsel of lobster-coral butter (to color them), and crown the whole with a large crayfish, trimmed, having one prong of each claw stuck into its tail; sauce neatly with the remainder of the sauce, and serve quickly.

769. TOURTE OF GODIVEAU, AU MADERE.

PREPARE about 1 lb. of *godiveau* (No. 250), and make it into small *quenelles* in the following manner :—Shake a handful of flour over a pastry-slab or kitchen-table; drop the *godiveau* thereon with a tea-spoon in small quantities; then roll each of these with the fingers dipped in flour to the size and form of a common cork; set them in regular order upon a baking-sheet, and put them to bake in the oven for about ten minutes; when done, remove them into a stewpan containing some Madeira sauce (No. 8) in sufficient quantity for the *entrée,* and also two artichoke-bottoms, cut into angular pieces, a few scollops of sweetbreads, some ox-piths cut into inch-lengths, and a few large button-mushrooms—set the whole to boil on the stove-fire for three minutes : garnish the *tourte,* and on the top of the ragout place eight trimmed crayfish, in the centre of which put a large truffle, or small sweetbread, larded and glazed; pour in the remainder of the sauce, and serve.

770. TOURTE OF OX-PALATES, A LA FRANCAISE

PREPARE the ox-palates as directed in the first part of the article treating of the *Pâté chaud* of ox-palates. Put the scollops into a stewpan containing one-fourth part of their quantity of red tongue cut into round scollops, and a like proportion of button-mushrooms and scollops of truffles; to which add enough *Poivrade* sauce (No. 29) for the *entrée;* boil the whole together, and garnish the *tourte* with this *ragout,* put the cover on, and serve.

771. TOURTE OF SCOLLOPS OF LOBSTER, A LA CARDINAL.

PICK the lobster out of the shell, and cut it into neat scollops; put these into a stewpan containing enough good *Béchamel* sauce (No. 6) for the *entrée*, mixed with about two ounces of lobster coral butter (No. 182), a little cayenne, and the juice of half a lemon; toss the whole together over the fire until sufficiently hot, and with it garnish the *tourte:* put the cover on, and serve.

TIMBALES OF MACARONI,

COMPRISING

Timbale of Macaroni, *à la Milanaise.*	*Timbale* of Soft Roes of Mackerel, *à l'Alle-*
„ *à la Mazarin.*	*mande.*
„ of *Nouilles, à la Chas-*	„ of *Raviolis, à la Romaine.*
seur.	

Timbale Cases.

772. TIMBALE* OF MACARONI, A LA MILANAISE.

THE *timbale* case should be left in the mould to be made hot in the oven, and when just on the point of sending it to table, garnish it with macaroni dressed with cheese, some *Béchamel* sauce, scollops of fowl, truffles, tongues, and mushrooms; turn the *timbale* out on its dish, glaze it, pour some *Béchamel* sauce round the base, and serve.

773. TIMBALE OF MACARONI, A LA MAZARIN.

BOIL one pound of macaroni in two quarts of water, with a pat of butter, eight pepper-corns, and a little salt; when done, and cold, put

---

* The mode of preparing the *timbale* case will be found described under the head of Pastry for *Entrées*.

about half of it to drain upon a napkin. Butter the inside of a plain round oval or square mould, according to the shape of the dish; cut the macaroni into half-inch lengths, and cover the bottom of the mould with these, placing them on end; cover this with a thick layer of chicken *quenelle* force-meat; then line the sides of the mould in the same way, and as soon as this is completed, smooth the inside with the back of a spoon dipped in hot water; fill this cavity with a *blanquette* of fowl (No. 204), the sauce of which must be thick, and cover the whole with a layer of force-meat, to be applied as follows:—

Spread some force-meat upon a round of buttered paper to fit the mould; smooth the surface with a knife dipped in hot water, then take hold of the paper with both hands, and turn it upside down upon the *timbale;* the paper is to be left on, as that can be easily removed when the force-meat has become set by steaming. About an hour and a half before dinner-time, place the *timbale* in a stewpan twice its size upon a trivet or ring to prevent it from touching the bottom, so that the water contained in the stewpan, which must only reach half-way up the mould, may circulate freely under it. The stewpan must be covered with its lid, containing some live embers of charcoal, and placed after it has boiled, upon a slow fire to simmer gently but continually, in order to keep up the steam during the whole of the time. Just before sending to table, remove the piece of paper from the *timbale*, and take a firm hold of the bottom of the mould with the left hand; place the dish upside down upon the mould with the right hand; then, with the left hand uppermost, place the dish on the table, and carefully lift the mould off the *timbale*. Pour some *Suprême* sauce (No. 38) over the *entrée*, garnish the base with white cock's-combs, truffles, and mushrooms, and serve.

774. TIMBALE OF NOUILLES, A LA CHASSEUR.

PREPARE about one pound of *nouilles* (No. 679), parboil these in water for ten minutes; drain, and put them into a stewpan with a quart of good *consommé*, a pat of butter, a little grated nutmeg, and a pinch of mignionette pepper; cover the whole with a round piece of buttered paper, put on the lid, and set the stewpan on the stove-fire to boil very gently until the *consommé* is reduced; add a gravy-spoonful of *Allemande sauce*, two ounces of grated Parmesan cheese, and two dozen very small *quenelles* of game, previously poached; toss the whole together lightly over the fire until the cheese is well mixed with the other ingredients; garnish the *timbale* case, previously prepared for this purpose, turn it out of the mould into its dish, glaze it over, pour a little half glaze round the base, and serve.

775. TIMBALE GARNISHED WITH SOFT ROES OF MACKEREL.

FIVE minutes before sending to table, garnish the *timbale* case, which must be quite hot, with a *ragout* of soft roes of mackerel (No. 199); then turn the *timbale* out of the mould into the dish, glaze it nicely, pour a little *Suprême* or *Béchamel* sauce round the base, and serve.

776. TIMBALE OF RAVIOLIS, A LA ROMAINE.

PREPARE four dozen *raviolis* (No. 375), and after they have been boiled in *consommé*, drain them upon a sieve and put them into a stew-pan containing four ounces of truffles cut into scollops, the like quantity of scollops of red tongue, and about twenty mushrooms; to these add two glasses of Madeira, and one ounce of game glaze, and set the whole to boil down quickly over a brisk fire; when the wine is absorbed, add two ounces of grated Parmesan cheese, and a large gravy-spoonful of reduced *Espagnole* sauce; toss these together over the stove-fire until quite hot, then garnish the *timbale* case, turn it out into its dish, glaze it, pour a little brown sauce or half glaze round the base, and serve.

CASSEROLES, OR BORDERS OF RICE.

COMPRISING

Casserole of Rice.
    „   *à la Polonaise.*
    „   *à la Reine.*

Casserole of Rice, garnished with a *Purée* of
    Game, *à la Belle-vue.*
    "   garnished with wings of Fowl, *à l'Allemande.*

777. CASSEROLES, OR BORDERS OF RICE.

A *casserole* of rice is justly considered one of the most elegant *entrées*: it requires great care throughout its preparation, especially in the treatment of the rice, that being its basis, and upon the success of this much of the beauty of the *casserole* depends. If the rice be not sufficiently boiled, and effectually worked into a smooth paste, it becomes a difficult matter to mould it: and any apparent roughness would spoil the look of the *casserole*.

For a *casserole* of ordinary size, wash about a pound and a half of Carolina rice in three waters, drain it on a sieve, and put it into a stew-pan with nearly twice its quantity of water, six ounces of butter, a small ladleful of stock-pot toppings and a piece of raw ham; cover with a circular piece of buttered paper and the lid, and set the rice to boil on the stove, after which it must be put in the oven, or on a smoth-ered stove-fire, to simmer very gently.   During the time that the rice remains on the fire, it should be carefully turned over with a spoon twice or thrice.   When all the grains become perfectly soft, the rice must be worked into a firm, compact paste, with the bowl of a large wooden spoon; it should next be rolled into the form of a ball, and placed on a baking-sheet, previously covered with a circular piece of buttered paper, and shaped to the height and circumference desired.   Next, for the purpose of imprinting upon the *casserole* the ornamental mouldings represented in the annexed illustrations, it will be necessary to cut a piece of turnip, carrot, or raw potato, in the form of a chisel, to be used for indenting or moulding the design.

When the *casserole* is moulded, it must be sprinkled over with a paste-brush dipped in clarified butter, and afterward baked of a fine yellow color; the interior must then be removed with a spoon, leaving the walls of the crust about half-an-inch thick; smooth the inside of the rice with the back of a table-spoon dipped in water, and keep the *casserole* in a dry place till it is wanted for use.

778. CASSEROLE OF RICE, A LA POLONAISE.

PREPARE a *purée* of fowls (No. 1009), and when on the point of sending to table, stir it over the fire until it is sufficiently hot, care being taken to prevent its becoming rough; then fill the *casserole* with the *purée*, place eight eggs (previously boiled four minutes, and the shells removed), round the top of the *purée;* between each egg, put a small fillet of fowl, decorated with tongue or truffle, sauce the surface of the *purée* with some *Suprême* (No. 38), and serve.

779. CASSEROLE OF RICE, A LA REINE.

THIS must be garnished with a *purée* of fowls in a similar manner to the foregoing, and a border of *quenelles* of fowl placed round the inner edge of the surface; sauce with *Suprême*, glaze the *casserole* with light-colored glaze, and serve.

780. CASSEROLE OF RICE, GARNISHED WITH A PUREE OF GAME, A LA BELLE-VUE.

JUST before dinner-time, warm the *purée* of game (No. 1090) pre-pared for the purpose, garnish the *casserole* of rice with it, place round the inner edge of the surface a border of very small fillets (decorated *contisés* with truffles or tongues), of the kind of game the *purée* is made from, pour a little *Allemande* sauce over the centre of the *purée*, glaze the *casserole* lightly, and serve.

781. CASSEROLE OF RICE, GARNISHED WITH WINGS OF FOWL, A L'ALLEMANDE.

THE *casserole* of rice must be garnished with a *ragout* of wings of fowls (No. 208), to which may be added some small truffles and mushrooms; ornament it with a border of large cocks'-combs, and scollops of red tongue cut in the form of cocks'-combs, placed alternately round the inner edge of the *casserole*, glaze it lightly, and serve.

Note.—*Casseroles*, or *Borders* of rice may also be garnished with *fricassée* of chickens, lamb's-feet, *blanquettes* of sweetbreads or fowls, and with all kinds of scollops whether of poultry, game or fish.

ORNAMENTAL BORDERS OF POTATO PASTE,

COMPRISING

Border of Potato-paste, garnished with Scollops of Larks and Truffles.

" garnished with Lamb's-Feet, *à la Pascaline.*

" garnished with Ox Palates, *à l'Indiénne.*

Border of Potato-paste, garnished with Scollops of Sheep's tongues, with fine-herbs.

" garnished with Calf's Brains, *à la Ravigotte.*

782. BORDER OF POTATO-PASTE, GARNISHED WITH SCOLLOPS OF LARKS AND TRUFFLES.

A BORDER of potato-paste resembles in a great measure a *casserole* of rice, and is prepared as follows :—

For an ordinary size *entrée*, fifteen large potatoes should be baked, and their pulp afterward rubbed through a fine wire-sieve upon a dish; this must be put into a middle-sized stewpan with four ounces of butter, the yolks of six eggs, a little grated nutmeg, pepper and salt. Stir the whole with a wooden spoon over a slow fire until the mixture becomes a smooth compact paste; it should then be rolled into a ball, placed on a baking-sheet, and shaped to the height and circumference designed. The border should now be moulded in the same way as a *casserole* of rice, for which purpose consult the mouldings represented in the designs of *casseroles* of rice (No. 777), and are to be executed with a piece of raw carrot or turnip, cut in the form of a chisel. When the border is moulded, it should be egged over with a soft paste-brush, and baked in an oven, of a light yellow color; when done, part of the inside must be removed, and the cavity smoothed over with the back of the bowl of a spoon. The border ought to be kept in a dry place till wanted for use. Put the border in the screen or hot closet to get warm, five minutes before sending to table; garnish it with a *ragout* of scollops of larks and truffles (No. 205), place a border of small *quenelles* of fowl round the edge, lightly glaze the border, pour a little of the sauce round the base and serve.

783. BORDER OF POTATO-PASTE, GARNISHED WITH LAMBS' FEET, A LA PASCALINE.

PROCURE a dozen lamb's-feet ready scalded, remove the shin-bone, parboil them for five minutes, immerse them in cold water, drain them on a napkin to absorb the water, then stick them one at a time upon the point of an iron skewer, and singe off the hair (if not already removed by scalding), over the flame of a charcoal fire. Next, braize them gently in some *blanc* (No. 236), for about three-quarters of an hour. When the feet are done, drain them on a napkin, cut out the black substance to be found between the cushions of the hoof, trim them neatly without waste, and put them into a stew-pan with a little of their own liquor. Five minutes before sending to table, pour off the liquor from the feet, previously warmed, then add half a pottle of prepared button-mushrooms, and enough *Pascaline* sauce (No. 15) for the *entrée;* toss the whole together over the stove-fire for two minutes, and garnish the border of potato-paste with this *ragout;* glaze the border lightly, and serve.

784. BORDER OF POTATO-PASTE, GARNISHED WITH SCOLLOPS OF OX-PALATES, A L'INDIENNE.

PREPARE the ox-palates according to the directions contained in (No. 209), add enough well-reduced Indian curry sauce (No. 47) for the *entrée*, warm the *ragout* and garnish the border of potato with it, just before sending to table.

Some plain boiled patna must be served in a plate.

785. BORDER OF POTATO-PASTE, GARNISHED WITH SCOLLOPS OF SHEEP'S-TONGUES, WITH FINE-HERBS.

SCALD eight sheep's tongues effectually, so as to be able to remove the outer skin easily; then trim them, and afterward put them into a stew-pan with a carrot, an onion stuck with four cloves, a garnished faggot of parsley, and a dozen pepper-corns; moisten with a quart of broth, and set them to braize gently for about an hour. When done, drain them on a dish, and set them in the larder to get cold, afterward to be cut into neat circular scollops; put these into a stewpan with half a pottle of prepared button-mushrooms, and enough well-reduced fine-herbs sauce (No. 14), for the *entrée;* toss these together over the stove-fire to warm them thoroughly, then garnish the border of potato-paste with this *ragout*, glaze it round, and serve.

786. BORDER OF POTATO-PASTE, GARNISHED WITH CALF'S BRAINS, A LA RAVIGOTTE.

STEEP two sets of calf's-brains in tepid water for several hours to cleanse them, and as soon as the thin membrane which covers the brains becomes loosened, detach it gently with the fingers; change the water frequently, and when the brains have become comparatively white, put them into a stewpan with a quart of boiling water, half a gill of vinegar, some sliced carrot, onion, parsley, thyme, bay-leaf, mignionette-pepper, and salt; alllow them to boil gently by the side of the fire for twenty minutes, then remove the brains carefully with a large spoon into another stewpan, pass their liquor through a sieve on them, and set them aside till within twenty minutes of dinner-time. The brains must then be warmed in their liquor, and afterward cut into thick scollops lengthwise, and placed in the border of potato in circular order, overlapping each other; pour a *Ravigotte* sauce (No. 21) over the brains, glaze the border, and serve.

CHARTREUSES OF VEGETABLES,

Chartreuse of Vegetables, with Partridges. *Chartreuse* of Vegetables, with Tendons of
    ,,   ,,   with Quails.   Veal.

787. CHARTREUSE OF VEGETABLES, GARNISHED WITH PARTRIDGES.

Scrape eight large carrots, and parboil them in water with a little salt for ten minutes; then put them to boil in some broth with a little sugar and salt, and a small pat of butter; when done, place them on a dish in the larder to get cold. In the mean time, eight large turnips should be peeled, and boiled in the same way as the carrots, and then put on a dish to cool. Next, a plain round mould must be lined with buttered paper, and the prepared carrots and turnips cut into appropriate forms or shapes for the purpose of arranging them over the bottom and round the inside of the mould, taking care that they fit in with each other, so as to represent any of the foregoing designs. Meanwhile parboil three large savoy cabbages in water; then immerse them in cold water, after which squeeze the moisture from them; spread them upon a napkin on the table, take out the cores, season with mignionette-pepper and salt, and tie each up with a string. Then, put the cabbages into a large stewpan with three partridges trussed with their legs inside, one pound of streaky bacon (previously parboiled), and two large saveloys; season with two onions stuck with four cloves, two carrots, and a garnished faggot; moisten with three pints of stock, cover with a buttered paper, put on the lid, and set them to braize gently for about two hours, if the birds are young, or three hours if not. When done, drain the cabbage into a colander, put the partridges, bacon, and saveloys on a dish to cool; squeeze the broth from the cabbage by pressing it tightly in a strong kitchen rubber; then chop it and afterwards put it into a stewpan with a spoonful of brown sauce, and stir it quickly over a brisk fire until it resembles a somewhat firm paste. Use this preparation to garnish the bottom and sides of the *chartreuse*, about an inch thick. The partridges must be cut up neatly into small members, tossed in enough brown sauce to moisten them, and then placed in the cavity of the *chartreuse* in close order, so as to give it solidity when turned out of the mould on its dish; a layer of prepared cabbage should be placed over these, and the whole covered with a circular piece of buttered paper. An hour before dinner, the *chartreuse* must be placed in a stewpan with sufficient water to reach up only one-third the height of the mould; then set the lid on, and put the stewpan near or upon a slow fire to keep the water gently simmering, so that the steam may warm the *chartreuse* through. When about to serve, turn the *chartreuse* up-side-down in the dish, and draw the mould off with care, remove the paper, and garnish the base with a close border of the bacon and saveloys cut into scollops; pour some brown sauce (worked with essence of vegetables) round the *entrée*, glaze the *chartreuse* carefully, so as not to disturb the order of the vegetables, and serve.

These directions will serve for the preparation of several kinds of *chartreuses:* pheasants, ducklings, pigeons, &c., being substituted for partridges.

788. CHARTREUSE OF VEGETABLES, GARNISHED WITH QUAILS, ETC.

THE preparation of this kind of *chartreuse* is very similar to the foregoing, cabbage-lettuces being substituted for savoys; the following are the only alterations required : the mould required must be either oval or round, according to the shape of the dish intended to be used, and should be lined with buttered paper, and ornamented with carrots and turnips prepared according to the directions given in the first part of the previous article, and afterwards cut out, either with a small knife, or proper-shaped tin-cutters, to suit the design intended to be represented, from one of the patterns given in the foregoing designs. The cavity left in the mould, after it has been decorated with the vegetables, must be filled up with the braized cabbage lettuces warmed in the same manner as directed for the last-mentioned *chartreuse*.

When about to send to table, turn the *chartreuse* out on its dish, place the quails (prepared as for a *pâté-chaud*, No. 759, and kept warm) upon the upper part of the *chartreuse*, with their breasts outward; fill the centre of the *entrée* with a *Jardinière* of vegetables (No. 144), garnish the base with small scollops of the streaky bacon and saveloys, pour some thin bright *Espagnole* sauce round the *entrée*, glaze the *chartreuse* lightly, and serve.

789. CHARTREUSE OF VEGETABLES, GARNISHED WITH TENDONS OF VEAL AND STEWED PEAS.

IN this case the *chartreuse* should be prepared in the same manner as described in the foregoing recipe; and when turned out on its dish preparatory to serving it, the top of the *border* must be garnished with braized tendons of veal (No. 885), placed in the same way as cutlets are dished up; the well or centre of the *entrée*, must be filled with stewed peas, then pour some brown sauce round the base, glaze the *chartreuse*, and serve.

This kind of *chartreuse* may be garnished with scollops of pheasants, partridges, larks, &c. ; and also with *blanquettes* of fowls, lambs' sweet-breads, &c. The ornamental part of these *entrées* may be much varied, by using asparagus-heads, green-peas, French-beans, artichoke-bottoms, glazed button-onions, carrots, and turnips turned in fanciful shapes and forms. A good effect is produced by arranging a decoration in relief on the top of the *chartreuse* after it has been turned out of the mould on to its dish : its base may also be garnished with alternate groups of vegetables cut in small fanciful shapes and prepared in the usual manner.

FORCE-MEAT CHARTREUSES,

COMPRISING

Chartreuse, à la Parisiene.   Chartreuse, à la Cardinal.
    „   à la Belle Vue.

790. CHARTREUSE, A LA PARISIENNE.

FIRST prepare some *quenelle* force-meat (No. 242), with the fillets of three fowls ; trim the tails of sixty boiled crayfish, trim also eight inner or minion fillets of fowls, and then simmer these in a little clari-fied butter and lemon-juice over the fire till they are done; then put them on a plate covered with thin layers of fat bacon, to keep them moist, until they are wanted for fur-ther use.

Next butter a large-sized char-lotte-mould, and dispose round the inner angle of the bottom a close border of crayfish-tails ; while up the sides of the mould, some long strips, or pipes, of black truffle (cut out with a tin vegetable cutter), must be arranged alternately with the prepared fillets of fowls, so as to form a decoration representing the " Grecian-key border ;" round the top of this, which, when the mould is turned upside down, forms the base, place another close border of crayfish tails ; after which, the bottom and sides of the *chartreuse* must be lined with a coating of the prepared *quenelle* force-meat, thus :—Butter a circular piece of paper, cut exactly to the size of the mould, and spread thereon a layer of the force-meat an inch thick ; smooth this over with a knife dipped in hot water, and then, with great care, take hold of the sides of the paper with both hands, and turn it upside down into the mould : pass the bottom of a small *bain-marie* filled with hot water over the paper, that the butter may become melted, by which the paper will be easily removed. Next, cut three pieces of paper to fit in with each other, so as effectually to line the mould ; butter these, and then spread them with force-meat, as directed for the bottom piece, and apply them in the same way.

Then smooth the cavity with a spoon dipped in hot water, and fill it to within an inch of its surface with a thickly-garnished *ragout à la Toulouse,* cold (No. 187). Cover in the top with force-meat, leaving the piece of paper on, and keep the *chartreuse* in a cool place till within two hours of dinner-time. It should then be put to steam in a deep stewpan, containing sufficient water to reach nearly half way up the mould. The water must be kept continually boiling by the side of a slow fire, and the stewpan covered with its lid containing live embers of charcoal.

When the *chartreuse* is done, turn it out of the mould carefully into its dish; cover the top with a border of button-mushrooms, placed near the edge, and in the centre put a star, formed with eight very small fillets of fowl, decorated with black truffles (previously turned in the form of a crescent, on a buttered sauta-pan, covered with very thin layers of fat bacon, and gently simmered in the oven for three minutes); garnish the base of the *chartreuse* with some thin *Toulouse ragout,* glaze the sides lightly, and serve.

791. CHARTREUSE, A LA BELLE-VUE.

BUTTER smoothly the inside of a plain cylinder mould, and dispose round the bottom and sides a bold decoration, formed with black truffles and red tongue; after which carefully fill up the interior of the mould with some very delicate *quenelle* force-meat, prepared from the fillets of three partridges. About an hour before dinner-time, the *chartreuse* must be put on to steam, as in the foregoing case; when done, turn it out on to its dish; fill the centre with a *ragout* of scollops of fillets of partridges, with the addition of some prepared truffles, cocks'-combs, and kernels in a rich Maderia sauce (No. 8); glaze the *chartreuse,* and serve.

792. CHARTREUSE, A LA CARDINAL.

FIRST, trim the fillets of three pairs of soles, and *contisés* them with scollops of the outside part of lobster-tails. Prepare some lobster *quenelle* force-meat (No. 246), in which mix the fillets of two whitings. Then, butter the inside of a plain charlotte-mould, and dispose therein the prepared fillets of soles, as represented in the annexed illustration; next, line the bottom and sides of the *chartreuse* with some of the lobster force-meat, in the same way as directed for the *chartreuse à la Parisiènne;* fill the cavity with a Parisian *ragout* (No. 303), the sauce of which must be kept stiff, and used cold for this purpose; cover in the top with a layer of force-meat, and steam the *chartreuses* for one hour and a half; when done, place it· upside down on its dish, and draw the mould off carefully, in order to avoid disturbing the fillets. Garnish the edges of the *chartreuse* with a close border of small round truffles, and in the centre arrange a neatly-formed group of trimmed crayfish-tails, previously warmed in a little glaze and lobster coral butter; pour some Parisian *ragout* (No. 203) round the base, and serve.

ORNAMENTAL CROUSTADES OF BREAD,

COMPRISING

Ornamental *Cróustades*.
Cróustades of Bread, garnished with Calves'
    tails, *à la Poulette*.
  „   „ with Lambs' brains,
    in *Matelotte* Sauce.

Cróustade of Bread, with Scollops of Fat
   Livers, a *à l'Epicuriènne*.
 „ „ with Quails, *à la Bour-*
   guignotte.

793. ORNAMENTAL CROUSTADES.

FOR a *cróustade* of ordinary dimensions, a 4lb. loaf of close bread should be procured two days before it is wanted for use, as it must be stale for this purpose. In order to prevent waste, the loaf should be baked in an oval, square, or round tin case, according to the intended form of the *cróustade;* and when this is required for a remove or flank dish, the loaf must be made of a proportionate size.

When the crust has been pared off the loaf with a sharp knife, it must be carved in the form of a fluted or chased vase or cup, according to the following patterns:

The *crôustade* thus carved, must next be fried of a light fawn color, in some clean hog's-lard, made quite hot for the purpose, the inside crumb carefully taken out, and the cavity smoothly covered with a thin coating of *quenelle* force-meat : the object of which is to prevent the escape or absorption of the sauce from the *entrée*, afterward placed in it : when this is done, the *crôustade* must be put in the oven for five minutes, to bake the *quenelle* force-meat, and to be kept hot until served.

794. CROUSTADE OF BREAD, GARNISHED WITH CALVES'-TAILS, A LA POULETTE.

SCALD two calves'-tails with the skin on, in the same way as calves-heads ; cut these up in joints, parboil them in water for five minutes, and then immerse them in cold water ; after which drain them on a napkin, trim and place them in a stewpan with some *blanc* (No. 235), or failing this, with a carrot, an onion, garnished faggot of parsley, four cloves, a blade of mace, and twelve peppercorns ; moisten with three pints of broth, or water, in which latter case add some salt ; and set them to boil gently for about an hour by the side of the stove-fire. When the tails are done, drain them on a napkin, trim them neatly, and place them in the *crôustade* in pyramidal form, pour over them a rich sauce *à la poulette*, containing two dozen button-mushrooms ; garnish the inner edge of the *crôustade* with a border of fluted scollops of red tongue, glaze a large black truffle, place it on the top, and serve.

795. CROUSTADE OF BREAD, GARNISHED WITH LAMBS' BRAINS, IN MATELOTTE SAUCE.

THE brains must be prepared as directed in No. 786, and when they are done, put to drain upon a napkin, preparatory to their being cut into scollops, and afterward placed in circular order in the *crôustade*. Pour a *matelotte* sauce (No. 31), made in this case of white wine with ·a little cayenne and lemon-juice, and containing some small button-onions, previously simmered in butter, 3 oz. of truffles cut in scollops, a dozen small *quenelles*, a few mushrooms, and trimmed cray-fish-tails ; crown the top with six large crayfish, between which place a fried *crouton* of bread, cut in the shape of a leaf ; in the centre of these, put a large truffle, and serve.

796. CROUSTADE OF BREAD, GARNISHED WITH SCOLLOPS OF FAT LIVERS, A L'EPICURIENNE.

WHEN about to send the *crôustade* to table, garnish it with a *ragout* of fat livers, prepared as follows :—

Wrap two Strasbourg livers in thin layers of fat bacon, and simmer them very gently in a wine *mirepoix* (No. 236) for half an hour ; then remove the stewpan from the fire, and allow the livers to cool in their liquor ; they must now be taken out, cut into scollops without waste, and placed in a small deep sautapan, containing 4 oz. of black Perigord truffles cut into scollops, a dozen small *quenelles* of game, and a few button-mushrooms ; to these add about half the *mirepoix*, freed from every particle of grease, and set the whole to boil briskly over the fire until the moisture be reduced to a glaze ; next, pour in some brown fine-herbs sauce (No. 14), in sufficient quantity for the *entrée*, toss the whole together over the fire, and use this *ragout* as directed above. A border of large double white cocks'-combs may be placed round the edge of the *crôustade*, and a fine large Perigord truffle in the centre.

797. CROUSTADE OF BREAD, GARNISHED WITH QUAILS AU GRATIN, A LA BOURGUIGNOTTE.

LET a *crôustade* be cut in the form of a cup, not more than five inches high, the carving of which must present eight bold fluted scollops at the upper part, and be brought to a tapering point toward the foot, as represented in one of the foregoing illustrations. When the *crôustade* has been fried, the inner crumb must be removed, and the cavities lined with a well-seasoned *farce* of fat livers (No. 249), previously prepared for the purpose, leaving sufficient room for the insertion, in each of the scolloped flutes, of a quail that has been boned and filled with some of the *farce*, then trussed and partially braized ; these must then be neatly garnished round with some of the *farce*, covered over with thin layers of fat bacon, and a thick band of buttered paper, secured with string, round the *crôustade*, to prevent it from acquiring more color while in the oven. About an hour before dinnertime, set the *crôustade* in a moderately-heated oven, to be baked. Just before sending it to table, remove the paper and bacon, absorb all the grease with the corner of a clean napkin, and place it carefully on its dish. On the breast of each quail place a very small fillet of fowl of circular form, *contisés* or decorated with black truffle, and then simmered in a buttered sautapan, covered with thin layers of bacon, to keep them white ; between each quail place a large white cocks'-comb, fill the centre with a *Bourguignotte ragout* (No. 195), finished with the addition of some extract made from the carcasses of the quails, reduced to glaze, and serve.

Note.—Ornamental *crôustades* of bread may also be garnished with *purée* of fowls *à la Reine*, ditto of game *à la Polonaise*, &c. ; and with almost every kind of *ragout* or garnish directed to be used for *pâtéschauds*, *vol'au'vents*, borders of rice and potato-paste, for which see those articles.

TURBANS AND MAZARINES,

COMPRISING

Turban of Ox-palates, *à la Périgueux*.	Turban of Fillets of Hares, *à la Conti*.
„ Fillets of Fowls, *à la Prince de Galles*.	„ Fillets of Soles, *à la Ximenes*.
	Mazarine of Whitings, *à la Venitiénne*.
„ Fillets of Rabbits, *à la Financière*.	„ Fat Livers, *à la Toulouse*.

798. TURBAN OF OX-PALATES, A LA PERIGUEUX.

BRAIZE eight ox-palates, and when done, place them between two dishes, to press them flat; prepare about 2 lbs. of *gratin* force-meat

(No. 249) ; decorate or *contisés* twelve minion fillets of fowls, and cover them with thin layers of bacon till wanted.

Next, roll out about 4 oz. of firm common paste, to the size of a dessert-plate, and bake it in a slack oven ; this is to serve for a foundation to raise the *entrée* upon. Next, trim the ox-palates, split each in two with a sharp knife, in the same way as thin layers of bacon are

cut ; trim eight of these, spread the rough side with a thin layer of the *gratin* force-meat, then roll them up ; put the piece of paste before alluded to on a round baking-sheet ; spread it with a layer of the force-meat, a quarter of an inch thick, and after having trimmed the rolled ox-palates, to make them fit in with each other in circular order, place them firmly together on the foundation of paste prepared to receive them, taking care to put a little force-meat between each, to fill up the fissures, and unite them ; upon each fissure, one of the decorated fillets must be neatly laid, and turned under to secure it. The remaining eight pieces of ox-palates must then be trimmed, garnished with force-meat like the former, and afterward cut to the size of two-thirds of the others, and with these smaller rolls of ox-palates, a second tier must be formed upon the first, in similar fashion, and upon each joining, a decorated fillet is to be placed likewise. Any roughness occasioned by the force-meat must be neatly smoothed over with a knife, dipped in water ; a thick carrot, or piece of bread, cut in the shape of a pillar, and covered with fat bacon, should be placed in the centre of the *entrée*, to support its shape while being baked. The whole of the turban must be covered in with thin layers of fat bacon, and these must be secured on by means of a thick band of buttered paper, cut in slits round the base (to enable it to fit closer), and secured round the *entrée* with string : this will serve also to keep the turban in shape. One hour and a half before dinner-time, put the turban in the oven to be baked ; when done, remove the paper, &c., and with the end of a large skimmer, place the turban on its dish, fill the centre with a *ragout* of small truffles, pour some *Périgueux* sauce (No. 23) round the base of the *entrée*, lightly glaze the palates, without touching the fillets—which must be kept as white as possible—and serve.

799. TURBAN OF FILLETS OF FOWLS, A LA PRINCE DE GALLES.

PREPARE some *quenelle* force-meat of fowls (No. 242) or veal ; and with part of it fill a plain cylindrical mould, measuring about four inches high and six in diameter, previously buttered inside. This must be steamed in a covered stewpan, with a little water in it ; and when done, turned out of the mould upon a plate, and allowed to cool ; it should then be placed upon a foundation of baked paste, the angles of the *quenelle* rounded, and the whole of it covered with a thin coating of force-meat : upon this turban of *quenelle*, six larded fillets of fowls should be placed, with the point made to turn over the top ;

between each of these, insert a decorated minion fillet; cover the latter with thin layers of fat bacon, and secure the *entrée* round with a band of buttered paper made fast with string. Three quarters of an hour before dinner-time, put the turban in the oven to be baked; when it is done, remove the paper and the bacon from the small fillets, glaze the larded fillets brightly, garnish the well of the *entrée* with a Parisian *ragout* (No. 203), pour some of the same round the base, and serve.

800. TURBAN OF FILLETS OF RABBITS, A LA FINANCIERE.

TAKE out the fillets from four rabbits, trim and lard them closely. With the flesh of the legs, prepare some *quenelle* force-meat, and use part of this to make a cylindrical foundation, as in the foregoing case; when cold trim the top of this round, and after it has been spread with a thin coating of the force-meat, lay the larded fillets round its sides in a slanting position, with the small end of each turned over at the top, and made to reach about an inch down the cylinder; between each fillet of rabbit, a closely-studded row of cock's-kernels must be deeply inserted in the coating of *quenelle* force-meat, and these should be covered with thin strips of fat bacon to keep them white. A buttered band of paper must be placed round the turban, and secured with string. An hour before dinner-time, put the turban in the oven to be baked; when it is done, remove the paper, glaze the larded fillets, and afterwards pick the bacon off the kernels without disturbing them; fill the centre of the *entrée* with a *Financière ragout* (No. 188), pour some round the base, and serve.

801. TURBAN OF FILLETS OF HARES, A LA CONTI.

TAKE out the fillets of three young hares, and by splitting each fillet into halves, lengthwise, of equal thickness, twelve fillets will be obtained; these must then be neatly trimmed and *contisés* from one end to the other with scollops of black truffles. Use the flesh of the legs to prepare some *quenelle* force-meat; and, as in the foregoing cases, a foundation must be made with part of this, to raise the turban upon it. When the cylinder of force-meat has been poached or steamed, and is cold enough, place it upon the foundation of paste, trim the top round, and spread it over with a coating of force-meat; lay the decorated fillets of hare slantingly round the sides with their tapering points secured inside the cylinder with a little force-meat, and cover the turban with thin layers of fat bacon, secured round with a band of paper in the usual way. An hour before dinner-time, put the turban in the oven to be baked, and when it is done, remove the paper and bacon, dish it up, fill the centre with scollops of black truffles and white mushrooms, pour some brown Italian sauce (No. 12) over and round the *entrée*, and serve.

Note.—The two foregoing *entrées* may be varied in their appearance, by larding one-half of the fillets, and decorating the remainder with truffles or red tongue.

802. TURBAN OF FILLETS OF SOLES, A LA XIMENES.

TRIM the fillets of four middle-sized soles, *contisés* half with red tongue, and the remainder with thin scollops of green Indian gherkins; prepare some *quenelle* force-meat with four whitings, with part of which make a cylindrical foundation in the manner described for the fillets of fowls *à la Prince de Galles*. Spread a coating of force-meat over

this, and then place the fillets of soles round it in a slanting position, alternating those decorated with tongue with the others; the fillets must be neatly turned under the base, and securely fastened inside the cylinder with the point of a knife and a little force-meat. Cover the turban with thin layers of fat bacon, and fasten a band of buttered paper round it with string. An hour before dinner-time, put the tuban in the oven to be baked; when it is done, remove the paper and bacon, place the turban carefully on its dish, garnish the centre with a *ragout* of muscles (No. 197), pour some Tomata sauce (No. 22) round the base, and serve.

803. MAZARINE OF WHITINGS, A LA VENITIENNE.

PREPARE some *quenelle* force-meat with the fillets of five whitings,

and mix therewith a large gravy-spoonful of *purée* of mushrooms (No. 122), some chopped parsley, two ounces of black truffles also chopped, and two whisked whites of eggs. Next, butter a plain round mould, line the inside with white paper, and then fill it with the force-meat. An hour before dinner-time, steam the *mazarine* in the usual way, and when done, turn it out of the mould on its dish; place a border of *contisés* fillets of whitings round the top, fill the centre with a *ragout* of crayfish-tails and muscles, pour some Venetian sauce (No. 26), round the sides of the *mazarine*, and serve.

804. MAZARINE OF FAT LIVERS, A LA TOULOUSE.

PROCURE two fine Strasbourg fat livers, cut therefrom twelve flat scollops in the form of flat fingers, and with the trimmings make some force-meat (No. 249). Next line a plain round mould with buttered white paper, and then fill it with the prepared ingredients thus: Spread a layer of force-meat half an inch thick at the bottom of the mould, then line the sides in a similar manner; place the scollops of fat livers in a perpendicular position, fill up the interstices with scollops of French truffles and the remainder of the force-meat, and cover the top with buttered paper. An hour and a half before dinner-time, steam the *mazarine* in a deep stewpan with a little water, and cover it with its lid containing live embers of charcoal. Care must be taken to prevent the water from boiling over into the mould. When the *mazarine* is done, turn it out of the mould on its dish, place a border of minion fillets of fowls decorated with truffles, curled round in rings, and simmered in butter, fill the centre with a rich *Toulouse ragout* (No. 187), pour some Madeira sauce (No. 8), over the *entrée*, and serve.

ENTREES OF BEEF,

COMPRISING

Plain Rump Steak,	Minced Beef, *à la Portugaise.*
Beef Steak, *à la Française.*	Hashed Beef, plain.
„ with Anchovy-butter.	Hashed Beef, and broiled Bones.
Fillets of Beef in their own glaze, &c.	Braized Beef, *à la Claremont.*
Minced Beef, with Poached Eggs.	Bubble and Squeak.

805. PLAIN RUMP STEAK.

THE steak should be cut rather thick, neatly trimmed, seasoned with a little pepper and salt, and boiled over a clear fire; when done, remove it carefully from the gridiron, in order to preserve the gravy which collects on its upper surface. Place the steak on its dish, rub a small pat of fresh butter over it, garnish round with grated horse-radish, and send some beef gravy separately in a sauce-boat. Epicures, however, prefer the gravy which runs out of a juicy steak when well broiled to any other addition.

Small ribs of beef, and especially steaks cut from between the small ribs, form an excellent substitute for rump-steaks; both, when nicely broiled, may be served with cold *Maître d'Hôtel* butter, anchovy ditto; and also with the following sauces: Brown oyster, muscles, Italian, *Piquante*, Poor-man's, *Poivrade*, Tomata, *Provençale*, Fine-herbs, &c.; for making which, see Special Sauces.

806. BEEFSTEAK, A LA FRANCAISE.

CUT one pound of trimmed fillet of beef across the grain of the meat into three pieces; flatten these with the cutlet-bat, and trim them of a round or oval form; tnen cut and trim three pieces of suet, half the size of the former: dip the steaks in a little clarified butter, season with pepper and salt, and place them on the gridiron over a clear fire to broil; when done, glaze them on both sides, dish them up on two ounces of cold *Maître d'Hôtel* butter (No. 44), garnish round with fried potatoes, and serve.

These potatoes must be cut or turned in the form of olives, and fried in a little clarified butter.

807. BEEFSTEAKS WITH ANCHOVY BUTTER.

THESE are prepared in the same way as the foregoing, but anchovy butter must be substituted for *Maître d'Hôtel*.

Note.—French beef-steaks are always cut from the fillet, and may be served with any of the savory butters described in this work; they may also be garnished with Indian pickle, water-cresses, turned olives, and with all the varieties of common pickles, or with either of the sauces named for small rib-steaks.

808. FILLETS, OR SCOLLOPS, OF BEEF IN THEIR GLAZE.

CUT one pound of trimmed fillet of beef into four pieces, flatten and trim these round or oval, season with pepper and salt, put them with a like number of smaller pieces of beef-suet in a sauta-pan containing two ounces of clarified butter. Ten minutes before sending them to table, set the sauta-pan on a brisk stove-fire, and fry the fillets of a brown color; when they are done on both sides, pour off the grease, add a table-spoonful of glaze and twice as much brown sauce, twenty mushrooms, with some of their liquor, and the juice of half a lemon; allow the whole to boil for one minute on the fire, dish the fillets with a piece of fat on each, place the mushrooms in the centre, and pour the sauce over all.

Note.—Fillets of beef prepared in this manner may be dressed with either oysters, muscles, olives, truffles, gherkins cut into scollops, fried onions, fine-herbs, morels, &c., added to the sauce after they have been fried, instead of the mushrooms, as in the foregoing case. They may also be served when finished, with the addition of a piece of glaze and enough brown sauce for the *entrée*, with every kind of *purée* of vegetables and vegetable garnish described in this work; as also with any of the sauces recommended to be served with broiled steaks.

In all cases, the garnish of these *entrées* must be placed in the centre of the fillets, in a conical form, and the sauce poured round the fillets.

809. MINCED BEEF WITH POACHED EGGS.

PARE the fat and skin off one pound of roast beef, cut it into thin small slices, and then mince these very fine by chopping them. Put the mince into a stewpan with two large gravy-spoonsful of brown sauce, and a small piece of glaze, stir the whole over the fire until quite hot, dish it up in a conical form, place six poached eggs round the mince, pour a little brown sauce round the base, and serve.

For those who like high seasoning, some grated nutmeg, lemon-peel, and Cayenne pepper may be added to the mince.

810. MINCED BEEF, A LA PORTUGUAISE.

TRIM one pound of roast or braized beef, cut it up in pieces the size of a finger, and then with a sharp knife mince these into small shavings, and put them into a stewpan. Next, put two glasses of Port wine into a stewpan with one chopped shalot, the rind of an orange cut into small shreds, a little grated nutmeg, Cayenne pepper, and the juice of half a lemon ; boil these ingredients down to one-third of their original quantity, add enough *Espagnole* sauce for the *entrée*, and mix the preparation with the minced beef ; dish this up in a conical form, shake some light-colored raspings of bread-crust over it ; place a border round the base consisting of six poached eggs, the same number of oval scollops of red tongue, and oval *croûtons* fried in butter of a light color and glazed. Pour some of the sauce reserved for the purpose round the base, and serve.

811. HASHED BEEF, PLAIN.

SLICE the beef up in very thin pieces, season with pepper and salt, and shake a little flour over it. Next, chop a middle-sized onion, and put it into a stewpan with a table-spoonful of Harvey sauce, and an equal quantity of mushroom catsup ; boil these together for two minutes, and then add half a pint of broth or gravy ; boil this down to half its quantity, throw in the beef, set the hash to boil on the stove-fire for five minutes longer, and then serve with sippets of toasted bread round it when dished up.

812. HASHED BEEF AND BROILED BONES.

SLICE the beef up as in the foregoing case, and set it aside on a plate. Cut the bones into pieces about two inches long or square, having a little meat left on them ; score them all over by making deep incisions across them, season with plenty of pepper and a little salt, and put them on a plate. Slice two onions and fry them brown, then add enough brown sauce for the hash, or if there be none ready, shake a table-spoonful of flour over the onions, stir this over the fire for a minute, then add half a pint of good broth or gravy and a table-spoonful of mushroom catsup ; stir the whole on the fire until reduced to two-thirds of the original quantity, and then rub it through a tammy into a *purée ;* mix this with the sliced beef, make the hash quite hot, dish it up with the broiled bones (glazed) round it, and serve.

813. SLICES OF BRAIZED BEEF, A LA CLAREMONT.

THIS *entrée*, with its undermentioned varieties, may be served when it happens that any braized beef remains from a previous day's dinner.

The beef must be cut in rather thin round, or oval slices, placed in a sautapan in neat order, and warmed with a gravy-spoonful of good stock ; these must then be dished up in a circle—overlapping each other closely—pour some Claremont sauce (No. 58) over them, and serve.

Note.—Slices of braized beef warmed and dished up, as in the foregoing case, may be greatly varied by being afterward garnished with macaroni prepared with grated cheese, a little glaze and tomata-sauce, also with all sharp sauces, with *purées* of vegetables, and with vegetable garnishes.

814. BUBBLE AND SQUEAK.

CUT some slices (not too thin) of cold boiled round, or edge-bone, of salt beef ; trim them neatly, as also an equal number of pieces of the white fat of the beef, and set them aside on a plate. Boil two summer or Savoy cabbages, remove the stalks, chop them fine, and put them into a stewpan with four ounces of fresh butter and one ounce of glaze; season with pepper and salt. When about to send to table, fry the slices of beef in a sauta or frying pan, commencing with the pieces of fat; stir the cabbage on the fire until quite hot, and then pile it up in the centre of the dish; place the slices of beef and the pieces of fat round it, pour a little brown sauce over the whole, and serve.

ENTREES OF OX-CHEEKS,

COMPRISING

Braized Ox-cheeks, with *Purée* of Green Peas.	Braized Ox-cheeks, *à la Provençale.*
„ „ *à la Flamande.*	„ „ with stewed Cabbage.
„ „ *à la Brêtonne.*	„ „ *à la Jardiniére.*

815. BRAIZED OX-CHEEK, WITH PUREE OF GREEN PEAS.

Bone an ox-cheek, and steep it in cold water for two hours; then parboil it in water for five minutes, immerse it in cold water, drain, and trim it, break up the bones, and put them at the bottom of an oval stewpan, place the cheek upon them, and garnish with carrot, onion, celery, garnished faggot of parsley, six cloves, a blade of mace, and twelve pepper-corns; moisten with two quarts of broth or water (if the latter, add some salt); set the ox-cheek to braize very gently by the side of a stove-fire for about two hours; when done, take it up carefully, and put it to press between two dishes. Half the broth may be used for preparing some brown sauce with, and the remainder boiled down to a half glaze. Next, cut the ox-cheek up into twelve pieces of equal size, shape them either round, square, oblong, or oval; trim them neatly, and place them in a sautapan with the half glaze. Ten minutes before sending to table, put the ox-cheeks, covered with the lid, to simmer gently on the stove-fire until they are warmed through, and then set them to boil quickly over a brisk fire for three minutes; roll them in their glaze, and afterward dish them up in a circle, closely overlapping each other; fill the centre of the *entrée* with some thick *purée* of green peas (No. 136), pour a little brown sauce round the base, and serve.

816. BRAIZED OX-CHEEK, A LA FLAMANDE.

This is prepared, cut, and dished up as in the foregoing. Between each scollop of ox-cheek insert a piece of carrot previously boiled in broth, and rolled in its own glaze; fill the centre with a garnish of Brussels-sprouts, round which place a neat border of prepared turnips cut in fancy shapes; pour a little thin *Espagnole* sauce round the *entrée*, and serve.

817. BRAIZED OX-CHEEK, A LA BRETONNE.

Prepare and dish up the pieces of ox-cheek as directed in the first case; and just before sending to table, fill the centre with some *purée* of potatoes (No. 116), pour some *Brêtonne* sauce (No. 27) over the pieces of ox-cheek, and serve.

818. BRAIZED OX-CHEEK, A LA PROVENCALE.

THIS when dished up must be garnished round the base with a border of ripe tomatas prepared *au gratin* (No. 1160); fill the centre of the *entrée* with some *Provençale* sauce (No. 25), and serve.

819. BRAIZED OX-CHEEK, WITH STEWED CABBAGES.

WHEN the ox-cheek is prepared for braizing, as directed in No. 816, about one pound of German sausage must be added, also half a pound of streaky bacon, and two savoy-cabbages, previously cut in halves, parboiled in water, the stalks removed, and afterward tied up with string. The whole must be covered with a round buttered paper, and set to braize gently for about two hours; as soon as it is done, the ox-cheek should be put in press, and when cold cut into scollops and placed in a sautapan with some half glaze; the bacon and sausage must be also cut in neat scollops and kept hot in a sautapan with a little half glaze. The cabbage must first be drained in a colander, and then pressed in a napkin, and afterward cut out in cork-shaped pieces. The scollops of ox-cheek should be dished up in a close circle, alternately placing a scollop of ox-cheek with the bacon and sausage: and so on, until the whole is used up. Next, place the cabbage round the base in a neat border, and upon each piece of cabbage set a ring of carrot, with a piece of turnip cut in the form of a very small pear, in its centre; fill the well of the *entrée* with a garnish of carrots and turnips, cut in very small fancy shapes, pour some *Espagnole* sauce round the base and serve.

The carrots and turnips, above alluded to, must, of course, be boiled in broth, with a little sugar, and afterward boiled down in their glaze.

820. BRAIZED OX-CHEEK, A LA JARDINIERE.

BRAIZE, cut up, and dish the ox-cheek as directed in the first article; then fill the centre of the *entrée* with a garnish of vegetables *à la Jardinière* (No. 144), pour some half glaze or thin *Espagnole* sauce round the base, and serve.

DRESSED OX-PALATES,

COMPRISING

Canelons of Ox-palates, with *Poivrade* sauce
Paupiettes of Ox-palates *à la Financiére.*
Ox-palates, *à la Tortuë.*

Curry of Ox-palates.
Ox-palates in cases, with fine-herbs.
Attereaux of Ox-palates, *à la D'Uxelles.*

821. CANELONS OF OX-PALATES, WITH POIVRADE SAUCE.

CLEANSE and braize six ox-palates, and put them in press, as directed in No. 209, between two dishes until they are cold. The ox-palates must then be trimmed and split in halves, lengthwise; each of these must be again divided across in two, crosswise; the twenty-four pieces thus produced should be laid upon a large dish, and covered on one side only with some thick cold *d'Uxelles* sauce (No. 16). The *canelons* must then be rolled up in the form of a cartridge, and each first dipped in beaten egg (seasoned with a little salt) and afterward bread-crumbed.

Just before sending to table, the *canelons* should be fried in some clean hog's-lard, made quite hot for the purpose; they must be piled up in the dish, in a pyramidal form, with green fried parsley in the centre, round the base, and on the top. Send some *Poivrade* sauce (No. 29) in a boat.

Note.—Instead of bread-crumbing the *canelons*, if preferred, they may be dipped in a light-made batter, and then fried.

822. PAUPIETTES OF OX-PALATES, A LA FINANCIERE.

BRAIZE and cut up the ox-palates as in the foregoing case; then trim the twenty-four pieces thus produced into oblong scollops, measuring about two inches by three and a half; lay these on an earthen dish, and spread upon each a thin layer of *quenelle* force-meat of veal or poultry, in which some fine-herbs have been mixed. The ox-palates should then be rolled firmly in the form of cartridges, and six of these, disposed lengthwise in a buttered sheet of writing paper, must be rolled up tightly in it, and placed in a deep sautapan: the remainder are to be finished in the same manner, and kept in the cool until wanted. Half an hour before dinner-time set the *paupiettes* on a stove-fire, at the same time adding to them about a quart of boiling broth or *consommé*; as soon as they begin to boil, put the lid on, and set them to simmer gently by the side of the stove-fire for twenty minutes. The *paupiettes* must be drained on a napkin, the ends of each neatly cut off, then placed in a sautapan with a little half glaze, and again set on the fire to be rolled in this as it boils down; after, they should be dished up in a pyramidal, or a conical form, and a *Financière ragout* (No. 188) poured over the *entrée*, and sent to table.

823. OX-PALATES, A LA TORTUE.

BRAIZE the ox-palates as before directed, put them in press, and when cold, stamp them out in scollops, with a circular tin cutter two inches in diameter, and put them in a small deep sautapan with a little of the sauce intended for the *entrée*. Twenty minutes before sending to table, make the scollops quite hot, and place them in neat order, in and round the base of an ornamental *croustade* of fried bread, previously prepared for the purpose, and made fast on the centre of the dish, with a little paste made of flour and white of egg; dispose the *ragout à la tortuë*, omitting the pieces of calf's-head (No. 189) tastefully about the *entrée*, and serve.

824. CURRY OF OX-PALATES.

PREPARE the scollops of ox-palates, as in the foregoing case, and put them in a good curry-sauce (No. 47). Just before sending to table make the curry quite hot, and dish it up with boiled rice pressed into a border-mould, and then turned out on its dish.

The above is the simplest manner of serving this *entrée*, but it looks much better when dressed with an ornamental rice border, in which case some plain boiled Patna rice must be served separately.

825. ATTEREAUX OF OX-PALATES, A LA D'UXELLES.

BRAIZE four ox-palates; when done put them in press between two dishes; as soon as they are cold, trim both sides, cut them into inch-square scollops, and place these on a large earthen dish, together with about half their quantity of square pieces of truffles and mushrooms; pour some reduced *D'Uxelles* sauce (No. 16) over the whole, and when the sauce has become set, run the scollops upon twelve small silver skewers, intermixing the truffles and mushrooms alternately with the ox-palates; gather the sauce from the dish with a knife, and spread it upon the *attereaux* to give them a square, smooth form. They must then be rolled in bread-crumbs, afterward dipped in beaten eggs, and again bread-crumbed. Half an hour before sending to table, fry the *attereaux* in clean hog's lard, made hot for the purpose; dish them up neatly with parsley, fried green and crisp, placed in the centre, and serve.

826. OX-PALATES IN CASES, WITH FINE-HERBS.

PREPARE the ox palates in small circular scollops, and put them into a stewpan containing about two-thirds of their quantity of scollops of truffles and mushrooms; to these add sufficient reduced fine-herbs sauce (No. 14) for the *entrée*, mix the whole, and with this fill twelve small square, or plaited circular paper cases, previously oiled and baked in the oven for five minutes; cover them with a layer of raspings of bread, or bread-crumbs, fried of a light color, and place them upon a baking-sheet covered with clean paper. About half an hour before sending to table, put these cases in the oven to be baked, or rather warmed through, and then dish them up on a folded napkin, with fried parsley round the base of the *entrée*, and serve.

OX-PITHS,

COMPRISING

Ox-piths, *à la Ravigotte.*   *Crôustades* of Ox-piths.
  „   in cases, with fine-herbs.

827. OX-PITHS,* A LA RAVIGOTTE.

PROCURE about 1 lb. of ox-piths, steep them in water for a couple of hours, wash them thoroughly, and then carefully remove the membranous covering, and change the water. Next, slice up an onion and a small carrot very thin, and put these into a stewpan with a quart of hot water, mignionette pepper, and salt, a little thyme and bay-leaf, three cloves, and a blade of mace, and half a gill of vinegar; set these to boil on the fire, drop in the ox-piths, and allow them to boil gently for ten minutes; then set them aside to cool. Drain them on a napkin, and cut them in three-inch lengths, then place them in a basin, with a few sprigs of parsley, three sliced shalots, some mignionette pepper, and salt, three table-spoonsful of salad-oil, and one of vinegar. The ox-piths must be left to steep in this pickle till within about ten minutes of dinner-time, when they must be drained upon a napkin, then dipped separately in some light batter, and fried in clean hog's-lard made quite hot for the purpose. Dish them up

---

* The pith consists of the spinal marrow, which is more generally taken from sides of beef; that taken from veal and mutton is also occasionally used.

with fried parsley, and send some *Ravigotte* sauce in a boat, to be handed round.

To save trouble, the piths, when fried, may be dished up without a napkin or fried parsley, and the sauce poured under them. But in this case, unless they are eaten as soon as dished up, the vapor arising from the sauce destroys much of their crispness.

Note.—Ox-piths, when fried according to the foregoing directions, may also be served with any of the following sauces, viz :—*Piquante, Poivrade*, Italian, Tomata, &c.

828. OX-PITHS IN CASES, WITH FINE-HERBS.

PREPARE these, in the first instance, according to the directions contained in the foregoing article. They must then be drained upon a napkin, cut into inch lengths, and placed in a small stewpan, with sufficient *D'Uxelles* sauce (No. 16) for the *entrée* they should then be gently mixed together, and put into about a dozen small square or round paper cases, the surfaces of which are to be strewn with raspings, or fried bread-crumbs, and then placed upon a clean baking-sheet. About twenty minutes before sending to table, put the cases in the oven to get thoroughly warmed ; dish them up neatly in a pyramidal form, and serve some fine-herbs, or brown Italian sauce, separately in a boat.

829. CROUSTADES, OR PATTIES OF OX-PITHS.

IN this case, the ox-piths must be prepared according to the first part of the directions for dressing them *à la Ravigotte ;* they must then be cut into half-inch lengths, and placed in a small stewpan, with about half their quantity of prepared mushrooms, and two artichoke bottoms, previously cut into small dice ; to this may be added some finished *Espagnole* sauce (No. 3), a little cayenne, and lemon-juice ; warm the whole together on the stove-fire, and garnish the *crôustades*, or patties, with it.

OX-TONGUES,

COMPRISING

Ox-tongues, with Spinach.	Ox-tongues, *à la Jardinière.*
„ with Brussels-sprouts.	„ *à l'Allemande.*
„ *à la Macédoine.*	„ with *Sauër-Kraut.*

830. OX-TONGUE, WITH SPINACH.

PROCURE a pickled tongue, run an iron skewer through it from the root to the pointed end, tie a piece of string on one ene of the skewer, and fasten it at the other, so as to keep it in shape. The tongue should then be put on the fire in cold water, and kept gently boiling for about three hours, when it must be taken up, and after removing the outer cuticle, should be placed in the larder to cool ; it should then be neatly trimmed, wrapped in a piece of buttered paper, and put into an oval stewpan, with a little common broth. Three-quarters of an hour before sending it to table, put the tongue in the oven, or on a slow fire, to get warmed through; then glaze it, and dish it up with some prepared spinach (No. 112) round it, pour a little *Espagnole* sauce, or some half-glaze round the base, and serve.

831. OX-TONGUE, WITH BRUSSELS SPROUTS.

THIS is prepared in the same manner as the foregoing, except that Brussels sprouts (No. 1192) must be substituted for spinach.

832. OX-TONGUE, A LA MACEDOINE.

PREPARE the tongue as in the foregoing cases, and when about to send to table, glaze and dish it up with a white *Macédoine* of vegetables (No. 143) placed neatly round it, and serve.

833. OX-TONGUE, A LA JARDINIERE.

THE tongue, when dished up, must be garnished round with groups of glazed carrots and turnips, cut in small fancy shapes, and boiled in broth, with a pinch of sugar and a little salt, previously to their being boiled down in their own glaze; these must be alternated with similar groups of flowerets of cauliflowers, heads of asparagus-peas, or French-beans cut in the form of diamonds and boiled green. Pour some half glaze or *Espagnole* sauce round the base, and send to table.

834. BRAIZED OX-TONGUE, A L'ALLEMANDE

SCALD a fresh ox-tongue in boiling water upon the fire for about ten minutes; then immerse it in cold water, remove the root and any superfluous fat. Next, place the tongue in an oval stewpan with a carrot, an onion, one head of celery, a garnished faggot, four cloves, and a blade of mace; add a glass of brandy and sufficient good broth or stock to cover the whole, and set it to braize gently for two hours and a half upon a slow fire. When the tongue is done, take it out of the braize, trim and put it into a stewpan with its own liquor, previously divested of all the grease, strained through a sieve, and boiled down to half its quantity. About half an hour before sending to table, set the tongue on a very slow fire to simmer until it is warmed through; roll it in its glaze, dish it up with some cherry sauce à la Victoria (No. 64) under it, garnish it round with a border of potato *quenelles* (No. 312), and serve.

835. OX-TONGUE, WITH SAUER-KRAUT.

FOR this purpose choose a smoked tongue, and let it soak in cold water for four-and-twenty hours previously to its being dressed. The tongue must now be parboiled for half an hour, and immersed in cold water; then remove the root, and truss it with a skewer and some string to keep it in shape; next, place it in an oval stewpan with one pound and a half of *sauër-kraut* (previously well washed in several waters), two carrots, two onions stuck with six cloves, and a garnished faggot of parsley; moisten with sufficient stockpot toppings to cover the whole; place a well-buttered paper on the top, and cover with a lid containing some live embers of charcoal; then set these to braize very gently on a slow fire for about three hours. When the tongue is done, take it up on a dish, trim it, and put it in a small oval stewpan with a little good stock, to be kept hot by the side of the stove.

Meanwhile, remove the carrot, onion, and faggot of parsley from the *sauër-kraut*, and afterward press it in a napkin, to absorb all the grease.   Then glaze the tongue, and place it in its dish, garnish it neatly round with the *sauër-kraut* and put a border of small turned carrots (previously boiled and glazed for the purpose) round the base; pour some *Poivrade* sauce over the whole, and serve.

Note.—Reindeer tongues may be dressed in the same manner as the foregoing; they must, however, be soaked in cold water for four-and-twenty hours previously to their being dressed.

ENTREES OF MUTTON.

1. Mutton Cutlets, sautees,

COMPRISING

Mutton Cutlets, plain.
,,   *à la Minute.*
,,   *à la Maintenon.*
,,   *à la Bourguignotte.*

Mutton Cutlets, with *Purée* of Endives, &c.
,,   *à la Nivernaise*, &c.
,,   with New Potatoes, &c.

836. MUTTON CUTLETS, PLAIN.

Choose a neck of mutton that has been killed at least four days, saw off the scrag end, and as much of the rib-bones as may be necessary in order to leave the cutlet-bones not more than three inches and a half long; the spine-bones must also be removed with the saw, without damaging the fillet.   Next, cut the neck of mutton thus trimmed into as many cutlets as there are bones; detach the meat from the upper part of each bone, about three-quarters of an inch, then dip them in water and flatten them with a cutlet-bat, trim away the sinewy part, and any superfluous fat.   The cutlets must then be seasoned with pepper and salt, passed over with a paste-brush dipped in clarified butter, and nicely broiled, over or before a clear fire. When they are done, dish them up neatly, and serve with plain brown gravy under them.

Cutlets prepared in this way may also be served with either of the following sauces—Poor-man's, *Piquante*, Italian, Tomata, *Provençale*, *Poivrade*, Shalot, Gravy.

837. MUTTON CUTLETS, A LA MINUTE.

Trim the cutlets as above, then season with pepper and salt, and place them in a sauta-pan with about two ounces of clarified butter. The cutlets must be fried over a rather brisk fire, of a brown color; then pour off the grease, and add a large gravy-spoonful of *Espagnole* sauce, a piece of glaze, and the juice of half a lemon; set the cutlets again on the fire to simmer gently for two minutes, dish them up, and pour the sauce over them.

The centre of this *entrée* may be filled with mashed potatoes, mashed turnips, spinach, potatoes *à la Maître d'Hôtel*, &c.

838. MUTTON CUTLETS, A LA MAINTENON.

THESE are prepared, in the first instance, according to the former part of the directions for cutlets *à la Minute ;* season with pepper and salt, add a table-spoonful of chopped mushrooms, the same quantity of parsley, and three shalots, also chopped. Fry the cutlets brown on both sides, pour off the grease, and two large spoonfuls of brown sauce, a very little grated nutmeg, and the juice of a lemon ; allow the whole to simmer together on the fire for five minutes, and then set them in the larder to cool. Meanwhile, take as many sheets of large-sized note-paper as there are cutlets, cut each somewhat in the form of a heart, and then let them be oiled. Next, place a cutlet with an equal proportion of the sauce in one of these papers, and with the fore-finger and thumb of the right hand, twist the edges of the paper tightly under into very close folds ; and repeat this with the remainder. A quarter of an hour before sending to table, put the cutlets in the oven in a sauta-pan, to get warm through ; then, with a heated iron skewer, mark the papers so as to make it appear that they have been broiled ; dish them up on a napkin with fried parsley in the centre, and send some brown Italian or fine-herbs sauce in a boat.

839. MUTTON CUTLETS, A LA BOURGUIGNOTTE.

TRIM the cutlets and arrange them in circular order in a sauta-pan with a little clarified butter. Then, fry them quickly on a brisk fire to brown them on both sides, and before they are quite done, pour off all the grease ; add half-a-pint of red wine (Port or Claret), about half a pottle of prepared mushrooms, and the same quantity of small button onions (previously simmered in a little butter, over a slow fire until nearly done) ; season with a pinch of mignionette pepper, and a little salt, some grated nutmeg, and a tea-spoonful of pounded sugar ; set the whole to boil on the stove for two minutes, and then add a small ladleful of brown sauce ; allow the cutlets (covered) to simmer very gently on a slow fire for twenty minutes, by which time they will be done, and the sauce sufficiently reduced. The cutlets must then be dished up closely, in a circle ; add half a glass of red wine and a dozen small *quenelles* to the sauce, boil the whole together for a minute, and garnish the centre of the *entrée* with the mushrooms, &c., pour the sauce over the cutlets, and serve.

840. MUTTON CUTLETS, WITH PUREE OF ENDIVES.

THESE are prepared and finished in the same manner as the cutlets *à la Minute;* and when they are dished up, the centre of the *entrée* must be filled with a *purée* of endives (No. 114).

Note.—Cutlets dressed in this way may be served with *purées* of vegetables of all sorts.

841. MUTTON CUTLETS, A LA NIVERNAISE.

TRIM and prepare the cutlets as in the the foregoing case, and when they have been fried brown, pour off the grease, and add a garnish of carrots and turnips *à la Nivernaise* (No. 137) ; allow the whole to simmer gently on a slow fire for a quarter of an hour, dish up the cutlets, and fill the centre with vegetables, pour the sauce over the *entrée,* and serve.

842. ANOTHER METHOD.

THE cutlets, when fried, may be glazed, then dished up, and the garnish *à la Nivernaise* placed in the centre. The advantage of the first method is, that the cutlets partake of the flavor of the vegetables by simmering with them.

843. MUTTON CUTLETS, WITH NEW POTATOES.

THESE are prepared in the same way as cutlets *à la Minute*, and when dished up, must be garnished with new potatoes *à la Maître d'Hôtel* (No. 1188).

Mutton cutlets, prepared in the same manner, may be garnished with any of the following vegetable garnishes, viz : *Jardinière*, *Macédoine*, asparagus-peas, stewed peas, Brussels-sprouts, &c.

---

2. MUTTON CUTLETS, BREAD-CRUMBED,

COMPRISING

Mutton Cutlets, Bread-crumbed and Broiled with Shalot Gravy.	Mutton Cutlets, Bread-crumbed, *à la Bretonne*.
„ „ with *Purée* of Mushrooms.	„ „ *à la Macédoine*.
„ „ with Cucumbers.	„ „ *à l'Indiènne*.
„ „ *à la Milanaise*.	„ „ with *Purée* of Chestnuts.

844. MUTTON-CUTLETS, BREAD-CRUMBED AND BROILED WITH SHALOT GRAVY.

TRIM the cutlets in the usual manner, and season them with pepper and salt; then egg them slightly over with a paste-brush dipped in two yolks of eggs, beaten up on a plate for the purpose; pass each cutlet through some fine bread-crumbs; then dip them separately in some clarified butter, and bread-crumb them over once more; put them into shape with the blade of a knife, and lay them on a gridiron, to be broiled over a clear fire, of a light-brown color; then, glaze and dish them up, and serve them with plain or shalot gravy. These cutlets may also be served with any of the sauces directed to be used for plain broiled cutlets.

845. MUTTON CUTLETS, WITH PUREE OF MUSHROOMS.

BREAD-CRUMB the cutlets as in the foregoing case; then place them in a sauta-pan with a little clarified butter, fry them over a brisk fire, of a light color, and when done, remove them on to a napkin or a sheet of paper, and glaze them; dish them up, fill the centre with a white *purée* of mushrooms (No. 122), pour some half glaze round the *entrée*, and serve.

846. MUTTON CUTLETS, WITH CUCUMBERS.

PREPARE these in the same way as the foregoing, and garnish them, when dished up, with some scollops of cucumbers (No. 138).

847. MUTTON CUTLETS, A LA MILANAISE.

IN this case, the bread-crumbs used for the cutlets must be mixed with 2 oz. of grated Parmesan cheese : in other respects they are to be bread-crumbed as before. When about to send to table, the cutlets should be fried of a light color, glazed, and dished up ; and the centre garnished with some macaroni, finished with grated Parmesan cheese, and a spoonful of *Béchamel,* or any other white sauce ; pour some *Provençale* sauce (No. 25) round the base of the *entrée* and serve.

848. MUTTON CUTLETS, A LA BRETONNE.

THESE are prepared and finished in the same way as cutlets, garnished with a *purée* of mushrooms, with this exception, that the centre must be filled with small potatoes previously cut or scooped in the form of olives, and fried in butter, of a yellow color ; pour some *Brétonne* sauce (No. 27) under the cutlets, and serve.

849. MUTTON CUTLETS, A LA MACEDOINE.

PREPARE these in the same way as the foregoing, and when they are dished up, garnish the centre with a *Macédoine* of vegetables (No. 143); pour some half glaze round the base of the *entrée,* and serve.

850. MUTTON CUTLETS, A L'INDIENNE.

BREAD-CRUMB, fry, glaze, and dish up the cutlets ; then garnish the centre with two dozen small *quenelles* of anchovies (No. 246), the force-meat of which must be mixed with a little strong curry sauce (No. 47) ; pour some mangoe sauce under the cutlets, and serve.

The mangoe sauce here alluded to is thus made :—Split a fine mangoe, and let the inside be reserved in a small stewpan ; then cut the outside part into narrow strips, and again mince these into shreds, or thin scollops, and place them in the stewpan ; add a small ladleful of *Espagnole* sauce (No. 3) ; boil the whole together for five minutes, when it will be fit for use.

851. MUTTON CUTLETS, WITH PUREE OF CHESTNUTS.

THESE, when dished up as in the foregoing cases, should be garnished with a *purée* of chestnuts (No. 115), and some thin *Espagnole* poured round them, then serve.

Note.—Bread-crumbed cutlets may be served with every sort of vegetable garnish described in this work, and with all the sauces directed to be served with plain cutlets.

BRAIZED MUTTON CUTLETS,

COMPRISING

Mutton Cutlets, *à la Soubise.*	Mutton Cutlets, *à la Pompadour.*
„ *à la Lyonnaise.*	„ *à la Provençale.*
„ with *Purée* of Artichokes.	„ *à la Russe.*
à la Chipolata.	

852. MUTTON CUTLETS, BRAIZED, A LA SOUBISE.

TRIM one or two necks of mutton (according to the size of the *entrée*) in the way described for plain cutlets ; the neck must then be cut up into thick cutlets, and placed on a dish without being further trimmed. Next, cut 1lb. of fat bacon into narrow strips, about the sixth of an inch square, and an inch and a half long, and with these the cutlets should be larded in the following manner:—Take a middle-sized larding-pin, and run it half through the lean of the cutlet : then place a strip of bacon in the open end, and draw the larding-pin through, leaving the bacon in the cutlet : repeat this, until the cutlet has been studded with eight strips of bacon, and proceed in the same manner with the remainder. Stew some of the trimmings over the bottom of a large stewpan, or *fricandeau* pan, and place the cutlets upon them in circular order, with the bone-end pointing to the centre; cover them with the remainder of the trimmings, and garnish with a couple of sliced carrots, a large onion, stuck with four cloves, a garnished faggot of parsley, and one head of celery ; season with a dozen pepper-corns and a blade of mace, moisten with a glass of brandy, and sufficient *fresh* broth or stock to cover the whole ; place a buttered paper on this, put on the lid, and set the cutlets to braize very gently on a slow fire, or in the oven, for about one hour and a half; when they are become nearly tender enough, draw the pan off the fire, and allow them to get partially cold in their own liquor. The cutlets must then be carefully taken out, one at a time, with a small slice or skimmer, and placed in rows on a large earthen dish : when the whole are thus removed, another dish must be placed upon these to press them slightly, in order to give them an even surface. As soon as they have become firm by getting quite cold, trim them neatly with a sharp knife, by paring off the surface of each cutlet (without waste), so as to show the bacon inserted in the lean ; put them into a deep sautapan with some half glaze, made with the broth they have been braized in, which must be strained, divested of all the grease, clarified, and afterward boiled down for the purpose. A quarter of an hour before sending to table, put the cutlets on a brisk fire to warm, allow them to boil quickly for five minutes, then roll the sautapan about carefully, so as to glaze them all over, and dish them up in a close circle ; fill the centre with some *Soubise* sauce, or *purée* (No. 119), pour the remainder of the half glaze round the base of the *entrée*, and serve.

853. MUTTON CUTLETS BRAIZED, A LA LYONNAISE.

PREPARE, finish, and dish up the cutlets, as in the foregoing case ; then fill the centre with some *Lyonnaise* sauce (No. 24), and serve.

854. MUTTON CUTLETS BRAIZED, WITH PUREE OF ARTICHOKES.

THESE are prepared exactly as for *Soubise*, and when dished up should be garnished with a *purée* of artichokes (No. 117); pour a little *Béchamel* sauce, or some half glaze round their base, and serve.

855. MUTTON CUTLETS BRAIZED, A LA CHIPOLATA.

PREPARE and dish up these in the same manner as the foregoing ; garnish them with a *Chipolata ragout* (No. 190), and serve.

856. MUTTON CUTLETS BRAIZED, A LA POMPADOUR.

THESE must be prepared, in the first instance, nearly in the same manner as the *Soubise* cutlets, except that, instead of the larding, they

must be studded with red tongue
and black truffles ; when the cutlets, after being braized, have been
trimmed, mask each of them with
a coating of reduced *Soubise* sauce
(No. 119) ; and when this has
become firmly set, by cooling on
the cutlets, dip them separately
in three whole eggs, seasoned with
a little salt, and beaten up for the
purpose, and afterward bread-
crumb them ; flatten the bread-crumbs on smoothly with the blade of
a knife, put the cutlets carefully away on a dish in a cool place until
within twenty minutes of dinner-time. The cutlets must then be
placed in rows, on the wire lining of a deep frying-pan ; when the
hog's-lard is sufficiently hot for the purpose, immerse the cutlets in
it, and fry them of a deep yellow color ; then drain them on a napkin, or a sheet of paper, in order to absorb all the grease, and dish
them up in a close circle upon a vegetable border. Fill the centre
with a *Macédoine* of vegetables (No. 143), pour some half glaze round
the base, and serve.

857. MUTTON CUTLETS BRAIZED, A LA PROVENCALE.

Braize and trim the cutlets as in the foregoing case ; except that
in the present instance the cutlets must be left plain, omitting altogether the larding or studding. While the cutlets are being braized,
set about making the following preparation :—Cut three Portugal
onions into very small dice, parboil these in water, drain them on a
sieve, and then place them in a small stewpan, with 1 oz. of fresh butter,
the same quantity of glaze, a little mignionette pepper and salt, and
some grated nutmeg ; set the lid on the stewpan, and place the onions
on a very slow fire, to be thoroughly stewed, without acquiring any
color. Next, add a gravy-spoonful of white sauce, a little grated garlic,
on the point of a knife, and stir the whole on the fire until reduced to
a paste ; then add the yolks of three eggs, and a little lemon-juice ;
mix well together, and use this preparation to cover the surface of
one side *only* of the cutlets ; shake a rather thick coating of bread-
crumbs and grated Parmesan cheese, in equal proportions, over this,
and then place the cutlets in a sauta-pan containing a little half glaze.
About twenty minutes before sending to table, put the cutlets in the
oven to be warmed through, pass the red-hot salamander over them,
to give them a deep yellow color, mash them with thin glaze, and
dish them up ; then pour some *Provençale* sauce (No. 25) under them,
and serve.

858. MUTTON CUTLETS BRAIZED, A LA RUSSE.

Cut twelve thick cutlets, as directed in the first article of this section ; insert eight strips of lean ham through the lean part, in a
circular form ; prepare them for braizing in the usual way, and in
addition to the customary complement of vegetables and seasoning,
add two cloves of garlic and a couple of capsicums ; moisten with a
pint of Madeira and a quart of good stock ; set the cutlets to braize
for an hour and a half, on a very slow fire, and when nearly done

remove them from the fire, that they may partially cool in their own liquor; and then put them in press between two dishes. When the cutlets are cold, trim them neatly, and cover one side only with a rather-thick coating of the following preparation :—Clean two large sticks of horse-radish, and grate them; put this into a small stewpan with a small pat of butter, two table-spoonfuls of French vinegar, a pinch of mignionette pepper, a little grated nutmeg, and a tea-spoonful of sugar; put the lid on, and set the whole to stew very gently for twenty minutes on a very slow fire; then add two gravy-spoonfuls of *Velouté* sauce, boil the whole well together for ten minutes, mix with this sauce the yolks of four eggs, and a small piece of glaze, and use this preparation as directed above.

Next, mask the coated side of the cutlets with a paste-brush dipped in some white of egg that has been beaten up, and sprinkle this surface over with very fine bread-crumbs, previously fried of a light color, with a little butter: place the cutlets in neat order in a sauta-pan, with a little half glaze, and a quarter of an hour before sending to table, put them in the oven to be warmed through, without allowing them to acquire any more color; dish them up with a very small paper ruffle on the bone of each cutlet, pour some half glaze (made with their own liquor, previously strained, divested of all grease, and afterward boiled down) under them, and serve.

Note.—Mutton cutlets, when braized according to any of the foregoing directions, may be served with all sorts of dressed vegetables, such as stewed peas, asparagus-peas, French-beans, broad-beans, *Macédoine* of vegetables, *Jardinière*, braized lettuces, &c., and also with all kinds of *purées* of vegetables : for making which, see those articles.

SCOLLOPS OF MUTTON,

COMPRISING

Scollops of Mutton, with Fine-herbs.	Scollops of Mutton, with Olives *farcies.*
„ *à la Claremont.*	„ with Mushrooms and
„ with Oysters.	Truffles.
„ *à l'Indiènne.*	

859. SCOLLOPS OF MUTTON, WITH FINE-HERBS.

BONE a loin of mutton, and with a sharp knife pare off the sinewy skin which lies beneath the fat of the upper and under or minion fillets. Next, cut these fillets into neatly-trimmed scollops, and place them in a circular order in a sauta-pan with two ounces of clarified butter; season with pepper and salt, and fry them over a brisk fire, until browned on both sides; then pour off the grease, and add sufficient fine-herbs sauce (No. 14) for the *entrée;* allow the whole to simmer together over the fire for three minutes, and then dish up the scollops, either in a pyramidal form, in a close circle, or else in an ornamental border of potato or rice. These scollops may also be garnished with a border of *croquettes* of mutton, mushrooms, potatoes or rice.

Note.—The garnishes here alluded to will serve for mutton scollops generally.

860. SCOLLOPS OF MUTTON, A LA CLAREMONT.

PREPARE the scollops as in the foregoing case, fry them brown, pour off all the grease, and add enough *Claremont* sauce (No. 58), for the *entrée*, set the whole to simmer briskly on the fire for three minutes, and serve.

861. SCOLLOPS OF MUTTON, WITH OYSTERS.

THESE are prepared according to the foregoing directions, and when the grease has been poured off, add as much brown oyster sauce (No. 51) as will suffice for the *entrée*, simmer the whole together on the fire for three minutes, and serve.

862. SCOLLOPS OF MUTTON, A L'INDIENNE.

PREPARE the scollops in the usual manner, fry them brown, pour off the grease, add then some curry sauce (No. 47) and a minced mangoe; simmer the whole together on the fire for five minutes, and send to table with some plain boiled rice served separately.

863. SCOLLOPS OF MUTTON, WITH OLIVES FARCIES.*

THESE are prepared in the same way as the foregoing, and when they have been fried and the grease poured off, add two dozen olives *farcies*, two large gravy-spoonfuls of *Espagnole* sauce (No. 3), a little cayenne and lemon-juice, and a small piece of glaze; toss the whole together, allow the scollops to simmer briskly on the stove-fire for three minutes, and then serve.

864. SCOLLOPS OF MUTTON, WITH MUSHROOMS AND TRUFFLES.

Sautez or fry the scollops brown, then pour off the fat, and add a small glass of Madeira, a dozen button-mushrooms, three ounces of truffles cut into scollops, a little cayenne, and a small piece of glaze; toss the whole together over the stove-fire until mixed, and then add enough finished *Espagnole* sauce for the *entrée*, and a little lemon-juice; set the scollops to simmer on the fire for three minutes, and serve.

BRAIZED CARBONNADES OF MUTTON,

COMPRISING

Carbonnades of Mutton, *à la Richelieu.*	Fillets of Mutton, larded, with *Chêvreuil*
„ „ *à la Dauphinoise.*	sauce, or Roebuck fashion, &c.
„ „ *à la Flamande.*	Haricôt of Mutton, *à la Nivernaise.*

865. BRAIZED CARBONNADES OF MUTTON, A LA RICHELIEU.

BONE two loins of mutton, leaving the small fillets adhering thereto; divest them of all the inside fat, season with pepper and salt, cut off the loose ends and flaps, and then roll them up tight, keeping the

---

* Olives *farcies*, or stuffed olives, are sold in small bottles, and may be procured at most Italian warehouses.

fillet in the centre; sew each of them up closely with string and a small trussing-needle, and tie them round with string to preserve their shape. Next, strew the trimmings over the bottom of an oval braizing-pan, place the *carbonnades* upon these, garnish with two carrots, two onions stuck with four cloves, two heads of celery, and a garnished faggot of parsely; moisten with a glass of brandy and sufficient broth or stock to cover the whole. Braize the *carbonnades* on a gentle fire for about two hours, and allow them partially to cool in their own liquor: they must then be put in press between two dishes, taking care that the sewn-up part is placed undermost. When cold, trim them neatly in the form of oblong cushions, remembering that nearly the whole of the fat which covers them must be left on: this, however, must be pared smooth. Strain their liquor, remove the grease, clarify it in the usual way, and then boil it down to half glaze, half of which is to be put with the *carbonnades* in a covered *fricandeau*-pan, to warm them in; the remainder being used to work the sauce with. Half an hour before sending to table, put the *carbonnades* in the oven to be warmed through; then take the lid off, allow their surface to dry, and baste them frequently with their own glaze, until they assume a bright shiny surface; they must then be placed side by side in their dish, garnished with potatoes previously cut in the form of olives, and fried in clarified butter; pour a *Richelieu ragout* (No. 210) under them, and serve.

866. BRAIZED CARBONNADES OF MUTTON, A LA DAUPHINOISE.

BONE two loins of mutton, remove all the inside fat and the small fillets; season with pepper and salt, and spread some highly-seasoned veal force-meat on the inside; they must then be rolled, sewn up, and afterward corded round with string to make them retain their shape. Braize the *carbonnades* in the same way as the foregoing, and when done, put them in press, and cut each into six pieces in the form of a pointed scollop; trim these neatly, put them on an earthen dish, and then cover them over with a thin coating of *d'Uxelles* sauce (No. 16). Next remove them to a cold place that the sauce may the sooner become firmly set; then dip each separately in some beaten egg, and bread-crumb them. About twenty minutes before sending to table, place the *carbonnades* upon the wire-lining of a frying-pan, immerse them in some clean hogs'-lard made quite hot for the purpose, and fry them of a light-brown color; drain them upon a napkin, and dish them up in a circular form, with the pointed ends placed toward the centre, so as to make them fit in with each other. Fill the centre with a group of small tomatas "*au gratin*" (No. 1160), and place also a border of these round the base; pour some *Provençale* (No. 25), under the *carbonnades*, and serve.

867. BRAIZED CARBONNADES OF MUTTON, A LA FLAMANDE.

PREPARE these as in the first case; and when they are become sufficiently cold, cut each into six pieces in the form of pointed scollops, trim them smoothly and neatly, and then place them in a deep sauta-pan with some half glaze made from their own liquor. Half an hour before sending to table, put them in the oven to be warmed and glazed, as before directed; dish them up as in the preceding case, fill the centre with some prepared Brussels sprouts (No. 156), over the part where the *carbonnades* join to each other ; place a crescent of turnip round the base of the sprouts, add a neat border of glazed carrots, and garnish the base of the *entrée* with a *Jardinière* (No. 144); pour some bright thin *Espagnole* sauce under the *entrée*, and serve.

Note.—Carbonnades, prepared and trimmed as directed in Nos. 865 and 867, may also be served with every sort of vegetable garnish, or *purée* of vegetables, described in this work.

868. FILLETS OF MUTTON LARDED, WITH CHEVREUIL SAUCE, OR ROEBUCK FASHION.

REMOVE the fillets from two loins of mutton, pare off all the sinewy skin that lies beneath the fat, and divide each fillet, lengthwise, into four, these, together with the smaller fillets thus trimmed also, will make up ten ; trim these and lard them closely with strips of fat bacon, in the usual way. The fillets must then be steeped in a cold *marinade* (No. 234) for about forty-eight hours ; after which, drain them upon a napkin to absorb any unnecessary moisture. Next, place the fillets in a sautapan thickly spread with butter, and turn them round in a semicircular form ; moisten with a little *mirepoix* (No. 236), or a glass of Sherry ; cover them with a buttered paper and set them in the oven to simmer for about twenty minutes ; they must then be glazed, trimmed neatly round the ends, and dished up in a close circle, overlapping each other ; fill the centre with potatoes cut in the form of olives, and fried in butter ; pour some *Poivrade* sauce (No. 29) under the fillets, and serve.

*Note.—*Fillets of mutton prepared as the foregoing, may also be garnished with *quenelles* of potatoes, with *Chêvreuil* sauce (No. 69), Victoria sweet sauce, Tomata, *Piquante*, Gherkins, or *Provençale* sauce.

869. HARICOT OF MUTTON, A LA NIVERNAISE.

CUT a neck of mutton into untrimmed cutlets, pare off any super-fluous fat, put them into a large stewpan with four ounces of butter, and fry them over a brisk fire until they become brown ; then pour off the greater portion of grease, and shake in a good handful of flour, stir the whole over the fire for about five minutes, moisten with three pints of broth, and stir the *haricôt* on the fire till it boils. Meanwhile, prepare some carrots and turnips, cut in the form of small pears, olives, half-moons, or any other fancy shape, and throw these into the *haricôt ;* a dozen small onions may also be added ; season with a garnished faggot of parsley, and some mignionette pepper. Keep the *haricôt* gently boiling by the side of the fire for about one hour and a half ; skim off all the grease, remove the faggot of parsley, place the cutlets and vegetables in another stewpan, and after having boiled the sauce down (if necessary), pass it through a tammy upon the cutlets. When about to send to table, warm the *haricôt*, dish the cutlets in the usual manner, fill the centre with the vegetables, pour the sauce over all, and serve.

*Note.—*Breasts of mutton with the superfluous fat removed, and cut into small square pieces, make a very good *haricôt*, or stew.

The foregoing may be varied by substituting green-peas, young carrots, turnips, or new potatoes for the vegetables directed to be used.

SHEEP'S-TONGUES,

Sheep's-tongues *à l'Ecarlate*, with Spinach, &c.　　Sheep's-tongues, *à la Napolitaine.*
　　" 　　　*à la Maintenon.* 　　　　　　　　　　" 　　　　with Gherkin sauce.

Sheep's-tongues should first be pickled in the manner directed for briskets of beef, &c.; for the preparation of which, see No. 564.

870. SHEEP'S-TONGUES, A L'ECARLATE, WITH SPINACH.

FROM six to a dozen tongues suffice for an *entrée ;* these must be braized in some wine *mirepoix* (No. 236), or common broth, garnished with the usual complement of vegetables, &c. : after about three quarters of an hour's gentle boiling, they will be done : they must then be placed upon a dish, on their sides, and another dish with a weight in it should be laid upon them to press them evenly. When the tongues are cold, trim them neatly, and place them in a deep sautapan with some half glaze, and about twenty minutes before sending to table, put them in the oven, to be warmed through, covered with a circular piece of buttered paper, to prevent their being dried up ; roll them in their glaze, dish them up in the same manner as cutlets, fill the centre with spinach (No. 112), mix a spoonful of *Espagnole* with the re- mainder of their glaze, pour it round the tongues, and serve.

871. SHEEP'S-TONGUES, A LA MAINTENON.

THESE must first be braized, and when done, put in press between two dishes, and afterwards neatly trimmed. The tongues must then be finished in every respect the same as mutton cutlets *à la Maintenon* (No. 838).

872. SHEEP'S-TONGUES, A LA NAPOLITAINE.

BRAIZE and trim the tongues as above, cover them all over with a thin coating of *d'Uxelles* sauce (No. 16), and when this has become firmly set by cooling, dip each tongue in some beaten egg, and roll it in bread-crumbs ; flatten them smoothly with the blade of a knife, and then place them on a dish in the larder, until within about twenty minutes of dinner-time. The tongues must then be fried of a light- brown color, in clean hog's-lard made hot for the purpose, then drained upon a napkin, and dished up in the form of a close circle, the centre of which must be filled with macaroni dressed with cheese and a little *Béchamel* sauce ; pour some Napolitaine sauce (No. 63), under them, and serve.

873. SHEEP'S-TONGUES, WITH GHERKIN SAUCE.

PREPARE, finish, and dish up the tongues according to the directions in the first case, pour some gherkin sauce (No. 19) in the centre of the *entrée*, and serve.

Note.—Sheep's-tongues prepared after the foregoing directions, may be served with every kind of brown sauce or *ragout ;* and also with any of the vegetable garnishes or *purées* described in this work.

SHEEP'S-HEAD AND KIDNEYS,

COMPRISING

Sheep's Kidneys, *à la Brochette.*	Sheep's Kidneys, with Fine-herbs.
„ bread-crumbed, *à l'Epicu-riénne.*	„ *à la Claremont.*
	Sheep's Head, *à la Gallimaufre.*

874. SHEEP'S-KIDNEYS, A LA BROCHETTE.

SLIT the kidneys lengthwise, without cutting through the sinew; remove the thin skin which covers them, and place them in a small dish; season with pepper and salt, and a table-spoonful of salad oil, and allow them to steep in their seasoning until broiled. They must then be run on a small silver or any other kind of skewer (two or three on each), and placed upon a gridiron over a clear fire to be broiled, with the open side downwards; when done brown they must be turned up, as, from the heat of the fire, their sides become contracted, which causes them to form a sort of cup to hold the gravy in when the kidneys are done: care must be taken not to spill this gravy in dishing them up: fill each with a small piece of cold *Maître-d'Hôtel* butter (No. 44), pour a little half glaze under them, and send to table quite hot.

Broiled kidneys may also be served with anchovy butter, plain gravy, or a pat of fresh butter and a spoonful of Harvey sauce.

875. SHEEP'S-KIDNEYS, BREAD-CRUMBED, A L'EPICURIENNE.

SPLIT the kidneys as before directed, season them with pepper and salt, dip them in clarified butter, and roll them in fresh-made bread-crumbs; place them on the skewers, and broil them on both sides: when done, dish them up with a small piece of epicurean butter (No. 186) in each, the juice of a lemon and a little half glaze under them, and serve quite hot.

876. SHEEP'S-KIDNEYS, WITH FINE-HERBS.

PREPARE some fine-herbs sauce (No. 14), slit the kidneys lengthwise quite through; remove the skin, and then slice them into thin scollops. Place a sauta or frying pan, with two ounces of butter in it, on a brisk fire; fry the kidneys brown, then add a glass of Sherry or Madeira; let this boil till reduced, then pour in the sauce prepared for the purpose; allow the whole to simmer together on the stove for three minutes; dish them up with some pastry *fleurons* round them, and serve.

877. ANOTHER METHOD.

PREPARE the kidneys in thin scollops, season with pepper and salt, and fry them brown in a little butter; then throw in a table-spoonful of chopped mushrooms, the same of parsley, and two shalots, also chopped; after allowing the whole to fry a few minutes longer, shake in a table-spoonful of flour, mix together, and moisten with a glass of sherry; let this boil for two minutes, then add a large spoonful of brown gravy or broth; allow the whole to simmer on the fire for five minutes, add a little lemon-juice, and serve.

878. SHEEP'S-KIDNEYS, A LA CLAREMONT.

Scollop and fry the kidneys as directed for those dressed with fine-herbs; and when they are browned, add some *Claremont* sauce (No. 58); simmer the whole together for three minutes, and serve with a border of potato *croquettes.*

879. SHEEP'S-HEAD, A LA GALLIMAUFRE.

Procure the head and pluck of a fresh-killed sheep, split the head into halves, remove the brains, steep the whole in water, and wash them thoroughly. Next, place the head, heart, and liver in a stewpan, with carrot, onion, garnished faggot of parsley, and green onions, two blades of mace, a dozen cloves, and a tea-spoonful of pepper-corns; moisten with a glass of brandy, and sufficient broth or water—if the latter be used, salt must be added; cover the whole with buttered paper and put the lid on, then set the stewpan on a gentle fire to braize for about one hour and a half. When the head, &c., are done, take them up carefully on a dish, strain the broth, and after having divested it of all grease, boil down one-half to thin glaze, and with the remainder make some brown sauce. The pieces of the head should be trimmed, seasoned with pepper and salt, chopped parsley, and two shalots, then rubbed over with a paste-brush dipped in beaten egg, well-covered with bread-crumbs, and placed on a dish in the larder. The liver and heart must be minced up fine, and when the sauce has been reduced to the usual consistency, add it to the mince, together with a spoonful of fine-herbs and a little lemon-juice. When about to send to table, make the mince quite hot, and turn it out on its dish; place the pieces of the head—previously broiled on both sides, of a bright yellow color, and afterward nicely glazed—upon the mince, pour some of the thin glaze round the *entrée*, and serve.

Note.—Sheep's or lamb's heads, when braized and bread-crumbed, may also be served with any kind of sharp sauce.

ENTREES OF VEAL,

COMPRISING

Fricandeau, with *Purée* of Green-peas.   Veal Cutlets, *à la Dreux.*
     „   *à la Macédoine*, &c.   „   *à la Périgord.*
Noix of Veal, *à la Régence.*   „   *à la Zingara.*
     „   *à la Toulouse.*   „   *à la Duchesse.*
Grenadins of Veal, with Spinach, &c.   „   in *Papillotes.*
Tendons of Veal, with stewed Peas.   *Blanquette* of Veal, with Mushrooms, &c.
        „   *à la Villeroi*, with *Purée* Croquettes of Veal.
                 of Celery.   Veal and Ham Scollops, with Italian sauce.
Veal Kernels, with *Purée* of Artichokes.   Scotch Scollops.
      „   *à la Talleyrand.*   Minced Veal, and Poached Eggs.
Veal Cutlets, *à la Financiére.*   „   *à la Portuguaise.*

880. FRICANDEAU, WITH PUREE OF GREEN PEAS.

The *fricandeau* piece consists of that part of the leg of veal generally called the *cushion*, and is found on the inner side of the leg, lying immediately under the udder or fatty covering. This part must be carefully cut out, by making a semicircular incision from one end round to the other, following the evident natural indication. Flatten the piece of veal slightly with a cutlet-bat, and then pare off the upper and under sinewy covering, leaving the surface perfectly smooth. The *fricandeau* must then be closely larded with the strips of fat bacon in the usual manner. Next, strew the bottom of a *fricandeau* pan with sliced carrot, onion and celery, and a well-garnished faggot of parsley and green onions; cover these over with thin layers of fat bacon, and then place the *fricandeau* on the top of all; moisten with good stock or broth of sufficient quantity to reach up to the larding, but not to cover it under; place a round of paper well buttered on the top, and cover with the lid. The *fricandeau* should be allowed to braize very gently for about three hours, either in the oven or upon a very slow stove-fire, during which time it must be frequently basted with its own liquor; when nearly done, the paper and the lid must be altogether removed, in order to enable the larding to dry, and it should be frequently basted with its own glaze, to give it a bright shiny appearance. Care must be taken to prevent the *fricandeau* from acquiring too much color during the latter part of the process. Put some *purée* of green peas (No. 106) in the centre of the dish, and with two forks carefully lift up the *fricandeau*, and place it upon the *purée;* pour a little half glaze round the base, and serve.

Note.—*Fricandeaux* prepared as above may also be served with every kind of vegetable *purée* or garnish described in this work.

881. FRICANDEAU, A LA MACEDOINE.

THIS must be trimmed and larded as in the foregoing case; then an incision of about three inches in length should be cut through its entire thickness, and a round or oval tin-cutter placed therein to distend the hollow part, so as to give it the appearance of a circle. Prepare and braize the *fricandeau* as before, and when done place it in its dish upon a base of *quenelle* force-meat; fill the centre of the *fricandeau* with a well-prepared *Macédoine* of vegetables (No. 143), round which place a neatly-arranged border of small spring turnips split into halves, turned in the shape of deep cuts, and filled with green peas : ornament the base of the *fricandeau* with a border of young spring carrots, nicely glazed : pour some thin *Espagnole* round the *entrée*, and serve.

882. NOIX* OF VEAL, A LA REGENCE.

IN this case the udder must be left adhering to the *noix*, or cushion of veal; it must be neatly trimmed, and the udder made to represent the form of a half-moon, with the lean part (within the inner semicircle) smoothly pared, and larded in the same manner as a *fricandeau*. This should then be placed in an oval stewpan upon a bed of vegetables, covered with layers of fat bacon, moistened with half a pint of Sherry or Madeira, and about a pint of good stock. The udder must be covered with layers of fat bacon, to preserve it white; then place a thickly-buttered paper over all, and cover with the lid. The *noix* must be very gently braized on a slow-fire, or in the oven, and fre-

* *Noix* is the French technical term for that part of a leg of veal generally used for *fricandeaux;* the English term for which is *cushion*, or *mouse-piece*.

quently basted with its own liquor,—care being taken that the larding is nicely glazed ; when nearly done the bacon must be removed from the udder, and the *noix* placed in its dish ; garnish it round with a *Financière ragout* (No. 188), incorporated with the glaze from the *noix*, stick three ornamental silver skewers, previously garnished with a large truffle, cock's-comb, and a cray-fish, in the udder ; glaze the larding, and serve.

883. NOIX OF VEAL, A LA TOULOUSE.

PREPARE this as in the foregoing case, and when dished up, garnish with a white *Toulouse ragout* (No. 87), using *Allemande* sauce for the purpose ; stick in three ornamental silver skewers, garnished with a large cock's-comb, a truffle, and a decorated *quenelle ;* keep the udder white, glaze the larding and serve.

Note.—This *entrée* may also be served with a garnish of prepared vegetables *à la Macedoine* (No. 143).

884. GRENADINS OF VEAL, WITH SPINACH, ETC.

Trim a *fricandeau* piece of white veal, and cut this into eight or ten fillets, beginning at the thick end ; these must be flattened with a cutlet-bat dipped in water, and trimmed somewhat in the shape of fillets of fowl.   They should then be closely larded with fat bacon, placed in neat order in a deep sauta or *fricandeau* pan, upon a bed of sliced vegetables covered over with layers of fat bacon ; moisten with sufficient good stock, just to reach up to the larding, place the buttered paper, and cover with the lid.   The *grenadins* will require to be braized for about one hour and a quarter, during which time they must be frequently basted ; when nearly done, remove the paper and glaze them.   Next, drain them on a napkin, trim them, and dish them on a foundation of force-meat, in close order ; fill the centre with some *purée* of spinach, pour some half glaze round the base of the *entrée* (made with the liquor from the *grenadins*), and serve.

Note.—*Grenadins* may also be garnished with all kinds of *ragouts* and vegetable garnishes directed to be served with *fricandeaux.*

885. TENDONS OF VEAL, WITH STEWED PEAS.

TENDONS of veal consist of that part which lies along the breast end of the ribs, forming an opaque gristly substance, which in the ox becomes bone.   To extract these, an incision must be made right down the extreme edge of the breast of veal, without damaging the tendons, which should then be laid quite bare with the knife up to the commencement of the ribs, where they must be divided from them. The bony part, if any remain, must be pared away, and the tendons put to steep in water for an hour or so.   They must then be tied up securely with string, and put to boil in the stockpot for about four hours ; or else, if there be no stockpot boiling at the time, place them in a stewpan, with the usual complement of vegetables and seasoning, covered over with a buttered paper ; moisten with three quarts of fresh broth or water, set them to braize on a slow fire, for about four hours, and when done, put them in press between two dishes, until they are cold.   The tendons must then be cut slantwise, into rather large scollops, measuring about two inches in diameter, and when neatly trimmed, should be placed in a sauta-pan with some half glaze to warm them in. Twenty minutes before sending to table, put the tendons in the oven, or on the stove-fire, to simmer for ten minutes; then allow them to boil briskly, so as to reduce the glaze, in which they must be gently rolled, to make it adhere to them; dish them up in a close circle upon a base of *quenelle* force-meat, fill the centre with stewed peas, pour a little thin *Espagnole* sauce into the sauta-pan, to be mixed with the glaze by boiling, use this to put round the *entrée*, and serve.

Note.—Tendons of veal prepared as above, may also be served with every other kind of dressed vegetable garnishes, as well as with all sorts of *purées* of vegetables; for making which, see those articles.

886. TENDONS OF VEAL, A LA VILLEROI, WITH PUREE OF CELERY.

PREPARE, braize, and trim the tendons, as directed in the foregoing case; put them on a large earthen dish, and mask them over with a coating of stiffly-reduced *Allemande* sauce; when this has become firmly set upon the tendons, by cooling, let them be dipped in beaten egg, and bread-crumbed, and afterward fried of a light color in clean hog's lard, made quite hot for the purpose. Let them be dished up in a close circle, overlapping each other, fill the centre with some *purée* of celery (No. 110), pour some half glaze, or a little *Suprême* or *Béchamel* sauce round the *entrée*, and send to table.

Note.—Tendons prepared in this manner may also be garnished as the former.

887. VEAL KERNELS, WITH PUREE OF ARTICHOKES.

VEAL kernels are an oblong fatty substance, containing a kind of small kidney of great delicacy, lying to the left of the blade-bone of the shoulder; these must be steeped in water for about half an hour, then parboiled for five minutes, immersed in cold water, drained upon a napkin, and put in press between two dishes. From ten to sixteen kernels suffice for an *entrée*. The kernels must be trimmed without waste, and placed in a deep circular *fricandeau* pan, upon thin layers of white veal; then moisten with some white wine *mirepoix* (No. 236), and set them on a slow fire to braize very gently for about three-quarters of an hour, bearing in mind that the heat of the stove is to be so regulated as to cause their liquor to be reduced to one half its original quantity. The kernels must then be carefully removed into a sauta-pan, and their half glaze, when strained and divested of all grease, poured upon them. Place them on a brisk fire, and let them boil quickly till their moisture is reduced to a glaze, roll them gently in this, causing as much of it as possible to adhere to them, to give them a bright appearance. Then dish them up in a close circle upon a base of force-meat of veal, with a *crôuton* of fried bread of the same shape between each kernel; fill the centre with some *purée* of arttichokes (No. 117), pour some half glaze round the *entrée*, and serve.

Note.—Veal kernels, prepared and dished up in this manner, may be garnished with all kinds of dressed vegetables and *purées*.

887. VEAL KERNELS, A LA DUCHESSE.

WHEN the kernels have been braized, pressed, and trimmed, as directed in the foregoing part of the preceding article, let them be smoothly masked over with some well-reduced *Allemande* sauce; and after the sauce has been allowed sufficient time to become firm by cooling, bread-crumb the kernels, fry them in properly-heated frying-fat, of a light color, and, having dished them up as directed in the preceding case, let the *entrée* be garnished and sauced similarly.

888. VEAL KERNELS, A LA TALLEYRAND.

PARBOIL and trim the kernels, then place them in a *fricandeau* pan between thin layers of fat bacon; moisten with some wine *mirepoix* (No. 236), and braize them gently for three-quarters of an hour; when done, put them on an earthen dish to cool, and mask each of them all over with a coating of stiffly-reduced *Allemande* sauce, mixed with 1 oz. of truffles, chopped fine; when the sauce has become firmly set, as it cools, dip each in some beaten egg, and bread-crumb them carefully. About twenty minutes before sending to table, fry them of a bright-yellow color, with clarified butter, in a deep sauta-pan; drain them upon a napkin, dish them up in a circle, garnish the centre with a *ragout* composed of small scollops of fat livers, truffles, mushrooms and cock's kernels, the whole of which must be tossed in good *Allemande* sauce; pour some thin *Espagnole* sauce (finished with some of the *mirepoix*) under the kernels, and serve.

889. VEAL CUTLETS, A LA FINANCIERE.

PROCURE a neck of very white veal, saw off the chine-bone and the upper end of the ribs, leaving the cutlet-bones about three inches and a half long; then, divide it into cutlets; flatten these with a bat dipped in water, trim them neatly and lard the lean of the cutlets closely with bacon, in the usual way. Next, prepare the cutlets for braizing in the same manner as directed for a *fricandeau;* about one hour and a quarter will suffice to braize them, when they must be nicely glazed, dished up with the larded part of the cutlet uppermost, and the centre of the *entrée* filled with a rich *Financière ragout* (No. 188); pour some of the sauce round the base of the cutlets, and serve.

890. VEAL CUTLETS, A LA DREUX.

THESE should be cut rather thicker than usual, but neither flattened nor trimmed; they must be interlarded or studded through the lean part with about a dozen oblong pieces of red tongue, or ham, and black truffles about an inch long and a quarter of an inch in depth and thickness; these must be placed in a braizing-pan, upon a bed of sliced vegetables covered with thin layers of fat bacon, some mace, four cloves, twelve pepper-corns, and a garnished faggot of parsley and green onions in the centre, and the whole again covered with layers of bacon; moisten with two glasses of Sherry and as much good stock as will suffice to cover the surface of the cutlets, and set them to braize on a slow fire for about one hour and a half, with the lid on; when done, allow them partially to cool in their own liquor. Then put them in press between two dishes, and when cold, let them be trimmed smooth, so as to show the truffle and tongue-studding.

They should next be placed in a sautapan with some half glaze, made from their own liquor, and put away in the larder. Twenty minutes before sending to table, put the cutlets in the oven to be warmed through, then place them on the stove-fire to glaze ; dish them up in a close circle, fill the centre with a white *Toulouse ragout* (No. 187), pour some thin *Espagnole* sauce round the base of the *entrée*, and serve.

891. VEAL CUTLETS, A LA PERIGORD.

TRIM the cutlets neatly, season with pepper and salt, then dip them in some whipped white of eggs, and afterward in some black truffles chopped very fine ; flatten this on securely with the blade of a knife, and place them in clarified butter in a sautapan, in circular order. Twenty minutes before sending to table, fry the cutlets over a gentle fire, on both sides, until done through—taking care that the chopped truffles do not burn ; when done, drain them on a piece of paper, glaze, and dish them up, fill the centre with scollops of red tongue and truffles ; pour some *Pèrigueux* sauce (No. 23), and serve.

892. VEAL CUTLETS, A LA ZINGARA.

TRIM the cutlets neatly, season with pepper and salt, and place them in a sautapan with some clarified butter. In another sautapan prepare a similar number of thin oval scollops of raw ham. When about to send to table, fry the cutlets and the ham, glaze both, and dish them up—alternately placing a cutlet and a piece of ham ; fill the centre with scolloped mushrooms and truffles, pour some thin *Espagnole* sauce into the sautapan the cutlets have been fried in, to this add a little cayenne and lemon-juice ; simmer these together on the fire, pour the sauce over the cutlets and serve.

893. VEAL CUTLETS, A LA DUCHESSE.

PREPARE these in the same way as the cutlets, *à la Dreux ;* and when they have been trimmed, mask them all over with a coating of *Atelet* sauce (No. 36) and bread-crumb them as for a *Villeroi.* Fry the cutlets of a bright-yellow color in clarified butter, dish them up, and fill the centre with circular scollops of red tongue and button-mushrooms tossed in a little thick *Allemande* sauce ; pour some Tomata sauce (No. 22) round the base of the *entrée,* and serve.

894. VEAL CUTLETS, IN PAPILLOTES.

TRIM the cutlets neatly, season with pepper and salt, and fry them in a little clarified butter ; when they are nearly done, add some mushrooms, parsley, and three shalots, the whole chopped fine ; fry these together over the fire for five minutes, and then add two gravy-spoonfuls of *Velouté*, or any other white sauce, a little nutmeg, lemon-juice, and a small piece of glaze ; simmer the whole together over a gentle fire for a few minutes, then add a leason of four yolks of eggs, toss the cutlets about to mix the leason in with the sauce, and let them become cool. In other respects, finish in the same way as directed for mutton cutlets, *à la Maintenon* (No. 838).

895. BLANQUETTE OF VEAL, WITH MUSHROOMS.

THE veal for this purpose must first be roasted, and when cold, cut into round thin scollops about an inch in diameter ; to these add some button-mushrooms also cut into scollops, and enough *Allemande* sauce (No. 7) for the *entrée*. Just before sending it to table, warm the *blanquette*, **and** dish it up with a border of *croquettes* of veal, of rice or potatoes. This dish may be varied by substituting scollops of truffles, cucumbers, or red tongue, for the mushrooms.

896. CROQUETTES OF VEAL.

CUT about 1 lb. of roasted veal into very small dice, or mince it into very fine shreds; add this to about half its quantity of mushrooms, truffles or red tongue, cut up in the same manner. Next, reduce by boiling enough *Allemande, Béchamel, Velouté* or *Suprême* sauce for the *entrée;* and when it has become rather stiff, throw in the mince; season with a little pepper and grated nutmeg; stir the whole well together, and then spread the preparation on a dish, about an inch thick; smooth it over with the blade of a knife, cover with buttered paper, and put it into the larder to cool. It must then be divided into about two dozen pieces, and each of these rolled in bread-crumbs in the form of a common-sized cork or a round ball, or in the shape of a pear, and after being dipped in some beaten egg, must again be rolled in bread-crumbs, and placed on an earthen dish till within twenty minutes of dinner time; the *croquettes* must now be fried in clean hog's-lard made quite hot for the purpose, and when done, drained upon a napkin to absorb all the grease, then dished up with fried parsley, and served immediately.

Note.—When *croquettes* are shaped in the form of pears, some parsley stalks of equal lengths should be stuck in at the pointed ends, before they are fried, to imitate the stalk of a pear.

897. VEAL AND HAM SCOLLOPS, WITH ITALIAN SAUCE.

PROCURE about 1 lb. of veal, either from the leg, the chump-end of the loin, or best end of the neck; cut this into round or oval scollops, season with pepper and salt, and place them in a sautapan with some clarified butter: an equal number of similarly-cut scollops of ham may either be put with these, or separately. Fry the veal and ham scollops nicely brown, pour off the grease, add the brown Italian sauce (No. 12) and some button-mushrooms; simmer the whole together for three minutes, dish them up, alternately placing a scollop of veal with the ham; fill the centre with the mushrooms, pour the sauce round the *entrée*, and serve.

898. SCOTCH SCOLLOPS.

TRIM the scollops as in the foregoing case, season with parsley and shalots chopped fine, pepper and salt; place the scollops after they have been bread-crumbed in the usual way, in a sautapan with a little clarified butter: mark the scollops of ham separately; prepare also two dozen small round *quenelles* with some highly seasoned veal forcemeat. When about to send to table, fry the scollops of veal and ham of a light color, glaze them, and dish them alternately in a close circle—first placing a scollop of veal and then one of ham; fill the centre with the *quenelles* (previously poached), pour a little thickened brown gravy with a little glaze in it, or some well-finished *Espagnole* sauce, round the *entrée*, and serve.

899. MINCED VEAL, AND POACHED EGGS.

PARE off the outside part of 1 lb. of veal, and then let it be chopped very fine, or cut it into thin shreds. Put about half a pint of *Béchamel* sauce (No. 5) into a stewpan and reduce it by boiling, until it becomes rather thick, then add the minced veal, and a little cream ; season with pepper and salt, and a very little nutmeg ; stir the whole well together over the fire until warm, and dish it up in a conical form ; place six poached eggs round it with a circular scollop of glazed red tongue or ham between each egg ; pour a little *Béchamel* sauce (No. 5) round the base of the *entrée*, and serve.

900. ANOTHER METHOD.

PUT a pat of butter into a stewpan on the fire, and when melted, throw in a table-spoonful of flour ; stir this with a wooden spoon over the fire for two minutes ; then gradually mix in half a pint of broth, put the sauce on the fire, stirring it until reduced to the thickness of *Béchamel* sauce ; then add the minced veal, a gill of cream, a small piece of glaze, and a little nutmeg, pepper, and salt ; stir this on the fire for three minutes, and serve as in the foregoing case.

Note.—Mushrooms, truffles, tongue, or ham, either minced or cut into shreds, may be added to the veal, in either of the two foregoing cases.

901. MINCED VEAL, A LA PORTUGUAISE.

SEE the directions for dressing beef in this method (No. 810).

HEART SWEETBREADS,*

COMPRISING

Sweetbreads, larded, with Stewed Peas, &c.	Sweetbreads, larded, *à la St. Cloud.*	
„ „ *à la Monarque.*	„ „ *à la Parisiènne.*	
„ „ *à la Conti.*		

902. SWEETBREADS LARDED, WITH STEWED PEAS.

THREE heart sweetbreads generally suffice for a dish. They must be procured quite fresh, otherwise they are unfit for table, and should be steeped in water for several hours, and the water frequently changed ; the sweetbreads are then to be scalded in boiling water for about three minutes, and immersed in cold water for half an hour ; after which they must be drained upon a napkin, trimmed free from any sinewy fat, and put between two dishes to be slightly pressed flat, and then closely larded with strips of bacon in the usual manner. The sweetbreads must next be placed in a deep sauta-pan on a bed of thinly-sliced carrot, celery, and onions, with a garnished faggot of parsley and

---

* Sweetbreads, or Pancreas, are the two white glands found in calves ; the one being placed immediately below the throat,. and the other, of a rounder form, lying nearer the heart ; hence they are designated heart and throat sweetbreads : the former is the most delicate, and when in perfection, is white and fat ; the latter is of an elongated form, not so fat as the other, and is only used for secondary purposes.

green onions placed in the centre, and covered with thin layers of fat bacon.   Moisten with about a pint of good stock, place a round of buttered paper on the top, cover with the lid, and after having put the sweetbreads to boil on the stove-fire, remove them to the oven or on a moderate fire (in the latter case live embers of charcoal must be placed on the lid), and allow them to braize rather briskly for about twenty minutes—frequently basting them with their own liquor.   When done, remove the lid and paper covering, and set them again in the oven, to dry the surface of the larding ; glaze them nicely, and dish them up on some stewed peas (No. 1175).

Sweetbreads, prepared in this way, may also be served with dressed asparagus peas, French-beans, scollops of cucumbers, braized lettuces, celery, *Macédoine* of vegetables, *Jardinière*, and also with every kind of vegetable *purée* described in this work.

To raise the sweetbreads above the garnish or sauce served with them, it is necessary to place as many foundations as there are sweetbreads in the dish ; these may be made, either by boiling some rice in broth until it becomes quite soft, then working it into a paste ; after this has been spread on a dish about an inch thick, a circular tin-cutter must be used to stamp it out.   They may also be prepared from veal force-meat, or even fried *croûtons* of bread will serve the purpose.

903. SWEETBREADS, A LA MONARQUE.

THESE must be larded and braized as the foregoing ; then cut a kind of pillar out of a piece of stale bread, of angular shape, about three inches high, each side of the angle measuring about two inches ; this should be fried in hog's lard, of a bright-yellow color, and stuck in a perpendicular position in the centre of the dish with a little paste made of flour and egg.   The sweetbreads are to be so arranged as to have one end resting up against this *croustade*, and between each a decorated minion fillet of fowl is to be placed ; crown the top with a row of white double cocks'-combs, stick in an ornamental silver skewer garnished with a large cocks'-comb, a mushroom, a large crayfish, and a truffle ; pour a *Financière ragout* (No. 188) round the *entrée*, and serve.

904. SWEETBREADS, A LA CONTI.

AFTER the sweetbreads have been scalded and pressed flat, make about a dozen incisions round the sides of their upper surface with the point of a small knife, in a slanting direction, to the depth of half an inch ; in these incisions insert circular scollops of black truffle, and repeat this so as to form an inner circle in the same manner.   Next, prepare the sweetbreads for braizing, placing them upon a bed of thinly-sliced carrot, onion, and celery, covered with thin layers of bacon, layers of the same being placed also over the sweetbreads ; moisten with good white stock, and braize the sweetbreads about twenty minutes.   When the sweetbreads are done, drain them on a napkin, and glaze them lightly, without drying the glaze on ; when about to dish them up, garnish with a *ragout* composed of small *quenelles* of fowl, button mushrooms, cocks'-combs, and kernels, crown the whole with a large truffle, place a crayfish between each sweetbread, pour some *Périgueux* sauce (No. 23) under the *entrée*, and serve.

Note.—The sweetbreads may be varied by scolloping, or *contiser,* one-half with truffle, and the remainder with red tongue, or mixing the latter with green gherkins.

905. SWEETBREADS, A LA ST. CLOUD.

THESE should be scalded and pressed in the usual way, and studded over in neat circular order with pieces of black truffle or red tongue, cut out in the form of large hob-nails ; then make twelve openings with a blunt wooden skewer in each sweetbread, and introduce in these the nail-like pieces of tongue perpendicularly. Braize them according to the directions for the foregoing, and when done, dish them up with a white *Toulouse ragout* (No. 187) ; garnish the *entrée* round the base with a border of small *quenelles* decorated with truffles, and place a group of trimmed crayfish-tails, previously tossed in a little glaze, colored with lobster-coral ; slightly glaze the sweetbreads, and serve.

906. SWEETBREADS, A LA PARISIENNE.

AFTER the sweetbreads have been scalded and pressed, let them be larded in the following manner : one with shreds of very black truffles, another with shreds of the tip of a red tongue, and the third with some green stalks of parsley ; braize them between layers of fat bacon, and moisten with a wine *mirepoix* (No. 236). When they are done, dish them up against a triangular *croûstade*, garnished with a well-arranged Parisian *ragout* (No. 203) ; stick an ornamental silver skewer, garnished with a double comb, a large truffle and a decorated *quenelle*, in the centre of the *croûstade*, and round the base of the skewer, stud a border of crayfish-tails, slightly glaze the sweetbreads, and serve.

Note.—Sweetbreads may also be served roasted for persons of delicate health, being very nutritious, and easy of digestion. In such cases they may be served with a little plain gravy, *Suprême* or brown sauce.

THROAT SWEETBREADS,

COMPRISING

Epigramme of Sweetbreads.	Scollops of Sweetbreads *à la Maréchale.*
Scollops of Sweetbreads, with Shalot Gravy.	„ „ *à la Soubise.*
„ „ *à la Dauphine.*	„ „ *à la Poulette.*
„ „ *à la d' Uxelles.*	*Croquettes* of Sweetbreads.

907. EPIGRAMME OF SWEETBREADS.

PROCURE four throat sweetbreads, and steep them in water for several hours, changing the water frequently, until they are freed from redness : they must then be scalded for five minutes in boiling water, and after being immersed in fresh water to cool them, should be put in press between two dishes, to flatten. Next, put one of the sweetbreads to braize in some white broth : when done, set it aside to get cool, and let it be afterwards cut into small circular scollops, and placed in a small stewpan, with an equal quantity of scollops of red tongue and mushrooms. Cut the three remaining sweetbreads, in a slanting direction, into oval scollops a quarter of an inch thick ; bread-crumb one-half with two coatings of bread-crumbs, by dipping them the first time in beaten egg, and the second in clarified butter; place these in a sautapan with a little clarified butter, and prepare the other half separately in a similar manner, without bread-crumbing them; both must be seasoned with pepper and salt. When about to send to table, fry the bread-crumbed scollops of a light-color, but the others should be merely simmered over a slow fire, in order to keep them as white as possible; glaze the former and toss the latter in a little *Béchamel* sauce, dish them up, alternately placing a bread-crumbed scollop with a white one; fill the centre with the small scollops of tongue, &c., previously warmed in a little *Béchamel* sauce, pour some of the sauce round the base, and serve.

908. SCOLLOPS OF SWEETBREADS, WITH SHALOT GRAVY.

BREAD-CRUMB the whole of the scollops, as directed in the foregoing case, fry them of a light color, drain them on a piece of paper, and glaze; dish them up in a close circle, pour some rich shalot gravy (No. 167) under them, and serve.

909. SCOLLOPS OF SWEETBREADS, A LA DAUPHINE.

CUT the sweetbreads into oval scollops, place them in a sautapan, with a little clarified butter, season with pepper and salt, a little nutmeg and some chopped parsley, squeeze the juice of half a lemon over them, and simmer them gently over the fire for ten minutes; they must then be removed into a dish, and when partially cold, covered with a thin coating of *purée* of fowl, mixed with an equal proportion of reduced *Allemande* sauce, and when this has become firmly set by cooling, dip them in beaten egg, and bread-crumb them. Twenty minutes before sending to table, let them be carefully fried in plenty of hog's-lard, made hot for the purpose; drain them on a napkin to absorb all the grease, dish them up in a close circle, pour some *ourée* of mushrooms (No. 122) in the centre, and serve.

910. SCOLLOPS OF SWEETBREADS, A LA D'UXELLES.

THESE are prepared in almost every particular just as the foregoing except that *D'Uxelles* sauce (No. 16) must be substituted for the *purée* to mask the scollop with. After having simmered, let them be masked with the sauce, and afterwards bread-crumbed; then fried, dished up and served with either of the following sauces :—Brown or white Italian, *Poivrade*, half glaze, scollops of mushrooms or truffles, *purée* of truffles, plain gravy, or *purée* of mushrooms.

911. SCOLLOPS OF SWEETBREADS, A LA MARECHALE.

THESE must be seasoned with a little pepper and salt, masked over with a thin coating of reduced *Allemande* sauce, and afterwards bread-crumbed upon this; they should then be placed in circular order in a sautapan with some clarified butter, and fried of a bright-yellow color. When done, dish them up in close order, and let the centre be filled with *Toulouse ragout* (No. 187).

912. SCOLLOPS OF SWEETBREADS, A LA SOUBISE.

PREPARE and dish up these, as the foregoing; fill the centre with *Soubise* sauce (No. 119), and serve.

They may also be scored with all kinds of garnishes of dressed vegetables, *purées* of vegetables, or any kind of sauce served with cutlets.

913. SCOLLOPS OF SWEETBREADS, A LA POULETTE.

WHEN the sweetbreads have been scalded in the usual manner, cut them into circular scollops, place them in neat order in a sautapan with a little clarified butter, and season with pepper and salt, chopped parsley and lemon-juice; simmer them over a moderate fire for about ten minutes, and when done remove them into a stewpan, containing enough sauce *à la Poulette* for the *entrée*, add some scollops of mushrooms or truffles, toss the whole together gently over the stove-fire until sufficiently hot, and then dish them up in a pyramidal form, and serve with a border of *croquettes* of potatoes round the *entrée*.

Note.—Scollops of sweetbreads, *à la Russe* and *à la Provençale*, are prepared in the same manner as veal cutlets under these names.

914. CROQUETTES OF SWEETBREADS.

WHEN the sweetbreads have been scalded, put them into a small stewpan with two shalots, a little mignionette-pepper and salt, half a bay-leaf and a sprig of thyme; moisten with some stock-pot toppings, and set them to braize gently for about twenty minutes; when done, drain them on a plate to get cold, after which let them be cut up into very small dice, and mix with some stiff-reduced *Allemande* sauce; season with a little pepper and salt and grated nutmeg; stir the whole gently over the stove-fire for two minutes, spread the preparation on a dish about an inch thick, and put it in the larder to get cold. The *croquettes* then must be shaped, bread-crumbed, and fried in the same manner as directed for veal *croquettes*.

Note.—Some red tongue, mushrooms, or truffles, cut into small dice, may also be mixed in with the sweetbreads.

CALF'S EARS, FEET, LIVER, AND BRAINS,

COMPRISING

Calf's Ear, *à la Tortuë*.	Calf's Liver, fried, with Fine-herbs Sauce.
„ fried, with Tomata sauce.	Calf's Brains, with *Matelotte* Sauce.
Calf's Feet, *à la Pascaline*.	„ with Nutbrown Butter.
„ fried, with Italian sauce.	„ fried, *à la Provençale*.
Calf's Liver, braized, with Vegetables.	„ Scolloped.

915. CALF'S EARS, A LA TORTUE.

PROCURE four white calf's ears (cut with a broad base), scald them in boiling water for five minutes, after which plunge them in cold water and let them be wiped dry; then hold them on the point of a skewer over the flame of a charcoal fire to singe off any remaining hairs; wipe them clean, rub them over with lemon-juice, and braize them in some *blanc* (No. 235) for about an hour and a half or two hours. When the ears are done, drain them on a wet napkin, and with the back of the blade of a small knife scrape off all the soft skin; trim them neatly, and with the point of a knife cut the white gristle of each into slits—taking particular care not to draw the knife through—so that when the thin part of the ears is turned down, the stripes may form themselves into loops or curls. When the ears are ready to dish up, fill each with a decorated *quenelle* or a round truffle, garnish with a *ragout à la Tortuë* (No. 189), and serve.

916. CALF'S EARS FRIED IN BATTER, WITH TOMATA SAUCE.

PREPARE the ears as directed in the foregoing, and when done let them be trimmed ; scrape off the soft skin from the upper part, and cut each ear into four pieces lengthwise; put them to steep in a basin with two spoonsful of salad oil, one of vinegar, two sliced shalots, parsley, bay-leaf, and thyme, and a little mignionette-pepper and salt. About twenty minutes before dinner time, drain the pieces of ears on a cloth, dip them in some light batter, and fry them in plenty of hog's-lard, heated to the proper degree for the purpose. When fried, dish them up in a pyramidal form, pour some *Tomata* sauce (No. 22) under them and serve.

Note.—Calf's ears prepared in this manner may also be served with any of the following sauces: *Piquante, Poivrade,* Italian, Gherkin, Poor-man's, *Provençale,* or *Richelieu.* If, however, this kind of fritter is not eaten as soon as served, it would be better to send the sauce separately.

917. CALF'S FEET, A LA PASCALINE.

SEPARATE each foot into halves by splitting the hoof with a knife, take the bone out, and scald these in boiling water for five minutes ; the feet must then be braized in *blanc* (No. 235), and when done, drained upon a cloth, cut into pieces about two inches square, and put into a stewpan containing some button-mushrooms and *Pascaline* sauce (No. 15) ; toss them in this over the stove-fire until sufficiently hot, and serve with a border of *fleurons* or potato *croquettes* round the *entrée.*

918. CALF'S FEET FRIED IN BATTER, WITH ITALIAN SAUCE.

THESE are prepared in all respects the same as calf's ears fried, but substituting Italian sauce (No. 12) for *Tomata* sauce.

919. CALF'S LIVER BRAIZED, WITH VEGETABLES.

CHOOSE a liver of a bright pinky color, entirely free from any whitish spots : wash and wipe it dry, and then lard it through with strips of ham and fat bacon—previously seasoned with chopped parsley, pepper, and a very little salt ; cover the bottom of a stewpan with veal or other trimmings of meat, place the liver upon them, garnish with two carrots, two onions stuck with four cloves each, two heads of celery, and a garnished faggot of parsley ; moisten with two glasses of Sherry and a quart of strong stock ; place a buttered paper on the top, cover with the lid, and set the liver to braize very gently on a slow fire for about two hours and a half, frequently basting it with its own liquor while it is being braized. When done, remove the liver into a deep santapan with part of its liquor, previously reduced to half-glaze ; use the remainder to work some brown sauce for the *entrée;* put the liver in the oven to be glazed with its own liquor, and when done dish it up with groups of small carrots, turnips, and glazed onions round its base, pour the sauce under it, and serve.

920. FRIED CALF'S LIVER, WITH FINE-HERBS SAUCE.

CUT the liver up into neat scollops about a quarter of an inch thick, season with pepper and salt, and fry them brown in a sautapan with a little clarified butter; when this is done, pour off all the grease, add some fine-herbs sauce (No. 14), simmer the whole together on the fire for about three minutes, and serve.

921. CALF'S BRAINS, WITH MATELOTTE SAUCE.

STEEP three sets of brains in water for several hours, care being taken to change the water frequently—and remove the loose skin that contains them; after being washed, and placed in a stewpan, containing some boiling water, and seasoned with a gill of vinegar, some thinly-sliced carrot and onion, thyme and bay-leaf, pepper and salt, let them boil gently for about twenty minutes. The brains must then be drained upon a cloth, and six *croûtons* cut in the shape of large cocks'-combs previously stuck on the bottom of an *entrée* dish, so as to form as many compartments; place a lobe of brains in each of these, make a slight incision in each portion of the brains, and insert in it a scolloped circular piece of red tongue; pour a *Matelotte ragout* (No. 193) over the *entrée*, and serve.

922. CALF'S BRAINS, WITH NUTBROWN BUTTER.

PREPARE, and dish up the brains as in the foregoing case; pour some nutbrown butter (No. 93) over them, place a bouquet of fried parsley in the centre, and serve.

923. CALF'S BRAINS FRIED IN BATTER, A LA PROVENCALE.

THESE must be cleaned, gently boiled in water, vinegar, &c.; and when drained, cut into oval scollops, and steeped in a basin with a little oil, vinegar, pepper and salt. When about to send to table, fry them in batter in the usual way (see directions for calf's ears No. 916), after which dish them up with some *Provençale* sauce (No. 25) under them, and serve.

Note.—They may also be served with *Tomata*, Italian, *Piquante*, or *Poivrade* sauce.

924. CALF'S BRAINS SCOLLOPED.

WHEN the brains have been dressed, cut them into rather small scollops, and put them into a sautapan with a few scolloped mushrooms and truffles, season with a little cayenne and grated nutmeg, pour in some *Allemande* sauce (No. 7) and juice of half a lemon; toss the whole gently together over the fire, and with this preparation fill as many silver scollop shells as will hold it; cover these over with a coating of fried bread-crumbs or raspings, place them for two minutes in a hot oven to *gratinate*, dish them up on a napkin, and serve.

ENTREES OF LAMB,

COMPRISING

Shoulder of Lamb, larded, *à la Financière.*
Neck of Lamb, *à la Régence.*
Epigramme of Lamb, with Mushrooms.
    „   „ *à la Villeroi,* with Peas.
Breasts of Lamb, *à la Maréchale,* with New Potatoes.
Lamb Cutlets (plain), with Cucumbers, &c.

Lamb Cutlets, bread-crumbed, with Asparagus Peas.
    „   *à la Chêvreuse.*
Braized *Carbonnades* of Lamb.
Lamb's Sweetbreads, *à la Toulouse,* &c.
Blanquette of Lamb's Sweetbreads.
Lamb's Sweetbreads Scolloped.

925. SHOULDER OF LAMB LARDED, A LA FINANCIERE.

SAW off the upper part of the shank-bone of a shoulder of lamb, then bone it entirely—with the exception of about three inches of the shank or leg bone, which must be left in. Spread the shoulder open, season with pepper and salt, garnish it with a thick layer of veal or fowl forcemeat; then with a small trussing-needle and some fine string draw the outer edges of the skinny part of the shoulder into a purse-like form, and tighten the strings so as to give it the appearance of a cushion; and, after removing the superficial skin in a circular shape, lard it closely. Next, strew the bottom of a stewpan with sliced carrot, onion, celery, and a garnished faggot of parsley; cover this with thin layers of fat bacon, and place the shoulder of lamb upon it; moisten with sufficient good stock to reach up to the larding, place a buttered paper on the top, and cover with the lid; then set it to braize very gently upon a slow fire for about an hour and a half,—with some live embers of charcoal on the lid—and take care to baste it frequently. When done, remove it into a deep sautapan, and after having strained the liquor, free it from all grease, boil it down to half glaze, pour this on to the lamb, and put it in the oven to glaze, repeatedly basting the larding till the moisture is lessened. The *ballotine** or shoulder of lamb must then be placed upon its dish, and garnished with a *Financière ragout* (No. 188); put a paper ruffle on the bone, and serve.

926. NECK OF LAMB, A LA REGENCE.

PREPARE this in exactly the same way as directed for necks of mutton larded *en chevaux-de-frise* (No. 611). When braized, glaze it nicely, and place it upon its dish, garnish it with a white *Toulouse ragout* (No. 187), and serve.

Note.—Necks of lamb prepared as the foregoing, may also be served with a *Macédoine* of vegetables, or a *Jardinière.*

927. EPIGRAMME OF LAMB, A LA TOULOUSE.

TRIM a neck of lamb into cutlets, and place them into a sautapan with some clarified butter; then braize a breast of lamb until quite tender, take it up, remove the bones and put it in press between two dishes; when cold, cut it into as many cutlet-shaped pieces as there are

* Shoulders of Lamb, prepared in the foregoing manner—called, in French, "*Ballotines*"—may also be served with every kind of dressed vegetables, or *purées* of vegetables.

cutlets from the neck, insert a small piece of bone in each, and bread-crumb them over a coating of *Allemande* sauce, dip them in some beaten egg, bread-crumb them again, and place them in a sautapan with clarified butter. When about to send to table, fry the cutlets in both sautapans; as soon as they are done, glaze them lightly, and dish them up—alternately placing a plain cutlet and one that is bread-crumbed; fill the centre with a white *Toulouse ragout* (No. 187), pour some *Espagnole* half-glaze round the *entrée*, and serve.

Note.—*Epigrammes* of lamb may also be garnished with a *blanquette*, with scollops of cucumbers, stewed peas, asparagus-peas, &c.

928. BREASTS OF LAMB, A LA VILLEROI, WITH PEAS.

BRAIZE two breasts of lamb, in the stock-pot, or in any kind of white broth; when done, take them up carefully, remove all the bones, and reserve these for the purpose of making cutlet bones with; put the breast in press between two dishes, and when cold, cut them into about twelve pieces, in the form of an elongated heart, or of a cutlet; stick a small bone in at the narrow end, and spread a coating of re-duced *Allemande* sauce over them; when this is set firm by cooling, roll them first in bread-crumbs, and then dip them in beaten egg, and bread-crumb them over again. When about to send to table, fry these cutlets in plenty of hog's-lard quite hot, dish them up, garnish them with stewed peas, pour some half-glaze round the base, and serve.

Note.—Breasts of lamb prepared *à la Villeroi* may also be served with spinach, endives, cucumbers, asparagus-peas, *Macédoine*, &c.

929. BREAST OF LAMB, A LA MARECHALE, WITH NEW POTATOES.

TRIM and prepare these in the same way as the foregoing, but the coating of sauce must be thinner in this case; bread-crumb them twice over the sauce, first dipped in beaten egg and then in clarified butter, over which bread-crumb them the second time; put them in shape with the blade of a knife, and place them in a sautapan with a little clarified butter. When about to send to table, fry the cutlets of a light color, drain them on a sheet of paper and glaze them lightly; dish them up, and serve some white Italian sance (No. 13) under them. They may also be served with all kinds of vegetable garnishes.

930. LAMB CUTLETS PLAIN, WITH CUCUMBERS.

IN trimming these cutlets, care must be taken not to pare off any more of the fat than is positively necessary to give them shape. When trimmed, place the cutlets in a sautapan with clarified butter, season with pepper and salt, fry them on both sides of a light-brown color, pour off the grease, throw in a little glaze, toss them over the fire in this, and dish them up; garnish the centre with prepared scollops of cucumbers (No. 138), pour a little *Espagnole* or half-glaze round the *entrée*, and serve.

931. LAMB CUTLETS, BREAD-CRUMBED, WITH ASPARAGUS-PEAS.

TRIM the cutlets, season with pepper and salt, rub them over with a paste-brush dipped in yolks of eggs, and roll them in bread-crumbs;

then dip them in some clarified butter, and bread-crumb them over
again ; put them in shape with the blade of a knife, and place them in
neat order in a sautapan with some clarified butter. When about to
send to table, fry the cutlets of a light color, drain them upon a
sheet of paper, glaze and dish them up ; fill the centre with asparagus-
peas (No. 148), pour some thin *Espagnole* or half-glaze round them,
and serve.

932. LAMB CUTLETS, A LA CHEVREUSE.

THESE must be cut rather thick, allowing two ribs for each, but they
should not be trimmed ; prepare and braize them in the same manner
as veal cutlets *à la Dreux* (No. 890); and when done, pressed, and
trimmed, mask them over with a *purée* of onions mixed with two ounces
of grated Parmesan cheese; when cold they should be dipped in beaten
egg, and afterward rolled in bread-crumbs ; put them into shape with
the blade of a knife, and place them in order upon a dish or sautapan,
until dinner-time. Then fry them in heated hog's-lard, of a bright-
yellow color, dish them up, put a small paper frill on the bone of each
cutlet; fill the centre with small circular scollops of truffles, mushrooms, and fat livers, tossed in some *Suprême* sauce (No. 38), pour
some of the sauce round the base of the *entrée*, and serve.

Note.—In addition to the foregoing methods for dressing lamb
cutlets, they may also be served in every variety of form in which veal
or mutton cutlets are prepared.

933. BRAIZED CARBONNADES OF LAMB.

LOINS of lamb are used for this, and should be prepared and finished
according to the directions for *carbonnades* of mutton (No. 865).

934. LAMB'S SWEETBREADS, A LA TOULOUSE.

ABOUT ten heart sweetbreads are necessary for an *entrée ;* steep these
in cold water for a couple of hours, and then scald them slightly to set
them, for the purpose of being afterward larded ; they must next be
placed in a deep sautapan, covered with thin layers of fat bacon or else
spread with butter; moisten with sufficient strong *consommé* to reach

nearly up to the larding ; place a buttered paper upon them, and put them
to boil briskly on a stove-fire for
five minutes, then set them in the
oven, or cover them with a lid containing live embers of charcoal, and
place them on a moderate stove-fire
to simmer gently for a quarter of an
hour, frequently basting them with
their own liquor. When the sweetbreads are nearly done, remove the
lid and the paper, put them in the
oven, or pass the red-hot salamander over them to dry the larding, and
then glaze them. When dished up, each sweetbread should be placed
in the dish upon a base, formed of *quenelle* force-meat made of fowl or
veal, and shaped to resemble a *dariole*-mould : these of course should

be previously poached. Fill the centre of the *entrée* with steweu peas, pour some *Espagnole* sauce round the base, and serve.

Note.—Lambs' sweetbreads prepared as the foregoing, may also be served with asparagus, *Macédoine* or *Jardinière* of vegetables; also with *Toulouse* or *Financière ragouts;* and indeed in every form directed for other sweetbreads.

935. BLANQUETTE OF LAMB'S SWEETBREADS.

THROAT sweetbreads will serve for this purpose, about eight being sufficient for a dish; steep them in water, scald them, and then braize them in a small stewpan with very little moisture; they will be done in about a quarter of an hour; put them on a dish to cool, cut them into scollops, and put them into a stewpan containing some sauce *à la Poulette,* toss the whole together till warm, then dish up the *blanquette* in a conical form, garnish it round' with a border of potato *croquettes* made in the form of pears and serve.

Note.—Mushrooms, truffles, cucumbers, or asparagus-peas may be added.

936. SCOLLOPED LAMB'S SWEETBREADS.

BRAIZE the sweetbreads, when cold cut them into rather thin small scollops, and finish these according to the directions for scolloped calf's brains (No. 924).

LAMBS' HEADS, EARS, AND FEET,

COMPRISING

Lamb's Head, *à la Pascaline.*	Lamb's Ears, fried in Batter.
Lamb's Ears, *à la Financière.*	Lamb's Feet, *à la Poulette.*
" *à la Dauphine.*	" *à la d'Uxelles.*
" *à la Venitiènne.*	" fried in Batter.

937. LAMB'S HEAD, A LA PASCALINE.

THE lamb's head must be scalded in the same way as a calf's head for mock turtle, then boned, and filled up with force-meat made of the liver, as for a *gratin* (No. 249); sew the the head up with a trussing needle and small twine, secure it in shape by fastening it in a napkin previously spread with butter, and set it to braize in a stewpan seasoned with a carrot, an onion, one head of celery, a garnished faggot of parsley, six cloves, and a blade of mace; moisten with good stock, and allow it to boil gently for about an hour and a half.

While the above is in preparation, four lambs' sweetbreads should be larded and prepared ready for glazing; two sets of lambs' brains must also be cleansed, and boiled in a little vinegar and water, with sliced carrot and onion, pepper and salt, afterward drained, cut and made into *croquettes.* Four lamb's tongues, after being braized, must be cut into scollops, and placed in a stewpan with an equal quantity of scolloped mushrooms, and enough of *Pascaline* sauce (No. 15), for the *entrée.*

When about to send to table, place the head with the ears curled upon its dish, and the larded sweetbreads at its four corners ; between these put the *croquettes* of brains, previously fried, pour the scollops of tongue, mushrooms, and sauce round the head, glaze it and serve.

938. LAMBS' EARS, A LA FINANCIERE.

PROCURE a dozen lambs' ears, scald these, then immerse them in cold water ; when cold, wipe them dry, and singe them over the flame of a charcoal fire ; they must then be gently braized in some *blanc* (No. 235) for about three-quarters of an hour, and when done drain upon a napkin ; the thin part of the ears should be carefully scraped with the back part of the blade of a knife to remove the skin, leaving the white cartilaginous part entire ; this last must then be slit in narrow bands, without cutting through the ends, so that when the ears are turned down, these bands by curling over should appear like a row of loops ; place the ears as they are trimmed in a deep sautapan or stewpan containing some of their own liquor, cover them with a buttered paper and the lid, and set them aside till dinner-time.

While the ears are braizing, prepare some veal force-meat, and fill a plain low cylinder border mould (previously buttered) with the force-meat ; poach this in the usual way, and when about to send to table, turn it out upon its dish, place the lambs' ears all round the top of it and in each of these put a round ball of black truffle ; fill the centre with a rich *Financière ragout* (No. 188), pour some of the sauce round the base and serve.

Note.—This *entrée* may also be served with a *ragout à la Tortuë* (No 189).

939. LAMBS' EARS, A LA DAUPHINE.

SCALD, singe, braize, and trim the lambs' ears as in the foregoing case, but they must not be slit. Fill them with force-meat made with the fillets of a fowl, or some veal, in which has been mixed a spoonful of white sauce and some chopped mushrooms ; mask the ears over with a coating of reduced *Allemande* sauce, and when this has become firmly set upon them, roll them in bread-crumbs, and dip each separately in some beaten egg seasoned with a little salt, then bread-crumb them over again, place them upon a dish, and set them aside in the larder. When about to send to table, fry the ears in plenty of heated hog's-lard, of a fine light color, dish them up in a circular row, or pyramidally, pour some *Suprême* or *Béchamel* sauce, containing a few mushrooms cut into shreds or scollops, round and under them, and serve.

940. LAMBS' EARS, A LA VENITIENNE.

PREPARE these exactly in the same manner as for *à la Financière* (No. 938), dish them up in a circle on the dish, fill the centre with small round balls, or *croquettes* of rice, prepared as follows : Boil four ounces of rice in white broth till done quite soft, then season with a pat of butter, two ounces of grated Parmesan cheese, a little nutmeg, Cayenne pepper and salt ; mix the whole well together, and form it into small round balls the size of marbles, roll these in flour, and fry them in clarified butter in a sautapan. Pour some Venetian sauce (No. 26) over the ears, and serve.

941. LAMB'S EARS, FRIED IN BATTER.

SEE Calf's-ears so prepared (No. 916).

942. LAMB'S FEET, A LA POULETTE.

REMOVE the shank-bones from a dozen lambs' feet, without tearing or cutting through the part that covers the bone; scald them for about five minutes in boiling water, and then immerse them in cold water; wipe and singe them over the flame of a charcoal fire, rub them over with lemon-juice, and braize them in some *blanc* (No. 235) for about an hour; then drain them upon a cloth, trim off the extremities neatly, make an incision in the hoof, and remove the round tuft of wool; place the lamb's feet in a stewpan containing some button-mushrooms and enough sauce *à la Poulette* for the *entrée*, toss them in this over the stove-fire until quite warm; then dish them up neatly, aud serve with a border of *fleurons*, or *croûtons* of fried bread.

943. LAMB'S FEET, A LA D'UXELLES.

BRAIZE and trim the feet as in the foregoing case, cover them with a coating of *D'Uxelles* sauce (No. 16), and when this has become firmly set by cooling, bread-crumb them twice over in the usual manner, and fry them in hog's lard; when done, drain them upon a cloth, dish them up with fried parsley upon a napkin, and serve some Italian sauce (No. 12) separately in a boat.

944. LAMB'S FEET, FRIED IN BATTER.

SEE Calf's feet (No. 918).

ENTREES OF PORK,

COMPRISING

Griskin, or Spare-rib, of Pork, *à la Soubise.*	Pig's Feet, *à la Ste. Ménehould.*
„ „ *à la Lyonnaise.*	„ *à la Périgord.*
„ „ *à la Périgueux.*	„ *à la Richelieu.*
Pork Cutlets, with plain gravy, &c.	Black Puddings, *à la Française.*
„ *à la sauce Robert, &c.*	„ *à l'Anglaise.*
„ *à l'Aurore.*	White Puddings, *à la Royale.*
„ *à l'Indiénne.*	

945. GRISKIN, OR SPARE-RIB OF PORK, A LA SOUBISE.

TRIM a griskin of pork, and lard it closely, then put it in a deep dish with sliced onion and carrot, parsley, a gill of salad oil, some slices of peeled lemon, and a little mignionette pepper; allow the griskin to steep in this for several hours, or a whole day, if possible. When about to dress the griskin, twist it round, run a stout iron skewer through, and fasten it upon the spit tightly with string; cover the larding with buttered paper, and roast it before the fire for about an hour; as soon as a kind of vapor arises, and it sputters toward the fire, it is time to take it up. When the griskin is placed upon its dish, pour some *Soubise* sauce (No. 119) round it, garnish with a border of potatoes fried in clarified butter, glaze the griskin, and serve.

946. GRISKIN OF PORK, A LA LYONNAISE.

PREPARE and roast this in the same way as the foregoing, and when done, dish it up with some *Lyonnaise* sauce (No. 24) round it; garnish with a border of tomatas *au gratin* (No. 1160), glaze the griskin, and serve.

947. GRISKIN OF PORK, A LA PERIGUEUX.

THIS must be prepared and roasted as the foregoing; when done, serve with some *Périgueux* sauce (No. 23), and a border of mushrooms *au gratin* (1161) aound it.

948. PORK CUTLETS, PLAIN BROILED, WITH GRAVY, ETC.

THESE cutlets must be cut from the neck or loin of dairy-fed pork, not too fat; they should be trimmed but very little, the rough part of the chine-bone only requiring to be removed; the skin must be left on, and scored in six places. Season the cutlets with pepper and salt, and broil them on a gridiron over a clear fire; coke makes a better fire than coal for broiling, as it emits no gas, and causes less smoke. Take care that they are thoroughly done and not scorched; dish them up with any of the following gravies or sauces, and serve:—Plan sage and onion, shalot, onion, fine-herbs, gravies, or essences: *Piquante*, Gherkin, Tomata, *Poivrade*, Poor-man's, *Richelieu*, and *Gasconne* sauces.

949. PORK CUTLETS, A LA SAUCE ROBERT, ETC.

TRIM the cutlets neatly, observing, however, that nearly half an inch of the fat must be left on, to encircle the fillet of the cutlet; place them in an earthen dish with a table-spoonful of salad oil; season with a little salt and pepper, and strew some parsley over them. When about to send to table, broil the cutlets nicely with the gravy in them, glaze and dish them up; pour under some sauce *à la Robert* (No. 67), and serve.

950. PORK CUTLETS, A L'AURORE.

TRIM the cutlets neatly, season with pepper and salt, and place them in a sautapan with some clarified butter. About twenty minutes before sending to table, fry the cutlets over a brisk fire, so as to lightly color them on both sides before they are done, then pour off all the grease, leaving the cutlets neatly arranged in the sautapan, and glaze them. Next rub the yolks of six eggs, previously boiled hard, equally over all the cutlets, and pass the red-hot salamander over them to color the yolk of egg a shade darker; then dish up the cutlets with some essence of anchovies (No. 176) poured under them, and serve.

951. PORK CUTLETS, A L'INDIENNE.

FRY the cutlets brown on both sides, then pour off all the grease, adding about half a pint of *Espagnole* sauce, and a table-spoonful of Cook's curry paste; put the lid on the sautapan, and simmer the cutlets on the fire very gently for ten minutes longer; then add a small piece of glaze, toss the whole together, dish them up in a close circle, fill the centre with rice boiled in plain broth, pour the sauce over the cutlets, and serve.

952. PIGS'-FEET, A LA STE. MENEHOULD.

FOR this purpose procure the feet of bacon hogs, as the feet of porkers are not large enough to be worth dressing for the table. They must first be pickled in common salt brine, for about ten days, and then, after being washed, should be gently braized in common broth, seasoned with carrot, onion, celery, and garnished faggot of parsley; if the feet are large, they will require about four hours gentle boiling. When done, drain them on an earthen dish, cut them into halves, and remove all the large bones, press them into shape with the hands, and put them in the larder to cool. Next, season the pieces of pigs'-feet with pepper and salt, rub them over with a paste-brush dipped in clarified butter, then roll them in fresh made bread-crumbs, and pat these closely on with the blade of a knife; broil them on a gridiron over a clear fire, taking care that they are frequently turned until warmed through: they are then to be dished up and served with *Piquante* sauce (No. 18).

953. PIGS'-FEET, A LA PERIGORD.

THESE should be braized and the bones taken out, and before they become quite cold, filled inside, and partially covered, with some force-meat of fat livers, in which has been mixed some chopped truffles; and when this is placed on the feet, some scollops of truffles must also be intermixed with it. The feet must next be wrapped up in appropriate-sized pieces of pigs' caul, and then bread-crumbed over this. When about to send to table, broil the feet upon oiled paper placed upon the gridiron, to prevent them from burning or falling to pieces, which, from the delicacy of the force-meat (if properly prepared), they are liable to. When nicely broiled on both sides, glaze and dish them up, and serve with some *Périgueux* sauce (No. 23) under them.

954. PIGS'-FEET, A LA RICHELIEU.

BRAIZE the feet, remove all the bones, and cut each foot in halves, lengthwise; spread them all over with a coating of *D'Uxelles* sauce (No. 16), and when this has become firmly set by cooling, bread-crumb them twice over, the first time dipped in egg, and the second in clarified butter: place them in a sauta-pan with clarified butter, and fry them over a stove-fire of moderate heat, so as to allow them time to warm through before they acquire much color. When done, dish them up, and serve with some *Richelieu* ragout (No. 207) under them.

955. BLACK-PUDDINGS, A LA FRANCAISE.

TO one pint of pig's blood, add rather more than half a pint of boiled double cream, three-quarters of a pound of the fat from the inside of a pig, cut into rather small pieces, and four large onions chopped and fried in a little butter without becoming colored; season with a little chopped bay-leaf and thyme, nutmeg, pepper, and salt; mix well together, and stuff the linings, prepared perfectly clean for the purpose, with the above, taking care to allow room for tying them into lengths of about six inches. Some water must be kept nearly at the boiling-point, and then removed from the fire down to the side, and the puddings immersed, and allowed to remain in it

until they become somewhat firm to the touch ; they must not, however, be kept in the water longer than will suffice to set the preparation. The puddings, when taken out of the water, should be hung up in the larder to cool.

956. BLACK-PUDDINGS, A L'ANGLAISE.

THE chief difference from the foregoing, in making black-puddings according to the English method, lies in the omission of the nutmeg, bay-leaf, and thyme, and in the addition of boiled Embden grits or rice ; in all other respects, the same directions must be followed.

When about to dress the black-puddings, they should be scored all over to prevent them from bursting while being broiled, and when done, are to be dished up with strips of dry toast placed between each piece of pudding : the centre of the dish should be filled with mashed potatoes to keep them quite hot.

957. WHITE-PUDDINGS, A LA ROYALE.

To half a pound of the breast of roast fowl thoroughly pounded and passed into a *purée*, add half a pint of boiled double cream, half a pound of fresh made and very fine bread-crumbs, one onion chopped fine, and boiled down in some white broth, and four ounces of butter and eight yolks of eggs ; season with pepper and salt, and grated nutmeg ; mix well together, put this preparation into the linings, and finish them in the same manner as the black-puddings. When about to send to table, score the puddings before they are broiled, and place them on the gridiron upon a sheet of oiled paper ; when nicely broiled, serve them, dished up, with either of the following sauces :— *Suprême, Richelieu, Poivrade,* essence of shallots, of truffles, or of mushrooms.

ENTREES OF VENISON,

COMPRISING

Haricôt of Venison.	Cutlets of Roebuck, *à la Chasseur.*
Civet of Venison.	Fillets of Roebuck, *à la Kinnaird.*
Venison Scollops.	„ with *Poivrade* sauce.
Venison Chops.	Civet of Roebuck.
Venison Fry.	

958. HARICOT OF VENISON.

TRIM a neck of venison into cutlets without paring off any of the fat, season them with pepper and salt, and fry them quickly brown on both sides before they are more than half done ; then pour off all the grease, shake a handful of flour over the cutlets, and toss them about over the fire for three minutes, moisten with a pint of red wine and a quart of good stock ; add half a pint of small button-onions, and twice that quantity of turnips and carrots, cut into small fanciful shapes of the size of the onions, and a garnished faggot of parsley ; stir the haricôt over the stove-fire with a wooden spoon until it boils, and then remove it to the side of the stove to continue gently boiling for about an hour and a half; when, if the cutlets are found to be done tender, remove them into a deep sautapan; then add the vegetables with a *ragout* spoon (with holes in it), and after the sauce has boiled up and been skimmed, reduce it, if necessary, to its proper consistency, and pass it through a tammy into a sautapan containing the cutlets, &c. ; then add a little salt, if needed ; simmer the whole together on the stove-fire, dish the cutlets in the usual way, fill the centre with the vegetables pour the sauce over the *entrée*, and serve.

959. ANOTHER METHOD.

FRY the cutlets brown, pour off all the grease, add a pint of red wine, a pint of *Espagnole*, and the same proportion of *consommé*, season with a carrot, an onion, head of celery, and a garnished faggot of parsley; allow the whole to simmer gently by the side of the stove-fire until the cutlets are tender; they must then be removed into a sautapan, with a little of the sauce to warm them in, the lid put on, and kept warm. The remainder of the sauce must then be strained through a sieve into a smaller stewpan ; and after it has been clarified, by gently boiling it by the side of the stove-fire, and thoroughly skimming all that rises to the surface, reduce it by boiling to its proper consistency, and pass it through a tammy into a *bain-marie*. When about to send to table, dish the cutlets up, fill the centre with some glazed carrots and turnips, previously prepared for the purpose; place some groups of small glazed button-onions round the *entrée*, pour the sauce over the cutlets, and serve.

Some neat frills of paper may be put on the bone of each cutlet.

960. CIVET OF VENISON.

THIS dish, although not very choice, is often served at the tables of wealthy epicures ; in general, the inferior parts of venison,—such as the shoulder and scrag end of the neck—are used for this purpose. The venison must be cut up into pieces, and for its preparation follow the directions for making a civet of hare (No. 1070).

961. VENISON SCOLLOPS.

VENISON for this purpose ought to be kept until it has become quite tender: a piece of the end of the neck may be used. Cut the fillet from the bones, with all the fat adhering to it, remove the outer skin, and then cut it into scollops—taking care not to trim off more of the fat than is necessary ; place them in a sautapan with clarified butter, season with pepper and salt, and fry them brown on both sides; pour off all the grease, add some scollops of mushrooms, a piece of glaze, and a glass of Port wine ; simmer the whole together over the stove-fire for about three minutes, and then pour in some *Poivrade* sauce (No. 29) ; toss the scollops in the sauce on the fire until quite hot, and then dish them up with a border of *quenelles* of potatoes (No. 312), and serve.

These scollops may also be served with Portarlington sweet sauce (No. 66), in which case the mushrooms must be omitted.

962. VENISON CHOPS.

CUT the chops about an inch thick, from the end of the haunch or the best end of the neck, flatten them a little with a cutlet bat, trim them without waste, season with pepper and salt, and broil them on a gridiron, over a clear fire of moderate heat; turning them over every three minutes while on the fire; when done through with their gravy in them, lift them carefully off the gridiron without spilling the gravy that may be swimming on the surface, dish them up with a little rich brown gravy under them, and serve some currant-jelly or venison sweet sauce (No. 65), separately, in a boat.

963. VENISON FRY.

Cut the fry into appropriate-sized pieces, season with pepper and salt, place them in a napkin, and shake them up with a handful of flour, then fry them brown and crisp in a sautapan or frying-pan with some butter; when done, dish them up in a pile with fried parsley round, pour either of the following sauces under it, and serve quite hot: rich brown gravy, essence of anchovies, *Poivrade*, *Espagnole*, Italian, or *Piquante* sauce.

964. CUTLETS OF ROEBUCK, A LA CHASSEUR.

Trim the cutlets in the usual way, and place them in a sautapan with clarified butter, season with pepper and salt, and set them in the larder. Put the shoulder on the spit, wrap it in buttered paper, and roast it before a fire of moderate heat until done; all the meat must then be cut from the bone, chopped fine, and thoroughly pounded in a mortar with a spoonful of sauce and a pat of butter, then rubbed through a tammy or very fine wire sieve, into a *purée;* this must be gathered up into a small stewpan and placed with the cutlets. When about to send to table, fry the cutlets brown, pour off the grease, add a piece of glaze, two large spoonfuls of *Espagnole* or *Poivrade* sauce (if the former, add some lemon-juice also); allow the cutlets to simmer over the fire for a few minutes, and then dish them up; fill the centre with the *purée*—previously warmed with care, and to which a piece of glaze has been added—pour the sauce over the *entrée*, and serve.

965. FILLETS OF ROEBUCK, A LA KINNAIRD.

Cut out the fillets from two necks of roebuck, trim these neatly, and lard them closely; steep them for about two days and nights in some cold *marinade* (No. 234), and when about to dress the fillets, drain them upon a cloth, place them in a sautapan spread with butter, and moisten with some wine *mirepoix* (No. 236) in sufficient quantity to reach up to the larding; place a buttered paper on the top, and put them to braize in the oven; baste them frequently with their own liquor, and when done, glaze them nicely, and place them on their dish; garnish with groups of *quenelles* made with roebuck, and small potatoes cut in the form of large olives and fried in clarified butter; pour some *Napolitaine* sauce (No. 63) under the *entrée*, glaze the fillets, and serve.

966. FILLETS OF ROEBUCK, WITH POIVRADE SAUCE.

These are prepared in the same manner as the foregoing; when done and glazed, dish them up with a border of potatoes, cut in the form of olives, and fried in clarified butter, pour some *Poivrade* sauce (No. 29) under them, and serve.

967. CIVET OF ROEBUCK

Is prepared in the same way as civet of hare (1070).

ENTREES OF POULTRY,

COMPRISING

Fricassee of Chickens, with Mushrooms, &c.
   ,,   *à la St. Lambert.*
   ,,   *à la Dauphine.*
   ,,   *à la Financière.*
   ,,   *à la Chevalière.*
   ,,   *à la Romaine.*
Chickens, *à la Marengo.*
  ,, with Oysters, &c.
  ,, with Truffles, &c.
  ,, *à la Provençale.*

Chickens, *à la Lyonnaise.*
  ,, *à la Diable.*
  ,, *à la Tartare.*
  ,, *à l'Algériènne.*
  ,, *à la Florentine.*
Curry of ditto, *à l'Indiènne.*
Fritôt of Chickens, with Tomata Sauce, &c.
Capilotade of Chickens, *à l'Italiènne.*
Chickens, *à la Toscane.*
Marinade of Chickens, fried in Batter.

968. FRICASSEE OF CHICKENS, WITH MUSHROOMS, ETC.

PROCURE two fat, plump chickens, and after they have been drawn, singe them over the flame of a charcoal fire, and then cut up into small members or joints, in the following manner :—First, remove the wings at the second joint, and the legs at the knotty bend of the first joint; then take hold of the chicken with the left hand, and with a sharp knife make two parallel cuts, lengthwise, on the back, about an inch and a half apart, so as partly to detach or at least to mark out where the legs and wings are to be removed ; the chicken must next be placed upon its side on the table, and, after the leg and fillet (with the pinion left on the upper side) have been cut, the same must be repeated on the other, and the thigh-bones must be removed. Then, separate the back and breast, trim these without waste, and cut the back across into two pieces : steep the whole in a pan containing clear tepid water for about ten minutes, frequently squeezing the pieces with the hand to extract all the blood. Next, strew the bottom of a stewpan with thinly-sliced carrot, onion, and a little celery, three cloves, twelve pepper-corns, a blade of mace, and a garnished faggot of parsley ; place the pieces of chicken in close and neat order upon the vegetables, &c., moisten with about a quart of boiling broth from the stockpot, or failing this, with water, cover with the lid, and set the whole to boil gently by the side of the stove-fire for about half an hour, when the chickens will be done. They must then be strained in a sieve, and their broth reserved in a basin ; next, immerse the pieces of chicken in cold water, wash and drain them upon a napkin, and afterward trim them neatly and place them in a stewpan in the larder. Then put 2 oz. of fresh butter to melt in a stewpan, to this add two tablespoonfuls of flour, and stir the *roux* over the fire for three minutes without allowing it to acquire any color ; it should then be removed from the stove, and the chicken-broth being poured into it, the whole must be thoroughly mixed together into a smooth sauce ; throw in some trimmings of mushrooms, and stir the sauce over the fire until it boils, then set it by the side to continue gently boiling to throw up the butter and scum. When the sauce has boiled half an hour, skim it, reduce it by further boiling to its proper consistency, and then incorporate with it a leason of four yolks of eggs, mixed with a pat of butter and a little cream ; set the leason in the sauce by stirring it over the fire until it nearly boils, then pass it through a tammy into the stewpan containing the pieces of chicken, and add thereto half a pottle of prepared button-mushrooms. When about to send to table, warm the fricassee without allowing it to boil, and dish it up as follows :

First, put the pieces of the back in the centre of the dish, place the legs at the angles, the bones pointed inwardly ; next, place the fillets upon these, and then set the pieces of breast on the top ; pour the sauce over the *entrée*, and place the mushrooms about the fricassee in groups ; surround the *entrée* with eight or ten glazed *croûtons* of fried bread cut in the form of hearts, and serve.

Note.—Truffles cut into scollops, or shaped in the form of olives ; crayfish-tails, button-onions, or artichoke-bottoms, cut into small pointed quarters, may also be served with a fricassee of chickens.

969. FRICASSEE OF CHICKENS, A LA ST. LAMBERT.

CUT into small dice the following vegetables, &c. : one carrot, an onion, one head of celery, and 4 oz. of raw ham ; put these into a stewpan with a small piece of butter, half a bay-leaf, a sprig of thyme, three cloves, a blade of mace, and a few pepper-corns ; stir these over a slow fire for about ten minutes, without allowing them to acquire any color, then moisten the whole with a pint of French white wine, and the same quantity of common broth ; boil this gently for half an hour, and then strain it through a sieve into a basin. Next, cut the chickens up as directed in the foregoing case; melt 3 oz. of butter in a stewpan, throw in the pieces of chicken, and toss them over the fire until they become set and feel firm to the touch, without, however, acquiring any color ; then shake in two table-spoonfuls of flour, toss the whole together over the fire for two minutes, and pour in the broth prepared for the purpose ; stir the fricassee over the fire until it boils, and finish it in the same way as the foregoing. When about to send to table, warm and dish up the fricassee, place about it small groups of glazed carrots, turnips, and French-beans, cut into small fanciful shapes, and garnish the base by placing a border composed of about eight small artichoke-bottoms, nicely turned and boiled, each filled alternately with glazed carrots and green-peas ; pour the sauce round the *entrée*, and serve.

970. FRICASSEE OF CHICKENS, A LA DAUPHINE.

PREPARE a fricassee in the same manner as described in No. 968, and place the pieces of chicken, when trimmed, on an earthen dish ; after having reduced the sauce to the consistency of *Allemande*, incorporate the leason, &c., and when this is set in the sauce, pass it through a tammy into a small basin ; dip each of the pieces of chicken in this, and replace them on the dish ; when the sauce has become set upon them by cooling, roll them in bread-crumbs, let them be dipped in beaten egg, and bread-crumbed over again. When about to send to table, place the pieces of chicken thus prepared carefully upon the wire lining of a frying-pan, immerse them all at once in plenty of clean hog's lard heated for the purpose, fry them of a light color; and when done, drain them upon a cloth, dish them up on a clean napkin with fried parsley, and serve some white Italian sauce (No. 13), separately in a boat.

Note.—This *entrée* may also be dished up without a napkin, and some *Allemande* or *Béchamel* sauce, containing a few scollops of mushrooms or truffles, may be poured under, and round it.

971. FRICASSEE OF CHICKENS, A LA FINANCIERE.

PREPARE this as directed in No. 968, and when it is dished up, garnish it with groups of cocks'-combs, mushrooms, truffles, and some small *quenelles* of fowl; place eight large crayfish in an upright position round the *entrée*, and a larded sweetbread on the top.

972. FRICASSEE OF CHICKENS, A LA CHEVALIERE.

WHEN the chickens have been drawn and singed, remove the legs and wings, and then, with the point of a knife, slit the skin of the breast, spread it off the fillets, and remove these with the pinion-bone left on them; each fillet must be trimmed, then closely larded, and placed in a small sauta-pan upon thin layers of fat bacon; the minion fillets should also be trimmed (the sinew being first extracted), then decorated or *contisés* with black truffle and placed in a sauta-pan with butter; the remainder of the chickens must be cut up and made into a fricassee in the ordinary way.  When this is done, the four legs must be neatly trimmed and set aside in the larder, and the smaller pieces placed in a stewpan with a few button mushrooms, cocks'-combs and kernels and truffles; then, reduce the same by boiling it to the consistency of *Allemande* sauce, incorporate these with a leason of four yolks of eggs, a little grated nutmeg, mignionette pepper, a small piece of glaze, and the juice of half a lemon; when this has become set in the sauce by stirring it over the fire for two minutes, pass two thirds of it through a tammy on to the fricassee, and reserve the remainder for the purpose of masking the legs with it. These must be afterwards bread-crumbed and fried of a light color. The larded fillets should be moistened with a little half-glaze, and put in the oven, or on a slow stove with fire on the lid, to braize or simmer for about twenty minutes; they are then to be glazed. In dishing up this *entrée*, first place all the small members of the chicken in the bottom of the dish in neat and square order; the legs are next to be added, and then the larded fillets must be placed between these with the taper end pointing upward; the four minion fillets (turned round in the form of rings) should be placed so as to rest upon the upper part of each of the legs, and the whole surmounted with a large truffle, and a border of large crayfish, and white double cocks'-combs should be placed round the *entrée;* add the remainder of the sauce, and serve.

973. FRICASSEE OF CHICKENS, A LA ROMAINE.

WHEN the chickens have been cut up and trimmed in the usual way, place the pieces neatly in a sauta-pan with a gill of salad oil, bay-leaf and thyme, four shalots, mignionette pepper and salt, a little grated nutmeg, one clove of garlic, and a dozen small pimentos; fry the chickens over a rather brisk fire until the pieces become firm to the touch, but without allowing them to acquire any color; shake in two spoonfuls of flour, toss the whole over the fire for three minutes, and moisten with a pint of *Chablis* or *Sauterne* wine, and a pint of white *consommé;* stir the fricassee on the fire till it boils, then remove it to the side to continue gently boiling for half an hour. Skim off the oil, &c., that has risen to the surface, drain the pieces of chicken on a sieve, reserving the sauce in a stewpan to be reduced and finished in the ordinary manner; trim the pieces of chicken neatly, and put them into a stewpan with the sauce, some button-mushrooms or morels, trimmed crayfish-tails and cocks'-kernels. When about to send to table, warm the fricassee, and add the juice of half a lemon and a pat of butter, previously pounded with six small red pimentos and a piece of lobster coral, and passed through a sieve. Dish this in the same manner to the first, garnish it round with a border of *Raviolis* (No. 375), and serve.

974. CHICKENS, A LA MARENGO.

CUT up the chickens or fowls into small joints, as for a fricassee; place them in a saucepan with half a gill of salad oil, and half a pound of truffles cut into the form of olives, a garnished faggot of parsley and green onions, a bruised clove of garlic, mignionette pepper, and salt; set the sauta-pan on a moderate fire, and put some live embers of charcoal on the lid. Allow the chickens to fry rather briskly, so as to acquire a deep-yellow or brown color; about twenty minutes will suffice to do them. Then pour off nearly all the oil, and remove the faggot of parsley; add half a pottle of prepared button-mushrooms, a small ladleful of worked *Espagnole* sauce (No. 3), and a piece of glaze; simmer the whole together on the fire for five minutes, add the juice of a lemon, and dish up the *entrée* in the following order. First, place the pieces of the backs and the wings, next the legs, the fillets, and lastly the pieces of the breasts, then pour the sauce, &c., over the *entrée*, garnish it round with *croûtons* of bread, and large crayfish, and serve.

975. CHICKENS SAUTES, WITH OYSTER SAUCE, ETC.

THESE must be cut up in the ordinary way, and after being neatly trimmed, should be placed in a sauta-pan with some clarified butter, seasoned with pepper and salt, and fried of a light-brown color. Pour off the butter, add three dozen parboiled oysters with their liquor (previously reduce in quantity by boiling), and two large gravy-spoonfuls of *Espagnole* sauce, a piece of glaze, and the juice of half a lemon; set the whole on the fire to simmer for five minutes, and then dish up the *entrée* with fried *croûtons* of bread round it.

Note.—This method of dressing chickens or fowls may be varied by substituting muscles, cockles, olives, truffles, mushrooms, or morels, for the oysters.

976. CHICKENS WITH TRUFFLES, A LA FINANCIERE.

PREPARE these as in the foregoing case, and when they are fried brown, pour off the grease; add a rich *Financière ragout* (No. 188), and half a pound of truffles cut into scollops or round balls; simmer the whole together on the fire for five minutes, and then dish up the *entrée* as directed in the foregoing cases; pour the *ragout* over it, garnish with *croûtons* and crayfish, and serve.

977. CHICKENS, A LA PROVENCALE.

CUT four large onions into rings, put them into a sautapan with a gill of salad-oil, and fry them of a light-brown color; then add two chickens cut up and trimmed as for a fricassee; season with mignionette pepper, and salt, a garnished faggot of parsley, and a clove of garlic; cover with the lid containing some live embers of charcoal, and set the chickens to simmer briskly over a moderate fire for about half an hour. Put about two dozen morels or mushrooms into a small stewpan with some chopped truffles, shalots, mushrooms, and parsley; moisten with a table-spoonful of salad-oil, and a glass of Madeira; stew these on the fire for five minutes, and then boil the whole down to a glaze. When the chickens are done, pour off all the grease, add the morels, &c., a piece of glaze, and some Tomata sauce (No. 22); simmer the whole together for five minutes over the fire, then dish up the *entrée* in a conical form, pour the *ragout* over it, and serve.

978. CHICKENS, A LA LYONNAISE.

CUT these up and fry them in butter, as directed for the chickens with oysters; when they are done, pour off all the grease, add some *Lyonnaise* sauce (No. 24), simmer the whole together on the stove-fire for ten minutes, and serve.

979. CHICKENS, A LA DIABLE.

FIRST draw and singe the chickens, and then twist their legs inside neatly through the sides without tearing the skin; next cut them through the breast-bone, lengthwise, into halves; take out all the bones, season with pepper and salt, rub them over with a paste-brush dipped in clarified butter, and broil them on both sides, of a light color; when done, dish them up and glaze them over, pour some sauce *à la Diable* (No. 17) under them, and serve.

980. CHICKENS, A LA TARTARE.

BONE the chickens as in the foregoing case, season with pepper and salt, rub tham over with a paste-brush dipped in yolks of eggs, breadcrumb them, then spread on some clarified butter, and bread-crumb them over again; pat the bread-crumbs closely together with the blade of a knife, broil them carefully to prevent their acquiring much color, and when done, glaze them lightly, and serve with some half glaze under them. Send some *Tartare* sauce (No. 96) separately in a boat.

981. CHICKENS, A L'ALGERIENNE.

CUT these up as for a fricassee, place the pieces in a deep sautapan with some clarified butter, and about one pound of raw ham cut into neat scollops; season with cayenne, a garnished faggot of parsley and green-onions, and a clove of garlic; fry the chickens over a brisk fire until they acquire a fine yellow color; then pour off the grease, and add a glass of Madeira, a teaspoonful of curry-paste, a piece of glaze, two gravy-spoonfuls of *Espagnole* sauce, and half a pottle of mushrooms; simmer the whole together over the fire for ten minutes, then add a pat of butter and the juice of half a lemon. Dish up the *entrée* in a pyramidal form, reserving the pieces of breast and the fillets to be placed uppermost; garnish with the ham and mushrooms, pour the sauce over all, place twelve *croutons* of bread round the base, and serve.

982. CHICKENS, A LA FLORENTINE.

FOR this purpose, choose two very small spring chickens, bone them in halves, trim them neatly, season with mignionette pepper and salt, and place them in a deep sautapan with half a gill of salad-oil, and a garnished faggot of parsley and green-onions containing a clove of garlic; then add half a pound of raw ham or streaky bacon, cut up into square pieces and parboiled in water for ten minutes, a table-spoonful of the powder of sweet red pimento, half a pint of small button-onions, also parboiled in water for five minutes, the same quantity of small carrots turned in the form of olives, and half a pottle of mushrooms. Set the whole over a moderate fire until the pieces of chicken, &c., acquire a light color, then pour off all the grease, add a glass of Malaga wine and a piece of glaze; simmer the whole together over a brisk fire until the moistening is reduced to a glaze; toss the pieces of chicken. &c., about in this to make it adhere to them, and immediately dish up the *entrée*, reserving the mushrooms, &c., to be placed in groups about the dish; next, pour a spoonful of *Espagnole* sauce into the sautapan, add the juice of half a lemon, allow this sauce to simmer, pour it over the *entrée*, and serve.

983. CURRY OF CHICKENS, A L'INDIENNE

CUT these as for a fricassee, trim them neatly, place them in a sautapan with some clarified butter, and fry them over a stove-fire until they become firm to the touch; then pour off all the grease, add sufficient curry-sauce (No. 47) for the *entrée*, and set the curry to simmer very gently over a slow stove-fire until the pieces of chicken have become perfectly tender; the *entrée* may then be dished up, and sauce poured over it, and with some plain boiled rice separately.

984. ANOTHER METHOD.

FRY the pieces of chicken or fowl in butter, until they are brightly browned all over, and remove them into a stewpan; then slice up three large onions and two heads of celery, and put these into a stew-pan, together with a clove of garlic, a garnished faggot of parsley, a blade of mace, and four cloves. Fry the whole over a slow fire until they acquire a light-brown color; add a' large table-spoonful of Cook's meat-curry-paste, and a similar proportion of flour: mix all the above together, and moisten with a pint of good broth or gravy; stir the sauce over the fire and keep it boiling for about twenty minutes, then rub the whole through a hair-sieve or tammy, and afterward pour it to the pieces of chicken. Set the curry to simmer gently over a slow fire until the pieces of chicken become tender, when the *entrée* may be served as in the former case.

985. FRITOT OF CHICKENS, WITH TOMATA SAUCE, ETC.

THE chickens must be cut up as for a fricassee, and the pieces neatly trimmed; then place them in a basin with some slices of onion, parsley, bay-leaf, and thyme, mignionette pepper and a little salt, three table-spoonfuls of salad-oil, and the juice of a lemon; steep them in this for several hours; and when about to send to table, drain the pieces of chicken upon a cloth, shake some flour over them, so as to entirely cover the pieces with a coating of it, form them into shape, drop them into some hog's-lard made hot for the purpose, and fry them of a yellow color. When done, drain the pieces of chicken on a sieve, covered with paper, lay them upon a sautapan, and glaze them over slightly; dish them up in a pyramidal form, garnish the *entrée* round with a border of fried eggs and *croûtons* of bread, placed alternately; pour some Tomata or *Poivrade* sauce (Nos. 22 and 29) under the *fritôt*, and serve.

986. CAPILOTADE OF CHICKENS OR FOWLS, A L'ITALIENNE.

THIS *entrée* is mostly served when there happens to be roast fowl or poultry of any kind in reserve. This should be cut up into small joints neatly trimmed, and placed in a stewpan containing some Italian sauce (No. 12), and scollops of mushrooms and truffles; when about to send to table, allow the *capilotade* to simmer gently on a slow fire until the pieces of chicken have become thoroughly impregnated with the sauce: about ten minutes will suffice for this purpose. The *entrée* may then be dished up, and garnished round with *croûtons* of bread; pour the sauce over it, and serve.

987. CHICKENS, A LA TOSCANE.

PREPARE these in the first instance as for a *fritôt*, and after the pieces of chicken have been sufficiently steeped, drain them upon a cloth to absorb all the moisture from the exterior, rub each piece over separately with a paste-brush dipped in yolks of egg, and bread-crumb them upon this; they must then be dipped in, or sprinkled over with clarified butter, and again bread-crumbed upon this; they should next be patted into shape with the blade of a knife, and placed in order in a sautapan with some clarified butter. About twenty minutes before sending to table, fry the pieces of chicken of a fine yellow color, and when done, drain them upon a napkin, glaze them over lightly, and dish them up; garnish with *mâcaroni* dressed with cheese, pour some essence of fowl under them, and serve.

Note.—This dish may also be served without the *macaroni*, and is then called *à la Viènnoise,* in which case some *quenelles* of potatoes may be added.

988. MARINADE OF CHICKENS, FRIED IN BATTER.

ROAST one or more chickens or fowls; when done, cut them into neatly-trimmed joints, and put these to steep for several hours in the following preparation:—Cut into thin slices a large onion, carrot, celery, parsley-root, a few green onions, some parsley, and a clove of garlic, and put them into a stewpan with two ounces of butter, a bay-leaf, sprig of thyme, blade of mace, and four cloves; fry all these of a light-brown color, moisten with half a pint of Sherry, and an equal proportion of French vinegar, add a very little salt, and a pinch of mignionette pepper, and allow the whole to simmer gently until the vegetables are thoroughly done; the *marinade* must then be strained through a tammy with considerable pressure, in order to extract the flavor of all the ingredients. When about to send to table, drain the pieces of chicken in a napkin, and afterward dip them into some light batter, fry them in hog's-lard of a light color, made hot for the purpose, dish them up on a napkin with fried parsley, and serve with some Italian, *Piquante, Poivrade, Provençale,* or Tomata sauce; or some essence of anchovies (No. 176), of truffles (No. 168), of shalots (No. 167), or of fine-herbs (No. 170), in a boat separately.

ENTREES OF FILLETS OF FOWLS,

COMPRISING

Suprême of Fillets of Fowls, *à l'Ecarlate.*	Fillets of Fowls, *à l'Indiènne.*	
„ „ *à la Toulouse.*	„ *à la Maréchale.*	
„ „ with Truffles, &c.	„ *à la Valençay.*	
„ „ *à la Parisiènne.*	„ *à la Royale.*	
„ „ with Cucumbers, *à la Belle-vue.*	„ *à la Financière,* &c.	
„ „ *à la Périgord.*	„ *à la d'Uxelles.*	

IT should be observed that the whole of the following *entrées* are expensive; with good management, however, much of the cost may be reduced, by subsequently using the remains of the fowls here required in the preparation of a variety of other dishes; such as those comprised in the last section of *entrées* of poultry, and also for making *galantines, ballotines,* cutlets, *croquettes,* pies, &c.

989. SUPREME OF FLLETS OF FOWLS, A L'ECARLATE.

TAKE out the fillets of three or four young fowls, in the following manner:—First, slit the skin on the centre of the breast in a straight line, so that, by folding it down on both sides, the fillets will be left bare. Next, draw the point of a knife along the edge of the breast-bone, cut through the centre of the merry-thought, and then remove the fillets by dividing them from the breast and ribs, carefully running the point of a knife close to the bones, while the fillet is held up with the fingers of the left hand, so as to prevent the knife from injuring it. The fillets being thus removed entire, divide the minion fillets from the large ones, and after the sinew which runs along these has been carefully extracted without tearing them, they should be trimmed and placed in a small sautapan with some clarified butter, covered with a round piece of paper, and placed in the larder; the larger fillets must also be trimmed in the following manner:—Place the fillet upon the edge of the table, with the pointed end to the right, and the smooth side downwards; then bear moderately with the fingers of the left hand upon the pointed end of the fillet, and at the same time slip the edge of a sharp knife (dipped in water) into that part, and slide the knife under the hand, closely bearing toward the skin so as not to waste any more of the fillet than is positively necessary for the purpose of removing it; it must then be trimmed neatly round at the thick end, and nearly to a point at the thin end. The fillets should now be arranged, all in the same direction, in a sautapan with some clarified butter; then seasoned with a little salt, covered with a circular piece of buttered paper, and placed with the others. It is necessary to observe that if the large fillets incline from right to left when placed in the sautapan, the minion fillets should be curved in the opposite direction: the latter may be decorated, or *contisés* with truffles or tongue; in which case they must be covered with thin layers of fat bacon. When about to send to table, place the sautapan containing the large fillets over a stove-fire, and as soon as they become set and whitened on one side, turn them over immediately on the other, and do not let them acquire any color; then, quickly pour off all the butter, add a large spoonful of *Suprême* sauce (No. 38), and having tossed the fillets in it over the fire without allowing them to boil or simmer, dish them in a close circle with a round scollop of red tongue (previously warmed in a little half glaze for the purpose) between each of them; fill the centre with scollops of button-mushrooms tossed in a little of the sauce, place the minion fillets, in a similar row to the others, upon the top of them; pour some *Suprême* sauce round the *entrée*, and upon each of the fillets, without masking the pieces of tongue, and serve.

990. SUPREME OF FILLETS OF FOWLS, A LA TOULOUSE.

PREPARE the large fillets as in the foregoing case, and when the smaller ones have been trimmed, lard them closely, and place them in a sautapan upon thin layers of fat bacon, in a curved form. A quarter of an hour before sending to table, finish the large fillets as in the foregoing case, substituting *Allemande* for *Suprême* sauce, and this should be incorporated with some reduced essence of fowls, a pat of butter, a little cream and lemon-juice. The larded fillets must be moistened with a little half-glaze, placed in the oven for about six minutes, and nicely glazed; then, dish up the large fillets in a close circle with a *croûtons* of bread, cut in the form of a deep crescent, fried in butter, and glazed; fill the centre with a *ragout* of cock's-combs, truffles, mushrooms, small *quenelles*, and cock's-kernels, tossed in some of the sauce; dress the larded fillets round the top of the others, pour some of the sauce round the *entrée*, and serve.

991. SUPREME OF FILLETS OF FOWLS, WITH TRUFFLES.

PREPARE this in the same way as in No. 989; decorate the small fillets with truffles, finish and dish up the *entrée* as therein directed, and fill the centre with scollops of truffles tossed in a small stewpan with a little glaze, and a very small piece of fresh butter; pour the *Suprême* sauce (No. 38) round the base, and on the fillets, and serve.

992. SUPREME OF FILLETS OF FOWLS, A LA PARISIENNE.

TRIM eight or ten large fillets of fowls, and decorate them with black truffles, in the following manner:—First, spread the bottom of a sautapan large enough to contain the fillets, with fresh butter; then place the fillets therein, all curved in the same direction, with the smooth side uppermost. Next, rub each fillet over slightly with a paste-brush, dipped in white of egg slightly beat up; the truffles, after being first cut into thin scollops, and stamped out with tin fancy cutters in various forms, should then be stuck upon this prepared surface, according to taste, forming therewith stars, scrolls, palms, mosaics, &c. When all the fillets are decorated, run some clarified butter over them, in sufficient quantity to cover their surface; place a covering of buttered paper upon them, and set the sautapan aside in the

larder. The minion fillets must also be decorated with red tongue, in the same way as the others. When about to send to table, simmer the fillets on both sides, carefully preventing them from becoming at all colored; when done, drain them upon a napkin, and dish them up in a close circle, placing a fillet of red tongue between each of the large fillets; next place the minion fillet in a close border on the top of the inner edge of these, fill the centre with a *ragout à la Parisiénne* (No. 203), pour some of the sauce round the base of the *entrée*, without in any way masking the decoration of the fillets, and serve.

993. SUPREME OF FILLETS OF FOWLS WITH CUCUMBERS, A LA BELLE-VUE.

In this instance the fillets must be prepared and finished in exactly the same way as stated in No. 989; but when dishing them up, instead of the fillets of tongue, place between the fillets a scollop of cucumber, prepared as follows:—

Cut two large well-shaped cucumbers into slanting scollops of about a quarter of an inch in thickness; trim these neatly in an oval form, scooping out the seeds, and after having parboiled these oval rings, or links, in salt and water, drain them upon a napkin, and place them in order at the bottom of a sautapan previously spread with butter; then proceed to fill up the centre of these with some *quenelle* force-meat of fowl, mixed with some chopped and parboiled parsley, to color it green; smooth the surfaces over, place a circular piece of buttered paper upon them, and poach them by pouring some boiling *consommé* in at the side of the sautapan, so as not to disturb the rings. Let them simmer gently by the side of a stove-fire for about ten minutes, then be carefully drained upon a napkin, lightly glazed, and used as directed above. Fill the centre of the *entrée* with prepared scollops of cucumbers (No. 138), previously tossed in some of the sauce; mask the fillets, without covering the links of cucumbers, with some *Suprême* sauce, and serve.

994. SUPREME OF FILLETS OF FOWLS, A LA PERIGORD.

Prepare this according to the directions for *Suprême à l'Ecarlate* (No. 989); the minion fillets, however, must be decorated with black truffle. When about to send to table, dish up the fillet as usual in a close circle round the base of a small ornamental *crôustade* of bread, previously fried of a light color, and stuck in the centre of the dish by means of a little flour-paste; fill this *crôustade* with some *purée* of truffles (No. 121), pour some *Suprême* sauce (No. 38) over the plain fillets, and round the base of the *entrée*, and serve.

995. FILLETS OF FOWLS, A L'INDIENNE.

Trim the fillets of three young fowls, and form the minion fillets into three large ones, by patting them together; when trimmed in shape, place them and the others in a sautapan, with some clarified butter, and a similar number of thin slices of raw ham (previously soaked in water) cut in the shape and size of the fillets. When about to send to table, fry the fillets of fowls and the ham of a light-brown color, pour off all the grease, then add a spoonful of glaze, a pat of fresh butter, the juice of a lemon, and a little grated nutmeg; toss the whole together gently over the stove-fire until mixed; dish them up, alternately placing a fillet, a piece of ham, and then a fried *crôuton* of bread, of the same shape. Pour some *Espagnole* sauce (No. 3) and some small scollops of mangoes into the sautapan containing the fillets and ham, simmer this over the fire for five minutes, then pour it over the *entrée*, and serve.

996. FILLETS OF FOWLS, A LA MARECHALE.

Trim the fillets of three or four fowls, and with the minion fillets form three or four large ones; make a slight incision down the centre of each fillet, so as to hollow it out a little: this must be done on the rough side. Then, chop a truffle, one shalot, and a little parsley very fine, and simmer these for five minutes in a small stewpan, with a bit of butter, pepper and salt, nutmeg, and a small piece of glaze, add the yolks of two eggs, and with this preparation fill the hollow made in the fillets, and then mask them over on both sides with a little stiffly-reduced *Allemande* sauce No. 7), when this has become firmly set upon them by cooling, bread-crumb the fillets twice over: having once after dipped them in beaten eggs, and again after they have been sprinkled over with clarified butter; put them gently into shape with the blade of a knife, and place them upon a dish in the larder. Twenty minutes before sending to table, cover the gridiron with a piece of oiled paper, place the fillets upon this, and broil them (on both sides) over a clear coke fire, of a bright-yellow color; when they are done, glaze them lightly, and dish them up in a close circle; fill the centre with a white *Toulouse ragout* (No. 187), pour some reduced essence of fowls under them, and serve.

Note.—Fillets of fowls *à la Maréchale* may also be served with every kind of delicate vegetable garnish; with white or brown Italian sauce; with *Maréchale, Suprême,* Venetian, *Provençale, Perigueux,* or Crayfish sauce: and also with either of the following essences:—Anchovy, truffle, fine-herbs, or shalot.

997. FILLETS OF FOWLS, A LA VALENCAY.

Trim eight fillets of fowls, and lay them flat upon an earthen dish. Prepare a sufficient quantity of *purée* of truffles (No. 121), in which incorporate two yolks of eggs, and then spread this over the fillets on both sides; when the coating has become firmly set by cooling, bread-crumb the fillets over twice: once with egg, and the second time, after being sprinkled over with clarified butter. Then, place the fillets in neat order in a sautapan with some clarified butter; and when about to send to table, fry them of a light color on both sides, drain them upon a napkin, and then dish them up closely in a circle; place the minion fillets (which should be decorated with truffle, and simmered in butter), in a row upon the top of the inner edge of the others; fill the centre with scollops of truffles, previously simmered in a little glaze and a very small piece of butter; pour some *Suprême* sauce (No. 38) under the *entrée*, and serve.

998. FILLETS OF FOWLS, A LA ROYALE.

TRIM the fillets of four fowls without removing the small fillets, then closely lard one-half of them, and decorate the other four with black truffle, in the same way as described for fillets *à la Parsiènne* (No. 992); place these fillets in separate sautapans, the larded ones upon thin layers of fat bacon, and moistened with some half-glaze, and the decorated fillets covered with clarified butter. Just before sending to table, put both in the oven for about five minutes; then withdraw the decorated fillets, glaze the larded ones, put them back for two minutes, and glaze them again. Dish them up, placing alternately a larded fillet with a decorated one; fill the centre with a *ragout* of scollops of fat livers and truffles tossed in a little *Allemande* sauce (No. 7); pour some of the sauce round the *entrée*, and serve.

999. FILLETS OF FOWLS, A LA FINANCIERE.

CUT out the fillets of four fowls, with the pinion-bones left adhering thereto, trim them in the usual way, and lard the whole of the fillet closely; then place them in order in a sautapan upon thin layers of fat bacon; moisten with some strong *consommé*, and set them to braize in the oven, or else covered with a lid containing some live embers of charcoal: about ten minutes will suffice to do them; they must next be glazed, and placed into the oven to dry the larding, and then glazed a second time. The fillets must then be dished up, and arranged in their natural order, that is, the right hand fillets to the right, and the left hand to the left. Fill the centre with a rich *Financière ragout* (No. 181), pour some of the sauce round the *entrée*, and serve.

Note.—Fillets of fowls, larded and prepared as the foregoing, may also be served with *pureés* of endive, green-peas, asparagus, *à la Macédoine ;* with stewed peas, scollops of cucumbers, asparagus-peas, &c.

1000. FILLETS OF FOWLS A LA D'UXELLES.

TRIM the fillets of three or four fowls, removing the minion fillets, which should be decorated with black truffles as described in No. 992, and afterwards placed in a sautapan with clarified butter. Cover the larger fillets with a coating of *D'Uxelles* sauce (No. 16), over which, when it has become firmly set upon the fillets by cooling, breadcrumb them twice; once after dipping them in beaten eggs, and the second time after they have been sprinkled over with clarified butter. They must then be gently patted into shape with the blade of a knife, and placed in a sautapan with some clarified butter. When about to send to table, fry the fillets on both sides, of a bright-yellow color;

then drain them upon a napkin, glaze lightly and dish them up in a close circle : place the decorated minion fillets in a row on the top of the inner edge of these, fill the centre with scollops of button-mushrooms tossed in a little *Allemande* sauce (No. 7), pour some half-glaze under the fillets, and serve.

ENTREES OF QUENELLE-FORCE-MEAT OF FOWL,

COMPRISING

Quenelles of Fowl, *à l'Essence.*	*Boudins* of Fowls *à la d'Artois.*
" *à la Toulouse.*	" *à la Cardinal.*
" *à la Maréchale.*	" *à la Soubise.*
Boudins of Fowls, *à la Richelieu.*	" *à la Reine.*
" *à la Perigueux.*	*Bouchées à la Pompadour.*
" *à la Sefton.*	

1001. QUENELLES OF FOWL, A L'ESSENCE.

PREPARE some *quenelle* force-meat (No. 242), with the fillets of two fowls, in which should be incorporated a spoonful of reduced *Allemande* sauce (No. 7) ; this should then be moulded into *quenelles* in the following manner: First, take up as much of the force-meat as will fill a silver table-spoon, then smooth it over the top in a dome-like form with the blade of a knife dipped in hot water ; next with another spoon of the same size and shape which must be dipped in hot water, scoop the *quenelle* out of the spoon, and lay it upon the under side at the bottom of a deep sautapan, previously spread with butter for the purpose ; repeat this until the whole of the force-meat that is meant for the *entrée* be used up, and then place a covering of buttered paper over them, and pour sufficient boiling *consommé* in at the side of the sautapan to float the *quenelles*. About ten minutes' gentle simmering by the side of the stove-fire will suffice to do them ; they must then be drained with care upon a napkin, dished up in a close circle ; pour some bright *consommé* of fowl (boiled down to nearly the consistency of half-glaze) under them, and send to table.

Note.—*Quenelles* of fowl prepared in this manner, may also be served with the following sauces : *Suprême, Italiènne, Perigueux, Allemande, Béchamel, Richelieu.*

1002. QUENELLES OF FOWL, A LA TOULOUSE.

FOR this *entrée* it will be necessary when about to mould the *quenelles*, first to shake some flour over a slab or table, and then to take up six spoonfuls of the force-meat and drop them separately upon the slab ; next shake a little flour over them, and proceed to roll each into the form of an egg ; these must then be placed in rows in a deep sautapan (previously spread with butter), about two inches distant from each other, and flattened to a quarter of an inch in thickness, by gently pressing them down with the fingers ; after which pour in some boiling broth, and set them by the side of the fire to poach. When the *quenelles* are done, drain them upon a napkin, trim them neatly, still retaining their oval shape, and place one half of them in a sautapan with a little white *consommé ;* bread-crumb the remainder, first masking them over with a coating of *Allemande* sauce. When about to send to table fry the bread-crumbed *quenelles* of a light color, in hog's-lard heated for the purpose, and having warmed the plain ones, and drained them upon a napkin, dish up the *entrée*, alternately placing one of each sort of *quenelle;* fill the centre with a white *Toulouse ragout* (No. 187), pour some of the sauce round the base and serve.

1003. QUENELLES OF FOWL, A LA MARECHALE.

PREPARE the *quenelles* as in the foregoing case; shape them in the form of cutlets, oval, oblong, circular, or like a heart; taking care not to make them more than a quarter of an inch thick. When they have been poached and trimmed, place them upon a dish, and mask them over with some *Allemande* sauce; when this has become firmly set upon the *quenelles* by cooling, bread-crumb them over twice in the usual way: once with egg, and the second time, after they have been sprinkled over, with clarified butter. They must then be broiled upon oiled paper, and when done of a light color on the one side, great care must be used in turning them over, to be equally broiled on the other. When done, dish them up in a close circle, fill the centre, either with scollops of truffles, mushrooms, fat livers, cock's-combs, and kernels; with *Allemande* or *Suprême* sauce, or with essence of fowl, and serve.

1004. BOUDINS OF FOWL, A LA RICHELIEU.

PREPARE some *quenelle* force-meat with the fillets of two fowls, in the usual manner (No. 242), form this into a dozen flat oblong *quenelles*, and poach them delicately in broth, as directed in the foregoing cases; when this is done drain them upon a napkin, and after making an opening on the surface to the extent of two inches long, by one inch wide, and then carefully scooping out the inside of the *quenelles* to the depth of two-thirds of their thickness, fill this cavity with the following preparation: cut a large onion into very small dice, and fry these in a small stewpan with a little butter, of a light-yellow color; then add an equal proportion of truffles, also cut into very small dice and some mushrooms in the same manner; next, add a spoonful of *Allemande* sauce (No. 7), a little nutmeg, mignionette pepper, and a small piece of glaze; stir the whole over the fire for about five minutes, and then use it as directed above. When the preparation with which the *quenelles* have been filled up has cooled, spread a layer of force-meat over the entire service of each; then place them in a sautapan previously spread with butter to receive them, rub them over carefully with a paste-brush dipped in white of egg and decorate them with truffle and tongue. When about to send to table, poach the *boudins* by pouring some boiling *consommé* on them, taking care not to disturb the decoration; when they have been allowed to simmer gently by the side of a stove-fire for about ten minutes, drain them upon a napkin, glaze them lightly, and dish them up in a close circle; pour some *Richelieu ragout* (No. 207) under them and serve.

Note.—This *entrée* may also be served with a *purée* of mushrooms, truffles, or with scollops of fat livers.

1005. BOUDINS OF FOWL, A LA PERIGUEUX.

THESE must be prepared, in the first instance, in the same manner as the foregoing : after the centre has been scooped out, the cavity of these should be filled up with some *purée* of truffles (No. 121) ; then, the *boudins* must be closed in with a thin coating of the force-meat, and after being rubbed over with a paste-brush, and dipped in some beaten white of egg, should be sprinkled over with black truffles, chopped very fine, and must be poached and afterward dished up in a close circle. Pour some *Périgueux* sauce (No. 23) under them, and serve.

1006. BOUDINS OF FOWL, A LA SEFTON.

PREPARE the force-meat in the usual way, and before using it, incorporate therewith about two table-spoonfuls of *purée* of mushrooms (No. 122) ; then divide the force-meat into three equal parts, roll these, with the aid of a little flour shaken over them, into square oblong shapes,* measuring about six inches in length ; place these in a deep sautapan, previously spread with butter to receive them, and poach them as directed in former cases ; when done, drain them upon a napkin, dish them up in the form of an angle, or in a row, side by side ; place two minion fillets that have been larded and glazed across the ends of each, garnish with a white *Financière ragout* (No. 188), and serve.

1007. BOUDINS OF FOWL, A LA D'ARTOIS.

PREPARE about twelve small oval or oblong flat *quenelles* of force-meat of fowls, and when they have been poached, drained, trimmed, and then scooped out as directed for the *quenelles à la Maréchale*, fill the cavities with a *salpicon*† composed of truffles, mushrooms, and red tongue mixed with a little reduced *Allemande* sauce ; spread a thin layer of force-meat over the surface, bread-crumb the boudins carefully, and place them with this side uppermost in a sautapan with clarified butter. When about to send to table, fry the *boudins* of a light color, on both sides, drain them upon a sheet of paper and glaze them lightly, and then dish them up in a close circle ; fill the centre with a *Financière ragout* (No. 188) in some Madeira sauce (No. 8), pour some of the sauce round the base, and serve.

1008. BOUDINS OF FOWL, A LA SOUBISE.

FIRST, prepare some force-meat with the fillets of two fowls (No. 242), and in finishing this, instead of sauce, add two table-spoonfuls of *purée* of onions (No. 119) ; form this force-meat into about sixteen small oblong *quenelles*, by rolling them upon the table or slab with a little flour : then cut each of these in two, lengthwise, spread out the

* There are fancy copper or tin moulds made for this purpose, and may be had at all braziers' shops. Previously to filling the moulds with the force-meat, they must be carefully and thinly spread with butter. These must be merely steamed in water, in the same manner as a pudding, and, when done, turned out of the moulds, and finished as directed for the others.

† *Salpicon* means, literally, anything savory, such as truffles, tongue, mushrooms, sweetbreads poultry, or game, that has undergone the process of mincing, preparatory to being mixed with some *Béchamel, Allemande,* or *Espagnole* sauce ; to be afterward used for such purposes as the above, and also for garnishing patties with.

sides of these halves a little with the point of a small knife, and then insert between them a small portion of *salpicon*, prepared as for the *boudins à la d'Artois;* this, after being spread out to the thickness of rather less than a quarter of an inch, and allowed to become cold and firm, must then be cut up into small strips, or bands, for the purpose of being inserted in between two halves of the *quenelles* or *boudin;* the sides of these should then be securely closed in, and patted smooth all over with the blade of a knife, dipped in flour, and are then to be placed in a sautapan, previously spread with butter to receive them. Pour some boiling broth to the *boudins*, and poach them in the usual way; then drain, trim, and bread-crumb them with beaten egg, and place them carefully in a sautapan with some clarified butter. When about to send to table, fry the *boudins* of a light color, glaze them lightly, dish them up in a close circle, fill the centre with some *Soubise* sauce (No. 119), pour some half-glaze or essence of fowls, under the *entrée*, and serve.

1009. BOUDINS OF FOWL, A LA REINE.

ROAST two fowls, remove all the brown skin, cut off all the meat from the bones, and use the latter to make some essence with. Chop the meat fine, and then pound it in a mortar with a pat of butter and a large spoonful of reduced *Béchamel* sauce; season with a little pepper and salt and grated nutmeg, and rub the whole through a very fine wire-sieve, or tammy cloth; then put this *purée* into a small stewpan, and after adding thereto half a gill of scalded double-cream, and a piece of glaze as big as a walnut, stir it over the fire until the whole is mixed, and spread this preparation on a dish, in a square form about two inches in thickness, and set it in the larder to become cold. Then, cut the square into two oblong pieces, and divide these again, each into about eight small oblong slices, about three inches long by two in width, and a quarter of an inch thick. Spread each of these over with a thin coating of some very delicate force-meat of fowl; flour them over, then dip them separately in some beaten egg, bread-crumb them, and set them on a dish in the larder until dinner-time. The *boudins* must then be placed upon the wire drainer of a frying pan, and immersed in some clean hog's-lard made quite hot for the purpose, and fried of a light-fawn color; they should be drained, and dished up in a close circle, with some *Béchamel* or *Suprême* sauce poured under them, and then sent to table.

1010. BOUCHEES OF FOWL, A LA POMPADOUR

PREPARE some very delicate force-meat with the fillets of two fowls; when finished, incorporate therewith two spoonfuls of *purée* of mushrooms, made with double cream (No. 122). Form this into about sixteen small oval, or circular flat *quenelles*, or *boudins*, about a third of an inch in thickness; place them in a buttered sautapan, and poach them delicately : that is, let them be only two parts done; drain them upon a napkin, then place them on a dish, covered over with a sheet of buttered paper, and put them in the larder until dinner-time. The *bouchées* should then be dipped in some very light batter, mixed with whipped cream, instead of water, and fried in plenty of clean hog's-lard, made hot for the purpose; they must then be dished up in circular order, and the centre filled either with stewed peas, asparagus-peas, or *purée*, a *Macédoine* of summer vegetables, *Poivrade*, or Tomata sauce. If garnished with dressed vegetables, some essence of fowl should be poured round the base of the *entrée*.

ENTREES OF FOWLS OR CHICKENS,

COMPRISING

Galantines of Legs of Fowl, *à la Financière*.
    "   "   *à la Jardinière*.
Minced and Grilled Fowl.
Minced Chicken, and Poached Eggs.
Minced Fowl, with Macaroni.

Minced Fowl, with Rice.
Scollops of ditto, *au gratin*.
Kromeskys of Fowl, *à la Russe*.
Croquettes of Fowl, with Mushrooms, &c.
Mince, or *Salpicon*, for Patties.

1011. GALANTINES OF LEGS OF FOWLS, A LA FINANCIERE.

THE legs must be carved from the carcasses of the fowls with the whole of the skin from the back left adhering thereto; then bone these entirely without dividing the leg, or, as it is commonly called, the drum-stick part. The feet should be cut with part of the leg-bones left on, scalded, and the outer skin carefully removed, without tearing them; trim these neatly, leaving only part of the claws in, and stick them into the small aperture of the legs, whence the drum-stick bones have been removed: when properly done, this gives them a neat and plump appearance. They must then be spread out upon the table, seasoned with pepper and salt, and about a dessert-spoonful of force-meat, in which has been mixed some fine-herbs, placed in the centre; a large needle and some coarse thread should be used to draw the skinny part of the legs up into a purse, and must then be fastened to secure them in shape. The *galantines* must next be larded closely on the plump part of the thigh, in the same manner as a sweetbread, and then placed in a deep sautapan, the bottom of which should be strewn with sliced carrot, onion and celery, and a garnished faggot of parsley, and covered with some thin layers of fat bacon, upon which the *galantines* are to be placed. Moisten with sufficient *consommé* or broth to reach nearly up to the larding: place a buttered paper on the top, cover with the lid containing some live embers of charcoal, and set them to braize gently for about half an hour over a moderate stove-fire, or else in the oven, frequently basting them with their own liquor. When they are done, remove the lid and the paper, and put them in the oven for a couple of minutes to dry the larding; then glaze them nicely, drain them upon a napkin, and dish them up in a close circle similarly to cutlets; fill the centre with a *Financière ragout* (No. 188), pour some of the sauce round the *entrée*, and serve.

Note.—*Galantines* dressed in this manner may also be served with endive, sorrel, *purée* of green-peas or asparagus, stewed peas, or *à la Macédoine*.

1012. GALANTINES OF LEGS OF FOWLS, A LA JARDINIERE.

IN this case, the legs of the fowls should be entirely laid open with the knife, and all the bones removed; they must then be spread out upon the table, seasoned with pepper and salt, and a table-spoonful of force-meat, mixed with fine-herbs, placed in the centre of each; then sew them up in an oblong or oval form, and place them in a stewpan on a bed of sliced carrot, onion, and celery, covered with thin layers of fat bacon, and braized as directed in the foregoing case. When the *galantines* are done, put them in press between two dishes until they become cold; they should then be trimmed and placed in a sautapan with a little *consommé* covered with a buttered paper. When about to send to table, put the *galantines* in the oven to simmer gently for a quarter of an hour; then glaze and dish them up in a close circle, with a braized lettuce, nicely trimmed (No. 164), placed in between each; fill the centre with a *Jardinière* (No. 144), pour some half-glaze or *Espagnole* sauce round the base of the *entrée*, and serve.

1013. MINCED AND GRILLED FOWL.

Cut off the legs of a roast fowl, trim and score them over on both sides, and season them with pepper and salt; then cut the meat off the breast, &c., into fine shreds, and put this into a small stewpan, with a little *Béchamel* sauce (No. 5). When about to send to table, broil the legs of a fowl over a clear fire, glaze them, and having previously warmed the mince, pour it out into the centre of the dish, place the legs upon it, and serve.

1014. ANOTHER METHOD.

Trim the legs and cut up the mince as in the foregoing case. Next, put an ounce of fresh butter into a small stewpan over the fire to melt, incorporate therewith a spoonful of flour, and stir these together for two minutes; then add about a gill of broth, and the same proportion of cream; season with pepper and salt, grated nutmeg, and a small piece of glaze: stir this sauce on the stove, keep it boiling for ten minutes, and then add it to the minced chicken. In all other respects, serve this *entrée* in the same way as the foregoing.

1015. MINCED CHICKEN, AND POACHED EGGS.

Cut up all the white meat of a roast or boiled fowl into mince or shreds, and put these into a small stewpan with a gravy-spoonful of good *Béchamel* sauce; when about to send to table, warm the mince, dish it up, and place the poached eggs round it with a scollop of glazed tongue or of ham, and a fried *crôuton* of bread in between each egg; pour a little white sauce round the *entrée*, and serve.

1016. MINCED CHICKEN, WITH MACARONI.

In this case prepare the chicken or fowl in small thin scollops, and add to them some *Béchamel:* when about to dish them up, first place some macaroni (dressed with grated Parmesan cheese and a spoonful of *Béchamel* sauce) round the bottom of the dish in the form of a border, and put the mince in the centre piled up like a cone; pour a little white sauce round the *entrée*, and serve.

1017. MINCED CHICKEN, WITH RICE.

Prepare the mince as directed in the foregoing instance. Put six ounces of Carolina rice, after it has been well washed, into a stewpan with a pat of butter and a pint of broth, a little salt and mignionette pepper: set the lid on and place it over a slow fire to boil very gently until the grains are become quite soft, and all the moisture is absorbed; then add the yolks of two eggs and a spoonful of sauce;

work the rice with a wooden spoon, then fill a circular border mould (previously buttered inside) with it, and turn it out upon its dish; fill the centre of this with the mince, and serve.

1018. MINCE, OR SCOLLOPS, OF FOWL AU GRATIN

Cut the meat off the breast and other white parts of a roast or boiled fowl, either into shreds or scollops; put these into a small stewpan with some *Allemande* sauce (No. 12), about a table-spoonful of grated Parmesan cheese, a little nutmeg, pepper, and salt, a small piece of glaze, and half a gill of cream; toss the whole together over the fire until well mixed, and then place the scollops in the dish, piled up in a dome; cover this entirely with a coating of fried bread-crumbs mixed with grated Parmesan cheese, in the proportion of two-thirds of the former with one-third of the latter; sprinkle a very little clarified butter over the surface, place round the *entrée* a border of neatly cut fancy *croûtons* of bread, of *fleurons*, of *croquettes* of rice, or of potatoes (previously fried), and then put it into the oven for about ten minutes, taking care that it does not get burnt. Next pour some *Béchamel* sauce round the base of the *entrée*, and serve.

1019. KROMESKYS, A LA RUSSE

Cut the fillets of a roast fowl into very small neat dice, and put them on a plate with half their quantity of mushrooms and truffles, also cut into small dice. Stir the *Béchamel* or *Allemande* sauce over the fire until stiffly reduced, and then throw in the minced chicken, &c., mix the whole well together, to spread it out upon a dish about an inch thick, and put it to cool in the larder. Next, cut this preparation into small pieces somewhat in the form of a common cork, and place them on an earthen dish. A calf's udder, previously braized for the purpose, must be cut, when cold, into very thin layers, just large enough to wrap one of the *Kromeskys* round with; they must then be dipped in some light batter, and fried crisp in plenty of hog's-lard made hot for the purpose. Dish them up with fried parsley in the centre and round the base, and serve them the moment they are done.

1020. CROQUETTES OF FOWL AND MUSHROOMS.

The mince for these is prepared in the same way as for *Kromeskys*, and when it has become cold, must be cut up in pieces about the size of a plover's egg, and rolled with a little bread-crumb, either in the form of corks, pears, or very small cutlets; they must next be dipped in beaten eggs and bread-crumbed a second time; roll them smooth, and if they have been shaped like pears, a stalk of green parsley should be stuck into each to imitate the stalk of pears. Just before sending to table, fry the *croquettes* of a light color in hog's-lard made quite hot for the purpose, dish them up on a napkin with fried parsley, and serve.

1021. MINCE, OR SALPICON FOR PATTIES.

Cut the fillets of a roast fowl into small dice, then take two dozen mushrooms, one truffle, and a small piece of red tongue, and cut these also in a similar way; mix all these with the fowl, add enough sauce, either *Béchamel, Allemande,* or *Espagnole,* and use this for garnishing patties, or *croûstades.*

ENTREES OF PIGEONS AND DUCKLINGS,

COMPRISING

Pigeons, *à la Gauthier.*
  „ *à la Crapaudine.*
  „ *à la Duchesse.*
  „ *à la Séville.*
  „ *au gratin*, in a case.
  „ *à la Maintenon.*
Compote of Pigeons, with Mushrooms.
  „ with Peas.
Fillets of Pigeons, *à la Villeroi.*

Fillets of Pigeons, *à la Borghese.*
  „ *à la Bourguignotte.*
  „ *à l'Allemande.*
Ducklings, *à la Rouennaise.*
  „ stewed with Olives.
  „ with stewed Peas.
Fillets of Ducklings, *à la Bigarrade.*
  „ *à la Macédoine.*
Salmis of Fillets of Ducklings.

1022. PIGEONS, A LA GAUTHIER.

PROCURE four young fat pigeons, draw, singe, and truss them with their legs thrust inside. Next, put a half pound of fresh butter into a small stewpan with the juice of a lemon, a little mignionette pepper, and salt; place this over a stove-fire, and when it is melted, put the pigeons, with a garnished faggot of parsley, in it, cover the whole with thin layers of fat bacon and a circular piece of buttered paper, and set them to simmer very gently on a slow fire for about twenty minutes, when they will be done. The pigeons must then be drained upon a napkin, and after all the greasy moisture has been absorbed, place them in the dish in the form of a square, with a large *quenelle* of fowl (decorated with truffles) in between each pigeon; fill the centre with a *ragout* of crayfish-tails (No. 196), pour some of the sauce over and round the pigeons, and serve

1023. PIGEONS, A LA CRAPAUDINE.

AFTER the pigeons have been cut in halves, lengthwise through the breast, flatten each of these with a cutlet-bat, and then remove the bones from the breasts and legs; season with pepper and salt, and simmer them in a sautapan with some clarified butter over the fire until they become partly set; they must then be put in press betwwen two dishes, and when they have become cold, should be bread-crumbed twice : first after being dipped in the beaten egg, and the second time in clarified butter. When about to send to table, broil the pigeons of a light color over a clear fire; then glaze them lightly, and dish them up, pour some *Poivrade* sauce (No. 29), to which must be added some chopped and parboiled shalots and parsley, and serve.

1024. PIGEONS, A LA DUCHESSE.

REMOVE the bones entirely from six very young pigeons; stuff them with some *quenelle* force-meat of veal mixed with a spoonful of sauce and some chopped mushrooms; sew them up neatly so as to give them an appearance of plumpness; put them in a stewpan with some white *poële* (No. 230), and braize them very gently over a slow fire for about twenty minutes; the pigeons must next be removed on to a dish and allowed to become partially cold; they should then be covered all over with a thin coating of reduced *Allemande* sauce (No. 7), and when this is become set upon them by cooling, roll them first in bread-crumbs, then dip them in beaten egg and bread-crumb them over again, and place them on a dish in the larder. About twenty minutes before dinner-time, place the pigeons carefully upon the wire lining of a frying-pan, and immerse them in plenty of clean hog's-lard, made quite hot for the purpose; as soon as they have acquired a light-brown color, remove them from the frying-pan on to a napkin to absorb any grease. Then pile up some *Macédoine* of vegetables (No. 143) in the centre of the dish, place the pigeons round this in circular order, with the breasts resting on the bottom of the dish; put a decorated fillet of chicken in between each pigeon, surmount the *entrée* with a group of nicely-turned small vegetables, pour some *Allemande* or *Béchamel* sauce round the base of the *entrée*, and serve.

1025. PIGEONS, A LA SEVILLE.

THESE are prepared, in the first instance, in the same way as the foregoing, excepting that they must be braized in some wine *mirepoix* (No. 236), and they should be also covered with thin layers of fat bacon, and only moistened half their depth; braize them gently for about twenty minutes, frequently basting them with their own liquor. When the pigeons are done, drain them upon a napkin, remove the strings, and dish them up with their backs resting up against a small *croustade* of fried bread, previously made fast on the bottom of the dish; garnish with a Spanish *ragout*, place a large crayfish between each pigeon, and a decorated minion fillet of fowl upon their breasts, surmount the whole with a small larded sweetbread, and serve. The *ragout* above alluded to consists of small truffles, carrots, pieces of ham, mushrooms, and a few boiled *garbanças*, or yellow peas; these must be first slightly fried in a little oil, and a spoonful of Tomata sauce, a glass of Malaga or Madeira, with a pinch of the powder of the sweet red Pimento, and a piece of glaze added; simmer the whole together over a slow fire until the carrots are done; then skim off all the grease, add a small ladleful of finished *Espagnole* sauce (No. 3), and two dozen cloves of garlic, previously boiled in water; the *ragout* must be allowed to boil gently by the side of the stove for five minutes longer; then, after it has been skimmed, add the juice of half a lemon and use it as directed.

1026. PIGEONS, AU GRATIN, IN A CASE.

REMOVE all the bones from six young pigeons, then make some force-meat of fat livers (No. 249), and stuff the pigeons with this; they must next be trussed and gently braized for about a quarter of an hour in a small quantity of moistening, after this removed on to a dish and placed in the larder to become cold. Make a circular case of stout paper, oil it over, and place it in the oven for a few minutes to make it firm; line this case with some of the force-meat, and place the pigeons in it in neat order; fill up the cavities with the remainder of the force-meat, cover them over with very thin layers of fat bacon, and then set the case in the oven to be baked for about half an hour. The bacon must then be removed, and all the grease absorbed by gently pressing a clean napkin upon it, and put on its dish. Place some scollops of mushrooms and truffles, simmered wtth a spoonful of fine-herbs on the top, pour some brown Italian sauce (No. 12) over the *entrée*, and serve.

1027. PIGEONS, A LA MAINTENON.

SPLIT four young pigeons lengthwise, flatten and bone them, and then season with pepper and salt; fry them in a sautapan with a little butter, some chopped mushrooms, parsley, and two shalots, and when this is done, add a large spoonful of *Allemande* sauce, a little essence of mushrooms, grated nutmeg, and lemon-juice; simmer the whole together for five minutes, and allow them partially to cool. Next, trim off the corners from as many sheets of note-paper as there are pieces of pigeon, and after the paper has been oiled over with a paste-brush, place the pigeons in them—dividing the sauce equally; twist the edges of the paper neatly and firmly, so as to secure the sauce from oozing out, and broil them over a very moderate fire; dish them up in close circular order upon a napkin, and send to table with some brown Italian sauce (No. 12), separately in a boat.

1028. COMPOTE OF PIGEONS, WITH MUSHROOMS.

TRUSS and then braize four pigeons with three quarters of a pound of streaky bacon. Peel half a pint of button onions, and after they have been parboiled in water, drain and fry them in a little butter over a very slow fire without allowing them to acquire any color; they must then be drained upon a sieve, and afterward placed in a small stewpan with half a pottle of mushrooms, and the bacon cut up in square dice. With the broth from the pigeons, make enough brown sauce for the *entrée*, and as soon as it has been sufficiently worked, add this as well as a glass of white wine to the onions, &c., and set the whole to boil very gently by the side of a stove-fire for about ten minutes : then skim off the grease, and place this *ragout* in a stewpan with the pigeons. When about to send to table, make the *compôte* of pigeons hot, dish up the pigeons with a *crôuton* of fried bread between each, put the pieces of bacon in the cavities formed between the pigeons, group the mushrooms and onions in the centre, pour the sauce over the *entrée*, and serve.

1029. COMPOTE OF PIGEONS, WITH PEAS.

TRUSS the pigeons as for boiling. Parboil three quarters of a pound of streaky bacon in water for a quarter of an hour, and then cut it into rather large dice-shaped pieces; put these into a middle-sized stew-pan and fry them of a light color over a stove-fire, remove these on to a plate, and then throw in the pigeons and fry them also, until they acquire a light-brown color, and place them with the bacon. Next, add two table-spoonfuls of flour to the fat in the stewpan, and stir this *roux* over the fire until it acquires a light color, then gradually mix in with it a quart of broth ; stir the sauce over the fire until it boils, add the pigeons, bacon, a quart of green-peas, a faggot of parsley, and green onions, and a little mignionette pepper, and keep the *compôte* gently boiling by the side of a stove-fire for about three quarters of an hour ; then skim off all the grease, and remove the faggot, and if the sauce is not sufficiently reduced, place the pigeons in another stewpan, and with a colander-spoon remove the peas and bacon also ; allow the sauce to boil briskly on the fire, stirring it the while, until reduced to its proper consistency, and then pour it to the *compôte*. When about to send to table, make the *compôte* quite hot, and dish it up in the same way as the foregoing.

1030. ANOTHER METHOD.

BRAIZE the pigeons together with a piece of streaky bacon (after it has been parboiled); when these are done, prepare a quart of young peas for stewing in the usual way, to which add about half a pint of the liquor from the pigeons to moisten and flavor them with, and when these have been stewed, and all their moisture boiled down to a glaze, thicken them by adding two ounces of fresh butter kneaded with a dessert-spoonful of flour; cut the bacon into fluted oval scollops, dish up the pigeons, first placing some of the peas in the centre of the dish to support them upright, then place the scollops of bacon in rows between the pigeons, or round them, pile the peas up in the centre; pour some bright *Espagnole* sauce, worked with some of the liquor from the pigeons, round the *entrée*, glaze the pigeons and the bacon, and serve.

1031. FILLETS OF PIGEONS, A LA VILLEROI.

FILLET six pigeons, remove the thin skin from them, and also the sinew from the under fillet, which must, however, be left adhering to the upper; flatten them slightly with a small bat, or the handle of a knife, dipped in water, and trim them; they must then be covered entirely with a coating of *D'Uxelles* sauce (No. 16), and when this has become firmly set upon the fillets by cooling, they should be bread-crumbed twice; once, after being dipped in beaten egg, and then after being dipped in clarified butter. Use the bones from the legs to imitate the bones of cutlets; and place the fillets carefully in a sauta-pan lined with clarified butter. Just before sending to table, fry the fillets of a light color on both sides, drain them on paper, glaze them lightly and dish them up in a close circle; fill the centre with a *Macédoine* of vegetables, asparagus-peas, French beans, or stewed peas; pour some bright half-glaze (made from the carcasses of the pigeons) round the *entrée*, and serve.

1032. FILLETS OF PIGEONS, A LA BORGHESE.

TRIM the fillets, insert the cutlet-bone in each, as in the foregoing case, and put them on an earthen dish: next, bone the carcasses of the pigeons, and remove the skin and sinews from the flesh, and with this make some *quenelle* force-meat (No. 244). Season the fillets of pigeons with a little pepper and salt, and neatly mask them over with a coating of the force-meat, thus increasing their size about one-half; cover the bottom of a sauta-pan with some clarified butter, about one-eighth of an inch thick, and having allowed this to become quite cold, put in the fillets thus prepared in circular rows, and cover them with some clarified butter, which, however, should not be poured over them until it has become nearly cold. About a quarter of an hour before sending to table, place a sauta-pan containing the fillets upon a rather brisk fire, and allow them to simmer quickly; and when they are done on both sides, drain them upon a napkin, and glaze them brightly; dish them up in close circular order, in the same way as cutlets, fill the centre with scollops of truffles, previously tossed over the fire with a small piece of glaze, half a pat of fresh butter, and a spoonful of sauce; pour some Madeira sauce (No. 8) round the base of the *entrée*, and serve.

1033. FILLETS OF PIGEONS, A LA BOURGUIGNOTTE.

PREPARE these in the same way as the foregoing, and when about to send to table, simmer them briskly over a stove-fire, and when done, drain, glaze, and dish them up in a close circle; fill the centre with a *ragout à la Bourguignotte* (No. 195), pour some of the sauce round the *entrée*, and serve.

1034. FILLETS OF PIGEONS, A L'ALLEMANDE.

PREPARE these in all respects according to the foregoing directions, and when the fillets have briskly simmered over a sharp fire, so as to become firmly set before they are more than half done, they must be immediately removed from the sauta-pan on an earthen dish, and after being separately dipped in some light-made batter, mixed with good cream, should be fried crisp in plenty of clean hog's-lard, made quite hot for the purpose; when done, drain them upon a napkin, and dish them up in a close circle; fill the centre with a *purée* of green peas, artichokes, or asparagus, with either a *Jardinière*, or *Macédoine*, stewed peas, or dressed young Windsor beans; pour some bright half-glaze (made from the carcasses) under the *entrée*, and serve.

1035. DUCKLINGS, A LA ROUENNAISE.

TRUSS two fat ducklings for boiling, put them in a stewpan, with about three-quarters of a pound of streaky bacon (previously parboiled), a carrot, an onion, and a garnished faggot of parsley, and cover them with thin layers of fat bacon and a round of buttered paper; moisten with a quart of white broth, and then set them to braize gently for about three-quarters of an hour. Cut a bunch of young turnips into the shape of large olives, or half-moons, and fry these in a stewpan with two ounces of clarified butter, and a dessert-spoonful of pounded sugar, over the fire, until they acquire a deep yellow color; then strain off the butter, and put the turnips into a smaller stewpan containing sufficient bright *Espagnole* sauce (No. 3) for the *entrée;* add a little of the liquor from the ducks to flavor them, and set them to boil gently by the side of a stove-fire until they are done, at the same time attending to the reduction of the sauce to its proper consistency. When about to send to table, the ducks may either be served whole, or cut up into small joints and neatly trimmed; pile these in the same manner as for a fricassee, keeping the fillets and breasts for the top; garnish the *entrée* with the turnips, place a border of scollops of streaky bacon round the base, pour the sauce over the ducks, and serve.

1036. DUCKLINGS, STEWED WITH OLIVES.

PREPARE these as in the foregoing case, and when done, cut each up into neatly-trimmed small joints, consisting of two legs, and two fillets with the pinions left on them; then cut the breast into two pieces, and also the back; clarify the liquor, and after it has been reduced by boiling to half-glaze, warm the pieces of ducklings in it, and dish them up as before directed; garnish the *entrée* with a *ragout* of olives, place the scollops of streaky bacon round the *entrée*, pour the sauce over the ducklings, and serve.

1037. DUCKLINGS, WITH STEWED PEAS.

PREPARE these as directed in the foregoing cases. Stew a quart of young peas (No. 146), and finish them with a little of the glaze made from the liquor in which the ducklings have been braized; the members or small joints of the ducklings must also be warmed in some of the same glaze, and dished up in a pile upon some of the stewed peas; garnish the base of the *entrée* with the remainder; place a row of scollops of the streaky bacon upon these, pour some bright *Espagnole* sauce (No. 3) over the *entrée*, and serve.

1038. FILLETS OF DUCKLINGS, A LA BIGARRADE.

DRAW and singe these, and pick out any remaining stubble-feathers on the ducklings; then separate the breast from the legs and backs, by running the knife in just above the thighs and cutting through the upper part of the back under the wings; roast the backs and use them for making the *Bigarrade* sauce with (No. 33). Place the breasts in a deep earthen dish, season with a little mignionette pepper, salt, parsley, bay-leaf, thyme, three table-spoonfuls of salad oil, and the juice of a lemon, and allow them to steep in this for several hours; about three-quarters of an hour before dinner, run a large iron skewer through the breasts of the ducklings, and tie them on a spit, then place the whole of the seasoning upon them, wrap them up with a large sheet of oiled paper, and set them before the fire for about twenty minutes: at the end of that time, remove the paper and seasoning, and allow the ducklings to acquire a bright color; then remove them from the spit, observing that they should be done with the gravy in them. The fillets must then be taken out, slightly trimmed and scored, and placed in a sautapan with a little half-glaze or some of the sauce, and allowed barely to simmer over a stove-fire to warm; they should then be dished up in a close circle with a fried *crôuton* of bread in between each fillet; pour the *Bigarrade* sauce over the *entrée*, and serve.

1039. FILLETS OF DUCKLINGS, A LA MACEDOINE.

THESE must be prepared in the same manner as the foregoing; when the fillets are trimmed, place them in a sautapan with some half-glaze made from the carcasses, and when about to send to table, warm them without allowing them to boil, as that would make them tough; dish them up in a close circle with a *crôuton* of fried bread in between each fillet, fill the centre with a *Macédoine* of vegetables (No. 143), pour some bright half-glaze round the base, and serve.

1040. SALMIS OF FILLETS OF DUCKLINGS.

PREPARE the breasts of the ducklings, and roast them off in the manner directed for those *à la Bigarrade;* cut them out, trim and score them, and place them in a sautapan with a little half-glaze. Next, roast the legs of a light-brown color, and when done, break them up, and put them into a stewpan with four shalots, a handful of parsley, a dozen pepper-corns, some mushroom trimmings, a bay-leaf, and sprig of thyme; moisten with a pint of Claret or Sauterne wine, and set this to boil very gently over a slow fire for about half an hour; then, strain it off through a sieve, add this extract or essence to an equal proportion of *Espagnole* sauce (No. 3), and work it in the ordinary manner: when it has been cleared by gentle ebullition, and afterward reduced by boiling to its proper consistency, strain it through a tammy into a *bain-marie*. When about to send to table, warm the fillets carefully, dish them up as in the former cases, fill the centre with scollops of truffles and mushrooms, pour the sauce over the *entrée*, and serve.

Note.—In addition to the foregoing methods for dressing ducklings for *entrées*, they may also, if intended to be served whole, be treated according to the directions for dressing ducks for removes and flanks; for which, see those articles.

ENTREES OF QUAILS,

COMPRISING

Quails, with stewed Peas.	Cutlets of Quails, *à la Bordelaise.*
„ *à la Périgueux.*	Fillets of Quails, *à la Talleyrand.*
„ *à la Financière.*	„ *à la Parisiènne.*
„ *à la Royale.*	Scollops of Quails, with Truffles.
Cutlets of Quails, *à la Maréchale.*	„ with Cucumbers.

1041. QUAILS, WITH STEWED PEAS.

TRUSS eight quails in the same manner as chickens are trussed for boiling, put them into a stewpan with half a pound of streaky bacon, and a garnished faggot of parsley in the centre, cover them with thin layers of fat bacon, moisten with some wine *mirepoix* (No. 236), and braize the quails gently for about three-quarters of an hour. Prepare about a pint of stewed peas, and finish them with a little of the *mirepoix* reduced to a glaze; dish up the quails in a circle with their breasts placed outward, fill the centre with the stewed peas, place a scollop of streaky bacon in between each quail, pour some *Espagnole* sauce, finished with some of the *mirepoix*, round and over the *entrée*, and serve.

1042. QUAILS, A LA PERIGUEUX.

DRAW eight fine fat quails, taking care not to tear the pouch, or skin of the throat; fill each with some truffles cut into very small olives, and prepared as for stuffing fowls, &c., *à la Périgueux* (No. 660); then truss them in the same manner as fowls for boiling. Next, cover the bottom of a stewpan with thin layers of bacon, and place the quails thereon; put a garnished faggot of parsley, and a clove of garlic in the centre, cover them with layers of bacon, and moisten with some wine *mirepoix* (No. 236): braize them gently for about three-quarters of an hour, and when done, dish them up with their backs resting upright against a small ornamental *croûstade* of fried bread previously fastened on the centre of the dish; place a large white cock's-comb between each quail, and some double cocks'-combs in the centre, with a large truffle to crown the whole; pour some *Périgueux* sauce (No. 23) over the *entrée*, and serve.

1042. QUAILS, A LA FINANCIERE.

REMOVE the bones entirely from eight fat quails, reserve the livers, and add to them half a pound of fat livers of fowl, with which prepare some force-meat (No. 249), and stuff the quails with part of this;

they must then be trussed in the usual manner, and placed in a stewpan with thin layers of fat bacon under them, a garnished faggot of parsley in the centre, and covered with layers of fat bacon ; moisten with some wine *mirepoix* (No. 236), and braize them gently for about three-quarters of an hour. Prepare a rich *Financière ragout* (No. 188), the sauce of which must be finished with some of the liquor in which the quails have been braized. When about to send to table, warm the quails, drain and dish them up, garnish the centre with the *Financière*, pour some of the sauce round the *entrée*, and serve.

1044. QUAILS, A LA ROYALE.

BONE eight quails, then stuff them with some *quenelle* force-meat, and truss them in the usual manner ; place them in a stewpan with some sliced carrot, an onion, two cloves, and a garnished faggot of parsley ; moisten with a pint of white broth, cover with a round of buttered paper, put the lid on, and set them to braize very gently by the side of a stove-fire for about three-quarters of an hour ; then allow them partially to cool in their own liquor, after which they must be taken out and placed upon a dish in the larder to become cold ; the  strings should then be removed, and the quails entirely covered with a coating of *d'Uxelles* sauce (No. 16) ; when this has become firmly set by cooling, roll them in bread-crumbs, afterwards dip them in beaten egg, and bread-crumb them over again. When about to send to table,. place the quails upon the wire-lining of a frying-pan, and immerse them in plenty of clean hog's-lard made quite hot for the purpose ; fry them of a light-brown color, then drain and dish them up on a border of *quenelle* force-meat previously turned out on the dish ; fill the centre with a white *Toulouse ragout* (No. 187), place a decorated minion fillet of chicken between each quail, pour some *Allemande* sauce round the base of the *entrée*, and serve.

1045. CUTLETS OF QUAILS, A LA MARECHALE.

SPLIT the quails into halves, remove the breast, pinion, and part of the back-bones, leaving the leg entire, which must be passed through the skin of the thigh to give them the appearance of cutlets ; flatten them slightly with a small bat, season with pepper and salt, then mask them over with a thin coating of *Allemande* sauce (No. 7), and bread-crumb them twice upon this : once after being dipped in beaten egg, and then in clarified butter : pat them into shape with the blade of a knife, and place them in neat order in a sautapan with some clarified butter. Fry the cutlets of a light color over a rather brisk fire ; when done, drain and glaze them lightly, and dish them up in the same way as other cutlets ; fill. the centre with either a *Macédoine* of vegetables (No. 143), or scollops of cucumbers, stewed peas, asparagus-peas, or a *purée* of artichokes ; pour some half-glaze, or a little *Suprême* sauce, round the *entrée*, and serve.

1046. CUTLETS OF QUAILS, A LA BORDELAISE.

TRIM the quails into cutlets in the same way as directed in the fore-going case, season them with pepper and salt, and place them in a sautapan with a little clarified butter ; fry them over a brisk fire, and as soon as they have acquired a light color on both sides, pour off all the grease, add a spoonful of glaze, and toss them in it over the fire ; then dish them up in a close circle with the legs uppermost, fill the centre with scollops of truffles and mushrooms, pour some *Bordelaise* sauce (No. 57), over the cutlets, and serve.

1047. FILLETS OF QUAILS, A LA TALLEYRAND.

FILLET eight quails, and with the carcasses make some essence (No. 218) ; trim the fillets, and stick a short bone (reserved from the legs) into them, to imitate cutlets ; then place them in a sautapan with some clarified butter. Prepare sixteen fried *croûtons* of bread cut in the shape and size of the fillets, and fill these with some *farce* made from the quails' livers ; prepare also some scollops of fat livers, truffles and mushrooms, and put them into a small stewpan with a little *Alle-mande* sauce (No. 7); finish some *Suprême* sauce (No. 38) by incorpo-rating therein the reduced essence of quails, and keep it in a small *bain-marie.* Just before sending to table, simmer the fillets over a moderate stove-fire, and when done, pour off all the grease, add a little of the *Suprême* sauce, toss the fillets in it, and dish them up as follows :—

First, place eight of the *croûtons* (previously warmed in the oven) at the bottom of the dish, so that the points meet in the centre ; then place a fillet upon each of these, after which repeat the *croûtons*, and then place the last row of fillets ; fill the centre with the scollops, pour the *Suprême* sauce over the fillets, and serve.

1048. FILLETS OF QUAILS, A LA PARISIENNE.

PREPARE the fillets and the *croûtons* as directed in the foregoing case, and finish and dish them up in the same way ; fill the centre of the *entrée* with a *Parisian ragout* (No. 203), pour some of the sauce over the fillets, and serve.

1049. SCOLLOPS OF QUAILS, WITH TRUFFLES.

FILLET eight quails ; trim each fillet into two scollops, and place the whole of these into a sautapan with some clarified butter ; season with a little pepper and salt, and place a round of buttered paper over them. Use the carcasses to make some extract or essence with, which when done must be clarified, boiled down to glaze, and incorporated with some finished *Espagnole* sauce (No. 3), and put into a small *bain-marie.* Simmer the scollops over a moderate fire, and as soon as they are done, pour off all the butter, and add half the sauce with about half a pound of truffles cut into scollops ; toss them over the stove-fire for two minutes without allowing them to boil ; pile them up in the centre of the dish, pour the remainder of the sauce over them, garnish the *entrée* with a border of potato *croquettes* or *fleurons*, and serve.

1050. SCOLLOPS OF QUAILS, WITH CUCUMBERS.

THESE are prepared in the same manner as the foregoing. When about to send to table, simmer them over the stove-fire, and when done, pour off the butter, add some scollops of cucumbers (No. 138), and some of the essence made from the carcasses boiled down to a glaze ; toss them over the fire for two minutes, and pile them up in the centre of the dish ; garnish the *entrée* round with a border of *croquettes* made with the legs, and serve.

ENTREES OF LARKS,

COMPRISING

Larks, *à la Minute.*	Larks, with Fine-herbs.
„ *à la Chipolata.*	„ with Truffles, *à l'Italiènne.*

1051. LARKS, A LA MINUTE.

Cut off the legs, and pick out the gizzards with the point of a small knife ; then place the larks in a deep sautapan previously spread with butter ; season with pepper and salt, and fry them over a brisk fire until they have acquired a brown color, and are nearly done ; all the grease must be poured off, and a large gravy-spoonful of *Espagnole* sauce, half a pottle of mushrooms, a small piece of glaze, a pat of butter, and the juice of half a lemon, should then be added ; toss them over the stove-fire until the whole is well mixed, then dish up the larks with fried *croûtons* of bread round them, pour the mushrooms and sauce over the *entrée*, and serve.

1052. LARKS, A LA CHIPOLATA.

Prepare and fry the larks as directed in the foregoing case, and when done, pour off the grease, and add some *Chipolata ragout* (No. 190) ; toss and simmer this over the stove-fire for five minutes, then dish up eight of the larks upon as many small oval *croûtons*, place eight more *croûtons* on these, and set a like number of larks upon them ; fill the centre with the *ragout*, pour the sauce over the *entrée*, and serve.

1053. LARKS, WITH FINE-HERBS.

Trim the larks and draw the gizzards, place them in a sautapan with a little butter, pepper and salt ; fry them of a light brown color over a brisk fire, and then add a table-spoonful of chopped mushrooms, an equal proportion of parsley, and two shalots also chopped ; simmer these with the larks for five minutes longer, then add a gravy-spoonful of *Espagnole* sauce (No. 3), a small piece of glaze, a pat of butter, the juice of half a lemon and a little grated nutmeg ; toss the whole well together over the fire for two minutes, and dish them in a neat pyramidal form, place some *croûtons* of fried bread round the *entrée*, pour the sauce over it, and serve.

1054. LARKS, WITH TRUFFLES, A L'ITALIENNE.

Fry these as directed in the foregoing cases, and when they have acquired a light-brown color, pour off the grease, add some brown Italian sauce (No. 12), half a pottle of mushrooms, and about two ounces of truffles cut into scollops ; toss the whole together over the fire for five minutes, dish up the larks in double rows, with *croûtons* of bread in between each row, fill the centre with the truffles and mushrooms, pour the sauce over the *entrée*, and serve.

ENTREES OF RABBITS,

COMPRISING

Rabbit, *à la Chasseur.*	Fillets of Rabbits, larded, *à la Toulouse,* &c.
„ fried in Batter, with *Poivrade*	„ *à la Maréchale,* &c.
sauce.	*Blanquette* of Rabbit, *à l'Ecarlate.*
„ *à la Bourguignonne.*	*Polpettes* of Rabbit, *à l'Italiènne.*
„ *à la Périgueux.*	

1055. RABBIT, A LA CHASSEUR.

CUT up the rabbit into small joints, as follows :—first, take off the hind legs even with the loins, then remove the shoulders, split the head into halves, and divide the loins into six pieces ; trim these neatly without waste, and place them in a sautapan with two ounces of clarified butter, pepper and salt. Fry them of a light-brown color over a rather brisk fire, and add a table-spoonful of chopped fine-herbs, consisting of mushrooms, truffle, parsley, and shalot ; then put the lid on, and set the rabbit over a slow fire for about ten minutes longer ; next pour off all the grease, add a large gravy-spoonful of *Espagnole* sauce, some scollops of mushrooms and truffles, two dozen small *quenelles* of rabbit, a small piece of glaze, a little nutmeg, and the juice of half a lemon ; simmer the whole together on the stove-fire for three minutes, then pile up the pieces of rabbit in the dish, arrange the *ragout* over this in neat groups, pour the sauce over the *entrée*, place some *croûtons* of fried bread round it, and serve.

1056. RABBIT FRIED IN BATTER, WITH POIVRADE SAUCE.

CUT the rabbit up as in the foregoing case, and then follow the directions given for dressing chickens in this manner (No. 988).

1057. RABBITS, A LA BOURGUIGNONNE.

CUT the rabbits up into small joints, season with pepper and salt, and fry them slightly over the fire, without allowing them to acquire much color, adding half a pint of button-onions previously parboiled in water, a very little grated nutmeg and half a pottle of mushrooms ; toss these over the fire for five minutes, then add a tumblerful of French white wine (Chablis or Sauterne), and set this to boil sharply until reduced to half the quantity ; next, add two large gravy-spoonfuls of *Velouté* sauce (No. 4), simmer the whole together gently for ten minutes longer, and finish by incorporating a leason of four yolks of eggs, the juice of half a lemon, and a dessert-spoonful of chopped parboiled parsley ; dish up the pieces of rabbit in a pyramidal form, garnish the *entrée* with the onions, &c., placed in groups round the base, pour the sauce over it, and serve.

1058. RABBITS, A LA PERIGUEUX.

CUT these up, and fry them with a little butter of a light-brown color : pour off the grease, add some *Périgueux* sauce (No. 23), four ounces of truffles cut into scollops, and two dozen small *quenelles* of rabbit, and simmer the whole together over the stove-fire for five minutes; dish up the *entrée* with *croûtons* round it, garnish with the *ragout*, pour the sauce over it, and serve.

1059. FILLETS OF RABBITS LARDED, A LA TOULOUSE.

FILLET four or six rabbits (according to the number of guests), trim the fillets and lard two-thirds of each—beginning at the thick end; then place them in a circular row, all curved in the same direction, in a sautapan, the bottom of which should be lined with thin layers of fat bacon. About twenty minutes before sending to table, pour a little strong *consommé* or thin half-glaze to the fillets, place a round piece of buttered paper upon them, and set them in the oven to simmer for ten minutes; then remove the paper, dry the larding and glaze it, frequently basting the fillets with their own glaze; next, drain them upon a napkin, trim and dish them up in a close circle, fill the centre with *ragout à la Toulouse* (No. 187), pour some of the sauce round the base, glaze the larding of the fillets, and serve.

Note.—Fillets of rabbits larded, may also be garnished with either a *ragout à la Parisiènne*, or *à la Financière;* with small *quenelles*, scollops of truffles, of mushrooms, or of cucumbers; and with any kind of dressed vegetables or *purées*.

1060. FILLETS OF RABBITS, A LA MARECHALE.

FILLET four rabbits, slightly flatten, and then trim the fillets, making an incision round the interior part of them; fill this with some *d'Uxelles* sauce (No. 16); mask them over with a thin coating of *Allemande* sauce, and when this has become firmly set by cooling, bread-crumb them twice: once dipped in beaten egg, and then, after being sprinkled over with clarified butter; broil the fillets over a clear fire of moderate heat, with a sheet of oiled paper placed upon the gridiron; when done of a light color on both sides, dish them up in a close circle, fill the centre with scollops of the kidneys and inner fillets, mixed with truffles and mushrooms, and tossed in a little *Allemande* sauce; glaze the fillets, pour some bright *Espagnole* sauce, worked with essence made from the carcasses, round the base of the *entrée*, and serve.

Note.—These fillets may also be served with some bright aspic, with cucumbers, a *purée* of celery, or white Italian sauce.

1061. BLANQUETTE OF RABBITS, A L'ECARLATE.

FILLET three rabbits, cut off the hind-quarters, place them upon an iron skewer; lay this upon a large sheet of thickly-buttered paper, season with pepper and salt, and strew upon it some thinly-sliced carrot, an onion, parsley, thyme, and bay-leaf; wrap the paper round them, and then tie the skewer upon a spit, and roast them before the fire for about twenty minutes; then take them up on a dish, and leave them in the paper till they have become cold; the meat must next be peeled off, cut into small dice, and made up into *croquettes* (No. 1020). Trim the fillets, and place them in a sautapan with a little clarified butter, pepper and salt, and simmer them in the oven or over a slow fire for about ten minutes, without allowing them to acquire any color; then drain them, and cut them into sloping scollops; put these into a stewpan with one-third of their proportion of scollops or red tongue and some mushrooms; add two gravy-spoonfuls of *Allemande* sauce (No. 7), warm the *Blanquette*, gently tossing it over the fire, and dish it up in the form of a dome; garnish it round with the *croquettes*, previously fried, mask the *Blanquette* with a spoonful of the sauce, and serve.

1062. POLPETTES OF RABBITS, A L'ITALIENNE.

ROAST two rabbits, and when they are cold, cut off all the meat and chop it up fine; put this into a stewpan with a tablespoonful of chopped mushrooms, an equal proportion of parsley and two shalots, also chopped, four ounces of grated Parmesan cheese, a little grated nutmeg, and two gravy-spoonfuls of reduced *Velouté* sauce; stir these together over the fire until well mixed, then add the yolks of four eggs, and spread the preparation out in a square, about half an inch thick, upon an earthen dish; when this has become cold, stamp the *Polpettes* out with a circular tin-cutter about an inch and a half in diameter; bread-crumb them twice in the usual manner, place them in a sautapan with some clarified butter, and fry them of a light color over a brisk fire; when done, drain them upon a napkin, dish them up in double circular rows, pour some brown Italian sauce under them, and serve.

Note.—Besides the foregoing methods of dressing rabbits for *entrées*, they may also be served in almost every variety of form in which chickens or fowls (previously cut up into small joints) are directed to be prepared; *purées*, minces, *salpicons*, and every kind of *quenelles* and *boudins*, may also be made with rabbits; for which consult those articles in that part of the work treating of *entrées* of chickens and fowls, and proceed in the same manner.

ENTREES OF HARE,

COMPRISING

Fillets of Hare, larded, with *Poivrade* Sauce.	Cutlets of Hare, *à l'Ancienne.*
„ *à la Chasseur.*	Scollops of Hare, with Fine-Herbs.
„ *à l'Allemande.*	„ *à la Périgueux.*
Cutlets of Hare, *à la Portuguaise.*	*Civet* of Hare, with Mushrooms.

1063. FILLETS OF HARE LARDED, WITH POIVRADE SAUCE.

IF the hares used for this purpose are full grown, three will suffice; they must be filleted, and each fillet split into halves; these should be trimmed and larded, and placed in a curve at the bottom of a sautapan lined with thin layers of fat bacon. Moisten with some *mirepoix* (No. 236), place a round of buttered paper upon the fillets, and set them in the oven to simmer for twenty minutes, frequently basting them with their own liquor; when they are nearly done, remove the paper, dry the larding and glaze it; drain the fillets upon a napkin, trim and dish them up in a close circle, pour some *Poivrade*, Tomata, or Italian sauce under them, and serve.

Note.—These fillets may also be garnished in the same way as directed for fillets of rabbits.

1064. FILLETS OF HARES, A LA CHASSEUR.

PREPARE the fillets and place them in a sautapan as directed in the foregoing case. Use the carcasses for making some extract, or *fumet*, reserve the hind-quarters, run them on a large iron skewer, place them on a large sheet of paper thickly buttered, season with pepper and salt, and strew over them some thinly-sliced carrot and onion, parsley, bay-leaf, and thyme; wrap the paper round the legs, and fasten the skewer on the spit with string, then roast them before the fire for about half-an-hour, basting them frequently. When done, pare off all the meat, chop it very fine, and pound it in a mortar with a pat of butter and a spoonful of *Espagnole* sauce; rub it through a fine wire sieve or a tammy, and put the *purée* into a small stewpan. When about to send to table, braize and glaze the fillets as directed in the foregoing case, dish them up in a close circle, fill the centre with the *purée*, pour round the base of the *entrée*, and mask the *purée* with some bright *Espagnole* sauce worked with the *fumet;* glaze the larding of the fillets, and serve.

1065. FILLETS OF HARE, A L'ALLEMANDE.

LARD the fillets as in the foregoing cases, steep them in some *marinade* (No. 234) for six hours at least; drain and put them in a sautapan lined with thin layers of fat bacon, moisten with some wine *mirepoix*, braize and glaze them in the usual manner, and when done, dish them up in a close circle; fill the centre with large prunes stewed in red wine with a small stick of cinnamon, pour some cherry sauce *à la Victoria* (No. 64) round the base, place a border of *quenelles* of potatoes (No. 312) round the *entrée*, and serve.

1066. CUTLETS OF HARE, A LA PORTUGUAISE.

FILLET three hares, cut each fillet across into halves, flatten these slightly with a bat, trim them into the shape of cutlets, and scrape some of the ribs to resemble cutlet-bones; season with a little pepper and salt, mask them over with a thin coating of *Allemande* sauce, and bread-crumb the cutlets twice; once dipped in beaten egg, and afterwards sprinkled with clarified butter; pat them gently into shape, and place them in a sautapan with clarified butter. When about to send to table, fry the cutlets of a light colour, drain, glaze and dish them up in a close circle, fill the centre with yams previously cut into the form of olives, and fried in butter; pour some Portuguese sauce (No. 59) round the base, and serve.

1067. CUTLETS OF HARE, A L'ANCIENNE.

These must be trimmed as directed in the foregoing case, and placed in a buttered sautapan without being bread-crumbed; then season with pepper and salt, pour a little clarified butter over them, and with half the hind-quarters make some *purée* in the usual way— keeping this rather thick. Use the carcasses to make some *fumet* with, to be worked into some *Espagnole* sauce for the *entrée*. Cut as many *crôutons* of bread as there are cutlets, and of the same shape; draw the point of a small knife round the inside of the edge of the *crôutons*, and when they are fried of a light colour, remove the inner piece, fill the cavities of the *croûtons* with the *purée*, and place them in a sautapan with a round of buttered paper upon them. Just before dinner-time, simmer the cutlets over a gentle fire for about five minutes, turn them over when done on the under side, and allow them to remain two minutes longer ; pour off the butter, add a little glaze and a spoonful of the sauce, toss them in this, and dish them up in a close circle ; placing one of the *croûtons* (previously warmed) in between each cutlet; fill the centre with scollops of the kidneys and small fillets, truffles and mushrooms tossed in a little of the sauce, pour the sauce round the base of the *entrée*, and serve.

1068. SCOLLOPS OF HARE, WITH FINE-HERBS.

CUT the fillets of three hares into scollops, flatten them slightly with the handle of a knife dipped in water, trim them neatly and place them in a sautapan with clarified butter, season with pepper and salt, and fry them on both sides over a brisk fire for about five minutes ; pour off the butter, add some fine-herbs sauce (No. 14) and half a pottle of mushrooms ; simmer the scollops over the fire for two minutes, pile them up in the centre of the dish, pour the sauce over them, garnish round with *croquettes*, made with the hind-quarters, as in No. 1020, and serve.

1069. SCOLLOPS OF HARE, A LA PERIGUEUX.

PREPARE the scollops and fry them as directed in the foregoing case; pour off the butter, add some *Périgueux* sauce (No. 23) and some scollops of truffles ; simmer them over the stove-fire for three minutes, dish them up in the form of a dome, garnish round with *croquettes* in the form of pears, and serve.

Note.—Scollops of hares may also be finished with the following sauces :—*Poivrade*, Italian, Tomata, *Espagnole*, and *Bourguignotte ;* in either case scollops of truffles, tongue, or mushrooms, may be added.

1070. CIVET OF HARE, WITH MUSHROOMS.

CUT the hare into small joints, then parboil one pound of streaky bacon, and cut it into square pieces the size of small walnuts; fry these in a stewpan until they acquire a light-brown colour, then take them out on a plate, and fry the pieces of hare brown also. Next, shake a handful of flour over them, and toss them over the fire for three minutes ; add the fried bacon, a pottle of mushrooms, an onion stuck with four cloves, a carrot and a garnished faggot of parsley ; season with pepper and salt, moisten with a pint of port wine, and a quart of good broth, stir the *civet* on the fire till it boils, and then remove it to the side that it may clarify itself by gentle ebullition. Fry half a pint of button onions in a small stewpan with a little butter, for five minutes, and when the *civet* has boiled about half an hour, throw these in ; as soon as the pieces of hare become tender, remove the scum and grease from the surface, take out the onion, carrot, and faggot; and if there appear to be too much sauce, pour it into another stewpan, and reduce it by boiling, stirring it with a wooden spoon to prevent its burning, then pass it through a tammy upon the *civet*. Pile up the pieces of hare in the centre of the dish, and garnish round with the mushrooms, &c.; pour the sauce over it, place a dozen *croûtons* of fried bread cut in the shape of a heart round the base, and serve.

LEVERETS, when cut up in small joints, may be dressed in the same manner as rabbits; which see.

ENTREES OF PHEASANTS,

COMPRISING

Salmis of Pheasant, *à la Bourguignotte.*   Scollops of Pheasant, *à la Richelieu.*
    „   *à la Brésilienne.*   „   *à la Victoria.*
    „   *à la Paysanne.*   „   *à la Palerme.*
    „   *à la Chasseur.*

1071. SALMIS OF PHEASANT, A LA BOURGUIGNOTTE.

ROAST the pheasant, let it become cold, and then cut it up as follows:—First, remove the legs, then cut off the fillets with the pinion-bones adhering thereto, separate the breast from the back, trim them both, cut them crosswise into halves, and place all the pieces in a stew-pan. Next, chop up the trimmings and put them into a stewpan with three shalots sliced up, a small bay-leaf and sprig of thyme, a few pepper-corns, a blade of mace, and a pat of butter; fry these over a stove-fire until they are slightly browned, moisten them with half a pint of Claret or Burgundy, and set the whole to boil upon the stove until reduced to half the quantity; then add half a pint of white *con-sommé*, and after the *fumet* has simmered by the side of the stove for a quarter of an hour, pass it through a sieve into a stewpan containing sufficient *Espagnole* sauce for the *entrée*, and work it in the usual manner (by clarifying and reducing it), then pass it through a tammy into a basin. Pour one-third of the sauce over the pheasant, and put the remainder into a *bain-marie* containing some button-mushrooms, small truffles, glazed button-onions, and about twenty very small *que-nelles*. When about to send to table, warm the members of pheasant without allowing them to boil; dish them up, first placing the pieces of back, then the legs, and the fillets, surmounting the whole with the breast; garnish the *salmis* with the *ragout* disposed in groups round the base, place some heart-shaped *croûtons* between these, pour the remainder of the sauce over the *entrée*, and serve.

1072. SALMIS OF PHEASANT, A LA BRESILIENNE.

ROAST the pheasant, and afterwards cut it up into small joints as in the foregoing case. Make a little *farce* with four pheasants' livers (or these failing, fowls' livers may be substituted), and use this to fill eight heart-shaped *croûtons* of fried bread. Chop the trimmings, and put them into a stewpan with two cloves of garlic, some chopped mushrooms, a blade of mace, bay-leaf, sprig of thyme, twelve pepper-corns, and a tea-spoonful of the powder of sweet red pimento, four ounces of lean ham, and a good table-spoonful of salad oil; fry these over a moderate stove-fire for five minutes, then add six ripe tomatas, and after these ingredients have been stirred over the fire until the tomatas are melted, pour in half a tumblerful of Madeira; boil this down to half its quantity, add half a pint of *consommé*, allow the *fumet* to boil gently for twenty minutes, and pass it through a tammy with pressure into a stewpan containing a small ladleful of *Espagnole* sauce; work this in the usual manner and pass it through the tammy into a basin; add one-third to the pieces of pheasant, and pour the remainder into a *bain-marie* containing some button-mushrooms and small truffles. Dish up the pheasant as usual, place the *crôutons* (warmed in the oven and glazed), round the *salmis*, garnish with the *ragout* and sauce, and serve.

1073. SALMIS OF PHEASANTS, A LA PAYSANNE.

ROAST the pheasant, just before dinner, with some *crôutons* of toast placed under it, cut it up into small joints and dish them up immediately; place the *crôutons* of toast round the *salmis*, and pour the following sauce over it:—Chop three shalots, some parsley and mushrooms, put these into a stewpan with a dessert-spoonful of oil, thyme and bay-leaf, and a little Cayenne pepper; fry these ingredients over a moderate fire for five minutes, add two glasses of white wine, a small piece of glaze and half a pint of good *consommé;* boil the sauce briskly until reduced to half its original quantity, then add the juice of half a lemon, and use it as directed.

1074. SALMIS OF PHEASANT, A LA CHASSEUR.

ROAST two young hen-pheasants, cut them up as usual, and put the fillets, the pieces of the breasts and backs, into a stewpan; using the legs to make some *purée* with. Prepare the *salmis* sauce (No. 108), with four shalots and some parsley, chopped and parboiled, which are to be added, together with the juice of half a lemon when sending to table. Warm the *salmis* in the sauce, dish it up in a pyramidal form, garnish it round with a dozen small *crôustades* of fried bread, about a inch and a half high, and the same in diameter, filled with the *purée;* pour the sauce over the *entrée*, and serve.

1075. SCOLLOPS OF PHEASANTS, A LA RICHELIEU.

FILLET two pheasants, pare away the sinews without trimming, and simmer the fillets in a sautapan with a little butter, pepper and salt; then cut them into scollops, and put these into a stewpan with some *Richelieu ragout* (No. 207). Just before sending to table, warm the scollops without letting them boil; dish them up, garnish round with *croquettes* made with the legs, and serve.

1076. SCOLLOPS OF PHEASANTS, A LA VICTORIA.

FILLET two young pheasants, and prepare the scollops as directed in the foregoing case. Make some *purée* with the legs; this must be kept stiff, and mixed with one third of its quantity of reduced *Allemande*, then spread out half an inch in thickness upon a dish, and when cold, cut into small heart-shaped *croquettes* and bread-crumbed in the usual manner. Use the carcasses to make some essences with, which, after being reduced to glaze, must be mixed with some *Suprême* sauce (No. 38), and poured on the scollops. Ten minutes before sending to table, fry the *croquettes* of *purée*, dish up the scollops in the form of a dome, place the *croquettes* in a close circle round the *entrée*, and serve.

1077. SCOLLOPS OF PHEASANTS, A LA PALERME.

PREPARE some scollops with the fillets of two hen-pheasants, use the legs to make some *purée* with (No. 1062), finish some *Poivrade* sauce (No. 29) with the essence made from the carcasses, and pour this to the scollops, and add to these some scolloped tongue, mushrooms, and truffles. Prepare also a dozen small *crôustades* of *nouilles* (No. 1266), fry them of a light-yellow colour, empty them, and fill them with the *purée;* dish up the scollops, place the *crôustades* round the *entrée*, and serve.

Note.—Fillets of full-grown pheasants are too large to dress for *entrées;* but when young pheasants are used for such a purpose, the fillets may be treated according to the various methods directed for dressing fillets of fowls.

For the preparation of *boudins* and *quenelles* of pheasant, follow the directions given for making *boudins* and *quenelles* of fowl.

ENTREES OF PARTRIDGES,

COMPRISING

Salmis of Partridges, *à la Financière.*	Fillets of Partridges, *à l'Anciènne.*
„ *à la Provençale.*	„ *à la Parisiènne.*
„ *à la Périgord.*	Scollops of Partridges, with Truffles.
„ with Mushrooms, &c.	„ with Fine-herbs, in
Fillets of Partridges, *à la Lucullus.*	cases.
„ *à la Prince Albert.*	

1078. SALMIS OF PARTRIDGES, A LA FINANCIERE.

TRUSS three partridges, run them upon an iron skewer, wrap them round with a large sheet of buttered paper, fasten the skewer upon a spit with string, and roast the partridges before a moderate fire for about five-and-twenty minutes; then take them up, place them on their breast in a dish, without removing the paper, and when cold, cut them up into small joints: first taking off the legs, next the fillets with the pinion-bones left on, then dividing the breast and back, and trimming these whole; place these joints in a stewpan, beginning with the pieces of breasts, the fillets, and then the legs and back. Make some essence with the trimmings, to be used for working the sauce with; pour a little of this to the pieces of partridges, and warm them without boiling; dish them up with the inferior joints under, garnish the *salmis* with a *Financière ragout* (No. 188) finished with the essence, place a dozen heart-shaped *crôutons* of fried bread round the *entrée*, and serve.

1079. SALMIS OF PARTRIDGES, A LA PROVENCALE.

ROAST, cut up, and trim the partridges as in the foregoing case, chop the trimmings, and put them into a small stewpan with three shalots, a clove of garlic, bay-leaf and thyme, a few pepper-corns, and a small blade of mace, two ounces of chopped lean of ham, and two table-spoonfuls of salad oil; fry these ingredients over a moderate fire for five minutes, and then add half a pint of French white wine. Boil this until reduced to half its original quantity, then add half a pint of good *consommé* and a ladleful of *Espagnole* sauce (No. 3), stir the sauce over the fire till it boils, then remove it to the side to clarify by gentle ebullition; after a quarter of an hour's simmering, remove the grease and scum, pass the same through a tammy, and boil it down over a brisk stove-fire; then incorporate a small piece of anchovy butter and the juice of half a lemon, and pass it again through a tammy into a basin; pour one-third to the partridges, and put the remainder into a *bain-marie* containing some scollops of truffles and mushrooms. When about to send to table, warm the *salmis* without boiling, dish it up in the usual order, mask it with the *ragout* and sauce, garnish round with glazed *croûtons*, and serve.

1080. SALMIS OF PARTRIDGES, A LA PERIGORD.

PREPARE the partridges as before directed; chop the trimmings and use them to make the sauce as directed in No. 1078. Cut out a dozen small heart-shaped *croûtons* of bread about a quarter of an inch thick, make an incision round the inside of the edges, fry them in butter, empty them, and then fill the cavities with some *purée* of truffles (No. 121); warm the *salmis* with a little of the sauce, and dish it up so as to form a well in the centre; place six of the *croûtons* round the top of the *entrée*, fill the centre with small *quenelles* of partridges, pour the sauce over the *salmis*, garnish the base with the remainder of the *croûtons*, and serve.

1081. SALMIS OF PARTRIDGES, WITH MUSHROOMS.

ROAST and trim the partridges as usual, use the trimmings to make the sauce (No. 10), then pour it to the partridges, and add some button-mushrooms or truffles; warm the *salmis*, dish it up in a pyramidal form, pour the sauce over it, garnish with *croûtons*, and serve.

1082. FILLETS OF PARTRIDGES, A LA LUCULLUS.

FILLET four young partridges, trim the large fillets and place them in a sautapan with some clarified butter; season with a little salt, and place a round of buttered paper upon them; remove the sinew from the minion fillets without tearing them, trim them neatly, and place them in a small sautapan spread with butter; dip a soft paste-brush in some beaten white of egg, and pass it over their surface, and then decorate them with black truffles. After this is completed, mask them with clarified butter, and place some very thin layers of fat bacon upon them. Use the carcasses to make some *fumet*, which must be boiled down to half glaze, and part of it incorporated with some white *purée* of mushrooms * (No. 122); place the fillets on the stove-fire for five minutes, then turn them over, and when done on both sides, without having acquired any colour, drain off the butter, add a little of the *purée* of mushrooms, toss the fillets over the fire for a minute, and dish them up with a heart-shaped *croûton* of fried bread between each; sauce the fillets with the *purée*, place the decorated fillets (previously simmered in the oven for about five minutes) across the *croûtons*, fill the *centre* with scollops of truffles, pour the sauce or *purée* round the base, and serve.

* This *purée* must be of the consistency and colour of *Suprême* sauce.

1083. FILLETS OF PARTRIDGES, A LA PRINCE ALBERT.

FILLET four young red-legged partridges, leaving the pinion bones on the fillets; trim these neatly, lard them closely, and place them in a sautapan lined with thin layers of fat bacon; moisten with some white-wine *mirepoix* (No. 236), place a round of paper upon them, and braize the fillets over a moderate fire or in the oven, and when they are nearly done, glaze them nicely. Dish them up in a close circle, with a decorated minion fillet between each; fill the centre with a *ragout* of crayfish-tails tossed in a little partridge glaze with some lobster coral; pour some *Allemande* sauce mixed with some *fumet* of partridges round the *entrée*, and serve.

1084. FILLETS OF PARTRIDGES, A L'ANCIENNE.

RUN an iron skewer through four young partridges, place them on a double sheet of thickly-buttered paper, cover them with some reduced *mirepoix* (No. 236), with the vegetables left in it; wrap the paper round, fasten them on a spit, and roast them before a brisk fire for about half an hour; then, take them up on a dish, and set them to cool without removing the paper. Cut the fillets out of the partridges, remove the skins, and trim them neatly without waste; place them in a sautapan with a little half-glaze made with the carcasses. Make some *purée* with the meat from the legs, and use the gravy that runs from the birds after roasting, to moisten it with. Warm the fillets without boiling, dish them up with a heart-shaped *crôuton* of fried bread between each, fill the centre with the *purée*, pour some *salmis* sauce (No. 11) over the *entrée*, and serve.

1085. FILLETS OF PARTRIDGES, A LA PARISIENNE.

TRIM the fillets of four young partridges, mask them over with a coating of *Allemande* sauce (No. 7), dip them in beaten eggs, and bread-crumb them; then, sprinkle them over with clarified butter, and bread-crumb them again; pat them gently into shape, and place them in circular order in a sautapan with some clarified butter. *Contises* the minion fillets with black truffles, lay them in a buttered sautapan in the form of crescents, and cover them with clarified butter. Fry the large fillets of a bright-yellow colour, drain them on a napkin, glaze them slightly, and dish them up with a circular scollop of red tongue between each; fill the centre with some Parisian *ragout* (No. 203), place the minion fillets round this, pour some of the sauce round the base, and serve.

1086. SCOLLOPS OF PARTRIDGES, WITH TRUFFLES.

FILLET the partridges, remove the sinews from the fillets and place them in a sautapan with some clarified butter; season with a little salt, and simmer them in the oven or over a stove-fire for five minutes; then, turn them over, and when done on both sides, drain them upon a napkin and cut them into scollops; place these in a stewpan with four ounces of truffles (previously simmered with a small piece of butter and glaze), and to these add some *Espagnole* sauce worked with a *fumet* made from the carcasses. Warm the scollops without boiling, dish them up in the form of a dome, garnish round with some *croquettes* made with the legs; or, the minion fillets may be reserved, and when decorated or fried in batter, used to place round the scollops.

1087. SCOLLOPS OF PARTRIDGES, IN CASES.

FILLET three young partridges, cut the fillets into small scollops, and place them neatly in a large sautapan with two small pats of very fresh butter, merely melted in the sautapan without being clarified; season with mignionette-pepper, salt, and nutmeg, chopped mushrooms, parsley, truffles, and two shalots; simmer the scollops briskly over the stove-fire, and when done, add two large gravy-spoonfuls of *Espagnole* sauce worked with some *fumet* or extract (made from the carcasses), and the juice of half a lemon; toss the whole together over the fire for a few minutes, and fill eight or ten small plaited circular, or heart-shaped, paper cases that have been oiled and baked in the oven for five minutes to make the paper firmer. Place the cases upon a baking-sheet lined with clean paper, and lay a thin circular layer of fat bacon upon each case. Twenty minutes before sending to table, put the cases of scollops in the oven to be warmed through, then dish them up, pour a little of the same sauce in each, and serve.

Note.—Scollops of partridges may be dressed as directed for scollops of pheasants; fillets may also be served in every variety of form directed for the treatment of fillets of fowls.

1088. CUTLETS OF PARTRIDGES, A L'ALGERIENNE.

SPLIT four young partridges into halves; remove the breast and backbones, and pass the legs through the skin of the thighs, so as to give them the form of cutlets; trim them without waste, and place them in circular order in a sautapan with two pats of fresh butter simply melted; season with mignionette-pepper, salt, and a little nutmeg, and then finish them as directed for spring chickens, *à la Algérinne* (No. 981).

1089. CUTLETS OF PARTRIDGES, A LA MAITRE D'HOTEL.

PREPARE these as in the foregoing case, then mask them with *d'Uxelles* sauce (No. 16), bread-crumb them twice, in the usual manner, pat them into shape, and place them in a sautapan with some clarified butter; fry them of a bright yellow colour, drain them upon a sheet of paper, glaze them slightly, and dish up; pour some *Maître-d'Hôtel* sauce (No. 43), mixed with a piece of partridge glaze, under them, and serve.

Note.—Cutlets of young partridges may also be dressed *à la Pompadour*, *à la Maréchale*, or *à la Valençay* (see No. 997).

1090. PUREE OF PARTRIDGES, WITH PLOVER'S EGGS.

ROAST the partridges, remove the skin, pare off all the meat, and use the bones to make some *fumet* or extract (No. 218); chop the meat quite fine, pound it in a mortar with a pat of butter and a spoonful of sauce, and rub this through a tammy or a very fine wire sieve. Put the *purée* into a stewpan, add some of the *fumet*, (boiled down to glaze,) and, if necessary, a little *Allemande* or *Béchamel* sauce; warm the *purée* with care, to prevent it from becoming rough, which would be the case if allowed to boil; dish it up in a conical form, place some poached eggs or plover's eggs (if in season) round the base, with a scollop of red tongue cut in the form of a cock's-comb between each egg; pour a little bright *Espagnole* sauce over the *purée* without masking the eggs, and serve.

1091. MINCED PARTRIDGES, WITH POACHED EGGS.

THIS *entrée* is mostly served when there happens to be any roast partridges or pheasants in reserve from a previous day's dinner: the same remark may in some degree apply to *salmis*: although it must be admitted that a *salmis* made with fresh-roasted game is preferable.

Cut the meat from the birds, either into shreds, or very small thin scollops or dice; add a little pepper and salt, and as much *salmis*, *Allémande*, *Béchamel*, or *Suprême* sauce, as will suffice to moisten the mince; some truffles, mushrooms, or red tongue, cut up in the same manner, may also be added if approved of. Warm the mince, dish it up, garnish it round with poached eggs, or potato *croquettes*, and serve.

BOUDINS, QUENELLES, AND SOUFFLES OF PARTRIDGES,

COMPRISING

Boudins of Partridges,	à la d'Orsay.	*Crépinettes* of Partridges,	à la d'Estaing.
„	à la Printanière.	*Soufflés* „	à la Royale.

1092. BOUDINS OF PARTRIDGES, A LA D'ORSAY.

PREPARE some *quenelle* force-meat with the fillets of three partridges (No. 243). Take two ounces of French truffles, about the same proportion of mushrooms, red tongue, and dressed calf's-udder; cut all these into even-shaped and very small dice, and add them together with a large spoonful of *purée* of mushrooms (No. 122) to the force-meat; mix thoroughly, and mould this preparation into three oblong *boudins*, about six inches in length, and two inches square: place these upon similar-sized pieces of buttered paper laid on a stewpan-lid, and slip them off into a stewpan containing some boiling broth; allow them merely to simmer gently by the side of the stove-fire for about twenty minutes, and when done through, drain them upon a napkin, trim them square, mask them over with some reduced *Suprême* sauce, place three larded minion fillets across each *boudin*, garnish the *entrée* with a *ragout à la Parisiènne* (No. 203), and serve.

1093. BOUDINS OF PARTRIDGES, A LA PRINTANIERE.

PREPARE some force-meat with the fillets of three partridges (No. 243), and mould this into three *boudins*, as directed in the foregoing case, poach them in the same manner, and when done, mask them with some *Printanière* sauce (No. 21), mixed with some partridge glaze: place a decorated minion fillet at each end of the *boudins*, and a larded lamb's-sweetbread in the centre of these; fill the well of the *entrée* with some prawns' tails tossed in a little glaze and lobster coral, pour some *Printanière* sauce round the base, and serve.

1094. CREPINETTES OF PARTRIDGES, A LA D'ESTAING.

To the quantity of *quenelle* force-meat named in the foregoing article, add half that proportion of fat bacon (previously boiled), and four ounces of French truffles, both cut into small dice, also a table-spoonful of *Espagnole*, and a similar quantity of partridge glaze (in a liquid state), and season with a little cayenne; mix well together, and then drop this preparation in table-spoonfuls upon a slab or table, over which some flour has been previously sprinkled; mould the *crépinettes* into the form of so many eggs, and wrap each of these in a proportionate-sized piece of pig's-caul; flatten them slightly by press-ing upon them with the fingers, dip them in clarified butter, and fry them over a brisk stove-fire to a light color; drain them upon a napkin, dish them up in a close circle, pour some half-glaze of par-tridges mixed with a small pat of butter, and the juice of half a lemon, and serve.

1095. SOUFFLES OF PARTRIDGES, A LA ROYALE.

PREPARE some *purée* of partridges (No. 1090), warm it, then add five yolks of eggs, whisk the five whites and mix them in lightly also. Fill a dozen small plaited fancy-paper cases with this preparation, pass a soft paste-brush dipped in half-glaze over their surfaces, put them on a baking-sheet, and bake them in a moderately-heated oven for about twenty minutes; then dish them up on a napkin, and serve.

These *soufflés* may be served in lieu of patties, after the fish.

Note.—Partridges dressed whole are also served for *entrées*, for which see Removes (No. 724).

ENTREES OF WOODCOCKS AND SNIPES,

COMPRISING

Woodcocks, *à la Financière.*	Salmis of Woodcocks, *à la Minute.*
„ *à la Périgord.*	„ *à la Bourguignotte.*
Fillets of Woodcocks, *à l'Ancienne.*	„ *à la Bordelaise.*
„ *à la Périgueux.*	

1096. WOODCOCKS, A LA FINANCIERE.

TRUSS three woodcocks in the usual way, and lard the breasts closely; place them in a stewpan lined at the bottom with thin layers of fat bacon; moisten with some wine *mirepoix* (No. 236), place a round of buttered paper upon them, cover with the lid containing live embers of charcoal, and set them to braize gently for about three-quarters of an hour over a moderate fire, or in the oven; frequently basting them with their own liquor. When the birds are nearly done, remove the lid and paper, to dry the larding for a minute or so, then glaze the woodcocks, and drain them upon a plate; remove the strings, and place them in the dish with their backs resting upright against a *croûstade* of fried bread, about four inches high, and cut in an angular form ; place a decorated *quenelle* between each woodcock, a large truffle on the top of the *croûstade*, and a border of white cocks'-combs round this ; garnish the *entrée* with a *Financière ragout* (No. 188), glaze the larding, and serve.

1097. WOODCOCKS, A LA PERIGORD.

DRAW three fine fat woodcocks, reserving the livers and trail ; stuff them with the usual preparation of truffles (No. 660), and truss them as for roasting ; then, run an iron skewer through the birds, and place them upon a double sheet of paper thickly spread with butter ; cover them with some reduced *mirepoix* (No. 236), having the vegetables left in it ; wrap the paper round them and secure it with string ; tie the woodcocks both ends upon a spit, and roast them before a rather brisk fire, for about three-quarters of an hour : they must then be taken off the spit, and dished up in the form of an angle ; fill the centre with small *quenelles*, pour some *Périgueux* sauce (No. 23) over the woodcocks, place a dozen *croûtons* round the *entrée*, and serve.

The above-named *croûtons* are thus prepared :—Fry the trail, &c., in a small stewpan with a little butter, a table-spoonful of chopped mushrooms, parsley, and half a shalot ; season with pepper, salt and nutmeg, and then add a table-spoonful of reduced *Espagnole* sauce (No. 3) ; rub this through a tammy, and spread it upon twelve heart-shaped *croûtons* of fried bread. These *croûtons* should be placed in the oven for three minutes, to warm them.

1098. FILLETS OF WOODCOCKS, A L'ANCIENNE.

SEE "Fillets of Partridges" (No. 1084). Add the trail to the legs of the woodcocks ; prepare an essence with the carcasses, and use this to work the sauce ; in all other respects proceed in the same manner.

1099. FILLETS OF WOODCOCKS, A LA PERIGUEUX.

TRIM the fillets of three woodcocks, using the under or minion fillets to form three more, by patting them together with the handle of a knife ; place them in a sautapan with clarified butter, and season with pepper and salt. Prepare some *farce* with the trail, as in No. 1097, and spread it upon as many *croûtons* of fried bread as there are fillets. Simmer the fillets over the fire without allowing them to acquire any color ; drain off the butter, then add a little of the *Périgueux* sauce (No. 23), worked with the essence made from the carcasses, toss the fillets in this, and dish them up in a close circle round a small *croûstade* of fried bread, cut in the form of a vase ; place one of the *croûtons* (previously warmed in the oven for three minutes) between each fillet ; fill the *croûstade* with some *purée* of truffles (No. 121), pour the *Périgueux* sauce over the fillets, and serve.

1100. SALMIS OF WOODCOCKS, A LA MINUTE.

ROAST three woodcocks just before dinner-time ; cut them up into small joints in the usual manner, reserving the trail, which must be made into a *purée* and spread upon a dozen small heart-shaped *croû-*

tons. Prepare the sauce as directed in No. 11, and add it to the woodcocks. Warm the *salmis* without boiling, dish it up in a pyramidal form, and place the *croûtons* round the base; add a dessertspoonful of chopped and boiled parsley to the sauce, pour it over the *entrée,* and serve.

1101. SALMIS OF WOODCOCKS, A LA BOURGUIGNOTTE.

ROAST the woodcocks, cut them up, and prepare the *croûtons* as in the foregoing case; make an essence with the trimmings, and add this to a *Bourguignotte ragout* (No. 195). Warm the *salmis* with a little of the sauce, dish it up, garnish with the *ragout* and sauce, place the *croûtons* round the base, and serve.

1102. SALMIS OF SNIPES, A LA BORDELAISE.

ROAST six fat snipes, split them into halves, and prepare a dozen *croûtons* with the trail, as directed in No. 1097; dish up the snipes in double circular rows, first placing a row of *croûtons,* then six pieces of snipes upon these, and again the *croûtons,* closing with the remainder of the snipes; fill the centre with a *ragout* of button-mushrooms, truffles, and small *quenelles,* pour some *Bordelaise* sauce, (No. 57) over the *entrée,* and serve.

ENTREES OF WILD FOWL.

COMPRISING

Salmis of Wild Duck.	Fillets of Widgeon, *à la Provençale.*
" Widgeon, or Teal.	Widgeons, *à l'Américaine.*
Fillets of Widgeon, *à la Bigarrade.*	Fillets of Teal, *à l'Anglaise.*

1103. SALMIS OF WILD DUCK.

ROAST a wild duck before a brisk fire, for about five-and-twenty minutes, so that it may retain its gravy; place it on its breast in a dish to get cool; then, cut it up into small joints—comprising two fillets, two legs with the breast and back, each cut into two pieces—and place the whole in a stewpan. Put the trimmings into a stewpan with half a pint of red wine, four shalots, a sprig of thyme, and a bay-leaf; the rind of an orange, free from pith, the pulp of a lemon, and a little cayenne; boil these down to half their original quantity; then add a small ladleful of worked *Espagnole* sauce (No. 3), allow the sauce to boil, skim it, and pass it through a tammy on to the pieces of wild duck. When about to send to the table, warm the *salmis* without boiling, dish it up, pour the sauce over it, garnish the *entrée* with eight heart-shaped *croûtons* of fried bread, nicely glazed, and serve.

1104. SALMIS OF WIDGEON, OR TEAL.

TRUSS three of these for roasting, place them in an earthen dish, and strew about them thinly-sliced carrot and onion, parsley, thyme, and bay-leaf; season with mignionette-pepper, a little salt, the juice of a lemon, and a gill of salad oil, and allow them to steep in this *marinade* for twelve hours (time permitting), frequently turning them over, that they may become thoroughly impregnated with its flavor. When about to dress the widgeons, run them upon an iron skewer, placing the vegetables, &c., on their breasts; wrap them round with two sheets of oiled paper, fastened on with string; tie them on the spit at both ends, and roast them before a brisk fire for a space of time proportionate to their size, in comparison to wild ducks, observing that they must be roasted with the gravy in them; allow them to cool, cut them in the ordinary way for *salmis*, use the trimmings and the gravy that has run from the wild fowl into the dish, to make the sauce with, which is to be prepared as directed in No. 28. Pour the sauce, when finished, on to the pieces of wild fowl, adding some button-mushrooms; warm the *salmis* without boiling, dish it up in a pyramidal form, garnish with *croûtons*, pour the sauce over it, and serve.

1105. FILLETS OF WILD DUCKS, WIDGEON, OR TEAL, A LA BIGARRADE.

PREPARE these, in the first instance, as directed in the foregoing article; spit them, and cover the breasts with their seasoning, wrap them up securely with paper, and roast them before a brisk fire; when nearly done, remove the paper, &c., and set them closer to the fire, that they may acquire a light-brown color. Take them up, and fillet them, leaving the pinion-bones on; score, trim, and dish them up at once, placing a *croûton* between each fillet; add the gravy that runs from the wild fowl to some *Bigarrade* sauce (No. 33), pour this over the fillets, and serve.

1106. FILLETS OF WILD FOWL, A LA PROVENCALE.

PREPARE the fillets as above, dish them up in the same manner, pour some *Provençale* sauce (No. 25), to which has been added a glass of Madeira, over the *entrée*, and serve.

1107. WIDGEON, A L'AMERICAINE.

ROAST these quite plain, basting them frequently with fresh butter while roasting: when done, cut them up into small joints, and place these in a stewpan with half a pound of red-currant jelly, the juice of a lemon, and two glasses of Port wine; allow the whole to simmer gently over a moderate stove-fire for ten minutes; dish up the *entrée* with fried *croûtons* round it, pour the sauce over the widgeon, and serve.

1108. FILLETS OF TEAL, A L'ANGLAISE.

ROAST the teal quite plain; when done, cut the fillets out, score them across, and dish them up with *croûtons* of fried bread; pour some essence of orange (No. 171) over the fillets, and serve.

372

ENTREES OF ORTOLANS AND WHEATEARS,

COMPRISING

Ortolans, in Cases, with Madeira sauce.   Wheatears, in Cases, with Fine-herbs.
in *Crôustades, à la Provençale.*

1109. ORTOLANS IN CASES, WITH MADEIRA SAUCE.

THESE very delicious birds are a great rarity in England; they are
in season in September, and are to be had only of first-rate poulterers,
who mostly import them from Belgium.

Cut four fat livers of fowls, and an equal quantity of fat bacon,
into square pieces; first fry the bacon in a sautapan over a brisk fire,
then add the livers, with a tablespoonful of fine-herbs, and season with
pepper, salt, and a little nutmeg; when all this is fried brown,
add to it half its quantity of *panada* (No. 239), and pound the whole
together in a mortar until well mixed; add three yolks of eggs, then
mix the above well together by pounding, and take the *farce* up into
a basin. Next, cut eight small oval *crôustades* of bread, just large
enough to hold an ortolan each, making a slight incision round the
inside of the edge of each *crôustade*, and fry them in butter, of a light
color; remove the inside crumb, line them with a thin coating of the
farce, place an ortolan in each, then put them on a baking-sheet with
a little oil, and bake them in the oven. When they are done, glaze
and dish them up, pour over them some Madeira sauce (No. 8) mixed
with a small pat of anchovy-butter, and the juice of half a lemon, then
serve.

1110. ORTOLANS IN CROUSTADES, A LA PROVENCALE.

PLACE the ortolans in a sauta-pan with three table-spoonfuls of salad
oil, a bruised clove of garlic, some chopped truffles, mushrooms, and
parsley; season with mignionette-pepper, salt, nutmeg, and the juice
of a lemon; fry them in this over a brisk fire for about ten minutes,
adding a small piece of glaze and a spoonful of *Espagnole* sauce when
done; toss the whole together, and then put the ortolans into small
oval *crôustades* of bread, fried in oil. Pour the fine-herbs over them,
and place them upon a baking-sheet in the oven for about a quarter of
an hour, that they may acquire a bright light-brown color; then,
dish them up, pour some *Provençale* sauce (No. 25) over them, and
serve.

1111. WHEATEARS IN CASES, WITH FINE-HERBS.

THESE are in season in August, and are seldom exposed for sale in
the London markets; they are more plentiful at Brighton, being chiefly
caught in that neighborhood: wheatears are not more than two-thirds
of the size of larks, but when in good condition, are so unctuous as to
resemble small lumps of butter, and are esteemed by epicures as very
choice eating. Cut the legs off the wheatears, chop some truffles,
mushrooms, and one shalot, and fry these in a sautapan with two pats
of butter; season with pepper and salt, and grated nutmeg; then add
a spoonful of sauce, two yolks of eggs, the juice of half a lemon, a small

piece of anchovy-butter, and a little glaze ; place two wheatears in each case (previously oiled and baked to stiffen the paper), pour the sauce over them, and bake them in the oven upon a sautapan for about a quarter of an hour ; pour a little bright *Espagnole* sauce over them, and serve.

FISH ENTREES,

COMPRISING

Boudins of Lobster, à *la Cardinal.*	Fillets of Soles, à *la Dieppoise.*
Quenelles „ à *la Vertpré.*	„ à *la Maître d'Hôtel.*
Boudins of Whitings, à *la Suprême.*	„ à *la Vénitiènne.*
Quenelles „ à *la Princesse.*	„ à *la Provençale.*
Boudins of Salmon, à *l'Italiènne.*	„ à *l'Horlg.*
Quenelles „ à *la Ravigotte.*	„ à *la Royale.*
Blanquette of Sturgeon.	*Paupièttes* of Soles, à *la Cardinal.*
Scollops of Sturgeon, with Fine-herbs.	Dolphins of Whitings, à *la Parisienne.*
Cutlets „ à *la Bourguignotte.*	Fillets of Whiting, &c.
Fillets of Salmon, à *l'Aurore.*	Fillets of Trout, à *la Chevalière.*
„ à *la Parisiènne.*	„ à *la Régence.*
„ à *la Maintenon.*	*Epigramme* of Fillets of Trout.
Fillets of Turbot.	Fillets of Perch, &c.
Fillets of Gurnet, with Caper Sauce.	„ of Mackerel.

1112. BOUDINS OF LOBSTER, A LA CARDINAL.

CHOP the meat of two good-sized lobsters very fine, put this into a mortar with the pith, and part of the coral, reserving the remainder for the sauce ; add two-thirds of its proportion of butter, pound the whole thoroughly, and rub the produce through a fine wire sieve upon a plate ; put the lobster back in the mortar with half its quantity of *Panada* (No. 239), and pound these until well mixed ; add three yolks of eggs, with pepper, salt, and nutmeg, mix thoroughly by pounding, add one whole egg, and then try the force-meat, by poaching a small portion of it in boiling water ; when done, cut it through the middle, and if the inside presents a smooth compact surface, take the force-meat up into a basin, but if it appears soft and rough, add a little more *Panada*, and another egg ; divide the force-meat into three parts, roll these upon a slab with a little flour into oblong *boudins*, about six inches in length by two inches square ; poach them with boiling water in a deep sautapan by the stove-fire, for about twenty minutes, turning them over carefully when done on one side ; drain them upon a napkin, trim the sides, and mask them with some *Cardinal* sauce (No. 48) ; place across them some small fillets of soles, *contisés* with truffles, and dish them up in a triangular form ; fill the centre with a *ragout à la Cardinal* (No. 200), and serve.

1113. QUENELLES OF LOBSTER, A LA VERTPRE.

MOULD eighteen table-spoonfuls of *quenelles* with some lobster force-meat prepared as directed in the foregoing case ; place them in circular order, in a sautapan spread with butter, and poach them with boiling water, which must be poured upon a stewpan-cover held in a sloping direction against the side of the sautapan ; put a round of buttered paper over the *quenelles*, and set them to simmer gently by the side of a stove-fire for about twenty minutes. When done, drain them upon a napkin, stick some thick pieces of the antennæ, or horns, of the lobsters in one end of the *quenelles*, dish them up in close circular order, pour some *Vertpré* sauce (No. 21) over them, fill the centre with picked prawns'-tails (previously warmed in a little glaze and lobster coral), and serve.

1114. BOUDINS OF WHITINGS, A LA SUPREME.

POUND the fillets of four skinned whitings, and rub them through a fine wire sieve; put the produce in a mortar, with two-thirds of its quantity of fresh butter, and an equal proportion of bread *panada* (No. 239); pound these until well mixed, season with pepper, salt, and nutmeg, adding three yolks of eggs, and continue pounding for five minutes, then add two whole eggs, and after these have been thoroughly mixed in by pounding, take the force-meat up into a basin. Previously to using the force-meat, add a spoonful of *Allemande* or *Béchamel* sauce; next, shake some flour over a slab or table, divide the force-meat with a table-spoon into fourteen equal parts, roll these with the hand dipped in flour into small oval shapes, and place them immediately in a sautapan spread with butter; mask them over with a soft paste-brush dipped in beaten white of egg, and decorate them with black truffles. Poach the *boudins* with boiling water, in the usual manner; when done, drain them upon a napkin, and dish them up in a close circle, so as to show the decorated part; fill the centre with a *ragout* consisting either of muscles, oysters, shrimps, crayfish, or mushrooms; pour round some *Suprême* sauce (No. 38), finished with some reduced essence made from the bones of the fish, and serve.

1115. QUENELLES OF WHITINGS, A LA PRINCESSE.

MOULD sixteen *quenelles* in table-spoons, with some force-meat of whitings prepared as directed in the above case, mixed with a spoonful of *purée* of mushrooms (No. 122); place the *quenelles* in a sautapan spread with butter, poach them in the usual manner, and when done, drain, and dish them up in close circular order; pour some *Princesse* sauce (No. 45) over the *entrée*, fill the centre with a *ragout* of soft roes of mackerel (No. 199), and serve.

1116. BOUDINS OF SALMON, A L'ITALIENNE.

POUND about one pound of fresh salmon, and pass it through a fine wire sieve; then put it again into a mortar with two-thirds of its quantity of fresh butter, and an equal proportion of bread *panada* (No. 239); pound these thoroughly for about five minutes, season with pepper, salt, and nutmeg, adding three yolks of eggs; mix these well together, then add one whole egg, and a spoonful of reduced *Allemande* sauce, continue pounding for ten minutes longer, after which take the force-meat up into a basin. Mould four large *quenelles* with *ragout*-spoons, and place them in a deep sautapan spread with butter; lay a small fillet of sole *contisé* with black truffles round the edge of each *quenelle*, poach them in the usual way, and when done, drain them upon a napkin, then dish them upright against a narrow *croustade* of fried bread, previously fastened in the centre of the dish; place a large crayfish between each *quenelle*, garnish the top of the *crôustade* with scollops of mushrooms, pour some white *Italian* sauce (No. 13) round the *entrée*, and serve.

1117. QUENELLES OF SALMON, A LA RAVIGOTTE.

MOULD a dozen *quenelles* in table-spoons, with some force-meat of salmon prepared as directed above; poach them in the ordinary way, and when done, drain and dish them up in close circular order; pour some *Ravigotte* sauce (No. 21) over them, fill the centre with scollops of whitings tossed in a little *Allemande* sauce, and serve.

1118. BLANQUETTE OF STURGEON.

BRAIZE about two pounds of sturgeon in some wine *mirepoix* (No. 236) for about three quarters of an hour, and set it to cool in its own liquor; then drain and cut it up into scollops, and place these in a stewpan with some scollops of truffles and button-mushrooms, to which add some *Allemande* sauce finished with part of the *mirepoix* reduced for the purpose : warm the *blanquette*, dish it up in the form of a dome, garnish round with lobster *croquettes*, and serve.

1119. SCOLLOPS OF STURGEON, WITH FINE-HERBS.

PROCURE about two pounds of sturgeon, place it in an earthen pan, strew over it sliced carrot and onion, parsley, bay-leaf, and thyme, and season with mignionette pepper and salt, lemon-juice, and a gill of salad-oil; allow this to remain for a day or two, frequently turning the fish over in the seasoning. When about to dress the sturgeon, drain it upon a cloth to absorb all the moisture, and cut it up into heart-shaped or oval scollops, about the thickness of a quarter of an inch; place these in a sautapan with some clarified butter, six ounces of scollops of truffles, some mushrooms, parsley, and two shalots chopped fine, and season with a little cayenne and grated nutmeg; fry the whole on a moderate fire, turning the scollops over when lightly browned on one side. When they are done, drain off the grease, pour in some finished sturgeon sauce (No. 56), toss the whole together over the fire for three minutes, dish the scollops up in the form of a dome, garnish round with a border of crayfish tails, and serve.

1120. CUTLETS OF STURGEON, A LA BOURGUIGNOTTE.

FIRST steep the sturgeon as directed in the foregoing case; then, cut it up into heart-shaped fillets, about the size and rather thicker than fillets of fowls: stick the claw of a crayfish into the pointed end of each cutlet, and place them in a curved form in a sautapan with some clarified butter : season with pepper, salt, nutmeg, and a little lemon-juice. Fry the cutlets of a light-brown color on both sides ; pour off the grease, toss them in a little glaze, and dish them up in a close circle; fill the centre with some *Bourguignotte ragout* (No. 195), pour some of the sauce round the base, and serve.

1121. FILLETS OF SALMON, A L'AURORE.

CUT about two pounds of salmon into oval fillets; place these in a sautapan with some clarified butter, season with pepper, salt, a little chopped parsley, and lemon-juice; fry them over the stove-fire for five minutes, pour off nearly all the butter, and then mask each fillet with a thin coating of *Allemande* sauce (No. 7) ; rub eight hard-boiled yolks of eggs through a wire sieve, and spread this kind of vermicelli equally over all the fillets ; then pass the hot salamander over them to deepen the color of the yolk of egg, dish the fillets up in a close circle, fill the centre with a *ragout* of mushrooms, small *quenelles*, and muscles, tossed in some Aurora sauce (No. 41), pour some of it round the base, and serve.

1122. FILLETS OF SALMON, A LA PARISIENNE.

CUT these into the shape of fillets of fowls, season with a little pepper and salt, and mask them over with a coating of reduced *Allemande* sauce ; when this has become cold, bread-crumb them twice over in the usual manner, and put them in a sautapan with some clarified butter ; fry the fillets over a brisk stove-fire, of a light color, and when done, drain, and dish them up in a close circle ; fill the centre with some *ragout à la Parisiènne* (No. 203), pour some of the sauce round the base, and serve.

1123. SALMON CUTLETES, A LA MAINTENON.

TRIM the salmon into fillets, as above, and place them in a sautapan with some clarified butter ; season with pepper and salt, grated nutmeg, chopped mushrooms, truffles, parsley, and two shalots, and fry them over a stove-fire for five minutes ; then add two gravy-spoonfuls of *Allemande* sauce (No. 7), a small piece of glaze, and the juice of half a lemon ; simmer the whole together for two minutes longer and remove them from the fire. Cut as many sheets of small note-paper, into the shape of hearts, as there are cutlets ; oil them over with a paste-brush, place one in each, divide the sauce equally, and then fold the edges down all round, by neatly and firmly twisting them under in pleats, so as thoroughly to prevent the sauce from escaping ; place the cutlets upon a clean gridiron, over a clear fire of coke, of very moderate heat, and broil them without allowing the paper to burn ; dish them up in a close circle, fill the centre with fried parsley, and send some brown Italian sauce (No. 12) separately in a boat.

1124. FILLETS OF TURBOT.

THESE are described in the section treating of turbots dressed for removes, &c. (No. 405).

1125. FILLETS OF GURNETS, WITH CAPER SAUCE.

FILLET the gurnets, remove the skin, and if the fish are large, divide each fillet into several pieces, so that they may not be larger than fillets of fowls ; place them in a sautapan with clarified butter, season with pepper and salt, and place them in the oven, or over a stove-fire, to simmer for about five minutes, then turn them over, and when done on both sides, drain them upon a napkin, and dish them up in a close circle ; fill the centre with small *quenelles* of the same kind of fish, pour some caper sauce (No. 90) over the *entrée*, and serve.

Note.—Fillets of gurnets prepared and dished up as the above, may also be served with any of the following sauces :—Italian, *Ravigotte*, *Maitre-d'hôtel*, Oyster, Muscles, or Crayfish.

1126. FILLETS OF SOLES, A LA DIEPPOISE.

TRIM the fillets, and spread them on the outside with a preparation of fine-herbs, mixed with three yolks of eggs; then double them up, put them together, and insert the claw of a crayfish into the narrow end of each. Place the fillets in a sautapan thickly spread with butter, moisten with the liquor from the oysters used for the sauce, and season with a little mignionette-pepper and salt; cover these with a circular piece of paper spread with butter, and set them to simmer gently over a stove-fire for about ten minutes; when they are done, drain the fillets on a napkin, and dish them up in a close circle, showing the crayfish claws; fill the centre, garnish the base of the *entrée* with some Norman *matelotte ragout* (No. 194), and serve.

1127. FILLETS OF SOLES, A LA MAITRE D'HOTEL.

TRIM the fillets neatly, take hold of both ends (keeping the whitest side uppermost), and bring them together, one overlaying the other; then place them in a sautapan with some clarified butter, season with pepper and salt, chopped parsley, and a little lemon-juice, simmer them over the fire for ten minutes, and when done, drain and dish them up in a close circle; pour some *Maitre-d'hôtel* sauce (No. 43) over them, and serve.

Note.—Fillets of soles prepared as the foregoing, may also be served• with either of the following sauces:—*Ravigotte*, Italian, Aurora, *Pascaline*, Crayfish, Oyster, Shrimp, and Dutch.

1128. FILLETS OF SOLES, A LA VENITIENNE.

FILLET four soles, trim the fillets, and place one half in a sautapan, with some clarified butter, lemon-juice, pepper and salt, in the manner directed in the foregoing case; simmer the remainder (without trimming them) also with the same seasoning; when they are done, drain them upon a plate, and allow these to cool. Then, cut up the latter into small dice, mix them with some reduced *Allemande* sauce, and season with two ounces of grated Parmesan cheese, mignionette-pepper and grated nutmeg; spread this preparation out upon an earthen dish about the sixth part of an inch thick, and when it has become firm by cooling, cut it out into pieces about the size and shape of the fillets, and bread-crumb these in the usual manner. Just before sending to table, simmer the fillets over the stove, and fry the *croquettes* in plenty of clean hog's-lard, made hot for the purpose; when done, drain both upon a napkin, and dish them in a close circle, placing alternately the *croquettes* and fillets; fill the centre with small *quenelles* of whitings, pour some Venetian sauce (No. 26) over these and the white fillets only, and serve.

1129. FILLETS OF SOLES, A LA PROVENCALE.

TRIM the fillets of soles, divide each, and steep them for several hours in a basin with mignionette-pepper, a little salt, lemon-juice, salad-oil, thyme, bay-leaf, and two shalots. Then, drain the fillets on a cloth to absorb all the moisture, flour them over, dip them in some light batter (No. 231), and fry them in clean hog's-lard; when they have acquired a light color, drain them upon a napkin, dish them up, pour either some *Provençale*, Dutch, Fine-herbs, *Ravigotte*, or *Maître d'H tel* sauce under them, and serve.

1130. FILLETS OF SOLES, A LA HORLY.

TRIM the fillets of soles, and steep them for several hours in the same kind of seasoning directed to be used for No. 1129—substituting two spoonfuls of tarragon vinegar for the lemon-juice. Drain the fillets on a cloth, in order to absorb the moisture, then shake them in some flour, drop them in some clean hog's-lard, and fry them of a light color; drain the fillets upon a sieve covered with paper, dish them up in a pile, pour either some Tomata, Italian, *Piquante*, *Ravigotte*, or *Provençale* sauce round them, and serve.

1131. FILLETS OF SOLES, A LA ROUENNAISE.

FILLET three large soles, divide each across, and trim them in the shape of fillets of fowls; mask them over with a coating of *d'Uxelles* sauce (No. 16), and when this has become firm upon them by cooling, bread-crumb them twice over in the ordinary way; stick a piece of the horns of a lobster into the narrow end of each fillet, so as to give them the appearance of cutlets, and place them in a sautapan, with some clarified butter. Fry the fillets of a bright-yellow color, on both sides; drain, and then dish them up in a close circle, fill the centre with a *Rouènnaise ragout* (No. 197), and serve.

1132. PAUPIETTES OF FILLETS OF SOLES, A LA CARDINAL.

TRIM the fillets of four large soles, spread them upon a napkin, garnish each with a layer of *quenelle* force-meat of whitings, mixed with some lobster coral, and roll each fillet up in the form of a small barrel; spread four sheets of letter-paper with butter, then place four *paupièttes* in each, squeeze some lemon-juice over them, and roll them up tightly to keep them in shape. Place these rolls of *paupièttes* in a sautapan, and put them in the oven to bake for about twenty minutes; then remove the papers, drain the *paupièttes* upon a napkin, pare off the ends with a sharp knife, and dish them up on their ends, side by side, in a close circle, so as to show the coral; fill the centre with some *Cardinal ragout* (No. 200), pour some of the sauce over the fillets, and serve.

1133. DOLPHINS OF WHITINGS, A LA PARISIENNE.

SKIN four fine fresh whitings, and remove the back-bones without detaching the fillets from the head; roll out, and bake a circular piece of common paste, nearly the size of the bottom of the dish; fasten thereon a pillar-shaped *croustade* of fried bread three inches high, and one inch in diameter. Prepare some force-meat of whitings, colored with lobster coral, and mask the heads and fillets of whitings entirely with it, smoothing them over with a knife dipped in hot water; then turn the tail-ends of the fish, inwardly, down upon the centre of the head—giving to each the form of a heart; place them upright against the *croustade*, with their heads resting flat upon the foundation of paste, and decorate them over with half-moons of black truffles, placed thereon so as to represent scales of fish; cover them with very thin layers of fat bacon, and encircle the *entrée* with a band of buttered paper, fastened with two pins : this must not touch the whitings. Bake the dolphins in a moderately-heated oven, for about forty minutes ; ascertain whether they are done through, and then remove the paper and bacon ; absorb all the grease, place them carefully upon their dish, garnish the *entrée* with a *ragout* of button-mushrooms, oysters, and crayfish-tails ; surmount the whole with a large truffle, glaze the dolphins with a little lobster coral diluted in the glaze, pour some *Suprême* sauce (No. 38), finished with an essence made from the bones and trimmings, round the *entrée*, and serve.

Note.—Fillets of whitings may also be prepared according to the several directions given for dressing fillets of soles.

1134. FILLETS OF TROUT, A LA CHEVALIERE.

DIVIDE the fillets of two good-sized trout into moderate-sized oval scollops or fillets ; mask them over with reduced *d'Uxelles* sauce (No. 16), and bread-crumb them twice over this with bread-crumbs mixed with grated Parmesan cheese in the proportion of one-third ; the fillets must be first dipped in beaten egg, and then sprinkled with clarified butter, preparatory to their being bread-crumbed a second time. Fry them of a bright-yellow color, drain, and dish them up in a close circle, fill the centre with a *ragout* of soft roes of mackerel or herrings, and crayfish tails ; pour some Crayfish sauce (No. 54) round the *entrée*, and serve.

1135. FILLETS OF TROUT, A LA REGENCE.

TRIM the fillets into pieces resembling fillets of fowls ; place them in a sautapan with clarified butter, and season with pepper and salt, chopped parsley, and lemon-juice ; simmer the fillets over the fire for five minutes, turn them over, and when done on both sides, drain and dish them up in a close circle ; fill the centre with a *ragout à la Régence* (No, 210), pour some of the sauce round the base, and serve.

1136. EPIGRAMME OF FILLETS OF TROUT.

TRIM the fillets as above, bread-crumb one half, in the ordinary manner, and place these in a sautapan, with clarified butter ; put the remainder into another sautapan, with clarified butter, without being bread-crumbed, and season with pepper and salt. Fry the fillets, drain and dish them up in a close circle, placing one of each kind alternately ; fill the centre with some scollops of fillets of soles, tossed in a spoonful of *Béchamel* sauce, and some chopped and parboiled parsley ; pour some *Aurora* sauce (No. 41), over the plain fillets (taking care not to smear those that are bread-crumbed), pour some of it round the base, and serve.

Note.—Fillets of plaice, flounders, and perch, may be dressed in the same manner as directed for fillets of soles or whitings.

1137. FILLETS OF MACKEREL.

SEE Mackerel (No. 480).

SECOND-COURSE ROASTS,

COMPRISING

Roast Hare.   Roast Larks.
  ,,   Rabbits.   ,,   Woodcocks, &c.
  ,,   Pheasants.   ,,   Capons.
  ,,   Partridges.   ,,   Poulards.
  ,,   Quails.   ,,   Green Goose.
  ,,   Ruffs and Reeves   ,,   Ducklings.
  ,,   Ortolans.   ,,   Pigeons.
  ,,   Wheatears.   ,,   Black Game.
  ,,   Guinea-fowls.   ,,   Pea-fowl.

1138. ROAST HARE.

SKIN and draw the hare, leaving on the ears, which must be scalded, and the hairs scraped off; pick out the eyes, and cut off the feet or pads, just above the first joint; wipe the hare with a clean cloth, and cut the sinews at the back of the hind-quarters, and below the fore-legs. Prepare some veal stuffing, and fill the paunch with it; sew this up with string, or fasten it with a wooden skewer, then draw the legs under, as if the hare was in a sitting posture, set the head between the shoulders, and stick a small skewer through them, running also through the neck, to secure its position; run another skewer through the four legs gathered up under the paunch, then take a yard of string, double it in two, placing the centre of it on the breast of the hare, and bring both ends over the skewer, cross the string over both sides of the other skewer, and fasten it over the back. Spit the hare, and roast it before a brisk fire for about three-quarters of an hour, frequently basting it with butter or dripping. Five minutes before taking the hare up, throw on a little salt, shake some flour over it with a dredger, and baste it with some fresh butter; when this froths up, and the hare has acquired a rich brown crust, take it off the spit, dish it up with water-cresses round it, pour some brown gravy under, and send some currant-jelly in a boat, to be handed round.

1139. ROAST RABBITS.

TRUSS these in the same manner as hares, then spit and roast them before a rather brisk fire, frequently basting them; ten minutes before taking them up, baste the rabbits with the following preparation :— Mix a gill of cream with a table-spoonful of flour, some chopped pars-ley, two yolks of eggs, pepper, salt, and nutmeg; mask the rabbits entirely with this, and as soon as it has dried on them, baste them with some fresh butter. This not only adds to the attractive appear-ance of the rabbits, but it concentrates their gravy, and prevents them from becoming dry, which too generally occurs when roasted accord-ing to the common practice. When done, take the rabbits up with care, to avoid breaking off the light-brown crust formed upon them; dish them up, pour some sauce prepared as follows, under them, and serve.

Boil the livers, chop them fine, and put them into a small stewpan with chopped parsley, a small piece of glaze, a pat of butter, a spoon ful of sauce, pepper, and salt, grated lemon-peel, nutmeg, and a spoonful of gravy ; stir this over the fire until it boils, and use it as directed above.

1140. ROAST PHEASANT.

DRAW the pheasant by making a small opening at the vent, make an incision along the back-part of the neck, loosen the pouch, &c., with the fingers, and then remove it ; singe the body of the pheasant and its legs over the flame of a charcoal-fire, or with a piece of paper ; rub the scaly cuticle off the legs with a cloth, trim away the claws and spurs, cut off the neck close up to the back, leaving the skin of the breast entire, wipe the pheasant clean, and then truss it in the following manner : Place the pheasant upon its breast, run a trussing-needle and string through the left pinion, (the wings being removed), then turn the bird over on its back, and place the thumb and fore-finger of the left hand across the breast, holding the legs erect ; thrust the needle through the middle joint of both thighs, draw it out and then pass it through the other pinion, and fasten the strings at the back ; next, pass the needle through the hollow of the back, just below the thighs, thrust it again through the legs and body, and tie the strings tightly : this will give it an appearance of plumpness. Spit and roast the pheasant before a brisk fire, for about half an hour, frequently basting it ; when done, send to table with brown gravy under it and bread sauce (No. 80), separately, in a boat.

1141. ROAST PARTRIDGES.

THESE should be trussed, roasted, and served in the same manner as pheasants. Sometimes, for the sake of variety, both pheasants and partridges are larded in the same way as sweetbreads, but the practice is not generally liked.

1142. ROAST QUAILS.

DRAW and truss these in the manner directed for pheasants ; cut some thin square layers of fat bacon, just large enough to cover a quail, spread a vine-leaf over each of these, cut it to their size, and then tie them neatly on the breasts of the quails. Run an iron skewer through the quails, fasten this on to a spit, and roast them before a brisk fire, for about a quarter of an hour, then dish them up with water-cresses round them, glaze the layers of bacon, pour some gravy under the quails, and serve.

1143. RUFFS AND REEVES.

THESE birds must not be drawn, neither do they require much trussing, being very plump ; a small wooden skewer should be run through the thighs and pinions, with a string passed round it, and fastened ; cover these also with a layer of bacon and a vine-leaf, run them upon a lark-spit, and roast them before a brisk fire for about twenty minutes, frequently basting them with butter, and set some toasted bread under them, to receive their droppings. When done, dish them up on square pieces of the toast, garnish with water-cresses, pour some gravy under them, and serve the following sauce separately in a boat :—A *ragout*-spoonful of good butter-sauce (No. 70), a piece of glaze, Cayenne pepper, and lemon-juice.

ORTOLANS and WHEATEARS are served in the same manner as the foregoing.

1144. ROAST LARKS.

CUT off the heads and legs, and pick out the gizzards at the sides with the point of a small knife; season with chopped parsley, pepper and salt, and nutmeg; rub the larks over with beaten yolks of eggs, bread-crumb them, sprinkle them with clarified butter, and roll them in bread-crumbs a second time; then run them on a lark-spit; fasten this on a common spit, and roast them before a very brisk fire, for about a quarter of an hour, basting them with fresh butter melted in a spoon before the fire. When done, dish them up in rows, or in a circle, fill the centre with bread-crumbs fried of a light-brown color in a sautapan with butter, and serve them with the sauce recommended for ruffs and reeves.

1145. WOODCOCKS AND SNIPES.

THESE are both trussed and roasted in the same manner. First, pick them entirely, neck and head, then twist the legs at the joints, so as to bring the feet down upon the thighs; run their bill through the thighs and body, and fasten a noose with string round the bend of the joints, across the lower part of the breast; bring both ends round the head and tip of the bill, and fasten it on the back. Cover the woodcocks with layers of bacon, and tie these round with string; roast them before the fire, for about five-and-twenty minutes, frequently basting them with butter or dripping; place some toasted bread under the birds, to receive the droppings from the trail, and when they are done, dish them up with a piece of the toast under each, and water-cresses round them. Serve some extract of woodcocks (No. 173) separately, in a boat.

1146. ROAST CAPONS.

DRAW and truss these as directed for trussing pheasants; place them upon a spit, fasten the feet to it with string, to prevent the capon from twisting round while roasting: about three quarters of an hour will suffice to roast them. When done, dish them up with water-cresses, pour some bright gravy under them, and serve with bread-sauce in a boat.

Poulards, fowls, chickens, and turkey poults, are treated in the same manner as the foregoing.

1147. GREEN-GOOSE.

DRAW the goose, pick off all the stubble-feathers, scald the legs, and rub off the skin with a cloth; cut the tips of the feet, and twist the legs round so as to let the web of the feet rest flat upon the thighs; then truss the goose in the ordinary way, as directed for pheasants. Place it on a spit, and roast it before a brisk fire, for about three quarters of an hour; when done, dish it up with water-cresses round it, pour some gravy under, and serve.

Ducklings are roasted and served in the same way as the above.

1148. ROAST PIGEONS.

TRUSS these with thin layers of fat bacon and a vine-leaf over the breasts; roast them before the fire for about twenty minutes, and when done, dish them up with a sauce made with the livers, in the manner directed for making liver-sauce for rabbits (No. 1139).

1149. ROAST BLACK-GAME, AND GROUSE.

BOTH these should be trussed in the same manner as pheasants, then roasted before a brisk fire, and five minutes before taking them up should be frothed with flour and butter, according to the directions for roast hare; when done, dish them up with gravy under them, and send to table with fried bread-crumbs, and bread-sauce, in separate sauce-boats.

1150a. PEAHENS.

TRUSS these in the same way as pheasants, except that the head must be left adhering to the skin of the breast, and fastened at the side of the thigh; let the peahen be closely larded all over the breast, and roasted before a moderate fire for about an hour; when nearly done, glaze the larding, and on removing the fowl from the fire, dish up with water-cresses, pour some gravy under, and serve with bread-sauce separately, in a sauce-boat.

1150b. GUINEA-FOWLS.

TWO of these are generally served for a dish, one of which should be larded, and the other covered with a layer of fat bacon; roast them before a brisk fire for about forty minutes, glaze and dish them up with water-cresses: pour some gravy under, and serve bread-sauce separately, in a boat.

VEGETABLES FOR ENTREMETS, OR SECOND-COURSE DISHES,

COMPRISING

Braized Celery, with *Espagnole* sauce.
Celery, *à la Villeroi*.
Salsifis, *à la Crême*.
    „ fried in Batter.
Spinach, with Butter.
    „ with Cream.
Endive, with Cream.
Cauliflowers, with White Sauce.
    „ with Parmesan Cheese.
Tomatas, *à la Provençale*.
Mushrooms, *au gratin*.
Large Truffles, *à la Serviètte*.
Truffles, *à la Piémontaise*.
Portugal Onions, *à l'Espagnole*.
Artichokes, with Butter Sauce.
    „ *à la Barigoule*.
    „ *à la Lyonnaise*.
    „ *à l'Italiènne*.
Asparagus, with White Sauce.
Asparagus Peas, *à la Crême*.
French Beans, *à la Maître-d'hôtel*.

French Beans, with Fine-herbs.
Broad Beans, *à la Crême*.
Green Peas, plain.
Stewed Peas.
Peas, *à la Française*.
Turnips *glacés*, with Sugar.
Young Carrots, *à l'Allemande*.
Vegetable Marrow.
Another Method.
Cucumbers, *à la Poulette*.
    „ *à l'Espagnole*.
Jerusalem Artichokes, *à la Sauce*.
    „ *à l'Italiènne*.
White Haricot Beans, *à la Maître-d'hôtel*.
    „ *à la Brêtonne*.
American Yams, *à la Française*.
Potatoes, *à la Maître-d'hôtel*.
New Potatoes, *à la Crême*.
Potatoes, *à la Crême, au gratin*.
Seakale, *à la Sauce*.
Brussels Sprouts.

1151. BRAIZED CELERY, WITH ESPAGNOLE SAUCE.

CLEAN twelve heads of celery, cut them about six inches in length, and trim the roots neatly; parboil them in water for ten minutes, and then immerse them in cold water; drain them on a sieve, and afterward place them in a stewpan with some *blanc* (No. 235), and braize them gently over a slow fire for about an hour; when done, drain them upon a napkin, trim and dish them up in the following order :—First, place five heads of celery the same way in the dish, then four, two, and one, respectively; garnish round with some small circular *croustades* of fried bread, about an inch in diameter, and filled with beef marrow, previously boiled for three minutes in water with a little salt, and afterward tossed in a stewpan with a little liquid glaze, lemon-juice, pepper, and salt; pour some bright *Espagnole* sauce (incorporated with a pat of butter and a little lemon-juice) over the celery, and serve.

1152. CELERY, A LA VILLEROI.

BRAIZE eight heads of celery in the manner described in the previous article, and when done, drain it upon a napkin to absorb all the moisture; split each head into halves, mask them with some reduced *Allemande* sauce (No. 7), and place them upon an earthen dish to become cold. They must then be rolled in bread-crumbs, afterward dipped in beaten eggs, and bread-crumbed over again. Just before sending to table, place the pieces of celery carefully upon the wire lining of a frying-pan, immerse them in plenty of clean hog's-lard heated for the purpose, and fry them of a bright-yellow color; drain them upon a cloth, dish them up on a napkin with some fried parsley, and serve.

1153. SALSIFIS, A LA CREME.

SCRAPE off the outside part until the salsifis become white, and throw them into a pan containing cold water, mixed with a twentieth part of vinegar or lemon-juice, to prevent them from losing their whiteness, then boil them in hot water, with a little butter, mignionette-pepper, salt, lemon-juice, or vinegar. When done, drain them on a sieve, cut them up into inch lengths, and put them into a stewpan with a *ragout*-spoonful of cream *Béchamel* sauce (No. 6), a pat of butter, a little mignionette-pepper and lemon-juice; toss them over the fire, and dish them up in the form of a dome; place some *croutons* of fried bread or *fleurons* round the dish, and serve

1154. SALSIFIS, FRIED IN BATTER.

PREPARE the salsifis as above, and when done, drain and cut them into pieces about three inches long; put these into a basin with two table-spoonfuls of oil, one of French vinegar, some mignionette-pepper and salt; allow them to steep in this until within about ten minutes before sending them to table; they must then be drained upon a napkin, dipped in some light-made batter, and fried in hog's-lard made hot for the purpose; when done, drain them on a cloth, dish them up on a napkin with fried parsley, and serve.

1155. SPINACH, WITH BUTTER.

PICK all the stalks from the spinach, wash it in several waters, and drain it upon a sieve; throw it into a stewpan of hot water with a handful of salt, and keep it boiling until it becomes thoroughly tender and soft to the touch; then drain it in a colander, immerse it in cold water, and afterward squeeze all the water from it. The spinach must next be carefully turned over with the point of a knife, to remove any straws or stalks that may have been overlooked; it should then be chopped or pounded in a mortar, rubbed through a coarse wire sieve, and placed in a stewpan with about two ounces of butter, a little salt, and grated nutmeg; stir the spinach over a stove-fire with a wooden spoon until it becomes quite warm, then add a gravy-spoonful of good sauce, a small piece of glaze, and about four ounces of fresh butter. Work the whole together, with a wooden spoon, until well mixed, then pile the spinach up in the centre of the dish, garnish it round with *croûtons*, and serve.

1156. SPINACH, WITH CREAM.

PREPARE the spinach as above, season with a little nutmeg, salt, and two ounces of fresh butter; stir it over a stove-fire until quite warm, then add a gill of double cream, two pats of butter, and a good dessert-spoonful of pounded sugar; work the whole well together over the fire, and dish up the spinach as directed in the foregoing article.

1157. ENDIVE, WITH CREAM.

PICK off all the outer leaves, leaving only the white; trim the roots, and wash the endive in several waters, carefully removing any insects that may be concealed in the inner folds of the leaves. Put a large stewpan half filled with water on a brisk fire, and when it boils, throw in the endives, with a handful of salt, and allow them to continue boiling fast until they become quite tender; drain them in a colander, immerse them in plenty of cold water, then squeeze all the moisture from them, and place them on a sieve. Next, take each head of endive separately, cut off the root, and again look over the leaves, spreading them on the table with the point of a knife; when this is completed, chop them very fine, and pass them through a coarse wire sieve. Then, place them in a stewpan with a quarter of a pound of fresh butter, a little grated nutmeg, and salt; stir this over the fire for ten minutes, add half a pint of double cream, a gravy-spoonful of *Béchamel* or *Velouté* sauce, and a dessert-spoonful of pounded sugar; keep the endives boiling on a stove-fire until sufficiently reduced so as to be able to pile them on a dish when sending to table; garnish round with *croûtons* or *fleurons*, and serve.

1158. CAULIFLOWERS, WITH WHITE SAUCE.

REMOVE the green stalks, divide them, if large, into quarters, and with the point of a small knife pick out all the small leaves; wash the cauliflowers, and boil them in hot water, with a little mignionette-pepper, a pat of butter, and some salt: when done, drain them upon a sieve. Next, take a round-bottomed quart basin, and fill it with the cauliflowers, placing the flowerets next the sides, that the white only may show when dished up; previously to turning them out upon the dish, drain them again on a napkin, by turning the basin upside down upon it; after which, turn the cauliflowers out into their dish, pour some white sauce (No. 71) over them, garnish with *fleurons*, and serve.

1159. CAULIFLOWERS, WITH PARMESAN CHEESE.

PREPARE and dish up the cauliflowers as directed above. Put a large *ragout*-spoonful of *Béchamel* or *Velouté* sauce, into a stewpan, with four ounces of grated Parmesan cheese, two ounces of fresh butter, the yolks of four eggs, a small piece of glaze, some lemon-juice, nutmeg, pepper and salt; stir this preparation over a stove-fire, until it be well mixed, without boiling; then, pour it on to the cauliflowers, so as to mask them entirely with it. Smooth the dome over with the blade of a knife, and cover the top with a coating of grated Parmesan cheese; place them in the oven to gratinate for about a quarter of an hour; when they have acquired a bright-yellow color, put a border of *croûtons* of fried bread round the base, and serve.

The *croûtons* may be stuck round the bottom of the dish in the form of a coronet, previously to dishing up the cauliflowers, so as to prevent them from spreading.

1160. TOMATAS, A LA PROVENCALE.

SLICE off that part of the tomata that adheres to the stalk, scoop out the seeds without breaking the sides of the fruit, and place this in circular order in a sautapan, containing about a gill of salad oil. Next, chop up half a pottle of mushrooms, a handful of parsley, and four shalots; put these into a stewpan with two ounces of scraped fat bacon, and an equal proportion of lean ham, either chopped or grated fine; season with pepper and salt, and a little chopped thyme. Fry these over the stove-fire for about five minutes; then, mix in the yolks of four eggs, fill the tomatas with this preparation, shake some light-colored raspings of bread over them, and place them over a brisk stove-fire, holding a red-hot salamander over them for about ten minutes, by which time they will be done; dish them up in the form of a dome, pour some brown Italian sauce (No. 12) round the base, and serve.

1161. MUSHROOMS, AU GRATIN.

PUNNET, or large mushrooms, must be used for this purpose. Cut the stalks, trim the edges, and remove the skin, then fill each mushroom with a similar preparation to that directed to be used for tomatas *à la Provençale;* shake some raspings of bread over them, place them in a sautapan, thickly spread with butter; put them in the oven for about a quarter of an hour to gratinate, and then dish them up in a pyramidal form; pour some brown Italian sauce round them, and serve.

1162. LARGE TRUFFLES, A LA SERVIETTE.

WHEN the truffles have been thoroughly cleansed by brushing the mould off in water, drain them in a sieve, then place them in a stewpan lined with thin layers of fat bacon; pour some wine *mirepoix* (No. 236) on them, place some layers of bacon on the top, and set them to boil on the stove-fire; the lid must then be put on, and hermetically closed round with stiff flour-and-water paste to concentrate the flavor of the truffles. Allow them to simmer gently by the side of a slow fire, or in the oven, for about three-quarters of an hour, then dish them in the folds of a napkin, and send the following sauce separately in a sauce-boat :—Mix a gill of the finest salad-oil with a table-spoonful of chopped parsley, the juice of a lemon, some mignionette-pepper, a little salt, and two table-spoonfuls of half-glaze (made by boiling down about a gill of the *mirepoix* in which the truffles have been boiled), which send to table in a sauce-boat.

1163. TRUFFLES, A LA PIEMONTAISE.

CUT half a pound of fresh truffles into scollops, place them in a sautapan with two table-spoonfuls of Lucca-oil, one of chopped parsley, a little chopped thyme, a clove of garlic, some mignionette-pepper and salt ; fry them over a brisk stove-fire for five minutes, remove the garlic, then add a gravy-spoonful of Italian or *Espagnole* sauce, a small piece of glaze, and the juice of half a lemon ; toss the whole together over the fire, and pour it over the hollow crusts of two French rolls, from which the top crust part has been removed, then thickly spread with butter, and afterward placed in the oven for ten minutes to become crisp.

1164. PORTUGAL ONIONS, A L'ESPAGNOLE.

PEEL the onions, and stamp out the cores with a long vegetable-cutter about a quarter of an inch in diameter ; parboil them in water, for ten minutes, and then drain them upon a cloth. Spread the bottom of a deep sautapan with butter, place the onions in it, moisten with broth sufficient to just cover them, and set them to boil gently over a slow fire, occasionally turning them in their liquor ; when they are nearly done, add a dessert-spoonful of pounded sugar, boil them down quickly to a glaze, and when this is done, roll the onions in it, and dish them up in a close circle. Next, pour a gravy-spoonful of *purée* of fresh tomatas, and an equal quantity of bright *Espagnole* sauce into the remainder of the glaze, boil this together over the stove-fire, pour it round the onions, and serve.

Note.—These onions are better adapted for garnishing removes of braized beef, &c., than for being served as a second-course dish.

1165. ARTICHOKES, WITH BUTTER SAUCE.

TRIM the bottoms of six artichokes, cut off the tips of the leaves, and boil them in water with a little salt, for about three-quarters of an hour ; when done, drain them upon a sieve, and immerse them in cold water for five minutes ; loosen the fibrous substance in the inside with the handle of a table-spoon, and after this has been all removed from the artichokes, put them back into some hot water for a few minutes to warm them through ; drain them upside down upon a napkin to absorb all the moisture, and then dish them up on a napkin ; pour a little butter sauce (No. 71) inside each, and send up some of the sauce in a boat.

1166. ARTICHOKES, A LA BARIGOULE.

TRIM six small artichokes, and with the handle of an iron table-spoon, scoop out all the fibrous part inside. Put about a pound of clean hog's-lard into a frying-pan on the fire, and when quite hot, fry the bottoms of the artichokes in it for about three minutes, then turn them upside-down, and fry the tips of the leaves also; drain them upon a cloth to absorb all the grease, and fill them with a similar preparation to that directed for tomatas *à la Provençale* (No. 1160); cover them over with layers of fat bacon, tie them up with string, and place them in a large stewpan or *fricandeau* pan lined with thin layers of fat bacon; moisten with half a tumbler of white wine, and a little good *consommé*, or with some wine *mirepoix* (No. 236); put the lid on, and after they have boiled up on the stove-fire, place them in the oven to simmer very gently for about an hour. When done, drain them upon a cloth, remove the strings and the bacon, fill the centre of each artichoke with some Italian sauce (No. 12), dish them up with some of the sauce in a boat, and serve.

1167. ARTICHOKES, A LA LYONNAISE.

PULL off the lower leaves without damaging the bottoms of the artichokes, which must be turned smooth with a sharp knife; cut the artichokes into quarters, remove the fibrous parts, trim them neatly and parboil them in water with a little salt, for about five minutes; then drain them in a colander, and immerse them in cold water, after which drain them upon a cloth, and arrange them in circular order in a sautapan thickly spread with about four ounces of fresh butter; strew a dessert-spoonful of pounded sugar over this, season with mignionette-pepper and salt, moisten with a glass of white wine, and a gravy-spoonful of good *consommé*, and place them on a slow fire to simmer very gently for about three-quarters of an hour, taking care that they do not burn. When done, they should be of a deep yellow color and nicely glazed; dish them up in the form of a dome, showing the bottom of the artichokes only; remove any leaves that may have broken off in the sautapan, add a *ragout*-spoonful of bright *Espagnole* sauce, two pats of butter, and some lemon-juice; simmer this over the stove-fire, stirring it meanwhile with a spoon, and when the butter has been mixed in with the sauce, pour it over the artichokes, and serve.

1168. ARTICHOKES, A L'ITALIENNE.

THESE are prepared in the manner described in the foregoing article, except that when about to finish them, brown Italian sauce (No. 12) must be substituted for *Espagnole*.

1169. ASPARAGUS, WITH WHITE SAUCE.

PICK the loose leaves from the heads, and scrape the stalks clean, wash them in a pan of cold water, tie them up in bundles of about twenty in each, keeping all the heads turned the same way; cut the stalks even, leaving them about eight inches long. Put the asparagus in hot water with a small handful of salt in it, to boil for about twenty minutes, and when done, drain them carefully upon a napkin to avoid breaking off the heads; dish them up on a square thick piece of toasted bread dipped in the water they have been boiled in, and send to table with some white sauce (No. 71) separately in a sauce-boat.

1170. ASPARAGUS-PEAS, A LA CREME.

BOIL a quart of asparagus-peas in plenty of water and a handful of salt : the water must boil before the peas are put in ; when they are done, drain them in a colander, immerse them in cold water for three minutes, and then drain them upon a sieve. Next place the asparagus-peas in a stewpan with a small faggot of green onions and parsley, two ounces of butter, a table-spoonful of pounded sugar, a little grated nutmeg, and salt; put the lid on and set them to simmer gently over a slow fire for ten minutes. Then remove the faggot of parsley and if there be any liquor in the peas, boil it down quickly, and incorporate with them two small pats of fresh butter, and a leason of four yolks of eggs, mixed with half a gill of cream ; toss the peas over a stove-fire to set the leason in them, and dish them up in the form of a dome, with a border of *fleurons* round them, and serve.

1171. FRENCH-BEANS, A LA MAITRE D'HOTEL.

PICK and string the beans, cut them up, and shred each bean into three or four strips ; wash them in plenty of water, drain them in a colander, and throw them into a stewpan containing boiling water and a handful of salt, and boil them briskly until they become tender : they must be drained in a colander, then immersed in cold water for five minutes, and drained upon a napkin to absorb all the moisture. Next, put a gravy-spoonful of *Béchamel* or *Suprême* sauce into a stewpan with four ounces of fresh butter, a table-spoonful of chopped and parboiled parsley, a very little nutmeg, mignionette-pepper, salt and the juice of half a lemon ; stir these well together over the stove-fire, and when perfectly mixed throw in the beans, and toss the whole together over the fire until quite hot ; then dish them up with a border of *croûtons* round them and serve.

1172. FRENCH-BEANS, WITH FINE HERBS.

BOIL the beans as directed in the foregoing case. Put two pats of fresh butter into a stewpan with a table-spoonful of chopped and parboiled parsley, and two shalots also chopped, a little nutmeg, mignionette-pepper and salt, and the juice of a lemon ; simmer this over a stove-fire until melted, and then throw the beans in, toss the whole together, and dish them up with *croûtons* round them.

1173. BROAD-BEANS, A LA CREME.

FOR this purpose the beans must be young. Boil them in water, with a faggot of parsley and some salt ; when done, drain them in a colander, put them into a stewpan with four ounces of fresh butter, some chopped parsley, and as much chopped winter-savory as will cover the tip of a spoon, with pepper, salt and nutmeg; toss the beans over the fire for five minutes, and then incorporate with them a leason of four yolks of eggs and the juice of half a lemon ; when the leason has become set in the beans, dish them up with *fleurous* round them and serve.

1174. GREEN PEAS, PLAIN.

PUT the peas into boiling water with some salt and a bunch of green mint; keep them boiling briskly for about twenty minutes, and when done, drain them in a colander, dish them up with chopped boiled mint on the top, and send some small pats of very fresh butter separately on a plate.

1175. STEWED PEAS.

PUT a quart of young peas into a pan, with four ounces of butter and plenty of cold water; rub the peas and butter together with the fingers, until well mixed, then pour off the water, and put the peas into a stewpan, with a couple of cabbage-lettuces shred small, a faggot of green-onions and parsley, a desert-spoonful of pounded sugar, and a little salt; put the lid on, and set the peas to stew very gently over a slow fire for about half an hour; when done, if there appears to be much liquor, boil it down quickly over the fire. Next put about two ounces of fresh butter on a plate, with a dessert-spoonful of flour, and knead them together; put this into the peas, and toss the whole together over the stove-fire until well mixed; dish the peas up, garnish round with *fleurons*, and serve.

1176. PEAS, A LA FRANCAISE.

THESE must be prepared as above (No. 1175), omitting the lettuces; stew them in the same manner, and when done, add a little light colored glaze, and finish with four ounces of kneaded butter and flour, with a little more sugar than in the foregoing case.

1177. TURNIPS, GLACES WITH SUGAR.

TURN about two dozen pieces of turnips into the form of rings, about two inches in diameter, or else in the shape of small pears; put them into a deep sautapan, thickly spread with fresh butter, and strewn with about two ounces of pounded sugar; moisten with about half a pint of good *consommé,* and set the turnips to simmer very gently over a moderate stove-fire for about forty minutes; when they are nearly done, remove the lid, and place them over a brisk fire to boil the moisture down to glaze, gently rolling the turnips in this, with great care, to avoid breaking them. They must then be dished up in neat order, and the glaze poured over them.

1178. YOUNG CARROTS, A L'ALLEMANDE.

Turn two bunches of spring carrots, keeping their original shape, but making them equal in size; parboil them in water with a little salt for about ten minutes; then drain them into a colander, and immerse them in cold water, afterward drain them again, and lay them upon a napkin. Next place the carrots in a deep sautapan with two ounces of fresh butter, an equal proportion of loaf sugar, and about a pint of good *consommé;* put the lid on, and set the carrots to boil very gently over a moderate stove-fire for about half an hour; then set them to boil briskly until their liquor is reduced to glaze, when they must be gently rolled in this, and dished up in a round-bottomed quart basin, so as to form a perfect dome when turned out upon the dish; pour round some *Allemande* sauce (No. 7) mixed with some chopped and parboiled parsley, also the remainder of their glaze over the carrots, and serve.

1179. VEGETABLE-MARROW.

Cut the vegetable-marrows, according to their size, into four, six, or eight pieces, just as oranges are divided ; peel, and trim them neatly, place them in a deep sautapan thickly spread with butter, and season with a very little nutmeg, mignionette-pepper, salt, and a tea-spoonful of pounded sugar ; moisten with half a pint of white broth, and set them to boil gently over a stove-fire for about ten minutes ; then boil them down in their glaze ; toss them gently in this, and dish them up neatly in a conical form. Pour a little *Espagnole* sauce into the sautapan, and simmer it with the remainder of the glaze ; mix in a pat of butter and the juice of half a lemon, pour this over the vegetable-marrow, and serve.

1180. ANOTHER METHOD.

Trim the vegetable-marrows as above, boil them gently in water with a pat of butter and a little salt, drain and dish them up, pour some white sauce (No. 71) or *Béchamel* (No. 5) over them, and serve.

1181. CUCUMBERS, A LA POULETTE.

Cut the cucumbers into scollops about an inch in diameter, put them into a basin with a table-spoonful of salt, and twice that proportion of vinegar, and allow them to steep in this for several hours. Then, pour off all the moisture from the cucumbers, and put them into a stewpan with two ounces of fresh butter, a very little grated nutmeg, and a dessert-spoonful of pounded sugar, and set them to simmer very gently over a slow fire until they become quite tender ; this will require about half an hour. The butter must then be poured off, and a gravy-spoonful of *Velouté* sauce (No. 4) added ; simmer the cucumbers over the fire for a few minutes, finish by incorporating with them a leason of four yolks of eggs, mixed with half a gill of cream, a spoonful of chopped and parboiled parsley, and the juice of half a lemon ; dish them up with a border of *fleurons*, and serve.

1182. CUCUMBERS, A L'ESPAGNOLE.

Cut the cucumbers into lengths of about two inches, scoop out all the seeds, pare off the skins, and trim them round and smooth at the ends ; parboil them in water and salt for five minutes, and then drain them upon a napkin. Fill each piece of cucumber with some *quenelle* force-meat of chicken (No. 242) ; then, place them in neat order in a deep sautapan, lined with thin layers of fat bacon, and cover them also with the same ; moisten with *consommé*, and set them to simmer very gently over a slow fire for about half an hour ; when they are become quite tender, drain them upon a cloth, dish them up in a pyramidal form, pour some bright *Espagnole* sauce (No. 3) over them, and serve.

1183. JERUSALEM ARTICHOKES, A LA SAUCE,

Wash them thoroughly in plenty of water, peel or turn them in the form of large olives or small pears ; boil them in water with a pat of butter and a little salt, for about a quarter of an hour ; when done, drain them upon a cloth, dish them up neatly, pour some butter sauce (No. 71) over them, and serve.

1184. JERUSALEM ARTICHOKES, A L'ITALIENNE.

TURN the artichokes into any fancy shape, place them in circular order in a deep sautapan thickly spread with butter; season with mignionette-pepper, nutmeg, salt, and lemon-juice; moisten with a little *consommé*, put the lid on, set them to simmer very gently over a slow fire for about half an hour,—during which time they will, if properly attended to, acquire a deep-yellow color. Boil them up in their glaze, dish them up, pour some Italian sauce (No. 12) round them, and serve.

1185. WHITE HARICOT-BEANS, A LA MAITRE D'HOTEL

THESE are seldom to be met with in England, except in a dried state; wnen procurable, they should be treated in the following manner :—

Put a large stewpan, half filled with water, on the stove-fire to boil; then throw in the beans, with a pat of butter and a little salt, and allow them to boil until they are become quite tender; drain them in a colander; then put them into a stewpan with about 6 oz. of fresh butter, a little pepper and salt, some chopped parsley, and lemon-juice; toss them whole well together over a stove-fire, until well mixed; then dish them up with *croutons* round them, and serve.

Note.—When the haricot-beans are in a dried state, they should be steeped in cold water for six hours at least, previously to their being dressed for the table, and must be boiled in cold water; in all other respects, finish them in the above manner.

1186. WHITE HARICOT-BEANS, A LA BRETONNE.

BOIL the haricot-beans as directed above, and when done, drain them in a colander, put them into a stewpan with some *Brétonne* sauce (No. 27), and set them to simmer over the stove-fire for five minutes; toss them together, and dish them up as the above.

1187. AMERICAN YAMS, A LA FRANCAISE.

CUT the yams into slices about half an inch thick, trim them into rather large oval-shaped scollops, and throw them into a panful of water; wash and drain them upon a cloth, then place them in circular order in a deep sautapan, thickly spread with 4 oz. of fresh butter, and season with a little grated nutmeg and salt; moisten with a pint of broth or warer, put the lid on, and set them to simmer gently over a slow fire for about three-quarters of an hour, taking care to turn them over, in order that they may acquire a bright-yellow glazed color on both sides; dish them up in close circular order, piled up in rows; pour the following sauce under them and serve :—Knead two pats of fresh butter with a dessert-spoonful of flour, put it into a stewpan with a gill of cream, a spoonful of pounded sugar, a very little salt, and a tea-spoonful of orange-flower water; stir this over the fire until it thickens, and then use it as directed.

1188. POTATOES, A LA MAITRE D'HOTEL.

THE small French kidney, or *Vitelotte*-potatoes, are best adapted for this purpose; boil or steam them in the ordinary way, and when done, cut them into slices about the eighth of an inch thick, put them into a stewpan with a *ragout*-spoonful of white sauce or broth, 4oz. of butter, some pepper and salt, chopped parsley, and lemon-juice ; toss them over the stove-fire until the butter, &c., is mixed in with the potatoes, then, dish them up with *cróutons;* round them, and serve.

1189. NEW POTATOES, A LA CREME.

CUT some recently-boiled new potatoes in slices, put them into a stewpan with a gill of cream, 4oz. of fresh butter, a very little nutmeg, pepper and salt, and the juice of half a lemon ; set them to boil on the stove-fire, toss them well together, and dish them up with *cróutons*.

1190. POTATOES, A LA CREME, AU GRATIN.

CUT some boiled potatoes in slices, about an inch in diameter, prepare the same kind of mixture as directed for cauliflowers *au gratin* (No. 1159) : stick some neatly-cut pointed *cróutons* of fried bread round the bottom of the dish, in the form of a coronet ; place a close circular row of the slices of potatoes within this border of *cróutons;* spread a layer of the mixture over them : then, repeat the row of potatoes and the mixture until the dish is complete. Smooth the top over with some of the sauce, shake some fried bread-crumbs and grated Parmesan cheese over the surface, so as entirely to cover it : put the potatoes in the oven for about twenty minutes, to be warmed through, and serve.

1191. SEAKALE, A LA SAUCE.

TIE the seakale up in small bundles, and put it in boiling water with a little salt : about twenty minutes will suffice to boil it tender : drain and dish it up on a piece of toast, and send some butter sauce (No. 71) separately in a boat.

Note.—Seakale may also be served with *Espagnole* or *Béchamel* sauce, in which case it must be placed in the dish, and the *Béchamel* or *Espagnole* sauce poured over it : if the latter, a pat of butter and a little lemon-juice should be first worked in with it.

1192. BRUSSELS-SPROUTS.

BOIL the sprouts green, put them into a stewpan with 4oz. of fresh butter, some mignionette-pepper, nutmeg, salt, and lemon-juice, and a *ragout*-spoonful of *Velouté* sauce (No. 4) ; toss the whole well together over a stove-fire until the butter is incorporated with them ; then, dish them up with a border of *fleurons*, and serve.

ENTREMETS OF EGGS, ETC.,

COMPRISING

Eggs, *à la Tripe*.
   ,,   *au gratin*.
   ,,   *Brouillés* with Truffles, &c.
Omelet, with Fine-herbs.
   ,,   with Shalots.
   ,,   with Parmesan Cheese.
   ,,   with Kidneys.
   ,,   with Oysters.
Poached Eggs, with Anchovy Toast.
   ,,   with Ham.
Eggs, *à la Dauphine*.
   ,,   *l'Aurore*.
   ,,   with Nutbrown Butter.

Eggs, *à la Suisse*.
Maccaroni, *à l'Italiènne*.
   ,,   with Cream.
   ,,   *au gratin*.
   ,,   *à la Florentine*.
Nouilles, à la Palerme.
   ,,   *à la Vanille*.
Indian Sandwiches.
Anchovy Sandwiches.
Italian Salad.
Russian Salad.
German Salad.
Noukles, or *Niochi, à la Viènnoise*.

1193. EGGS, A LA TRIPE.

BOIL eight eggs hard, immerse them in cold water for three minutes, take off the shells, cut them in rather thick slices, and put these into a stewpan. Next, cut three small onions in slices, separating the folds in rings; these must be first parboiled in water, and then after being boiled in white broth, should be drained on a sieve and placed with the eggs; add two *ragout*-spoonfuls of good *Béchamel* sauce (No. 5), as much garlic as can be held on the point of a knife, a pinch of mignionette pepper, a little nutmeg, and the juice of a lemon : toss the whole together over the stove-fire, and when the eggs are quite hot, dish them up in a conical form; garnish round with *crôutons* or *fleurons*, and serve.

1194. EGGS, AU GRATIN.

BOIL the eggs hard, and when done, take off the shells, cut them in slices, and set them aside on a plate. Next, put a large *ragout*-spoonful of white sauce into a stewpan to boil over the stove-fire, and when it is sufficiently reduced, add two ounces of grated Parmesan cheese, a small pat of butter, a little nutmeg, mignionette-pepper, the yolks of four eggs, and the juice of half a lemon; stir this quickly over the stove until it begins to thicken, and then withdraw it from the fire. Place the eggs in close circular rows in the dish, spread some of the preparation in between each layer, observing that the whole must be dished up in the form of a dome; smooth the surface over with the remainder of the sauce, strew some fried bread-crumbs mixed with grated Parmesan cheese over the top, put some fried *crôutons* of bread or *fleurons* round the base, and set them in the oven to bake, or *gratinate* for about ten minutes, then send to table.

1195. EGGS, BROUILLES, WITH TRUFFLES.

BREAK eight new-laid eggs into a stewpan, to these add four ounces of fresh butter, two ounces of truffles (cut up in very small dice, and simmered in a little butter), a gill of cream, a small piece of glaze, a little nutmeg, mignionette-pepper, and salt; stir this quickly with a wooden spoon over the stove-fire until the eggs, &c., begin to thicken, when the stewpan must be withdrawn; continue to work the eggs with the spoon, observing, that although they must not be allowed to become hard, as in that case the preparation would be curdled and rendered unsightly, yet they must be sufficiently set, so as to be fit to be dished up: to effect this it is necessary to stick the *croûtons* or *fleurons* round the inner circle of the dish with a little flower and white-of-egg paste; dish up the eggs in the centre of these, and serve.

1196. OMELET, WITH FINE-HERBS.

BREAK six eggs in a basin, to these add half a gill of cream, a small pat of butter broken in small pieces, a spoonful of chopped parsley, some pepper and salt; then put four ounces of fresh butter in an omelet-pan on the stove-fire; while the butter is melting, whip the eggs, &c., well together until they become frothy; as soon as the butter begins to fritter, pour the eggs into the pan, and stir the omelet, as the eggs appear to set and become firm; when the whole has become partially set, roll the omelet into the form of an oval cushion, allow it to acquire a golden color on one side, over the fire, and then turn it out on its dish; pour a little thin *Espagnole* sauce, or half-glaze under it, and serve.

1197a. OMELET, WITH SHALOTS.

PREPARE and finish this omelet, in all respects like the foregoing, except that some chopped shalots must be added to the parsley.

1197b. OMELET, WITH PARMESAN CHEESE.

BREAK six eggs into a basin, then add a gill of cream, four ounces of grated Parmesan cheese, some mignionette-pepper and a little salt; beat the whole well together, and finish the omelet as previously directed.

1198. OMELET, WITH KIDNEYS.

FIRST prepare the kidneys with fine herbs (No. 876); then, make an omelet as directed for "Omelet with Fine-herbs" (No. 1196), and when it is fried, before folding it up, place the prepared kidneys in it; roll it up into shape, dish it up with a little half-glaze round the base, and serve.

1199. OMELET, WITH OYSTERS.

THIS is made in the same manner as the foregoing, merely substituting some oysters, prepared as for scollops (No. 538), for the kidneys.

1200. POACHED EGGS, WITH ANCHOVY TOAST.

FIRST, break some new-laid eggs into separate small cups, or *dariole*-moulds; then, drop them one after the other into a stewpan containing boiling water mixed with a table-spoonful of white vinegar, and a little salt; keep this boiling while the eggs are being dropped in at the side of the stewpan, and when they have boiled for two minutes, drain them on a napkin, trim them and place each egg upon a square or oval piece of dry toast, spread with anchovy butter (No. 179), over which have been laid some thin fillets of anchovies; dish these up in a close circle, pour a little half-glaze under them, place a pinch of mignionette-pepper in the centre of each egg, and serve.

1201. POACHED EGGS, WITH HAM.

POACH the eggs as in the foregoing case, and when done, dish them up on thin oval scollops of fried ham ; pour some thin *Poivrade* sauce (No. 29) under them, and serve.

1202. EGGS, A LA DAUPHINE.

BOIL ten eggs hard, take off the shells, and cut each egg into halves, lengthwise; scoop the yolks out and put them into the mortar, and place the whites on a dish.   Add four ounces of butter to the yolks of eggs, also the crumb of a French-roll soaked in cream, some chopped parsley, grated nutmeg, pepper and salt, and two ounces of grated Parmesan cheese; pound the whole well together, and then add one whole egg and the yolks of two others; mix these well together by pounding, and use this preparation for filling the whites of eggs kept in reserve for the purpose: smooth them over with the blade of a small knife dipped in water, and as they are filled, place them on a dish. Next, with some of the remaining part of the preparation, spread a thin foundation at the bottom of the dish, and proceed to raise the eggs up, in three or four tiers, to a pyramidal form, a single egg crowning the whole : four hard-boiled yolks of eggs must then be rubbed through a wire sieve, over the *entremêts*, for them to fall upon in shreds, like vermicelli ; place a border of fried *croûtons* of bread round the base, and set the eggs in the oven for about twenty minutes, that they may be baked of a bright-yellow color; when done, withdraw them, pour some thin *Béchamel* round the *entremêts*, and serve.

1203. EGGS, A L'AURORE.

BOIL the eggs hard, remove the shells, and cut each egg into halves, lengthwise; take the yolks out and place them on a dish, shred the whites up in fine strips and put these into a stewpan with some Aurora sauce (No. 41), toss them over the fire until quite hot, and then dish them up in the centre of a border of *croûtons* previously stuck round the bottom of the dish.   First place a layer of the whites, then shake a little grated Parmesan cheese, after which rub some of the yolks through a wire sieve upon this, and so on, repeating the same until the whole is used up, finishing with the yolks of eggs, resembling vermicelli. Put the *entremêts* in the oven to be baked of a bright-yellow color, and then serve.

1204. EGGS, WITH NUTBROWN BUTTER.

PUT four ounces of butter into an omelet-pan over the fire : as soon as it begins to fritter, break the eggs into it, without disturbing the yolks ; season with pepper and salt, fry the eggs over the fire for five minutes, and then remove them gently on to their dish.   Next, put two ounces more butter into the pan, fry it of a brown color, then add two table-spoonfuls of French vinegar, boil the whole together for two minutes, pour it over the eggs, and serve.

1205. EGGS, A LA SUISSE.

SPREAD the bottom of a silver dish with two ounces of fresh butter, cover this with rather thin slices of fresh Gruyere cheese, break eight whole eggs upon the cheese, without disturbing the yolks; season with grated nutmeg, mignionette-pepper, and salt; pour a gill of double cream on the surface, strew the top with about two ounces of grated Gruyere cheese, and set the eggs in the oven to bake for about a quarter of an hour: pass the hot salamander over the top, and serve with strips of very thin dry toast separately on a plate.

1206. MACCARONI, A L'ITALIENNE.

BREAK up the maccaroni in three-inch lengths, and put it on to boil in hot water, with a pat of butter, a little mignionette-pepper and salt; when done, drain it on a napkin, and as soon as the moisture is absorbed, dish it up in the following manner:—First, put two large *ragout*-spoonfuls of good tomata sauce into a stewpan, and boil it over the stove-fire; then add two pats of fresh butter with as much glaze, and work the whole well together; next, strew a layer of the maccaroni on the bottom of the dish, then pour some of the sauce over it, and strew some grated Parmesan cheese over this: and so on, repeating the same until the dish is full enough; strew some grated cheese over the top, put the maccaroni in the oven for five minutes, and then serve while it is quite hot.

1207. MACCARONI, WITH CREAM.

BOIL one pound of maccaroni, and when done, cut it up in three-inch lengths, and put it into a stewpan, with four ounces of fresh butter, four ounces of grated Parmesan cheese, and a similar quantity of Gruyere cheese also grated, and a gill of good cream; leason with mignionette-pepper and salt, and toss the whole well together over the stove-fire until well mixed and quite hot, then shake it up for a few minutes to make the cheese spin, so as to give it a fibrous appearance, when drawn up with a fork. The maccaroni, when dished up, must be garnished round the base with *fleurons* of pastry, and then served.

1208. MACCARONI, AU GRATIN.

CUT the maccaroni up as above, put it into a stewpan with three-quarters of a pound of grated cheese (Parmesan and Gruyere in equal quantities), four ounces of fresh butter, and a *ragout*-spoonful of good *Béchamel* sauce; season with mignionette-pepper and salt, toss the whole together over the fire until well mixed, then pile it up in the centre of a border of fried *croutons* of bread (previously stuck round the bottom of the dish); strew the surface with fine bread-crumbs and grated Parmesan cheese, in equal proportions; run a little melted butter through the holes of a spoon, over the top of the maccaroni, and then put it in the oven to be baked of a bright-yellow color: it should then be served quite hot.

1209. TIMBALE OF MACCARONI, A LA FLORENTINE.

DECORATE a plain mould with some *nouilles* paste (No. 1256), mixed with a little sugar; then line the mould with some thin strips of fine short paste (No. 1253), which must be placed exactly in the same manner as when lining a charlotte-mould with bread; fill the *timbale* with flour, cover it in with some of the paste, and bake it for about one hour; it must then be again emptied, and all the flour brushed out with a paste-brush, put back into the mould, and kept in the screen until wanted.

While the *timbale* is being made, parboil half a pound of Naples maccaroni in water for a quarter of an hour, then drain it on a sieve, and afterwards put it into a stewpan with a pat of butter, a pint of milk, and the same quantity of cream, four ounces of sugar, a stick of vanilla, and a very little salt; then set the maccaroni to boil very gently over a slow fire until it is thoroughly done—by which time the maccaroni will have entirely absorbed the milk, &c., then add about one ounce of grated Parmesan cheese; toss the whole well together over the fire, remove the stick of vanilla, and fill the *timbale* with the maccaroni; then turn it out of the mould on to its dish, shake over it some finely-pounded sugar, glaze it with the hot salamander, and send to table.

1210. NOUILLES, A LA PALERME.

MAKE three-quarters of a pound of *nouilles* (No. 1367), parboil them in water with a pat of butter and a little salt for about ten minutes; then drain them on a sieve, and afterwards put them in a stewpan with a pint of chicken-broth, a pat of butter, a little grated nutmeg, mignionette-pepper and salt; place a circular piece of buttered paper on the top, put the lid on, and then set the *nouilles* over a slow fire, to boil very gently until the whole of the broth has been absorbed. Next, add a gill of cream, four ounces of grated Parmesan cheese, two pats of butter, and a small piece of glaze; toss the whole well together over the fire, and then pile them up in the centre of a border of *croûtons* previously stuck round the bottom of the dish; shake some vermicellied yolks of eggs, and some grated Parmesan cheese over the surface, put the *entremêts* in the oven to be baked of a fine bright-yellow color, and send to table.

1211. TIMBALE OF NOUILLES, A LA VANILLE.

PARBOIL the *nouilles* in water for ten minutes, then drain them on a sieve, and afterward put them in a stewpan with a pint of cream, a table-spoonful of pounded vanilla, a pat of butter, six ounces of sugar, and a little salt; cover them with a circular piece of buttered paper, and put on the lid; then set them on a slow fire to boil gently for about three-quarters of an hour, by which time the cream will be absorbed by the *nouilles;* add the yolks of six eggs, and mix the whole well together. Next, spread a plain round oval mould with butter, roll some *nouilles* paste out on the slab with the fingers, and use this for the purpose of lining the mould with—coiled round as closely as possible, thus forming a kind of *timbale;* fill this with the prepared *nouilles,* place it on a baking-sheet, and put it in the oven to be baked of a fine light color; when it is done, turn the *timbale* out of the mould on to its dish, shake some fine-sifted sugar over it, glaze it with the red-hot salamander, and serve.

1212. INDIAN SANDWICHES.

CUT the breast of a roast fowl or pheasant in very small square, dice-like pieces, and place these on a plate; take about four ounces of red tongue or lean ham, and four anchovies (previously washed and filleted), cut these also in small dice, and place them with the chicken. Next, put two *ragout*-spoonfuls of *Véloute* sauce, and a dessert-spoonful of curry-paste into a stewpan, boil these over the stove, stirring it meanwhile, until reduced to the consistency of a thick sauce; then add the chicken, &c., and the juice of half a lemon, mix the whole well together, and use this preparation in the following manner :—

Cut some thin slices of the crumb of a sandwich-loaf, and with a circular tin-cutter, about an inch and a half in diameter, stamp out two dozen *croutons;* fry these in clarified butter to a bright-yellow color, drain them on a napkin, and place one-half on a baking-sheet covered with clean paper; spread a thick layer of the above preparation on each of these, and then cover them with the remaining twelve *croutons.* Next, grate four ounces of fresh Parmesan, and mix these with a pat of butter into a paste, divide it in twelve parts, roll each into a round ball, and place one of these on the top of each sandwich; about ten minutes before sending to table, put them in the oven to be warmed thoroughly, pass the red-hot salamander over them, to color them of a bright yellow, dish them up on a napkin, and serve.

1213. ANCHOVY SANDWICHES.

ORDER a dozen very small round rolls, rasp them all over, cut off the top, remove all the crumb, place them on a dish, and set them aside. Next, chop four hard-boiled eggs very fine, and put this into a small basin with a table-spoonful of chopped tarragon, chervil, chives, and burnet; season with four table-spoonfuls of salad-oil, one ditto of French-vinegar, pepper, and a little salt; mix the whole well together, and use this preparation for filling the rolls with; then, place some small fillets of anchovies (previously prepared) over the sandwiches, at about one-eighth of an inch distant from each other, and place another row of fillets across these at a similar distance. Dish the sandwiches up on a napkin, in the form of a pryamid, and serve.

1214. ITALIAN SALAD.

BOIL two heads of fine white cauliflower, a similar portion of asparagus-points, French-beans cut in diamonds, a few new potatoes, (which after being boiled must be stamped out with a small vegetable cutter), half a pint of green-peas, and three artichoke-bottoms, also cut up in small fancy shapes when boiled. All these veegtables must be prepared with great attention, in order that they may retain their original color; the cauliflowers should be cut up in small buds or flowerets, and the whole, when done, put into a convenient-sized basin.

Next, boil two large red beetroots, six large new potatoes, and twenty large-sized heads of very green asparagus, or a similar quantity of French-beans; cut the beetroot and potatoes in two-inch lengths, and with a tin vegetable cutter, a quarter of an inch in diameter, punch out about two dozen small pillar-shaped pieces of each, and put these on a dish, with an equal quantity of asparagus heads or French-beans, cut to the same length. Then, take a plain border-mould, and place the green vegetables in neat and close order all round the bottom of the mould; observing that a small quantity of aspic-jelly must be first poured in the mould, for the purpose of causing the pieces of French-beans to hold together. Next, line the sides of the mould, by placing the pieces of beetroot and potatoes alternately, each of which must be first dipped in some bright aspic-jelly, previously to its being placed in the mould; when the whole is complete, fill the border up with aspic-jelly.

Preparatory to placing the vegetables, the mould must be partially immersed in some pounded rough ice, contained in a basin or pan.

When about to send this *entremêt* to table, turn the vegetable border out of the mould on to its dish; after the vegetables before alluded to have been seasoned, by adding to them a *ragout*-spoonful of aspic-jelly, three table-spoonfuls of oil, one of tarragon-vinegar, some pepper and salt; and when the whole have been gently tossed together, they should be neatly placed in the centre of the border, in a pyramidal form. Ornament the base of the *entremêts* with bold *croûtons* of bright aspic-jelly, and serve.

1215. RUSSIAN SALAD.

FIRST, cut a lobster in neat thin scollops, and place them in a basin; to these add some scolloped fillets of anchovies, about one pound of thunny cut up into scollops, the tails of two dozen crayfish, a similar quantity of prawns' tails, two dozen olive *farcies* and a good table-spoonful of French capers; then add a sufficient quantity of red *Mayonnaise* sauce (No. 99), to moisten these ingredients; mix the whole together gently, and use this preparation to fill a border of vegetables similar to that described in the foregoing article. Finish the *entremêts* in the same manner, and serve.

1216. GERMAN SALAD.

REMOVE the skin from the fillets of three Dutch herrings, cut these up into pieces an inch long and a quarter of an inch wide, and put them into a basin; with a sharp knife shave some very thin slices from one pound of Hambro' beef (previously parboiled in water for about half an hour), and add them to the pieces of herrings; to these must also be put two dozen turned olives, some white and red beetroot (baked), cut or stamped out in fancy shapes, in the proportion of one-fourth part of the whole of the ingredients, two dozen crayfish-tails, and some curled celery; then add sufficient *Rémoulade* sauce (No. 95) to moisten the whole, and use this preparation to fill a vegetable border as directed in the foregoing articles.

1217. NOUKLES, A LA VIENNOISE.

PUT half a pint of *consommé* into a stewpan with four ounces of butter, and a little pepper and salt; set this over the stove, and as soon as it begins to simmer, throw in about six ounces of sifted flour to thicken the preparation into a soft paste, and keep stirring this over the fire for about three minutes, by which time the paste will cease to adhere to the sides of the stewpan; add two whole eggs, and four ounces of grated Parmesan cheese, and work the whole thoroughly together until well mixed, then add a gill of whipped cream and another egg; mix these in with the paste, and mould it with two tea-spoons into small *quenelles;* when this is done, place them in close order on a stewpan-cover previously spread with butter, and when about to poach them, they must be slipped off into some boiling *consommé*, after gently boiling for about ten minutes, drain them on a sieve, and place them in a deep silver dish, or souffle-lining. Pour sufficient thin bright *Espagnole* sauce over them to reach the surface, sprinkle some grated Parmesan cheese over the top, and set the *noukles* in the oven to simmer for about twenty minutes; just before sending to table, pass the red-hot salamander over the surface to give them a bright-yellow color, and serve.

Noukles are mostly served immediately after the fish, but are also suited for the second course; they may also be dressed with *Allemande* sauce instead of *Espaguole*, when preferred.

COLD ENTREES FOR BALL SUPPERS, &c.,

COMPRISING

Aspic-Jelly.	Potted Pheasants, *à la Royale.*
Fricassee of Chickens, with Aspic-Jelly.	Potted Fowl and Tongue.
Salmis of Partridges.	„ Lobster.
Mayonaise of Fillets of Soles, &c.	„ Prawns or Shrimps.
„ of Chickens.	„ Yarmouth Bloaters.
Darne, or Slice of Salmon, *à la Montpellier.*	Galantine of Poulard, with Jelly.
Trout, *à la Vertpré.*	Boar's Head, with Aspic-Jelly.
Chicken Salad.	Chickens, *à la Belle-Vue.*
Lobster Salad.	Lamb Cutlets, *à la Princesse.*
Tongue, with Aspic-Jelly.	Fillets of Fowls, *à la Victoria.*
Ham, with ditto.	Sandwiches, *à la Régence.*
Aspic of Fowl, *à la Reine.*	„ of Fillets of Soles, &c.

1218. ASPIC JELLY.

TAKE about thirty pounds of knuckle of fresh veal, wash the meat in plenty of water, and put it into a stock-pot, with four hens, and eighteen calves'-feet previously boned, and parboiled in water for ten minutes; fill up the stock-pot with about four gallons of spring water, and set it on a stove-fire to boil; as the scum rises to the surface, remove it with a skimmer, and keep pouring in small quantities of cold water, to check the boiling occasionally, so as to enable the albumen (which forms the white scum), when effectually dissolved by the heat of the water, to be thrown up in larger quantities than would be the case if the process is hurried; otherwise the aspic so prepared would be more difficult to clarify. The aspic, being well skimmed, should then be garnished with four carrots, three large onions stuck with two cloves each, four heads of celery, two cloves of garlic, a large faggot of parsley and green onions, with two bay-leaves, and a large sprig of thyme; four blades of mace, and a teaspoonful of pepper-corns. Next, set the stock-pot down by the side of the stove-fire, to boil very gently for about six hours; all the grease should then be carefully removed from the top, and the aspic strained through a broth napkin into large kitchen basins, and put away in the larder to cool. When the aspic has become firm, scrape off the grease from the surface, and run a little boiling water upon the top, to wash away any that remains, throw this water off, and with a clean cloth absorb all the remaining moisture. The aspic must now be put into a large stewpan, and set to boil on a brisk stove-fire, and then removed to the side that it may throw up its scum for ten minutes ; this should be removed as it rises and the aspic must afterward be allowed partially to cool, preparatory to its being clarified ; for which purpose, put into a stewpan the whites of six eggs, four whole eggs, about one pound of fresh veal, as much game or fowl, perfectly free from bone, sinew, or fat, and thoroughly pounded in a mortar ; to these add a bottle of French or Rhenish white wine, and a little spring water ; whisk the whole well together until thoroughly mixed, then add this preparation to the aspic, and continue whisking the whole together over a brisk stove-fire until the eggs, &c., begin to coagulate ; then immediately pour in the juice of six lemons, mixed with a little spring water, and remove the aspic to the side of the stove-fire ; put the lid on the stewpan, place some live embers of charcoal upon it, and leave it to simmer very gently for about half an hour. Next, pour it into a flannel jelly-bag, prepared in the usual way to receive it, and keep pouring the jelly through the bag for a few minutes, when it will become perfectly bright, then allow it to run into the basin until the whole has passed. Pour the aspic into deep sautapans or stewpans, and set it in the larder to become firm. Care should be taken throughout the process to avoid putting any thing into the aspic that would be likely to prevent it from becoming of a pale straw color : half may be colored of a darker shade, by mixing in with it a few drops of *caramel* or browning.*

Previously to mixing the eggs, &c., with the aspic, a small quantity should be put into a *dariole*-mould upon the ice to prove its strength ; as although it is necessary (especially during hot weather) that all jellies should contain a large proportion of gelatine, yet, if this predominate, the jelly becomes very difficult to clarify..

1219. FRICASSEE OF CHICKENS, WITH ASPIC JELLY.

PREPARE a fricassee of chickens, as directed in No. 968 ; keep the pieces of chickens separate from the sauce, which must be rather stiffly reduced, previously to incorporating the leason of eggs in it ; and when this has been done, add about one-third of its quantity of aspic jelly ; stir them together on the ice, and when well mixed, dip the pieces of chicken in it, and dish them up as you proceed. The *entrée* should be raised in a conical form, and neatly masked with the remainder of the sauce, so as to detach each piece of chicken in relief. Place some fine cocks'-combs, white button-mushrooms, and glazed truffles in the cavities ; surmount the whole with a large truffle, in which a large white cock's-comb has been inserted, garnish the base with some chopped jelly, rolled with the blade of a knife in the form of a thick cord, and place a border of angular or fancy-shaped *croutons* of bright aspic jelly round this.

---

* This is made by baking some sugar in a small copper pan, and allowing it to boil down very gradually over a slow fire, until it becomes a very dark brown in color ; some cold water must then be added to melt the *caramel*, and after it has boiled up it should be kept in a small bottle for use.

1220. SALMIS OF PARTRIDGES, WITH ASPIC JELLY.

PREPARE the salmis as directed in No. 1078, keep the pieces of partridges separate from the sauce, which, when partially cold, must be mixed with one-third of its quantity of aspic jelly, and gently stirred on the ice, until it assumes sufficient body to admit of its being used for masking the pieces of partridges with: these must be raised on their dish in a pyramidal form; pour the remainder of the sauce over the *entrée*, which should be garnished in the same manner as the foregoing.

Note.—*Salmis* of pheasants, woodcocks, quails, &c., are prepared for ball-suppers, and similar entertainments, in the same way as partridges.

1221. MAYONAISE OF FILLETS OF SOLES, ETC.

TRIM the fillets of the three soles, simmer them in a sautapan with 2 oz. of butter, pepper, salt, and lemon-juice; when done, put them in press between earthen dishes, and as soon as they are cold, divide each fillet into three scollops, trim the ends round, put them into a basin with a little oil, vinegar, pepper, and salt, and let them steep in this. Next, prepare an aspic border-mould, in the following manner:— Pound some rough ice fine, and put it into a deep pan; imbed the mould partially in this, pour a small quantity of aspic-jelly in the bottom of the mould, to the depth of about the eighth of an inch, and upon this place a decoration, made as follows:—Cut some black truffles and boiled white of eggs, in very thin slices; stamp these out into the form of rings, diamonds, leaves, &c., and arrange them with taste on the surface of the jelly; when this is complete, the decoration must be covered in with a spoonful of aspic jelly, poured over with great care, so as not to disturb it: as soon as this has become set, fill the mould up with aspic, and when that also has become set, turn the border out of the mould on its dish. Fill the centre with the fillets of soles (previously drained upon a napkin), neatly piled up in a conical form, pour some green *Mayonaise* sauce (No. 98) over them, garnish the base of the fillets with a neat border of trimmed prawn's-tails, and crown the *Mayonaise* with the white-heart of a cabbage-lettuce, stuck into half an egg, boiled hard.

Note.—Fillets of turbot, salmon, trout, mackerel, or gurnets, may be treated as the above; the sauce can be varied according to Nos. 97 and 99, and may also be garnished round the base of the fillets, either with plover's-eggs cut, crayfish-tails, or quarters of the white-hearts of cabbage-lettuces. Some shred lettuce, seasoned with oil, vinegar, pepper, and salt, may first be placed at the bottom of the aspic-border, to pile the fillets upon.

1222. MAYONAISE OF CHICKENS.

ROAST two chickens, and when cold, cut them up into small joints; remove the skin, trim them neatly, and steep them in a basin with oil, vinegar, pepper, and salt. Prepare a decorated aspic-border, as directed in the preceding article; when this has been turned out on its dish, pile up the pieces of chickens in the centre upon some shred lettuces in a conical form; mask them with some white *Mayonaise* sauce (No. 97), garnish with lettuce-hearts and quarters of egg boiled hard, or with plover's-eggs; crown the *Mayonaise* with some chopped aspic or a *crôuton* of jelly.

1223. DARNE, OR SLICE OF SALMON, A LA MONTPELLIER.

PROCURE a prime cut (four inches thick) from an unsplit salmon of good size; slip the blade of a sharp knife under the skin, and detach this without removing it; fill out the vent with a piece of carrot covered with fat bacon; wrap the slice of salmon in layers of fat bacon, and tie them on with string. Place the fish on its drainer in a stewpan, moisten with some *mirepoix* (No. 236), and set it to boil very gently over a moderate fire for about three-quarters of an hour; then remove it, and allow the fish to remain in its own liquor until it is nearly cold; drain it upon an earthen dish, and set it aside to become firm. The *darne* must then be freed from its skin, &c., trimmed, and lightly masked over with glaze mixed with some lobster-coral. Cut out a round or oval piece of crumb of bread, about the size of the salmon, and an inch thick, and fry it of a light color; spread this all over with some Montpellier butter (No. 183), smooth the surface with a knife dipped in warm water, and put it on the bottom of the dish intended to receive the salmon. Next place the *darne* of salmon upon this, and spread the upper part with rather a thin coating of the Montpellier butter, which, after being smoothed over, must be decorated with a bold wreath of roses or laurels, composed of black truffles. Ornament the *entrée* with aspic-jelly, by placing fancy-shaped *crôutons* of this round the base.

1224. TROUT, A LA VERTPRE.

BOIL three small trout in some *mirepoix* (No. 236), and when cold, remove the skins; spread them over completely with a thin coating

of Montpellier butter (No. 183),
and mark out the mouth, gills, and
the eyes, with some narrow strips
of black truffles; then, cut some
of these into thin slices, and afterwards stamp them out with a circular tin-cutter, in the form of
half-moons, and proceed so to arrange them upon the trout, as to
imitate fish scales. Prepare a
foundation of fried bread, covered
with Montpellier butter, as directed
in the preceding case; place it on
the dish, arrange the trout upon it
in a row, and ornament them with
a rich border of aspic *croûtons*.

1225. CHICKEN SALAD.

PREPARE the chickens as directed for a *Mayonaise* (No. 1222. Pile
the pieces of chicken up in the dish, upon a bed of seasoned shred
lettuces, in a conical form; pour some white *Mayonaise* sauce (No. 97)
over the pieces, place a border of hard eggs cut in quarters, and hearts
of cabbage-lettuces round the base; stick a white heart of a lettuce on
the top, and serve.

Note.—Chicken-salads may also be ornamented and garnished with
plover's-eggs, decorated with truffles; and with eggs boiled hard, cut
in quarters, and ornamented either with thin fillets of anchovies and
capers, or colored butter, either lobster coral (No. 182), or green *Ravigotte* (No. 185), or with tarragon or chervil-leaves, laid flat on the
eggs, or else stuck in the point.

1226. LOBSTER SALAD.

BREAK the shells, and remove
the meat whole from the tails and
claws of the lobsters; put this into
a basin, with a little oil, vinegar,
pepper and salt, and reserve the
pith and coral to make some lobster-butter (No. 182), which is to
be thus used:—First, spread a circular foundation of the lobster-
butter upon the bottom of the
dish, about seven inches in diameter, and the fourth part of an
inch thick; then, scoop out the
centre, leaving a circular band.
Drain the lobster on a cloth, cut
the pieces in oval scollops, and
with some of the butter (to stick
the pieces firmly together), pile the
lobster up in three successive rows,

the centre being left hollow; fill this with shred lettuce, or salad of any kind, seasoned with oil, vinegar, pepper, and salt; pour some scarlet *Remoulade* (No. 95) or *Mayonaise* sauce (No. 100) over the salad, without masking the pieces of lobster; garnish the base with a border of hearts of lettuces, divided in halves, and around these place a border of plover's-eggs, having a small sprig of green tarragon stuck into the pointed end of each; place a white-heart of lettuce on the top, and serve.

1227. TONGUE, WITH ASPIC-JELLY.

RUN an iron skewer through the root of a pickled tongue; tie some string round the point of the skewer, and fasten it at the other end, thus giving to the tongue the form of an arch. Boil the tongue for about three hours; when done, immerse it in cold water, and pull off the outer skin. Then, truss the tongue afresh, in the form of an arch, put it in press, sideways, between two dishes, and when cold, trim it smooth; or with a small sharp knife, carve the surface, so as to represent leaves and flowers; glaze it over brightly, and place it upon its dish. Finally, garnish and ornament the tongue with aspic-jelly (No. 1218), and serve.

1228. HAM, WITH ASPIC-JELLY.

BRAIZE a ham as directed in (No. 646), trim and glaze it accordingly, dish it up, and garnish with aspic-jelly, according to the design represented in the above wood-cut.

1229. ASPIC OF FOWL, A LA REINE.

ROAST off two fowls, and use them to make some *purée à la Reine* (No. 779); mix this with a *ragout-*spoonful of good *Béchamel* sauce (No. 5), and about one-third part of strong aspic-jelly (No. 1218), and work the whole well together in a stewpan upon some rough ice. While this is going on, a plain round or oval mould should be decorated with black truffles and red tonge, in the following manner:—First, place the mould upon some pounded rough ice, quite straight; then, pour about a tablespoonful of bright aspic-jelley over the bottom, and when this has become set, place on it a bold decoration, formed with leaves, rings, dots, crescents, &c., cut out of truffles and tongue, and arranged so as to represent a circular wreath, with a star or scroll in the centre. Decorate the sides of the mould in the same manner, dipping each piece of the decoration in a little melted aspic-jelly, to make it adhere to the mould; when the decoration is completed, fill the mould up with the prepared *purée*, and imbed the mould in ice to set the aspic. When it has become quite firm, dip the mould in tepid water for a few seconds, instantly withdraw it, wipe it with a clean cloth, and turn it out upon its dish. Garnish the aspic round with a roll of chopped aspic-jelly, place some *croûtons* round the base, and serve.

Note.—The above may be made also with pheasant, partridge, or any other kind of game.

1230. POTTED PHEASANTS, A LA ROYALE.

TRUSS a pheasant as for boiling, and braize it with 1 lb. of ham, in some well-seasoned wine *mirepoix* (No. 236); when done, drain them upon a dish, strain their liquor into a stewpan, and when divested of all the grease, boil it down to glaze. Meanwhile, chop and pound all the meat from the pheasant with the ham, and add to these 6 oz. of clarified fresh butter, a *ragout*-spoonful of good sauce, and the glaze; season with Cayenne pepper, a little nutmeg and salt, pound the whole thoroughly, and rub this preparation through a fine wire-sieve on to a dish. Next, fill some small round or oval earthenware potting pans with this preparation, smooth the surface over with a spoon dipped in water, place them in a covered stewpan, and submit them to the action of steam for about half an hour. The potted pheasant must then be allowed to cool; then, with the bowl of a spoon, press down the meat in the pots, wipe them clean, and run a little clarified fresh butter over the surface.

Note.—All kinds of game should be potted in the above manner, and will then keep fresh-flavored for months. For those who approve of it, more spice and aromatic herbs may be added; but it should be observed, that an immoderate use of these impairs the flavor of the game.

1231. POTTED FOWL AND TONGUE.

PARE off all the meat from a roast fowl, chop and pound it thoroughly with about one pound of boiled red tongue or dressed ham; add six ounces of clarified fresh butter, three ounces of good glaze (made with the bones of the fowl), and a gravy-spoonful of good *Béchamel* sauce (No. 5); season with Cayenne pepper, nutmeg, and salt; and when the whole has been thoroughly mixed by pounding, rub the produce through a fine wire-sieve, and then finish this as directed for the potted pheasant.

1232. POTTED LOBSTER.

LOBSTERS for potting must be quite fresh. Take the meat, pith, and coral out of the shells; cut this up in slices, and put the whole into a stewpan with one-third part of clarified fresh butter, and to every pound of lobster, add four whole anchovies (washed and wiped dry); season with mace, pepper-corns, and a little salt, then put the lid on the stewpan, and set the lobster to simmer very gently over a slow fire for about a quarter of an hour. After this, it must be thoroughly pounded in a mortar, rubbed through a sieve, put into small pots, steamed, and when cold, should be pressed down with the bowl of a spoon, and the surface covered with a little clarified butter.

1233. POTTED PRAWNS, OR SHRIMPS.

PICK one pound of fresh-boiled prawns or shrimps, and reserve the heads and shells; pound them in a mortar with four anchovies (previously washed and wiped dry for the purpose), and then rub the whole through a hair-sieve, and put the produce, with the picked shrimps, into a stewpan with six ounces of clarified fresh butter; season with some grated nutmeg, Cayenne pepper, and a little salt; simmer the whole together over a slow fire for about ten minutes, then toss the shrimps in the seasoning occasionally, until they become nearly cold; they must then be put into pots, with a little clarified butter poured over the surface, and set aside in a cool place, for use.

1234. POTTED YARMOUTH BLOATERS.

TAKE six fresh-cured bloaters, immerse them in scalding water, and remove the skins; wipe them dry, take out the bones, and put the fillets of the herrings into a stewpan with half a pound of clarified fresh butter, a blade of mace, and enough cayenne to season them; set this on a slow fire to simmer for about ten minutes, then thoroughly pound the whole well together in a mortar, and rub it through a sieve. Put this preparation into pots, run a little clarified butter over the surface, and keep them in a cool place for use.

Note.—Smoked, or kippered salmon, or Finnan haddocks, may be potted in the same way as the foregoing. By submitting any of the above described potted shell-fish, &c., to the action of steam, a sufficient time for the meat to be thoroughly penetrated by the heat, they may keep good for months. Much will, however, depend on the freshness of the butter used in this preparation; should it become rancid, as frequently happens after keeping for a few weeks, it will, of course considerably impair the flavor of the potted fish.

1235. GALANTINE OF POULARD, WITH ASPIC-JELLY.

CHOP up one pound of white veal, with the same quantity of fat bacon, and season with chopped mushrooms, parsley, nutmeg, pepper, salt, and aromatic seasoning (No. 1250); when these are chopped quite fine, pound the whole in a mortar, with the yolks of three eggs, and remove the force-meat into a basin. Peel one pound of truffles, and cut up a boiled red tongue, and about one pound of fat bacon or boiled calf's udder, into long narrow fillets, about a quarter of an inch square. Next, bone a fine *poulard*, and draw the skin from the legs and pinions, inside; then, spread the *poulards* out upon a napkin, and with a sharp knife, pare off some part of the fillets, to cover the thinner parts of the skin; season slightly with pepper, salt, and aromatic spices; spread a layer of the prepared force-meat, about an inch thick, then place the fillets of tongue and bacon upon this, about an inch apart, and insert rows of truffles between these; after which, spread another layer of force-meat over the whole, then repeat the tongue and truffles, and so on, until a sufficient quantity of both has been placed in the *poulard*.

It must then be sewn up the back, placed upon a napkin thickly spread with butter, rolled up tightly, and fastened at each end with string : thus giving to the *galantine* the appearance of a cushion. This must be then put into an oval stewpan with the carcasses and any trimmings of veal or poultry that may be at hand, also two calves'-feet, two carrots, two onions stuck with four cloves, a faggot of parsley, garnished with green onions, two bay-leaves, sweet basil and thyme, two blades of mace, and a dozen pepper-corns; moisten with two glasses of brandy, and set the pan over a stove-fire to simmer for five minutes, then moisten the *galantine* with as much white stock as will suffice to cover it, and put it back on the stove-fire to boil ; it must then be placed on a very slow stove-fire, or in the oven, to continue gently braizing (not boiling) for about two hours and a half. It should then be removed from the fire, and the *galantine* taken carefully out of the napkin ; the latter, after being washed in clean hot water, must be spread out upon the table, and the *galantine*, after being placed in it again, and bound up tightly as before, should be put back into its braize, and left in to become partially cold ; it must then be put in press between two dishes with a heavy weight upon it. Strain the stock, remove all the grease from the surface, and clarify it in the usual manner, then pass it through a napkin or a jelly-bag, and place it on some rough ice to become firmly set. When the *galantine* is quite cold, take it out of the napkin, and use a clean cloth to absorb any moisture or grease there may be on the surface ; it must then be glazed, and placed upon its dish. Decorate it with aspic-jelly, as represented in the foregoing wood-cut, and serve.

Note.—*Galantines* of turkeys, geese, capons, fowls, pheasants, partridges, &c., are made in the same way as the above.

1236. BOAR'S HEAD. WITH ASPIC JELLY.

Procure the head of a bacon hog,* which must be cut off deep into the shoulders; bone it carefully, beginning under the throat, then

* For this purpose, the head must be cut off before the pig is scalded, and the bristles singed off with lighted straw ; by this means, it will have all the appearance of a wild boar's head.

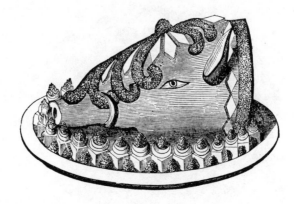

spread the head out upon a large earthenware dish, and rub it with the following ingredients :—Six pounds of salt, four ounces of saltpetre, six ounces of moist sugar, cloves, mace, half an ounce of juniper berries, four cloves of garlic, six bay-leaves, a handful of thyme, marjoram, and basil. When the head has been well rubbed with these, pour about a quart of port-wine lees over it and keep in a cool place for a fortnight, observing that it must be turned over in its brine every day during that period.

When about to dress the head, take it out of the brine, and wash it thoroughly in cold water; then absorb all the exterior moisture from it with a clean cloth, and spread it out upon the table. Next pare off all the uneven pieces from the cheeks, &c., cut these into long narrow fillets, and put them with the tongue, fat bacon, and truffles, prepared as directed for the *galantine;* then, line the inside of the head with a layer of force-meat (the same kind as used for *galantines*) about an inch thick, and lay thereon the fillets of tongue, bacon, truffles, and here and there some pistachio kernels (the skin of which must be removed by scalding); cover these with a layer of force-meat, and then repeat the rows of tongue, &c., and when the head is sufficiently garnished to fill it out in its shape, it should be sewn up with a small trussing-needle and twine, so as thoroughly to secure the stuffing. The head must then be wrapped up in a strong cloth, previously well spread with butter, and sewn up in this, so as to preserve its original form; it should next be put into a large oval braizing-pan, covered with any carcasses of game (especially of grouse, from its congenial flavor), or any trimmings of meat there may be at hand, and also four cow-heels, or six calves' feet; then moisten with a copious wine *mirepoix* (No. 236), in sufficient quantity to cover the surface of the head. Set the brazier on the stove-fire; as soon as it boils, skim it thoroughly, then remove it to a slow fire (covered with the lid containing live embers), that the head may continue to simmer or boil very gently, for about five hours; as soon as it appears to be nearly done, remove the braizier from the fire, and when the heat of the broth has somewhat subsided, let the head be taken up on a large dish; if it appears to have shrunk considerably in the wrapper, this must be carefully tightened, so as to preserve its shape : it should then be put back into its braize, there to remain, until the whole has become set firm by cooling. The head must then be taken out of the braize or stock, and put in the oven, upon a deep baking dish, for a few minutes, just to melt the jelly which may adhere to the wrapper ; it must then be taken out quickly, and the wrapper carefully removed, after which, glaze the head with some dark-colored glaze ; place it on its dish, ornament it with aspic-jelly, and serve.

Note.—On the Continent it is usual to decorate boars' heads with colored gum-paste, and sometimes with natural flowers : the latter produce a very pretty effect, when arranged with taste ; the former method is objectionable, from the liability of the gum-paste to give way, and run down the sides of the head : it has, moreover, a vulgar and gaudy look.

1237. CHICKENS, A LA BELLE VUE.

TRUSS two chickens or fowls for broiling, and braize them in white broth in the usual manner ; when done, set them to cool, and mask them completely with some reduced *Béchamel* sauce (No. 5), in which should be mixed a fourth part of aspic-jelly. Previously to saucing the chickens, the *Béchamel* thus prepared must be stirred in a stewpan imbedded in rough ice, until it just begins to get firm ; it should then be immediately poured over the chickens ; these should be decorated, upon the breast with black truffles or red tongue, and placed upon their dish with a trimmed and glazed tongue in the centre ; ornament them by placing a roll of chopped aspic-jelly round the base, then outside this, some bold *croutons* of aspic-jelly, and serve.

1238. LAMB-CUTLETS, A LA PRINCESSE.

THESE must be prepared, in the first instance, in the same way as cutlets of veal *à la Dreux* (No. 890) : then braized, pressed and trimmed. Next, cover the bottom of a sautapan with some bright aspic-jelly, not quite a quarter of an inch deep ; when this has become set firm by cooling, place the cutlets flat upon it, in circular order, then run a little aspic-jelly over them, just enough to cover them, and place the sautapan in ice to set the jelly; as soon as this has become quite firm, use a tin-cutter (in the form of a cutlet) dipped in hot water, to stamp the cutlets out; dish them up in close circular order upon a little aspic-jelly, placed on the bottom of the dish, to raise the cutlets, and garnish the centre with a well-prepared *Macédoine* of vegetables (No. 143), tossed in some bright aspic-jelly, instead of sauce ; ornament the base with a border of bold *croutons* of jelly, and serve.

1239. FILLETS OF FOWL, A LA VICTORIA.

PREPARE the fillets of three young fowls as for a *Suprême* (No. 989) ; when they have been simmered, drain them upon a napkin, and put them in press between two dishes ; when cold, trim them neatly, dip each fillet either in some *Suprême* (No. 58) or *Béchamel* (No. 5), mixed with one-fourth part of aspic-jelly, place them with the smoothest side uppermost in a dish or sautapan, and set them on some rough ice. Next, cover the bottom of a large sautapan with some bright aspic-jelly, to the depth of about the eighth of an inch ; when this has become firm, by cooling on the ice, place the fillets upon it in circular order, and decorate the upper part of each with black truffles; the fillets must then be covered with a little bright aspic-jelly, to produce the same thickness upon the upper surface as the under. While this is going on, a border of vegetables should be prepared as follows : first cut some carrots and turnips with vegetable cutters as for a *chartreuse*, and boil them separately in broth; prepare also some French-beans or asparagus-heads and green-peas, which, when boiled, must be used to ornament a border-mould in exactly the same manner as a *chartreuse :* observing that each piece of vegetable must be first dipped in some aspic-jelly, previously to its being placed in the mould. When the mould is lined, the void left must be filled up with some sort of vegetables cut smaller, and tossed in aspic-jelly, seasoned with a little mignionette-pepper and salt, a very little salad-oil and tarragon vinegar; it must then be imbedded in pounded rough ice, until set quite firm. The border should now be turned out upon its dish, and the fillets of fowls, previously stamped out with a tin-cutter dipped in hot water, must be placed on the top of the border, in close circular order, each one over-laying the other; fill the centre of the *entrée* with a copious *Macédoine* of vegetables (No. 143), tossed in a little glaze and aspic-jelly; garnish the base of the *entrée* with bold *croûtons* of jelly, and serve.

Or, when the border is dished up, fill the center with the *Macé-doine,* and place the fillets, with the broad ends resting full on the top of the border; thus causing the pointed ends to meet at the summit; crown this with a bouquet of chopped jelly, insert a narrow slip of red tongue, cut in the form of a cock's-comb, between each fillet, and place an angular *croûton* of jelly so as apparently to support the tongue : garnish the base with *croûtons* of jelly, and serve.

1240. SANDWICHES, A LA REGENCE.

FOR this purpose, it is necessary to order one or more dozens of very small round or oval rolls about the size of an egg; cut a small piece off the top of each, about the circumference of half-a-crown piece, and remove all the crumb from the inside. These rolls must then be filled with the following preparation. First, shred the white meat from the breast of a roast fowl, and put this in a basin; then shred the fillets of six washed anchovies, and some red tongue or dressed ham in equal proportion to the fowl, and place these with the latter; add about one-sixth part of the whole, of Indian gherkins or mangoes, also shred fine ; season with a little chopped tarragon and chervil, add sufficient *Rémoulade* sauce (No. 95) to moisten the whole, and use the preparation as directed above. The rolls must then be covered with the circular pieces reserved for the purpose, and dished up on a napkin.

Note.—These sandwiches may also be prepared with lobster; in which case, neither ham nor tongue should be used.

1241. SANDWICHES OF FILLETS OF SOLES.

SIMMER the fillets of soles in a sautapan with a little clarified butter, pepper, salt and lemon-juice ; when done, put them in press between two dishes, and afterwards divide each fillet into four scollops ; trim, and put them into a basin with a little mignionette-pepper, salt, oil and vinegar. Some small oval rolls must be ordered for this purpose; after the tops are cut off, and the crumbs removed, first strew the bottom of each roll with small salad, then place a scollop of sole upon this, add a little *Mayonaise* sauce (No. 97), then strew some small salad on the surface, cover with the tops, and dish them up.

Note.—Sandwiches of lobster or salmon are prepared in a similar manner.

1241*a*. BADMINTON SANDWICH.

CUT some square pieces from a half-quartern loaf of stale bread, barely a quarter of an inch thick; toast these of a light color, and immediately on their being taken from the fire, let them be split or divided with a sharp knife, the inner or untoasted sides must be spread with anchovy butter, and over this place closely some fillets of anchovies; cover the whole with the other piece of toast previously spread with anchovy butter, press down the sandwich with a knife, and after having cut the preparation into small oblong shapes, dish them up, and serve.

1241*b*. BRETBY SANDWICH.

FIRST cut some thin slices of white bread and butter; then, cover half these, first, with finely-shred white-heart lettuce, then, with very thin slices of roast or boiled fowl; these to be placed alternately side by side with fillets of anchovies; strew some shred lettuce over this, place a slice of bread and butter over the whole, and after slightly pressing the sandwich with the blade of a knife, proceed to cut the preparation into oblong shapes, about two and a half inches long, by one inch in width. Dish up the sandwiches neatly, and serve.

1241*e*. SUMMER SANDWICH.

BETWEEN thin slices of white or brown bread and butter, place some very thin slices of any of the following kind of meats: ham, tongue, boiled or roast beef, roast mutton, poultry or game; season with pepper and salt, and a little mustard; strew some mustard and cress, small salad, or, if preferred, some finely-shred lettuce, over the meat; press the sandwich together with the blade of a knife, cut it into small oblong shapes, which, having dished up neatly, send to table.

COLD RAISED PIES AND PRESERVED GAME,

COMPRISING

Veal and Ham Pie, or *Timbale*.	Leicestershire Pork Pie.
Capon Pie.	Eel Pie, *à l'Anglaise*.
Pheasant Pie.	Salmon Pie. *à la Russe*.
Yorkshire Pie	Preserved Hare, and other Game.
Devonshire Squab Pie.	Aromatic Spices, for Seasoning.

1242. VEAL AND HAM PIE, OR TIMBALE.*

FIRST *daube* or interlard about three pounds of white veal (from the leg) with *lardoons* or square strips of fat bacon or ham ; cut this in thick slices across the grain of the meat, and put them on a dish with an equal quantity of dressed ham, cut also in thick slices. Next, spread the inside of a plain mould with butter, and line it with short paste (No. 1253), about a quarter of an inch thick ; line the inside of this with rather a thick layer of force-meat (No. 247), then place the veal and ham in alternate layers, season between each with aromatic spices, pepper and salt, fill up the hollow places and cover in the surface with some of the force-meat ; place some thin layers of fat bacon over the whole, and cover in the top with some of the paste, previously rolled out to the thickness of the eighth part of an inch ; this must be applied after the edges of the pie have been wetted with a paste-brush dipped in water, and made fast by pressing both pieces of paste together with the fore-finger and thumb, so as to cause them to adhere closely together. The edges should then be neatly trimmed, and pinched round with pastry-pincers ; decorate the top of the *timbale* with thin strips of paste, cut out in the form of leaves, &c., arranged according to the upper part of the design represented in No. 1244. Egg the surface over with a paste-brush, make a small hole in the centre of the top of the pie, for the steam to escape, and bake it in the oven for about three hours ; when it is done, withdraw it from the oven, and about twenty minutes afterwards, place the point of a funnel in the hole at the top of the *timbale*, and through this pour in about a pint of good, well-seasoned strong *consommé*, reduced to the consistency of half-glaze ; stop up the hole with a small piece of paste, and keep the *timbale* in a cool place until wanted for use.

1243. CAPON PIE, WITH TRUFFLES.

FIRST, bone a capon, spread it out on the table, and season the inside with prepared spices and a little salt ; then spread a layer of force-meat of fat livers (No. 247), and place upon this, in alternate rows, some square fillets or strips of fat bacon, tongue, and truffles ; cover these with a layer of the force-meat, repeat the strips of bacon, then fold both sides of the skin over each other, so as to give to the capon a plump appearance, and set it aside on a dish.

* The difference between a raised pie and a *timbale* consists principally in the former being raised (by hand or otherwise) with a stiff paste, while the latter is prepared in a mould, lined with a more delicate kind of short crust, which is made edible.

Next, pare off the sinewy skin from the mouse-piece, or inner part of a leg of veal, *daube* it with seasoned lardoons of fat bacon, then place this, and an equal quantity of dressed ham, with the capon.

Prepare four pounds of hot-water paste (No. 1251); take two-thirds of this, mould it into a round ball on the slab with the palm of the hand, and then roll it out in the form of a band, about two feet long and six inches wide; trim the edges, and pare the ends square, taking care to cut them in a slanting direction; wet them with a paste-brush dipped in water mixed with a little flour, and wrap them over one another neatly and firmly, so as to show the joint as little as possible. Next, roll out half the remainder of the paste, either in a circular or oval form, about a quarter of an inch thick, to the size the pie is intended to be made; place this, with buttered paper, under it, on a baking-sheet, wet it round the edge with a paste-brush dipped in water, and stick a narrow band of the paste, about half an inch high, all round it, to within about an inch of the edge; the wall or crust of the pie is to be raised up round this, and by pressing on it with the tips of the fingers, it should be made to adhere effectually to the foundation. Then by pressing the upper part of the pie with the fingers and thumbs of both hands, it will acquire a more elegant appearance, somewhat resembling the curved lip of a vase. The base must be spread out in proportion to the top, by pressing on it with the thumb. The bottom and sides of the pie should now be lined with a coating of force-meat of fat livers (No. 247), or, if preferred, with veal and fat bacon, in equal proportions, well-seasoned, chopped fine and pounded; next, place in the veal and ham, previously cut up in thick slices and well-seasoned, and fill up the cavity with some of the force-meat; then add the capon and cover it over, and round, with the remainder of the force-meat, placing some truffles in with it, and cover the whole with thin layers of fat bacon. Roll out the remainder of the paste, and after wetting this, and the pie round the edges, use it to cover in the pie, pressing the edges of both tightly with the fingers and thumb, in order to make them adhere closely together; trim the edge neatly and pinch it round with the pastry pincers. The pie should then be egged over, and decorated, for which latter purpose a similar kind of paste must be used, being first rolled out thin, then cut out in the form of leaves, half-moons, rings, &c., and arranged according to the designs contained in No. 249: or, if preferred, a moulding raised from decorating boards with some of the paste may be used instead. The pie must then be placed in the oven, and baked for about four hours, and when done, should be withdrawn, and about a pint of strongly-reduced *consommé* (made from the carcasses of the capons, two calves' feet and the usual seasoning), should be introduced within it through a funnel: it must then be kept in a cold place until wanted for use; when the cover should be carefully removed without breaking it, and after the top of the pie has been decorated with some bright aspic-jelly, it may be put on again and sent to table.

Note.—For making pies of turkeys, fowls, pheasants, grouse, partridges, &c., follow the above directions.

1244. YORKSHIRE, OR CHRISTMAS PIE.

First, bone a turkey, a goose, a brace of young pheasants, four partridges, four woodcocks, a dozen snipes, four grouse, and four

widgeons; then boil and trim a small York ham and two tongues.
Season and garnish the inside of the fore-named game and poultry, as

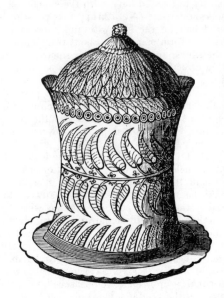

directed in the foregoing
case, with long fillets of
fat bacon and tongue,
and French truffles; each
must be carefully sewn
up with a needle and small
twine, so as to prevent
the force-meat from escaping while they are being
baked. When the whole
of these are ready, line
two round or oval braiz-
ing-pans with thin layers
of fat bacon, and after
the birds have been ar-
ranged therein in neat
order, and covered in with
layers of bacon and but-
tered paper, put the lids
on, and set them in the
oven to bake rather slowly,
for about four hours:
then withdraw them, and
allow them to cool.

While the foregoing is in progress, prepare some highly-seasoned
aspic-jelly with the carcasses of the game and poultry, to which add six
calves-feet, and the usual complement of vegetables, &c., and when
done, let it be clarified: one-half should be reduced previously to its
being poured into the pie when it is baked.

Make about sixteen pounds of hot-water paste (No. 1251), and use
it to raise a pie of sufficient dimensions to admit of its holding the
game and poultry prepared for the purpose, for making which follow
the directions contained in the foregoing article. The inside of the
pie must first be lined with thin layers of fat bacon, over which spread
a coating of well-seasoned force-meat of fat livers (No. 247); the birds
should then be placed in the following order:—First, put the goose at
the bottom with some of the small birds round it, filling up the cavities with some of the force-meat; then, put the turkey and the
pheasants with thick slices of the boiled ham between them, reserving
the woodcocks and widgeons, that these may be placed on the top:
fill the cavities with force-meat and truffles, and cover the whole with
thin layers of fat bacon, run a little plain melted butter over the surface, cover the pie in the usual manner, and ornament it with a bold
design. The pie must now be baked, for about six hours, in an oven
moderately heated, and when taken out, and after the reduced aspic
above alluded to has been poured into it, stop the hole up with a small
piece of paste, and set it aside in the larder to become cold.

Note.—The quantity of game, &c., recommended to be used in the
preparation of the foregoing pie may appear extravagant enough, but
it is to be remembered that these very large pies are mostly in request

at Christmas time. Their substantial aspect renders them worthy of appearing on the side-table of those wealthy epicures who are wont to keep up the good old English style, at this season of hospitality and good cheer.

1245. DEVONSHIRE SQUAB PIE.

FIRST, make two pounds of short paste (No. 1253), roll it up in a clean cloth, and set it aside till wanted. Then, cut about two pounds of griskin of pork in slices, season these with a little chopped onion, sage and thyme, pepper and salt, and place them on a dish; cut one pound of streaky bacon (previously parboiled for a quarter of an hour) also in slices, and put them with the pork; to these add about a dozen good apples, which, when peeled, and the cores taken out, must be cut in thick slices and put on a plate. Next, take rather more than half the paste, roll it out, and line an oblong tin mould, about two inches deep, with it; then, arrange the pork, bacon, and apples in this, in alternate layers, commencing with the bacon, over this put slices of apples, and then the pork, and so on until the whole is used up. The remainder of the paste must now be rolled out, and used to cover the pie with; fasten it securely round the edges, trim it, and pinch it round boldly with the pincers; ornament the top with leaves, &c., egg it over and bake it in an oven of moderate heat, for about two hours, and serve it hot.

1246. LEICESTERSHIRE PORK PIE.

CUT the pork up in square pieces, fat and lean, about the size of a cob-nut, season with pepper and salt, and a small quantity of sage and thyme chopped fine, and set it aside on a dish in a cool place. Next, make some hot-water-paste, using for this purpose (if desired) fresh-made hog's-lard instead of butter, in the proportion of eight ounces to the pound of flour. These pies must be raised by hand, in the following manner :—First, mould the paste into a round ball upon the slab, then roll it out to the thickness of half an inch, and with the back of the right hand indent the centre in a circle reaching to within three inches of the edge of the paste; next, gather up the edges all round, pressing it closely with the fingers and thumbs, so as to give to it the form of a purse; then continue to work it upwards, until the sides are raised sufficiently high; the pie should now be placed on a baking-sheet, with a round of buttered paper under it, and after it has been filled with the pork—previously prepared for the purpose, covered in with some of the paste in the usual manner. Trim the edges, and pinch it round with the pincers, decorate it, egg it over and bake it until done : calculating the time it should remain in the oven, according to the quantity of meat it contains.

1247. EEL-PIE, A L'ANGLAISE.

BONE two good-sized Thames eels, spread them out on a dish, and sprinkle them over with a little pepper and salt. Make some quenelle force-meat with either perch, tench, or carp : and after having mixed some chopped mushrooms, parsley, one shalot, spread a thick layer of it inside each eel, roll them up, cut the eel into four-inch lengths, and place them on a dish until wanted. Next, line a plain mould with short paste (No. 1253), arrange the pieces of eels in it, in neat order, season between each layer with chopped parsley and mushrooms, pepper and salt, and a spoonful of good *Béchamel* sauce ; cover in the pie, in the usual manner, with some of the paste, pinch the edge round, ornament the top, egg it over, and bake it in the oven for about an hour and a half : when done, dish it up on a napkin, and send to table.

Note.—When eel-pies are intended to be eaten cold, the top should be carefully removed, and the pie ornamented with aspic-jelly.

1248. SALMON-PIE, A LA RUSSE.

MAKE two pounds of short paste (No. 1253), roll it up in a cloth, and keep it in a cool place till wanted. Cut two pounds of fresh salmon in slices about half an inch thick, and set them aside on a plate ; fillet six anchovies, turn two dozen olives (removing the stone, by paring off the outer part without altering the shape), boil six eggs hard, and place the whole of these on a dish. Chop a pottle of mushrooms, two shalots, a handful of parsley, a little green-thyme, sweet basil, and tarragon ; put these ingredients into a stewpan with two ounces of butter, a little nutmeg, pepper, and salt, and simmer them over the stove-fire for about five minutes ; then add about half a pint of good brown sauce, and the juice of a lemon, stir the whole together over the stove-fire for five minutes longer, and then take it off. Next, roll out two-thirds of the paste to the thickness of the sixth of an inch, and after having thinly spread the inside of an oblong mould with butter, line it with this, and fill it with alternate layers of the slices of salmon, hard eggs, olives, and fillets of anchovies, at the same time spreading some of the fine-herbs sauce in between each layer ; the pie must be covered with the remainder of the paste in the usual manner ; bake it in a moderately-heated oven for about one hour and a half, and when done, dish it up on a napkin, and send to table.

Note.—These pies may also be made with sturgeon, trout, mackerel, char, gurnets, eels, soles, &c.: the addition of some sliced thunny* tends considerably to improve the flavor.

1249. PRESERVED HARE, AND OTHER GAME.

BONE a hare, lard it with narrow square strips of fat bacon, well seasoned with aromatic spices (No. 1250), and salt : then garnish the inside with some force-meat of fat livers (No. 247), and fold the hare so as to give to it a plump oval form ; then place it in an oval stewpan with a small glass of brandy ; cover it with thin layers of fat bacon, put the lid on the stewpan, and set it in the oven, in order that the hare may be sufficiently baked to set the meat : it should be then withdrawn.

Meanwhile, line the bottom and sides of an oval white earthen pan (sufficiently large to contain the hare) with thin layers of fat bacon, over these spread a coating of the force-meat about an inch thick, and place the hare in it, press it down tight, spread a thick layer of the force-meat on the top, cover this with layers of fat bacon, and place a covering of common paste over the whole ; then, set the pan on a

---

* Thunny is a fish abounding in the Mediterranean, and which is procurable, preserved in oil, at all the Italian warehouses.

baking-sheet, and put it in the oven to bake slowly for about two hours: it should then be withdrawn and allowed to cool. Let the paste be removed, the edges and sides of the pan washed, and the contents of the pan pressed down tight, so as to exclude any confined air, and after pouring over the surface some well-reduced glaze (made from the carcass), to the depth of about a quarter of an inch, keep the pie in a cool place until wanted for use.

When this kind of pie is intended to be kept for any length of time, some clean hog's-lard should be run over the surface to the depth of about an inch; when this has become set firm by cooling, the pan should be covered in with strong white paper pasted over it, or in lieu of this, a bladder (soaked in water, and well washed) may be tied over it.

Note.—All kinds of game should be preserved in the above method; but, if preferred, game may be used instead of livers for making the force-meat. Indeed, this is by far the best plan when the preserved game is intended for keeping, as force-meat, when made with livers of any kind, is more liable to fermentation than when made with fresh-killed game.

1250. AROMATIC-SPICES, FOR SEASONING.

TAKE of nutmegs and mace, one ounce each; of cloves and white pepper-corns, two ounces each; of sweet-basil, marjoram, and thyme, one ounce each, and half an ounce of bay-leaves: these herbs should be previously dried for the purpose: roughly pound the spices, then place the whole of the above ingredients between two sheets of strong white paper, and after the sides have been twisted or folded over tightly, so as to prevent as much as possible the evaporation of the volatile properties of the herbs and spices, place them on a baking-sheet in the skreen to become perfectly dry; they must then be pounded quickly, sifted through a fine hair-sieve, corked up tightly in a dry bottle, and kept for use.

DIFFERENT KINDS OF PASTE,

VIZ.,

Hot-water-Paste, for Raised Pie.	*Nouilles*-Paste.
French Paste, for do.	Office do.
Short Paste, for *Timbales*, &c.	Almond do.
Short Puff-Paste.	Gum do,
Tart-Paste.	Puff do.

1251. HOT-WATER PASTE, FOR RAISED PIES.

INGREDIENTS:—One pound of flour, four ounces of butter, a tea-spoonful of salt, about a gill and a half of hot water.

Place the flour on the pastry-table, spread it out with the back of the hand, so as to form a well or hollow in the centre, into this put the salt. Next, put the butter and water into a stewpan over the fire, and when they are sufficiently heated, so that one can just bear the finger in, pour them both gradually in upon the flour, and mix them quickly together with the hand, taking particular care to knead the whole firmly, and at once, into a compact paste : then press this smoothly together in a napkin, and afterward keep it covered up in a stewpan in a warm place till used.

1252. FRENCH PASTE, FOR RAISED PIES.

INGREDIENTS :—One pound of flour, four ounces of butter, a teaspoonful of salt, a gill and a half of cold water.

Place the flour on the slab, spread it out in the centre, then add the salt, water, and butter, and proceed to work the whole together with the hands into a very firm paste in the following manner :—When the ingredients have been worked into a paste, this must be brought to the edge of the slab ; then use the palms of both hands, applying them alternately, with great force, to spread and divide the paste into small parts; sprinkle a few drops of water over the paste, and knead it together : this is called breaking and kneading, and must be repeated three or four times. The paste must then be gathered up, placed in a clean rubber, and finally kneaded together by pressing upon it with the elbow. It will then be ready for use.

1253. SHORT-PASTE, FOR TIMBALES, ETC.

INGREDIENTS :—One pound of flour, half a pound of butter, a teaspoonful of salt, the yolks of two eggs, and nearly half a pint of water.

Make a well in the centre of the flour, place in this the yolks of eggs, salt, butter, and two-thirds of the water, then work the whole together with the hands into a somewhat firm paste; dip the fingers into the flour, to separate any of the paste that may adhere to them, sprinkle a little water over it, and then work the whole together into a ball, and keep it in a cloth till wanted for use.

1254. SHORT PUFF-PASTE.

INGREDIENTS :—One pound of flour, twelve ounces of butter, a little salt, one egg, and about half a pint of water.

Spread the flour out in the usual manner, place the egg, salt, half the butter, and two-thirds of the water at first, adding as much of the remainder as may be necessary afterward; work these together into a smooth and somewhat firm paste, then spread this out with the hand, and after the remaining half of the butter has been placed in the centre, the sides should be folded over so as to entirely enclose the butter. When the paste has stood five minutes, shake some flour with the hand over the slab and on the paste, then roll it out to the length of about two feet and a half, and about a foot wide ; this must be then folded into three, and after turning the paste round so as to bring the sides to face you, roll it out again in a similar manner ; after an interval of about ten minutes, repeat the rolling* twice more : the paste will then be fit for use.

* Each time that the paste undergoes the process of rolling, as here described, it is termed by cooks, " giving it a turn." This kind of paste requires only four turns.

1255. SHORT-PASTE FOR TARTS.

INGREDIENTS :—One pound of flour, half a pound of butter, two ounces of pounded sugar, a very little salt, two whole eggs, and about a gill of water.

Spread the flour out on the slab with a hollow in the centre, then add the butter, sugar, salt, and the water, and break in the two eggs ; work the whole together with the hands into a firm paste, and use it for covering fruit tarts, and lining tartlets, &c.

1256. NOUILLES-PASTE.

INGREDIENTS :—One pound of flour, about ten yolks of eggs, a tea-spoonful of salt, and merely sufficient water to melt the salt.

Place the flour on the slab, form a hollow in the centre, then put the salt in, with a little water to melt it, and add the yolks of eight eggs ; work the whole well together, at first rubbing the ingredients between the hands, and then, if necessary, add two more yolks of eggs, and finish working the paste by pushing it from you with the palms of the hands, using considerable pressure ; sprinkle a few drops of water over it, then knead the paste into a ball, and keep it wrapped up in a cloth until wanted for use. This paste must be kept very stiff.

1257. OFFICE-PASTE.

INGREDIENTS :—One pound of flour, eight ounces of pounded sugar, two whole eggs, and two yolks.

Place the flour on the slab, forming a hollow in the centre, then add the sugar and the eggs, and proceed to work the whole up into a stiff, compact body. If, however, the paste should appear dry, and present any difficulty in kneading, another yolk or two may be added.

This paste is mostly used for making ornaments for the second course.

1258. ALMOND-PASTE.

INGREDIENTS :—Eight ounces of Jordan almonds, a pound and a half of sugar, with half an ounce of gum-dragon.

First, scald the almonds, remove the skin, wash them, and allow them to steep in cold water for about twelve hours. Next, put the gum into a galley-pot, adding to it rather more than a gill of water, cover this over with paper twisted round the edge of the galley-pot, and allow the gum to steep until it has absorbed all the water ; it must then be placed in the centre of a strong cloth, which should be twisted round at each end by two persons (in the manner practised in wringing wet cloths) with considerable pressure, so as to squeeze the gum through the cloth, which must then be gathered up into a small basin. Pound the sugar and sift it through a very fine lawn-sieve.

The almonds must now be drained on a napkin, afterwards placed in a mortar, and pounded into a very smooth paste ; in order to prevent them from turning oily, while they are being pounded, it will be necessary to add a few drops of water or lemon-juice occasionally. As soon as the almonds present the appearance of a smooth paste, rub this through a very close hair-sieve, on to a plate. Next, place the pounded almonds in a convenient-sized sugar boiler, with about one-third part of the sugar, and stir these together over a stove-fire with a new wooden spoon, working the paste briskly and carefully the whole time, in order to prevent it from burning or acquiring the least color. As soon as the paste ceases to adhere to the sides of the pan, turn it out on to the slab, and begin to work in the remainder of the sugar and the gum; the latter must be previously worked on the marble slab with the hand, and some of the sugar should be added at intervals. When the whole of the ingredients have been worked together, the paste should form a white, stiff, and smooth compact body.

Note.—Almond paste, prepared as the above, is mostly used for making *croquantes,* small baskets filled with whipped cream and strawberries, &c. : it may also be used for making second-course ornaments ; being preferred by many for that purpose on account of its transparency.

1259. ALMOND-PASTE, ANOTHER METHOD.

INGREDIENTS :—Two pounds of fine-sifted sugar, eight ounces of pounded almonds, and one ounce of steeped gum-dragon.

When the ingredients have been prepared as directed in the foregoing case, work about half the sugar in with the gum ; then work the almonds with part of the remainder, add both together, and manipulate them with the remaining portion of the sugar, until the whole is thoroughly incorporated. If the paste is not stiff enough, a little more fine-sifted sugar should be filled in. In order to obtain this paste of a pure and dazzling whiteness, a very small quantity of cobalt blue, in powder, may be worked in with it, the color must be first mixed on a plate with a drop of water, preparatory to its being used.

Note.—About one-third part of starch, or hair powder, may be used to work in with this kind of almond paste ; this addition makes it less brittle, and consequently increases the facility of using it to cast mouldings, cutting out borders, &c. When, however, starch powder is introduced, double the usual quantity of gum-dragon is required.

1260. GUM-PASTE.

INGREDIENTS :—Two ounces of gum-dragon, one pound of fine-sifted sugar, and one pound of starch powder.

First, steep the gum-dragon in a small basin with nearly half a pint of water, cover it over with paper, and put the basin in a warm place : when the gum has absorbed all the water, press it through a cloth as directed for the almond paste, then work it on the marble slab with the palm of the hand, mixing in the sugar at intervals ; when the gum has absorbed all the sugar, the powder must be gradually worked in with it. The whole, when finished, should have the appearance of a very stiff compact smooth paste. Then gather it up into a round ball, put it on a plate covered with a basin, and keep it in a damp place, to prevent its becoming dry and hard.

1261. PUFF-PASTE.

INGREDIEETS :—One pound of flour, one pound of butter, the yolk of an egg, a tea-spoonful of salt, and about half a pint of water.

Place the flour on the pastry-slab, spread it out in the centre, so as to form a well, in which place the salt, a small piece of butter, the yolk of an egg, and about two-thirds of the quantity of water required to mix the paste; spread out the fingers of the right hand, and mix the ingredients together gradually with the tips of the fingers, adding a little more water, if necessary; when the whole is thoroughly incorporated together, sprinkle a few drops of water over it, and work the paste to and fro on the slab for two minutes, after which it should be rather soft to the touch, and present a perfectly smooth appearance.

The paste, thus far prepared, must now be spread out on the slab with the hands, and after the butter has been pressed in a cloth, to extract any milk it may contain, it should be placed in the centre of the paste, and partially spread, by pressing on it with the cloth; the four sides should then be folded over so as entirely to cover the butter; a little flour must next be shaken under and over it, and the paste should be shaped in a square form, measuring about ten inches each way, by pressing it out with the hand; it should then be placed on a clean baking-sheet, laid on some pounded rough ice,* and a deep sautapan also filled with ice should be placed upon it : by these means the paste will be kept cool and firm. About ten minutes after the paste has been made, take it from the ice and place it on a marble slab, shake a little flour over and under it, and then roll it out about two feet long, and ten inches wide; observing that the paste must be kept square at both ends, as much of the success depends on due attention being paid to the turning and folding. The paste should then be laid in three equal folds, and after these have been rolled over to cause them to adhere together, the paste must next be turned round in the opposite direction and rolled out again in the same manner as before; it should then be put back on the ice, and after allowing it to rest for about ten minutes or a quarter of an hour, roll it out again, or, as it is technically termed, give it two more turns; the paste must now be put back on the ice, and again rolled twice or three times, as the case may require, preparatory to its being cut out for whatever purpose it may be intended.

* In the summer season it is impossible to insure success in making puff-paste, unless rough ice be used to further that end, it being a matter of the first necessity that it should be kept cool and firm : two requisites that tend materially to facilitate the working of the paste, and also contribute very considerably to give to it that extraordinary degree of elasticity, when exposed to the heat of an oven, so well known to experienced pastrycooks. A piece of puff-paste, a quarter of an inch thick, when baked, will rise to the height of two inches—thus increasing in volume eight times. To effect this properly, it is necessary to procure three oblong tin pans, of the following dimensions : the first should measure 20 inches by 16, depth 3 inches ; the second, 18 inches by 14, depth 2 inches ; and the third, 16 inches by 12, depth 3 inches. Place some pounded rough ice in the largest, then set the second-sized tin on this, with the puff-paste in it; lastly, put the smallest pan, also filled with ice, on the top of the paste : by this method puff-paste may be easily made to perfection during the hottest days of summer.

In winter, the use of ice may, of course, be dispensed with. In extreme cold weather, when the butter is very hard, it will be necessary to press it in a cloth or on the slab, to give it more expansion, and thus facilitate its incorporation with the paste. Care must be taken, in mixing the paste, not to make it too stiff, especially in summer, as, in that case, it becomes not only troublesome to work, but it also affects its elasticity in baking.

VOL-AU-VENT, TOURTE, AND PATTY CASES

Vol-au-vent Cases, for an *Entrée.*   *Timbale* of *Nouilles* Cases.
Tourte   ditto   ditto.   Patties, *à la Mazarine.*
Puff-paste Patty Cases.   Mutton Patties, *à la Windsor.*
Crôustade   ditto.

1262. VOL-AU-VENT CASES, FOR AN ENTREE.

For this purpose, one pound of puff-paste will be required, and when mixing it, the juice of one lemon must be added. The paste must be rolled perfectly square at the ends, and folded likewise with the greatest correctness, in order to ensure the *vol-au-vent's* rising perfectly straight all round, which cannot be the case if it is rolled unevenly. Five turns and a half must be given to the paste, allowing about seven minutes to elapse between each turn: observing that previously to folding up the last turn and a half, the paste must be passed over with a paste-brush dipped in water or a little lemon-juice; attention must be paid, in giving the last two turns, to roll the paste out, and also to fold it, especially when giving the last turn on spreading it to the size the *vol-au-vent* is intended to be made, so as to be able to cut it as thick as the quantity of paste will admit of; just before cutting out the *vol-au-vent*, the piece of paste must be wetted on one side with the brush dipped in water. Next, roll out about four ounces of common paste to the diameter of a dinner-plate, lay this on the puff-paste, just passing the rolling-pin over to cause it to adhere, and then place it on the baking-sheet, previously wetted in the centre to receive it. For the purpose of guiding the hand when cutting it out, the cover of a stewpan or *bain-marie* should be placed on it; then with a small sharp-pointed knife proceed to cut round the edge of the cover, forming perpendicular flutes or scollops; the knife must be held comparatively loose, yet securely, with the tips of the fingers only. Remove the trimmings and the cover, egg over the surface, and be careful not to smear the edges of the paste, as that would prevent it from rising evenly; then with the point of the small knife, held slanting, make a slight incision all round the surface, within about three-quarters of an inch of the edge, and with the point notch round the extreme edge of the inner circle, so as to separate it entirely from the inner edge of the outer circle. The *vol-au-vent* should now be put into the oven (not too hot, as excess of heat prevents the paste from rising); as soon as it begins to rise, let a trivet be quickly slipped under it, and the oven immediately closed. When it has risen about two inches, and before it has acquired any color, a broad band of double paper (or a wooden hoop from an old sieve), measuring two inches more in circumference than the *vol-au-vent*, about eight inches high, and fastened in the form of a hoop, must be placed round it to protect the sides from being suddenly caught by the heat, which otherwise would not only scorch it, but also check its full development: it should remain in the oven quite an hour to be thoroughly baked. When the *vol-au-vent* is done, withdraw it from the oven; instantly remove the cover, and after carefully detaching all the greasy crumb from the centre, without in any way injuring the sides of the case, lift it out, taking particular care to stop up any thinly-covered places in the inside of the case with small flakes of the crumb which has been removed : this precaution is necessary in order to prevent the sauce from escaping through any fissures that may exist.

1263. TOURTE CASES, FOR AN ENTREE.

FIRST, prepare half a pound of puff-paste, and give it four turns, in the usual manner; make also half a pound of common short paste, take half of this, knead it into a round ball, roll it out to the size of a dinner-plate, put it on a round baking-sheet, and place a tampoon* of paper in the centre. The puff-paste must then be rolled out about twenty inches long, wetted over with the brush dipped in water, and folded lengthwise in three; this must be rolled again in its width, just sufficient to make it about four inches wide : the paste should then be slightly wetted over, and then folded as before : by this time, it should form a band, measuring about twenty inches long by nearly two inches wide, and about half an inch thick. The edges of the paste must now be pared away, with a small sharp knife, held perpendicularly in the right hand, whilst the paste must be slightly pressed on the slab with the fore-part of the fingers. Next, add the trimmings of the puff-paste to the remaining half of the common paste, knead both together, roll this out to the size of a plate, and after having first wetted the foundation round the edge, place it over the tampoon and press it down all round with the thumb; then wet the edge of the *tourte* round again, and apply the band in the following manner. Take hold of the band at both ends, and begin by fastening that held in the right hand round the edge of the *tourte*, and continue fixing the band all round as fast as it is dropped in its place with the left hand; press the first end down so as to thin it, wet this part with the brush, and after paring away a little of the other end, so as to thin that also, fasten both together by effectually joining them. Press the band down all round with the thumb, and flute it round the edge by jagging it slightly with the back of a knife.

The *tourte* must then be edged over with a paste-brush, so as to carefully avoid smearing the edges of the band. Place it in a moderately-heated oven, and let it be baked of a light color; when done,

* From the French word *tampon*, a kind of small, hard cushion : in the present case, it should consist of a large sheet of rather soft paper, twisted in the form of a circular cushion, about four inches in diameter.

withdraw it, make an incision with a small knife all round the bottom of the crown, inside the band, remove the crown or top, take out the tampoon, and the case will then be ready for garnishing.

1264. PUFF-PASTE, PATTY-CASES.

MAKE one pound of puff-paste in the manner described in No. 1261, and give it seven turns, wetting the last turn before folding it; then roll the paste out so as to leave it scarcely a quarter of an inch thick, and about three minutes afterwards, take a fluted circular tin-cutter about two inches in diameter, and use this to stamp out as many patties as may be required; previously to stamping out each patty, the cutter should be first dipped in very hot water, as the heat thus imparted to the cutter causes it to slip easily through the paste, and produces the same effect as if it were cut with a sharp knife; in consequence of there being little or no pressure on the edges, the paste has thus a much better chance of rising while baking, especially in the summer season. As soon as the patties are cut out, they should be immediately placed in rows, on a baking-sheet previously wetted over, about two inches apart from each other; then egg them over with a soft brush dipped in beaten egg, being careful not to smear the edges, and stamp them in the centre, making a slight incision through their surface, with a plain circular tin-cutter about one inch and a half in diameter (this cutter must also be dipped in hot water each time it is used). The patties should then be quickly put in the oven and baked of a light color; when done, let the covers or tops be removed, pick out the inner crumb carefully with the point of a small knife, and then place the patties with their tops on a baking-sheet lined with clean paper.

1265. CROUSTADE CASES.

ROLL out half a pound of *timbale* paste (No. 1253) to the thickness of a penny-piece, then take a circular tin-cutter, about four inches in diameter, and stamp out a dozen flats; next, press one of these on the end of a circular piece of wood, about six inches long by about one and a quarter in diameter (or failing this, cut a carrot to that shape). Line a *dariole*-mould, previously slightly spread with butter, with the paste so prepared: use the thumb to make the paste lie evenly in the mould, trim away the edges, raise the sides a little, then fill each *croustade* so finished with flour, mixed with a fourth part of chopped suet, and bake them of a light color; when done, empty them, brush them out, and place them on a dish. The tops must be stamped out with a small circular fluted cutter, from some puff-paste, rolled seven turns; put these on a baking sheet previously wetted to receive them, egg them over with a soft brush, place a much smaller circular piece of paste on the top of each, egg these over, and then bake them of a bright light color; when done, trim them, and place each on the top of one of the *croustades* after they are garnished.

1266. TIMBALE OF NOUILLES CASES.

PREPARE the *nouilles* as directed in No. 774, and parboil them in water for ten minutes, then drain them thoroughly on a sieve; afterward toss them with two ounces of butter, a spoonful of good *Béchamel* sauce (No. 5), and a little grated nutmeg, in a stewpan over the stove-fire for five minutes; then, throw them into a sautapan, full two inches deep, previously slightly spread with butter; cover them down evenly with a circular piece of buttered paper, and allow them to become perfectly cold. The preparations must then be turned out of the sautapan on the table, upon a sheet of paper; and the *croûstades* or *timbales* should be stamped out of this with a plain circular tin-cutter about an inch and a half in diameter, and placed on a dish; they must next be rolled in very fine fresh-made bread-crumbs, afterwards dipped in beaten egg, and then bread-crumbed over again: smooth the bread-crumbs on the *timbales* by rolling and patting them, place them in neat order on a dish, and with a plain circular cutter, an inch in diameter, stamp out the surface of each, exactly in the centre, making only a slight incision. When about to send the *timbales* to table, place them carefully in neat order on the wire lining of a deep frying-pan (half filled with clean hog's-lard, made quite hot; immerse them in the fat, and fry them of a bright yellow color; when done, drain them on a cloth, and empty them carefully with a fork.

Note.— *Croûstades* or small *timbales* may also be made of vermicelli, prepared in the same way as *nouilles*. Rice may also be used for the same purpose.

1267. PATTIES, A LA MAZARIN.

GIVE seven turns to half a pound of puff-paste, roll it out to the thickness of a penny-piece, and stamp out two dozen tops with a plain circular tin-cutter, about one inch and a half in diameter; then gather up the trimmings, knead them together, roll them out, and stamp two dozen more; place these on a baking-sheet, about an inch and a half apart from each other, and wet them over with a soft brush; garnish the centre of each with a little force-meat of any kind, place the tops on them, and use the upper part of a smaller cutter to press them down, so as to fasten the two parts together; they must then be egged over, and baked in a rather brisk oven; when done, dish them up on a napkin, and serve.

1268. MUTTON PATTIES, A LA WINDSOR.

TRIM the lean parts of a loin of mutton, free from fat and sinew; cut this up into small scollops, mix these with some fine-herbs, consisting of chopped mushrooms, parsley, and shalot; season with pepper and salt, and add a *ragout*-spoonful of reduced *Espagnole* sauce; use the preparation to fill some *croûstades* lined with short paste, cover them with some of the same kind of paste, and bake them of a light color. When done, remove the tops from the patties, pour a little thin *Espagnole* or Italian sauce in each, cover them with puff-paste tops (made similar to *croûstade* tops), and serve.

Note.— *Croûstades* and patties are garnished with scollops or *ragouts* of chicken, game, all kinds of fillets of fish, the tails of crayfish, prawns and shrimps, with oysters in scollops, small dice, and also with lobster cut up in small dice. They may be sauced either with *Suprême, Béchamel,* or *Allemande,* Lobster, Oyster, or Crayfish sauces.

CAKES IN GENERAL,

COMPRISING

Brioche Paste.
Baba, or Polish Cake.
Compiègne Cake.
German Kouglauff.
Parisian Cake.
Victoria Cake.
Savarin.
Savoy Cake.
Finger, or Naples Biscuit.
Plum Cake.
Scotch Bread.
Plain Seed Cake.
Brussels Biscuits, or Rusks.
Pound Cake.
Flemish Gauffres.
French Gauffres.
Almond Gauffres.
Nougats.
Parisian Nougats.
Small Nougats, à la Chantilly.
Genoese Cakes.
Genoese Cakes, with Almonds.
Madeleines.
Spanish Cake (Petite-choux).

Duchess Loaves.
Petite-choux, with Caramel.
Profitrolles.
Mecca Loaves.
Queen's Cakes.
Almond Cakes.
Meringues.
Italian Biscuits.
Venetian do.
Swedish Macaroons.
Brown-Bread Biscuits.
Ginger Cakes.
Champagne Biscuits.
Orange do.
Peach do.
Apricot do.
Chocolate Glacés.
Varieties of other Glacés.
Suisse Lecrelets.
Sicilian Biscuits.
Russian do.
Albert do.
Victoria do.

1269. BRIOCHE PASTE.

INGREDIENTS:—One pound of flour, ten ounces of butter, half an ounce of German yeast, a tea-spoonful each of salt and sugar, and about seven eggs.

Put one-fourth part of the flour on the slab, spread it out to form a well, then place the yeast in the centre, and proceed to dissolve it with a little tepid water; when this is effected, add sufficient water to mix the whole into a rather soft paste; knead this into the form of a round ball, put it into a stewpan capable of containing three times its quantity, score it round the sides with a knife, put the lid on and set it to rise in a rather warm place; in winter it may be put in the skreen, but in hot weather the fermentation will proceed more satisfactorily if it is merely placed on the kitchen table, or in some such place of moderate warmth. This part of the operation is termed setting the sponge. Next, put the remainder of the flour on the slab, and spread it out in the centre to form the well; then place the salt and sugar, and a tea-spoonful of water to dissolve these, after which the butter must be added; break in six eggs, and work the whole together with the hands until well mixed, first working it between the hands, and then rubbing it with both fists held flat on the slab, and moving them to and fro, so as to thoroughly reduce any remaining lumps in the paste. By the time the paste is mixed, the sponge will probably have risen sufficiently; to be perfect, it must rise to three times its original size; when spread out on the paste prepared to receive it, it should present the appearance of a sponge, from which it takes its name.

Both the above should be then immediately, gently, but thoroughly mixed. A napkin must be spread in a wooden bowl, or a basin, some flower shaken over it, and the *brioche*-paste lifted into it; then shake a little flour over the paste, and after throwing the ends of the napkin over all, set the bowl containing the paste in a cool place, free from any current of air.

It is usual to make this kind of paste late in the evening previously to the day on which it is required for use. The first thing on the following morning, the *brioche*-paste must be turned off the napkin on to the slab; then shake some flour under and over it, and fold the paste over half a dozen times, pressing it down with the knuckles each time; put the paste back again into the bowl in the same way as before; and about three hours afterwards, knead it again in a similar manner, previously to its being baked.

If the paste, when finished, appears to be full of small globules of air, and is perfectly elastic to the touch, it is certain to be well made, and, when baked, will be both light and of a bright clear color.

If the paste is intended to be made into one *brioche* only, take five-sixths of it, mould this into the form of a round ball or cushion, and place it in a plain mould or paper-case* (previously spread with butter) with the smooth surface uppermost; press it down in the case with the knuckles, and, after moulding the remaining piece of paste in a similar manner, first, wet the surface of the other part over with the paste-brush dipped in water, and then, after inserting the pointed end of this into the centre of that portion of the *brioche* which has been already placed in the case, press the head down upon it with the back of the hand; egg the *brioche* over with a paste-brush, score the sides slightly, in a slanting direction, place it on a baking-sheet and put it in the oven (at moderate heat). As soon as the *brioche* begins to rise, and has acquired a slight degree of color, let it be covered over with a sheet of paper: about two hours will suffice to bake a large *brioche* of double the quantity of paste described in this article.

Note.—*Brioches* may be varied in their form, when intended to be served as fancy bread, for breakfast, &c.; in which case they should be moulded in the shape of twists, fingers, rings, &c. When served on the refreshment table, at routs, public breakfasts, balls, &c., dried cherries, citron, candied orange or lemon-peel, pine-apple or angelica, steeped in some kind of liqueur, may be introduced; in either of these cases, previously to mixing in the fruit, part of the paste must be

---

* The case is thus made. For a large *brioche*, intended to be served as a second-course remove, take a large sheet of Bristol-board, and cut a band from this, measuring about two feet long by eight inches broad; the two ends should be sewed together with strong thread, and some small bands of paper, smeared over with flour-and-water paste, should be stuck over the sewing to make it more secure. This hoop should then be placed upon a circular piece of the pasteboard, cut to fit its circumference, and both these must be securely fastened together by placing small strips of paper (pasted over) all round the angle of the bottom part of the case; these must be placed close together and crosswise, with one end fastened under the case, while the other is lapped round the angle and fastened at the side. These strips of paper, after becoming very dry, should receive another row over them, to make the case stronger.

reserved, which, after being rolled out, must be used to enclose the other part of the *brioche*. This precaution is necessary to prevent the fruit from protruding through the paste, as it becomes calcined by the heat of the oven, and gives an unsightly appearance to the sponge. When fruit has been mixed in a *brioche*, it should be (when baked) glazed with fine sugar by the salamander.

Gruyere or Parmesan cheese, in equal proportions, are sometimes introduced in a *brioche* for a second-course remove; the first should be cut up in dice, the latter grated. As in the above cases, this kind of *brioche* must be enclosed in a portion of the paste reserved for that purpose.

1270. BABA, OR POLISH CAKE.

INGREDIENTS :—Two pounds of flour, twenty ounces of butter, four ounces of sugar, six ounces of muscatel raisins, four ounces of currants, two ounces of candied citron, a good pinch of saffron, two wine-glasses of brandy, and the same quantity of rum, half an ounce of salt, about fifteen eggs, and one ounce of German yeast.

First, set the sponge with one-fourth part of the flour and the yeast, in the same way as directed for preparing *brioche*. Then, spread out the remainder of the flour so as to form a hollow in the centre: place in this the butter and salt previously dissolved with a drop or two of water, four ounces of pounded sugar, and break in fifteen eggs : mix the whole thoroughly, working the paste with the hands on the slab. When this is effected, gather the paste up closely, and take up portions of it with the hands, and jerk or throw these down again on the other part of the paste ; continue working it in this fashion for five minutes, then, if the sponge is sufficiently risen, spread it out over the paste and mix both together lightly. A large mould should now be spread with butter, and lined not more than half through with a thin coating of the paste, and as soon as this has been effected, all the fruit, the rum, the brandy, and an infusion of the saffron, must be added ; the whole of which must be instantly well mixed and lifted into the mould.

The *baba* should next be set, to rise gradually, in a place where the temperature is moderate and free from any current of air ; and as soon as it has risen in a satisfactory manner, which may easily be known by its increasing sufficiently in quantity (through fermentation), to nearly fill the mould,—although at first only half filled, the *baba* should be immediately placed in the oven on a thick baking-sheet, with a thick roll of paper round the bottom of the mould to protect the *baba* from receiving too much heat at first. From one hour and a half to two hours will suffice to bake it.

Particular care should be taken in baking the *baba*, to prevent its acquiring a deep color ; to obviate this, it must be baked in an oven of moderate heat.

1271. COMPIEGNE CAKE.

INGREDIENTS :—Two pounds of flour, twenty-two ounces of butter, half a pint of double cream, six ounces of pounded sugar, two wine-glasses of maraschino, one ounce of German yeast, fifteen eggs, and half an ounce of salt.

Set the sponge with one-fourth part of the flour and the yeast in the usual way (see *Brioche* No. 1269), and while it is rising, prepare the paste at follows :—

Place the remainder of the flour on the marble slab, spread it out in the centre to form the well, place in this the salt, and sugar (with a very little water to dissolve the salt), the butter and eggs, and proceed to mix these thoroughly in the same way as *brioche ;* just before adding the sponge, mix in the maraschino and the whipped cream. The paste must be instantly lifted into an appropriate-sized mould, previously spread with butter, and deposited in a comparatively-cool place to rise, or ferment in the usual manner : as soon as it has nearly reached the surface of the mould, stick a band of paper round the edge, and put it in the oven to bake, at a very moderate heat ; remembering that an essential characteristic of this kind of cake, is a light color.

It is customary to eat the *Compiègne* cake hot, and it is served in various ways. When turned out of the mould, a small piece should be taken out of the centre of the top, and a few glasses of maraschino poured in through the opening; or, the cake may be cut up in horizontal slices half an inch thick, and previously to putting them together again, some apricot marmalade may be placed between each. Dried cherries and angelica may be introduced in the composition of these cakes, previously to their being baked.

1272. GERMAN KOUGLAUFF.

INGREDIENTS :—Two pounds of flour, one pound and a quarter of butter, eight whole eggs, and eight yolks ; one and a quarter ounce of German yeast, four ounces of sugar, half an ounce of cinnamon powder, and grated lemon-peel, or the rind of lemon rubbed on lump sugar, and afterwards scraped off, half an ounce of salt, half a pint of single cream, and six ounces of Jordan almonds.

First, place the butter in a convenient-sized white kitchen pan, and work it with a clean wooden spoon for about ten minutes, by which time the butter should present the appearance of a thick cream ; the cinnamon, lemon and sugar, the pounded sugar, about one-fourth part of the flour, and three eggs should then be added, and the whole quickly worked together for a few minutes ; then add the remainder of the flour and eggs gradually, still continuing to work the paste with the wooden spoon. When the whole has been used up, spread the paste out in the centre, and add the yeast (previously dissolved with the salt in the cream made tepid for the purpose); work the whole thoroughly, then pour this batter into a large mould, previously spread with butter, split the almonds, and place them round the inside of the mould in close order. Bake the *kouglaüf* in an oven of moderate heat. Its color should be of a bright reddish yellow.

In Germany, it is customary to shake some cinnamon sugar all over this kind of cake as soon as it is turned out of the mould.

1273. PARISIAN CAKE.

INGREDIENTS.—Two pounds of flour, twenty ounces of butter, six ounces of sugar, eight whole eggs and eight yolks, one pint of single cream, eight ounces of Jordan almonds, and two ounces of bitter ditto, eight ounces of pistachio kernels, four ounces of candid orange-peel, half an ounce of salt, one and a quarter ounce of yeast.

First, let the pistachio kernels be scalded, remove the hulls, split each kernel into four strips, and place these aside in a small basin. The candied orange-peel must then be shred into small thin narrow strips, and put with the pistachios. Next, remove the hulls from the almonds, wash and pound them into a very soft paste (adding a few drops of water to prevent them from becoming oily), then mix them with the cream, and after they have steeped for half an hour, let the whole be rubbed through a tammy, the same as a *purée*, and kept in very cool place until wanted for use.

For mixing this cake, follow in all respect the directions given for the German *kouglaüff* (No. 1272), adding the pistachios and orange-peel after lining the mould with the plain paste; the yeast must be dissolved in a little tepid water, and the almonds and cream added cold. It should be baked nearly of the same color as a Savoy cake.

Note.—It is necessary to put all these cakes back in the oven for two or three minutes, after they are turned out of the mould, to prevent them from becoming shriveled on the surface, or from otherwise shrinking and falling in, which is unavoidably the case when any steam has collected upon them.

1274. VICTORIA CAKE.

INGREDIENTS :—Two pounds of flour, twenty ounces of butter, twelve eggs, six ounces of pounded sugar, six ounces of ground or pounded almonds, also a few bitter ditto, eight ounces of dried cherries, four ounces of green citron cut up in shreds, half an ounce of cinnamon powder, half a pint of whipped cream, one ounce and a quarter of German yeast, two wine-glasses of brandy, and half an ounce of salt.

Mix the above ingredients according to the directions given for the German *kouglaüff:* except that the yeast must be dissolved in a spoonful of tepid water, and the cream whipped previously to its being added the last thing. When the cake is mixed, it should be placed in a tin hoop, measuring about ten inches in diameter by four inches deep. A double sheet of paper, spread with butter, should be first placed on a stout copper baking-sheet, and the hoop, also lined with paper, next placed upon it, ready to receive the mixture. As soon as the fermentation of the paste has taken place in a satisfactory degree, causing it to increase to twice its original quantity, let it be immediately put in the oven (at moderate heat), and baked of a light color.

This kind of cake may be served as a second-course remove; some apricot marmalade, diluted with a little lemon-juice and warmed, should be sent to table with it separately in a sauce-boat, or, if preferred, instead of the apricot, some German custard sauce, made in the following manner :—

Put four yolks of eggs in a middle-sized *bain-marie*, and add two ounces of pounded sugar, two wine-glasses of Sherry, and the rind of an orange or lemon grated on sugar. Place the *bain-marie* containing these ingredients in a larger stewpan with water sufficient to reach about one inch up the outside of the *bain-marie;* set this on a slow stove-fire, and commence whisking or milling the contents briskly, until it appears like a rich-looking frothy custard. Be careful not to allow the cream to become too hot, as that would set the yolks of eggs, and thereby decompose the custard.

1274a. SAVARIN CAKE.

INGREDIENTS :—Two pounds of flour, four ounces of sugar, twenty ounces of fresh butter, fifteen eggs, half an ounce of salt, one ounce of German yeast, and four ounces of blanched and shred almonds.

First, set the sponge, with one-fourth part of the flour, and the yeast, in the same manner as directed for making *brioche*. Then, while the sponge is placed in a moderate temperature, to admit of its rising gradually and satisfactorily, place the remainder of the flour in a large white pan or basin, hollow out the centre, and having first placed therein the salt, moistened with a tea-spoonful of water, the butter, sugar, and ten whole eggs broken, proceed to manipulate the whole with the right hand, beating up the paste until it easily leaves the sides of the pan ; you then break in the remainder of the eggs, two at a time, until the paste has absorbed the whole ; and, after having continued to work it five minutes longer, proceed to fill an appropriate-sized mould with it in manner following :—First, let the inside of the mould be well buttered, after which, strew the shred almonds equally over and about the surface of the interior ; next, work the paste up again for a minute or two, and put a sufficient quantity thereof into the mould to rather more than half fill it. You now place the *Savarin* in a moderate temperature to rise until it has nearly filled the mould ; when, after first sticking a broad band of thick paper round the upper part of the mould, so as effectually to prevent the batter from running over the sides of the mould, while it is being baked, put it into an oven of moderate heat, and bake it for about two hours. When done, turn the *Savarin* out of the mould, and after first running a knife into several parts of the surface, pour gently a rather thick orange syrup, containing a glassful of curaçao, over and into the *Savarin*, and send to table quite warm.

This kind of cake is sometimes, in order to vary its appearance, after being first well soaked with a warm rich syrup, rolled all over in orange or lemon sugar.

1275. SAVOY CAKE.

INGREDIENTS :—One pound of the finest quality of sugar (pounded), fourteen eggs, four ounces and a half of the finest flour, and four ounces and a half of potato flour.

First, separate the yolks from the whites of the eggs, taking care not to drop the least portion of the yolks into the whites, as any mixture of these renders it impossible to whisk the whites firm. The yolks must be put into a kitchen basin, and the whites into an egg bowl, to be kept in a cool place until used. Add the sugar to the yolks, throw in as much salt as will stand on a sixpence, and either some vanilla, lemon, or orange sugar, or else a few drops of any kind of essence, such as orange, lemon, orange-flowers, vanilla, or bitter almonds. Work these together with a wooden spoon, until the whole presents the appearance of a thick creamy batter. The whites must now be whisked into a firm substantial snowy froth ; while this is going on, let both the wheaten and potato flour be well mixed in with the batter. As soon as the whites are satisfactorily whisked,* proceed to mix them also in with the batter : they must be added in small quantities at first, until it has become smoothly diluted ; the whole of what remains should then be added, and gently yet thoroughly mixed. The batter thus prepared, must now be gently poured into a mould previously prepared for the purpose in the following manner :—

About one pound of beef or veal suet should be first chopped very fine, then melted down in a stewpan ; after it has been strained through a napkin, pour this into the mould, turn it round in all directions, so that the fat may touch all the angles and recesses ; it must then be poured out, and the mould should be turned upside down on a plate, and allowed to stand in a warm place, for a few minutes, that the fat may be entirely drained off. About one pound of the finest sifted sugar should now be immediately put into the mould, and shaken about in it, in order that it may effectually cover the whole of the inside of the mould with a perfectly smooth white surface. Care must be taken to avoid leaving a greater quantity of fat adhering to the sides of the mould than is positively necessary ; for if there be too thick a coating of sugar in the mould, the Savoy cake will be more difficult to bake of a light color ; the heat of the oven being liable to partially calcine the sugar, and thus darken its hue.

When the Savoy cake is ready to be baked, tie a broad band of paper (folded in three) round the base, and put a few wood-ashes on the baking-sheet, previously to placing the cake on the latter, before putting it in the oven, which must be of very moderate heat ; particular care must be taken to keep it closed as mush as possible while the cake is baking, and also not to increase its temperature afterwards : this may be easily avoided, if the oven be substantially built,† by its being properly heated at first, it will then retain for some time an even temperature.

It is impossible to determine on the exact length of time that this, or, indeed, any other cake should remain in the oven before it is done ; this will mainly depend upon the construction of the oven, and partly on the necessity there may be for occasionally opening it during the process of baking the cake.

---

* The whites must be whisked slowly at first, increasing the motion of the hand gradually until it reaches the greatest possible speed : the motion of the whisk must be kept up at this rate, until the whites are become sufficiently firm, when they must be instantly mixed in with the batter,—otherwise they are liable, by partial decomposition, to lose their consistency.

† Brick ovens are best adapted for baking all kinds of large cakes, pies, &c.: the reason of this is chiefly owing to their being generally constructed of a superior kind of bricks and tiles, requiring, from their compactness, one or two hours to heat them thoroughly ; such an oven is, therefore, capable of retaining its heat a much longer time than one built of iron ; unless, indeed, when the latter happens to be very substantially made, which is too seldom the case. Iron-built ovens are also desirable, as well for their economy of fuel, as for the short time in which they may be heated ; and, further, on account of the celerity and convenience with which *one person* may prepare large quantities of small pastry, and bake it also. This could not so easily be done with a brick oven by only one person ; as, when it happens that a large oven is full of pastry, some one must be in constant attendance, in order to watch and regulate the different degrees of heat or baking which the several articles require, and determine their stay and position in the oven accordingly. All this needs the most vigilant care and attention, in order to secure success in the baking of delicate pastry ; for, however well it may have been prepared, if it is not equally well baked, the result will be unsatisfactory.

The best way to ascertain whether the cake be done is to run a wooden skewer down the centre, and if, when withdrawn, the skewer is dry, and free from any portion of the cake in an unbaked state, it will be safe to turn it out of the mould; it should then be of a light color and smooth surface.

Note.—Savoy cakes may also be made by using twelve, sixteen, or even twenty eggs to one pound of sugar; but when a cake of large size is required, the proportions must be at the rate of twelve, fourteen, or at the utmost sixteen eggs to one pound of sugar; even in the latter case, such batter would not prove successful where four pounds are required to fill one mould. Savoy-cake batter made in the proportion of sixteen or twenty eggs to one pound of sugar, is best adapted for small sponge cakes, finger biscuits, drops, &c.

1276. FINGERS, OR NAPLES BISCUITS.

PREPARE the batter as directed in the foregoing case; then fill a biscuit-forcer with some of it, and after securely folding down the open end, proceed to use the batter in the following manner:—Cut a sheet of foolscap paper in two, fold these lengthwise, in order to mark a straight line along the centre of the half-sheets; the forcer must then be held in the right hand, pressing the batter out by working the thumb upon it, while the pointed end must be guided with the left hand. In this manner the biscuits must be spread, or rather dropped in straight lines, resembling fingers, about three inches long by half an inch wide: they should form two rows, being divided by the line in the centre of the paper. When the sheet is full, place it upon a large sheet of kitchen paper (or demy) containing about one pound of the finest sifted sugar, placed in the form of a ridge along the upper part of the paper as it lies on the table before you; the sheet containing the biscuits being placed just below the sugar, it will only be necessary to lift up the other paper at each corner with the hands, and by given it a slight jerk, the sugar will be thrown on. to the biscuits: then, by taking hold of the paper, holding the biscuits at each upper corner, and gently shaking it as it is held up in a perpendicular position, the sugar will be made to slide over the whole at once. By this means the biscuits are effectually glazed without waste. The finger biscuits must be immediately placed on a baking-sheet, and put in the oven (at very moderate heat); about a quarter of an hour will suffice to bake them. When done, they should be of a very light yellow color.

Note.—With the same kind of batter, and by using a biscuit-forcer,* the shape of these small biscuits may be easily varied according to taste or fancy.

1277. PLUM CAKE.

INGREDIENTS required:—One pound and a half of flour, one pound and a half of butter, one pound of fine sugar, one pound of dried

---

* These biscuit-forcers are also made of tin, resembling a funnel in shape; they have a bag of wash-leather, or canvas cloth, affixed round the upper part, with a string running through the top, which, when the bag is filled with batter, is drawn tight, thus effectually preventing it from escaping at the upper end, while it is forced out at the point below. The use of this utensil, however, is objectionable, from the leather or canvas contracting a nauseous odor. In other respects it answers the purpose well enough.

cherries (slightly chopped), one pound and a half of currants, one pound and a half of candied orange, lemon, and citron peel, in equal quantities,—all these must be cut in small shreds; eight ounces of ground or pounded almonds, eight whole eggs, the zest or rind of four oranges (rubbed on a piece of sugar and afterwards scraped off), half an ounce of ground spices, consisting of cinnamon, cloves, and nutmeg, mixed in equal proportions, half a pint of Cognac brandy, and a tea-spoonful of salt.

Place the butter in a large white earthen pan, and work it with a wooden spoon until it presents the appearance of a creamy substance; next add gradually the flour, sugar, and the eggs, still continuing to work the batter the whole of the time. When these have been thoroughly mixed, the cherries, currants, candied-peel, ground almonds, brandy, spices, and salt, must also be added gradually, and as soon as these ingredients are incorporated with the batter, let the preparation be poured into a convenient-sized tin hoop (previously lined with double bands of buttered paper), and placed on a stout-made copper baking-sheet, with two sheets of buttered paper under the cake, to prevent the composition from becoming calcined by the heat of the oven. A moderate heat will be sufficient to bake this cake, and care must be taken not to put any fire under the oven while it is baking, so as to increase the heat.

These cakes, when baked, should be iced over with sugar in the following manner :—

First, mix eight ounces of very fine pounded almonds with double that quantity of fine sifted sugar, a little orange-water, and sufficient whites of eggs to form the whole into a soft paste; spread a coating of this all over the surface of the cake (after it has become cold); and when it is hardened by drying, let the whole be iced over with the following preparation :—

Place about six whites of eggs in a convenient-sized basin, add about one pound and a half of the finest sifted loaf sugar, and work these well together, with a clean wooden spoon, adding occasionally a little lemon-juice, until the whole presents the appearance of a very thick yet comparatively liquid shiny substance of a pure white. Use this icing to mask the entire surface of the cake, with a coating about a quarter of an inch thick; allow this to become firmly set, by drying, for which purpose the cake should be placed in a warm temperature, and kept covered with a large sheet of paper, to preserve it from dust, &c. When the icing has become perfectly hard, decorate the top and sides of the cake with raised ornaments of gum paste, (stamped out from boards cut for the purpose) and arranged with taste, either in the form of garlands, wreaths, scrolls, &c.; or else, the cake may be decorated with piping, using for that purpose some of the icing worked somewhat thicker, by adding to it more sugar and a little prepared gum-dragon.

When intended for a wedding cake, the ornaments must be all white, and some blossoms or sprigs—or, even wreaths of orange-flowers, should also be introduced.

1278. SCOTCH BREAD.

INGREDIENTS :—One pound of flour, one pound of sugar, one pound of butter, eight eggs, half a pound of candied lemon, orange, and citron peel in equal proportions, a gill of Cognac brandy, a very little salt and four ounces of white comfits.

Put the butter in a basin, work it with a wooden spoon until it presents the appearance of thick cream; then add the flour, sugar, eggs, and salt, gradually, throwing in a handful of each, and two eggs at a time; when the whole is thoroughly mixed, the candied peel (cut in shreds), also the brandy and the rind of two oranges or lemons (rubbed on sugar) must next be added. This paste should now be poured into tins of an oblong shape, about two inches deep, spread with butter, and after the comfits have been strewn over the surface, a little fine sugar should be shaken over the top previously to placing them in the oven on baking-sheets: they must be baked of a very light color.

Note.—This kind of cake is a general favorite in Scotland, being served on most occasions, at breakfast, luncheon, or for casual refreshment, and also with the dessert.

1279. PLAIN SEED CAKE.

INGREDIENTS :—One quartern of dough, six eggs, eight ounces of sugar, eight ounces of butter, half an ounce of caraway-seeds, and a teaspoonful of salt.

Spread the dough out on the pastry-slab, then add the whole of the above-named ingredients, work them well together with the hands, so as thoroughly to incorporate them with the dough: the eggs should be added two at a time.

When the paste is ready, put it into a plain mould (previously spread with butter), and set it to rise in a warm place. As soon as the fermentation has taken place in a satisfactory manner, the cake should be immediately put into the oven and baked of a light color. When done, serve it cold for luncheon, or otherwise.

This kind of cake may be varied by introducing raisins, currants, or candied orange or lemon peel.

1280. BRUSSELS BISCUITS, OR RUSKS.

INGREDIENTS required :—One pound of flour, ten ounces of butter, half an ounce of German yeast, four ounces of sugar, four whole eggs, and four yolks, a teaspoonful of salt, and a gill of cream.

Mix the paste in the manner described for the preparation of the Compiegne cake, excepting that this must be beaten with the hand on the slab until it presents an appearance of elasticity; the sponge should then be added, and after the whole has been well worked once more, the paste must be placed in long narrow tins, about two inches deep, and of about the same width: preparatory to placing the paste in the moulds, these should be first well floured inside (to prevent the paste from sticking), then the paste rolled out to their own length, and about one inch and a half thick, dropped into them, and set in a warm place to rise. When the paste has sufficiently risen, it must be gently turned out on a baking-sheet previously spread with butter, then egged all over with a soft paste-brush, and baked of a bright deep-yellow color. When done, cut them up in slices about a quarter of an inch thick, place them flat on a baking-sheet, and put them again in the oven to acquire a light-yellow color on both sides.

These form a superior kind of rusks, and are well adapted for the refreshment table at evening parties, or for the breakfast table.

Note.—Rusks may also be made with *brioche*-paste, pound cake, or Savoy cake; in the latter case a few caraway seeds are sometimes added.

1281. POUND CAKE.

INGREDIENTS required :—One pound of flour, one pound of butter, one pound of sugar, eight eggs, a wine glass of brandy, a little salt, and the rind of two oranges or lemons rubbed on sugar.

Place the butter in a basin, and work it with a wooden spoon until it assumes the appearance of thick cream; then add the flour, sugar, and the eggs gradually; when the whole is thoroughly incorporated, add the brandy, sugar, and salt; mix well together, and bake the cakes in any kind of mould (previously spread with butter), or in a tin hoop lined with buttered paper.

Plumbs, currants, almonds, pistachio-kernels, candied peel, or dried cherries may be added.

1282. FLEMISH GAUFFRES.

INGREDIENTS required :—Eight ounces of flour, six ounces of butter, six eggs, one ounce of yeast, half a pint of milk, half a pint of cream (whipped), the rind of two oranges rubbed on sugar, or a stick of vanilla pounded with half an ounce of sugar, and a little salt.

Put the flour into a gallon-sized basin, spread it out in the centre, then add the milk (with the yeast dissolved in it over the fire until the whole becomes tepid); mix these gradually and thoroughly; then take the spoon out, scrape the sides of the basin with a knife, cover it with paper, and set the batter to rise in the screen. When the sponge has increased to twice its quantity, the butter should first be merely melted by the fire, and then added with the salt, orange sugar, and two whole eggs; mix these well in with the sponge, then add the whipped cream and the yolks of the four eggs, and lastly, after having whipped the four whites into a substantial froth, mix them lightly in with the batter, and again set it to rise in a warm place, either on the top of the screen or on the kitchen table, that it may rise to twice its original quantity.

While the batter is being prepared, let the *gauffre*-irons be heated over the flame of a charcoal fire, and when sufficiently hot to admit of their baking the *gauffres*, run a little clarified butter through them with a paste-brush, then fill one side of the irons with some of the batter, handling it gently with a spoon; close the irons, and then turn them upside down (that the batter may run into the opposite side), and set them over the flame of the charcoal fire, and when done of a bright-yellow color on one side, turn the irons over, that the *gauffres* may be baked also on the other side. They must then be turned out of the irons, and after the edges have been trimmed with a pair of scissors, set them in the oven or before a fire on a baking-sheet covered with paper. Repeat this until the whole of the batter be used up; then, shake some orange, lemon, or vanilla sugar over them, pile them up neatly on a napkin, and serve.

These *gauffres* are generally served as a remove in the second course.

1283. FRENCH GAUFFRES.

INGREDIENTS required:—Eight ounces of flour, four ounces of pounded sugar, one pint of whipped cream, eight eggs, one stick of vanilla, a little salt, and a glass of caraçao.

Place the flour, sugar, and salt in a basin, then add the yolks of eggs, the pounded vanilla, and the caraçao, and mix these well together, gradually adding the whipped cream : just before using the batter, add the whipped whites of eggs, and mix them in lightly so as to thoroughly incorporate them with it.

Bake these *gauffres* in the same way as the foregoing, observing, however, that the iron be very carefully heated, and the superfluous heat allowed to go off previously to filling them with the batter ; as, owing to the presence of sugar in their composition, they readily acquire color. When done, shake some vanilla-sugar over them, and send to table.

These *gauffres* may be spread with some kind of preserve ; such as apricot, currant-jelly, &c.

284. ALMOND GAUFFRES.

INGREDIENTS required :—Eight ounces of Jordan almonds (either chopped extremely fine, or else cut into very fine shreds), four ounces of pounded sugar, a good table-spoonful of flour, two whole eggs, and a very little salt; flavor with orange flower-water, or flowers (candied).

Mix the almonds, sugar, flour, and the flavoring together in a basin, with a wooden spoon. Then heat a baking-sheet in the oven, rub it all over equally with a piece of white wax, and when this has cooled, spread the *gauffres* very thinly over it with a fork ; put them in the oven (at a slow heat), and when they are about half-baked, withdraw them, and with a circular tin-cutter about two inches in diameter, stamp out as many *gauffres* as the sheet will admit of, and put them back again in the oven that they may acquire a light-fawn color ; they should then be instantly taken out and formed in the shape of small cornucopiæ—two or three persons assisting,—so as to finish them off before they have time to get cold, as in that case they become brittle, and consequently unmanageable. But when it happens that one person only is able to attend to them, it will be necessary to keep the *gauffres* at the entrance of the oven while they are shaped, and, as they are finished, to place them on another baking-sheet.

These *gauffres* may also be cut into pieces two inches square, and coiled round a small roller in the form of barrels ; the ends of these, after being first covered with whipped white of egg mixed with a little sugar, should then be dipped in some finely chopped pistachios, and placed on a baking-sheet to dry in the skreen. In either case they may be filled with whipped cream seasoned with vanilla, orange flowers, or maraschino, and some strawberries placed on the top of this : they are sometimes also garnished with vanilla cream-ice.

Note.—This kind of *gauffres* may be varied in their appearance, by strewing some currants, or finely shred or chopped pistachios over the surface, previously to their being placed in the oven.

1285. NOUGATS.

INGREDIENTS required :—Two pounds of Jordan almonds, and one pound of sifted sugar.

Scald the almonds, remove the skins, and after they have been washed and dried in a napkin, split each almond into halves ; then place them on a baking-sheet, and put them in a slow oven to acquire a very light fawn color. While the almonds are undergoing this process in the oven, place the sugar in a convenient-sized sugar-boiler, and stir it with a wooden spoon over a slow fire to melt it : as soon as it is entirely dissolved, and begins to form small purling bubbles on the surface, the almonds (which by this time should be ready and quite hot) must be instantly thrown in, and very gently mixed with the sugar, care being taken not to break or bruise them. The vessel containing the *nougat* should be kept at the entrance of the oven or near the stove-fire, so as to prevent its becoming cold before it is used up. The mould intended to be used must then be first carefully oiled inside with a paste-brush, and set to drain on a plate that the superfluous oil may run off. Some of the *nougat* should now be dropped on a slightly-oiled baking-sheet, and spread out with a lemon to the thickness of about the eighth of an inch ; and as these pieces are thus spread or pressed out, they must be immediately placed in the mould, and pressed into its form with the assistance of the fingers and a lemon, and made to adhere effectually to each other ; great celerity must be used in this part of the operation, as in the event of the *nougat* being allowed to become brittle by cooling, it would be found impossible to build it up, unless by melting it, which is seldom found to succeed. When the *nougat* has become set by cooling, turn it out of the mould, and serve it on a napkin or upon an ornamental stand.

The foregoing proportions, as well as the directions for splitting the almonds, refer only to large *nougats ;* when it is intended to make a smaller one, the almonds should be shred. In all cases, the proportion of almonds and sugar should be as two of the former to one of the latter. For the purpose of varying their appearance, as soon as the *nougat* is turned out of the mould, some shred pistachio-kernels and rough granite-sugar,* should be strewed over its surface.

1286. PARISIAN NOUGATS.

INGREDIENTS required :—Eight ounces of pistachio-kernels, four ounces of sugar, and one stick of vanilla.

Scald the pistachios, remove the skins, absorb all the moisture by gently rubbing them in a napkin, then split each kernel into halves, and put them to dry on a baking-sheet in the screen. Pound the vanilla with one ounce of sugar, sift it, and then put this and the four ounces of pounded sugar into a small sugar-boiler, together with a tea-spoonful of the prepared extract of cochineal : stir these over the stove-fire with a wooden spoon until the sugar is entirely melted, and as soon as it begins to purl on the surface, immediately add the pistachios, and gently mix the whole together, taking care not to

---

* Granite-sugar is generally prepared by breaking up some loaf-sugar of the finest quality into very small pieces with the end of a rolling-pin ; after sifting away all the fine-sugar, the pieces are then passed through a colander with large holes. All that passes through this may be used for the above purpose. But when the granite is required finer, it must be riddled through a wire sieve.

bruise the pistachios. The *nougat* must now be spread out in the form of a square on a baking-sheet or marble slab (previously oiled), to the thickness of about the eighth part of an inch ; some roughly-broken granite sugar should be strewed over the surface, and before it becomes cold, the square must be divided into two bands, and then again each of these cut in about a dozen small oblong *nougats.* When about to send to table, pile them up in close circular rows on a napkin, and serve.

1287. SMALL NOUGATS, A LA CHANTILLY.

INGREDIENTS required :—Three-quarters of a pound of ripe filberts, and six ounces of pounded sugar.

Scald the nuts, remove the skin, then split each kernel in four—lengthwise, and put them to dry on a baking-sheet in the oven ; meanwhile, stir the sugar in the boiler over the fire in the usual manner, and as soon as it is ready, mix in the above ; have half a dozen small *dariole*-moulds ready, oiled inside, put some of the *nougat* into each of the moulds, and use a small stick made of hard wood (about half an inch in diameter) to work the *nougat* up the sides, or into the flutes of the moulds ; pare away all that may rise above the edge of the moulds, and then turn them out on to a baking-sheet. About eighteen will suffice for a dish. Several persons should assist in moulding these *nougats*, in order to insure their all being of one color ; otherwise, from being frequently obliged to warm the *nougat*, it is liable to become dark.

When about to send these *nougats* to table, each should be filled with some whipped cream flavored with vanilla or maraschino, and a few strawberries (when in season) placed on the top ; dish them up neatly in a pyramidal form on a napkin.

1288. GENOESE CAKES.

INGREDIENTS required :—Half a pound of flour, half a pound of sugar, half a pound of butter, four eggs, a small glass of brandy, and a little salt.

Mix the flour, sugar, eggs, brandy, and salt well together in a basin with a wooden spoon ; then add the butter (merely melted by the side of the fire), and when this is thoroughly incorporated with the batter, pour it into an appropriate-sized baking-sheet, previously spread with butter, to the thickness of about a quarter of an inch, and bake this in an oven moderately heated.

When the Genoese paste is done, it should be turned out upon a sheet of paper, and cut or stamped out, either in circular, oblong, oval, angular, leaf-like, or any other fancy shapes that taste may suggest. These may then be decorated with white of egg and sugar prepared as for *meringues* (No. 1298), or with icing prepared as directed for wedding cakes (No. 1277), and ornamented with pistachio-kernels, currants, &c. Those cut in the form of leaves, rings, oblongs, &c., may be ornamented by forming a design composed of leaves and pearls (using for that purpose some *meringue*-paste in a paper *cornet*, or small biscuit-forcer) ; when the Genoese cakes are ornamented in this manner, shake some fine sugar over them with a dredger, and dry them either in the screen or at the entrance of the oven ; then, finish decorating them by placing some neat stripes or dots of any kind of bright

preserve, such as red-currant jelly, apple jelly, apricot jam, green-gage
jam, &c., between the leaves or pearls of the white of egg decoration.
By these means a very pretty effect is produced, and as no artificial or
unwholesome substance is used in the composition, it may be partaken
of with safety.

1289. GENOESE CAKES, WITH ALMONDS.

PREPARE these as directed in the foregoing case, and when they are
nearly done, mask the surface with the white of an egg beat up with
an ounce of sifted sugar; then strew four ounces of chopped almonds,
mixed with two ounces of sugar, and a few drops of orange-flower
water, all over the coating of egg; shake a little sugar on the top of
this, and put the Genoese cakes back again in the oven, to finish baking. When done, the coating of almonds should be of a light-fawn
color; they must then be carefully removed from the baking-sheet, cut
or stamped out in shapes, according to fancy, and dished up on a napkin, in a pyramidal form.

1290. MADELEINES.

THESE are made with the same kind of batter as Genoese cakes, to
which currants, dried cherries, candied peel, or angelica may be added.
When the batter is ready, let it be poured into a sufficient number of
small fluted or plain *dariole* or *madelaine* moulds (previously buttered
inside); these must be placed on a baking-sheet spread with some
charcoal ashes, to the depth of half an inch, and then baked in an oven
of a moderate heat. When they are done, turn them out of the moulds,
and dish them up in a pyramidal form.

These cakes may also be partially emptied, then filled up with some
kind of preserve, and the small circular piece, removed previously to
taking out the crumb, should be replaced.

1291. SPANISH CAKES, PETITS-CHOUX.

INGREDIENTS required :—Half a pint of milk or water, four ounces
of butter, two ounces of sugar, five ounces of flour, three eggs, a few
drops of essence of orange, a very little salt, and two ounces of chopped almonds.

Put the water, butter, sugar, and the salt into a stewpan on the fire,
and as soon as these begin to boil, withdraw the stewpan from the fire,
and add the flour; stir the whole well together with a wooden spoon
over the stove-fire for about three minutes, by which time the ingredients should present the appearance of a soft compact paste. The
essence of orange (or any other kind of flavor) should now be added,
and also one egg; incorporate these with the paste, then mix in the
other two eggs, and if the paste should be stiff, another egg, or a yolk
only, may be added. This paste should now be laid out on a baking-
sheet in small round balls, the size of a pigeon's egg, egged over with
a paste-brush, some chopped almonds (mixed with a spoonful of
pounded sugar, and a very small quantity of white of egg) strewn
upon them, with some sifted sugar shaken over, and then baked of a
very light color.

These cakes may be served plain, or garnished inside with cream, or
some kind of preserve.

1292. DUCHESS LOAVES.

THESE are made of the same kind of paste as the foregoing; this must be laid out on the pastry-slab, in small pieces about the size of a pigeon's egg, then rolled out with a little flour, in the form of a finger, and placed in order upon a baking-sheet spread with butter; they should now be egged over, and baked of a bright light color. Just before they are quite done, shake some finely-sifted sugar over them, set them back again in the oven until the sugar is nearly melted, and then pass the red-hot salamander over them, to give them a bright glossy appearance; the loaves must now be immediately withdrawn from the oven, and allowed to cool. Just before sending this kind of pastry to table, make an incision down the sides, and fill the small loaves with apricot-jam, then dish them up in a pyramidal form on a napkin, and serve.

1293. PETTITS-CHOUX,* WITH CARAMEL.

PREPARE these as the above, except that they must be rolled and baked in the form of round balls, which, when done, should be about the size of an egg. About two ounces of roughly-chopped pistachios, a few cleaned currants, and an equal proportion of loaf sugar, chopped small, should be mixed together on a plate; then boil about four ounces of sugar, first dipping each *petit-choux* slightly in this, then gently roll in the prepared pistachios, &c., so as to mask its surface with these. When the whole have been thus passed in the sugar-*caramel*, allow them to cool previously to dishing them up.

1294. PROFITROLLES

PREPARE two dozen *petits-choux* as directed in the first part of the foregoing article; when they are baked and have become cold, cut a circular piece from the top of each, about the size of a shilling; then fill them with some custard, prepared as follows:—Put the yolks of four eggs into a small stewpan, with two ounces of pounded sugar, a good table-spoonful of flour, two ounces of grated chocolate, and a very little salt; mix these well together with half a pint of cream, add a small pat of butter, then stir the whole over the stove-fire, and allow it to boil for about ten minutes; this custard should now be passed through a tammy (with pressure) into a basin, and when it has become cold, three table-spoonfuls of whipped cream should be added; then serve.

This custard may also be flavored either with lemon, orange, vanilla, orange-flower, or any kind of liqueur; in which case the chocolate must be omitted.

1295. MECCA LOAVES.

THE paste for these is prepared as in the foregoing cases, with the addition, however, of a few spoonfuls of whipped cream, which must only be incorporated just previously to the loaves being laid out on the baking-sheet in the following manner:—

Take a table-spoon, and fill it half full from the stewpan, containing the paste; then dip the point of a knife in some beaten egg, and use it to force the paste from the spoon, gently dropping it on the baking-

* Pronounced by English cooks, "Petty-shoes."

sheet in the form of a gherkin, pointed at the ends, and elevated at the centre; fill the baking-sheet with these, placing them about two inches distant from each other; egg them over, shake some fine chopped loaf sugar (about the size of small hail stones) over them, then shake some sifted sugar upon them, and put them in the oven (at very moderate heat), to bake of a bright-yellow color. When the Mecca loaves are done, allow them to become cold; then after they have been dished up in double circular rows, fill the well or centre with some whipped cream seasoned with a little sugar, and a small glass of liqueur, and serve.

1296. QUEEN'S CAKES.

FIRST, prepare eight yolks of eggs of *nouilles* paste (No. 1256), roll this out as thin as paper, cut it into bands, and shred these extremely fine; after the *nouilles* have been allowed to dry upon a sieve for a short time, put them into a convenient-sized stewpan, with a pint of boiling cream, two pats of butter, six ounces of sugar, and a glass of brandy; set them to boil very gently over a slow stove-fire (covered with the lid), and when the cream has been absorbed by the *nouilles*, withdraw them, add the yolks of six eggs, and stir the whole well together; then place this preparation upon two baking-sheets (spread with butter), in layers about the eighth part of an inch thick, and bake these of a deep-yellow color. When done, spread one of them with apricot-jam, cover this over with the other, and then stamp the cakes out with a circular tin-cutter, in the form of half-moons; dish these up in double circular rows, so as to form a cone, and serve.

These cakes may also be garnished with any other kind of preserve, or even with pastry-custard (No. 1311); they may be cut out, either in oblong, circular, oval, leaf-like, or diamond shapes. In order to vary their appearance, their surface should be first lightly spread with a little *meringue*-paste (No. 1298), and then strewn with chopped or shred pistachios, granite-sugar, or small pink or white comfits.

1297. ALMOND CAKES.

INGREDIENTS :—Six ounces of flour, eight ounces of sugar, two ounces of ground or finely-powdered almonds (with a few bitter almonds), six yolks of eggs, two whole eggs, four whites whipped, a glass of brandy, a little salt, four ounces of chopped almonds mixed with two ounces of sugar, and half the white of an egg.

First, work the butter in a basin with a spoon, until it presents a creamy appearance; next, add the flour, sugar, almonds, brandy, eggs, and salt, gradually; then mix in the whipped whites of eggs, lightly; pour this paste on a baking-sheet about an inch and a half deep (previously buttered), and bake it of a light color. When the cake is nearly done, spread the prepared chopped almonds over the top, and then put it back again into the oven to finish baking; when done, the almonds should be of a light fawn-color. Turn the cake out carefully, and when cold, cut it up into bands about an inch and a half wide, then again divide these into diamond-shaped cakes, and dish them up pyramidally.

Some whipped cream may be placed in the centre of the dish, and the cakes neatly dished up round it.

Dried cherries, sultana raisins, currants, any kind of candied peel, pistachios or Spanish nuts, may be added. The cakes may also be flavored with any kind of essence or liqueur.

MERINGUES.

INGREDIENTS required :—One pound of sifted sugar, and twelve whites of egg.

Whisk the whites in an egg-bowl until they present the appearance of a perfectly white, smooth, substantial froth, resembling snow ; then substitute a spoon for the whisk, and proceed to mix in the whole of the sugar, lightly ; carefully avoid working the batter too much, for fear of rendering it soft, as in that case it becomes difficult to mould the *meringues ;* they can never be so gracefully shaped as when it is kept firm. Next, cut some stiff foolscap paper into bands about two inches wide ; then take a table-spoon, and gather it nearly full of the batter, by working it up at the side of the bowl in the form of an egg, and drop this slopingly upon one of the bands of paper, at the same time drawing the edge of the spoon sharply round the outer base of the *meringue,* so as to give to it a smooth and rounded appearance, in order that it may exactly resemble an egg. Proceed in this manner until the band is full, keeping the *meringues* about two inches and a half apart from each other on the paper; as each band is filled, place them close beside each other on the slab or table, and when all the batter is used up, shake some rather coarse sifted sugar all over them, and allow it to remain for about three minutes ; then take hold of one of the bands at each end, shake off the loose sugar, and place the band of *meringues* on the board :* and so on with the other bands, which when placed carefully on the boards closely side by side, must be put in the oven (at very moderate heat) and baked of a light-fawn color. When done, each piece of *meringue* must be carefully removed from off the paper, the white part of the inside scooped out with a dessert spoon, and then nicely smoothed over ; after this, they must be placed in neat order on a baking-sheet, and put back again in the oven to dry, taking particular care that they do not acquire any more color.

When about to send the *meringues* to table, whip some double cream, season it with a little pounded sugar, and either a glass of any kind of liqueur, a few drops of orange-flower water, or some pounded vanilla ; garnish each piece with a spoonful of this cream join two together, dish them up in a pyramidal form on a napkin, and serve.

Note.—*Meringues* may be made of all sizes, and may also be shaped in the form of small bunches of grapes : for this purpose it is necessary to use a *"cornet,"* or biscuit-forcer, of paper, to mould the berries. In order to vary their appearance, previously to shaking the sugar over them, some finely-shred pistachios or almonds, rough granite sugar, and small currants, may be strewn over them. They may also be garnished with preserve, or any kind of iced-creams.

---

* These boards must be made of seasoned wood, and should be about an inch thick ; their size must of course depend upon the dimensions of the oven, allowing sufficient room for them to be turned round in it.

1298*a*. ITALIAN BISCUITS.

INGREDIENTS :—Six eggs, eight ounces of pounded sugar, five ounces of flour, some orange or lemon sugar for flavoring, a pinch of salt, and six ounces of chopped almonds.

First, divide the yolks from the whites of the six eggs, placing the whites in an egg-bowl, and the yolks in a basin; add the sugar, the flavoring, and the salt, to the yolks, and with a wooden spoon continue working these until they present the appearance of a rather stiff creamy batter. Then add half the flour, and when this has been well mixed in, let the six whites previously whipped firm, be also lightly mixed in, together with the remainder of the flour, taking care to keep the batter as firm and light as possible.

You now fill a biscuit-forcer with some of the batter, and then proceed to gently force out the batter on to the baking-sheets (previously buttered and floured for the purpose), in round or oval shapes, twice the size of a five-shilling piece; and when the whole of the batter is used up in this manner, let the chopped almonds be equally strewn over the biscuits; and, after some sugar has been shook over their surface with a dredger-box, they must be baked of a very light color, in a rather slack oven.

These cakes are most appropriate for dessert; but, when made of the size of a five-shilling piece, by first spreading any kind of fruit, jam, on the under part, and sticking two of them together, they may be neatly dished up, for a second-course dish, with some whipped cream in the centre.

1298*b*. VENETIAN BISCUITS.

FIRST prepare some *Genoese* as directed at No. 1289, which, when cold, must be carefully split in convenient-sized pieces, and after spreading the insides with apricot-jam, let them be pressed together again. You next spread a thin coating of white icing on one square of *Genoese*, and then spread a similar coating of pink icing on the other square; after which, each square must be cut into small oblong shapes of equal sizes; and when the icing has become dry, may be dished up, either for a second-course dish, or for dessert.

1298*c*. SWEDES.

INGREDIENTS :—One pound of pounded sugar, twelve ounces of finely-shred almonds, four ounces of flour, a stick of vanilla (pounded and sifted), and one whole egg, and the white of another. Let the whole of the fore-named ingredients be well mixed together in a basin, and then with a tablespoon proceed to mould the preparation into round balls the size of a large walnut, which are to be placed on pieces of sheet-wafer, previously cut to the size of half-crown pieces; these must now be placed on baking-sheets, and after slightly shaking some fine sugar over them, are to be baked of a light color in a slack oven.

These cakes may also be finished in manner following: the preparation should be spread about half an inch thick upon sheet-wafer, and after being baked of a light color, and immediately on its being taken from the oven, should be cut into leaf-like shapes, and bent over a rolling pin, till the pieces become cold and crisp.

These cakes may be served either for dessert or a second-course dish ; in the latter case, some whipped cream must be placed in the centre of the dish.

1298*d*. BROWN BREAD BISCUITS.

INGREDIENTS :—One pound of pounded sugar, eight ounces of brown flour, six ounces of Jordan almonds, ground or pulverized without being blanched or divested of their brown pellicule, six drops of the essence of bitter almonds, and one dozen eggs.

Break the eggs, placing the yolks in a basin, and the whites in an egg-bowl; add the sugar, flour, almonds, and the flavoring to the yolks, and work these well together for twenty minutes with a wooden spoon ; then mix in the whites previously whisked firm for the purpose, and with this batter proceed to fill as many small oblong or square paper cases as you may require for the purpose ; which after they have been sugared over, should be baked in a very moderate oven.

These biscuits are adapted for dessert only.

1298*e*. GINGER CAKES.

INGREDIENTS :—One pound of flour, twelve ounces of fresh butter, twelve ounces of pounded sugar, two ounces of ground Jamaica Ginger, eight yolks of eggs.

Work the whole of the above-named ingredients together on a pastry-board or slab ; and, after having gathered the paste up into a compact mass, separate it into four parts, roll these out to the thickness of the sixth of an inch, one after the other, and with a tin-cutter, either oval, round, &c., &c., cut out as many cakes as the paste will produce, and place them on a slightly-buttered baking-sheet, pass a paste-brush over them when they are about half done, shake some sugar over them, and set them back in the oven to finish baking, of a very light color.

1298*f*. CHAMPAGNE BISCUITS.

INGREDIENTS :—Eight ounces of flour, eight ounces of pounded sugar, eight ounces of fresh butter, eight eggs, a quarter of an ounce of carraway seeds, a pinch of salt.

Place the butter in a basin, and work it with a wooden spoon until it presents the appearance of thick cream ; you then add the sugar, flour, yolks of eggs, the carraway seeds and the salt gradually ; after which mix in the eight whites of eggs previously whisked firm for the purpose. You now procure a sheet of stout cartridge-paper, which must be folded in reversed plaits so that when the paper is opened, it may present the appearance of the plaits of a fan, thus forming angular trenches about an inch deep. Next fill a biscuit-forcer with some of the batter, and proceed to force out some finger-like biscuits into the aforesaid paper trenches of about three inches long ; shake some sifted sugar over these, and bake them of a light color in a very moderate oven.

These cakes are fit only for dessert.

1298*g*. ORANGE BISCUITS.

THESE are made with the same kind of batter as described in the foregoing article, omitting in this case the carraway seeds, and substituting in their place some orange-sugar and candied-orange-peel cut into small shreds; some very small moulds must be slightly buttered, filled with some of the batter, some sugar sifted over them, and then baked of a very light color in a very moderate oven.

1298*h*. PEACH BISCUITS.

PREPARE some butter as directed for fingers (No. 1276), and, with this, proceed to form some small round biscuits (using a biscuit-forcer for that purpose) on a baking or sheet of paper ; if the former, it must be previously buttered and floured, shake some sugar over the biscuits, and bake them of a very light color ; and when they are done, and removed from the baking-sheet or paper, spread the under parts with some kind of preserved fruit (peach marmalade being most appropriate), stick two of these together; thus forming as nearly as possible the shape and size of a peach, these must now be very thinly covered all over with some white icing, which, when dry, must be *very* slightly brushed over with a soft pencil-brush dipped in a very small quantity of carmine, thereby giving to the cake merely a tinge of color similar to that displayed by the ripe peach. These cakes may be dished up with whipped cream in the centre of the dish.

1298*i*. APRICOT BISCUITS.

THESE are prepared in all respects according to directions given in the preceding article, excepting that they should be made smaller,— so that they may form a near resemblance to apricots in size and form, apricot jam being used to stick them together with ; and when so far prepared, are to be dipped in the following preparation :—To one pound of fine loaf sugar placed in a sugar-boiler, add half a pint of spring-water ; boil these over a brisk stove-fire until the sugar while boiling throws up pearl-like bubbles ; the degree of boiling required for glazing being ascertained by taking a small quantity of the boiling sugar between the fore-finger and thumb (previously dipped in cold water), and if the sugar when pressed with the fingers presents the appearance of strong glue, it should then be removed from the fire, and ten minutes afterward, whatever flavoring is intended to be used, must be in a liquid state, such as liqueurs, strong vailla, orange or lemon syrups or infusions : any one of the foregoing must be gradually mixed in with the boiled sugar, quickly stirring and working the sugar in the pan the while ; and when thoroughly mixed, the cakes should be dipped in—and being afterward placed on a wire drainer, placed in the hot closet for a few minutes to set.

The yellow tinge required for the *glacés* in this case may be given by using either some orange-sugar or a small decoction of saffron ; the latter is objectionable, on account of its flavor.

1298*k*. CHOCOLATE GLACES.

The foundation for these may be made either of pound-cake, Genoese, or song-cake ; the batter for making either of the foregoing may be first baked in a baking-sheet, and afterward cut out in shapes and sizes to suit taste or convenience ; or otherwise may be baked in appropriate moulds or cases for the purpose ; they must then be dipped in the following preparation :—First, boil the sugar as directed in the foregoing article, and when it has reached its proper degree, add six ounces of chocolate dissolved with a wine-glassful of water ; work the whole well together, and use it while hot ; but, if it should become cold, and set before the operation is terminated, the preparation may be easily liquified by stirring it over the fire.

Cakes both large and small may be *glacés*, or glazed, in this manner in almost infinite variety, by using any kind of liqueur, or a very strong infusion of tea or coffee instead of the chocolate here recommended.

1298*l*. SUISSE LECRELETS.

INGREDIENTS :—Eight ounces of honey, four ounces of sweet-almonds, blanched and shred, half an ounce of cinnamon-powder, a quarter of an ounce of ground cloves, half a nutmeg grated, six ounces of pounded sugar, half an ounce of carbonate of potash, six ounces of candied orange, lemon and citron, a wine-glassful of *Kirschen-wasser*, ditto of orange-flower-water, and the grated rind of two lemons, one pound of flour, including the quantity required to manipulate the paste on the slab.

Put the honey in a copper egg-bowl on the stove-fire, and when it is melted, skim off the froth, and immediately add the shred almonds, the ground spices, and the grated lemon-peel; mix these well together with a wooden spoon, and then add the sugar, the *Kirschen-wasser*, the orange-flower-water, and the candied peels ready shred for the purpose; and, after having mixed in these, then add the carbonate of potash dissolved in a table-spoonful of water, and also fourteen ounces of flour, leaving the remainder for manipulating the paste on the slab). This paste must now be gently stirred over the fire for three or four minutes longer, and then placed in a covered pan in a cool place for three days previously to its being used; the further process must be directed as follows :—

Cut the *Lecrelet*-paste into four equal parts ; and, after having first strewn the slab with some of the flour reserved for the purpose, roll out each of the four pieces to about the eighth part of an inch thick ; these squares must now be placed on baking-sheets, previously buttered and floured for the purpose ; and, after being deeply marked out or cut into small oblong-squares, must be rubbed over with a paste-brush dipped in water to remove the flour from the surface. Next, bake the *Lecrelets* in a rather slack oven of a light color, and when they are about three parts done, let them be nearly cut through into shape, and immediately they have been brushed over with some thin white icing, replace them in the oven to finish being baked. When the *Lecrelets* have been withdrawn from the oven a sufficient time to have become cold, break them up as marked out, and put them away in a tin box in a dry place.

These cakes are well adapted for dessert, luncheon, or as a pleasant adjunct for the supper-tray.

1298*m*. SICILIAN BISCUITS.

INGREDIENTS :—Four eggs, twelve ounces of pounded sugar, ten ounces of flour, a stick of vanilla pounded.

Whisk the eggs, the sugar, and the vanilla together in a copper egg-bowl, over a very slow stove-fire until the batter begins to feel warm ; it must then be removed from off the fire, and whisked briskly until the batter becomes cold; the flour must now be lightly added in, and when thoroughly mixed, must be shaped upon a prepared baking-sheets with the aid of a biscuit-forcer, in fingers, ovals or rounds; sugared over similarly to finger or Naples biscuits, and baked in a slack oven.

1298n. RUSSIAN BISCUITS.

INGREDIENTS :—Eight ounces of pounded sugar, ten eggs, six ounces of flour, four ounces of almonds pounded and dried over the fire in a sugar-boiler, quarter of an ounce of aniseed.

Let the yolks of the eggs and the sugar be whisked together in an egg-bowl over a slow-fire, until they present the appearance of a thick batter; the whites, previously whisked firm, must now be lightly added, as also the flour, pounded almonds, and the aniseed. The batter thus produced, may either be baked in small moulds, or as is most appropriate for these biscuits, they should be baked in long tin moulds, or, failing these, in stout paper cases, ten inches long by three inches deep, and two and a half inches wide. When the last named are baked, and have been allowed to become thoroughly cold, cut them into rather thin slices, which, being placed on baking-sheets, should be again baked of a very light color on both sides.

1298o. ALBERT BISCUITS.

INGREDIENTS :—Ten ounces of pounded sugar, eight ounces of finely-chopped almonds, six ounces of flour, twelve yolks and fourteen whites of eggs, two ounces of candied orange-peel shred fine, a tea-spoonful of cinnamon-powder, half that quantity of ground cloves, and a little grated lemon-rind.

Work the sugar and the almonds with the yolks and two whites of eggs, for twenty minutes, then incorporate the remaining twelve whites firmly whisked together with the flour, candied peel, and spices. Next, pour the batter into a convenient-sized paper case, and bake it in a moderate oven; and, when done and sufficiently cold, let it be cut up into thin slices for dishing up.

This preparation may also be baked in small moulds, or forced out upon paper or baking-sheets previously buttered and floured for the purpose.

1298p. VICTORIA BISCUITS.

INGREDIENTS :—One pound of pounded sugar, twelve ounces of dried flour, six ounces of pounded or ground bitter almonds, six ounces of fresh butter, a wine-glassful of *Kirschen-wasser*, and the rind of two lemons grated.

First, let the butter be worked up in a basin with a wooden spoon, until it assumes a creamy appearance; then add the remainder of the ingredients, finishing with the *Kirschen-wasser;* and when the batter is ready, pour it into small moulds, ready buttered and interiorly coated with potato flour. When these cakes or biscuits are baked of a very light color, first, spread the surface with orange marmalade, and over this glaze them according to directions given for finishing Apricot biscuits.

SMALL PASTRY IN GENERAL,

COMPRISING

Fanchonnettes.	Puff-paste Walnuts.
Cheesecakes.	Bread-and-Butter Pastry.
Mirlitons.	Puff-paste Rings, or Wreaths.
Pithiviers Cakes.	Polish Cakes.
D'Artois Cake.	Harry the VIII.'s Shoestrings.
German *Tourte* of Apricots.	Puff-paste Plaits.
Parisian Turnover of Apples.	Apple Tartlets.
Darioles.	Cherry Tartlets.
Condé Cakes.	Puff-paste Tartlets.
Royals.	Mosaic Tartlets.
D'Artois of Apricots.	Parisian Loaves.
Apricot *Nougats.*	Marygolds.
Pastry Custard, or Cream.	Filbert-cream Tartlets.
Talmouses.	Coventry Tartlets.
Talmouses, with Cheese.	Apple Tart, with Quince.
Florentines.	Pear Tart.
Cupid's or Love's Wells.	Fruit Tarts in general.

1299. FANCHONNETTES.

PREPARE some pastry custard in the manner directed for the *profitrolles* (No. 1294), season it either with two ounces of grated chocolate, an infusion of coffee, a glass of liqueur, or a few drops of some kind of essence, such as orange-flower, vanilla, bitter almonds, or lemon; when this is ready, fill two dozen plain-lined tartlets with it; bake these of a light color, and when done, take them out of the moulds, and lay them flat upon the marble slab to cool. Meanwhile, whip three whites of eggs quite firm, then mix in three ounces of pounded sugar, and use some of this to mask the *fanchonnettes* over with, giving to them a flat smooth surface; next, with a *cornet* filled with some of the whites of egg, form a star, or some other design on the top; when they are all done, shake some sifted sugar over them, put them on a baking-sheet, and bake them of a very light-fawn color. When they are baked, previously to dishing them up, ornament them, by placing some neat strips of bright currant or apple-jelly in between the folds of the decoration.

These *fanchonnettes* may be infinitely varied, by altering their form and design, when masking them with the whipped whites of eggs, according to taste and fancy. Strips of pistachios, almonds, or currants may also be used for this purpose.

1300. CHEESECAKES.

INGREDIENTS required:—Eight ounces of pressed curd, two ounces of ratafias, six ounces of sugar, two ounces of butter, six yolks of eggs, some grated nutmeg, a little salt, the rind of two oranges or lemons, rubbed on sugar, and afterward scraped off.

Press the curd in a napkin to absorb the superfluous moisture, then pound it thoroughly in a mortar, and mix in the above-named ingredients; when the whole is incorporated together into a kind of soft paste, take this up in a basin. Next, line two dozen or more tartlet-

pans with some well-worked trimmings of puff-paste, garnish these
with the cheese-custard, place a strip of candied peel on the top of each,
put them on a baking-sheet, and then set them in the oven (at moderate heat), to be baked of a very light-brown color; when done, shake
a little sifted sugar over them, and serve them quite hot.

Currants, dried cherries, sultanas or citron, may be used instead of
the candied peel.

1301. MIRLITONS.

INGREDIENTS required :—Puff-paste, trimmings, three whole eggs,
three ounces of sugar, one ounce of ratifias, half an ounce of candied
orange-flowers, one ounce of butter, and a little salt.

Put the above into a basin having a spout: the ratafias and orange-
flowers must be bruised, and the butter merely melted; work the
whole well together with a wooden spoon, until the batter presents
the appearance of a rich creamy-looking-substance, it must then be
instantly poured into two dozen small deep tartlets, lined with puff-
paste trimmings; shake a rather thick coating of sifted sugar over
the *mirlitons*, and when it has nearly melted on their surface, put
them in the oven (at very moderate heat), and bake them of a light-
fawn color. When the *mirlitons* are done, the centre should rise out
from the tartlet to the height of about half an inch, resembling the
crown of a boy's cap.

These cakes may also be flavored with chocolate, grated previously
to its being added to the preparation; or with pistachios or almonds,
both of these must be pounded first: they may also be flavored with
different essences. Previously to pouring the batter into the tartlets
a spoonful of apricot or pine-apple-jam may be placed in them.

1302. PITHIVIERS CAKES.

INGREDIENTS required :—Half a pound of puff-paste, eight ounces
of almonds or nuts, six ounces of sugar, four ounces of butter, two
ounces of ratafias, a spoonful of orange-flower-water, the yolks of four
eggs, and a very little salt.

First, pound the almonds with a little white of egg, until they become pulverized; then add the remainder of the ingredients, and
pound the whole well together until thoroughly incorporated, when it
should present the appearance of a rather soft creamy paste; take
this up in a basin.

While the above preparation is going on, half a pound of puff-paste
should be made, to which seven turns or foldings must be given;
take two-thirds of this, and knead, or rather fold it, by twisting over
the corners, so as to form it into a cushion; knead the other piece in
a similar manner, and then roll them both out in a circular or oval
form, to the size of a small dish or dessert plate; place the thinnest
piece on a baking-sheet, wet round the edges with a paste-brush
dipped in water, fill the whole of the centre with a layer of *Pithiviers*
cream, about an inch thick, and place the other piece of puff-paste
over the top of this; press it all round the edge, by bearing on it with
the thumb of the right hand; then trim the edges round neatly (in
the manner practised to cut a *vol-au-vent*), and with the point of a
small knife, handled lightly and freely, sketch or mark out some neat
or elegant design, such as a lyre, a vase of flowers, a helmet with flow-

ing mane or feathers, a wreath, or a star, &c. Shake some finely-sifted sugar over the cake, and bake it of the lightest possible color; indeed, it should be free from any color, the characteristic appearance of this kind of pastry being its whiteness. *Pithiviers* cake should be eaten cold.

These cakes may also be made in tartlet moulds, thinly lined with puff-paste, and after being neatly filled with the *Pithiviers* cream (the edges being previously wetted round), the mould must be covered in with circular pieces of puff-paste, stamped out with a cutter to fit them; then fastened down by pressing the two pieces of paste together with the forefinger and thumb of the right hand, and finished and baked as directed in the foregoing case.

1303. D'ARTOIS CAKE.

PUFF-PASTE or large D'Artois cakes, prepared as directed in the foregoing cases, may be garnished either with apple marmalade, mince-meat, or any kind of preserve; in this case, however, when the cake has been covered in with the puff-paste, previously to marking out the design on its surface, it must be egged over with a paste-brush; when it has been baked of a bright-yellow color, shake some finely-sifted sugar over it, after which put it back again in the oven for a minute or two, and then pass the red-hot salamander over it to give it a bright glossy appearance. The same direction applies to the smaller D'Artois cakes.

1304. GERMAN TOURTE OF APRICOTS.

CUT a dozen ripe apricots into quarters, and put them into a small sugar-boiler or stewpan, with the kernels extracted from the stones, four ounces of pounded sugar, and a spoonful of water; stir this over the stove-fire until the fruit is dissolved into a jam, and then withdraw the stewpan from the fire.

Roll out some trimmings of puff-paste, or else about half a pound of short paste, to the diameter of about eight inches, place this on a circular baking-sheet, and with the forefinger and thumb of the right hand, twist the paste round the edges so as to raise it in imitation of cording; then cut up a dozen ripe apricots into quarters, and place these in close circular rows on the paste, shake some sifted sugar (mixed with some rind of lemon) over the apricots, and then bake the *tourte* (at moderate heat); when it is done, pour the marmalade of apricots over the others; shake some sifted sugar mixed with a tea-spoonful of cinnamon-powder over the surface, dish the *tourte* on a napkin, and serve it either hot or cold.

This kind of *tourte* may be made of every kind of fruit, the process in each case being similar to the above—consisting in baking one-half of the fruit on the paste, while the remainder is added after the *tourte* is baked, being first boiled down into a kind of jam for that purpose. In all cases, some cinnamon-sugar must be strewn over the surface.

1305. PARISIAN TURNOVER OF APPLES.

PEEL about a dozen apples, cut them in quarters, and take out the cores; after which, put them into a stewpan with eight ounces of sugar, two ounces of butter, the rind of a lemon rubbed on a piece of sugar, and two table-spoonfuls of water; toss the apples over a slow fire until they are about half done, and then remove them from the fire. While the apples are being prepared, roll out a piece of short paste, in a circular form, the eighth part of an inch thick, and about the size of a dinner-plate; wet this round the edge, then fasten a rolled cord of paste, the thickness of a small finger, within an inch of the edge, and pile the prepared apples up in the centre in the form of a dome; then, spread some apricot marmalade over the surface, and cover the whole in with another circular piece of puff-paste; press them together round the edges, wet the extremities, then, with the forefinger and thumb of the right hand, twist or fold the edges over in the form of a cord; let the turnover now be egged all over with a soft paste-brush dipped in some beaten white of egg, then strew some rough granite-sugar over the entire surface, and bake it of a light color.

These turnovers may also be made with all kinds of plums; the only difference in their mode of preparation being, that they need not undergo any dressing previously to placing them in the paste, except that the stones should be removed: the plums, peaches, or apricots must be piled up in several rows forming a dome, with some pounded sugar between each layer, and some of the same kind of fruit the turnover is made of should be first boiled down to a jam, for the purpose of masking the fruit with, preparatory to its being covered in.

1306. DARIOLES.

INGREDIENTS:—One ounce of flour, two ounces of pounded sugar, one ounce of ratafias, three gills of cream, one whole egg and six yolks, one ounce of candied orange-flowers, a small pat of butter, a very little salt, half a pound of trimmings of puff-paste.

Place the flour, sugar, the bruised ratafias, and the eggs in a spouted basin, work the whole well together, and then add the cream, a very little salt, and a table-spoonful of orange-flower-water, and mix these in with the batter. Line a dozen *dariole*-moulds, with some trimmings of puff-paste, place these on a baking-sheet, put a very small bit of butter at the bottom of each *dariole*, and then, after stirring the batter well together, pour it into the moulds; strew the candied orange-flowers on the top of each, and set them in the oven (at moderate heat) to bake. When done, the *darioles* should be slightly raised in the centre, and of a light color; take them out of the moulds without breaking them, shake some finely-sifted sugar over them, and serve them hot.

Darioles may also be flavored with vanilla, lemon, orange, coffee, or chocolate.

1307. CONDE CAKES.

CHOP six ounces of Jordan almonds as fine as possible, mix them with four ounces of sifted sugar, some grated rind of lemon, and the white of an egg: the whole should present the appearance of a rather firm paste. Next, make half a pound of puff-paste, to which give eight turns or foldings, and roll this out to the thickness of the eighth part of an inch; then, with a tin cutter, of an oval, circular, crescent, diamond, or any other fancy shape, stamp out about eighteen *condés* and place them on a baking-sheet previously wetted over with a paste-brush to receive them; spread a coating of the prepared chopped almonds on the surface of each, shake some fine sugar over them with the dredger, and bake them of a very light-fawn color.

1308. ROYALS.

MIX the whites of two eggs with as much finely-sifted sugar as they will absorb, so as to form a kind of soft paste; this must be effected without working it more than is necessary to mix the ingredients together : a few drops of any kind of essence may be added to flavor the cakes.

Make half a pound of puff-paste, and to finish these cakes, proceed in all respects as directed in the foregoing article.

1309. D'ARTOIS OF APRICOT.

MAKE one pound of puff-paste, and give it seven turns or foldings; then, take one-third part of it, and after kneading this well together, roll it out to the size of a square baking-sheet, measuring about fourteen inches by twelve, and lay the paste upon it ; next spread a rather thick layer of apricot-jam over the paste to within about an inch of the edges ; then, roll out the remainder of the puff-paste to the size of the baking-sheet, and place it neatly over the surface of the apricot; fasten it round by pressing upon the edges with the thumb, and trim the edges by cutting away the superfluous paste from the sides with a knife. The *D'Artois* must now be marked out in small oblong shapes with the back part of a knife, and after the whole surface has been egged over, score them over neatly, forming a kind of feather pattern on each cake. Bake them of a bright light-brown color, and when they are done, shake some finely-sifted sugar over them out of the dredger, put them back again into the oven for a minute or two, to melt the sugar, and then pass the red-hot salamander over them to give to the pastry a bright glossy appearance. When the *D'Artois* have become sufficiently cold, cut them up, and serve them dished up in several circular rows piled on a napkin.

Note.—This kind of pastry may also be garnished with *Pithiviers*-cream, pastry-custard, apple marmalade, or any other kind of preserve.

1310. APRICOT NOUGATS.

ROLL out some trimmings of puff-paste to the thickness of the eighth of an inch; lay this all over the surface of a baking-sheet, spread it with a rather thick layer of apricot-jam, and then strew some shred pistachio kernels or Jordan almonds over this, shake some finely-sifted sugar over all, and bake them in a very moderately-heated oven. When done, allow the pastry to cool, and then use any kind of fancy tin-cutter to stamp them out.

1311. PASTRY CUSTARD, OR CREAM.

INGREDIENTS :—Four ounces of flour, four ounces of sugar, six yolks of eggs, two ounces of butter, one pint of cream or milk, one ounce of ratafias, a spoonful of orange-flower-water, and a very little salt.

Mix the flour, sugar, and salt with two whole eggs, in a stewpan with a wooden spoon; then add the cream and the butter, and stir the whole over the stove-fire until it boils ; it must then be well worked together, so as to make it smooth. Withdraw the spoon, and after putting the lid on the stewpan, place the cream in the oven, or on a slow stove-fire partially smothered with ashes, that it may continue to simmer very gently for about twenty minutes: the cream must then be put out into a basin, and the bruised ratafias, the yolks of eggs, and the orange-flower-water must be added; after which put four ounces of butter into a small stewpan on the fire, and as soon as it begins to fritter, and has acquired a light-brown color (which gives to it the sweet flavor of nuts), add this also to the cream, and let the whole be well mixed.

Use this cream to garnish various kinds of pastry, according to directions given in the several articles for which it is intended.

1312. TALMOUSES

INGREDIENTS required: Half a pint of milk, four ounces of flour, two ounces of sugar, two ounces of butter, six ounces of cream-curd, the rind of an orange rubbed on sugar, a very little salt, and half a pound of puff-paste.

Put the milk, butter, sugar, and salt, into a stewpan on a stove-fire, and as soon as these begin to simmer, fill in the flour by stirring the whole with a wooden spoon for two or three minutes over the fire; then add the curd (from which all the superfluous moisture must be extracted by pressing it in a napkin), and work in the eggs one after the other, remembering that this paste must be kept to about the same substance as for *petits-choux*.

Make half a pound of puff-paste, and give it nine turns; roll this out to the eighth of an inch in thickness, stamp out about two dozen circular pieces with a tin-cutter about two inches in diameter, and place them in neat order on a baking-sheet about an inch apart from each other; then place a good tea-spoonful of the preparation described above, in the centre of each, wet these round the edges, and then turn up the sides so as to form each of them in the shape of a three-cornered hat; egg them over with a paste-brush, bake them of a light-brown color, and when they are withdrawn from the oven, shake some fine sugar over them. These cakes may be served either hot or cold.

1313. TALMOÙSES WITH CHEESE.

THESE are prepared just as the foregoing, except that the sugar and rind of orange must be omitted, substituting in their stead four ounces of scraped Brie, or Neuchatel cheese: when these cannot be procured, Gruyère or Parmesan cheese may be used for the purpose.

1314. FLORENTINES.

ROLL out about half a pound of trimmings of puff-paste to the thickness of the eighth of an inch, and lay this on the entire surface of a rather large-sized baking-sheet; spread a thick layer of green-gage-jam over the paste, and then bake it in an oven of moderate heat; when done, let it be withdrawn and allowed partially to cool. Then spread it with a coating of whipped whites of egg mixed with sugar, about half an inch in thickness, and strew some shred pistachio kernels all over the surface; shake some finely-sifted sugar over the top, and finish baking the *Florentines* of a very light color, taking care that the *meringue*-paste is allowed sufficient time to become perfectly crisp. A few minutes after the *Florentines* are taken out of the oven, they must be stamped out with a tin-cutter or else cut out with a knife, in oblong or diamond-shapes.

1315. CUPID'S, OR LOVE'S WELLS.

GIVE seven turns to half a pound of puff-paste, then roll it out to the thickness of the sixth part of an inch; stamp out about eighteen circular pieces from this with a fluted tin-cutter, one inch and a half in diameter, and place these in rows on a baking-sheet previously wetted to receive them. Then, stamp out as many more pieces with a smaller fluted cutter only one inch in diameter, and after stamping out the centre of these, wet the surface of the others over with a paste-brush, and lay one of the smaller ones on each of the others; press them down with the fingers, egg over the tops, and bake them of a bright light color; when they are nearly done, shake some sugar over them with the dredger, put them back again into the oven for a minute or two, and then pass the red-hot salamander over them to give them a bright glossy appearance. Previously to serving these "love's wells," fill them either with preserved cherries, greengage-jam, or currant-jelly.

1316. PUFF-PASTE WALNUTS.

GIVE seven turns to half a pound of puff-paste, and roll it out to the thickness of the sixth part of an inch; then stamp out twenty circular pieces with a fluted cutter, about an inch and a half in diameter, and after wetting each of these with a paste-brush dipped in water, fold them up, at the same time pressing the two parts of the paste slightly, so as to cause them to adhere closely together; they must then be placed on baking-sheet in rows, egged over, and baked of a bright light color. Just before they are done, some fine sugar should be shaken over them with a dredger, and they must then be put back again into the oven for a little while to melt the sugar; pass the red-hot salamander over, and withdraw them. Previously to serving this kind of pastry, a broad strip of red currant or apple-jelly should be placed across the centre.

1317. BREAD-AND-BUTTER PASTRY.

GIVE six turns to half a pound of puff-paste, and roll it out to the thickness of a quarter of an inch; cut this into bands about three inches wide, then cut these again into strips rather better than a quarter of an inch wide, and place them (on the cut side) on a baking-sheet in rows, about two inches apart, so as to allow them sufficient room to spread out. Bake these strips of paste in a rather sharp oven, and just before they are done, glaze them; that is, shake some fine sugar over, and then salamander them. About two dozen of these are required for a dish: they must be spread with some kind of preserve, and stuck together in pairs, to imitate bread-and-butter; dish them up on a napkin, piled up in several circular rows, in a pyramidal form.

This kind of pastry may also be dished up with some stiffly-whipped cream, seasoned with a glass of liqueur, in the centre.

1318. PUFF-PASTE RINGS, OR WREATHS.

GIVE eight turns to half a pound of puff-paste, and roll this out to the sixth part of an inch in thickness; then stamp out twenty circular pieces with a fluted tin-cutter about one inch and three quarters in diameter, and stamp out the centre of these with a plain circular cutter about three quarters of an inch in diameter, then place the rings on a wetted baking-sheet, shake some fine sugar over them, and bake them of a very light color (at very moderate heat). When they are done, decorate them with some whipped white of egg and sugar, over which strew some coarse sugar; put them to dry in the screen, and then finish decorating them by placing or inserting some strips of currant or apple jelly in between the folds or dots of the decoration.

Note.—Puff-paste turned or folded eight times, then rolled out to the thickness of the sixth part of an inch, and stamped out with appropriate fancy-shaped tin cutters—either in the form of crescents, leaves, trefoil or shamrock, stars, &c., and after being baked as directed in the foregoing case, may also be decorated in the same manner; a *cornet* of paper should be used for this purpose.

1319. POLISH CAKES.

GIVE seven turns to half a pound of puff-paste, roll it out as in the foregoing cases, and then cut it up into square pieces measuring rather better than two inches each way; wet these in the centre, and then fold down the corners, so as to make them all meet in the middle of the piece of paste; place a dot of paste in the centre of each, pressing it down with the end of the finger, egg them over, and bake them in a rather sharp oven, of a fine bright light color, and just before they are done, shake some finely-sifted sugar over them; put them back again in the oven to melt the sugar, and then pass the red-hot salamander over them to give them a glossy appearance. Decorate this kind of pastry with bright red-currant or apple-jelly.

1320. HARRY THE VIII.'S SHOESTRINGS.

THIS kind of pastry is prepared in the first instance in exactly the same manner as the foregoing, as far as folding the corners down. Then cut out a small angle from each of the parts that have been folded down, which will then present the appearance of four bows joined together; place a small ring of puff-paste in the centre of each, which must be fastened on by first wetting the part; they should be then egged over and baked of a bright light color, and afterward glazed as directed in the foregoing cases. Previously to dishing them up, fill a *cornet* of paper with some firm red-currant jelly, and use this to draw rather bold lines all round the angular parts of the bows, and also round the ring that has been placed in the centre; then, with another paper *cornet* filled with bright apricot or green-gage-jam, fill in the centre of the bows; this kind of decoration produces a very brilliant effect.

1321. PUFF-PASTE PLAITS.

GIVE nine turns to half a pound of puff-paste, roll it out to the thickness of the eighth part of an inch, and then cut this into bands about five inches in width, and divide these into narrow strips a quarter of an inch wide. Take four of these strips, and after fastening them together at one end with a little egg or.water, plait them neatly but rather loosely together, and when finished, fasten the ends: as each plait is completed, place it on a baking-sheet, and when they are all ready, egg them over, and bake them of a light color, and when done, let them be glazed as usual. Just before sending these cakes to table, decorate them by placing in the small cavities some dots of bright currant or apple-jelly, and some greengage-jam.

1322. APPLE TARTLETS.

MAKE half a pound of tart-paste (No. 1255), roll it out rather thin; then stamp out twenty circular flats, with a fluted cutter suited to the size of the tartlets, and use them to line the moulds; fill each tartlet with a spoonful of apple-marmalade, cover them in with a mosaic* of paste, egg them over, place them on a baking-sheet, and bake them of a light color; when done, shake some fine sugar over them, and use the red-hot salamander, to give them a glossy appearance.

1323. APPLE TARTLETS, ANOTHER METHOD.

LINE the tartlet-pans as above, then garnish them with halves of small apples, previously turned and divested of the cores, and afterwards parboiled in a little syrup in which the juice of a lemon has been squeezed; bake the tartlets, and when they are done, dilute some apricot-jam with a little of the syrup; use this to mask the apples in the tartlets, and then place a preserved cherry on the centre of each.

1324. CHERRY TARTLETS.

TAKE the stones out of two pounds of Kentish cherries, put these into a small sugar-boiler with three quarters of a pound of pounded sugar, toss them in this, then set them on the stove-fire and allow them to boil for about five minutes: the cherries must then be strained on a sieve, and the syrup reduced to about one-third part of its quantity, then added to the cherries, and kept in a small basin.

Line two dozen small tartlet-pans with short paste or tart-paste (the flats being stamped out with a fluted cutter); knead as many small pieces of paste as there are tartlets, and after dipping them in flour, press one of them into each of the tartlets, place them on a baking-sheet, and put them in the oven (moderately heated) to be baked of a light color; when they are nearly done, withdraw them, and take out the pieces of paste, shake some fine sugar over them, and then glaze them with the red-hot salamander. Just before serving the tartlets, fill them with the cherries.

Note.—Raspberries, currants, gooseberries, and all kinds of plums, may be prepared for tartlets, by gently boiling them for a few minutes in about a pint of syrup; the fruit should then be drained on a sieve, and the syrup reduced to one-third of its original quantity, and kept

---

* Mosaic-boards, for tartlets, may be had of all sizes and patterns at any turner's shop. To cut out impressions from these, it is necessary to use small circular flats of raised pie-paste, which must be placed on the board, and pressed into the design, by rolling it with a paste-pin; the superfluous paste must then be cut or shaved away, and the mosaic of paste that remains in the design shaken out of the board.

with the fruit in a small basin, to fill the tartlets with as in the fore-going cases.

1325. PUFF-PASTE TARTLETS.

GIVE eight turns to half a pound of puff-paste (No. 1261), roll it out to the thickness of the sixth part of an inch, and then with a circular tin-cutter, about one inch and three quarters in diameter, stamp out twenty flats; again use a small cutter, measuring one inch in diameter, to stamp out the centre of these : next, gather up the trimmings, knead them together, and roll them out to the eighth part of an inch in thick-ness, and stamp out as many flats as there are rings ; place them on a wetted baking-sheet, moisten the edges with a soft brush dipped in water, stick the rings of paste on these, shake some sugar over them with the dredger, and bake them of a very light color (at very moderate heat). When the tartlets are done, mask the bands or rings with a little *meringue*-paste, dip them either in some chopped or very finely-shred pistachios or almonds, and place them in the screen to dry. Previously to serving these tartlets, they may be filled, either with cherries, currants, plums, &c., prepared as directed above, or else with any kind of preserve.

1326. MOSAIC TARTLETS.

PREPARE two dozen puff-paste tartlets as directed above, and fill each of them with a spoonful of apricot or greengage-jam ; wet round the edges, and place a mosaic of paste on the top of each, egg these over slightly, and bake them of a light color ; when they are done, shake some fine sugar over them, and glaze them with the red-hot salamander.

1327. PARISIAN LOAVES.

PREPARE some small slender finger-biscuits, spread them with apricot or greengage-jam, and stick two of these together ; then, hold one at a time on a fork, mask them over slightly with some *meringue*-paste, and with a paper *cornet* filled with some of the same, draw parallel lines across the cakes in a slanting direction ; when they are all com-pleted, shake some sugar over them, and put them in the oven to be baked, or rather dried, of a very light-fawn color. When done, insert some narrow strips of bright currant-jelly, greengage-jam, and apple-jelly between the bars of the decoration.

1328. MARYGOLDS.

GIVE eight turns to half a pound of puff-paste, roll it out to the thickness of the sixth part of an inch, stamp out twenty flats with a circular fluted tin-cutter, about one inch and three quarters in diameter, and place these on a wetted baking-sheet ; roll out the trimmings rather thin, and with two smaller cutters, stamp out as many rings of the size of a shilling as there are cakes, and place one of these on the centre of each of the marygolds, previously wetted all over the surface. Then, place some almonds split into four strips lengthwise, closely round the rings, in a somewhat slanting direction ; these must be slightly pressed into the paste to make them hold on, and should be arranged so as to give to the cake, as much as possible, the appearance of the flower they are intended to resemble. When they are all completed, shake some sugar over them with the dredger, and bake them of a light color. When done, insert some very narrow strips of bright firm red-currant or apple-jelly between each piece of almond, and place a piece of apricot or greengage-jam in the ring.

1328a. FILBERT CREAM TARTLETS.

LINE two dozen tartlet-moulds with some short-paste, and then fill them with the following preparation :—First, extract the kernels from a sufficient quantity of fresh filberts to produce half a pound of sound kernels; let these be first pounded in a mortar, adding a dessert-spoonful of water, in order to prevent them from turning oily; and when they are thoroughly bruised, add two ounces of fresh butter, four ounces of sugar, a liqueur-glassful of white noyeau, and the yolks of four eggs; and, having beaten the whole well together, use the preparation as directed above. Bake the filled tartlets in a moderate oven, and when done remove them from the moulds on to a clean baking-sheet, and let them be glazed on the surface of the cream with the following mixture :—To a small glassful of white noyeau, add about two ounces of glazing-sugar, work these well together until they form a rather thick icing, which use as directed above; and after this last part of the process is completed, place the tartlets in the screen to dry the icing.

1328b. COVENTRY TARTLETS.

LINE two dozen deep-fluted tartlet-moulds with some short-paste, and fill these with the following preparation :—Procure about twelve ounces of hard fresh curd, which place in a mortar with four ounces of pounded sugar, the yolks of four eggs, two ounces of fresh butter, as much grated nutmeg as would hold on a sixpence, a small pinch of salt, and a dessert-spoonful of orange-flower-water; bruise all these smoothly together until the whole forms a compact creamy substance, and then use it as directed above. Bake the tartlets of a light color, and, when done, turn them out upside-down upon a sheet of paper, and allow them to cool. Next, proceed to mask over the upper part of each tartlet with some apricot-marmalade, and place thereon a tasteful decoration formed with angelica, dried cherries, &c., &c.

These cakes may be varied in appearance by using currant or apple-jelly instead of apricot, &c., and ornamenting them with small cut fancy shapes or designs, made of worked puff-paste, or almond-paste.

1329. APPLE TART WITH QUINCE.

PEEL the apples, remove the cores, cut them in slices or quarters, and arrange them neatly in the pie-dish; then add the quince, which must be previously sliced up very thin, and stewed in a small stew-pan over a slow fire with a little water, sugar, and a small piece of butter; add sufficient pounded sugar to sweeten the quantity of apples the tart may contain, and strew some zest of lemon (*i. e.*, the rind rubbed on sugar, and then scraped off) over the top. Cover the tart with puff-paste, first placing a band of the same round the edge of the dish; scollop it round the edges by pressing them with the back of a knife, egg the tart over, then ornament the top by drawing out some fanciful design with the point of a knife, and bake it of a light color; when done, shake some sugar upon it, and use the red-hot salamander to glaze it.

1330. PEAR TART.

IF mellow pears be used for this purpose, the foregoing directions may be followed; but if stewing pears are made use of, these must be first stewed with some sugar, a little water, and some lemon-peel and cloves tied together. When the pears are nearly done, allow them to cool previously to making the tart, which, in this case, should be covered with tart paste (No. 1255); when so far finished, sprinkle it over with a paste-brush dipped in some beaten white of egg, and some sifted sugar strewn upon it, it should then be baked of a light color.

1331. FRUIT TARTS IN GENERAL.

WHEN peaches, apricots, or any of the larger kinds of plums are used for making tarts, the stones should be removed, and the kernels taken out and blanched; the fruit should be then neatly arranged in the tart-dish in the form of a dome, with the kernels amongst it, and some sifted sugar strewn over all. These tarts should invariably be covered with tart-paste, and finished as directed in the foregoing case.

For making cherry, damson, raspberry, and currant tarts, follow the same directions; except that the stones need not be removed from the two first of these.

FRITTERS,

COMPRISING

Apple Fritters.	Custard Fritters.
Pine Apple Fritters.	Princess Fritters.
Orange Fritters.	Portuguese Fritters.
Peach Fritters.	German Fritters.
Spanish Puffs.	Diavolini.

1332. APPLE FRITTERS.

CUT the apples in rather thick slices, scoop out the cores with a tin-cutter, then pare off the rind, and place the pieces of apples in a basin with a small glass of brandy, a table-spoonful of sugar, and some grated peel of lemon or orange, letting them steep in this for several hours, if possible. When about to send the fritters to table, throw the pieces of apple into a basin containing some light-made batter (No. 232), then take them out one at a time, and drop them into some heated hog's-lard, to be fried of a light color; when they are done, drain them on a sheet of paper, break off all the rough parts, place the fritters on a baking-sheet, shake some fine sugar upon them, glaze them with the red-hot salamander, and serve.

Note.—Pear fritters are made in the same manner as the above.

1333. CUSTARD FRITTERS.

PEEL the pine apple without waste; if it is small, cut it into slices in the same manner as apples; but if the fruit happens to be large, it should be cut up in pieces about the size of a finger; these must be then steeped with a glass of maraschino and a spoonful of pounded sugar, in a basin for several hours, previously to their being fried in batter; this should be mixed with cream. In other respects, finish these as directed for apple fritters.

1334. ORANGE FRITTERS.

CHOOSE some thin-skinned oranges, peel them, divide them into quarters, remove the pips, and then put them to steep in a basin with a glass of brandy, a spoonful of sugar, and some grated rind of orange. Previously to frying the fritters, drain the pieces of oranges from the brandy, &c., throw them into some light-made batter (No. 232), then take them out one by one, drop them gently into some heated hog's lard, and fry them of a light color; finish these in the usual manner.

1335. PEACH FRITTERS.

CUT the peaches into quarters, remove the skins, and put them to steep in a basin with a glass of noyeau and a spoonful of sugar; then fry them in batter, as directed in the foregoing cases.

Note.—Fritters of apricots and large plums are prepared as the above; brandy being used instead of liqueur, to steep the fruit in.

1336. SPANISH PUFFS.

PREPARE some *petits-choux* paste (No. 1291). Next, cut a sheet of foolscap-paper into four pieces, spread these with butter, and then take up as much of the paste as will stand in a small tea-spoon; press it out in rows on the paper, in the form of round balls: this should be done just before frying them. When about to send to table, take hold of the sheets of paper containing the puffs, at one corner, and as they are immersed in the hot hog's-lard, shake them gently off the paper; fry them of a light color, and when done, drain them on a wire-sieve covered with paper to absorb any grease: some fine sugar must then be shaken over them, previously to their being dished up on a napkin, in a conical form.

1337. CUSTARD FRITTERS.

INGREDIENTS :—One pint of cream, ten yolks of eggs, one ounce of potato-flour, six ounces of sugar, a little cinnamon and grated lemon-peel.

Mix the above ingredients together in a basin, after having first boiled the cinnamon and lemon in the cream; strain the whole through a sieve, and then pour the custard into a plain mould, previously spread with butter: steam the custard in the usual manner, and when done, allow it to become cold, preparatory to its being cut up into slices about half an inch thick, and then divided into squares of about two inches each: place these on a dish, and sprinkle them with a little cinnamon-powder, and a spoonful of brandy. When about to send to table, dip each piece of custard separately in some light-made batter (No. 232), then drop them into some hot hog's-lard, and fry them of a light color; when done, drain them on a sheet of paper, break off any rough parts, sugar them, glaze them over with the red-hot salamander, and dish them up on a napkin.

Note.—This kind of fritter may be varied by changing the flavoring, and also by adding a proportionate quantity of either grated chocolate, pulverized almonds essence of coffee, or lightly-burnt sugar.

1337 *a*. PRINCESS FRITTERS.

THIS kind of fritter is prepared from the remains of *Brioche, Baba, Savarin, Compiègne* cake, or *Kouglaüff;* which ever of the foregoing happens to be used for the specified purpose, should be first cut up into slices a quarter of an inch thick, and then again cut out into small circular shapes with a tin-cutter, about the diameter of a five-shilling piece; place these in a sautapan previously strewn with orange sugar, and pour over them sufficient cream to cover them, shake some more orange sugar over the entire surface, and when about to fry the fritters, dip each separately in very light and delicately-made frying-batter. When these fritters are fried crisp, let them be brightly glazed with sifted sugar and the red-hot salamander; and, after being dished up, pour some apricot-jam, diluted with a little orange flower-water, round the base, and serve.

1337 *b*. PORTUGUESE FRITTERS.

INGREDIENTS :—Eight ounces of Carolina rice, four ounces of sugar, two ounces of fresh butter, a quart of milk, a small stick of cinnamon, and a pound-pot of orange-marmalade, and six eggs. Thoroughly pick and wash the rice, and then place it in a convenient-sized stewpan, together with the sugar, butter, milk and cinnamon; allow the whole to simmer very gently by the side of a slow fire, until the whole of the milk is absorbed by the rice, when, if the simmering has been gradual and slow, the grains of rice will be satisfactorily done. Next add the orange-marmalade, and the yolks of the six eggs; stir the whole over a quick stove-fire until the eggs are set firm in the preparation; it must now be turned out upon a clean dish or baking-sheet, and spread equally to about a quarter of an inch in thickness, and when this has become cold, must be cut out in oblong shapes, which, after being first dipped in light frying-batter, are to be fried crisp, glazed with cinnamon-sugar, and dished up on a napkin.

1337 *c*. DIAVOLINI.

INGREDIENTS :—Eight ounces of ground rice, four ounces of sugar, a quart of milk, two ounces of butter, a tea-spoonful of essence of ginger, six eggs, one pound of preserved ginger.

Mix the rice, sugar, milk and butter together in a stewpan, and stir the produce over a stove-fire until it thickens; it must then be removed from the fire, and after being worked quite smooth, and the lid being put on the stewpan, set it either in the oven or over a slow ash-fire to finish doing; this will be effected in about half an hour. The rice must now be removed from the fire, and the preserved ginger previously cut into very small dice-like shapes, the essence of ginger and the six yolks of eggs, being added thereto, stir the whole over a quick fire until the eggs are set firm in the rice, and then finish the fritters as directed in the preceding article; using plain sugar to glaze them.

1337d. GERMAN FRITTERS.

DIVIDE one pound of Brioche-paste into twenty-four equal parts; next, mould these into small finger-shapes, and bake them of a very light color. These fingers must now be placed in a deep sautapan, and a pint of cream, previously boiled with a stick of vanilla in it, is to be poured over them, and they are to be allowed to soak therein until quite cold; after which they must be bread-crumbed by being first dipped in beaten egg, and then rolled in the bread-crumbs. About twenty minutes before the fritters are required to be served, fry them of a bright light color, in heated hog's-lard, shake some vanilla sugar over them, and when neatly piled on a napkin, send to table quite hot.

ICED PUDDINGS AND ORNAMENTED ENTREMETS,

COMPRISING

Iced Cake, à la Stanley.
Iced Rice Pudding, à la Cintra.
Iced Pudding, à la Cerito.
   „   à la Prince of Wales.
   „   à la Chesterfield.
   „   à la Kinnaird.
   „   à la Prince Albert.
   „   à la Parisiènne.
   „   à la Duchess of Kent.
Biscuit glacês, in small cases.
Nesselrode Pudding.
Iced Pudding, à la Princess Alice.
Millefeuilles Cake, à la Chantilly.
Apples and Rice, ornamented.

Apples and Rice, plain.
   „   à la Portuguaise.
   „   in the form of a Porcupine.
   „   à la Portuguaise, another way.
Flan of Peaches.
Napolitaine Cake, à la Chantilly.
Croquante of Oranges.
   „   of Fresh Walnuts.
   „   of Ratafias, à la Chantilly.
Meringue, à la Parisiènne.
Grosse-Meringue, with Pistachios.
Swan of Savoy Biscuit, à la Chantilly.
Savoy Cake, in the form of Glazed Ham

1338. ICED CAKE, A LA STANLEY.

FIRST, make a Parisian cake (in a fluted mould), as directed in No. 1273. Next, prepare a *compôte* of greengages in syrup; these must be kept whole, and of as green a color as possible. Then, prepare a custard in the following manner: —Mix ten yolks of eggs with a pint and a half of boiling cream, eight ounces of sugar, and sufficient cinnamon and lemon-peel to flavor it; add a very little salt, and stir the whole in a stewpan over the fire until it begins to thicken; the custard should then be immediately passed through a tammy or sieve, into a basin, and allowed to become cold. This custard must now be placed in a freezing-pot used for making ices, and should be occasionally worked with a spatula as it becomes set by freezing; when frozen sufficiently firm, scrape the custard from the sides of the pot, and gather it all up at the bottom; put the lid on with paper to exclude the hot air, pour off the water from the tub, and after the pot has been packed in with fresh ice and salt, place a damp cloth over the top, and keep it in a very cool place until wanted.

When about to send the cake to table, scoop out nearly the whole of the crumb from the centre, and fill it with the iced custard; place it on its dish, pile up the *compôte* of greengages on the top, as represented in the wood-cut, pour some of the syrup round the base, and serve.

1339. ICED RICE PUDDING, A LA CINTRA.

WASH and parboil eight ounces of Carolina rice; then, put it into a stewpan, with a quart of milk and a pint of cream, two sticks of vanilla, twelve ounces of sugar, and a little salt; allow the rice to simmer very gently over or by a slow stove-fire, until the grains are almost dissolved, stirring it over occasionally with a light hand. When the rice is done, and while it is yet in a boiling state, add the yolks of six eggs; then stir the whole well together for several minutes, in order to mix in the eggs, and also for the purpose of breaking up and smoothing the rice. Let this rice-custard be frozen in the same manner as directed in the foregoing case, and then put it into a plain mould; cover it with the lid, and immerse it in the ice in the usual way.

While the above part of the process is going on, a *compôte* of twelve oranges (Tangerene, if in season) should be prepared in the following manner:—First, cut each orange into halves, remove the pithy core and the pips with the point of a small knife; then, with a sharp knife, pare off the rind and white pith, so as to lay the transparent pulp of the fruit quite bare, taking care to trim them neatly, and without waste; when the whole of the fruit is ready, throw it into a convenient-sized sugar-boiler, or stewpan, containing about a pint of syrup (made with one pound of sugar, and nearly a pint of spring-water), allow the pieces of orange to boil up gently in this for two minutes, and then drain them on a sieve. Boil the syrup down to about one-half of its original quantity; then, add two wine-glasses of curaçao, and three table-spoonfuls of apricot-jam; mix the whole together, and pour it over the oranges in a basin.

When about to send the pudding to table, turn it out of the mould, and place it on its dish, dress the *compôte* of oranges on the top and round the base, as represented in the wood-cut, pour the syrup over it, and serve.

1340. PUDDING, A LA CERITO.

First, prepare about eighteen finger, and the same number of almond *cornet-gauffres* (No. 1284), and arrange the finger-*gauffres* round the inside of a plain circular charlotte-mould. Prepare also an iced custard, as directed for the Stanley cake, except that this must be flavored with vanilla. An iced *Macédoine* of fruits in a strawberry-water-ice must also be got ready.

About an hour before sending the pudding to table, garnish the sides of the *gauffres* (previously placed in the mould as directed above,) with a coating of the vanilla-cream ice, about an inch thick, and cover the bottom of the mould in the same manner; then fill up the centre with the iced *Macédoine* of fruits, place a round piece of paper on the top, and cover with the lid, next, immerse the pudding in rough ice, mixed with salt, in a pail or tub; cover this over with a damp cloth, and set it in a cool place till wanted. The pudding must then be turned out of the mould on to its dish, with the decorated top placed upon it, and garnished round the base, and on the centre, with the small *gauffres*, made in the form of *cornets* or cornucopiæ, each being filled with a little of the vanilla-cream ice, and a strawberry placed on the top; then serve immediately.

To prepare the decorated top above alluded to, a circular piece of *gauffre*, the size of the mould, must be ornamented with sugar-icing, pressed out of a *cornet* of paper, so as to imitate a scroll, as shown in the above wood-cut; the icing must be allowed to dry in the screen, and the decoration should then be completed by introducing some red-currant and bright apple-jelly in between the scrolls.

1341. ICED PUDDING, A LA PRINCE OF WALES.

FIRST, prepare eight yolks of eggs of custard, as for the Stanley cake (No. 1338); previously to passing this through a tammy, add two pottles of picked scarlet strawberries, tossed in a sugar-boiler with ten ounces of pounded sugar over a brisk fire, until they begin to simmer; when the whole has been passed into a *purée*, allow it to cool; then freeze it in the usual manner, and fill a cylindrical pudding-mould with it, stop it down with the lid, and immerse it in rough ice.

While the foregoing part of the process is in preparation, an iced

Macédoine of fruits must be made as follows :—First, extract the juice from one pound of muscatel grapes, and add a sufficient quantity of syrup, to give body to it ; this must then be put into the freezing-pot, and worked in the usual way. Just before using the ice, a proportionate quantity of light-coloured fruit must be added, and mixed in lightly with the ice, so as not to bruise them : these fruits should consist of small pieces of pine-apple, peach, apricot, white raspberries, strawberries, and bigaroon cherries; this *Macédoine* should be finished just before dishing up. The pudding must be turned out of the mould on to its dish, the centre filled with the *Macédoine*, as represented in the annexed wood-cut, and immediately served.

1342. ICED PUDDING, A LA CHESTERFIELD.

GRATE one pound of pine-apple into a basin, add this to eight yolks of eggs, one pint and a half of boiled cream, one pound of sugar, and a very little salt; stir the whole together in a stewpan over a stove-fire until the custard begins to thicken ; then pass it through a tammy, by rubbing with two wooden spoons, in the same manner as for a *purée*, in order to force the pine-apple through the tammy. This custard must now be iced in the usual manner, and put into a mould of the shape represented in the annexed wood-cut; and in the centre of the iced cream, some *Macédoine* ice of red fruits, consisting of cherries, currants, strawberries and raspberries in a cherry-water ice, must be introduced; cover the whole in with the lid, then immerse the pudding in rough ice in the usual way, and keep it in a cool place until wanted.

When about to send the pudding to table, turn it out of the mould on to its dish, ornament the dish with a kind of drooping feather, formed with green angelica cut in strips, and arranged as represented in the wood-cut; garnish the base with small *gauffres*, filled with some of the iced cream reserved for the purpose, place a strawberry on the top of each, and serve.

1343. ICED PUDDING, A LA KINNAIRD.

BLANCH eight ounces of Jordan almonds, and two of bitter ditto ; dry them in a cloth, put them into a sugar-boiler, and stir them over a slow fire, in order to roast them of a light color ; as soon as the almonds have acquired sufficient color, throw in six ounces of pounded sugar, and continue stirring the whole over the fire until the sugar has melted, and acquired a light-brown color ; they should now be withdrawn from the fire, and stirred about with the spoon until they have become nearly cold ; they must then be thoroughly pounded in the mortar, and added to eight yolks of eggs, eight ounces of sugar, and one pint and a half of boiled cream ; stir the whole with a wooden

spoon in a stewpan over the stove-fire, until the yolks of eggs are
sufficiently set in the custard, and
then pass it through a tammy in the
same way as a *purée*. This custard
must be iced in a freezing-pot in the
usual manner, and afterwards put
into a mould resembling that represented in the wood-cut, and after
being covered in with its lid, immersed in rough ice, there to remain
until it is sent to table. The pudding must then be turned out of the
mould on to its dish, the top garnished with a drooping feather,
formed of strips of green angelica,
and served.

Note.—The centre of this pudding may be garnished with apricot or
orange-marmalade, previously to its being again immersed in the
rough ice.

1344. ICED PUDDING, A LA PRINCE ALBERT.

PREPARE some rice custard ice, as directed for the pudding *à la
Cintra* (No. 1339) : about half that quantity will suffice. Slice up a
dozen ripe apricots, and boil them with twelve ounces of sugar, and
half a pint of water, until the fruit is dissolved ; then pass it through
a sieve—if it should be too thick, add a little thin syrup, and freeze
this in the usual manner. The two ices being ready, a pudding-mould
should be lined with a coating of the apricot-water ice, about half an
inch thick, and the centre filled up entirely with the iced rice-custard ;
cover the pudding with the lid of the mould, and immerse it in rough
ice until dishing-up time. The pudding must then be placed on its
dish, garnished with some wafer-*gauffres* filled with whipped cream
seasoned with noyeau, and served immediately.

1345. ICED PUDDING, A LA PARISIENNE.

PARBOIL and remove the skin from eight ounces of Jordan almonds,
and two ounces of bitter ditto, wash and dry them on a cloth, and then
thoroughly pound them with twelve ounces of sugar in a mortar, until
they present the appearance of a soft paste ; this must then be added
to eight yolks of eggs, and a quart of boiled cream ; stir the whole
together in a stewpan over a stove-fire, until the eggs are sufficiently
set in the custard, and then pass it through the tammy in the same
manner as a *purée*. Pour this into a freezing-pot—ready packed in
rough ice, and freeze it in the usual manner ; when this is effected, fill
an ice pudding-mould with it, cover it in with the lid, and immerse it
in rough ice until dishing-up time. The pudding must then be placed
on its dish, and the top and base garnished with a *compôte* of apricots ;
after mixing a glass of noyeau in with the syrup, pour it over the
pudding, and serve.

1346. ICED PUDDING, A LA DUCHESS OF KENT.

REMOVE the skins from one pound of filbert-kernels, and pound these
with ten ounces of sugar (adding a few drops of water), until they

become soft and pulpy ; take up this paste into a basin, add a pint of single cream, stir the whole well together, and pass it through a tammy into a *purée ;* then freeze this in the usual manner. While the above is being prepared, a pint of cherry-water-ice must be made as follows :— Remove the stalks from two pounds of Kentish cherries, and bruise them thoroughly in a mortar, so as to break the stones, then take them up into a sugar-boiler, add twelve ounces of sugar, and boil the whole together over a brisk stove-fire for five minutes ; rub this through a hair-sieve into a basin, and freeze it, adding a little thin syrup, if necessary. Use the cherry-water-ice to line the pudding-mould with, garnish the centre with the filbert-cream-ice, cover the mould with its lid, and immerse the pudding in rough ice until dishing-up time. The pudding must then be turned out on its dish, garnished round with wafer-*gauffres* filled with some of the filbert-cream reserved for the purpose, and served immediately.

1347. BISCUITS GLACES, IN SMALL CASES.

To eight yolks of eggs, add one pint of cream, four ounces of ratifias, ten ounces of sugar, and a very little salt ; stir the whole in a stewpan over a stove-fire until the egg is sufficiently set ; then pass the custard through a tammy into a basin, and when it has become cold, add two wine-glasses of maraschino, and freeze this in the usual manner. Just before dishing up the *biscuits,* half a pint of whipped cream must be lightly added to the iced custard ; the small paper cases must be filled with this, and afterwards sprinkled over with some finely-bruised high-colored ratifias, then dish the *biscuits* upon a napkin, and serve.

Note.—These iced *biscuits* may be also infinitely varied, by changing the flavorings : for which purpose, all kinds of liqueurs, and essences of almonds, vanilla, orange, lemon, coffee, chocolate, or orange-flowers, may be used : they may also be made by adding a *purée* of apricots, strawberries, raspberries, or pine-apple, to the custard.

1348. NESSELRODE PUDDING.

Boil three dozen chestnuts in water, and when done, peel, pound, and rub them through a sieve ; put this pulp into a stewpan with eight yolks of eggs, a pint of cream, two sticks of vanilla, previously pounded, half a pint of pine-apple syrup, and a very little salt ; stir these ingredients over a stove-fire until the eggs are sufficiently set in the custard, then rub the whole through a tammy, and put the cream into a basin. Cut four ounces of green citron, six ounces of pine-apple (previously simmered in the syrup above alluded to), and place these in a basin with six ounces of dried cherries, and four ounces of Smyrna raisins ; to these add two wine-glasses of maraschino, and allow the fruit to steep for several hours. Place the chestnut cream in a freezing-pot immersed in rough ice, and freeze it in the usual manner ; then add half a pint of whipped cream and the fruit. Mix the pudding, and continue working the freezing-pot for a few minutes longer ; when the pudding is thoroughly set firm, put it into the mould, cover it down and immerse it in ice until it is required to be sent to table.

1349. ICED PUDDING, A LA PRINCESS ALICE.

FIRST, remove the skins from the kernels of about fifty green walnuts, then pound these with ten ounces of sugar, until the whole forms
a kind of soft and pulpy paste; take this up into a basin, mix it with
a pint of single cream, then pass it through a tammy into a *purée*, and
let this be frozen in the usual manner.

While the above is in course of preparation, two dozen greengages
must be boiled with twelve ounces of sugar and half a pint of water,
until the fruit is dissolved, when the whole must be rubbed through a
tammy or sieve : this should then be frozen, adding, if necessary, a little
thin syrup. The pudding-mould must now be lined with the greengage
ice, and the centre filled with the walnut-cream ice; then place the lid
on the mould, and immerse the pudding in rough ice in the usual manner, until dishing-up time, when the pudding must be turned out on to
its dish, garnished round with small almond-*gauffres* filled with whipped
cream, with a preserved cherry placed on the top of each, and served
immediately.

1350. MILLE-FEUILLES CAKE,* A LA CHANTILLY.

GIVE ten turns to one pound of
puff paste (No. 1261), then divide
it into two pieces, and roll them
out to the thickness of the tenth
part of an inch; then, with a circular tin-cutter about five inches
in diameter, stamp out eight or ten
flats; place these on baking-sheets,
stamp out the centre part from
each of the flats, leaving only a
circular band about two inches
wide; shake some fine sugar over
them, and bake them of a very
light color, and when done, allow
them to become cold. The flats
must now be raised one upon
another, with layers of some kind
of preserve between each, and placed on a baking-sheet, in order that
the cake may be entirely covered with a thin coating of whipped
whites of eggs mixed with sugar; this must be smoothed over with
the blade of a knife, and should be then ornamented with a paper
cornet filled with some of the white of egg, as represented in the
wood-cut: as soon as this is completed, shake some fine sugar over it,
and dry it of a very light color in a slow oven, or else in the hot
closet. When the decoration of the cake has been dried, it must be
ornamented with bright red-currant and apple-jelly, placed tastefully
about the design so as to give it more effect. On sending to table,
fill the centre of the cake with whipped cream flavored with some
kind of liqueur, garnish the dome of cream with strawberries, and
serve.

The above may also be ornamented with spun sugar or with pista-

---

* Or "thousand-leaved" cake, so called from the lightness of the puff-paste with
which it is made.

chios. The centre of these cakes may also be filled with a *Macédoine* of fruit in jelly, or with any of the various kinds of creams; the latter should be whipped on the ice, until nearly set.

1351. APPLES AND RICE ORNAMENTED.

FIRST, turn or peel smoothly about two dozen golden pippins  (after the cores have been removed); boil these very gently in some light syrup for about ten minutes, when they will be sufficiently done. Then prepare some rice in the same manner as for a cake, observing that for this purpose, it must be kept firmer. Prepare also a circular or oval raised pie-case (No. 752), about three inches high, taking care that its diameter suits the dish it is meant for. When the case is baked, fill it with the prepared rice, and pile the apples up in a pyramidal form, as represented in the woodcut, placing some of the rice in the centre of these. Mask the whole with some diluted apricot-jam, place a preserved cherry in the hole of each apple, and insert some pieces of angelica, cut in the form of pointed leaves, in between the apples. This dish should be served hot, and must, therefore, be dished up only a short time previously to its being served.

1352. APPLES AND RICE, PLAIN.

DIVIDE a dozen apples in halves, take out the cores, peel them, and place them in neat order in a deep sautapan thickly spread with butter; strew some lemon-sugar over them, put the lid on, and then bake them without allowing them to acquire any color. Prepare some rice boiled with milk, sugar, a little butter, and some cinnamon; when thoroughly done, work this up with a spoon, and then dish it up in the form of a dome; arrange the apples neatly upon this, pour some melted apricot-jam over the whole, and serve quite hot.

1353. APPLES, A LA PORTUGUAISE.

PREPARE some apple marmalade with about a dozen apples. Split  a dozen apples into halves, peel them, and remove the cores, and then place them in a deep sautapan thickly spread with butter; shake some sugar and grated lemon-peel over them, and bake them in the oven. Prepare next a small quantity of pastry custard (No. 1311), also an ornamented case (No. 752), which should be partially baked.

When the foregoing articles are ready, nearly fill the case with the marmalade of apples, leaving an opening or well in the centre ; then pile the pieces of apples upon the marmalade in the form of a dome, leaving the centre hollow; fill this with the pastry-custard, and cover the whole with some orange marmalade. Next, whip four whites of eggs quite firm, mix in four ounces of sifted sugar, and use this *meringue*-paste to finish the apples, according to the design placed at the head of this article : this is done by first masking over the entire surface of the dome, formed by the apples, with a smooth coating of the prepared whites of eggs, and then with a paper *cornet* filled with some of the same, marking out the design : when this has been effected, shake some sifted sugar upon it, and bake the *meringue* of a very light-fawn color. Just before sending this *entremet* to table, finish ornamenting it by filling up the inner part of the cross with alternate strips or layers of red-currant and apple-jellies, and also with greengage or apricot-jam ; these must be arranged so as to show their colors distinctly, which will produce a very pretty effect.

This *entremets* should be served hot.

1354. APPLES IN THE FORM OF A PORCUPINE.

PREPARE some marmalade with about eighteen apples ; place this in an oval case of raised pie-paste previously baked for the purpose ; leave a hollow in the centre of the marmalade, fill this up with some pastry custard (No. 1311), and spread some apricot-jam over the whole. Next, prepare some *meringue*-paste as directed in the foregoing article, and spread this over the surface of the apples, giving it at the same time the form of a porcupine ; when this has been effected, about six ounces of Jordan almonds, previously shred in strips, must be regularly inserted in close rows, to imitate the quills of porcupine, and the head and feet should be marked out with angelica cut out in imitation of these. Shake some sifted sugar upon the whole, and bake the *meringue* covering of a very light-fawn color. Just before sending to table, fill out the circle of the eyes with apple-jelly, with a currant inserted in the centre of each to form the pupils, and use a paper *cornet* filled with red-currant-jelly, to draw some stripes lengthwise, between the rows of almonds placed on the back.

1355. APPLES, A LA PORTUGUAISE, ANOTHER WAY.

REMOVE the cores from a dozen golden pippins, or small russets ; peel them smoothly, and then simmer them in a pint of light syrup until they are nearly done ; they must then be drained on a sieve. Next, spread the bottom and sides of a baked pie-case raised in a mould about two inches high (tart-paste should be used for this purpose), with apple marmalade mixed with one-third part of orange-jam, and arrange the apples in close circular order in this ; each apple must be filled with orange-jam, and the entire surface then masked over with a rather thick coating of transparent red-currant or apple-jelly. Some tasteful design should be formed on the layer of jelly in the form of a wreath or scroll ; this should be done either with almond paste, or with puff-paste to which ten turns have been given, then stamped out with appropriate tin-cutters, and placed on a baking-sheet, sugared over and baked, without allowing it to acquire any color. The latter style of ornamenting is preferable.

1356. FLAN OF PEACHES.

FOR this purpose, a crust or case should be prepared in the following manner. First, make one pound of short paste (No. 1255); then spread with butter the inside of a fluted circular or oval mould, about two inches high, and eight inches in diameter; line this with the paste, cut the edges level, and then raise them all round, and pinch the part that rises above the mould with a pair of pastry pincers. Next, fill the case with flour, mixed with one-sixth part of chopped suet, and bake it until it is about three parts done; the flour must then be removed, and the case brushed out clean, with a paste-brush; after which it must be nearly filled with halves of peaches, previously skinned and simmered in some thin syrup for about five minutes; the *flan* must now be placed again in the oven for about a quarter of an hour, and when withdrawn, a close row of halves of peaches (previously simmered in syrup added to the juice of a pint of red currants) should be neatly arranged, and a peach kernel being placed on each piece of peach, let the jelly be poured over the whole, and serve.

Note.—For the preparation of *flans* of apricots, and all kinds of plums, follow the above directions; except that in either of these cases, the currant juice is to be omitted.

1357. NEAPOLITAN CAKE, A LA CHANTILLY

FIRST, weigh one pound of flour, eight ounces of sifted sugar, eight ounces of pounded almonds, and eight ounces of butter; place these

ingredients on the pastry slab, add five yolks of eggs, the zest of the rind of two oranges extracted by rubbing on a piece of sugar, and a very little salt; work these well together, and when they are thoroughly mixed, knead the paste into the form of a rolling-pin, and divide it into twelve equal parts; these must be again kneaded into round balls, rolled out to the diameter of about seven inches, placed upon baking-sheets, spread with butter; after having cut them all of the same size with a circular tin-cutter, let them be egged and pricked all over with a fork, and baked of a light color, and when done, placed on a level slab or table, with a baking-sheet upon them, to keep them straight as they become cold. These flats must then be laid one upon another, with a layer of some kind of preserve spread between each: apricot, greengage, strawberry, orange, or raspberry-jam, may be used for the purpose. Previously to placing the last piece on the top of the cake, it should be first decorated with *meringue*-paste or sugar-icing; the sides must be masked with some kind of bright preserve,—such as greengage, apricot, red-currant, or apple-jelly, and afterwards ornamented with a design similar to that represented in the wood-cut, formed either of almond or gum-paste (raised from carved boards used for such purposes) ; or else with piping, as used for wedding-cakes. The cake should then be placed on its dish, the centre filled with whipped cream, and some strawberries piled on the top ; when these are not in season, preserved cherries, verjuice, or angelica may be substituted.

1358. CROQUANTE OF ORANGES.

LET the peel and all the white pith be carefully removed with the fingers from about a dozen sound, and not over-ripe oranges ; then divide them by pulling them into small sections with the fingers, taking care not to break the thin skin which envelopes the juicy pulp, then place them on an earthen dish. Next, put about one pound of the finest lump-sugar into a sugar-boiler with sufficient spring water to just cover it, and boil it down until it snaps or becomes brittle,  which may be easily ascertained thus : take up a little of the sugar, when it begins to boil up in large purling bubbles, on the point of a knife, and instantly dip it into some cold water ; if the sugar becomes set, it is sufficiently boiled, and will then easily snap in breaking.* The sugar should now be withdrawn from the fire. The pieces of orange stuck on the points of small wooden skewers must be slightly dipped in the sugar, and arranged at the bottom and round the sides of a plain circular mould (previously very lightly rubbed with salad-oil), according to the foregoing design. When the whole is complete, and the sugar has become firm by cooling, just before sending to table, fill the inside of the *croquante* with whipped cream, seasoned with sugar, a glass of maraschino and some whole strawberries, and then turn it out on to a napkin, and serve.

1359. CROQUANTE OF FRESH WALNUTS.

THE fittest season for making this, is when the walnuts are just ripe enough to be easily taken out of the shell ; about sixty will be required for the purpose. They must be carefully shelled and divided into halves, then freed from the thin whitish skin which covers the kernels, and kept in a clean napkin until used. In all other respects, this kind of *croquante* must be finished as in the preceding case.

1360. CROQUANTE OF RATIFAS, A LA CHANTILLY.

PROCURE one pound of small ratafias ; boil down one pound of the finest loaf-sugar as directed in the foregoing case. Then, slightly rub the inside of a basket-shaped mould with oil, and proceed to line this with the ratafias lightly dipped in the sugar—taking care to arrange them in neat and close order ; when the *croquante* is completed, and the sugar has become firmly set, turn it out of the mould. With the remainder of the sugar, form the handles, and a scroll-pattern border, which is to be placed round the join of the basket, and also

---

* When boiling sugar for this purpose, it is customary to add a pinch of cream of tartar and calcined alum mixed, or, a few drops of acetic-acid.

round the edge: this is effected by dipping the pointed end of the bowl of a spoon into the hot sugar, and then drawing it ont, and dropping the sugar from the bowl, in the form of the intended design, on a baking-sheet slightly oiled; before it becomes set, fix it round the part it is to ornament. Just before sending the *croquante* to table, fill the inside with whipped cream, arrange some strawberries, preserved cherries, or cut angelica, neatly on the surface, and serve.

1361. MERINGUE, A LA PARISIENNE.

FIRST, make half a pound of office-paste (No. 1257); then, slightly rub the outside of a tin vegetable-cutter, about one and a quarter

inch in diameter, and cover this to the extent of about three and a half inches in length, with some of the office-paste rolled out rather thin; fasten the joint neatly with egg, and place it on a baking-sheet; roll out the remainder of the paste to the thickness of the eighth part of an inch, and, out of this cut two circular pieces or flats, one measuring about six inches, and the other four inches in diameter; place them on a buttered baking-sheet, egg them over, prick them with a fork, and bake them of a light color, in a slow oven. When they are done, and have become cold, file or scrape their edges even and smooth, and cut the ends of the pillar even, that it may stand perfectly level; then fasten the base of the pillar on to the centre of the largest flat, with a little white of egg and fine sugar mixed together; next, fasten the smaller flat on the top of the pillar in like manner, taking care that it is quite straight, and put the whole to dry in the screen.

Whip twelve whites of eggs into a firm substantial froth, and then mix in one pound of finely-sifted sugar; use part of this to mask the entire surface of the foundation already described, and set this to dry at the entrance of the oven; when it has become comparatively hard, fill a paper *cornet* or biscuit forcer, with some of the *meringue*-paste, and use this to form the design round the pedestal of the *meringue*, as represented in the wood-cut: when this is done, shake some sugar over it, and put it into the oven to be baked of a very light-fawn color. With part of the *meringue*-paste, a kind of cup or deep saucer, measuring about seven inches in diameter, must be formed, by covering a flat dome (made of tin) with the paste to the thickness of about an inch; this must be well sugared over and baked firm, without allowing it to acquire much color. When this is done, take the *meringue* carefully off the dome, and place it upside down in a soup plate, and after the white of egg has been partially removed from the interior, smoothed with a spoon, and then sugared over, set it to dry in the hot-closet, or at the entrance of the oven, if the latter is not too hot. As soon as the *meringue* has become dry and hard, fasten it on the pedestal with a little of the paste, and use a paper *cornet* filled

with *meringue*-paste, to finish ornamenting the edge and sides, as represented in the wood-cut ; shake some sifted sugar over the unbaked
part, and put the *meringue* to dry in the hot-closet, taking particular
care that it does not acquire any color. Just before sending to
table, place the *meringue* on a napkin in its dish, fill it with whipped
cream flavored with orange-flower or some liqueur, and strew some
strawberries on the surface ; garnish round the base with quarters of
lemons or oranges filled with jelly (No. 1429), and serve.

1362. GROSSE-MERINGUE WITH PISTACHIOS

PREPARE the *meringue*-paste as directed in (No. 1298) ; then cut
six circular pieces of writing-paper to the size of a dinner-plate and
proceed to cover each of these with a kind of wreath formed with the
meringue-paste. This is effected in the following manner :—First, draw
a rather thick circle, about five inches in diameter, round the inner
part of one of the pieces of paper above alluded to ; then, with a
dessert-spoon mould the paste in the form of very small elongated
ovals, and place these crosswise, closely to each other upon the circle
already mentioned, thus forming a kind of wreath : fill the remaining
five papers in the same way, and then, after the *meringues* have been
well covered with sifted sugar, shake off the loose sugar, place them
on square pieces of board, and bake them of a very light color.
When done, turn the wreaths of *meringue* upside down upon plates,
shake sone sifted sugar over the unbaked part, and set them to dry
in a very slow oven.

Just before sending to table, pile the wreaths or rings of *meringue*
one upon another, with a layer of apricot-jam spread in between each ;
fill the centre with whipped cream, flavored with a glass of liqueur,
and serve.

1363. SWAN OF SAVOY BISCUIT, A LA CHANTILLY.

PREPARE sixteen eggs of Savoy-cake batter (No. 1275), and bake
it in a plain oval mould,—or failing this, in a deep oblong paper case ;
when it is done, and has become quite cold, shape it with a sharp
knife in the rough outline of the body of a swan ; the wings, tail-
piece, and the neck and head, must be made of office-paste (No. 1257) ;
the bill should be dipped in rather high-colored boiled sugar, and
the eyes may be formed with a little of the same, with a currant stuck
in the centre for the pupil. Just before sending the swan to table,
stick the neck into the breast-part, insert the wing-pieces in the sides,
and the fan-like piece into the tail-part ; cover the bird entirely with
a thick coating of whipped-cream ; first smooth this over with the
blade of a knife, and then, with the point of a small knife, imitate the
feathers about the wings, tail, and body. Place some spun-sugar
round the swan—in imitation of waves, and put a border of *petits
choux*, glazed with rough sugar and pistachios, round the base, and
serve.

1364. SAVOY CAKE IN THE FORM OF A GLAZED HAM.

BAKE sixteen eggs of Savoy-cake batter in an oblong paper case ;
when this has become quite cold, shape it in the form of a nicely-
trimmed ham, with a sharp knife, and hollow it out underneath.
That part of the rind which is usually left adhering to the knuckle

as an ornament must be imitated by spreading a layer of chocolate-icing over it, in the form of a scollop shell; the remaining part of the surface of the ham should be masked with a coating of diluted bright apricot jam, to imitate glaze.

Just before sending the ham to table, fill the hollow part with some *Macédoine* of fruit in jelly, or else with some kind of cream; then place the ham on its dish, fix a handsome paper ruffle on the knuckle with a small silver skewer; garnish the ham round the base with *croutons* of some kind of sweet jelly, pink and white; place an ornament of the same on the top, and serve.

RICE CAKE AND TIMBALES,

COMPRISING

Rice Cake with Almonds.	Macaroni Cake.
Timbale of Rice.	Semolina Cake.
Nouilles Cake, *à l'Allemande.*	Potato Cake.
Vermicelli Cake.	

1365. RICE CAKE, WITH ALMONDS.

WASH twelve ounces of rice, put it into a stewpan with four ounces of butter, eight ounces of sugar, half an ounce of bitter, and four ounces of sweet almonds (pounded), one quart of milk, and a very little salt; set the whole to boil very gently by the side of a slow stove-fire, and by the time the milk has become absorbed by the rice, the latter will be sufficiently done,—or, if not, a little more milk should be added previously to setting it to boil a little longer. When the rice is done, mix in the yolks of six eggs, and the whites of three whipped. Next, shred four ounces of sweet almonds, and strew them equally over the inside of a plain mould, previously rather thickly spread with butter; then pour in the prepared rice, and bake the cake for about one hour and a half; when done, turn it out on to its dish, pour some diluted apricot-jam round the base, and serve.

Note.—Rice cakes may also be flavored with vanilla, orange-flower, lemon and cinnamon, coffee, or any kind of liqueur; dried cherries, currants, sultana-raisins, candied-orange, lemon or citron or pistachio-kernels may be added.

1366. TIMBALE OF RICE.

THE only difference between this and a rice cake consists in the mould being lined either with short or puff-paste: *nouilles*-paste, however is sometimes used for the purpose: it should be rolled in the form of very small pipes, and the mould closely lined with them. The prepared rice should then be poured into the mould, and baked for about an hour and a half. When done, turn the *timbale* out of the mould on its dish, glaze it over with sugar, and with the salamander, then pour some kind of diluted preserve (warm), round the base.

1367. NOUILLES CAKES, A L'ALLEMANDE.

PREPARE about six yolks of *nouilles* (No. 1256), put them into a stewpan with one quart of milk of almonds,* eight ounces of sugar, four ounces of butter, two sticks of vanilla and a very little salt; cover with the lid, and set them to simmer very gently by the side of a slow stove-fire; by the time that the *nouilles* have absorbed all the milk they will be sufficiently done, and must then be withdrawn from the fire and emptied into a basin. Add the yolks of six eggs, and the whipped whites of three, mix the whole lightly together, and pour it into a mould previously spread with butter, and strewn with shreded almonds. The cake must then be baked in the usual manner, and when done, turned out of the mould on its dish, and served with some Victoria cherry sauce (No. 64).

Note.—This kind of cake may also be made with maccaroni, vermicelli, or semolina, and it may be flavored in the same manner as rice cakes or *timbales.*

1368. VERMICELLI CAKE.

PARBOIL twelve ounces of vermicelli, drain it on a sieve, and then put it into a stewpan with a pint of cream, four ounces of butter, eight ounces of sugar, the zest or essence of the rind of two oranges extracted by rubbing on a piece of sugar, and a little salt; cover with the lid, and set the stewpan to simmer very gently on a slow fire until the vermicelli has entirely absorbed the cream. Then, add the yolks of six eggs and the whipped whites of three, mix the whole lightly together, and put this preparation into a mould previously spread with butter, and strewn with bread-crumbs; bake the cake in the oven for about an hour and a half, and when done, turn it out on its dish; pour some damson sauce round the base, and serve.

1369. MACCARONI CAKE

Is prepared in the same way as a vermicelli cake.

1370. SEMOLINA CAKE.

THIS is also made in the same manner as a vermicelli cake, except that it does not require to be parboiled.

Sago and tapioca are treated in a similar way.

1371. POTATO CAKE

TAKE eighteen large York potatoes, and when done, rub their pulp through a wire sieve; put this into a large basin, add four ounces of butter, eight ounces of sifted sugar, a spoonful of pounded vanilla, a gill of cream, the yolks of six eggs, and the whipped whites of two, and a little salt; work the whole well together, and then place it in a mould previously spread with butter, and strewn with bread-crumbs;

---

* Milk of almonds is prepared in the following manner:—First, remove the skins from eight ounces of Jordan almonds, and one ounce of bitter almonds, then pound them thoroughly in a mortar, adding occasionally a few drops of water; when they are well pulverized, place them in a basin, add a quart of spring-water, mix well together, and allow this to stand for about an hour; the milk may then drawn off by straining it through a napkin.

bake the cake for about an hour, and when done, dish it up with a fruit sauce poured round the base, made in the following manner :—

Pick one pound of either currants, raspberries, cherries, damsons, strawberries, or apricots; place them in a stewpan with eight ounces of sifted sugar and half a gill of water; boil the whole down to the consistency of a thick *purée*, and then rub it through a sieve or tammy.

SOUFFLES IN GENERAL,

COMPRISING

Potato-flour *Soufflé*.
Soufflé of Rice.
Chocolate *Soufflé*.
Coffee *Soufflé*.
Ginger *Soufflé*.
Pine-apple *Soufflé*
Soufflé of Apricots.

Soufflés of Raspberries.
Brown bread *Soufflé à l'Allemande*.
Omelette *Soufflée*.
Pancakes, plain.
    „   *à la Celestine*.
Pancakes *Soufflés*.

1372. POTATO FLOUR SOUFFLE.

INGREDIENTS :—Six ounces of potato-flour, ten ounces of sugar, four ounces of butter, one pint of cream or milk, twelve eggs, two sticks of vanilla, and a little salt.

Put the milk or cream to boil, then throw in the vanilla, cover the stewpan with its lid, and allow the infusion to stand for about half an hour, in order to extract the flavor of the vanilla. Next, put the potato-flour, the sugar, butter, salt, and one egg into a stewpan, and mix the whole well together; then add the milk and the vanilla, and stir the preparation on the stove-fire until it boils, when it must be worked with the spoon to make it perfectly smooth; after adding the yolks of ten eggs, set it aside, while the ten whites are being whipped quite firm, and then add these in with the *soufflé* batter: pour the whole lightly into a *soufflé* dish, having a broad band of buttered cartridge paper round the outside, and then set it in the oven to bake : this will take about three-quarters of an hour. When the *soufflé* is done, place it (on its baking-sheet) upon another baking-sheet covered with hot embers of charcoal, and let it be thus carried to the dining-room door; just before dishing it up, remove the bands of paper, shake some sifted sugar over the top, place it in the *soufflé* dish, and serve immediately.

Note.—*Soufflés* of flour, ground rice, semolina, arrow root, tapioca, *tous-les-mois* (a kind of potato-flour), should all be prepared as the above; substituting either of these for the potato-flour. *Soufflés* may be flavored with orange, lemon, cinnamon, orange-flowers, or with any kind of essence or liqueur.

1373. SOUFFLE OF RICE.

INGREDIENTS :—Six ounces of rice, ten ounces of sugar, four ounces of butter, ten eggs, two lemons, a quart of milk, and a little salt. Wash the rice and parboil it in water for five minutes; then put it into a stewpan with the sugar, butter, milk, and salt, and set this to simmer very gently on a slow fire for about an hour, by which time the grains of the rice will have become quite soft; the whole should now be well worked with a wooden spoon, and the ten yolks of eggs, with the rind of the lemons rubbed on sugar, should then be added, and if the rice be too firm, a little cream also. The ten whites of eggs must be whipped very firm, then lightly mixed in with the preparation, and poured into the *soufflé* case or crust, baked for about three-quarters of an hour, and served immediately.

1374. CHOCOLATE SOUFFLE.

THIS is made by adding eight ounces of finely-scraped vanilla chocolate to two-thirds of the same kind of preparation directed to be used in making a potato-flour *soufflé*. The same number of eggs are also required.

1375. COFFEE SOUFFLE.

PUT eight ounces of Mocha coffee into an untinned stewpan or sugar-boiler, and roast it of a light color, by stirring it continually over a charcoal fire. When the coffee has acquired a light-brown color, toss it up in the pan, blow away the small burnt particles, and then throw it into a pint of boiling cream; put the lid on the infusion, and allow it to stand for about half an hour, in order to extract the flavor. Then, strain the infusion away from the coffee-berries, in a basin, and use it to mix up the *soufflé*, in exactly the same manner as described for the potato-flour *soufflé*.

1376. GINGER SOUFFLE.

PREPARE a potato-flour *soufflé*, and add to it eight ounces of preserved ginger cut up into small dice-like pieces. The vanilla must of course be omitted.

1377. PINE-APPLE SOUFFLE.

FOLLOW the directions for making a potato-flour *soufflé*, adding to it about one pound of preserved pine-apple, cut up into small pieces; the syrup of this should also be added.

1378. SOUFFLE OF APRICOTS.

REMOVE the stones, and peel eighteen ripe apricots, then put them, together with the kernels, into a stewpan wita twelve ounces of pounded sugar; stir this over the fire with a wooden spoon, and as soon as the fruit is boiled down to a jam, withdraw it from the fire, and mix it with dalf the usual quantity of the preparation for a potato-flour *soufflé*. The same number of eggs are required, and in all other respects the same directions should be followed.

Note.—*Soufflés* of peaches, nectarines, and all kinds of plums, are prepared in the same manner as the above.

1379. SOUFFLE OF RASPBERRIES.

PUT one pound of picked raspberries into a small preserving pan, with twelve ounces of pounded sugar, stir the whole over a charcoal fire until it has boiled for about five minutes, and then rub it through a sieve. Use this preparation as directed for making a *soufflé* of apricots.

Note.—*Soufflés* of currants, strawberries, or gooseberries, are made in the same way.

1380. BROWN-BREAD SOUFFLE, A L'ALLEMANDE.

PUT one pound of brown bread-crumbs into a stewpan, with a pint of cream, ten ounces of pounded sugar, four ounces of butter, and a little salt, and flavor it with some cinnamon-powder and lemon-sugar. Stir this over the stove-fire until it boils, then remove it, and add the yolks of ten eggs; next, whip the whites quite firm, and mix them in lightly with the preparation, then pour it into the *soufflé*-case, and bake it in the usual manner: when done, shake some cinnamon-sugar over it, and serve.

1381. OMELETTE SOUFFLE.

PUT the yolks of six eggs into a large basin, add six ounces of pounded sugar, a dessert-spoonful of potato-flour, ditto of orange-flower-water (or any other kind of essence or liqueur used for such purposes), and a very little salt; stir these together with a wooden spoon for about ten minutes; then whip the six whites, and mix them in lightly with the batter. Next, put two ounces of butter into an omelet-pan, set it on a stove-fire, and as soon as the butter begins to sputter, pour the whole of the omelet-batter into it; set the pan over the fire, and as the battter becomes partially set round the sides and at the bottom of the pan, toss it over and over gently, and then turn the *omelette* out neatly, and as much as possible in the form of a dome, on to a silver dish previously spread with butter; put it in the oven, and bake it for about twelve minutes, when it will be ready to send to table. Shake some sugar on the *omelette*, and serve it immediately.

1382. PANCAKES, PLAIN.

MIX four ounces of flour with four ounces of pounded sugar, two ounces of bruised ratafias, a dessert-spoonful of orange-flower-water, four yolks and two whole eggs, a pint of cream, and a very little salt. When milk is used instead of cream, two ounces of butter should be added, and must be melted previously to its being mixed in with the batter.

When about to fry the pancakes, melt about two ounces of butter in a small stewpan, and keep this by the side of the stove; before throwing any of the batter into the pan, first pour a little of the butter over the bottom: fry the pancakes on both sides of a very light-brown color, pile them one upon another on the dish, and serve immediately. Plain pancakes should be eaten with a little lemon-juice and some pounded sugar.

1383. PANCAKES, A LA CELESTINE.

PREPARE the pancakes as above, and as each is fried, spread some apricot-jam upon it, then roll it up, and place it on a baking-sheet in the oven; when a sufficient number is ready, shake some sifted sugar over them, glaze them with a red-hot salamander, and then dish up the pancakes on a napkin in close circular order, in double or treble rows, and serve them quite hot.

1384. PANCAKES SOUFFLES.

PREPARE some potato-flour *soufflé*-batter (No. 1372)—about half the usual quantity will suffice; make also the usual quantity of pancake-batter. Then fry the pancakes, and as they are done, spread them over with apricot-jam, and pile them up one upon another in the form of a dome, with a thick layer of the *soufflé*-batter in between each pancake. When the whole is complete, put them in the oven to bake for about half an hour; when done, shake some sugar over the top, and serve immediately.

PUDDINGS IN GENERAL,

COMPRISING

Brown-bread Pudding, à la Gotha.	Ginger Pudding.
Cherry Bread.	Pine Apple „
Mehl Prie.	Lemon „
Krapfen, or German Puffs.	Orange „
Semolina Puddnig, à la Baden.	Bread „ plain.
Dampfnudeln, or German Dumplings.	Rusk „
Pudding, à la Coburg.	Apple „
„ à la Française.	Biscuit „ à la Prince Albert.
„ à la Viènnoise.	Plum „
Cabinet Pudding.	Tapioca „
Chestnut „	

1385. BROWN-BREAD PUDDING, A LA GOTHA.

GET ready the following ingredients:—Twelve ounces of brown bread-crumbs, six ounces of pounded sugar, six eggs, half a pint of whipped cream, some grated lemon-rind, a little cinnamon-powder, one pound of morello cherries, and a little salt.

Mix the bread-crumbs, sugar, the yolks of eggs, and whipped cream, the lemon, the cinnamon, and the salt, together in a large basin; then add the whipped whites of six eggs, and set this aside. Next, spread a plain mould with butter, and strew it with brown bread-crumbs; then, spread a large spoonful of the preparation at the bottom of the mould, and arrange a layer of cherries (with the stones left in) upon it; cover this with some of the preparation, and upon it place more cherries, and so on until the mould is filled. The pudding must now be placed on a baking-sheet, and put in the oven (moderately heated), to be baked for about an hour; when done, turn it out of the mould on its dish, pour a *purée* of cherry-sauce round the base, and serve.

In Saxony, it is customary to eat this kind of pudding as a cake, when cold; in this case it should be entirely covered with sifted sugar, mixed with one-fourth part of cinnamon-powder.

1386. CHERRY BREAD.

PICK the stalks from two pounds of Kentish-cherries, and pound them in a mortar so as to bruise the stones; they must then be placed in a small preserving-pan with about a pint of claret or port-wine, and twelve ounces of sugar; allow this to boil upon the stove-fire, remove the scum as it rises, and after the cherries have boiled for about ten minutes, rub the whole through a sieve, and then pour it into a silver *soufflé*-case.

While the above part of the *entremets* is in course of preparation, a dozen pieces of crumb of bread, or French rolls, shaped in the form of eggs with a sharp knife, should be fried of a light-fawn color, in some clarified butter. After these have been drained on a clean cloth, place them in close circular rows in the *purée* of cherries ; shake some cinnamon sugar over the surface, set the cherry-bread on a baking-sheet in the oven, to simmer slowly for about half an hour, and when done, send to table.

1387. MEHL PRIE.

INGREDIENTS required :—Six ounces of flour, eight ounces of pounded sugar, two sticks of vanilla, a very little salt, a quart of cream, and a pint of milk.

Put the flour, sugar, and salt, into an appropriate-sized stewpan, and mix in with these the cream and milk with the vanilla ; then, stir the whole with a wooden spoon over a brisk charcoal-fire, until it has boiled down to about one-half of its original quantity ; the *mehl prie* should then be withdrawn from the fire, and kept hot by the side of the stove, the stewpan containing it being kept covered with its lid. Next, place an untinned baking-sheet on a trivet over a charcoal stove-fire, and when it has become too hot for the hand to remain upon it, spread the centre over with a thin coating of the *mehl prie* (which may be done with the back of a wooden spoon), and as this becomes browned, it will detach itself from the baking-sheet ; it must then be removed, and before it has cooled, should be cut or stamped out with a tin-cutter. This must be repeated until the process has furnished a plateful of crisp chips. When about to send the *mehl prie* to table, the custard pudding should be poured into a *soufflé*-dish, and the chips sent up separately on a plate ; when served at table, a small ladleful of the custard should be first poured on the guest's plate, and then a spoonful of the chips placed upon this.

1388. KRAPFEN, OR GERMAN PUFFS.

INGREDIENTS required :—One pound of flour, ten ounces of butter, six eggs, a gill of cream, one ounce of sugar, one ounce of German yeast, a very little salt, with the rind of two oranges rubbed on a piece of sugar and the zest then scraped off.

First, set the sponge, with one-fourth part of the flour and the yeast, in the usual manner, and let it rise in a warm temperature ; meanwhile spread the flour out in the form of a ring, and place the sugar, salt, butter, eggs, and cream in the centre ; then work the whole well together with both hands ; gather it up in a heap towards the edge of the slab ; and with the knuckles of both hands bent under, rub the paste quickly before you on the slab ; then gather it up again in a heap by taking up small portions at a time with both hands held together, and fling it down on the slab with some force. This must be constantly repeated for about five minutes. As soon as the sponge has sufficiently risen, let it be added to the paste, and thoroughly incorporated with it. The *krapfen*-paste should now be gathered up, and placed in a clean napkin previously strewn over with flour to prevent the paste from adhering to it, and set it in a rather cool place to rise : this will require about four hours. The paste must then be kneaded on the slab, and after it has been again placed in the cool for about half an hour, let it be cut up into about thirty pieces of equal size ; knead these in the form of round balls, and place them by half-dozens, on separate sheets of paper spread with butter ; the sheets of *krapfen* must now be placed on baking-sheets, and set to rise in a warm part of the kitchen : when the *krapfen* have risen, immerse them in some clean hogs'-lard made quite hot for the purpose, and fry them of a light color; as soon as they are done, drain them on a clean cloth, shake some cinnamon and orange sugar over them, dish them up in a pyramidal form on a napkin, and serve them with some warm apricot-jam diluted with a little water or syrup.

1389. SEMOLINA PUDDING, A LA BADEN.

INGREDIENTS required :—Twelve ounces of semolina, six ounces of pounded sugar, eight ounces of butter, eight eggs, a pint of cream, a table-spoonful of orange-flower-water, two ounces of ratafias, and a little salt.

Mix the semolina with the sugar, the orange-flower-water, half the butter, two eggs, the cream, and salt, in a stewpan ; stir this over a stove-fire until it boils, then work it perfectly smooth, and keep working the paste over the stove-fire until it ceases to adhere to the sides of the stewpan ; then, withdraw it from the fire, and gradually mix in the remainder of the eggs and butter, and also the bruised ratafias. Next, spread the inside of a plain mould with butter, and fill it with the preparation of semolina ; put the bottom of the mould in a deep sauta-pan, half filled with hot water, and place it in the oven to bake for about an hour and a quarter ; when done, turn the pudding out on to its dish, pour either a fruit or custard sauce over it, and serve.

1390. DAMPFNUDELN, OR GERMAN DUMPLINGS.

THESE are made with the same kind of paste as the *krapfen* (No. 1388), but half the quantity will suffice for this purpose. When the fermentation of the paste has properly taken place, let it be laid on the pastry-slab, kneaded into a dozen small rolls, and then placed in a deep sautapan, about an inch apart from each other : as much warm milk must be poured over them, as will suffice to cover their surface, and as soon as they have risen to nearly twice their original size, put them in the oven to be baked of a light color; just before withdrawing them from the oven, see that the milk is not absorbed by *dampfnudeln*, and let them be glazed over with sugar and the red-hot salamander. Dish them up on a napkin, and send some vanilla-custard sauce separately in a sauce-boat.

1391. PUDDING, A LA COBURG.

FOR this purpose it is necessary to have some ready-baked *brioche*. This should be cut in circular slices, about an inch less in diameter than the mould intended to be used for the pudding; the slices of *brioche* must be placed on a dish, and soaked in maraschino. The sides of the mould should be spread with butter, and ornamented with dried cherries and candied citron ; and previously to placing the pieces of *brioche* in the mould, let each of them be spread with apricot-jam ;

the mould must then be filled up with some vanilla-custard prepared for the purpose, part of which must, however, be reserved for the sauce. The pudding should be steamed in the usual way for about an hour and a quarter, and when done, turned out on its dish, and the sauce poured over it.

1392. PUDDING, A LA FRANCAISE.

TAKE the following ingredients :—Twelve ounces of chopped marrow, eight ounces of flour, eight ounces of apricot-jam, four ounces of chopped apples, six ounces of dried cherries, six ounces of candied orange-peel and citron, four ounces of sugar, a little grated nutmeg, six cloves (pounded), a tea-spoonful of cinnamon-powder, the zest of the rind of two oranges on sugar, five whole eggs, a glass of brandy, a little salt, and about half a pint of cream.

Put the above ingredients into a large basin, and mix them well together; spread a mould with butter, shake a little flour about the inside, fill it with the pudding, and after tying it up in a cloth, boil it for about four hours, and when done, dish it up with a German custard-sauce, made as follows :—

Put four yolks of eggs into a *bain-marie* or stewpan, together with two ounces of pounded sugar, a glass of Sherry, some orange or lemon peel (rubbed on loaf sugar), and a very little salt. Whisk this sharply over a very slow fire, until it assumes the appearance of a light frothy custard.

1393. PUDDING, A LA VIENNOISE.

INGREDIENTS required :—Twelve ounces of *brioche*, or crumb of bread cut up into small dice, two glasses of Madeira, the rind of two lemons, two ounces of sweet, and half an ounce of bitter almonds pounded, six ounces of sultana raisins, a burnt-sugar custard, made with eight yolks of eggs, a pint of cream, two ounces of burnt-sugar, and sweetened with six ounces of loaf-sugar.

Put the *brioche*, almonds, rind of lemon (rubbed on sugar), and the sultanas, into a large basin ; pour the Madeira to this, and when it has been absorbed by the *brioche*, &c., pour as much of the burnt-sugar custard on it as will suffice to complete the quantity required to fill the mould. Then, spread the inside of the mould with butter, decorate it with candied orange-peel, and fill it with the above preparation. This pudding must be steamed for about an hour and a half, and when done, turned out on its dish, some custard or arrow-root-sauce poured over it, and sent to table.

1394. CABINET PUDDING.

SPREAD the inside of a plain mould with butter, and ornament the sides with dried cherries and candied citron ; fill the mould with alternate layers of slices of sponge-cakes and ratafias or macaroons ; then fill up the mould with a lemon custard made with eight yolks of eggs, a pint of milk or cream, six ounces of sugar, a glass of brandy, and the grated rind of a lemon. This custard must not be set, but merely mixed up. Steam the pudding in the usual way, for about an hour and a half, and when done, dish it up either with arrow-root-sauce or a custard.

1395. CHESTNUT PUDDING.

BAKE or boil fifty fine chestnuts, rub their pulp through a sieve, and place this in a stewpan with a pint of cream, four ounces of butter, six ounces of sugar, a pounded stick of vanilla, and a very little salt; stir these ingredients over a stove-fire until the preparation thickens, and then quicken the motion of the spoon, so as to prevent the paste from adhering to the bottom of the stewpan. As soon as it leaves the sides of the stewpan, remove it from the fire, add eight yolks, and the whites of six eggs whipped firm; pour the pudding mixture into a plain mould, previously spread with butter, and then steam it for about an hour and a half. When the pudding is done, turn it carefully out of the mould on its dish, pour some warm diluted apricot-jam over it, and serve.

1396. GINGER PUDDING.

INGREDIENTS required :—Six ounces of flour, six ounces of sugar, six eggs, eight ounces of preserved ginger, a pint of cream, six ounces of butter, a little salt.

Put the cream, sugar, butter, and salt into a stewpan on the fire, and as soon as these begin to simmer, take off the stewpan, throw in the flour, and stir the whole together quickly; then put this paste back again on the fire, and continue stirring it for about five minutes; it must then be withdrawn, and the six eggs mixed in gradually with it. The ginger, cut into small pieces, must now be added to the preparation, which must then be poured into the mould previously spread with butter. Steam it for an hour and a half, and when done, dish up the pudding with a custard-sauce made with the syrup from the ginger.

1397. PINE-APPLE PUDDING.

THIS is made in the same manner as the above, pine-apple being substituted for ginger.

1398. LEMON PUDDING.

INGREDIENTS required :—The juice and grated rind (rubbed on sugar) of six lemons, a pint of cream, six ounces of bruised ratafias, twelve yolks and the whites of four eggs, whipped, half a nutmeg grated, a little cinnamon powder, twelve ounces of pounded sugar, and a very little salt.

Mix the above altogether in a large basin, and work the ingredients together with a whisk for about ten minutes. Next, put a border of puff-paste round the edge of a tart dish, spread the dish with butter, pour the batter into it, strew some shred pistachio kernels on the top, and bake it for about half an hour (at moderate heat). When done, shake some sifted sugar over it, and serve.

1399. ORANGE PUDDING.

THIS is made as the above; double the quantity of oranges may be used for this purpose, owing to their not containing so much acid as lemons; but the rind of three will suffice for the zest.

1400. BREAD PUDDING, PLAIN.

INGREDIENTS :—Twelve ounces of bread-crumbs, six ounces of sugar, two ounces of butter, a pint of milk, the rind of a lemon rubbed on a piece of sugar, six yolks of eggs, and two whites whipped, and a little salt.

Put the bread-crumbs into a basin with the sugar, butter, lemon-sugar, and salt; then pour in the milk boiling, cover up the whole, and leave it to steep for about ten minutes; the eggs may then be added, and after the whole has been well mixed together, pour the preparation into a mould, or pudding basin, previously spread with butter. Steam the pudding for about an hour, and when done, dish it up with some arrow-root sauce made as follows : Mix a dessert-spoonful of arrow-root with twice that quantity of sugar, half the juice of a lemon, a little nutmeg, and a gill of water, and stir this over the fire until it boils.

1401. RUSK PUDDING.

INGREDIENTS :—A dozen rusks, a plain custard of six eggs, a pint of cream, six ounces of sugar, a glass of maraschino, a little salt, and four ounces of dried cherries.

Spread a plain mould with butter, arrange the cherries round the sides and bottom, dip the rusks in the custard, and place them in the mould with a layer of raspberry-jam between each layer of rusks; fill up the mould with the custard, and steam the pudding in the usual manner. When done, dish it up with a German custard-sauce (No. 1392).

1402. APPLE PUDDING.

PEEL two dozen grey russets, remove the cores, and cut them up in slices; then put the apples into a deep sautapan with four ounces of butter, the rind of two lemons, twelve ounces of pounded sugar, and one pound of apricot-jam; toss the whole over a slow stove-fire until the apples begin to dissolve, and then set them aside to cool. Next, line a good-sized pudding basin with some light-made suet paste, fill this with the prepared apples, place a covering of paste on the top, fasten it down securely, and then steam it in the usual manner for about two hours. When the pudding is done, dish it up, pour some warm apricot jam over it, and serve.

1403. BISCUIT PUDDING, A LA PRINCE ALBERT.

INGREDIENTS :—Twelve ounces of crumbled Savoy cake, a pint of cream, the yolks of six eggs and the whipped whites of two, the rind of a lemon rubbed on sugar, four ounces of pounded sugar, and a little salt.

Pour the pint of cream (boiling) on to the crumbled Savoy cake and let it steep for a few minutes : then add the sugar, the eggs, the lemon-sugar, and the salt; mix the whole lightly together, pour the preparation into a mould spread with butter, and steam the pudding for about an hour and a quarter. When done, dish it up with a *purée* of currants and raspberries for the sauce, or else serve a custard-sauce over it.

1404 PLUM PUDDING.

INGREDIENTS :—Three-quarters of a pound of raisins, three-quarters of a pound of currants, half a pound of candied orange, lemon, and citron, one pound and a quarter of chopped beef suet, one pound of flour, three-quarters of a pound of moist sugar, four eggs, about three gills of milk, the grated rind of two lemons, half an ounce of nutmeg, cinnamon, and cloves (in powder), a glass of brandy, and a very little salt.

Mix the above ingredients thoroughly together in a large basin several hours before the pudding is to be boiled; pour them into a mould spread with butter, which should be tied up in a cloth. The pudding must then be boiled for four hours and a half; when done, dish it up with a German custard-sauce spread over it (No. 1392).

1405. TAPIOCA PUDDING.

INGREDIENTS.—Ten ounces of tapioca, a quart of milk, six ounces of sugar, six yolks of eggs and two whipped whites, the grated rind of a lemon, two ounces of butter, and a little salt.

Put the tapioca, sugar, butter, salt, grated lemon, and the milk into a stewpan, stir this over the fire until it boils; then cover the stewpan with its lid, and set it on a very slow stove-fire (partially smothered with ashes), to continue gently simmering for a quarter of an hour. The tapioca should then be withdrawn from the fire, and after the six yolks and the two whipped whites of eggs have been thoroughly incorporated in it, pour the preparation into a mould or pudding basin previously spread with butter; steam the pudding for about an hour and a half, and when done, dish it up with either a plain arrow-root or custard-sauce over it.

Sago or semolina may be prepared in the same manner.

Note.—In addition to the foregoing, puddings may also be made with every kind of preparation described for making *timbales* or cakes of rice, vermicelli, maccaroni, *nouilles*, &c. These may be either steamed in a mould or pudding-basin, or baked in a pie-dish.

1406. FONDU OF PARMESAN CHEESE.

INGREDIENTS :—Twelve ounces of fresh Parmesan cheese grated, four ounces of flour, twelve eggs, four ounces of butter, a pint of milk or cream, a pinch of mignionette-pepper, and a very little salt.

Mix the flour, butter, pepper and salt, well together with the milk, and then stir this over the fire until it boils; work the batter quickly with the spoon to render it perfectly smooth, then add the grated cheese and the twelve yolks of eggs; whip the whites quite firm, and add them also, very lightly. Fill the *soufflé* case with the *fondu*, bake it for about three-quarters of an hour, and send it to table as soon as it is ready.

Note.—Half the quantity of Gruyère with the other half of Parmesan cheese is sometimes used. It is also customary to season *fondus* with mustard, lemon-juice, Cayenne pepper, and essence of anchovies, for those who prefer high seasoning to the more delicate flavor of the Parmesan cheese: the latter is most likely to be approved of by a true epicure.

JELLIES,

COMPRISING

Calf's-foot Jelly, with Wine.
Clarification of Calf's-foot Jelly, for general purposes.
Orange Jelly, made with Calf's-foot Stock.
Clarified Syrup, for Jellies.
To clarify Isinglass.
Preparation of Paper for filtering Orange or Lemon Juice for Jellies.
Orange Jelly, à l'Anglaise.
Lemon Jelly, à l'Anglaise.
Orange Jelly, à la Française.
Pomegranate Jelly.
Pine Apple Jelly.

Currant and Raspberry Jelly.
Strawberry Jelly.
Cherry Jelly.
Mulberry Jelly.
Macédoine of Fruits.
Orange Jelly, garnished with quarters of Oranges.
Maraschino Jelly.
Variegated Jelly, à la Victoria.
Panachée Jelly.
Russian Jelly.
Punch Jelly.
Oranges filled with transparent Jelly.

1407. CALF'S-FOOT JELLY, WITH WINE.

SPLIT four calf's feet, break up the bones, and put the whole into a gallon-sized stewpan or stock-pot; then fill it up with cold water, and set it on the fire to boil; remove the scum as it rises to the surface, and when the stock has been thoroughly skimmed, set it down by the side of the fire, to continue gently boiling for about five hours. The stock must then be strained off through a sieve into a basin or pan, and set aside in a cool place until it has become firm. The grease should be scraped off the surface with a spoon, and a little boiling water thrown over it, in order to wash away any that may remain; it should then be wiped with a clean cloth and put into a stewpan to melt over the fire. Next, add two pounds of loaf sugar, a pint of sherry, two glasses of brandy, twelve cloves, a stick of cinnamon, the rind of four lemons peeled very thin, and without any of the pith, as this is bitter; then pour in the whites of six eggs and two whole eggs whipped up with a little cold water and the bruised shells; whip this well together over the fire, and when it is near boiling, throw in the juice of eight lemons, stir the jelly with the whisk for a minute or so, and then set the stewpan down by the side of the fire; put on the lid with some live embers upon it, and allow the jelly to stand by the side of the stove-fire for a quarter of an hour longer, to set the eggs. Next, throw the jelly into a jelly-bag, fixed on a stand, ready with a basin placed under, to receive it as it passes through the bag; continue pouring the jelly back again through the bag several times, until it runs quite bright and clear; then cover over the stand with a cloth, and leave the jelly to run until the whole is passed.

This kind of jelly may either be served in glasses, or set in moulds imbedded in rough ice: when it has become quite firm, dip the mould in hot water, wipe it, and then turn the jelly out carefully on its dish.

1408. CLARIFICATION OF CALF'S-FOOT JELLY, FOR GENERAL PURPOSES.

PUT the prepared stock of four calf's feet into a stewpan with two pounds of sugar, the rind of four lemons, and the juice of eight; whip six whites and two whole eggs together, with half a pint of spring-water; throw this in with the stock, and whisk the whole together over the stove-fire, until it is on the point of boiling, then add the juice of another lemon and a little spring-water; withdraw the jelly from the stove, and set it down by the side, to continue gently simmering for about ten minutes longer, covered with the stewpan lid containing some live embers of charcoal. The jelly may then be passed through the bag in the usual way, and when it has run through perfectly bright, let it be kept in a cool place to be used as occasion may require.

This kind of foundation or stock-jelly, prepared without any decided flavor, may be used for making all kinds of jellies; it will then only be necessary to add, to the quantity required to fill a mould, a gill and a half of any kind of liqueur, and if the jelly be too stiff, a little thin syrup may also be added. It may be used likewise for making fruit jellies, with the addition of a pint of the filtered juice of currants, raspberries, cherries, or strawberries, or half a pint of the clarified in-fusion syrup of peaches, apricots, or pine-apples.

1409. ORANGE JELLY, MADE WITH CALF'S-FOOT STOCK.

To the stock produced from four calf's feet, add two pounds of loaf-sugar, the juice of six lemons and a dozen oranges, and the rind of eight oranges; put the stewpan on the fire to melt the stock, and then pour in the whipped whites of eggs, and continue whisking the jelly on the stove-fire until it begins to simmer; it must then be set down by the side of the stove-fire, covered with the stewpan lid, and allowed to continue simmering until the egg is set; the jelly must then be passed through the bag in the usual way, and just before putting it into the mould, a few drops of prepared cochineal should be added to give it an orange-pink tinge.

Note.—Lemon jelly is prepared in the same way as the above, sub-stituting lemons for oranges.

1410. CLARIFIED SYRUP, FOR JELLIES.

To every pound of the finest loaf sugar, whatever quantity may be required, add rather more than a pint of spring-water; and when the sugar is dissolved, add half the white of an egg whipped up with a little water; whisk the whole well together, set the stewpan on the stove-fire, and as soon as the syrup begins to boil, set it down by the side of the fire to continue gently boiling, until it has thrown up all the scum; remove this as it rises to the surface, and then strain the syrup through a napkin into a basin, and keep it in a cool place for use.

1411. TO CLARIFY ISINGLASS.

FIRST wash the isinglass in cold water, to free it from the dust that is apt to gather about it; then put it into a stewpan, and to every two ounces add half a pint of spring-water, and about one ounce of sugar; stir this on the stove-fire till it boils, then throw in the juice of half a lemon, and set the stewpan by the side of the stove, to continue gently boiling for about ten minutes, in order to dissolve the shreds of isin-glass, and that it may thereby throw up all the scum, which should be removed as it rises to the surface; the isinglass may then be strained through a napkin into a basin, and used for the required purpose.

Isinglass may also be clarified by adding a very small quantity of whipped white of egg, after it has been dissolved in water as directed above, and then allowed to cool previously to mixing in the white of egg; it must then be allowed to boil gently by the side of the stove-fire, and when perfectly cleared of all the scum, should be strained through a napkin.

Note.—There are several kinds of *gelatine* in use, which serve the same purpose as isinglass, with more or less success; all these may be clarified in the same way as the above.

1412. PREPARATION OF PAPER FOR FILTERING ORANGE OR LEMON-JUICE, FOR JELLIES.

WASH several sheets of white blotting-paper (of the best quality) in cold water; then boil them in two quarts of water for about twenty minutes, strain the water from the paper, and pound it in a mortar until reduced to a fine pulp; mix this with a spoonful of washed white sand, then add both to the juice intended to be filtered, and throw the whole into a clean beaver jelly-bag. Pass the juice through the filtering bag until it drops as bright as spring-water.

1413. ORANGE JELLY, A L'ANGLAISE.

RUB the rind of six oranges upon twelve ounces of the best loaf sugar, and put this into a basin; then squeeze the juice from a dozen ripe oranges and four lemons, and add this to the sugar. Next, clarify two ounces of isinglass as directed in No. 1411, and mix this with the juice and sugar in a sugar-boiler, add six drops of prepared cochineal, and stir the whole over the stove-fire till the jelly becomes tepid; then strain it through a hair-sieve into a basin, and when it has become quite cold, and is commencing to congeal on the surface and sides of the basin, stir it well together, and pour it into a mould previously imbedded in rough ice. When the jelly is set firm, dip the mould in rather warm water, wipe it with a cloth, and turn it out carefully on its dish.

1414. LEMON JELLY, A L'ANGLAISE.

THIS is prepared in the same way as the above, substituting lemons for oranges; it will be necessary, however, to add four ounces of sugar on account of the acidity of the lemons.

1415. ORANGE JELLY, A LA FRANCAISE.

PEEL off the rind from six oranges, as thin as possible, and put it into a pint basin. Then clarify one pound of the finest loaf-sugar with a pint of spring-water and half the white of an egg, and strain it through a napkin on to the rind; cover the basin down with a sheet of paper twisted tightly round the edges, to prevent the volatile essence of the essential oil contained in the rind from escaping. Extract the juice from twelve oranges and four lemons (by pressure) into a basin, remove the pips, and filter the juice as directed in No. 1412; this being done, strain the infusion syrup through a napkin into a basin, add the filtered juice, two ounces of clarified isinglass and six drops of prepared cochineal; stir these together, and then pour the jelly into the mould previously imbedded in rough ice.

Note.—Lemon jelly *à la Française* is prepared in the same manner as the foregoing, except that the cochineal must be omitted, and four ounces of sugar added to qualify the acidity of the lemons.

1416. POMEGRANATE JELLY.

EXTRACT the bright pips from six ripe pomegranates, bruise these in a basin, with one pound of roughly-pounded sugar, add thereto a gill of spring-water, and then filter the preparation through a beaver jelly-bag, without the aid of paper pulp, in order to preserve the delicate flavor of the fruit : when either paper or sand is made use of for the purpose of filtering the juice of any kind of delicate flavored fruit, although the juice is rendered brighter, it certainly loses much of its original flavor.

The filtered juice of the pomegranates must then be mixed with two ounces of clarified isinglass, six drops of cochineal, and, if necessary to make out the quantity of jelly required to fill the mould, some thin clarified syrup may be added. Set a jelly mould in a basin of rough ice, and fill the mould with alternate layers of jelly and the bright pips of this fruit.

Note.—A glass of noyeau or maraschino may be added, if approved of.

1417. PINE-APPLE JELLY.

PEEL a pine-apple of about one pound weight, cut it into slices about a quarter of an inch thick, and put these into a basin. Clarify one pound of loaf-sugar with a pint of spring-water, the juice of two lemons, and half the white of an egg whipped with a little water; when thoroughly skimmed, strain the syrup on to the pine-apple, allow it to boil for three minutes, then cover it down with a sheet of paper twisted round the basin, and allow the infusion to stand for several hours, in order to extract the flavor. When about to mix the jelly, strain the syrup through a napkin into a basin, and put the pieces of pine-apple to drain upon a sieve; add two ounces of clarified isinglass to the pine-apple syrup, and then pour the jelly into a mould previously imbedded in rough ice.

1418. CURRANT AND RASPBERRY JELLY.

PICK the stalks from one quart of red currants and a pottle of raspberries, then put these into a large basin with half a pound of pounded sugar and a gill of spring-water; bruise them thoroughly, by squeezing them with the back part of the bowl of a wooden spoon against the sides of the basin, then throw the whole into a beaver jelly-bag, and filter the juice, pouring it back into the bag until it runs through perfectly bright; next, add half a pint of clarified syrup, and two ounces of clarified isinglass to the juice, and pour the jelly into a mould placed in rough ice to receive it.

Note.—This kind of jelly serves for the foundation of several others : for instance, it may be garnished with a *Macédoine* of fruits, with white raspberries, with currants, strawberries, peaches, or cherries; either of these fruits, when mixed with currant and raspberry jelly, prepared according to the foregoing directions, will make it most delicious.

1419. STRAWBERRY JELLY.

PICK the stalks from two pottles of scarlet strawberries, put these into a basin, and then pour one pint of clarified boiling syrup and half a pint of red-currant juice on to them; cover them down with a sheet of paper, tightly twisted round the edges of the basin, and allow the infusion to stand in a cool place until it becomes cold; then, filter it through a beaver jelly bag in the usual way, and when the whole has run through perfectly bright, mix it with two ounces of clarified isinglass, and set the jelly in a mould, immersed in rough ice.

Note.—This jelly should be garnished with a pottle of fine "British Queen" strawberries.

1420. CHERRY JELLY.

PICK the stalks from two pounds of Kentish cherries and a handful of red currants, and pound them in the mortar in order to bruise the stones and kernels; then take them up and place them in a small preserving pan, with one pound of fine loaf-sugar and half a pint of spring-water; set this to boil on the stove-fire for about five minutes, taking care to remove the scum as it rises to the surface: the whole must then be poured into a beaver jelly-bag, and filtered in the usual way. The juice should next be mixed with two ounces of clarified isinglass, and poured into a mould imbedded in rough ice. The jelly may be garnished with cherries from which the stones must be removed.

1421. MULBERRY JELLY.

THIS is prepared in the same way as strawberry jelly (No. 1419).

1422. MACEDOINE OF FRUITS.

THIS may be made with every kind of jelly, which should be mixed with a variety of the most delicate fruits in season: these should be arranged with taste, so as to show their forms and colors to the best advantage. The fruits most appropriate for this purpose are peaches, nectarines, apricots, all kinds of plums, strawberries, raspberries, mulberries, red, white, and black currants, cherries, pears, oranges, pomegranates, grapes, &c.

1423. ORANGE JELLY, GARNISHED WITH QUARTERS OF ORANGES.

PEEL six oranges with a sharp knife, leaving the transparent pulp quite bare; divide each into six, cutting the orange lengthwise, thus giving an angular form to the pieces; put these into a small preserving pan, with a pint of clarified syrup, and set the whole to boil on the stove-fire for not more than two minutes, then pour the pieces of oranges and their syrup into a basin, and set them aside in a cool place. Prepare about a pint of bright orange jelly in the manner directed in No. 1412, using the syrup from the pieces of oranges, which must be drained upon a sieve for that purpose. Next, imbed a plain mould in some pounded rough ice contained in an earthen pan, and proceed to garnish it with the pieces of oranges and the jelly, first pouring a little jelly on the bottom of the mould, then, when the jelly is set, arrange a layer of the pieces of oranges upon it in close circular order, one resting upon another; pour sufficient jelly upon these to reach their surface, and when this has become firm, place another layer of oranges upon it, and so on, until the mould is filled.

1424. MARASCHINO JELLY.

To one pint of clarified syrup, add two ounces of clarified isinglass, the filtered juice of two lemons, and a gill and a half of genuine maraschino; pour this into a jelly-mould ready set in rough ice.

Note.—Jellies flavored with noyeau, kirschen-wasser, Dantzic brandy, cedratti, and all kinds of liqueurs, when made with isinglass, are prepared as the above.

1425. VARIEGATED JELLY, A LA VICTORIA.

PREPARE some jelly, with Dantzic brandy (sometimes named "gold-and-silver-water"). Parboil and remove the skin from six ounces of pistachios, and shred each kernel into six strips. Set a jelly-mould in some pounded rough ice contained in a pan, pour a little of the jelly into the bottom of the mould, and then strew some of the prepared pistachios in it; when this has become firm, pour in a little more of the jelly and strew a few of the pistachios in it; as these layers become set, repeat the same until the mould is filled, and allow the jelly to remain imbedded in the ice for a sufficient time to congeal it properly.

1426. PANACHEE* JELLY.

THIS may be prepared with any kind of light-colored jelly, which must be divided into two equal parts: add a few drops of cochineal to one-half, and leave the remainder plain. Then, imbed the mould in rough ice, pour enough of the pink jelly into the mould to reach about a quarter of an inch up the sides, and when this has become set, pour as much of the plain jelly upon it; when this has congealed, repeat another layer of the pink jelly, and go on alternating the different colored layers of jelly until the mould is filled.

The design for this kind of jelly may be varied according to taste, by attending to the following directions:—

Fill two small plain moulds with different colored jelly, such as pink and white noyeau, or amber and very light pink-orange jelly, and when these are become firm, turn the jellies out of their respective moulds upon a clean napkin. Next, imbed a plain mould in some rough ice, and then cut the different colored jellies into strips, or any kind of fancy shaped ornaments, which must be so managed as to admit of their being fitted into each other, thus entirely covering the bottom of the mould with the design so formed; a little of the jelly must first be poured at the bottom of the mould, to cause the decoration to adhere together. The sides of the mould should then be ornamented by placing alternate strips of the different jellies in a perpendicular

---

* Derived from another French word, *panache*, a plume—a graceful feather. This jelly first received its name at the period of the first French Revolution, when it was customary for the representatives of the French people to wear a tri-colored plume in their hats.

position, and these must first be dipped in a little liquid jelly. The mould being lined according to the foregoing directions, the hollow may be filled up with either a *Macédoine* jelly of fruits, with any kind of cream, or with the remainder of the same, so arranged in it as to have the appearance of marble when cut.

1427. RUSSIAN JELLY.

PUT about two-thirds of either of the fore-mentioned kinds of jelly into a basin, partially imbedded in rough ice, then whip the jelly with a whisk, until it assumes the appearance of a substantial froth, and begins to thicken; it must then be immediately poured into a mould, and kept in ice until required to be served.

1428. PUNCH JELLY.

PUT the prepared stock from four calves'-feet into a stewpan, to melt on the stove-fire; then withdraw it, and add thereto the following ingredients :—Two pounds of loaf-sugar, the juice of six lemons and four oranges, the rind of one Seville orange and of four lemons, half a nutmeg, twelve cloves, and two sticks of cinnamon, a small cup of strong green tea, a pint of rum, half a pint of brandy, and a glass of arrack. Stir these well together, then add six whites and two whole eggs whipped up with a little Sherry and spring-water, and continue whisking the punch on a brisk-stove-fire until it begins to simmer, then set it down by the side of the fire, and cover the stewpan with its lid containing some live embers of charcoal ; about ten minutes after, pour the jelly into a flannel or beaver filtering-bag, keep pouring the jelly back into the bag until it becomes quite clear and bright, and when the whole has run through, set it in a mould in ice in the usual way.

1429. ORANGES FILLED WITH TRANSPARENT JELLY.

SELECT half a dozen oranges without specks on the rind, make a hole at the stalk-end with a circular tin cutter, about half an inch in diameter, and then use a small teaspoon to remove all the pulp and loose pith from the interior ; when this is effected, soak the oranges in cold water for about an hour, then introduce the spoon through the aperture, and scrape the insides smooth, and after rincing them again in cold water, set them to drain on a cloth. Next, stop up any holes that may have been made in them while scooping out the pulp, and set the oranges in some pounded rough ice contained in a deep sautapan ; fill three of them with bright pink-orange-jelly, and the remainder with plain jelly. When the jelly has become firm, wipe the oranges with a clean cloth, cut each into four quarters, dish them up tastefully on an ornamental pastry-stand, or upon a napkin, and send to table.

Note.—Lemons may be prepared in the same way as the above.

1429a. LEMONS FILLED WITH JELLY A LA BELLEVUE.

THESE are to be prepared in this instance as directed in the preceding article ; and are afterwards to be filled with alternate layers of lemon-jelly and *Blanc-manger*. Cut them up in the same way as oranges.

CREAMS,

COMPRISING

Blanc-Manger.
Maraschino Bavarian Cream.
Strawberry ditto.
Apricot ditto.
Coffee Cream.
Chocolate ditto.
Burnt ditto.
Orange-flower ditto.

Pistachio Cream.
Italian ditto.
Russian *Charlotte.*
Celestine Strawberry Cream.
Currant and Raspberry transparent
    Cheese.
Apricot Cheese, *à la Chantilly.*

1430. BLANC-MANGER.

PARBOIL twelve ounces of Jordan, and two ounces of bitter almonds, in a quart of water for about two minutes; drain them on a sieve, remove the skins, and wash them in cold water; after they have been soaked in cold water for half an hour, pound them in a mortar with four ounces of sugar, until the whole presents the appearance of a soft paste. This must then be placed in a large basin, with twelve ounces of loaf sugar, and mixed with rather more than a pint of spring-water; cover the basin with a sheet of paper, twisted round the edges, and allow the preparation to stand in a cool place for about an hour, in order to extract the flavor of the almonds more effectually. The milk should then be strained off from the almonds through a napkin, with pressure, by wringing it at both ends. Add two ounces of clarified isinglass to the milk of almonds, pour the *blanc-manger* into a mould imbedded in rough ice, and when set quite firm, turn it out on its dish with caution, after having first dipped the mould in warm water.

1431. MARASCHINO BAVARIAN CREAM.

WHIP a pint of double cream, until it presents somewhat of the appearance of snow, taking care not to overdo it, as it would then produce butter. When the cream is whipped, add one ounce and a half of clarified isinglass, a gill and a half of genuine maraschino, the juice of a lemon, and four ounces of pounded sugar; mix these well together and pour the cream into a mould, previously very slightly oiled inside with oil of sweet almonds; set the cream in rough ice, and when it has become firm, turn it out on its dish. The mould having been oiled prevents the necessity of dipping this delicate cream in warm water, previously to turning it out.

This kind of cream may also be flavored with all kinds of liqueurs; also with the essences of orange, lemon, orange-flowers, vanilla, roses and bitter almonds.

1432. STRAWBERRY BAVARIAN CREAM.

PICK the stalks from a pottle of scarlet strawberries, and bruise them in a basin with six ounces of pounded sugar; rub this through a sieve, and mix it with a pint of whipped cream, and one ounce and a half of clarified isinglass; pour the cream into a mould, previously oiled with oil of sweet almonds, set it in rough ice, and when it has become firm, turn it out on its dish.

Note.—Raspberries, mulberries, currants and raspberries may be prepared for making Bavarian creams, by following the above directions.

1433. APRICOT BAVARIAN CREAM.

SPLIT a dozen ripe apricots, and remove the stones; place the pieces in a small preserving-pan, with twelve ounces of pounded sugar, and a gill of spring water, then stir them on the fire and let them boil until the fruit is entirely dissolved; this *purée* must then be rubbed through a clean hair-sieve into a large basin, and mixed with a pint of whipped cream, and one ounce and a half of clarified isinglass; pour the cream into an oiled mould, and set it in rough ice, in the usual way.

This sort of cream may be prepared with all kinds of plums, instead of apricots.

1434. COFFEE CREAM.

ROAST eight ounces of Mocha coffee-berries in a small preserving-pan over a stove-fire, stirring it the whole time with a wooden spoon, until it assumes a light-brown color; then blow away the small burnt particles, and throw the roasted coffee into a stew-pan containing a pint of boiling milk or cream, put the lid on the stewpan, and set it aside to allow the infusion to draw out the flavor of the coffee. Next strain this through a napkin into a stewpan containing eight yolks of eggs and twelve ounces of sugar, add a very small pinch of salt, stir the cream over the stove-fire until it begins to thicken, then quicken the motions of the spoon, and when the yolks of eggs are sufficiently set, strain the cream through a tammy or sieve into a large basin. Mix half a pint of whipped cream and one ounce and a half of clarified isinglass in with this, pour the whole into a mould ready set in rough ice for the purpose, and when the cream has become firm, dip the mould in warm water, and turn the cream out on its dish.

1435. CHOCOLATE CREAM.

GRATE eight ounces of vanilla chocolate, put this into a stewpan with eight ounces of sugar, eight yolks of eggs, and a pint of cream; stir the whole over a stove-fire until the preparation begins to thicken; and the yolks of eggs are sufficiently set without allowing them to curdle, strain them through a tammy, with pressure, into a basin; add half a pint of whipped cream, and one ounce and a half of clarified isinglass, mix the whole well together, and pour it into a mould previously imbedded in rough ice, to receive it.

1436. BURNT CREAM.

PUT two ounces of pounded sugar into a stewpan, with the grated rind of two lemons; stir these with a wooden spoon over a slow fire, until the sugar begins to assume a rather light-brown color; then pour in a pint of cream, add to this eight ounces of sugar, eight yolks of eggs, and a little salt, and stir the whole over a stove-fire until the eggs are set; then strain the cream through a tammy into a large basin, and mix in with it half a pint of whipped cream, and one ounce and a half of clarified isinglass. Pour the cream into a mould imbedded in rough ice.

1437. ORANGE-FLOWER CREAM.

PUT two ounces of candied orange-flowers into a stewpan, with two ounces of pounded sugar; stir these over a slow fire until the sugar is merely melted, and pour in a pint of cream, adding eight ounces of sugar, eight yolks of eggs, a table-spoonful of orange-flower water, and a very little salt; stir this preparation over the fire to set the yolks of eggs, and then strain the cream through a tammy into a basin; add half a pint of whipped cream and one ounce and a half of clarified isinglass to it, mix well together, and then pour the cream into a mould imbedded in rough ice.

Note.—The flavoring of this kind of cream may be varied according to taste, by substituting lemon, orange, vanilla, cinnamon and lemon, or any other kind of essence or liqueur, for the foregoing.

1438. PISTACHIO CREAM.

PARBOIL eight ounces of pistachio kernels for two minutes in boiling water; then remove the skin, wash and wipe the kernels, and pound them in a mortar with six ounces of sugar and a dessert-spoonful of orange-flower water; rub the whole through a fine hair-sieve, and place it in a large basin. Add to the pounded pistachios a spoonful of the green extract of spinach (No. 285), a pint of whipped cream, and one ounce and a half of clarified isinglass; mix well together, pour the cream into an oiled mould, and then set it in ice in the usual way.

1439. ITALIAN CREAM.

PUT eight yolks of eggs into a stewpan with four ounces of ratafias, eight ounces of sugar, the grated rind of an orange, a small stick of cinnamon, a wine-glassful of curaçao, and a pint of cream; stir this over a stove-fire, in order to set the yolks of eggs in it, and then strain it through a tammy into a basin. Add thereto half a pint of whipped cream, and one ounce and a half of clarified isinglass, and after having well mixed the whole together, pour it into a mould ready imbedded in rough ice to receive it.

1440. RUSSIAN CHARLOTTE.

TRIM about six ounces of finger-biscuits perfectly straight, so as to make them fit closely to one another, and line the bottom and sides of a plain mould with these; then fill the interior of the *charlotte* with any one of the foregoing creams. The same kinds of fruit as are used for making a *Macédoine* jelly may be introduced in the cream.

1441. CELESTINA STRAWBERRY CREAM.

IMBED a jelly-mould, or plain *charlotte*-mould, in some rough ice contained in an earthen pan; line the bottom and sides of the mould, with picked strawberries; which must first be dipped in some perfectly-cold liquid jelly; then fill the interior of this kind of *charlotte* with some strawberry-cream, prepared for the purpose.

1441a. CREAM A LA ROMAINE.

BLANCH four ounces of Jordan almonds with one ounce of bitter almonds, and when freed from their hulls, washed and wiped dry, let them be chopped rather fine. Next, place them in a sugar-boiler and stir them over a stove-fire with a wooden spoon until they have acquired a very light-brown color; these almonds should now be thrown into a pint of milk that has been kept boiling for the purpose; to this add six ounces of sugar and eight yolks of eggs, and stir the whole quickly over the fire until the yolks are set; when the cream must be immediately removed from the fire, and stirred for a few minutes longer, previously to its being rubbed through a tammy like a *purée*. The produce will present a light fawn-colored thick cream; this must be mixed first, with rather better than an ounce of clarified isinglass, and then, three gills of whipped cream are to be lightly yet well incorporated. Pour the cream into a mould, and set it in ice as usual.

1441b. CREAM A LA CHATEAUBRIAND.

SET a jelly-mould in ice, and then proceed to ornament the bottom and sides with blanched almonds that have been split and well soaked to whiten them, each being first dipped in some rather strong and perfectly colorless jelly, previously to its being stuck to the sides of the mould. When the mould is thus ornamented, pour some of the same jelly into it, and by gently and gradually moving the mould round (side-ways) in the ice, cause the jelly to form a thin coating over the almonds. When the latter part of the process is satisfactorily effected, proceed to effect another coating about the third of an inch thick, with some pistachio cream (No. 1438); and when this is firmly set, fill up the cavity with some cream *à la Romaine* (No. 1441a).

Note.—An infinite variety of creams, usually designated *"en surprise,"* may be thus produced by using two different preparations of different creams, such as currant and orange-flower, apricot and vanilla, peach and noyeau, chocolate and white coffee, &c.

1442. CURRANT AND RASPBERRY TRANSPARENT CHEESE.

PICK the stalks from a quart of ripe red currants and a pottle of raspberries; put these into a small preserving-pan with one pound of pounded sugar and a gill of water; stir the whole on a stove-fire and keep it boiling for about five minutes; remove the scum as it rises to the surface, and then rub the whole through a hair-sieve into a large basin; add two ounces of clarified isinglass, and then pour it into a jelly-mould, ready imbedded in rough ice to receive it. When this kind of cheese is set firm, dip the mould in warm water, wipe it, and turn the cheese out on its dish; fill the well or cylinder with some stiffly-whipped cream, and serve.

1443. APRICOT CHEESE, A LA CHANTILLY.

REMOVE the stones from eighteen ripe apricots, and put them into a small preserving-pan with one pound of loaf sugar, and a gill of spring water; stir this on a brisk stove-fire, until the whole of the fruit is entirely dissolved ; and then rub it through a hair-sieve into a large basin ; add two ounces of clarified isinglass, and fill a jelly-mould (ready imbedded in rough ice) with the preparation. When the cheese is set firm, turn it out on its dish, and fill the centre with whipped cream.

Note.—These cheeses may be made of every kind of fruit before directed to be used for both jellies and creams; and also with pears, apples, and quinces.

1444. MINCE-MEAT.

THOROUGHLY cleanse four pounds of currants, and remove the stones from four pounds of raisins ; cut up two pounds of candied citron, one pound of candied lemon, and one pound of orange-peel, into shreds, or very small dice; remove the skin, and then chop four pounds of fresh beef-suet, and place this with the currants and the candied peel in an earthen pan; next chop the raisins with four pounds of peeled apples, and add them to the other ingredients. Trim away all the sinewy parts from eight pounds of roasted sirloin of beef, and chop all the lean of the meat quite fine; this will produce about four pounds, which must also be placed in the pan. To the foregoing must now be added four pounds of moist sugar, four ounces of ground spice—consisting of nutmegs, cloves, and cinnamon in equal proportions, with the grated rind of twelve oranges, and of the same number of lemons; the whole must then be thoroughly mixed together, and pressed down to a level in the pan. Two bottles of brandy, and a like quantity of Madeira, sherry or port, should be poured into the mince-meat. Put the lid on the pan, place a cloth over it, and tie it down close, so as to exclude the air as much as possible, and also to prevent the evaporation of the brandy, &c. The mince-meat should be kept in a cool place, and will be fit for use a fortnight after it is made.

1445. LEMON MINCE-MEAT.

BOIL four lemons till quite tender, then pound them in a mortar or chop them up while warm, adding to them two pounds of pounded loaf sugar; let this stand till next day, then add two pounds of suet, two pounds of currants, one pound of raisins chopped, a little brandy, one ounce of mixed spice, and port wine, to taste, say half a pint of brandy and wine together.

1446. MINCE MEAT, A LA ROYALE.

To equal proportions of roast beef, raisins, currants, suet, candied citron, orange, lemon, spices and sugar, add a proportionate weight of stewed pears and preserved ginger, the grated rind of three dozen oranges and lemons, and also their juice, one bottle of old rum, one bottle of brandy, and two of old port.

1447. APPLE CHARLOTTE.

To prepare this *entremet* in great perfection it is necessary that a crumb-loaf of close-made bread should be ordered two days previous for the purpose ; this, it must be owned, is not positively necessary ; therefore, in its stead, a stale quartern loaf may answer the purpose well enough.

First of all, some apple marmalade must be prepared as follows :— Let two or three dozen apples be peeled, cored, sliced up, and placed in a stewpan with one pound of sugar, two ounces of butter, and some lemon-peel and cinnamon tied together ; moisten with half a pint of water, place the lid on the stewpan, and then set the apples to boil sharp on a quick stove until they are melted. You then remove the lid, and with a wooden spoon continue stirring the marmalade over a brisk fire until it is reduced to a rather stiff consistency.

A plain round *charlotte*-mould must now be lined at the bottom with small thin circular pieces of bread, dipped in clarified butter, and placed so as to overlap each other until the bottom of the mould is well covered. Next, cut some oblong-squares of thin bread, also dipped in clarified butter, and set these up the sides of the mould overlapping each other—in order that they may be thus enabled to hold firmly to the sides of the mould. Fill the cavity with the apple-marmalade, cover in the top with a thin circular piece of bread dipped in butter, place the *charlotte* on a baking-sheet, and bake it in a rather brisk oven, of a light color ; and when done, turn it out on its dish, glaze it on the top with sifted sugar and a red-hot salamander ; pour some diluted apricot-jam round the base, and serve.

1448. APPLE CHARLOTTE, ANOTHER WAY.

The apples in this case must be cut up thin, and placed in a deep sautapan containing three ounces of dissolved butter, six ounces of pounded sugar, the grated rind of a lemon, and a pinch of cinnamon powder ; toss the whole over a stove-fire until the apples begin to melt their angles ; then add a pound-pot of apricot-jam, toss the whole gently together, and place this preparation in the centre of a *charlotte*-mould, lined as directed in the foregoing article, and proceed in all other respects as therein prescribed.

1449. CHARLOTTE, A LA PARISIENNE.

First, bake a thin sheet of Genoese, and when this has become thoroughly cold, proceed to cut it out into twenty-four oblong-squares, measuring four inches long, by an inch wide ; also about twelve half-moon or crescent shapes, of an equal size, in order that these may closely fit in with each other, so as to effectually cover the bottom of a *charlotte*-mould ; a circular piece must also be prepared, with which to finish the centre. All these pieces must be glazed over with icing prepared of two colors in equal numbers ; as, for instance, one-half being pink, amber, green, or chocolate ; while the other half is to be white. With the foregoing, line the mould, and then fill the centre with any kind of cream described at No. 1431 and following numbers.

1450. PEAR CHARLOTTE, A L'ALLEMANDE.

Peel, quarter, and core a dozen baking-pears ; stew them in three pints of water with three quarters of a pound of sugar, some lemon-peel, and cinnamon, until done. The pears must then be drained upon a sieve, and when comparatively dry, must be tossed in a sauta-pan with a pound-pot of red-plum or damson-jam, and used to fill in the centre of a bread-lined *charlotte*-mould, and then baked; and, on the *charlotte* being dished up, some honey, diluted with orange flower-water (warm), poured round the base, and sent to table.

1451. PEACH CHARLOTTE, A LA FRANCAISE.

ABOUT one dozen not over-ripe peaches, cut into quarters, skinned, and the kernels taken from the stones, should be placed in a sautapan with a pound-pot of peach-marmalade; the whole to be tossed over a stove-fire until the pieces of peach are just barely warmed through; and with this preparation fill a lined *charlotte*-mould—brioche being used for the purpose instead of bread. When this *charlotte* is sent to table, some currant-jelly, diluted with a glass of noyeau, should be poured round the base.

1452. APRICOT CHARLOTTE.

THIS is prepared in the same manner as the foregoing, substituting apricots for peaches, and apricot-marmalade for peach ditto; and, when the *charlotte* is turned out on to its dish, pour some honey, diluted with a liqueur called *Ratafia d'Abricôts* round the base, and serve.

1453. CROUTES AUX PECHES.

WITH the remains of *Brioche, Compiêgne, Konglaüff,* or *Savarin* cakes, cut some oblong shapes, about three inches long, by one inch wide; sugar over, and glaze these with a heated salamander; then, spread each with some peach-jam, and, after having first made a ring on the dish with some of the jam, proceed to dish up these fingers, each resting upon the other in the form of a high wreath; on the top of this, some halves of peaches (previously boiled for about three minutes in syrup) must be closed, dressed: and, having filled the hollow centre of the *entremet* with whipped cream, stick a feather of green angelica in the summit, decorate the pieces of peach with preserved cherries, raspberries, strawberries, or currant-jelly; pour some maras-chino over the crusts and round the base, and serve.

1454. PEACHES, A LA RICHELIEU.

HALF a pound of rice boiled thoroughly tender in a quart of milk, six ounces of sugar, two ounces of butter, seasoned with a stick of vanilla, and a pinch of salt; which, when done, must be first worked together with a wooden spoon, and then, with some of this, proceed to form a circular base about two inches high, in the inner part of the dish; and, on the outer part of this base, dress some peaches prepared as for a *compote*, in a thick circle, each overlapping the other; fill the centre of these with a piece of the prepared rice about three inches high, and upon this eminence build up a pyramid of peaches; over the whole pour some strawberry jelly. Round the base of the *entremêt*, place a border of preserved greengages; stick a plume made of angelica on the summit, and finish by pouring some vanilla liqueur round the base.

1455. SUPREME OF FRUITS, A LA VICTORIA.

FOR this purpose, some Genoese cake about an inch thick should be first prepared, and, out of this, three or four graduated circular pieces should be cut; the largest, with which to form the basement, must be eight inches in diameter, the next six, the third four, and lastly finishing with a round piece an inch and a half in diameter; these being stuck one upon the other with some kind of fruit jam, will thus produce a kind of pyramid. Upon this elevation, closely connected rows of either peaches, apricots, pears, or apples, prepared as for *compotes*, must be placed; finishing at the summit with a vase or cup formed out of apple or pear, and filled with a *Macédoine* of fruits. Mask the rows of fruit with some apricot jam, diluted with maraschino; and with a paper *cornet* or biscuit-forcer, fill with whipped cream, ornament the base of the *entremet* in wave-like fashion, upon these place some plumed pieces of green angelica.

1456. POIRES OF CROQUETTES.

ABOUT twelve middle-sized pears of good quality must be turned smoothly in their own shape, and gently simmered in a little syrup until done. Some rice must be prepared as for a rice cake, which must be made rather stiff, and steamed in a plain border mould; this, when done, must be turned out on to its dish, the pears are to be placed upright thereon in a circular row, and masked all over with diluted apricot-jam; on the stalk-end place a *Mirabelle* plum, and through this a piece of green Angelica, so as to form the stalk; fill the centre with some of the rice (reserved for this purpose), mixed with an equal quantity of whipped cream, at the summit of which a plume of green angelica must be stuck; ornament the base with a *compote* of greengages, and serve.

1457. ICED SOUFFLE, WITH MARASCHINO.

INGREDIENTS:—One pint of clarified syrup, twelve yolks of eggs, and two whole eggs, a large wine-glassful of maraschino.

Mix the whole of the ingredients in an earthen basin; then pour the preparation into an egg-bowl that has been previously warmed with hot water and wiped dry; whisk the *soufflé* briskly (the egg-bowl being placed on a stove containing hot ashes) until it resembles a well-prepared firm sponge-cake batter. Next, fill a *soufflé*-dish-lining with the whisked preparation to an inch or two above the rim, a band of stout paper having been secured round the case with a pin or string, to prevent the preparation from flowing over. The *soufflé* must now be placed in a circular tin box with a tight-fitting lid; the box to be immersed in pounded ice mixed with salt and half a pound of saltpetre well mixed, a wet cloth being placed over the top, and allowed to remain thus in ice for about three hours before it is served; when previously to sending the *soufflé* to table, the band of paper must be removed, and some sifted macaroon powder or grated chocolate shook over the surface, in order to give it the appearance of a baked *soufflé*.

1458. ICED SOUFFLE, OR CAFE.

THIS is prepared in exactly the same manner as the foregoing, with the exception that either a white infusion of coffee, or a small cup of *very strong* coffee, made in the ordinary way, must be substituted for the maraschino.

These *soufflés* may be greatly varied by altering the flavor ; using for that purpose any kind of liqueur, orange-flower-water, vanilla, orange, lemon, &c., &c., &c.

1459. BISCUITS GLACES.

THE preparations described in the foregoing articles serve equally for this purpose; small square, oblong, or round paper cases being filled with the same, and afterwards placed in a tin or zinc box, made expressly for such purposes ; and which may be easily obtained at small cost, either at Ravey's, in Conduit street, or Temple's, in Motcomb street ; the only houses where culinary utensils are to be had in greatest perfection.

1460. LA SPONGADA DI ROMA.

INGREDIENTS :—One pint of clarified syrup, six ounces of dissolved chocolate, a table-spoonful of vanilla sugar, an equal quantity of cinnamon sugar, four ounces of shred pistachios, two ounces of *Diavolini*, or ginger comfits, six whites of eggs.

Mix the syrup, dissolved chocolate, the whites of eggs (previously broken up with a fork in a basin), the vanilla and cinnamon sugars ; and, when these are well mixed together, let them be strained through a sieve, and poured into the freezing-pot, previously set with ice, &c., in a pail for the purpose. Next, let the freezing-pot be worked or twirled round with the left hand, while the *spongada* is being at the same time worked with a *spatula* held in the right hand, bearing in mind that this method of working the ice, while it is being frozen, is requisite, in order to facilitate the addition of the fixed air, necessary to promote its lightness, and by means of which its volume is thus increased twofold. When the *spongada* has become firm, and at the same time light, the ginger comfits and the shred pistachios should be lightly mixed in with it ; and immediately after, let the *spongada* be moulded in any kind of iced-pudding-mould ; and after it has been properly immersed in rough ice prepared in the usual way, for about three hours, let the *spongada* be carefully turned out upon a napkin and served for a second-course remove.

1461. SPONGADA DI TOLEDO.

INGREDIENTS :—Eight ounces of sweet almonds, and two ounces of bitter almonds, pounded with half a pint of water, and strained through a sieve to produce half a pint of milk of almonds, one pint of strong clarified syrup, a wine-glassful of *Kirschen-wasser*, six whites of eggs, six ounces of burnt almonds, slightly bruised, and half a pint of cream whipped.

Mix the milk of almonds, the syrup, whites of eggs, and the *Kirschen-wasser* well together, and strain them through a sieve into a freezing-pot ready set in ice, work this as directed in the preceding article, and when it has increased to twice its original quantity, let the bruised burnt almonds and the whipped cream be lightly added in with the *spongada*. Mould as in the former case.

1462. LA SPONGADA DI VENEZZA.

First, line a spherical iced-pudding-mould with some apricot-water-ice, about the third of an inch thick ; and then fill the cavity with the following preparation :—

First, scald and then peel eight ounces of pistachios and one ounce of bitter almonds, and pound these into a smooth paste in a mortar—adding, by degrees, a gill of water; and when thoroughly pounded, rub the produce through a tammy. Next, let the *purée* of pistachios be placed in a basin with a pint of syrup, a table-spoonful of orange-flower-water, ditto of spinach-green, and six whites of eggs that have been pressed through a tammy for the purpose; mix well together, and having poured the preparation into a ready-prepared freezing-pot, proceed immediately to work it as directed in the former cases; and when finished, use it to fill the *bombe*-shell; which, being completed, and the mould being effectually closed, must be immersed in ice for three hours previously to its being turned out for table.

These *spongadi* are well qualified to form a rich variety of iced-puddings for the second course, and are capable of being greatly varied by introducing different kinds of flavoring; such as all kinds of liqueurs, essences, or pounded sugar impregnated with orange, lemon, vanilla, orange-flowers, cinnamon, bitter almonds, &c., &c. The body of the ice may also be altered by using *purées* of different kinds of fruits, instead of the milk of almonds or the *purée* of pistachios.

[*The following eight pages are reproduced from the London edition of 1883.*]

1. HOW TO PREPARE CAUDLE.

Mix four ounces of Robinson's Patent Groats with half a pint of cold ale, pour this into a stewpan containing a quart of hot ale, add a small piece of bruised ginger, a small stick of cinnamon, and six cloves; stir the caudle over the fire while gently boiling for ten minutes, and then strain it off free from the spices, into a jug; add sugar, and rum or brandy to taste.

2. ROYAL POSSET FOR A COLD.

Mix a table-spoonful of Robinson's Patent Groats with a wine-glassful of cold water, pour this into a stewpan containing nearly half a pint of ordinary French white wine, sweeten with honey, flavour with a few drops of essence of cloves, or failing this, a few cloves will do; stir the posset over the fire while boiling for six minutes, and drink it quite hot just before going to bed.

3. HOW TO MAKE GRUEL.

Take of Robinson's Patent Groats, one table-spoonful mixed with a wine-glassful of cold water, pour this into a stewpan containing nearly a pint of boiling water, stir the gruel on the fire while it boils for ten minutes; pour it into a basin, add a small pat of butter, and a pinch of salt; or if more agreeable, some sugar, and a small quantity of spirits may be added instead of the butter and salt.

Note.—When gruel is made for an invalid, and if the constitution be delicate, the butter must be omitted.

4. A PUDDING FOR INFANTS.

To two ounces of Robinson's Patent Barley add one ounce of sifted sugar, half an ounce of butter, a pinch of salt, and nearly a pint of milk mix thoroughly, and stir it over the fire till it boils; then add two yolks of eggs, and bake the pudding in a buttered pie-dish.

5. INFANT'S FOOD.

To a good table-spoonful of Robinson's Patent Barley mixed with a wine-glassful of cold water, add one and a half gills of boiling water; stir this over the fire while boiling for six minutes, and then feed the infant. The same proportion of milk may be used instead of water, when the baby is weaned.

6. SCOTCH PUDDING.

To six ounces of Robinson's Patent Barley add six ounces of sifted sugar, mix both together with one quart of milk in a stewpan, then add four ounces of fresh butter, a pinch of salt, the rind of a lemon rubbed on sugar, and a wine-glassful of whisky. Stir the whole on the fire until it boils, and then work the batter perfectly smooth; next, work in six yolks of eggs, and then lightly mix in six whites of eggs whisked into a firm froth: pour the batter into a slightly buttered pie-dish, and bake the pudding in moderate heat.

7. HOW TO MAKE BARLEY-WATER.

Take of Robinson's Patent Barley one ounce mixed with a wine-glassful of cold water, pour this into a stewpan containing nearly one quart of boiling water, stir this over the fire while boiling for five minutes; then flavour with a small bit of lemon-peel or cinnamon, and sweeten according to taste.

Note.—When the above Patent Barley is used to make a summer beverage, only half an ounce must be taken.

8. HOW TO PREPARE A SAVOURY CUSTARD.

To one table-spoonful of Robinson's Patent Barley add rather more than half a pint of good beef tea; mix and stir over the fire for five minutes, and you have a light yet invigorating kind of food for the debilitated stomach, which in its results will prove far more satisfactory than any preparation known.

Note.—This delicate custard may also be advantageously prepared with broths made from mutton, game, or poultry.

FRANCATELLI'S

INSTRUCTIONS FOR THE SERVICE OF WINES,

DENOTING THE ORDER IN WHICH THEY SHOULD BE DRUNK AT THE DINNER-TABLE.

———◆◇◆———

THE judicious service of wines at the dinner-table is essential to the complete success of a well-ordered and *recherché* dinner; for on the manner and order in which this service is conducted will chiefly depend the more or less favourable judgment awarded (independently of their real claims to superiority) to the wines put before the guests.

First, let it be remembered that all possible care should be taken in removing the bottles from their bins, and afterwards also, in handling them for the purpose of drawing the corks, and decanting the wines, not to disturb any deposit that may exist in the bottles, for that deposit, if shaken, destroys not only the brilliancy of the wine, but impairs its flavour and *bouquet*.

The different kinds of Sherries, Ports, Madeira, and all Spanish and Portuguese wines in general, are the better for having been decanted several hours before being drunk. During winter their aroma is improved by the temperature of the dining-room acting upon their volatile properties for an hour or so before dinner-time. By paying due attention to this part of the process, all the mellowness which good wines acquire by age, predominates to the delight of the epicure's grateful palate. The lighter wines, such as Bordeaux, Burgundy, and most of the wines of Italy, should be most carefully handled, and decanted an hour only before dinner-time. In winter, the decanters should be either dipped in warm water or else placed near the fire, to warm them, for about ten minutes previously to their being used. In summer, use the decanters without warming them, as the genial warmth of the atmosphere will be all-sufficient, not only to prevent chilling the wines, but to develop their fragrant *bouquet*. Moreover, let these, and all delicate wines, be brought into the dining-room as late as may be consistent with convenience.

And now, as regards the order in which wines should be served during dinner :—I would recommend all *bon vivants* desirous of testing and thoroughly enjoying a variety of wines, to bear in mind that they should be drunk in the following order: viz.—

When it happens that oysters preface the dinner, a glass of Chablis or Sauterne is their most proper accompaniment: genuine old Madeira, or East India Sherry, or Amontillado, proves a welcome stomachic after soup of any kind,—not excepting turtle,—

after eating which, as you value your health, avoid all kinds of punch—especially Roman punch. During the service of fish, cause any of the following to be handed round to your guests :—Amon- tillado, Hock, Tisane Champagne, Pouilly, Meursault, Sauterne, Arbois, vin de Grave, Montrachet, Château-Grillé, Barsac, and generally all kinds of dry white wines.

With the entrées, any of the following wines may be introduced : viz.—

BORDEAUX.

Saint Julien.
Leoville.
Laroze.
Haut-Brion.
Château-Lafitte.
Château-Margaux.
Mouton-Lafitte.
Latour.
Médoc.
Saint Emilion.
Saint Estèphe.

BURGUNDY, &c.

Macon.
Moulin-à-vent.
Thorins.
Beaune,
Chassagne.
Pale and brown Sherries.
Amontillado.
Bucellas.
Mancinillo.

SECOND-COURSE WINES.

RED WINES.

Pommard.
Volnay.
Nuits.
Richebourg.
Clos-Vougeot.
Romanée-Conti.
Chambertin.
Saint Georges.
Pouilly.
Meursault.
Saint Perray.

Rhenish wines (red).
Ermitage.
Hermitage.
Tavel.
Roussillon.
Château neuf du Pape.
Côte-rôtie.
Jurançon.
Monté-Fiascone.
Monté-Pulciano.
Vino di Pasta.

WHITE WINES.

Vin de Grave.
Sauterne.
Barsac.
Langon.

Aï pétillant,
Carbonnieux.
Champagnes.

RED CHAMPAGNES.

Bouzy.
Versy.
Volnay mousseux.
Veuve Cliquot.

Champagne.
Sillery.
Sparkling Moselle.

DESSERT WINES.

Muscat-Frontignan.
Muscat-Lunel.
Muscat-Rivesalte.
Grenache.
Vin de paille.
Malaga.
Rota.
Alicante.

Madeira.
Malmsey Madeira.
Syracuse.
Tokay.
Constance.
Carcavallos.
Picoli.
Schiras,

A question of the highest importance, but into which I may but briefly enter, is to determine to which of all these wines a decided preference should be given, both with regard to taste, and also in respect to their influence on the health of different temperaments. It is easier to settle the latter part of the question than the former, inasmuch as it is difficult, not to say impossible, to lay down rules for the guidance of the palate. Thus there are some who delight in the perfumed yet austere *bouquet* of Bordeaux, while others prefer the delicate fragrance of Champagne; some give the palm to the generous and mirth-inspiring powers of Burgundy; while the million deem that Madeira (when genuine), Port, and Sherry, from what are termed their generous natures, ignoring the plentiful admixture of alcohol, are the only wines worthy of notice. All these tastes are no doubt well enough founded on good and sufficient reasons, and may prove safe indicators for the preservation of health:—for instance, a person of sanguine temperament feels a necessity for a light sapid wine, such as *genuine* Champagnes and Rhenish wines; while the phlegmatic seek those of a more spirituous, generous nature—Burgundy, Port, Madeira, or Sherry. Those who are a prey to spleen—lowness of spirits—melancholy—are prone to select, as a sure and pleasant remedy for their frightful ailments, the wines of Italy, Spain, Portugal, Roussillon, and Burgundy. The bilious, who generally are blessed with a good appetite, provided always that they do not smoke, require a generous wine, which, while capable of acting both as an astringent and a dissolvent of the bile, is of facile digestion; such are the properties of all first-class Bordeaux wines. Bordeaux is said to be a cold wine; this false notion arises out of mere prejudice—nothing can be more contrary to truth: this health-restoring wine, as I have already stated, is of easy digestion, and possesses, moreover, the advantage of being very considerably less inebriating than any other first-class wine. In short, Burgundy is exciting, Champagne is captious, Roussillon restorative, and Bordeaux stomachic.

It now remains to show the order in which the several sorts of wines, enumerated above, should be served at table. Custom and fashion have ever had more to do with this practice than any real consideration for health or taste.

It is generally admitted by *real gourmets*, that red wines should precede the introduction of white wines,—those recommended as proper accompaniments to oysters and fish excepted. The custom most in vogue at the best tables in London and Paris is, to commence by introducing, simultaneously with the entrées, any of the following Burgundy wines:—Avallon, Coulanges, Tonnerre, Vermanton, Irancy, Mercurey, Chassagne, and, generally, all those wines known under the specific names of Macon and Auxerre: these may be varied or replaced by other wines, denominated Saint Denis, Saint Ay, and Beaugency: these again lead to the further libations of Beaune, Pommard, Volnay, Richebourg, Chambertin, Saint Georges, Romanée. With the second course, roasts and dressed vegetables, and savoury *entremets*, honour your guests by graciously ushering to their notice sparking Champagne and Moselle, the deliciously perfumed Cumières, the brilliant Sillery, the glorious Hermitage, Côte-rôtie, and Château-Grillé.

With the service of the *entremets de douceur*—or, as we have it, the sweets—let iced-creaming, sparkling Champagne or Moselle be handed round ; but far superior to them, I would recommend a trial of Aï *pétillant*, Arbois, Condrieux, Rivesaltes, Malaga, Frontignan, Grenache, Malmsey, Madeira, and East India Sherry.

So little wine is drunk at dessert in this country, that it would be superfluous to enter into particulars about the service further than to refer the reader to the list of wines appropriated to this part of a dinner. And what shall be said with respect to the class of wines best adapted to make their appearance on the table after dinner ? Why simply this ; if you have done reasonable honour to some of the good things which I will suppose your table to have been supplied with, pray let the wine alone for the present, and order up the coffee—*hot*, *strong*, and *bright !* Let it be made with pure — picked overland Mochà, — fresh roasted pale — coarsely ground,—and pray do forbid your housekeeper to clarify it with egg ; but tell her to use a bit cf genuine Russian isinglas, not the spurious filth made from all sorts of abominations, and sold at most Italian warehouses under the name of isinglas. The Cafetière à la Dubelloy, or one of Adams' Percolators, is best adapted for making good coffee without the trouble or necessity for clarifying it. And as to liqueurs? Try Eau de vie d'Andaye, Eau de la Grande Chartreuse, or ten-year-old Cognac.

Before I take my leave of you, dear reader, let me here acknowledge how much I feel indebted to the press generally for the flattering notices of my " Cook's Guide," which in a great measure through such favourable introduction has, in the short space of six months, gone through three large editions.

And as I now write at " the wee hour beyont the twal," as the Scots say, and we have entered on a new year, I will wish you all good fortune, and that you may possess the means of enjoying the delectable wines we have passed in review, and a dinner dressed by an Aberlin, a Brûnet-Montrose, a Jules Magdelin, a Georges Comte, a Sédille, or a Valentin :—and then, indeed, you will be of the most fortunate on this globe.

C. E. FRANCATELLI.

Boyne Terrace, Notting Hill,
     January, 1862.

1. CLARET CUP.

Ingredients :—One bottle of Claret, one pint bottle of German Seltzer-water, a small bunch of balm, ditto of burrage, one orange cut in slices, half a cucumber sliced thick, a liqueur-glass of Cognac, and one ounce of bruised sugar-candy.

Process :—Place these ingredients in a covered jug well immersed in rough ice, stir all together with a silver spoon, and when the cup has been iced for about an hour, strain or decanter it off free from the herbs, &c.

2. BADMINTON CUP.

Ingredients :—One bottle of red Burgundy, one quart of German Seltzer-water, the rind of one orange, the juice of two, a wine-glass of Curaçao, a bunch of balm, ditto of burrage, a sprig of verbina, one ounce of bruised sugar-candy, a few slices of cucumber.

Process :—Place these ingredients in a covered jug embedded in rough ice for about an hour previously to its being required for use, and afterwards decanter the cup free from the herbs, &c.

3. CHAMPAGNE CUP.

Ingredients :—One bottle of Champagne, one quart bottle of German Seltzer-water, two oranges sliced, a bunch of balm, ditto of burrage, one ounce of bruised sugar-candy.

Process :—Place these ingredients in a covered jug embedded in rough ice for an hour and a quarter previously to its being required for use, and then decanter it free from the herbs, &c.

4. SAUTERNE CUP.

Ingredients :—One bottle of Sauterne, one pint of Vichy-water, two oranges sliced, a bunch of balm, ditto of burrage, one ounce of bruised sugar-candy.

Process :—Place these ingredients in a covered jug embedded in ice for an hour and a quarter previously to the cup being required for use, and then decanter it.

5. MOSELLE CUP.

Ingredients :—One bottle of sparkling Moselle, one quart of German Seltzer-water, a bunch of balm, ditto of burrage, two oranges sliced, one ounce of bruised sugar-candy.

Process :—Place these ingredients in a covered jug embedded in rough ice for an hour and a quarter previously to the cup being required for use, and then decanter it free from the herbs, &c.

6. PINE-APPLE CUP.

Ingredients :—Eight ounces of pine-apple sliced very thin, one bottle of Aï wine, a sprig of verbina, a wine-glassfull of Maraschino, one quart bottle of double soda-water, one ounce of bruised sugar-candy.

Process :—Thoroughly embed the wine and the soda-water in rough ice for an hour previously to its being required for use; and then, first place the slices of pine-apple, the verbina, the Maraschino, and the sugar-candy in a glass jug, and afterwards add thereto the iced wine and soda-water.

7. CHABLIS CUP.

Ingredients :—One bottle of Chablis, one pint of German Seltzer-water, one bunch of balm, ditto of burrage, one orange sliced, one ounce of bruised sugar-candy.

Process :—Place these ingredients in a covered jug embedded in rough ice for an hour and a quarter previously to its being required for use, and then decanter the cup free from the herbs, &c.

8. BEER CUP.

Ingredients :—One quart of stout or porter, half an ounce of moist sugar, a small slice of bread toasted brown, and a small quantity of grated nutmeg and ginger. Mix these ingredients in a jug and allow the cup to steep for half an hour previously to its being drank.

Note.—Ale cup is made in a similar manner.

These cups are more particularly adapted for being handed round with cheese.

CYDER CUP.

Ingredients :—One quart of Cyder, one pint of German Seltzer-water, a small glass of Cognac, a bunch of balm, ditto of burrage, a sliced orange, one ounce of bruised sugar-candy.

Process :—Place the ingredients in a covered jug embedded in ice for an hour and a quarter, and then decanter the cup free from herbs, &c.

Note.—Any other aërated water may be substituted for Seltzer, or the cup may be prepared without the addition of any water.

PERRY CUP.

This is prepared in the same manner as Cyder cup, substituting, of course, Perry for Cyder.

A SERIES OF BILLS OF FARE

FOR EVERY MONTH THROUGHOUT THE YEAR.

DINNER FOR 6 PERSONS. *January.*

Julienne soup.

---

1 *Fish.*

Fried soles, anchovy sauce.

Fowl and rice.   [2 *Removes.*]   Roast leg of Welsh mutton.

2 *Entrées:*

Salmis of partridges, à l'ancienne.   Fricandeau with purée of sorrel.

SECOND COURSE.

Roast snipes.

---

3 *Entremêts:*

Spinach with cream.   Blanc-manger.

Apples à la Portuguaise.

DINNER FOR 6 PERSONS. *January.*

Palestine soup.

---

1 *Fish.*

Crimped cod and oyster sauce.

Roast griskin of pork, with ap-   [2 *Removes.*]   Braized pheasant, with cab-
ple sauce.   bages.

2 *Entrées:*

Patties of chicken, à la Béchamel.   Mutton cutlets sautées, with purée
                                      of potatoes.

SECOND COURSE.

Roast Hare.

---

3 *Entremêts:*

Fried salsifis in batter.   Apricot puffs.

Orange jelly.

(507)

DINNER FOR 6 PERSONS. *January.*
Ox-tail clear soup.

---

1 *Fish.*
Broiled Herrings, with mustard sauce.

Snipe pudding, à la D'Orsay.   [2 *Removes.*]   Roast saddle of mutton.

2 *Entrées :*
Blanquette of fowl with mushrooms.   Scollops of beef, à la Napolitaine.

SECOND COURSE.
Roast Pheasant.

---

3 *Entremêts :*
Brussels-sprouts, à la crême.   Meringues, with cream.
Pears and rice, à la Condé.

DINNER FOR 6 PERSONS. *January.*
Vermicelli soup, à la Windsor.

---

1 *Fish.*
Turbot, with lobster sauce.

Boiled neck of mutton, with   [2 *Removes.*]   Partridges, à la Séville.
mashed turnips.
2 *Entrées :*
Fillets of rabbits, à la Maréchale.   Fricasse of chicken, in a border of rice

---

SECOND COURSE.
Roast wild duck.

---

3 *Entremêts :*
Jerusalem artichokes, à l'Espagnole.   Custards in glasses.
Tourte of apples, à la Cobourg.

DINNER FOR 6 PERSONS. *January.*
Jardinière clear soup.

---

1 *Fish.*
Whitings au gratin.

Roast neck of venison.   [2 *Removes.*]   Braized pheasant, with Soubise sauce.
2 *Entrées :*
Quenelles of fowl, à l'essence.   Tendons of veal, with a purée of spinach.

SECOND COURSE.
Roast larks.

---

3 *Entremêts :*
Brown-bread pudding, à la Gotha (preserved cherries).
Turnips glacés à l'Espagnole.   Apple fritters.

DINNER FOR 10 PERSONS. *January.*

Bisque of lobster Soup.

1 *Fish.*

Crimpt cod, with oyster sauce, garnished with fried smelts.

Patties, à la Monglas.

2 *Removes.*

Roast turkey, à la Périgord.   Braized ham with spinach.

2 *Entrées :*

Fat livers, à la Financière.   Fillets of partridges, à la Lucullus.

SECOND COURSE.

Roast black-cock.   [2 *Roasts.*]   Roast Teal.

1 *Remove.*

Soufflé of apples, à la Vénitiènne.

4 *Entremêts.*

Mecca loaves, with apricot.   Braized celery.
Italian cream.   Macaroni au gratin.

DINNER FOR 10 PERSONS. *January.*

Purée of grouse, à la Condé.

1 *Fish.*

Soles à la Matelotte Normande.

Boiled Poulard with Nouilles.   [2 *Removes.*]   Roast saddle of mutton.

Croquettes of oysters

2 *Entrées :*

Blanquette of pheasant and truffles.   Cutlets of pork, Robert sauce.

SECOND COURSE.

Partridges.   [2 *Roasts.*]   Woodcocks.

[1 Remove.]
Fondu of Parmesan Cheese.

4 *Entremêts.*

Apples à la crême.   Seakale à la Béchamel.
Pethiviers cakes.   Punch-jelly.

DINNER FOR 10 PERSONS. *January.*

Giblet soup, clear.

Baked haddock.　[2 *Fishes.*]　Fillets of soles au gratin.

Capon, à la Chipolata.　[2 *Removes.*]　Boiled leg of mutton, à l'Anglaise.

Oyster patties.

2 *Entrées:*
Boudins of pheasant, à la d'Artois.　Mutton cutlets, à la Russe.

SECOND COURSE.

Lobster, au gratin.　[2 *Roasts.*]　Widgeon.

4 *Entremêts:*
Filbert-cream tartlets.　　Pears à la Condé.
Noyeau-jelly.　　Cardoons, à l'Espagnole.

DINNER FOR 10 PERSONS. *January.*

Soup, à la Juliènne.

1 *Fish.*
Turbot, with lobster and Dutch sauces.

Fowls, à la Macédoine.　[2 *Removes.*]　Fillet of Beef larded, à la Financière.

Patties, à la Reine.
2 *Entrées:*
Salmis of snipes, with truffles.　Fillets of pigeons, à la de Luynes.

SECOND COURSE.

Roast Hare.　[2 *Roasts.*]　Savarin, with cherries.

4 *Entremêts:*
Spinach, with croûtons.　　Orange-jelly, in small baskets.
Charlotte, à la Parisiènne.　Profitrolles au chocolat.

DINNER FOR 12 PERSONS. *January.*

Soup à la Xavier.	[2 *Soups.*]	Purée of fowl, à la Reine.
Fried smelts, with Dutch sauce.	[2 *Fishes.*]	Crimped cod, à la crême au gratin.
Braized ham, garnished with Brussels-sprouts.	[2 *Removes.*]	Roast loin of veal, à la Monglas.

4 *Entrées.*

Fillets of partridges, à la de Luynes.   Kromeskys of lobsters, à la Russe.
Mutton cutlets, à la Soubise.   Scollops of fowls, with truffles.

SECOND COURSE.

| Widgeon. | [2 *Roasts.*] | Woodcocks. |
| Fondu of Parmesan. | [2 *Removes.*] | Iced pudding, à la Cintra. |

6 *Entremêts:*

Italian salad.   Punch jelly.
Mushrooms, à la Provençale.   Damson tartlets.
Apples and rice plain, with apricot jam. Mecca loaves, with rasberry jam.

DINNER FOR 12 PERSONS. *January.*

Flemish clear soup.	[2 *Soups.*]	Mock turtle.
Soles in Norman matelotte.	[2 *Fishes.*]	Haddocks, with egg sauce.
Pheasants à la Dauphinoise.	[2 *Removes.*]	Roast saddle of mutton.

4 *Entrées:*

Oyster patties.   Boudins of fowl, à la Richelieu.
Salmis of woodcocks, à l'anciènne.   Scollops of sweetbreads, à la Villeroi.

SECOND COURSE.

| Larks. | [2 *Roasts.*] | Roast capon. |
| Ginger pudding. | [2 *Removes.*] | Soufflé of arrow root. |

6 *Entremêts:*

Braized celery, à l'essence.   Charlotte of apples.
Macaroni au gratin.   D'Artois of strawberry jam.
Maraschino jelly.   Italian cream.

DINNER FOR 12 PERSONS. *January.*

Macaroni clear soup.	[2 *Soups.*]	Purée of carrots, à la Crécy.
Fillets of whitings, à la Royale.	[2 *Fishes.*]	John-dory, with Dutch sauce.
Braized fillet of beef, with Madeira sauce.	[2 *Removes.*]	Poulards, à la Périgeux.

4 *Entrées:*

Boudins of pheasant, à la Reine.   Fillets of pigeons, à la D'Uxelles.
Mutton cutlets, à la Bour uignotte.   Marrow patties, with fine-herbs sauce.

SECOND COURSE.

Teal.	[2 *Roasts.*]	Hare.
Brown-bread soufflé.	[2 *Removes.*]	Ramequins, à la Sefton.

6 *Entremêts:*

Salsifis à la crême.   Vol-au-vent of greengages.
Potatoes au gratin.   Noyeau cream.
Lemon jelly.   Pithiviers cakes.

DINNER FOR 12 PERSONS. *January.*

Soup, à la Colbert.	[2 *Soups.*]	Purée of pheasant, à la Chasseur.
Torbay soles, with lobster sauce.	[2 *Fishes.*]	Fillets of gurnets, à la Maître d'hôtel.
Roast turkey, à la Financière.	[2 *Removes.*]	Baked ham, with Madeira sauce.

4 *Entrées:*

Mutton cutlets, à la Provençale.   Fillets of widgeon, Poivrade sauce.
Bouchées of rabbit, à la Pompadour.   Croquettes of oysters, à la Béchamel.

SECOND COURSE.

Partridges.	[2 *Roasts.*]	Black game.
Iced pudding, à la Duchesse de Kent.	[2 *Removes.*]	Pancakes soufflés.

6 *Entremêts:*

Portugal onions glazed à l'Espagnole.   Apple tartlets.
Spinach au jus.   Meringue à la Parisiènne.
Damson cheese à la Chantilly.   Eggs à la neige, flavored with coffee.

DINNER FOR 16 PERSONS. *January.*

Juliènne.   [2 *Soups.*]   Calf's-feet, à la Windsor.

Fillets of soles, à la Vénitiènne. [2 *Fishes.*] Haddocks broiled, Dutch sauce

Capon, à la Toulouse.   [2 *Removes.*] Rump of beef, à la Jardinière.

6 *Entrées :*

Crôustades of ox-piths, à la Monglas.   Mutton cutlets bread-crumbed, with
Border of rice garnished with a purée   a purée of chestnuts.
    of pheasants.   Fillets of fowls with truffles, Su
Boudins of rabbit, à la D'Artois.   prême sauce.
                                          Salmis of widgeon, à la Bigarrade.

SECOND COURSE.

Pheasants.   [2 *Roasts.*]   Snipes.

Apricot Soufflée.   [2 *Removes.*]   Parmesan fritters.

8 *Entremêts :*

Lobster salad.   Kirschen-wasser jelly.
Mushrooms, au gratin.   Chocolate cream.
Potatoes, à la maître d'hôtel.   Pears, à la Condé.
Brussels-sprouts sautés with butter. Darioles, à la Vanille.

DINNER FOR 16 PERSONS. *January.*

Purée of celery, à la crême.   [2 *Soups.*]   Quenelles of rabbit, in con
                                                  sommé.
Fillets of soles, à la Dièppoise. [2 *Fishes.*] Baked pike, Piquante sauce.

Calf's-head, à la Tortuë.   [2 *Removes.*] Fowls with Nouilles, à l'Al-
                                              lemande.

6 *Entrées :*

Pork cutlets, à la Robert.   Patties, à la Reine.
Woodcocks, à la Monarque.   Fillets of partridges, à la Maréchale.
Mince of chicken in a border, garnished Sweetbreads larded, with endives.
    with poached eggs.

SECOND COURSE.

Hare.   [2 *Roasts.*]   Wild ducks.

Pancakes with apricot.   [2 *Removes.*]   Iced pudding, à la Stanley

8 *Entremêts :*

Potato croquettes, à la Béchamel.   Panachée jelly.
Seakale, à l'Espagnole.   Pine-apple cream.
Crusts garnished with mushrooms.   Pastafrolle cake, à la Napolitaine.
Lobster, au gratin.   Tourte of greengages.

Dinner for 8 Persons. *February.*

Cream of barley, à la Reine.

Matelotte of eels.	[2 *Fishes.*] Crimped cod broiled, Dutch sauce.
Pheasants à la Financière.	[2 *Removes.*] Braized roll of beef, à la Fla-mande.

Noukles with Parmesan.

---

2 *Entrées:*

Scollops of fowls à l'écalarte.	Lamb cutlets bread-crumbed, with a purée of celery.

═══════════

Second Course.

Teal.	[2 *Roasts.*]	Macaroni, à l'Italiènne.

1 *Remove.*

Rice soufflée.

---

4 *Entremêts:*

Canapes of anchovies.	Tourte of pears, à la Cobourg.
Seakale, à la Béchamel.	Burnt cream, au caramel.

━━━━━━━━━

Dinner for 8 Persons. *February*

Soup à la Désclignac.

Crimped haddocks, Dutch sauce.	[2 *Fishes.*] Fillets of brill, à la Maréchale.
Roast haunch of mutton.	[2 *Removes.*] Braized goose, à la Jardinière.

Lobster patties.

---

2 *Entrées:*

Chickens, à la Marengo.	Salmis of Snipes, à la Talleyrand.

═══════════

Second Course.

Black game.	[2 *Roasts.*]	Salad, à la Russe.

1 *Remove.*

Nouilles cake, à l'Allemande.

---

4 *Entremêts:*

Celery, à la Villeroi.	Profitrolles, à la créme.
Poached eggs, on anchovy toast.	Apricot cheese, à la Chantilly.

Dinner for 10 Persons. *February.*

Purée of Carrots, à la Stanley.
Cod à la Crême, au gratin.　　[2 *Fishes.*] Water Souchet of Fillets of Soles.

Kromeskys of Lobster.

Boiled Turkey, with purée of [2 *Removes.*]　Braized Ham, au Madère.
Celery.

2 *Entrées:*

Suprême of fillets of Woodcocks,　　Cutlets of Sweetbreads, à la Dauphine.
à l'anciènne.

Second Course.

Roast Pheasants.　　[2 *Roasts.*]　　Timbale of Noukles.

4 *Entremêts.*

Brocoli, au gratin.　　　　Currant and Raspberry jelly (preserved).
Lobster salad.　　　　　Meringues filled with Orange ice.

Dinner for 10 Persons. *February.*

Soup of Sturgeon's Head, à la Chinoise.

Cod's Sounds, à la Gasconne.　　[2 *Fishes.*]　　Fried Soles.

Patties au jus.

Pheasants à la Périgueux.　　[2 *Removes.*] Boiled leg of Pork à l'Anglaise.

2 *Entrées:*

Tendons of veal in a Chartreuse.　　Fricassee of chicken, à la St. Lambert.

Second Course.

Suprême of fruits.　　[2 *Roasts.*]　　Wild Ducks.

4 *Entremêts.*

Apple tartlets.　　　　　Mushrooms, au gratin.
Chestnut pudding.　　　　Vanilla cream.

DINNER FOR 10 PERSONS.   *February.*
Bonne Femme Soup.

Whitings, au gratin.   [2 *Fishes.*]   Eels, à la Tartare.

Rissoles, à la Milanaise.

Capon à la Montmorency.   [2 *Removes.*]   Braized beef, à la D'Orleans.

2 *Entrées:*
Fillets of chicken, à l'Indiènne.   Paupièttes of Ox-palates, à la Financière.

SECOND COURSE.

Salad, à la Russe.   [2 *Roasts.*]   Larks, bread-crumbed.

4 *Entremêts:*
Apricots à la Conde.   Nesselrode pudding.
Maraschino jelly.   Mosaic tartlets.

DINNER FOR 10 PERSONS.   *February.*
Bisque of rabbits.

1 *Fish.*
Haddocks, à la Belle-vue.

Ox-piths fried in batter.

Calf's-head à la Financière.   [2 *Removes.*]   Small chickens, à la Vertpré.

2 *Entrées:*
Mutton cutlets à la Pompadour.   Scollops of fat livers, with truffles and
fine-herbs.

SECOND COURSE.

Scolloped oysters.   [2 *Roasts.*]   Pintail.

4 *Entremêts:*
Krapfen with apricot.   Pudding, à la Viennoise.
Seakale à la sauce.   Champagne jelly.

DINNER FOR 8 PERSONS. *February.*

Hare soup, à la Chasseur.

Turbot, lobster sauce. [2 *Fishes.*] Broiled whitings, capers' sauce.

Capon and rice. [2 *Removes.*] Braized leg of mutton, à la Soubise.

Patties, à la Mazarin.

2 *Entrées.*

Grenadins of veal larded, garnished   Fillets of pheasants, à la Marèchale.
with a Nivernaise.

SECOND COURSE.

Potato chips. [2 *Roasts.*] Ptarmegans.

1 *Remove.*
Apple pudding.

4 *Entremêts:*

Braized Celery, garnished with crôus-   Orange jelly, à l'Anglaise.
tades of marrow.   Bread-and-butter pastry.
Scolloped oysters.

DINNER FOR 8 PERSONS. *February.*

Ox-cheek soup, à la Flamande.

Brill, lobster sauce. [2 *Fishes.*] Baked Gurnets, Italian sauce.

Fillet of beef, Poivrade sauce. [2 *Removes.*] Braized Ducks, with turnips.

Tourte of godiveau, à la Ciboulette.

2 *Entrées:*

Boudins of pheasant, à la Victoria.   Veal cutlets, à la Régence.

SECOND COURSE.

German salad. [2 *Roasts.*] Woodcocks.

1 *Remove.*
Macaroni pudding.

4 *Entremêts:*

Jerusalem artichokes, à l'Espagnole.   Quarters of oranges filled with trans-
Eggs brouillés, with truffles.   parent jelly.
                               Almond Gauffres, à la crême.

Dinner for 20 Persons. *February.*

Soup à la Sévigné.   [2 *Soups.*]   Cream of rice, à la Chasseur.

Salmon, lobster sauce.   [2 *Fishes.*]   Slices of crimped Cod broiled,
                                     à la Maître d'hôtel.

Ham, à la Parisiènne   [2 *Removes.*]   Poulards, à la Royale.

Kromeskys of oysters.

8 *Entrées:*

Fillets of rabbits larded, à l'anciènne.   Lamb cutlets, with Macédoine of
Fricassée of chickens, à la St. Lambert.   vegetables.
Paté-Chaud of larks, à la Périgueux.   Fricandeau, with purée of artichokes.
Border of rice, with purée of fowl, à la   Fillets of partridges, with fumet.
    Polonaise.   Mazarine of fat livers, à la Financière.

Second Course.

Snipes.   [2 *Roasts.*]   Pheasants.

Iced pudding, à la Syriènne.   [2 *Removes.*]   Soufflè tartléts, à la D'Artois.

Nougat of almonds.   [2 *Flanks.*]   Savoy cake in the form of a swan.

8 *Entremêts:*

Aspic of lobsters, with mayonaise.   Charlotte of apricots.
Russian salad.   Orange jelly, garnished with oranges.
Spinach with cream.   Florentines, with pistachios.
Brocoli with Parmesan cheese.   Cherry tartlets.

Dinner for 20 Persons. *February.*

Purée of pheasant.   [2 *Soups.*]   Brûnoise soup.

Crimped soles, Dutch sauce.   [2 *Fishes.*]   Fillets of turbot, à la Parisiènne.

Turkey, à la Périgueux.   [2 *Removes.*]   Braized roll of beef, à la D'Or-
                                     leans.

Marrow patties.

8 *Entrées:*

Potato border, garnished with scol-   Mutton cutlets, à la Duchesse.
    lops of Larks.   Fillets of fowls à l'écarlate with Su-
Turban of ox-palates, au gratin.   prème sauce.
Fillets of widgeons, à la Gasconne.   Sweetbreads larded, à la Monarque.
Calf's-ears, à la Tortuë.   Quenelles of partridge, à l'Allemande.

Second Course.

Hares.   [2 *Roasts.*]   Black game.

Small fondus in cases.   [2 *Removes.*]   Polish Baba.

Sultana of spun sugar.   [2 *Flanks.*]   Meringue, à la Parisiènne.

8 *Entremêts:*

Truffles, à la Piémontaise.   Variegated jelly, à la Victoria.
Crayfish, à la Poulette.   Bavarian coffee cream.
Seakale with white sauce.   Apricot nougats.
Brussels sprouts with Maître d'hôtel   Mirlitons.
    sauce.

DINNER FOR 24 PERSONS. *February.*

Purée of turnips, à la Jardinière. [2 *Soups.*] Barley in consommé, à la Princesse.

John-Dory, Dutch sauce. [3 *Fishes.*] Salmon, à la Régence.
Fried smelts.

Calf's head, à la Financière. [2 *Removes.*] Chickens, à la Montmorency.

Fillet of beef, à la Napolitaine. [2 *Flanks.*] Grenada ham, with spinach.

8 *Entrées:*
2 Lamb Cutlets, à la Chêvreuse. 2 Fillets of Woodcocks, à la Valençay.
2 Scollops of fowls, with cucumbers. 2 Timbales of macaroni, à la Chasseur.

SECOND COURSE.

Partridges. [2 *Roasts.*] Wild Ducks.

Talmouses with cheese. [2 *Removes.*] Iced Pudding, à la Prince Albert.

Croquante of Ratafias. [2 *Flanks.*] Cake, à la Parisiènne.

12 *Entremêts.*
French truffles, au champagne. Braized celery, à l'Espagnole.
Scolloped oysters in small shells. Brocoli, with Béchamel sauce.
Aspic, à la Reine. Mayonaise of fillets of soles.
Bavarian cream of preserved rasberries. Pine-apple jelly.
Mosaic tartlets of apricots. Neapolitan cake, à la Chantilly.
Macédoine jelly. Charlotte à la Russe.

DINNER FOR 36 PERSONS. *February.*

Purée of partridges, à la Condé. [4 *Soups.*] 2 Turtle, Spring soup.

Fried smelts. Soles, à la Parisiènne. [4 *Fishes.*] Crimped turbot, lobster sauce, fried fillets of whiting.
Roast Baron of lamb, à la Macédoine. [2 *Removes.*] Pheasants, à la Dauphine.
Croquettes, à la Reine, and oyster croustades.

Paté-chaud of snipes, à la Périgueux. [2 *Flanks.*] Chartreuse of tendons of veal.

12 *Entrées:*
2 Mutton Cutlets, à la Soubise. 2 Fillets of rabbits, à la D'Uxelles.
2 Scollops of partridges, à la Victoria. 2 Boudins of fowl, à la Sefton.
2 Lamb's-ears, à la Financière. 2 Croustades of nouilles, with purée of woodcocks.

SECOND COURSE.

Black Game. [3 *Roasts.*] Teal, Ducklings.

Flemish gauffres, Fondu of cheese. [3 *Removes.*] Iced pudding, à la Kinnaird.
Millefeuilles cake, à la Chantilly. [2 *Flanks.*] Ham of Savoy cake, garnished with jelly.

16 *Entremêts.*
2 Croûtes of mushrooms. 2 Asparagus, with butter sauce.
2 Darnes of salmon, with Montpellier-butter. 2 Lobster salads.
2 Cherry cheeses with cream. 2 Punch jellies.
2 Vol-au-vents of apricots.
2 Darioles, with candied orange-flowers.

Dinner for 6 Persons. *March.*
Brown purée of turnips soup.

1 *Fish.*
Soles, à la Colbert.

Boiled fowl, with brocoli.   [2 *Removes.*]   Roast leg of lamb.

2 *Entrées :*
Mutton cutlets, sautées, with a purée   Vol-au-vent of godiveau, à la Financière.
of potatoes.

Second Course.
Roast widgeon.

3 *Entremêts :*
Eggs brouillés, with asparagus-peas.   Tapioca pudding, custard sauce.
German tourte of apples.

Dinner for 6 Persons. *March.*
Purée of vegetables, à la Croissy.

1 *Fish.*
Salt Fish, à la Béchamel.

Roast saddle of mutton.   [2 *Removes.*]   Partridge pie, à l'Anglaise.

2 *Entrées :*
Chickens, à la Lyonnaise.   Blanquette of sweetbreads, garnished
with croquettes.

Second Course
Roast larks.

3 *Entremêts :*
Salsifis with white sauce.   Bavarian cream of Noyeau.
Duchess loaves with rasberry jam.

Dinner for 6 Persons. *March.*
Soup à la Bonne-femme.

1 *Fish.*
Fillets of whitings, à la Provençale.

Roast fillet of beef, Poivrade [2 *Removes.*] Cushion of veal, à la Jardinière.
sauce.

2 *Entrées :*
Partridges, à la Bréziliènne.   Quenelles of fowl, à l'essence.

Second Course.
Roast wild duck.

3 *Entremêts.*
Brussels-sprouts sautés with butter.   Orange jelly, à la Française.
Genoese cakes with almonds.

DINNER FOR 6 PERSONS. *March.*

Potato soup, à la crême.

1 *Fish.*
Fillets of salmon, à la ravigotte.

Chickens, à l'Italiènne.　　[2 *Removes.*] Roast beef, horse-radish sauce.

2 *Entrées:*

Pigeons, à la Crapaudine, with Pi-　　Carbonnades of mutton, à la Jardi-
quante sauce.　　　　　　　　　　　　　nière.

SECOND COURSE.
Roast Plovers.

3 *Entremêts:*

Macaroni au gratin.　　　　　　　Lemon pudding.
Chocolate custards.

DINNER FOR 6 PERSONS. *March.*

Paysanne soup.

1 *Fish.*
Crimped skate fried, with capers' sauce.

Braized neck of mutton, à [2 *Removes.*] Lark pudding, à la Chipolata.
l'Irlandaise.
2 *Entrées:*
Timbale of raviolis, à la Romaine.　　　Chickens, à l'Allemande.

SECOND COURSE.
Roast Duckling.

3 *Entremêts:*

Scolloped muscles.　　　　　　Cranberry tart.
Lemon and cinnamon cream.

DINNER FOR 6 PERSONS. *March*

Cream of rice soup, à la Victoria.

1 *Fish.*
Fried Eels, à la Tartare.

Lamb's-head, à la Gallimauffré. [2 *Removes.*]　　Fowl, à la Dauphine.

2 *Entrées:*

Beefsteaks, à la Française.　　　　　Braized duck, à la Nivernaise.

SECOND COURSE.
Roast Pigeons.

3 *Entremêts:*

Jerusalem artichokes, à l'Espagnole.　　Cherry bread, à la Gotha.
Puff-paste tartlets of rasberry-jam.

DINNER FOR 12 PERSONS. *April.*

Spring soup.	[2 *Soups.*]	Bisque of crayfish, à la Malmesbury.
Crimped salmon, with parsley and butter sauce.	[2 *Fishes.*]	Perch, à la Stanley.
Calf's-head, à la Beauveau.	[2 *Removes.*]	Poulards and tongue, à la Macédoine.

4 *Entrées:*

Lamb cutlets, à la Duchesse.	Boudins of lobster, à la Cardinal.
Fillets of fowls with asparagus-peas, Suprême sauce.	Fritôt of spring chickens, with Poivrade sauce.

SECOND COURSE.

Guinea fowls, larded.	[2 *Roasts.*]	Ducklings.
Steamed soufflée.	[2 *Removes.*]	Compiégne cake.

6 *Entremêts:*

Brocoli with white sauce.	Gooseberry cream.
Spinach in small crôustades.	Flan of pears and rice, à la Condé.
Loaves, à la Parisiènne.	Cherry jelly.

DINNER FOR 12 PERSONS. *April.*

Quenélles of fowl in consommé.	[2 *Soups.*]	Purée of young carrots, à la Faubonne.
Spey trout, Dutch sauce.	[3 *Fishes.*]	Fillets of soles, à la Bagration.
Roast fore-quarter of lamb.	[2 *Removes.*]	Chickens, à la Printanière.

4 *Entrées:*

Veal cutlets, à a Dreux.	Fillets of mutton larded, with Tomata sauce.
Scollops of fowls with cucumbers.	Boudins of rabbit, à la Pompadour.

SECOND COURSE.

Pigeons.	[2 *Roasts.*]	Turkey poults.
Ramequins, à la Sefton.	[2 *Removes.*]	Biscuits glacés, in cases.

6 *Entremêts.*

Seakale with white sauce.	Gooseberry tartlets.
Mushrooms, au gratin.	Pudding, à la Viènnoise.
Vol-au-vent of Macédoine.	Marbled cream.

DINNER FOR 16 PERSONS. *April.*

Macaroni clear soup. [2 *Soups.*] Purée of spinach, à la Condé.

Crimped turbot, lobster sauce. [2 *Fishes.*] Matelotte of eels, à la Bordelaise.

Braized saddle of lamb, à la Jar- [2 *Removes.*] Poulards, à l'Estragon.
dinière.

Shrimp patties, to be handed round.

---

6 *Entrées:*

Mutton cutlets with new potatoes. Sweetbreads larded, à la Parisiènne.
Fillets of pigeons, à la Dauphine, with Fillets of ducklings, à la Bigarade
French-beans. Quenelles of fowl, à la Périgueux.
Quails, au gratin, with Financière sauce.

SECOND COURSE.

Peahen larded. [2 *Roasts.*] Green goose.

Brioche with cheese. [2 *Removes.*] Chocolate soufflée.

---

8 *Entremêts.*

Asparagus with white sauce. Vanilla cream.
French-beans, à la Poulette. Apricot tartlets.
Macédoine jelly. Porcupine of apples meringuée.
Pudding, à la Prince de Galles. Lobster salad.

DINNER FOR 16 PERSONS. *April.*

Clear turtle soup. [2 *Soups.*] Soup, à la Hollandaise.

Haddocks, egg sauce. [2 *Fishes.*] Turbot, à la crême, au gratin.

Lobster patties, to be handed round.

Fillet of beef, à l'Allemande. [2 *Removes.*] Capon, à la Perigueux.

---

6 *Entrées:*

Braized carbonnades of mutton, à la Fricandeau, with purée of spinach.
Macédoine. Casserole of rice, à la Reine, with
Lamb cutlets bread-crumbed, cucum- plovers' eggs.
ber sauce. Paté-chaud of quails, à la Bourguig-
Fillets of pigeons, à la de Luynes. notte.

SECOND COURSE.

Spring chickens. [2 *Roasts.*] Leverets.

Small fondus, in cases. [2 *Removes.*] Pine-apple fritters.

---

8 *Entremêts:*

Crôtes with mushrooms. Bavarian strawberry cream.
Asparagus-peas, à la Française. Cheese cakes.
Vol-au-vent of rhubarb. Calf's-feet wine jelly.
Savarin cake. Salade de volaille.

DINNER FOR 20 PERSONS. *April.*

Chiffonade spring soup. [2 *Soups.*] Bisque of crab, à la Fitzhardinge

John-Dory, Dutch sauce. [2 *Fishes.*] Salmon, à la Royale.

Kromeskys of fowl, à la Russe.

Braized rump of beef, à la Polo- [2 *Removes.*] Chickens, à la Chivry.
naise.

8 *Entrées:*

Mutton cutlets braized, with a purée   Vol-au-vent, à la Nèsle.
of chestnuts.   Fillets of fowls, à la Maréchale.
Scollops of leverets, à la Périgueux.   Lamb's-ears farcied, à la Dauphine.
Compôte of pigeons, à la Bourguignotte. Grenadins of veal, with purée of
                                        spinach.
Timbale of macaroni, à la Mazarin.

SECOND COURSE.

Quails. [2 *Roasts.*] Ducklings.

Vol-au-vent of damsons with   [2 *Removes.*]   Semolina soufflée.
iced custard.
Nougat, à la Parisiènne.   [2 *Flanks.*]   Brioche with candied citron.

8 *Entremêts:*

French beans, à la Maître d'hôtel.   Brocoli with Parmesan cheese.
Bastion of eels with Montpellier butter. Aspic of plovers' eggs.
Pine-apple cream.   Strawberry jelly.
Parisian loaves.   Green-currant tartlets.

DINNER FOR 20 PERSONS. *April.*

Spring soup. [2 *Soups.*] Bisque of quails à la Prince
                            Albert.
Mackerel, Fennel sauce. [2 *Fishes.*] Trout, à la Parisiènne.

Rissoleé, à la Milanaise.

Poulards, à la Printanière.   [2 *Removes.*] Roast fillet of beef larded, Ma-
                                            deira sauce.
8 *Entrées.*

Fillets of chickens, with a purée of Epigramme of Lamb, with aspara-
truffles.   gus-peas.
Cutlets of sweetbreads, à la D'Uxélles. Boudins of fowl, à la Reine.
Noix of veal, à la St. Cloud.   Fillets of rabbits larded, with a pu-
Timbale of nouilles, à la Chasseur.   rée of endives.
Border of potato, garnished with scollops of leverets.

SECOND COURSE.

Guinea fowls. [2 *Roasts.*] Pigeons.

Ramequins with Gruyère. [2 *Removes.*] Iced pudding, à la Princesse
                                        Alice.
Cake, à la Victoria.   [2 *Flanks.*] Large Meringue, à la Chantilly.

8 *Entremêts:*

Perigord truffles (boiled in mirepoix). Aspic of fillets of fowl, à la Belle-vue.
Asparagus with white sauce.   Pomegranate jelly.
Lobster salad with a border of plovers' Bavarian coffee cream.
eggs.   Tourte of apricots, à l'Allemande.
Croquante of Genoese cake.

DINNER FOR 8 PERSONS. *May.*

Bisque of Prawns.

Trout, Dutch sauce. [2 *Fishes.*] White bait.

Roast poulard, à l'Italiènne. [2 *Removes.*] Boiled leg of lamb and spinach.

Patties of ox-piths au jus.

2 *Entrées:*
Pigeon cutlets, à la Dauphine. Scollops of fillets of beef, à la Claremont.

SECOND COURSE.

Plovers' eggs, plain. [2 *Roasts.*] Green-goose.

1 *Remove.*
Apricot soufflé.

4 *Entremêts:*
Green peas plain. Burnt cream, au caramel.
New potatoes, au gratin. Strawberry tartlets.

DINNER FOR 8 PERSONS. *May.*

Purée of green peas, à la Victoria.

Scollops of fillets of gurnets, [2 *Fishes.*] Boiled mackerel, à la Maître
Dutch sauce.   d'hôtel.
Poulard and rice. [2 *Removes.*] Beefsteak pie.

Mazarine patties.

2 *Entrées:*
Lambs' sweetbreads larded, with purée Blanquette of fowls, garnished with
of asparagus.   cucumbers farcied.

SECOND COURSE.

Russian salad. [2 *Roasts.*] Leveret.

1 *Remove.*
Brown-bread pudding, cherry sauce.

4 *Entremêts:*
French beans, à la Poulette. Marygolds of puff-paste.
Macaroni, à la Crème. Célestine charlotte of strawberries.

DINNER FOR 8 PERSONS. *May.*

Purée of fowls, à la Célestine.

Crimped soles, Dutch Sauce.   [2 *Fishes.*]   Red mullets in cases with fine-
herbs.

Chickens, à la Reine.   [2 *Removes.*]   Ribs of beef, à la mode.

Lobster patties.

2 *Entrées:*

Boudins of rabbit, à la Richelieu.   Mutton cutlets with stewed peas.

SECOND COURSE.

Crayfish plain.   [2 *Roasts.*]   Ducklings.

1 *Remove.*

Pancakes with apricot.

4 *Entremêts:*

New potatoes, à la crème.   D'Artois of strawberry-jam.
Macaroni, au gratin.   Maraschino jelly.

DINNER FOR 8 PERSONS. *May.*

Désclignac soup, with asparagus points.

Small turbot, lobster sauce.   [2 *Fishes.*]   Epigramme of fillets of trout.

Braized green-goose, à la Fla- [2 *Removes.*]   Roast quarter of lamb, à la
mande.   Maître d'hôtel.

Soft roes of mackerel fried in batter, Gascony sauce.

2 *Entrées:*

Chickens, à la Florentine.   Tendons of veal, with a Macédoine of
vegetables.

SECOND COURSE.

Canapés of anchovies.   [2 *Roasts.*]   Turkey-poult larded.

1 *Remove.*

Flemish gauffres.

4 *Entremêts:*

Seakale, à la Béchamel.   Orange-flower cream.
New potatoes, àla Maître d'hôtel.   Raspberry tartlets.

DINNER FOR 36 PERSONS. *May.*

Turtle soup (clear).
Soup, à la Sevigné.   [4 *Soups.*]   Turtle soup.(full).
Purée of fowls, à la Princesse.

Crimped salmon, lobster sauce.
White bait.   [4 *Fishes.*]   Turbot, à la Vatel.
White bait.

Granada ham braized, garnished
with a Macédoine.   [4 *Removes.*]   Fillet of beef larded, à la Napolitaine.
Calf's-head, à la Tortuë.   Poulards, à la Godard.

Kromeskys oı lobsters, to be handed round.

---

12 *Entrées:*

2 Fillets of quails, à l'anciènne.
2 Scollops of Fowls with cucumbers.
2 Lamb cutlets bread-crumbed, garnished with purée of mushrooms.

2 Quenelles of fowl, à l'essence.
2 Patés-chauds of leverets, à la Perigueux.
2 Timbales of raviolis, à la Romaine.

===

SECOND COURSE.

Pigeons larded.   [3 *Roasts.*]   Spring chickens.
Peahen larded.

Krapfen with apricot.   [3 *Removes.*]   Fondu of Parmesan.
Iced pudding, à la Chesterfield.

Savoy cake, à la Vanille.   [2 *Flanks.*]   Sultana of spun sugar.

---

16 *Entremêts:*

2 Groups of large Périgord truffles.
2 Stewed peas, à la Française.
2 Asparagus with white sauce.
2 Cherry tartlets.

2 Aspics garnished with plovers' eggs.
2 Red currant and raspberry-jellies.
2 Pine-apple cheeses, à la Chantilly.
2 Peaches au riz, à la Condé.

Dinner for 28 Persons. *May*

Jardinière soup. [3 *Soups.*] Bisque of prawns, à la Cerito.
Turtle soup.

Crimped trout, lobster sauce. [3 *Fishes.*] Sturgeon à la Régence.
Fillets of whitings, à la Horly.

Marrow patties, with fine-herbs sauce.

Poulards, à la Dauphine. [2 *Removes.*] Baron of lamb, à la Montmorency.

Small ribs of beef braized, à [2 *Flanks.*] Braized ham, garnished with
la Milanaise. French beans.

8 *Entrées :*

2 Mutton cutlets braized, à la Russe. 2 Fillets of fowls larded and glacés,
2 Fillets of pigeons, à la Villeroi, gar- garnished with a Parisian ragout.
nished with a Bourguignotte ragout. 2 Veal kernels glacés, garnished with
a purée of green peas.

Second Course.

Turkey-poults larded. [3 *Roasts.*] Ducklings.
Quails.

Talmouses of cheese. [3 *Removes.*] Pancake soufflés.
Cabinet pudding.

Croquante of oranges. [2 *Flanks.*] Meringue, à la Parisiènne.

12 *Entremêts :*

2 French-beans sautés with butter. 2 Italian salads in decorated aspic-
2 Asparagus, white sauce. borders.
2 Macédoine jellies. 2 Célestine strawberry creams.
2 Red-currant and raspberry tartlets.

DINNER FOR 6 PERSONS. *June.*
Green-peas soup, à la Condé.

---

1 *Fish.*
Baked whitings, with fine-herbs.

Chicken pie, à l'Anglaise.   [2 *Removes.*] Breast of veal and stewed-peas.

---

2 *Entrées:*
Mutton cutlets, à la Milanaise.   Rabbit curry, in a border of rice.

===

SECOND COURSE.
Roast pigeons.

---

3 *Entremêts:*
Stewed-peas, à la Française.   Bavarian strawberry cream.
Puff-paste royals.

DINNER FOR 6 PERSONS. *June.*
Clear rice soup.

---

1 *Fish.*
Fillets of mackerel, à la Maître d'Hôtel.

Poulard, à l'Ivoire.   [2 *Removes.*] Braized neck of mutton, à l'Allemande.

---

2 *Entrées:*
Minced beef, à la Polonaise.   Tourte of godiveau, à la Financière.

===

SECOND COURSE.
Roast Duckling.

Cauliflowers with white sauce.   Duchess loaves with apricot-jam.
Timbale of ground rice.

DINNER FOR 6 PERSONS. *June.*
Bonne femme soup.

---

1 *Fish.*
Broiled trout, Dutch sauce.

Roast leg of Welsh mutton. [2 *Removes.*]   Noix of Veal, à la crème.

---

2 *Entrées:*
Mince of fowl, with poached eggs.   Fillets of beef in their glaze, garnished with stewed-peas.

===

SECOND COURSE.
Roast fowl.

---

3 *Entremêts.*
Asparagus with sauce.   Apricot nougats.
Maraschino jelly with strawberries.

Dinner for 8 Persons. *June.*

Macaroni soup, à la Royale.

---

1 *Fish.*
Soles with fine-herbs.

Pigeon pie, à l'Anglaise.   [2 *Removes.*] Roast fillet of beef, à la Provençale.

Croquettes of sweetbreads.

---

2 *Entrées:*
Lamb's-feet, à la Poulette.   Capilotade of fowl with mushrooms.

===

SECOND COURSE.
Lobster, au gratin.   [2 *Roasts.*]   Green-goose.

---

1 *Remove.*
Peach fritters.

---

4 *Entremêts:*
Cherry tart.   Green-peas plain.
Custards in glasses.   Aspic, à la Reine.

Dinner for 8 Persons. *June.*

Soup, à la Colbert.

---

1 *Fish.*
Paupiettes of fillets of gurnets, à la Cardinal.

Braized ham, with spinach.   [2 *Removes.*] Roast fillet of veal, à l'Anglaise.

Crôustades à la Monglas.

---

2 *Entrées:*
Fricassée of chickens, à la Bour-   Mutton cutlets, à la Maintenon.
guignonne.

===

SECOND COURSE.
Plovers' eggs plain.   [2 *Roasts.*]   Guinea fowls.

---

1 *Remove.*
Soufflé of rice.

---

4 *Entremêts:*
Stewed peas, à la Française.   Vol'au'vent garnished with a Macé-
Braized lettuces, à l'Espagnole.   doine of fruits.
Noyau cream.

DINNER FOR 8 PERSONS. *June.*

Soup, à la Ferney.

1 *Fish.*
Spitchcocked eels, with piquante sauce.

Ox-piths fried in batter, with Tomata sauce.

Chickens, à l'Espagnole. [2 *Removes.*] Boiled neck of mutton.

2 *Entrées.*
Lamb cutlets bread-crumbed, with Young rabbits sautés with fine-herbs.
stewed-peas.

SECOND COURSE.

Italian salad. [2 *Roasts.*] Quails.

1 *Remove.*
Fritters, à la Dauphine.

4 *Entremêts :*
French beans, à la crème. Peach jelly.
Crayfish, à la Poulette. Queen's cakes.

DINNER FOR 18 PERSONS. *June.*

Quenelles of rabbit in consommé. [2 *Soups.*] Bisque of lobsters, à la Stanley.

Crimped turbot, lobster sauce. [2 *Fishes.*] Mullets, à la Chesterfield.

White bait.

Chickens, à l'Allemande. [2 *Removes.*] Calf's-head, à la Marigny.

6 *Entrées :*
Crôustades of soft roes of mackerel, à Fillets of ducklings with green-peas-
la Ravigotte. Salmis of quails, à la Bordelaise.
Chartreuse, à la Parisiènne. Veal cutlets larded, with a purée of
Epigramme of lambs' sweetbreads, à endives.
la Macédoine.

SECOND COURSE.

Turkey-poult. [2 *Roasts.*] Leverets.

Ramequins in cases. [2 *Removes.*] Iced pudding, à la Prince of
Wales.
6 *Entremêts :*
Asparagus with sauce. Ginger cream.
New potatoes, à la crème. Vol'au'vent of strawberries and
Cherry jelly garnished with cherries. cream.
Parisian nougats.

DINNER FOR 18 PERSONS. *June.*

Consommé with lettuces and peas. [2 *Soups.*]   Macaroni, à la Medicis.

Salmon trout with parsley and   [2 *Fishes.*]   Sturgeon, à la Beaufort.
   butter sauce.
             Bouchées of whitings, à la Pompadour.

Poulards, à la Belle-vue.   [2 *Removes.*]   Haunch of venison.

6 Entrées:

Mazarine of fat livers, à la Toulouse.   Mutton cutlets braized, à la Niver-
Chartreuse of vegetables, garnished   naise.
   with tendons of veal.   Fillets of fowls, à la Valençay.
                      Lamb's-ears, à la Tortuë.
            Boudins of rabbit, à la Reine.

SECOND COURSE.

Green-goose.   [2 *Roasts.*]   Quails.

Large meringue with iced cream. [2 *Removes.*]   Compiègne cake.

8 Entremêts:

French-beans sautés with butter.   Pine-apple cheese, à la Chantilly.
Stewed-peas, à la Française.   Fanchonettes with vanille.
Red-currant jelly garnished with   Flan of cherries.
   peaches.   Aspic of prawns.
Plovers' eggs.

DINNER FOR 12 PERSONS. *July.*

Vermicelli clear soup.   [2 *Soups.*]   Brown purée of turnips. à la
                                        Condé.
Fried flounders.   [2 *Fishes.*]   Char, à la Génoise.

Noukles, with Parmesan.

Fillet of beef, Chêvreuil sauce. [2 *Removes.*] Chickens and tongue, à la Prin-
                                       tanière.

4 Entrées:

Cutlets of breasts of lamb, à la Ville-   Quenelles of lobster, à la Vertpré.
   roi, with French-beans.   Paté-chaud of young rabbits with
Compote of pigeons with peas.   fine-herbs.

SECOND COURSE.

Peahen larded.   [2 *Roasts.*]   Ducklings.

Parmesan fritters.   [2 *Removes.*]   Polish Baba.

4 Entremêts:

Young broad-beans, à la Poulette.   Peaches with rice, à la Condà.
Aspic of prawns, à la Russe.   Puff-paste platts.

DINNER FOR 12 PERSONS. *July.*

Consommé soup, à la Xavier.   [2 *Soups.*]   Green-peas soup, à la Fabert.

White bait.   [2 *Fishes.*]   Salmon, à l'Ecossaise.

Shrimp patties.

Poulard, à la Godard.   [2 *Removes.*] Necks of lamb larded, à la Macédoine.

4 *Entrées* :

Mutton cutlets bread-crumbed and broiled, with shalot gravy.	Tendons of veal on a border of vegetables, garnished with peas.
Vol'au'vent, à la Financière.	Blanquette of fowls, à l'écarlate.

SECOND COURSE.

Guinea fowls.   [2 *Roasts.*]   Quails.

Omelette soufflée.   [2 *Removes.*]   Coburg cake.

4 *Entremêts* :

Cucumbers farcied, à l'essence	Tourte of currants and raspberries.
Stewed-peas, à la Française.	Blanc-manger.

DINNER FOR 14 PERSONS. *July.*

Spring soup.   [2 *Soups.*] Cream of pearl-barley, à la Printanière.

Crimped pe.ch, Dutch sauce.   [2 *Fishes.*]   Salmon, à la Maréchale.

Rissoles of lamb's brains, à l'Allemande.

Chickens à la Florentine.   [2 *Removes.*] Small ribs of beef, à la Flamande.

4 *Entrées* :

Grenadins of veal with stewed-peas.	Boudins of whitings, with a ragout of crayfish tails.
Cutlets of pigeons, à la Dauphine, garnished with Bourguignotte ragout.	Fricassée of chickens, à la Paysanne.

SECOND COURSE.

Capon.   [2 *Roasts.*]   Leverets.

Puff-paste ramequins.   [2 *Removes.*] Soufflé pudding of semolina.

4 *Entremêts* :

Lobster salad, with plovers' eggs,	Artichokes, à la Lyonnaise.
Charlotte Russe, garnished with fruits.	Vol'au'vent of cherries.

DINNER FOR 14 PERSONS. *July.*

Brûnoise-Printanière.　　　[2 *Soups.*] Bisque of crayfish, à l'Anciènne.

John-Dory, lobster sauce.　　[2 *Fishes.*]　　Trout, à la Chevalière.

Croquettes of ox-palates.

Braized ham with broad-beans. [2 *Removes.*]　　Poulards, à la Périgord.

4 *Entrées:*

Mutton cutlets, à la Pompadour, gar-　Lamb's-sweetbreads larded, with pu-
nished with a Macédoine.　　　　　rée of artichokes.
Scollops of quails with fumet sauce　Fillets of fowls, à la Belle-vue with
and truffles, garnished with small　Suprême and cucumbers.
crôustades of purée.

SECOND COURSE.

Spring-chickens.　　　[2 *Roasts.*]　　　Ducklings.

Dauphine fritters.　　　[2 *Removes.*]　　Vanilla soufflés in cases.

4 *Entremêts:*

French beans, à a Maître d'Hôtel.　Strawberry jelly.
Aspic of plovers' eggs and prawns.　Profitrolles, à la vanille.

DINNER FOR 18 PERSONS. *July.*

Soup à la Dauphine.　　[2 *Soups.*] Purée of asparagus, à la St.
　　　　　　　　　　　　　　　　　George.
Crimped salmon, parsley and [2 *Fishes.*] Fresh-water trout in cases with
butter.　　　　　　　　　　　　　fine-herbs.
Chicken patties, a la Béchamel.

Capon, à la Toulouse.　　[2 *Removes.*] Saddle of lamb, à la Printanière.

6 *Entrées.*

Chartreuse of vegetables, garnished　Scollops of fowls with cucumbers
with braized quails, fumet sauce.　and Suprême sauce.
Turban of fillets of rabbits, à la Royale,　Mutton cutlets braized, garnished
Financière ragout.　　　　　　　with asparagus peas.
Veal kernels, à la Villeroi, garnished　Fillets of ducklings, with French-
with a purée of green-peas.　　　beans and half glaze

SECOND COURSE.

Pigeons.　　　　[2 *Roasts.*]　　　Turkey poults.

Flemish gauffres.　　[2 *Removes.*] Iced pudding, à la Nesselrode.

6 *Entremêts:*

Artichokes, à la Barigoule.　　　Raspberry tartlets.
Stewed-peas, à la Française.　　　Duchess loaves, garnished with
Pine-apple jelly.　　　　　　　　fresh currants.
Peach cheese, à la Chantilly.

DINNER FOR 18 PERSONS. *July.*

Consommé of fowl with que- [2 *Soups.*] Purée of green-peas, à la Ferney.
nelles.

Water-souchet of fillets of soles. [2 *Fishes.*]   Sturgeon, à la Cardinal.

Kromeskys of lobsters.

Poulards, à la Parisiènne.   [2 *Removes.*]   Haunch of venison.

6 *Entrées.*

Mazarine of fillets of whitings, à la Paté chaud of leverets, à la Perigueux.
  Venitiènne.   Scollops of sweetbreads, à la Maré-
Lamb-cutlets, breadcrumbed, with   chale, with purée of mushrooms.
  purée of artichokes.   Fricassée of spring chickens, à la
Fillets of pigeons, à la de Luynes,   urguignonne.
  with a Macédoine of vegetables.

SECOND COURSE.

Green-goose.   [2 *Roasts.*]   Quails.

Brioche with cheese (hot).   [2 *Removes.*] Vol'au'vent of currants and
                                    raspberries, with an iced
                                    custard-cream.

8 *Entreméts :*

Young broad-beans, à la Poulette.   Bavarian cream of pistachios.
Cucumbers farcied, with Espagnole Panachée jelly.
  sauce.   Almond gauffres, filled with straw-
Italian salad in a border of aspic-jelly.   berries and cream.
Darne of salmon, with Montpellier German tourte of apricots.
  butter.

BALL SUPPER FOR 300 PERSONS. *Summer.*

8 *Grosse-pieces, on ornamental stands.*

2 Raised pies of fowls and ham with truffles, garnished with jelly.
2 Gelantines of poulards, with aspic-jelly.

2 Hams ornamented with aspic jelly.
2 Boars'-heads, ornamented with as-pic-jelly.

48 *Cold entrées, dished up on silver plates:*

6 Groups of plovers' eggs, garnished with aspic jelly.
6 Plates of cold roast fowls with do. (cut up).
6 Plates of tongue, in slices, garnished with aspic-jelly.

6 Lobster salads.
6 Mayonaises of fowl.
6 Mayonaises of fillets of salmon.
6 Entrées of lamb-cutlets, à la Belle-vue.
6 Entrées of chaud-froid fricassées of chickens.

36 *Cold roast fowls, and 4 tongues, to be kept in reserve for the purpose of replenishing those entrées as they are eaten.*

8 *Grosse-pieces of pastry, on stands:*

2 Savoy cakes, à la vanille.
2 Nougats of almonds and pistachios.

2 Croquantes.
1 Baba.   1 Victoria cake.

16 *Entremêts of small pastry,*

Cherry tartlets,
Strawberry and apricot tartlets.
Fenchonnettes, with orange flowers.
Genoese cakes, with almonds.
Apricot nougats.
Florentines.
Madelines.
Duchess loaves.

Mecca loaves.
Polish cakes.
Cheese-cakes.
Queen's cakes.
Small meringues.
Almond gauffres.
Puff-paste mosaic tartlets.
Petits-choux, with pistachios.

36 *Moulds of jellies ana creams.*

6 Currant jellies, garnished with peaches.
6 Cherry jellies.
6 Russian Charlottes.

6 Pine-apple jellies.
6 Macédoine jellies.
6 Strawberry Charlottes.

3 *Soups, to be served from the buffet.*

Spring soup.   Vermicelli clear soup.
Purée of fowls or cream of barley.

24 *Hot roast fowls.*

French beans, new potatoes.

Public Dinner for 300 Persons. *Summer.*

Spring soup.   [3 *Soups.*]   Purée of fowls, à la Reine.
Turtle soup (full and clear).*

---

24 *Dishes of Fish.*

6 Turbots, with lobster sauce.   6 Fillets of mackerel, à la Ravigotte.
6 Salmon, Dutch and parsley sauces.   6 Fried fillets of soles.

---

8 Haunches of venison.   48 Roast fowls (hot).

---

48 *Hot Entrées :*

8 Of sweetbreads larded, with purée of artichokes.
8 Of beefsteaks, à la Française.
8 Of scollops of fowls with cucumbers.
8 Of lamb-cutlets breadcrumbed, with Macédoine.
8 Of cutlets of quails, à la Maréchale, with stewed peas.
8 Of chickens, à la Marengo.

---

48 *Cold Entrées :*

8 Of lobster salads.
8 Of fillets of fowls, à la Belle-vue.
8 Of salads of fillets of soles and salmon.
8 Of Mayonaises of chickens.
8 Of sliced galantine with jelly,
8 Of aspics of plovers' eggs.

---

12 *Grosse pieces, on ornamental stands :*

3 Raised pies, garnished with aspic-jelly.
3 Groups of large crayfish.
3 Groups of large périgord truffles.
3 Hams garnished with aspic-jelly.

---

12 *Grosse pieces of pastry, on stands :*

3 Brioches, with dried cherries and candied citron (hot).
3 Cobourg cakes (in high moulds), (hot).
3 Nougats, à la Parisiènne.
Grosse meringues, à la Chantilly.

---

48 *Entremêts of small pastry, on ornamental stands :*

8 Of Genoese cakes, with pistachios and apple-jelly.
8 Of apricot puff-paste tartlets.
8 Of Parisian loaves.
8 Of currant and raspberry tartlets.
8 of Profitrolles (half with coffee, half with chocolate).
8 Of Darioles, à la vanille.

---

48 *Moulds of jellies and creams :*

8 Peach jellies.
8 Cherry jellies.
8 Italian creams and blanc-mangers.
8 Macédoine jellies,
8 Bavarian strawberry creams.
8 Penachée jellies (with apricot cream in the centre).

---

48 *Entremêts of dressed vegetables :*

12 Of new potatoes, à la crème.
12 Of stewed-peas, à la Française.
12 Of artichokes, à l'Italiènne.
12 Of French-beans, à la Maître d'Hôtel.

---

* Serve 12 tureens of turtle, 6 of clear, and 6 of full-dressed turtle; 6 tureens of spring soup, and 6 of purée of fowl, à la Reine.

DINNER FOR 12 PERSONS. *August.*

Désclignac soup. [2 *Soups.*] Purée of carrots, à la Crécy.

Soles, à la Colbert. [2 *Fishes.*] Red mullets à l'Italiênne.

Anchovy patties, à la Mazarin.

Capon, à la Milanaise. [2 *Removes.*] Braized necks of mutton larded, à l'Allemande.

4 *Entrées:*

Blanquette of lamb's-sweetbreads, à   Salmis of grouse, à la Bordelaise.
la Paysanne.   Tourte of whitings, à la Dauphine.

Mutton cutlets, à la Provençale.

SECOND COURSE.

Chickens. [2 *Roasts.*] Wheatears.

Fondu of Parmesan. [2 *Removes.*] Viènnoise pudding.

4 *Entremêts:*

Vegetable marrow, à la crême.   Codling cheese, à la Chantilly.
Potatoes, à la Hollandaise.   Genoese cakes with pistachios.

DINNER FOR 12 PERSONS. *August.*

Macaroni in consommé. [2 *Soups.*] Purée of spinach, à la Beauveau.

Water-souchet of perch. [2 *Fishes.*] Slices of salmon broiled, with
capers sauce.
Patties, au jus.

Roast saddle of mutton. [2 *Removes.*] Grouse pié, à l'Ecossaise.

4 *Entrées.*

Fricassée of chickens, à la Financière. Members of ducks, à la Nivernaise.
Epigramme of lamb, with a purée of   Fillets of leverets larded, with Poi-
potatoes.   vrade sauce.

SECOND COURSE.

Guinea fowls. [2 *Roasts.*] Ruffs and Reeves.

Omelette with apricot. [2 *Removes.*] Cherry bread.

4 *Entremêts:*

French beans, à la Poulette.   Flan of peaches.
Artichokes with white sauce.   Coffee cream.

DINNER FOR 12 PERSONS. *August.*

Consommé of fowl with quenelles. [2 *Soups.*] Hodge-Podge, à l'Ecossaise.

Fried whitings, Dutch sauce. [2 *Fishes.*] Char, à la Parisiènne.

Oyster patties.

Roast haunch of venison. [2 *Removes.*] Capon au gros-sel.

4 *Entrées:*

Chartreuse, à la Cardinal.   Members of chickens, à la Maréchale.
Fricandeau, à la Jardinière.   Mutton cutlets with purée of turnips.

=====

SECOND COURSE.

Peahen larded. [2 *Roasts.*] Grouse.

Custard fritters. [2 *Removes.*] Apple pudding with apricot jam.

4 *Entremêts:*

Vegetable marrow, à l'Espagnole.   Blanc-manger.
Spinach with cream.   Florentines.

DINNER FOR 12 PERSONS. *August.*

Juliènne soup. [2 *Soups.*] Oyster soup, à la Plessy.

Brill and Shrimp sauce. [2 *Fishes.*] Trout, à l'Aurore.

Lobster patties.

Roast capon, à la Financière. [2 *Removes.*] Necks of red deer, à la St. Andrew.

4 *Entrées:*

Grouse. à la Richelieu.   Ox-cheek braized, à la Jardinière.
Quenelles of fowls, à la Toulouse.   Timbale of raviolis, à la Romaine.

=====

SECOND COURSE.

Ducklings. [2 *Roasts.*] Wheatears.

Pancakes with apricot. [2 *Removes.*] Iced biscuits in cases.

4 *Entremêts:*

Cucumbers, à la Poulette.   Kirschenwasser jelly.
Artichokes, à la Provençale.   Meringues with cream and strawberries.

DINNER FOR 12 PERSONS. *August.*

Brûnoise soup.   [2 *Soups.*]   Grouse soup, à l'Ecossaise.

Crimped salmon, Dutch sauce.   [2 *Fishes.*]   Matelotte of soles, à la Plessy.

Tourte of Godiveau, à la Ciboulette.

Capon, à la Chivry.   [2 *Removes.*]   Breast of veal, à la Windsor.

4 *Entrées*:

Crôustade- of bread, garnished with scollops of fat livers, à l'Epicuri-ènne.

Chickens sautés with fine-herbs.

Fillets of mutton larded, garnished with fried potatoes, Poivrade sauce.

Fillets of rabbits, à la D'Uxelles.

SECOND COURSE.

Turkey-poults.   [2 *Roasts.*]   Leveret.

Ratafia soufflé.   [2 *Removes.*]   Rice croquettes.

4 *Entremêts*:

Broiled mushrooms.   Eggs à la neige, flavored with orange-flowers.
Stewed peas, à la Française.
Pears in tartlets (whole).

DINNER FOR 12 PERSONS. *August.*

Consommé with Italian paste. [2 *Soups.*] Soup of gratinated crusts, à la Ferneuse.
Fried fillets of trout.   [2 *Fishes.*] Stewed carp, à l'Anglaise.

Oysters fried in batter.

Roast neck of venison.   [2 *Removes.*] Chicken pie, à la Reine.

4 *Entrées*:

Tendons of veal, à la Dauphine, with stewed peas.
Fillets of fowls with truffles, Suprême sauce.

Braized carbonnades of mutton à la Richelieu.
Salmis of grouse, à l'Anciènne.

SECOND COURSE.

Dottrel.   [2 *Roasts.*]   Guinea-fowls.

Ramequins.   [2 *Removes.*]   Krapfen with apricot.

4 *Entremêts*:

Macédoine of vegetables.   Condé cakes.
Russian salad.   Plum Charlotte.

DINNER FOR 24 PERSONS, RUSSIAN STYLE. *September.*

Macaroni, à la St. Piérre.   [3 *Soups.*]   Jardinière clear soup.
                                Turtle.

Fillets of salmon, à la Ravigotte. [3 *Fishes.*]   Pike, à la Chambord.
                                Turbot, lobster sauce.

Kromeskys of oysters.

Ham with French-beans.   [3 *Removes.*]   Chickens, à la Belle-vue.
                                Haunch of venison.

6 *Entrées:*

2 Of mutton cutlets, à la Soubise.   2 Of partridges with fine-herbs.
                2 Of quenelles of fowl with essence.

SECOND COURSE.

Quails.   [3 *Roasts.*]   Capon.
            Grouse.

Fondu of Parmesan.   [3 *Removes.*]   Brown-bread pudding.
                Iced cake, à la Stanley.

8 *Entremêts.*

2 Of artichokes, à la Provencale.   2 Of peach-jellies.
2 Of apricot tartlets.   2 Of Russian salads.

DINNER FOR 24 PERSONS, RUSSIAN STYLE. *September.*

Soup à la Colbert.   [3 *Soups.*]   White purée of turnips.
                        Giblet soup.

Fillets of gurnets, à l'Italiènne. [3 *Fishes.*]   Fried soles.
                Crimped cod with oyster sauce.

Patties, à la Béchamel.

Boiled leg of mutton.   [4 *Removes.*] Black game, à la Norwégienne.
                2 Roast geese, à l'Anglaise.

6 *Entrées.*

2 Of sweetbreads larded, with purée of   2 Of cutlets of young partridges, à
    endives.   la Maréchale.
            2 Of haricot of venison, à la Nivernaise.

SECOND COURSE.

Wheatears.   [3 *Roasts.*]   Pigeons.
            Poulard.

Parmesan fritters.   [3 *Removes.*]   Pancakes soufflés.
                Pudding, à la Nesselrode.

8 *Entremêts:*

2 Of French-beans sautés with butter.   2 Of pears with rice, à la Condé.
2 Of scolloped lobsters au gratin.   2 Of Vol'au'vents of greengages.

DINNER FOR 16 PERSONS. *September.*

Vermicelli, à la Royale.   [2 *Soups.*]   Ox-tail soup.

Cod, à la Béchamel.   [2 *Fishes.*]   Broiled haddocks, Dutch sauce.

Fowls and tongue with cauli- [2 *Removes.*] Haunch of red deer, à la Kin-
flowers.   naird.

6 *Entrées:*

Fillets of grouse, breadcrumbed, à la   Crôustade, garnished with lamb's-
Maître d'Hôtel.   brains, with Matelotte sauce.
Mutton patties, à la Windsor.   Tourte of scollops of lobsters, à la
Minced beef, à la Polonaise.   Cardinal.

Chickens sautés, à la Lyonnaise.

SECOND COURSE.

Black-game.   [2 *Roasts.*]   Partridges.

Sweet omelette.   [2 *Removes.*]   Chestnut pudding.

6 *Entremêts:*

Tomatas au gratin.   Bavarian chocolate cream.
Fried artichokes.   D'Artois of apple marmalade.
Lemon-jelly, à la Russe.   Petits-choux, with almonds.

DINNER FOR 16 PERSONS. *September.*

Purée of endives, à la crème.   [2 *Soups.*]   Giblet soup, à l'Irlandaise.

Eels, à la Tartare.   [2 *Fishes.*]   Salmon, with lobster sauce.

Veal and ham pie.   [2 *Removes.*]   Braized goose, à l' Estouffade.

6 *Entrées.*

Ox-piths in small cases, with fine-herbs.   Partridges, à la Périgueux.
Crôustades, à la Milanaise.   Quenelles of whitings, with crayfish
Vol'au'vent of lamb's-feet, à la Pou-   sauce.
lette.

Blanquette of fowl with mushrooms.

SECOND COURSE.

Capon.   [2 *Roasts.*]   Leveret.

Puff-paste ramequins.   [2 *Removes.*]   Tapioca pudding.

6 *Entremêts:*

Spinach au jus.   Noyau-jelly.
Vegetable marrow, à la Béchamel.   Burnt-almond cream.
Charlotte of apricots.   Cheese-cakes.

DINNER FOR 12 PERSONS. *October.*

Juliènne soup.	[2 *Soups.*]	Mock turtle soup.

Cod's head, baked.	[2 *Fishes.*]	Fillets of soles, à la Dièppoise.

Ham, with spinach.	[2 *Removes.*]	Roast fillet of veal, à la Macédoine.

4 *Entrées :*

Suprême of fowls, à la Talleyrand.   Mutton cutlets, à l'Indiènne.
Oyster patties, à la Sefton.   Fillets of woodcocks, à l'Anciènne.

SECOND COURSE.

Hare.	[2 *Roasts.*]	Pheasants

Brioche, with cheese.	[2 *Removes.*]	Soufflé of chocolate.

4 *Entremêts :*

Mushrooms, à la Provençale.   German apple tourte.
Scolloped crayfish.   Pine-apple jelly.

DINNER FOR 12 PERSONS. *October.*

Purée of spinach, à la Conti.	[2 *Soups.*]	Soup, à la Paysanne.

Fried soles, shrimp sauce.	[2 *Fishes.*]	Crimped cod, à la Séville.

Roast saddle of mutton.	[2 *Removes.*]	Partridge pie, à l'Anglaise.

4 *Entrées :*

Fillets of teal, à la Provençale.   Scollopes of beef sautées, with oyster sauce.
Ballotines of legs of chickens, à la Financière.   Croquettes of sweetbreads, à l'Allemande.

SECOND COURSE.

Larks.	[2 *Roasts.*]	Grouse.

Omelette, with Parmesan.	[2 *Removes.*]	Pancakes, with apricot.

4 *Entremêts :*

Crôutes, with mushrooms.   Damson cheese, à la Chantilly.
Macaroni, au gratin.   Apple mosaic tartlets.

DINNER FOR 12 PERSONS. *October*

| Consommé, with rice. | [2 *Soups.*] | Brown purée of turnips |

| Brill, with lobster sauce. | [2 *Fishes.*] | Cod's sounds, à la Provençale. |

| Braized ribs of beef, à la mode. | [2 *Removes.*] | Roast sucking pig, à l'Anglaise. |

4 *Entrées:*

Scollops of young rabbits in cases, with fine-herbs.   Salmis of partridges, with mushrooms.

Chickens, with Lasagnes, à l'Italiènne

Fricandeau, with purée of endives.

SECOND COURSE.

| Poulard. | [2 *Roasts.*] | Snipes. |

| Croquettes of chestnuts. | [2 *Removes.*] | Pine apple pudding. |

4 *Entremêts*

Brussels sprouts, dressed with butter.   Puff-paste Royals.

Scolloped mussels, au gratin.   Apple charlotte.

DINNER FOR 12 PERSONS. *October.*

| Consommé with Lasagnes. | [2 *Soups.*] | Calves'-tails soup, à la Royale. |

| Fried smelts, anchovy sauce. | [2 *Fishes.*] | Haddocks, egg sauce. |

| Boiled leg of mutton, à l'Anglaise. | [2 *Removes.*] | Braized pheasants, with cabbages. |

4 *Entrées:*

Kromeskys of oysters, à la Russe.   Boudins of rabbit, à la D'Artois.

Pork cutlets, à la sauce Robert.   Chickens sautés, à l'Algeriènne.

SECOND COURSE.

| Hare. | [2 *Roasts.*] | Partridges. |

| Spanish puffs. | [2 *Removes.*] | Apple pudding. |

4 *Entremêts:*

Potatoes, à la Maître d'Hôtel.   Nougats of apricot.

Tomatas, with fine-herbs, au gratin.   Coffee cream.

DINNER FOR 12 PERSONS. *October.*

Brûnoise soup. [2 *Soups.*] Hare soup, à la St. George.

Fillets of whitings, à la Royale. [2 *Fishes.*] Baked gurnets, with Piquante sauce.

Capon, with rice. [2 *Removes.*] Roast haunch of mutton.

---

4 *Entrées.*

Salmis of woodcocks, à la Minute.   Fillets of beef sautés in their glaze.
Polpettes of rabbit, à l'Italiènne.   Mince and grill of fowl, à la Béchamel.

SECOND COURSE.

Larks. [2 *Roasts.*] Pheasants.

Coburg cake. [2 *Removes.*] Iced pudding, à la Duchess of Kent.

---

4 *Entremêts:*

Spinach, au jus.   Apples, à la Portuguaise.
Eggs brouillés, with truffles.   Russian lemon-jelly.

DINNER FOR 12 PERSONS. *October.*

Flemish soup. [2 *Soups.*] Purée of pheasant, à la Condé.

Slices of Cod, broiled, à la Maî- [2 *Fishes.*] Fillets of gurnets, à l'Italiènne.
tre d'Hôtel.
Chickens, à l'Ivoire. [2 *Removes.*] Haunch of roebuck, à l'Alle-mande.

---

4 *Entrées:*

Veal cutlets, bread-crumbed, with pu- Partridges, à la Brésiliénne.
rée of spinach.   Quenelles of fowl, à la Maréchale.
Haricôt of mutton, à la Nivernaise.

SECOND COURSE.

Black game. [2 *Roasts.*] Golden plovers.

Parmesan fritters. [2 *Removes.*] Ginger pudding.

---

4 *Entremêts:*

Jerusalem artichokes, à la Béchamel.   Punch jelly.
Portugal onions, à l'Espagnole.   Genoese cakes, à la Chantillly.

DINNER FOR 18 PERSONS. *November.*

Juliènne. [2 *Soups.*] Bisque of snipes, à la Bonne-bouche.

Crimped skate fried, with capers' [2 *Fishes.*] Matelotte of carp and eels.
sauce.

Pheasants, à la Financière. [2 *Removes.*] Braized rump of beef, à la Fla-mande.

6 *Entrées:*

Pâté-chaud of partridges, à la Chasseur. Blanquette of fowl, with truffles.
Chartreuse, à la Parisiènne. Braized carbonnades of mutton, à la
Pork cutlets, à L'Aurore. Brêtonne.
Fillets of grouse, with fumet sauce.

SECOND COURSE.

Capon. [2 *Roasts.*] Teal.

Cheese fondu. [2 *Removes.*] Apple fritters.

6 *Entremêts:*

Macaroni, à la Napolitaine. Russian charlotte, à la vanille.
Turnips glacés, with sugar. Darioles, with ratafias.
Orange-jelly, à l'Anglaise. Bread-and-butter pastry.

DINNER FOR 18 PERSONS. *November.*

Consommé of pheasant, with [2 *Soups.*] Cream of pearl barley, à la Vic-
quenelles. toria.

Spitchcocked eels. [2 *Fishes.*] Crimped haddocks, Dutch sauce.

Roast haunch of mutton. [2 *Removes.*] Black game, à la Montagnarde.

6 *Entrées:*

Pâté-chaud of ox-palates, à l'Italiènne. Quenelles of fowl, à la D'Orsay.
Chartreuse of tendons of veal, gar- Mutton cutlets, à la Provençale.
nished with a Jardinière. Scollops of fowls, with truffles
Fritôt of chickens, with Tomata sauce.

SECOND COURSE.

Wild ducks. [2 *Roasts.*] Partridges.

Krapfen. [2 *Removes.*] Coffee soufflé.

6 *Eniremêts:*

Group of Périgord truffles. Mirlitons, with apricot.
Brocoli, with Parmesan cheese. Lemon-jelly in quarters.
Pear with rice, à la Condé. Maraschino Bavarian cream.

Dinner for 18 Persons. *November.*

Macaroni clear soup.   [2 *Soups.*]   Purée of celery, à la crème.

Fillets of perch, fried, Dutch   [2 *Fishes.*]   Carp, à la Chambord.
     sauce.
Poulards, à la Périgueux.   [2 *Removes.*] Fillets of mutton, larded with
                                 Poivrade sauce.

6 *Entrées:*

Crôustades of rice filled with purée of   Fillets of rabbits, à la D'Uxelles,
    woodcocks.   garnished with Soubise purée.
Tourte of Godiveau, à la Financière.   Suprême of fowls, à l'écarlate.
Scollops of pheasant, à la Victoria.   Mutton cutlets, with purée of potatoes.

Second Course.

Larks.   [2 *Roasts.*]   Grouse.

Custard fritters.   [2 *Removes.*]   Apple soufflé.

6 *Entremêts:*

Salsifis, with white sauce.   Calf's-feet jelly, with grapes.
Mushrooms, with fine-herbs, au gratin.   Timbale of ground rice.
Cuiraçao, Bavarian cream.   Puff-paste walnuts.

Dinner for 18 Persons. *November.*

Scotch broth.   [2 *Soups.*]   Hare soup, à l'Anglaise.

Fried slices of cod, oyster sauce. [2 *Fishes.*] Baked pike, with Italian sauce

Roast fillet of beef, Poivrade   [2 *Removes.*] Braized goose, à la Flamande.
     sauce.

6 *Entrées:*

Boudins of partridge, à la Périgueux.   Scollops of mutton, with oyster sauce
Pork cutlets, broiled, with Tomata   Widgeon, à l'Américaine.
     sauce.   Crôustades of marrow, with fine
Curry of rabbits, à l'Indiènne.   herbs.

Second Course.

Golden Plovers.   [2 *Roasts.*]   Pheasants.

Ramequins.   [2 *Removes.*]   Iced pudding, à la Parisiènne.

6 *Entremêts.*

Braized celery, à l'Espagnole.   Pine-apple cheese, à la Chantilly.
Scolloped muscles.   Mecca loaves.
Noyau jelly.   Apples and rice, with apricot.

DINNER FOR 8 PERSONS. *November.*

Soup, à la Paysanne.

Turbot, lobster sauce. 　[2 *Fishes.*] 　Salmon cutlets, à la Maintenon.

Roast leg of mutton. 　[2 *Removes.*] 　Lark pudding, à la Melton
　　　　　　　　　　　　　　　　　　　　　　　　　Mowbray.

Rissoles, à la Milanaise.

---

2 *Entrées:*

Pigs' feet, à la Ste. Ménéhould. 　　　Chicken sautés with fine-herbs.

======

SECOND COURSE.

Fried potatoes. 　[2 *Roasts.*] 　　　Pheasant.

Apricot soufflé, to remove the roast.

---

4 *Entremêts:*

Crôutes with truffles, à la Piémontaise. 　Pudding, à la Viènnoise.
German salad. 　　　　　　　　　　　　Almond cakes, à la crème.

DINNER FOR 8 PERSONS. *November.*

Purée of rabbits, à la Chantilly.

Broiled herrings, mustard sauce. [2 *Fishes.*] Scollops of cod, à la Hollandaise.

Capon, with nouilles. 　[2 *Removes.*] 　Braized neck of mutton larded,
　　　　　　　　　　　　　　　　　　　　　　　à la Soubise.

Calf's brains, fried in batter.

---

2 *Entrées.*

Kidneys bread-crumbed, à la Maître 　Cutlets of partridges, à l'Algéri-
d'Hôtel. 　　　　　　　　　　　　　　ènne.

======

SECOND COURSE.

Macaroni, au gratin. 　[2 *Roasts.*] 　　Wild ducks.

Orange fritters, to remove the roast.

---

4 *Entremêts:*

Celery, à la Villeroi. 　　　　　　　Pear cheese, à la crème.
Poached eggs, on anchovy toàst. 　Love's wells, garnished with preserve.

DINNER FOR 8 PERSONS. *November.*

Pearl barley soup, à la Princesse.

| Salmon, à la Tartare. | [2 *Fishes.*] | Paupièttes of fillets of soles, à la Ravigotte. |
| Roast neck of venison. | [2 *Removes.*] | Calf's-head, à l'Anglaise. |

Black puddings.

---

2 *Entrées:*

Boudins of pheasant, à la Dauphine with Soubise sauce. Fricassée of chickens, à la Romaine.

===

SECOND COURSE.

Scolloped oysters. [2 *Roasts.*] Woodcocks.

Iced rice pudding, à la Cintra, to remove the roast.

---

4 *Entremêts:*

Eggs, à l'Aurore. Apple cheese, with custard.
Spinach, with cream. Harry the Eighth's shoe-strings.

DINNER FOR 8 PERSONS. *November.*

Mulligatawny soup.

Fillets of haddock, à la Royale. [2 *Fishes.*] Cod, à la crême.

Boiled turkey, with oyster sauce. [2 *Removes.*] Roast sucking pig.

Croquettes of ox-palates.

---

2 *Entrées:*

Crépinettes of partridges à la D'Estaing. Fricandeau, with purée of tomatas.

===

SECOND COURSE.

Italian salad. [2 *Roasts.*] Hare.

Iced biscuits, in small cases.

---

4 *Entremêts:*

Brussels sprouts sautés, à la Maître d'Hôtel. Potatoes, à la Hollandaise.
Orange pudding.
Meringues, à la crême.

DINNER FOR 8 PERSONS. *November.*

Cream of rice, à la Chasseur.

| Fried Smelts. | [2 *Fishes.*] | Lampreys, à la Foley. |

| Goose, à la Dauphinoise. | [2 *Removes.*] | Fillets of red deer, à la Royale. |

Patties, au jus.

2 Entrées:

| Sheep's tongues, à l'écarlate, with spinach. | | Pigeons, à la Duchesse. |

SECOND COURSE.

| Pheasant. | [2 *Roasts.*] | Snipes. |

Pear fritters, to remove the roast.

4 Entremêts:

| Salsifis fried in batter. | Rice cake, with almonds. |
| Eggs, à la tripe. | Vol-au-vent of apricots. |

DINNER FOR 8 PERSONS. *November.*

Purée of lentilles, à la Soubise.

| Fried soles. | [2 *Fishes.*] | Tench, à la Hollandaise. |

| Ham, with spinach. | [2 *Removes.*] | Roast turkey, à l'Anglaise. |

Bouchées of larks, à la Pompadour.

2 Entrées:

| Fillets of partridges, à la Plessy. | Scollops of mutton sautées, with olives. |

SECOND COURSE.

| Russian salad. | [2 *Roasts.*] | Widgeon. |

Vol-au-vent of damsons, with iced cream, to remove the roast.

4 Entremêts:

| Eggs, à la Dauphine. | Pomegranate jelly. |
| Endives, with cream. | Macaroni cake. |

DINNER FOR 14 PERSONS. *December.*

Juliènne. [2 *Soups.*] Purée of rabbits, à la Maître
d'Hôtel.

Crimped slices of pike, Dutch [2 *Fishes.*] Broiled turbot, à la Provençale.
sauce.

Turkey, with celery sauce. [3 *Removes.*] Haunch of roebuck, à la Marie
Stuart.

Oyster patties, à la Sefton

4 *Entrées :*

Mutton cutlets, à la Russe. Fricassée of chickens, à la Dauphine.
Partridges, à la Périgueux. Noix of Veal, à la Macédoine.

SECOND COURSE.

Pheasants. [2 *Roasts.*] Snipes.

Ratifia soufflé. [2 *Removes.*] Chestnut pudding.

6 *Entremêts :*

Seakale, with white sauce. Vanilla Bavarian cream.
Group of large truffles. Millefeuilles cake, à la Chantilly.
Orange jelly, à la Françalse. Apricots, à la Conde (preserved).

DINNER FOR 14 PERSONS. *December.*

Consommé of game, with lasag- [2 *Soups.*] Purée of lentils, à la Brùnoise.
nes.

John Dory, with lobster sauce. [2 *Fishes.*] Whitings, with fine-herbs.

Ham, with Brussels sprouts. [2 *Removes.*] Roast turkey, à la Chipolata.

White Puddings, à la Royale.

4 *Entrées.*

Veal cutlets, à la Zingara. Fillets of grouse, à la Dauphine,
Timbale of raviolis, à la Napolitaine. with Piquante sauce.
Civet of hare, with mushrooms.

SECOND COURSE.

Wild ducks. [2 *Roasts.*] Partridges.

Iced pudding, à la Kinnaird. [2 *Removes.*] Mince pies.

6 *Entremêts :*

Jerusalem artichokes, à l'Espagnole. Lemon jelly, à la Française.
Croquettes of potatoes. Cherry tartlets.
Pistachio cream. Tourte of Frangipane.

DINNER FOR 14 PERSONS. *December.*

Brûnoise soup.   [2 *Soups.*]   Purée of grouse, à la Condé.

Baked pike, with Piquante sauce. [2 *Fishes.*]   Whitings, à la Maître d'Hôtel.

Capon, à la Périgueux.   [2 *Removes.*]   Roasted ham, à la St. James.

Rissoles of calf's brains

---

4 *Entrées :*
Cutlets of partridges, à la Maréchale,   Scollops of fat livers, with fine-herbs.
with an essence of garlic.   Boudins of fowl, à la D'Orsay.
Mutton cutlets, with purée of endives.

SECOND COURSE.

Pheasants.   [2 *Roasts.*]   Widgeon.

Arrow-root Soufflé.   [2 *Removes.*]   French gauffres.

---

6 *Entremêts :*
Potatoes, au gratin.   Bavarian rasberry cream (preserved).
Crôutes, with mushrooms.   Timbale of Nouilles, with vanilla.
Calf's-feet jelly, with grapes.   Florentines, with greengage jam.

DINNER FOR 14 PERSONS. *December.*

Macaroni, à la Royale.   [2 *Soups.*]   Soup of tendons of veal, à la
     Jardinière.
Fried fillets of gurnets, Shrimp [2 *Fishes.*]   Soles in Matelotte Normande.
sauce.
Roast pheasants, à l'Italiènne. [2 *Removes.*]   Mutton pie, à l'Anglaise.

Muscles, fried in batter.

---

4 *Entrées*
Tendons of veal, à la Villeroi, with a   Salmis of wild fowl, à la Provençale.
Nivernaise ragout.   Fillets of beef sautés, with an es-
Suprême of fowls, à l'écarlate, with a   sence of anchovies.
purée of truffles.

SECOND COURSE.

Hare.   [2 *Roasts.*]   Partridges.

Soufflés of vanilla, in small [2 *Removes.*]   Ginger pudding.
cases.

6 *Entremêts :*
Spinach, au jus.   Pine-apple jelly.
Fried potatoes.   Flân of pears.
Queen's cakes, with apricot.   Polish puff-paste cakes.

DINNER FOR 6 PERSONS. *December.*

Vermicelli clear soup.

———

1 *Fish.*
Brill, with shrimp sauce.

———

2 *Removes.*
Capon, with brocoli, à la Béchamel.   Roast fillet of beef, Poivrade sauce.

———

2 *Entrées:*
Purée of pheasant, with poached eggs.   Scollops of sweetbreads, with Soubise sauce.

═══════

SECOND COURSE.

Roast partridges.

———

3 *Entremêts:*
Omelette, with fine-herbs.   Lemon pudding.
Blanc-manger in glasses.

━━━━━━━

DINNER FOR 6 PERSONS. *December.*

Purée of peas, à l'Anglaise.

———

1 *Fish.*
Cod, à la crême au gratin.

———

Roast pheasant, à la Périgueux. [2 *Removes.*] Boiled leg of pork, à l'Anglaise.

———

2 *Entrées:*
Blanquette of fowl, garnished with po-   Scollops of beef, with oysters.
tato croquettes.

═══════

SECOND COURSE.

Roast snipes.

———

3 *Entremêts.*
Spinach, with poached eggs.   Plumpudding.
Almond cakes, à la Chantilly.

DINNER FOR 6 PERSONS.   *December.*

Purée of endives, à la crême (preserved).

1 *Fish.*

Fillets of whitings, à la Provençale.

Snipe pudding, à la D'Orsay.   [2 *Removes.*] Braized pheasant, with celery
sauce.

2 *Entrées:*

Chickens, à la Tartare.   Mutton cutlets, with purée of chestnuts.

SECOND COURSE.

Roast wild duck.

3 *Entremêts:*

Apricot omelette.   Apple Charlotte.

Brussels sprouts, with butter.

DINNER FOR 6 PERSONS.   *December.*

Consommé with nouilles.

1 *Fish.*

Smelts, au gratin.

Roast saddle of mutton.   [2 *Removes.*]   Partridges, à la Soubise.

2 *Entrées.*

Curry of rabbits, à l'Indiènne.   Ox-tail, à la Jardiniére.

SECOND COURSE.

Roast larks.

3 *Entremêts:*

Potatoes soufflées.   Mince pies.

Orange jelly, à l'Anglaise.

Diner de 24 Couverts. *Mai.*

3 Potages:

Le Printanier aux pointes. La Bisque de Prawns.

A la Tortuë.

---

3 Poissons:

Le Saumon à la Régence. Le Turbot a la sauce homard.

Les White Bait frits.

---

4 Assiètles de Hors-d'Œuvres:

2 de rissoles à la Monglas. 2 de petites crôustades de laitances.

---

2 Relevés:

La Tête de Veau à la Financière. Le Filet de Bœuf piqué,

garni de laitues farcies.

---

2 Flancs:

Les Langues à la Macédoine. Les petits poulets à la Vertpré.

---

8 Entrées:

La Bordure de riz à la Reine. Le Pâté Chaud de Cailles.
La Timbale à la Milanaise. La Chartreuse à la Parisiènne.
Les Filets de pigeons à la Duchesse. La Blanquette aux Concombres.
Les Ris de Veau à la Toulouse. Les Côtelettes d'agneau aux asperges.

===

Second Service.

2 Rôts:

Les Poulardes. Les Canetons.

2 Relevés:

Le Savarin. La Spongada di Roma.

2 Flancs:

Le Bastion d'auguilles sur Socle. La Galantine sur Socle.

---

16 Entremêts:

Les Haricôts verts au beurre. Les Asperges à la sauce.
Les Asperges à la sauce. Les Haricôts verts au beurre.
La Grosse meringue à la Chantilly. La Croquante de patiences.
Le Croqu'en'bouche d'oranges. Le Chateaubriant.
Le Bavaroix de Groseilles vertes. La Gélée de fraises.
La Gélée de Champagne rosé. Le Bavaroix en Surprise.
L'Aspic d'Œufs de pluviers. L'Aspic d'Œufs de pluviers.

CONCERT SUPPER.   *June.*

[2 *Soups.*]

La crême d'orge.   Le consommé de volaille.

24 *Entrées:*

6 of cold roast fowls, with aspic jelly.   3 lobster salads.
6 of ham and tongue, with aspic jelly.   3 chicken salads.
3 aspics of plovers' eggs,

12 *Dishes of Pastry:*

2 of strawberry tartlets.   2 of D'Artois cakes.
2 of Genoese cakes with almonds.   2 of Duchess loaves.
2 of Meringues, à la crême.   2 of Chocolate profitrolles.

12 *Jellies and Creams:*

2 Macédoines of fruits.   2 Russian Charlottes.
2 Celestina Charlottes.   2 pine-apple jellies.
2 cherry jellies.   2 Italian creams.

DINER DE 24 COUVERTS. *Juin.*

3 Potages :

A l'Impératrice. A la purée de pois verts.
A l'Esturgeon à la Chinoise.

---

3 Poissons :

Le Turbot à la Vatel. Les Truites à la Beaufort.
Le Water-Souchet de Limandes.

---

4 Hors-d' Œuvres :

2 de Niochi au Parmésan. 2 de White Bait frits.

---

2 Relevés :

Le Jambon à la Parisiènne. Les Poulardes à la Chivry.

---

2 Flancs :

La petite pièce de Bœuf à la d'Orléans. La Selle d'agneau à la Royale.

---

8 Entrées :

Les Boudins de homard Cardinal. La Chartreuse de Cailles.
Les Ris d'agneau à la Toulouse. Le Vol-au-vent à la Nèsle.
Les Filets de Canetons aux petits pois. Le Suprême de volaille asperges.
Les Noisettes de Veau à la de Luynes. Les Côtelettes de mouton à la Dreux.

SECOND SERVICE.

2 Rôts :

L'Oisillon. Les Lévrauts.

---

2 Flancs :

La Spongada Napolitana. Le Jambon en surprise.

---

16 Entremêts :

Les Asperges à la sauce. Les Asperges à la sauce.
Les petits pois à l'Anglaise. Les petits pois à la Française.
L'Aspic de homard sur socle. L'Aspic à la Belle-vue sur socle.
Des Œufs de pluviers sur socle. Le Buisson de prawns sur socle.
La Gélée à la Montmorency. La Gélée Macédoine.
La Charlotte d'ananas. Le Bavaroix au Chocolat.
Le Croqu'en-bouche à la Reine. Le Gateau de Millefeuilles.
Le Melon en Nougat. Le Biscuit à la Florentine.

HER MAJESTY'S DINNER. 25*th January*

(*Under the control of C. Francatelli.*)

Potages:

A la Tête de Veau en Tortuë.
Le Quenelles de Volaille au Consommé.

Poissons:

Le Saumon, à la sauce homard.
Les Soles frites, sauce Hollandaise.

Relevés:

Le Filet de Bœuf, piqué braisé aux pommes de terre.
Le Chapon à la Godard.

Entrées:

Le Bord de pommes de terre, garni de Palais de Bœuf.
La Chartreuse de Perdrix aux Choux.
Les Côtelettes d'Agneau panées.
La Blanquette de Volaille à l'écarlate.
Les Laperaux, sautés aux finès herbes.
Les Petits Pâtés aux huîtres.

Rôts:

Les Poulets.   Les Faisans.

Relevés:

Le pudding à l'Orange.   Les Omelettes Soufflées.

Entremêts:

Les pommes de terre à la Strasbourgeoise.
Les Epinards au jus.
La Gelée de Marasquin.
Le Petites Talmouses.
Les Feuillantines de Pommes.
La Crême aux Amandes Prâlinées.

Buffet.

Roast Beef and Mutton.   Boiled Round of Beef.

HER MAJESTY'S DINNER. 30*th June.*

(Under the control of C. Francatelli.)

4 *Potages :*

Printannier. A la Reine.

2 à la Tortuë.

4 *Poissons :*

Les Truites à la sauce Génévoise. Le Turbot, à la sauce homard.
Les Filets de merlans frits. Les white-bait frits.

4 *Hors d'œuvres :*
Les Petits pâtés de homards.

4 *Relevés :*
Les Poulardes trûffées à la sauce Périgueux.
Le Jambon glacé garni de fèves de marais.
La Selle d'agneau farcie à la Royale.
Le Filet de Bœuf piqué à la Napolitaine.

16 *Entrées :*
2 Les Nageoires de Tortuë sauce au vin de Madère.
2 Les Filets de poulets à l'écarlate aux concombres.
2 Les Côtelettes de mouton braisées à la purée d'artichauds.
2 Les Aiguillettes de canetons aux pois verts.
2 Les Riz de veaux piqués glacés à la Toulouse.
2 Les Côtelottes de pigeons panées à l'Allemande.
2 Les Chartreuse de tendons d'agneau à l'essence.
2 Les Timbales de macaroni à la Mazarine.

Side Board :
Haunch of Venison.
Roast Beef. Roast Mutton.
Vegetables.

SECOND SERVICE.

6 *Rôts :*
2 de Cailles. 2 Lévrauts. 2 de Poulets.

6 *Relevés :*
2 Les puddings à la Nesselrode. 2 Les soufflés à la fécule de
2 Les puddings de Cabinet. pommes de terre.

2 *Flancs :*
Le Pavillon Mauresque. La Tente Militaire.

4 *Contre-Flancs :*
Le Nougat aux amandes. Le Biscuit de Savoie à la vanille.
La Sultane Parisiènne. Le Croque-en-bouche historié.

16 *Entremêts :*

Les trûffes au vin de Champagne.
Les artichauts à la Lyonnaise.
Le Buisson de prawns sur socle.
L'anguilles en volute au beurre de Montpellier.
La gelée de groseilles garnie de pêches.
Les tartelettes de framboises.
Les Génoises aux fruits transparents.

Les petits pois à la Française.
Les haricôts verts à la poulette.
L'aspic de blancs de volaille à la Belle-vue.
La salade de légumes à l'Italiènne.
La Macédoine de fruits.
Le Bavaroix de chocolat panaché.
La crèmé aux amandes prâlinées.
Les petits pains à la Parisiènne.
Les gâteaux de Péthiviers.

Her Majesty's Dinner.   15*th* *August*,
(*Under the control of C. Francatelli.*)

Potages :

A la croûte gratinée à la Sévigné.   A la purée de Gélinottes.
A la Crème de Riz garni de quenelles au beurre d'Ecrivisses.

Poissons :

Le Brochet garni d'une Matelote d'Anguilles.   Lss Filets de Marlans frits.
Les Truites sauce à la Plûche.

Relevés :

Les Poulardes, au Macaroni.   Le Gigot de Mouton de sept heures.
Le Jambon aux Petits Pois.   Les Queux de Bœufs à la Jardinière.

Entrées :

Les Côtelettes d'Agneau sautées aux Concombres.
Les Filets de Lapereaux panés à l'Allemande.
Les Cervelles de Veau marinées frites sauce Tomates.
Les Escalopes de Gélinottes aux Trûffes.
Les Ris de Veau aux Petits Pois.
Les Fricassée de Poulets dans un bord de Riz.

Rôts :

Les Canetons.   Les Dindonneaux.

Relevés

Le Pudding de Sagou sauce au Fruit.   Le Soufflé au Citron.
Les Beignets de Pèches.

Flancs :

Le Schapska Polonais.   Le Melon en Nougat.

Entremêts :

Le Bastion d'Anguilles au beurre de Montpellier.
Le Buisson de Trûffes au Vin de Champagne.
Les Concombres à la poulette.
Les Haricôts Verts sautés au beurre.
La Gelée de Malaga.
La Macédoine de Fruit.
Les Tartelettes de Prûnes de Reine Claude.
Les Petits gâteaux feuilletés à l'Abricôt.
Le Pain de Gibier à la gelée.
La Salade à la Russe.
Les Pommes de Terre à la Maître d'Hôtel.
La Macédoine de Légumes.
Le Bavaroix aux Framboises.
La Crême au Café mocha.
Les Pains de la Mecque à la Chantilly.
Les Dauphines à la fleur d'Orange.

Side Board.

Roast Beef.   Roast Mutton.   Roast Venison.   Riz au Consommé.
Emincé de Poulet aux Œufs pôehes.   Haricôts Verts.   Currant Tart.

HER MAJESTY'S DINNER. *16th August.*

(Under the control of C. Francatelli.)

Potages

A la Cressy.   A la Tortuë.   A la Royale.

Poissons:

Le St. Pierre à la sauce Homard.   Les Filets de Soles à la ravigotte.
Les Gougeons frits sauce Hollandaise.   Le Saumon sauce aux Câpres.

Relevés:

Le Pièce de Bœuf à la Flamande.   Les Poulardes et Langue aux
La Pâté-chaud de Pigeons à l'Anglaise.   Chouxfleurs.
La Noix de Veau en Bédeau.

Entrées:

Les Côtelettes de Mouton à la purée d'Artichauts.
Les Boudins de Laperaux à la Richelieu.
Les Pieds d'Agneau en Canelons farcis à l'Italiènne
Les Filets de Poulardes à la Régence.
Les Tendons de Veau glacés à la Macédoine.
Les Petites Timbales de Nouilles à la Purée de Gélinottes.

Rôts:

Les Combattants.   Les Chapons.   L'Oie.

Relevés:

Le Pudding de Riz.   Le Baba au Rhum.   Les Beignets au Parmesan.

Flancs:

La Cascade ornée de sucre filé.   La Chaumiére rustique.

Entremêts:

La Darne d'Esturgeon au beurre de Montpellier.
Le Buisson d'Ecrivisses.
Les Petits Pois à la Française.
Les Haricôts Verts à la Maître d'hôtel.
Le Gélee au Vin de Champagne.
La Crême au Caramel.
Les Petits Gateaux de Crême à l'Anglaise.
La Tourte de Pêches.
L'Aspic de Volaille à la Belle-vue.
Les Fonds d'Artichauts à la Provençale.
Les Concombres farcis à l'Essence.
Les Choux-fleurs, à la sauce.
Le Bavaroix de Fraises.
La Gelée de Pêches.
Les Tartelettes de Cerises.
Le Gateau de Péthiviers.

Side Board:

Roast Beef.   Roast Mutton.   Hashed Venison.
Riz au Consommé.
Plum and Yorkshire Puddings.

HER MAJESTY'S DINNER. *20th August.*

(Under the control of C. Francatelli.)

Potages:

À la Tortuë.   À la Faubonne.   À la Xavier.

Poissons:

Le Saumon ciselé sauce Homard.   Les Eglefins sauce aux œufs.
Les Merlans frits sauce Hollandaise.

Relevés:

Le Jambon de Westphalia aux Hari-   La Pjèce de Bœuf à la Mazarine.
   côts Verts.   L'Oie braisée garni de racines.
Les Poulardes à la Belle-vue sauce Su-
   prême.

Entrées:

Les Côtelottes de Mouton à la purée de Pommes de Terre.
Les Ballottines de Volailles à la Jardinière.
Les Fricandeaux glacés à la purée de Pois.
Les Ailerons de Poulets panés à la Villeroy.
Les Petites Crôustades à la purée de Gélinottes.
Les Boudins à la Reine.

Rôts:

Wheatears.   Gélinottes.   Poulets.

Relevés:

Les Beignets Soufflés au citron.   Le Pudding roulé à l'Allemande.
Le Pudding Bavaroix.

Flancs:

Les Canards à la Chantilly.   La Gondole Vénitiènne.

Entremêts:

Les Anguilles en bastion.   L'Aspic de Galantine.
Les Ecrivesses au Vin.   Les Trûffes à la serviètte.
Les Artichauts à la Provençale.   Les Petits Pois à l'Anglaise.
La Macédoine de Légumes.   Les Haricôts Verts à la Mâitre d'hôtel.
La Gelée de Pêches.   Le Bavaroix de Framboises.
La Charlotte Russe.   La Chartreuse de Poires.
Les Tartelettes de Cerises à la Crême. Les Petits Puits d'Amour.
Les Génoises au Confitures.   Les Dauphines aux Pistaches.

Side Board.

Roast Beef.   Haunch of Venison.   Roast Mutton.
Riz au Consommé.   Marrow on toast.

HER MAJESTY'S DINNER. *August.*

(Under the control of C. Francatelli.)

Potages:
De Quenelles au Consommé.   A la purée de Gélinottes.
A la Garbure aux Laitues.

Poissons:
Les Brochets farcis au four.   Les Anguilles à la Tartare.
Le Turbot sauce Homard.

Relevés:
Les Carrés de Venaison en Cheveaux-   Le Pâté de Pigeons à l'Anglaise.
de-frize.

Entrées:
Les Petits Poulets aux choufleurs.
Les Poitrine d'Agneau à la Dauphine.
Les Blanquettes de Volaille aux Concombres.
Les Boudins de Volaille à la Sefton.
Les Chartreuses de Tendons de Veau.
Les Petits Pâtés aux huîtres.

Rôts:
Les Lévrauts.   Le Dindonneaux.
Wheatears.

Relevés:
Les Gauffres à la Flamande.   Le Pudding Soufflé au Citron.

Entremêts:
La Darne Saumon à la remoulade.
La Salade à la Russe.
Le Macaroni à l'Italiènne.
Les Œufs à l'Aurore.
Les Artichauts à la Lyonnaise.
Les Haricôts Verts à la poulette.
La Gelée de Citron garnie de Prûnes vertes.
Le Bavaroix à la Canelle.
Les Feuillantines aux Pommes.
Le Flan de Fruit.
Les Petits Biscuits aux Amandes.
Les Pêches au Riz à la Condé.

Side Board:
Roast Beef.   Roast Mutton.
Hashed Venison.
Riz au Consommé.   Petits Pôts de Volaille.
Greengage tart.

HER MAJESTY'S DINNER.   17*th September.*

(*Under the control of C. Francatelli.*)

Potages:

A la Purée de Volaille.   A la Xavier.

Poissons:

Les Tranches de Cabillaud aux huîtres.   Les Eperlans frits sauce Holland-
                                              aise.

Relevés:

Les noix de Veau à la Jardinière.   Le Jambon glacé aux Epinards.

Entrées:

Le Haricôt de Venaison.
Les Perdreaux braisés à la soubise.
Les Boudins de Volaille à la Sefton.
Les Petits Filets de Bœuf dans leur glace.
Les Tendons de Veau en kari.
La Poularde poêllée sauce Suprême.
Les Aiguillettes de Poulets à la chicorée.
Les Filets de Soles en Epigramme.

Rôts:

Les Gélinottes.   Le Lievre.   Les Dindonneaux.

Relevés:

Les Beignets de Crême frite.   La Charlotte de Pommes.

Entremêts:

La Gélee d'Ananas.
Le Pain de Pêches à la Chantilly.
Les Gâteaux à la Religieuse.
Les Madelines au Cédrat.
Les Pommes de Terre à la crême.
Les Choux-fleurs à la sauce.
Les Œufs à l'Aurore.
Les Huitres frites.
Les Coupes garnies de Partisserie.

Side-Board:

Roast Beef.   Roast Venison.   Roast Mutton.
                   Marrow on Toast.
                   Riz au Consommé.

HER MAJESTY'S DINNER. 18*th September.*

(*Under the control of* C. *Francatelli.*)

Potages:

A la Cressy aux Croûtons.   A la Royale.

Poissons:

Les Eglefins sauce aux Œufs.   Les Harengs sauce moutarde.

Relevés:

Le Filet de Bœuf braisé aux laitues.   Les Petits Poulets en Galantine.

Entrées:

Les Côtelettes de Porc frais sauce Tomates.
Les Boudins de Merlans à la Béchamel.
Les Croquettes de Volaille à l'Allemande.
Les Palais de Bœuf au gratin.
La Fricassée de Poulets à la Villeroy.
Le Sauté de Perdreaux à la Bourguignotte.
Les Cervelles de Veau au beurre noir.
Les Crôustades de Mouton aux fines herbes.

Rôts.

Les Perdreaux.   Les Poulardes.

Relevés:

Les Croquettes de Riz sauce au fruit.   Le Soufflé au Citron.

Entremêts:

Les Concombres à l'Espagnole.
Les Epinards au jus.
Les Œufs brouillés aux Trûffes.
La Salade à la Russe.
Le Pudding à la D'Orléans.
La Gelée de Fruits.
Le Flan de Poires.
Les Meringues à la Chantilly.
Les Cassolettes garnies de Patisserie.

Side Board:

Roast Beef.   Roast Venison.

Roast Mutton.
Riz au Consommé.

HER MAJESTY'S DINNER. *19th September.*

(*Under the control of C. Francatelli.*)

Potages:

A la Purée de Perdreaux.   Au Vermicelli clair.

Poissons:

Les Filets de Brochets panés à l'Allemande.   Le Turbot sauce Homard.

Relevés.

Les Filets de Mouton, piqués à la Jardinière.   La Tête de Veau en Tortuë.

Entrées:

Les Côtelettes d'agneau à la chicorée.
Les Poulets à l'Allemande.
La Suprème de Volaille aux Concombres.
Le Filet de Bœuf au Madère.
Les Gélinottes braisées aux Choux.
Les Boudins de Volaille à la Reine.
Le Vol-au-vent à la Nêsle.
Les Filets de Perdreaux à la Marèna.

Rôts:

Le Chapon.   Les Gélinottes.

Relevés

Le Pudding de Farine de Riz.   Les Pommes Meringuées.

Flancs:

Les Piéces montées.

Entremêts:

La Salade de Homards.
Les Trûffes à la Serviètte.
Les Haricôts Verts à la poulette.
Les Choux-fleurs au Parmesan.
La Gelée de Marasquin.
La Timballe de Raisins garnie d'un Bavaroix.
Le Gâteau de Crême à la moëlle.
La Charlotte de Pêches à l'Abricot.

Side Board:

Roast Beef.   Boiled Round of Beef.   Roast Mutton.
    Hashed Venison.   Riz au Consommé.

HER MAJESTY'S DINNER. 21st *September.*

(*Under the control of* C. *Francatelli.*)

Potages:

A la Purée de Volaille. A la Brûnoise.

Poissons:

Le Saumon sauce au persil.
Les Harengs, sauce Moutarde.
Le St. Pierre, sauce Homard.
Les Eperlans frits.

Relevés:

Le Rond de Veau, à l'Anglaise. Le Jambon glacé aux haricôts verts.

2 *Flancs:*

Les Petits Poulets, au gros sel. Les Filets de Mouton, à la Jardinière.

Entrées:

Les Poitrines d'Agneau, à la purée de pommes de terre.
Les Perdreaux, à la Périgueux.
Les Kromeskys de Volaille, à la Russe.
L'Emincé de Bœuf, à la Polonaise.
Les Ris de Veau, à la Financière.
Les Petites Quenelles de Volaille.
Les Amourettes frites, sauce Tomates.
Les Petits Vol-au-Vent, aux huîtres.

Rôts:

Les Poulardes. Les Perdreaux.

Relevés;

Les Omelettes soufflées, à la fleur d'Orange. Le Pudding Bavaroix.

Entremêts:

Les Epinards au jus.
Les Pommes de Terre frites.
La Gelée de Pieds de Veau au Vin.
Les Fenchonettes, à l'Abricôt.
La Charlotte, à la Parisiènne.
Le Gâteau de Compiègne.
Les Homards au gratin.
La Salade de Volaille.
La Crême au Caramel.
Les Nougats de Pommes au Citron.
La Gelée de Fruits.
La Grosse Meringue, à la Chantilly.
Les Corbeilles garnies de Noix.

Side Board:

Roast Beef. Roast Mutton.
Haunch of Venison.
Riz au Consommé. Hashed Venison.

HER MAJESTY'S DINNER.   24*th October.*

(Under the control of C. Francatelli.)

Potages:

A la Purée de Pois aux Croûtons.   Au Macaroni clair.

Poissons :

Le Turbot à la sauce Homard.   Les Eperlans frits sauce Hollandaise.

Relevés:

Le Filet de Bœuf, piqué sauce Poivrade.   Les Faisans, à la Financière.

Entrées:

Les Ris de Veau piqués, à la sauce Tomates.   Les Epaules de Lièvres, en civet.
La Fricassée de Poulets, à la Villeroy.   Les Filets de Soles, aux Huîtres.
Les Carbonnades de Mouton, à la Macédoine.   Les petits Poulets, aux Riz.

Rôts:

Les Mauvièttes.   Les Dindonneaux.

Relevés:

Le Soufflé, à la fécule.   Les Gauffres, à la Flamande.

Entremêts :

Les Artichauts, à la Barigoule.   Le Blanc-manger.
Les Salsifis, à l'Espagnole.   Les Gâteaux de Pommes.
La Gelée d'Ananas garnie.   Les Darioles, à la Fleur d'Orange.

Side Board:

Roast Beef.   Roast Mutton.
Hashed Venison.
Riz au Consommé.

HER MAJESTY'S DINNER. *25th October.*

(*Under the control of C. Francatelli.*)

Potages :

A la Bisque d'Ecrivisses. Au Vermicelli clair.

Poissons :

Les Eglefins, à la sauce aux Œufs. Les Soles frites, sauce aux Anchois.

Relevés :

Le Jambon aux Epinards. Le Filet de Veau, à l'Anglaise.

Entrées:

Le Salmi de Coqs de Bruyère.
Les Filets de Mouton piqués sauce Tomates.
Le Suprême de Volaille, a l'Ecarlate.
Les Petites Crôustades, à la purée de Faisans.
Les Tanches farcies au Vin de Sauterne.
Les Ris de Veau, à la Dauphine.

Rôts :

Les Bécassines. Les Poulets.

Relevés :

Le Pudding de Sémoule, à l'Abricôt. Les Caneions frits, garnis de Framboises.

Entremêts .

Les Pommes de Terre, à la Hollandaise.
Les Œufs brouillés aux Trûffes.
La Gelée des Fruits.
Les Gâteaux, à l'Anglaise.
Les Pains de la Mecque.
Le Bavaroix, à la Vanille.

Side Board:

Roast Beef. Haunch of Venison.
Riz au Consommé.
Plum and Yorkshire Puddings.

Her Majesty's Dinner.   *October 26th.*

(Under the control of C. Francatelli.)

Potages :

De Queues de Bœuf aux racines.   A la bonne femme.

Poissons :

Le Turbot, à la sauce Homard.   Les Filets de Brochets à la Dauphine.

Relevés :

La Pièce de Bœuf braisée, à la Flamande.   La Dinde rotie aux saucisses.

Entrées :

Les Escalopes de Mouton aux fines-herbes.
La Blanquette de Volaille, à l'Ecarlate.
Les Crépinettes de Faisans, à l'Essence.
Le Fricandeau glacé, à la chicorée.
Les petits vols'au'vent, à la Béchamel.
Les ailerons de poulardes, à la Macédoine.

Rôts :

Les Faisans.   Les Gélinottes.

Relevés :

Lés tartelettes soufflées, à la d'Artois.   Le Baba au raisin.

Entremêts :

Les choux de Bruxelles au beurre.
Les salsifis en Magnonnaise.
La gélée de citron.
Le bavaroix de Marasquin.
Le pudding de cabinet.
Le nougats de pommes.

Side Board :

Roast Beef.   Roast Mutton.
Hashed Venison.
Riz au Consommé

INDEX.

Albert sauce, 46.
Allemande sauce, 7.
Almond cakes, 1297.
  „   gauffres, 1284.
  „   paste, ·1258.
  „   „   another method, 1259.
American yams, à la Française, 1187.
Anchovies, essence of, 176.
Anchovy sandwiches, 1213.
  „   sauce, 72.
Apple, Charlotte, 1447.
  „   „   another way, 1448.
  „   „   à la Marialva, 1448.
  „ fritters, 1332.
  „ pudding, 1402.
  „ tart with quince, 1329.
  „ tartlets, 1322.
  „   „   another method, 1323.
Apples and rice, ornamented, 1351
  „   „   plain, 1352.
  „ à la Portuguaise, 1354.
  „   "   another method, 1355.
  „ in the form of a porcupine, 1354.
  „ Parisian turnover of, 1305.
Apricot Bavarian cream, 1433.
  „   Charlotte, 1452.
  „   cheese, à la Chantilly, 1443.
  „   nougats, 1310.
  „   soufflé, 1378.
Apricots, German tourte of, 1304.
Aromatic sauce, 34.
  „ spices for seasoning, 1250.
Artichoke-bottoms, garnish of, 153.
Artichokes, purée of, 117.
    „   with butter sauce, 1165.
    „   à la Barigoule, 1166.
    „   à l'Italiènne, 168.
    „   Jerusalem, with white sauce, 1183.
    „   „ à l'Italiènne, 1184.
    „   à la Lyonnaise, 1167.
    „   „ purée of, 126.
Asparagus-heads, garnish of, 147.
    „   peas, à la crême, 1170.
    „   „ garnish of, 148.
    „   purée of, 118.
    „   with white sauce, 1169.
Aspic of fowl, à la Reine, 1229.
Aspic-jelly, essence of, 172.

Aspic-jelly, or savory jelly, 1218.
Atelet sauce, 36.
Aurora sauce, 41.

Baba, or Polish-cake, 1270.
Badminton sandwich, 1241a.
Béchamel sauce, 5.
  „   cream sauce, 6.
Beef, braized roll of, à l'Allemande, 542.
  „   „   à la Claremont, 545.
  „   „   à la Dauphinoise, 549.
  „   „   à la Flamande, 539.
  „   „   à la Milanaise, 547.
  „   „   à la D'Orléans, 546.
  „   „   à la Polonaise, 541.
  „   „   à la Richelieu, 548.
  „   „   à la Royale, 543.
  „   „   à la Windsor, 544.
  „   „   garnished, 550.
  „ braized rump of, 551.
  „   „ à l'Allemande, 556.
  „   „ à la Printanière, 540.
  „ boiled brisket of, à l'Anglaise, 564.
  „   „ à l'Ecarlate, 565.
  „ stewed brisket of, à la Flamande 566.
  „ edgebone of, à l'Anglaise, 567.
  „ fillet of, à la Jardinière, 554.
  „   „ à la Macédoine, 553.
  „   „ à la Milanaise, 558.
  „   „ à la Napolitaine, 552.
  „   „ dressed roebuck fashion, 555.
  „   „ with Madeira sauce, 557.
  „ braized fillet of, à la Nivernaise, 560.
  „   „ à la Royale, 561.
  „ fillets of, dressed plain, 563.
  „ fillets or scollops of, in their own glaze, 808.
  „   „ with oysters or muscles, 808.
  „   „ with olives, truffles, or gherkins, 808.

Beef, fillets or scollops of, with purées of vegetables, 808.

„ „ with vegetable garnishes, 808.

„ roast fillet of, à l'Anglaise, 559.

„ „ à la Parasiènne, 562.

„ „ à la Provençale, 563.

„ stewed ribs of, à la Chasseur, 570.

„ braized ribs of, à la Piémontaise, 571.

„ small ribs of, à la Mode, 572.

„ „ à la Bourgeoise, 573.

„ ribs of, with Madeira sauce, 574.

„ „ à la Baden, 575.

„ boiled round of, à l'Anglaise, 568.

„ „ à la Chasseur, 569.

„ entrées of, 244.

„ minced, with poached eggs, 809.

„ „ à la Portuguaise, 810.

„ hashed, plain, 811.

„ „ and broiled bones, 812.

„ slices of braized, à la Claremont, 813.

„ „ with sharp sauce 813.

„ „ with macaroni, 813.

„ , with purées of vegetables, 813.

Beefsteak, à la Française, 806.

„ plain, 805.

„ with anchovy butter, 807.

„ with Indian pickles, &c., 807.

Beef-tea, 226.

Beurre-noir, or black-butter sharp sauce 93.

Bigarrade sauce, 33.

Biscuits, glacés, in small cases, 1347.

„ " another way, 1460a.

„ Albert, 1298o.

„ apricot, 1298i.

„ champagne, 1298f.

„ Italian, 1298a.

„ orange, 1298g.

„ peach, 1298h.

„ Russian, 1298n.

„ Sicilian, 1298m.

„ Venetian, 1298b.

„ Victoria, 1298p.

Black-puddings, à la Française, 955.

„ à l'Anglaise, 956.

Black currant-jelly sauce for venison, 66.

Black-game, à la Financière, 751.

„ à l'Italiénne, 748.

„ à la Montagnarde, 747.

„ à la Norwégiènne, 751.

„ à la Paysanne, 750.

„ à la Périgueux, 751.

„ à la Soubise, 751.

„ à la Suédoise, 749.

„ with a purée of celery, 751.

Blanc, or white braize, for calves'-heads, 236.

Blanquette of lambs' sweetbreads, 235.

„ of rabbits, à l'Ecarlate, 1061.

„ of sturgeon, 1118.

„ of veal with mushrooms, 895.

Blond de veau, or veal gravy, 222.

Boar's-head sauce, 103.

„ another method, 104.

„ with aspic-jelly, 1236.

Boiled marinade, 234.

Bordelaise sauce, 57.

Border of potato paste, garnished with scollops of larks, 1782.

„ „ with lamb's-feet à la Pascaline, 783.

„ „ with scollops of ox-palates, à l'Indiènne, 784.

„ „ with scollops of sheep's-tongues, 785.

„ „ with calf's-brains à la Ravigotte, 786.

Borders of potato-paste, for entrées, &c., 1782.

Borsch, or Polish soup, 380.

Bouchées of fowl, à la Pompadour, 1010.

Boudins of partridges, à la D'Orsay, 1092.

„ „ à la Printaniere, 1093.

„ of fowls, à la D'Artois, 1007.

„ „ à la Périgueux, 1005.

„ „ à la Reine, 2009.

„ „ à la Richelieu, 1094.

„ „ à la Sefton, 1006.

„ „ à la Soubise, 1008.

Bouillabaisse, or Provençale soup, 379.

Bourguignotte sauce, 28.

Braize for general purposes, 230.

Brawn sauce, 105.

Bread panada for quenelles, 240.

„ sauce, 80.

„ fried, sauce, 81.

Bredby sandwich, 1241b.

Brêtonne sauce, 27.

Brill, method of dressing, 410.

Brioche-paste, 1269.

Brocoli, garnish of, 155.

Broth, crayfish, for purifying the blood, 227.

„ Mucilaginous, for persons in delicate health, 229.

„ mutton, plain, 225.

„ pectoral chicken, 224.

„ plain chicken, 223.

„ snail, for inveterate coughs, 228.

Broths, medicinal, for invalids, 223.

Brown-bread biscuits, 1298d.

„ Italian sauce, 12.

Brown gravy, for roast veal, 82.
Brussels-sprouts, garnish of, 156.
Brussels-sprouts, for a second-course
     dish, 1192.
  " biscottes, or rusks,
    1280.
Bubble-and-squeak, 814.
Butter, Anchovy, 179.
 ,, Crayfish, 184.
 ,, Epicurean, for the table, 186.
 ,, Green-ravigotte, 185.
 ,, Lobster, 182.
 ,, Montpellier, 183.
 ,, Provençale, 181.
 ,, Ravigotte, 180.
 ,, sauce, 70.
 ,, for asparagus, &c., 71.

Cabbages, garnish of braized, 162.
 ,, ,, stewed red, 163.
Cabinet pudding, 1394.
Cake, Compiègne, 1271.
 ,, ginger, 1298e.
 ,, Parisian, 1273.
 ,, plain seed, 1279.
 ,, plum, or wedding, 1277.
 ,, pound, 1281.
 ,, Savarin, 1274a.
 ,, Savoy, 1275.
 ,, Victoria, 1274.
Calf's-brains, with matelotte sauce, 921.
 ,, with nutbrown butter, 922.
 ,, fried, à la Provencale, 923.
 ,, scolloped, 924.
Calf's-ears, à la Tortuë, 915.
 ,, fried, with Tomata sauce,&c.,
  916.
Calf's-feet, à la Pascaline, 917.
 ,, fried, with Italian sauce, 918.
Calf's-head, à l'Anglaise, 624.
 ,, à la Beauvaux, 627
 ,, à la Financière, 626.
 ,, à la Marigny, 629.
 ,, à la Tortuë, 628.
 ,, plain, with piquante sauce,
  625.
Calf's-liver, braized,with vegetables,919.
 ,, fried, with fine-herbs sauce,
  920.
Calf's-udder, prep. of, for forcemeats,
 242.
Cambridge sauce, 94.
Caper sauce, for fish, 90.
 ,, for boiled mutton, 91.
Capilotade of chickens, à l'Italiènne, 986.
Capon, stuffed with truffles, à la Perigord, 666.
 ,, à l'Anglaise, 669.
 ,, à la Chipolata, 668.
 ,, à l'Estragon, 675.
 ,, à la Godard, 667.
 ,, à l'Ivoire. 673.
 ,, à la Jardinière,670.
 ,, with macaroni, 678.

Capon, à la Macédoine, 671.
 ,, à la Milanaise, 677.
 ,, with nouilles, 679.
 ,, à la Printanière, 672.
 ,, with rice, 676.
 ,, au gros sel, 674.
Cardinal sauce, 48.
Carp, à l'Allemande, 517.
 ,, à la Bourguignotte, 514.
 ,, à la Chambord, 512.
Carp, à la Périgueux, 515.
 ,, à la Provençale, 516,
 ,, à la Royale, 513.
 ,, à la Venitiènne, 518.
 ,, small, fried, 520.
 ,, stewed, à l'Anglaise, 519.
Carrots, young, à l'Allemande, 1178.
 ,, à la Suèdoise, for garnishing
  removes, 749.
 ,, garnish of, in olives, &c., 135.
 ,, young, garnish of, 134.
 ,, ,, à la Flamande,
  142.
 ,, purée of, for cutlets, &c., 108.
 ,, and turnips, garnish of, à la
  Nivernaise, 137.
Casserole, or border of rice, 777.
Casserole of rice, à la Polonaise, 778.
 ,, à la Reine, 779.
 ,, garnished, with a pu-
  rée of game, 780.
 ,, garnished with wings
  of fowls, 781.
 ,, with fricassée of
  chickens, 230.
 ,, with blanquette of
  sweetbreads, 230.
 ,, with scollops of game,
  230.
Cauliflowers, purée of, for cutlets, &c.,
 111.
 ,, garnish of, for entrées,
  &c., 155.
 ,, with white sauce, 1158.
 ,, with Parmesan, au gratin,
  1159
Celery, purée of, garnishing entrées,
 110.
 ,, garnish of, à la crême, 140.
 ,, ,, à l'Espagnole, 141.
 ,, braized, à l'Espagnole, 1151.
 ,, " à la Villeroi, 1152.
Char, à la Beaufort, 496.
 ,, à la Génoise, 493.
 ,, à la Hollandaise, 495.
 ,, in Matelotte, 494.
Charlotte of apples, 1447.
 ,, another way, 1448.
 ,, à la Parisiènne, 1449.
 ,, à l'Allemande, 1450.
 ,, of peaches, à la Française,
  1451.
Chartreuse, à la Belle-vue, 791.
 ,, à la Cardinal, 792.

Chartreuse, à la Parisiènne, 790.
  ,,   of vegetables, garnished with part- ridges, 787.
  ,,   ,,   garnished with quails 788.
  ,,   ,,   with tendous of veal, 789.
  ,,   ,,   with scollops of pheas- ant, 789.
  ,,   ,,   with blan- quette of fowl, 789.
  ,,   ,,   with lambs' sweet- breads, 789
Cherry-bread, 1386.
Cherry-sauce, 62.
  ,,   à la Victoria, 64.
Cherry tartlets, 1324.
Cheese-cakes, 1300.
Cheese, apricot, à la Chantilly, 1443.
  ,,   greengage, &c., 1443.
Chestnut pudding, 1395.
Chestnuts, purée of, for cutlets, &c., 115.
  ,,   garnish of, for a roast tur- key, 157.
Chevreuil sauce, for roebuck, 69.
Chickens, à l'Africaine, 692.
  ,,   à l'Algériènne, 981.
  ,,   à l'Allemande, 690.
  ,,   à la Cardinal, 689.
  ,,   à la Chivry, 687.
  ,,   à la Dauphine, 684.
  ,,   à la Diable, 979.
  ,,   à l'Espagnole, 694.
  ,,   à la Florentine, 688, 982.
  ,,   à l Indiènne, 691.
  ,,   à l'Italiènne, 681.
  ,,   à la Lyonnaise, 978.
  ,,   à la Milanaise, 686.
  ,,   à la Montmorency, 685.
  ,,   à la Provençale, 977.
  ,,   à la Reine, 680.
  ,,   à la Tartare, 980.
  ,,   à la Turque, 693.
  ,,   à la Vénitiènne, 683.
  ,,   with Tomata sauce, 682.
  ,,   fricassée of, with mushrooms, &c., 968.
  ,,   ,,   à la St. Lambert, 969.
  ,,   ,,   à la Dauphine, 970.
  ,,   ,,   à la Financière, 971.
  ,,   ,,   à la Chevalière, 972.
  ,,   ,,   à la Romaine, 973.
  ,,   (cut up in small joints), à la Marengo, 974.
  ,,   with oysters, &c., 975.
  ,,   with truffles, &c., 976.

Chickens, fritôt of, 985.
  ,,   à la Toscane, 987.
  ,,   marinade of, fried in batter, 988.
  ,,   salad, 1225.
  ,,   à la Belle-vue, (cold entrée), 1237.
Civet of hare, 1070.
  ,,   roebuck, 967.
  ,,   venison, 960.
Claremont sauce, 58.
Clarification of calf's-feet jelly, 1408.
Cockles, scolloped, 538.
Cod-fish, fillets of, à l'Indiènne, 446.
  ,,   slices of, à la Séville, 445.
  ,,   scollops of, à la Béchamel, 450.
  ,,   and oyster sauce, 441.
  ,,   stuffed and baked, 442.
  ,,   à la crême, au gratin, 443.
  ,,   crimped slices of, and oyster sauce, 444.
  ,,   ,,   à la Hollandaise, 447.
  ,,   ,,   à la Colbert, 448.
  ,,   ,,   à la Maître d'Hôtel, 451.
  ,,   ,,   in matelotte Nor- mande, 449.
Cod's-head, baked, 452.
Cod's-sounds, and egg sauce, 461.
  ,,   à la Gasconne, 463.
  ,,   à la Ravigotte, 462.
  ,,   à la Royale, 464.
Cold marinade for pickling roebuck, &c., 235.
Cold Poivrade sauce, 102.
Common stock, for general purposes, 1.
  ,,   gravy, for roasts, &c., 221.
Consommé for preparing soups in gene- ral, 213.
  ,,   of fowls, for soups, &c., 214.
  ,,   of pheasants or partridges, (brown), 215.
  ,,   (white), 218.
  ,,   of fowl (white) for working sauces, 217.
  ,,   of rabbits (brown), 216.
Condés, 1307.
Coventry tartlets, 1328b.
Crayfish sauce, 54.
Crayfish, scolloped, 538.
Cream Apricot, 1433.
  ,,   Blanc-manger, 1430.
  ,,   Caramel, or burnt, 1436.
  ,,   Celestina strawberry, 1441.
  ,,   Chocolate, 1435.
  ,,   Coffee, 1434.
  ,,   Curaçao, 1431.
  ,,   Currant and raspberry transpa- rent, 1442.
  ,,   Italian, 1439.
  ,,   Maraschino Bavarian, 1431.
  ,,   Noyeau (pink or white), 1431.
  ,,   Orange-flower, 1437.

Cream, Pistachio-kernels, 1438.
,,   Russian Charlotte, 1440.
,,   Strawberry, Bavarian, 1432.
,,   à la Chateaubriant, 1441b.
,,   à la Romaine, 1441a.
Cream sauce, for roast necks of veal, 83.
,,   for salt fish, 92.
Croquante of oranges, 1358.
,,   of fresh walnuts, 1359.
,,   of ratafias, à la Chantilly, 1360.
Croquettes of fowl and mushrooms, 1020.
,,   of veal, 896.
Crôustade of bread, garnished with calves'-talls, à la Poulette, 794.
,,   garnished with lambs'-brains 795.
,,   with scollops of fat livers, à l'Epicuriènne, 796.
,,   with quails, à la Bourguignotte, 797.
,,   cases, for patties, 1265.
Cucumbers, purée of, 124.
,,   scollops of, for garnishing, 138.
,,   garnish of, farcis, 139.
,,   à la Poulette, 1181.
,,   à l'Espagnole, 1182.
Cupid, or love's wells, 1315.
Curry sauce (plain), 87.
,,   of chickens, à l'Indiènne, 983.
Cygnets, 202.
,,   à la Norwich, 202a.

Dampfnudeln, or German dumplings, 1390.
Darioles, 1306.
Darne of Salmon, with Montpelier butter, 1223.
D'Artois, of apricot-jam, 1309.
Duchess-loaves, 1292.
Ducks, for removes, 703.
,,   à la Macédoine, 703.
,,   braized, with turnips, 704.
,,   ,,   with stewed peas, 705.
,,   ,,   à la Provencale, 706.
,,   ,,   à la Jardinière, 706.
,,   ,,   à la Nivernaise, 706.
,,   ,,   with olives, 706.
,,   ,,   with sauërkraut, 706.
,,   ,,   for entrées, 1035.
Ducklings, à la Rouennaise, 1035.
,,   stewed with olives, 1036.
,,   with stewed peas, 1037.
,,   fillets of, à la Bigarrade,1038.
,,   "   Macédoine,1039
,,   with truffles and mushrooms, 1040.
Dutch sauce, 42.
,,   plain, 79.
D'Uxelles sauce, 16.

Eels, spitchcocked, 501.

Eels, plain broiled, 502.
,,   stewed, à l'Anglaise, 503.
,,   matelotte of, à la Bordelaise, 504.
,,   ,,   à la Génoise, 506.
,,   ,,   à la Parisiènne, 505.
,,   à la Dauphinose, 507.
,,   à l'Indiènne, 511.
,,   à la Poulette, 510.
,,   à la Tartare, 509.
,,   à la Venitiènne, 508.
Eggs, à la tripe, 1193
,,   au gratin, 1194.
,,   brouillés, with truffles, 1195.
,,   poached, with anchovy toast, 1200.
,,   ,,   with ham, 1201.
,,   à l'Aurore, 1203.
,,   à la Dauphine, 1202.
,,   à la Suisse, 1205.
,,   with nutbrown butter, 1204.
Egg sauce, 84.
,,   another method, 85.
Endive, purée of, for fricandeaux, &c., 114.
Endive, à la crème, 1157.
Entrées of fish, 1112.
Entrée, of boudins of lobster, à la Cardinal, 1112.
,,   of quenelles of lobster, à la Vert-pré, 1113.
,,   of boudins of whitings, à la Suprême, 1114.
,,   of quenelles of whitings, à la Princesse, 1115.
,,   of boudins of salmon, à l'Italiènne, 1116.
,,   of quenelles of salmon, à la Ravigotte, 1117.
,,   of blanquette of sturgeon, 1118.
,,   of scollops of sturgeon, with fine-herbs, 1119.
,,   of cutlets of sturgeon, à la Bourguinotte, 1120.
,,   of dolphins of whitings, à la Parisiènne, 1133.
,,   of fillets of salmon, à l'Aurore, 1121.
,,   ,,   à la Maintenon, 1123.
,,   ,,   à la Parisiènne, 1122.
,,   ,, of turbot, 1124.
,,   ,, of gurnet, 1125.
,,   ,, of soles, à la Dièppoise, 1126.
,,   ,,   à la Horly, 1130
,,   ,,   à la Maître d'hôtel, 1127.
,,   ,,   à la Provençale, 1129.
,,   of fillets of salmon, à la Royale, 1131.
,,   ,,   à la Venitiènne 1128.

Entrée, of paupiettes of soles, à la Cardinal, 1132.
  „ of fillets of whitings, 343.
  „   „ of trout, à la Chevalière, 1134.
  „   „ of mackerel, 1137.
  „   „ of perch, 343.
Epigramme of fillets of trout, 1135.
Espagnole, or brown sauce, 3.
Essence of anchovies, for broiled steaks, 176.
  „ aspic-jelly, 172.
  „ fine-herbs, for broiled meats, &c., 170.
  „ game, for broiled partridges, &c., 174.
  „ garlic, for broiled fowls, &c., 175.
  „ mushrooms, 169.
  „ onions, for broiled pork, 179.
  „ orange-zest, for wild fowl, 171.
  „ sage and onions, for geese, 178.
  „ shalots, 167.
  „ truffles, 168.
  „ woodcocks, 173.
Extract of hare or rabbit, 220.
  „ larks or quails, 219.

Fanchonnettes, 1299.
Farce, for preserving game in, 249.
  „ of fat-livers, for gratins, 250.
Fennel sauce, 75.
Filbert tartlets, 1328a.
Fillets of fowls, for entrées, 989.
  „ à l'Ecarlate, 989.
  „ Suprême of, à la Toulouse, 990.
  „   „ with truffles, 991.
  „   „ à la Parisiènne, 992.
  „ with cucumbers, à la Belle-vue, 993.
  „ à la Financière, 999.
  „ à l'Indiènne, 995.
  „ à la Maréchale, 996
  „ à la Périgord, 994.
  „ à la Royale, 998.
  „ à la D'Uxelles, 1000.
  „ à la Valençay, 997.
Finger, or Naples biscuits, 1276.
Financière sauce, 8.
Fine-herbs sauce, 14.
Flan of peaches, 1356.
Flemish gauffres, 1282.
  „ sauce, 89.
Florentines, 1314.
Flounders, fillets of, 1136.
Force-meat of liver and ham, 248.
French-beans, purée of cutlets, &c., 125.
  „ garnish of, 152.
  „ à la Maître d'Hôtel, 1171.

French-beans, with fine-herbs, 1172.
French gauffres, 1283.
Fricassée of chickens, with aspic-jelly, 1219.
Fritter, apple, 1332.
  „ pine-apple, 1333.
  „ orange, 1334.
  „ peach, &c., 1335.
  „ Spanish-puffs, 1336.
  „ custards, 1337.
  „ Princess, 1337a.
  „ Portuguese, 1337b.
  „ Diavolini, 1337c.
  „ German, 1337d.
Fruit tarts in general, 1331.
Frying-batter, for fillets of fish, &c., 232.
  „ for fruit-fritters, 233.

Galantine, of poulard, with aspic-jelly, 1235.
Galantines of legs of fowls, à la Jardinière, 1012.
  „   „ à la Financière, 1011.
  „   „ with endive, stewed peas, &c., 1011.
Garlic, garnish of cloves of, for entrées of game, &c., 159.
Gasconne, sauce, a la, 68.
Genoese cakes, 1288.
  „   „ with almonds, 1289.
Génoise sauce, 30.
German sweet sauce, 61.
Gherkin sauce, 19.
Glacés au chocolat, 1298k.
  „ another way, 1298k.
Godiveaux, in genéral, 251.
Goose, à l'Allemande, 691.
  „ à l'Anglaise, 695.
  „ à la Dauphinoise, 699.
  „ à l'Estouffade, 696.
  „ à la Flamande, 697.
  „ à la Normande, 700.
Gooseberry sauce, 76.
Grayling, 485.
Green Ravigotte sauce, 21.
Grey-Mullet, 485.
Grouse for removes (see Black-game), 751.
Gurnet, stuffed and baked, 474.
  „ à la Dauphine, 475.
  „ à la Génoise, 476.

Haddocks, fillets of, à l'Italiènne, 460.
  „   „ à la Maréchale, 459.
  „   „ à la Royale, 458.
  „   „ à la Royale, 453.
  „ stuffed and baked, 454.
  „ à la Belle-vue, 455.
  „ boiled with Dutch sauce, 456.
  „ broiled with egg sauce, 457.
Ham, braized, with spinach, &c., 646.

Ham, Grenada and Bayonne, 650.
„ Westphalia, à l'essence, 647.
„   „   baked, 648.
„   „   roasted, à la St. James 649.
„   „   à la Parisiènne, 650.
„ with aspic-jelly, 1228.
Hare, cutlets of, à l'Anciènne, 1067.
„ cutlets of, à la Portuguaise, 1066.
„ entrées of, or side dishes, 1063.
„ fillets of, à l'Allemande, 1065.
„   „ à la Chasseur, 1064.
„   „ larded, with Poivrade sauce, 1063.
„ scollops of, with fine-herbs, 1068.
„   „ à la Périgueux, 1069.
Haricôt-beans, à la Maître d'Hôtel, 1185.
„   à la Brétonne, 1186.
„   garnish of, for cutlets, &c., 160.
„   red, garnish of, 161.
Harry the VIII.'s shoe-strings, 1320.

Iced cake, à la Stanley, 1338.
„ Nesselrode pudding, 1348.
„ pudding, à la Cerito, 1340.
„   „ à la Chesterfield, 1342.
„   „ à la Duchess of Kent, 1346.
„   „ à la Kinnaird, 1343.
„   „ à la Prince Albert, 1344.
„   „ à la Prince of Wales, 1341.
„   „ à la Parisiènne, 1345.
„   „ à la Princess Alice, 1349
„ rice-pudding, à la Cintra, 1339.
Indian Curry-Sauce, 47.
John Dory, 411.

Kouglauff, or German cake, 1272.
Krapfen, or German puffs, 1388.
Kromeskys of fowl, à la Russe, 1019.

Lamb, removes of, 614.
„ baron of, à la Jardinière, 616.
„   „ à la Maître d'Hôtel, 617.
„   „ à la Montmorency, 614.
„   „ à la Printanière, 615.
„ braized carbonnades of, 933.
„ breasts of, à la Maréchale, with new potatoes, 929.
„ cutlets, plain, with cucumbers, &c., 930.
„   " bread-crumbed, with asparagus-peas, 931.
„   „ à la Chêvreuse, 932.
„   „ à la Princesse, 1238.
„ epigramme of, with mushrooms, 927.
„   „ à la Villeroi, with peas, 928.
„ hind-quarters of, 617.
„ neck of, à la Régence, 926.
„ saddle of, à la Dauphine, 618.
„   , à la Godard, 619.

Lamb. saddle of, à la Financière, 620.
„   „ à la Macédoine, 622.
„   „ à la Milanaise, 623
„   „ à la Royale, 621.
„ shoulder of, larded, à la Financière, 925.
Lambs' sweetbreads, à la Toulouse, &c., 934.
„   „ scolloped, 936
„ ears, à la Dauphine, 939.
„   „ à la Financière, 938.
„   „ à la Vénitiènne, 940.
„ feet, fried in batter, 941.
„ feet, à la Poulette, 942.
„   „ à la D'Uxelles, 943.
„   „ fried in batter, 944.
„ head, à la Pascaline, 937.
„ blanquette of, 935.
Lamperns, how to dress, 133.
„   à la Beauchamp, 499.
„   à la Foley, 498.
Lampreys, matelotte of, 497.
Larks, à la Minute, 1051.
„   à la Chipolata, 1052.
„ with fine-herbs, 1053.
„ with truffles, à l'Italiènne, 1054.
Lettuces, garnish of braized cabbage, 164.
Lobster salad, 1226.
„ sauce, 55.
„   „ plain, 73.
„ scolloped, 538.
Lyonnaise sauce, 24.

Macaroni, à l'Italiènne, 1206.
„ with cream, 1207.
„ timbale of, à la Florentine, 1209.
„ au gratin, 1208.
Macédoine of vegetables (white), 143.
„   „ (brown), 144.
Mackerel, boiled, with fennel sauce, 477.
„ broiled, à la Maître d'Hôtel, 478.
„   „ with nutbrown butter, 479.
„   „ à la Génoise, 480.
„   „ à l'Italiènne, 480.
„ fillets of, à la Maître d'Hôtel, 480.
„   „ à la Ravigotte, 480.
Madeleines, 1290.
Matelotte sauce, 31.
„ Norman, sauce, 32.
Mayonaise sauce, 97.
„   „ green, 98.
„   „ red, 99.
„   „ of savoury jelly, 100.
„ of chickens, 1222.
„ of fillets of soles, &c., 1221.
Mazarine of whitings, à la Vénitiènne, 803
„ of fat livers, à la Toulouse, 804,

Mecca loaves, 2195.
Meringues, 1298.
   ,,   à la Parisiènne, 1361.
   ,,   with Pistachios, 1362.
Millefeuilles cake, à la Chantilly, 1350.
Mince-meat, 1444.
   ,,   lemon, 1445.
   ,,   royal, 1446.
   ,,   and grilled fowl, 308, 1013.
   ,,   ,,   another way, 1014.
   ,,   or scollops of fowl, au gratin, 1018.
   ,,   or salpicon, for garnishing, 1021.
Minced chicken, and poached eggs, 1015.
   ,,   with macaroni, 1016.
   ,,   with rice, 1017.
Mirlitons, 1301.
Mirepoix, for braizing larded roebuck, 237.
Mosaic tartlets, 417, 1326.
Mullets, in cases, with fine-herbs, 481.
   ,,   au Ragout Cardinal, 484.
   ,,   à la Chesterfield, 485.
   ,,   à la Génoise, 483.
   ,,   à l'Italiènne, 482.
Mushrooms, au gratin, 1161.
   ,,   garnish of, in Allemande sauce, 132.
   ,,   ,,   in Espagnole sauce, 133.
   ,,   purée of, 122.
Muscle sauce, 52.
Mustard sauce for herrings, 86.
Mutton, removes of, 601.
   ,,   braized carbonnades of, à la Dauphinoise, 866.
   ,,   ,,   a la Flamande, 867.
   ,,   ,,   à la Richelieu, 865.
   ,,   ,, leg of, with roots, 602.
   ,,   ,, saddle of, à la Macédoine, 607.
   ,,   ,,   ,,   à la Bretonne, 605.
   ,,   ,,   ,,   à la Jardinière, 606.
   ,,   ,,   ,,   à la Provencale 603.
   ,,   ,,   ,,   à la Soubise, 604.
   ,,   boiled leg of, à l'Anglaise, 601.
   ,,   fillets of, larded, with Chêvreuil sauce, 868.
   ,,   haricôt of, à la Nivernaise, 869.
   ,,   necks of, à l'Allemande, 612.
   ,,   ,,   à l'Anglaise, 608.
   ,,   ,,   à l'Irlandaise, 609.
   ,,   ,,   à la Jardinière, 610.
   ,,   ,,   larded, with Poivrade sauce, 611.
   ,,   ,,   à la Soubise, 613.

Mutton, necks of, with purée of artichokes, 854.
   ,,   cutlets for entrée, or side dishes, 836.
   ,,   ,,   braized, à la Chipolata, 855.
   ,,   ,,   ,,   à la Lyonnaise, 853, 854.
   ,,   ,,   ,,   à la Pompadour, 856.
   ,,   ,,   ,,   à la Provençale, 857.
   ,,   ,,   ,,   à la Russe, 858.
   ,,   ,,   ,,   à la Soubise, 852.
   ,,   ,,   breadcrumbed, and broiled, 844.
   ,,   ,,   plain, 836.
   ,,   ,,   à la Bourguignotte, 839.
   ,,   ,,   à la Brêtonne, 848.
   ,,   ,,   à l'Indiènne, 850.
   ,,   ,,   à la Macédoine, 849.
   ,,   ,,   à la Maintenon, 838
   ,,   ,,   à la Minute, 837.
   ,,   ,,   à la Milanaise, 847.
   ,,   ,,   another method, 842.
   ,,   ,,   à la Nivernaise, &c., 841.
   ,,   ,,   with cucumbers, 846.
   ,,   ,,   with purée of chestnuts, 851.
   ,,   ,,   with purée of endives, &c., 840.
   ,,   ,,   with purée of mushrooms 845.
   ,,   ,,   with stewed peas, &c., 858.
   ,,   ,,   with new potatoes, &c., 843.
   ,,   scollops of, with fine-herbs, 859.
   ,,   ,,   à la Claremont, 860.
   ,,   ,,   à l'Indiènne, 862.
   ,,   ,,   with mushrooms and truffles, 864.
   ,,   ,,   with olive farcies, 863.
   ,,   ,,   with oysters, 861.
Neapolitan cake, à la Chantilly, 1357,
   ,,   sauce, 63.
Nougats, large, 1285.
   ,,   small, à la Chantilly, 1287.
   ,,   à la Parisiènne, 1286.
Nouilles, à la Palerme, 1210.
   ,,   timbale of, à la Vanille, 1211.
Noukles, à la Viennoise, 1217.
Nutritive soup, 22.

Omelette, soufflée, 437.
Omelet, with fine-herbs, 1196.
   ,,   with kidneys, 1198.
   ,,   with oysters, 1199.
   ,,   with Parmesan cheese, 1197a.
   ,,   with shalots, 1197.
Onions, purée of, à la Soubise, 119.

Onions, button, for Matelotte, 149.
„ White button, for garnishing, 150.
„ glazed for garnishing, 154.
Ortolans in cases, with fine-herbs, 1109.
„ in crôustades, à la Provençale, 1110.
Ox-cheeks, for removes or flank dishes, 630.
„ braized, à l'Allemande, 632.
„ „ à la Brêtonne, 817.
„ „ à la Flamande, 630.
„ „ à la Jardinière, 820.
„ „ à la Polonaise, 631.
„ „ à la Pompadour, 634.
„ „ à la Portuguaise, 633
„ „ à la Provençale, 818.
„ „ with purée of green peas, 815.
„ „ with stewed cabbage, 819.
OX-PALATES FOR ENTREES, 821.
Ox-palates, attereaux of, à la D'Uxelles, 825.
„ canelons of, with Poivrade, sauce, 821.
„ curry of, 824.
„ paupiéttes of, à la Financière, 822.
„ à la Tortuë, 823.
„ in cases, with fine-herbs, 826.
Ox-piths, for Entrées, 250.
„ à la Ravigotte, 827.
„ in cases with fine-herbs, 828.
„ crôustades of, 829.
OX-TONGUES FOR ENTREES, 251.
Ox-tongue with spinach, 830.
„ with Brussels-sprouts, 831.
„ à l'Allemande, 834.
„ à la Jardinière, 833.
„ à la Macédoine, 832, 252.
„ with sauërkraut, 835.
Oyster sauce (white), 50.
„ (brown), 51.

Pancakes, plain, 1382.
„ à la Celestine, 1383.
„ soufflés, 1384.
Parisian loaves, 1327.
„ nougats, 1286.
„ sauce, 40.
Parsley sauce, 77.
Partridges for removes, or top and bottom dishes, 209.
„ entrées of, 327.
„ „ à la Cerito, 726.
„ „ à l'Ellsler, 729.
„ „ à la Ravigotte, 727.
„ „ à la Seville, 724.
„ „ à la Soubise, 728.
„ red-legged, à la Plessy, 725.
„ cutlets of, à l'Algériènne, 1088

Partridges, cutlets of, à la Maître d'Hôtel, 1809.
„ fillets of, à la Lucullus, 1082.
„ „ à la Prince Albert, 1083.
„ „ à l'Anciènne, 1084.
„ „ à la Parisiènne, 1085.
„ minced, with poached eggs, 1091.
„ purée of, with plovers' eggs, 1090.
„ salmis of, à la Financière, 1078.
„ „ à la Provençale, 1079.
„ „ à la Perigord, 1080.
„ „ with mushrooms, 1081.
„ scollops of, with truffles, 1086.
„ „ in cases, 1087.
Pascaline, sauce, 15.
Paste, French, for raised pies, 1252.
„ Gum, 1260.
„ hot water, for raised-pies, 1251.
„ Nouilles, 1256.
„ Office, 1257.
„ short, for tarts, &c., 1255.
„ short, for timbales, &c., 1253.
Pastry-custard or cream, 1311.
Patés-chauds, for entrées, 219.
„ of godiveau, à la Ciboulette, 756.
„ of larks boned, à l'essence, 760.
„ of leverets, with truffles, à la Perigueux, 754.
„ of leverets, à la Financière, 755.
„ of ox-palates, à l'Italiènne, 758.
„ of young partridges, à la Chasseur, 757.
„ of quails, à la Financière, 759.
„ of young rabbits, with fine-herbs, 752.
„ „ à la Poivrade, 753.
„ of snipes, à la Bordelaise, 761.
Patties, à la Mazarin, 1267.
Peas, purée of, for garnishing entrées, &c., 106.
„ green, garnish of, for cutlets, &c. 145.
„ stewed, for do., 146.
„ green, plain, to boil, 1174.
„ stewed, à la Française, 1176.
„ stewed plain, 1175.
Perch, à la Stanley, 526.
„ à la Vénitiènne, &c., 528.
„ à la Wastrefische, 527.
„ fillets of, à la Cardinal, 529.

Perch, fillets of, à l'Italiènne, 529.
Perch, fillets of, à la Maître d'Hôtel,529.
,, ,, à la Ravigotte, 527.
,, ,, à la Vertpré, &c., 529.
Petits-choux, with almonds, 1291.
,, with caramel, 1293.
Perigueux sauce, 23.
Pheasants for removes, or top and bottom dishes, 204.
,, à l'Allemande, 719.
,, à l'Aspic, 722.
,, à la Beauvaux, 710.
,, à la Chipolata, 708.
,, à la Dauphine, 714.
,, à la Dauphinoise, 716
,, à la Financière, 711.
,, à la Flamande, 718.
,, à l'Italiènne, 709.
,, à la Monglas, 723.
,, à la Paysanne, 715.
,, à la Périgueux, 707.
,, à la Régence, 720.
,, à la Soubise, 713.
,, with purée of celery, 712.
,, with stewed cabbage, &c., 717.
,, with rice, à l'Espagnole, 721.
Pie, capon, with truffles, 1243.
,, eel, à l'Anglaise, 1247.
, Devonshire squab, 1245.
,, Leicestershire pork, 1246.
,, Salmon, à la Russe, 1248.
,, Yorkshire, 1244.
,, raised, of veal and ham, 1242.
Pies, meat, for removes, or entrées, 212.
Pie, beefsteak and oyster, 735.
,, chicken, à la Reine, 730.
,, fieldfare or blackbird, 739.
,, giblet, with fine-herbs, 734.
,, grouse, à l'Ecossaise, 732.
,, lark, à la Melton Mowbray, 740.
,, partridge, à la Chasseur, 733.
,, pigeon, à l'Anglaise, 731.
,, mutton, à l'Anglaise, 737.
, veal and ham, 736.
,, of woodcocks or snipes, à l'Irlandaise, 738.
Pig, sucking, roast, 641.
,, ,, roast, à la Chipolata, 643.
,, ,, ,, à la Napolitaine,645
,, ,, ,, à la Perigord, 642.
,, ,, ,, à la Provençale,644.
Pigeons, à l'Allemande, 1034.
,, à la Crapaudine, 1023.
,, à la Duchesse, 1024.
,, à la Gauthier, 1022.
,, à la Séville, 1025.
,, fillets of, à la Borghese, 1032.
,, ,, à la Bourguignotte, 1033.
,, ,, à la Villeroi, 1031.
,, au gratin, in a case, 1026.
,, à la Maintenon, 1027.
Pig's feet, à la Ste. Menehould, 952.
,, à la Perigord, 953.

Pig's-feet, à la Richelieu, 954.
Pike or Jack, stuffed and baked, 521.
,, à la Cardinal, 522.
,, à la Chamboard, 522.
,, à la Royale, 522.
,, fried à l'Allemande, 522.
,, ,, à la Hollandaise,523.
,, crimped in slices, à la Hollandaise, 524.
,, fillets of, 525.
Piquante sauce, 18.
Pithiviers cakes, 1302
Plaice, fillets of, 1136.
Poële, white, for poultry, 231.
Poires Croquettes, 1456.
Poivrade sauce, 29.
Polish cakes, 1319.
,, sauce, 37.
Polpettes of rabbits, à l'Italienne, 1062.
Poor-man's sauce, 17.
Portuguese sauce, 69.
Portugal onions, à l'Espagnole, 1164.
Pork, boiled leg of, à l'Anglaise, 635.
,, ,, à l'Allemande, 736.
,, roast leg of, à l'Anglaise, 637.
,, ,, loin of, 638.
,, ,, neck of, 639.
,, ,, griskin of, 640.
Pork cutlets. plain broiled, 948.
,, à l'Indiènne, 951.
,, à la sauce Robert, 949.
,, à l'Aurore, 950.
Pork, entrées of, 285.
,, griskin of, à la Soubise, 945.
,, ,, à la Lyonnaise, 946.
,, ,, à la Périgueux, 947.
Potatoes, purée of, for cutlets, &c., 116.
,, à la crême, au gratin, 1190.
,, à la Maître d'Hotel, 1188.
,, new, à la crême, 1189.
Potted bloaters, 1234.
,, fowl and tongue, 1231.
,, lobster, 1232.
,, pheasant, à la Royale, 1230.
,, prawns or shrimps, 1233.
Preparation of paper for filtering orange juice, &c., 1421.
Preserved hare, and other game, 1249.
Princess sauce, 45.
Provençale sauce, 25.
,, (cold) sauce, 101.
Profitrolles with chocolate, 1294.
PUDDINGS, MEAT, for REMOVES or ENTREES, page 222.
,, beefsteak and oyster, 741.
,, kidney, 743.
,, mutton, 742.
,, sausage, 746.
,, of small birds, à la Chipolata, 744.
,, snipe, à la D'Orsay, 745.
PUDDINGS for ENTREMETS, or SECOND-COURSE DISHES, page 451.

Puddings, brown bread, à la Gotha, 1385.
,, bread, (plain), 1400.
,, rusk, 1401.
,, biscuit, à la Prince Albert 1403.
,. ,, à la Coburg, 1391.
,, ,, à la Française, 1392.
,, ,, à la Viennoise, 1393.
,, cabinet, 1394.
,, chestnut, 1395.
,, ginger, 1396.
,, apple, 1402.
,, pine-apple, 1397.
,, plum, 1404.
,, lemon, 1398.
,, orange, 1399.
,, tapioca, 1405.
Puff-paste, 1261.
,, patty-cases, 1264.
,, platts, 1321.
,, rings or wreaths, 1318.
,, ,, marygolds, 1328.
,, royals, 1308.
,, short, 1254.
,, tartlets, 1325.
,, walnuts, 1316.

Quails, with stewed peas, 1041.
,, à la Financière, 1043.
,, à la Périgueux, 1042.
,, à la Royale, 1044.
,, cutlets of, à la Bordelaise, 1046.
,, ,, à la Maréchale, 1045.
,, fillets of, à la Parisiènne, 1048.
,, ,, à la Talleyrand, 1047.
,, scollops of, with cucumbers, 1050.
,, ,, with truffles,1049.
Queen's cakes, 1296.
Quenelle forcemeat, of fish, 246.
,, of fowl, 243.
,, of hare, 244.
,, of lobsters, 247.
,, of pheasants or partridges, 244.
,, of rabbit, 244.
,, of small birds, 245.
Quenelles, bread panada for, 240.
,, Pâte-a-choux, panada for, 241
,, Prep. of calf's udder, for, 242.
,, of fowls, à l'essence, 1001.
,, of partridges, à la D'Orsay,
,, ,, à la Printanière, 1093.
,, of pheasants, 1017.
,, of rabbit, 1062.
,, à la Maréchale, 1003.
,, à la Toulouse, 1002.

Rabbit, à la Bourguinonne, 1057.
,, à la Chasseur, 1055.
,, à la Périgueux, 1058.

Rabbit, fillets of, larded, à la Maréchale, 1060.
,, ,, à la Toulouse, 1059.
,, fried in batter, with Poivrade sauce, 1056.
Rabbits, entrées of, or side dishes, 1055.
,, how to dress, the same method as fowls, page 326.
Ragout, Bourguignotte, for entrées of game, 195.
,, Cardinal, for chickens, &c.,200.
,, Chipolata, for turkeys, &c.,190.
,, crayfish, for fish entrées, 196.
,, Financière, 188.
,, Matelotte, for fish, 193.
,, Norman Matelotte, for soles, &c., 194.
,, Parisian, for fillets of partridges, &c., 203.
,, Périgueux, for garnishing entrées, &c., 192.
,, Rouennaise, 197.
,, Regents, 211.
,, Richelieu, for bread-crumbed entrées, 207.
,, Strasbourg, of fat livers, for fillets, &c., 191.
,, à la Tortuë, for calf's-head,189.
,, Toulouse, for garnishing fowls, &c., 187.
,, of chickens' wings, 208.
,, of cocks' kernels, à la Soubise, 206.
,, of ox-palates, 209.
,, of sheep's-tongues, 210.
,, scollops of poultry or game,204
,, of scollops of larks for an entrée, 205.
,, of scollops of sweetbreads, 198.
,, of soft roes of mackerel, 199.
,, of scollops of soles to garnish fish entrées, 201.
,, of scollops of salmon, 202.
Ravigotte (white) sauce, 20.
,, (green) sauce, 21.
,, plain, 78.
Red-currant-jelly sauce, for venison, 65.
Regency sauce, 49.
Remoulade sauce, for cold meat, &c., 95.
Roast black game and grouse, 1149.
,, capons, 1146.
,, green-goose, 1147.
,, guinea fowls, 1150b.
,, hare, 1138.
,, larks, 1144.
,, peahens, 1150a.
,, partridges, 1141.
,, pheasant, 1140.
,, pigeons, 1148.
,, quails, 1142.
,, rabbits, 1139.
,, ruffs and reeves, 1143.
,, woodcocks and snipes, 1145.

582 INDEX.

Roasts, second course, 344.
Robert sauce, for pork cutlets, 67.
Roux white, for thickening Velouté sauce, 238.
,, brown, for thickening Espagnole sauce, 239.
Russian sauce, 35.

Salsifis, à la crême, 1153.
,, fried in batter, 1154.
Salmis of partridges, with aspic-jelly, 1220.
,, sauce, 10.
,, ,, à l'Anciènne, 11.
Salad, German, 1216.
,, Italian, 1214.
,, Russian, 1215.
Salmon, à l'Anglaise, 418.
,, à la Cardinal, 415.
,, à la Chamborg, 412.
,, à l'Ecossaise, 419.
,, à la Génoise, 414.
,, à la Maréchale, 417.
,, à la Règence, 413.
,, à la Tartare, 420.
,, à la Victoria, 416.
,, matelotte of, 421.
,, slices of, à la Vénitiènne, 422.
Sandwiches, Indian, 1212.
,, à la Régence, 1240.
,, anchovy, 1213.
,, of fillets of soles, &c., 1241.
,, Badminton, 1241a.
,, Bredby, 1241b.
,, Summer, 1241c.
Sauërkraut, German, 165.
,, French, 166.
Savoy cake in the form of a ham, 1364.
Scotch bread, 1278.
Seakale, purée of, 127.
,, à la sauce, 1191.
Shrimp sauce, 53.
,, plain, 74.
Sicilian sauce, 60.
Skate, crimped, boiled, 530.
,, fried, 531.
,, with nutbrown butter, 532.
,, fried, à l'Italiènne, 533.
,, with fine-herbs, au gratin, 534.
,, à la Pascaline, 535.
,, à la Royale, 536.
Smelts, fried, &c., 500.
Snipes, salmis of, à la Bordelaise, 1102.
Soles, fried, with shrimp sauce, 465.
,, boiled, with Dutch sauce, 466.
,, à la Colbert, 467.
,, au gratin, 468.
,, with fine-herbs, 469.
,, à la Parisiènne, 470.
,, à la Maréchale, 471.
,, matelotte Normande of, 472.
,, ,, à la Plessy, 473.
Sorrel, purée of, for fricandeaux, &c., 113.

Soufflé of rice, 1373.
,, apricot, 1378.
,, brown bread, 1380.
, chocolate, 1374.
,, coffee, 1375.
,, ginger, 1376.
,, pipe-apple, 1377.
,, raspberries, 1379.
,, potato-flower, 1372.
,, iced, with maraschino, &c., 1457.
,, ,, au café, &c., 1458.
Soufflés of partridge, à la Royale, 1095.
Soup, barley, à la Princesse, 260.
,, Borsch, or Polish, 380.
,, Bonne-femme, 315.
,, Bouillabaise, or Provençale, 379.
,, Brûnoise, 273.
,, calf's-feet, à la Windsor, 355.
,, Ceylon-moss, gelatinous chicken broth, 396.
,, chicken, or game custards, 392.
,, chicken panada, 390, 102.
,, chickens and rice, 268.
,, Chiffonnade, 625.
,, cocky-leeky, 269.
,, clear consommé with rice, 266.
,, clear rice, with asparagus heads, 267.
,, Dauphine, 259.
,, Crécy, with whole rice, &c., 309
,, deer's-head, à la Chasseur, 360.
,, Desclignac, 277.
,, eel, à la Richmond, 338, 81
,, Flemish, 275.
,, fillets of flounders, à l'Anglaise, 339.
,, giblet, à l'Anglaise, 352.
,, clear giblet, à l'Irlandaise, 353
,, grouse, à la Montagnarde, 361.
,, hare, à l'Anglaise, 356.
,, ,, St. George, 357.
,, hodge-podge, 271.
,, Italian-paste, 264.
,, Jardinière, 254.
,, Julienne, 255.
,, knuckle of veal and rice, 272.
,, Lasagnes, 265.
,, lettuce and whole peas, 274.
,, leveret, à la Russe, 358.
,, macaroni, 263.
,, ,, à la Medicis, 385.
,, ,, à la St. Pierre, 386.
,, ,, à la Royale, 384.
,, mulligatawney, 351.
,, nutritious liquid custards of chicken, 394.
,, ox-tail, 364.
,, ox-cheek, 359.
,, Ouka, or Russian, 381.
,, Olla Podrida, or Spanish, 382.
,, Nivernaise, 275.
,, oyster, à la Plessy, 336.
,, Palestine, 296.

Soup, Paysanne, 278.
,, pheasant or partridge, panada, 391
,, Pilaff, or Turkish, 383.
,, potato, à la crême, 310.
,, ,, ,, Victoria, 311.
,, quenelles of fowl in consommé, 261
,, Raviolis à la Napolitaine, 375.
,, rice, à la Florentine, 376.
,, à la Piémontaise, 377.
,, à la Béarnaise, 378.
,, of fillets of Soles, à la Bagration, 337.
,, ,, Game, 395.
,, spring, 252.
,, ,, à la Vertpré, 253.
,, sportsman's clear, 276.
,, Semolina, à la Palerme, 387.
,, ,, à la Pisane, 339.
,, ,, à la Vénitiènne, 388.
,, Scotch broth, 270.
,, turtle, 347.
,, ,, clear, 348.
,, ,, mock, 349.
,, ,, ,, clear, 350.
,, clear vermicelli, 262.
,, à la Fabert, 304.
,, à la Faubonne, 302.
,, à la Ferney, 301.
,, à la Hollandaise, 316.
,, of bisque of crabs, à la Fitzhard-inge, 332.
,, ,, crayfish, à l'Ancienne, 331.
,, ,, ,, à la Malmesbury, 332.
,, ,, lobsters, à la Stanley, 334.
,, ,, prawns, à la Cerito, 335
.,, ,, quails, à la Prince Al-bert, 328.
,, ,, rabbits, au Velouté, 329
,, ,, snipes, à la bonne-bouche, 330.
,, cream of pearl barley, à la Duch-esse, 327.
,, ,, ,, à la Princesse 326.
,, ,, ,, à la Printan-ière, 323.
,, ,, ,, à la Reine, 322.
,, ,, ,, à la Royale, 324, 325.
,, cream of rice, à la Cardinal, 319.
,, ,, à la Royale, 317.
,, ,, à la Chasseur, 321.
,, ,, à la Juvenal, 320.
,, ,, à la Victoria, 318.
,, of gratinated crusts, à la Beaujon, 283.
,, ,, à la Ferneuse 282.
,, ,, à la Jardin-ière, 279.

Soup of gratinated crusts, à la Princesse 280.
,, ,, à la Royale, 281.
,, purée of asparagus, à la Condé, 313.
, ,, ,, à la St. George, 314.
,, ,, of artichokes, 297.
,, ,, of carrots, à la Crécy, 293.
,, ,, à la Stanley, 308.
,, brown purée of chestnuts, 299.
,, white purée of chestnuts, 300.
,, ,, of endives, 208.
,, purée of fowl, à la Reine, 362.
,, ,, à la Printanière, 363
,, ,, à la Princesse, 364.
,, ,, à la Célestine, 365.
,, ,, French partridges, à la Conti, 266.
,, ,, hare, à la Conti, 572.
,, ,, partridges, à la Beaufort, 370.
,, ,, lentils, à la Reine, 288.
,, ,, ,, à la Soubise, 289.
,, ,, ,, à la Brûnoise, 290
,, ,, green peas, 291.
,, purée of peas, à l'Anglaise, 284.
,, ,, green split peas, 285.
,, ,, red haricôt-beans, 286
,, ,, white haricôt, 287.
,, ,, green peas, à la Victo-ria, 306.
,, ,, ,, à la Prin-cesse, 307
,, ,, pheasants, à la Royale, 367.
,, ,, ,, à la Dauph-ine, 368.
,, ,, ,, à l'Anglaise, 369.
,, ,, ,, à la Balzac, 371.
,, ,, rabbits, à la Maître d'Hôtel, 373
, ,, ,, à la Chantilly, 374.
,, ,, roots, 292.
,, ,, spinach, à la Beauvaux, 301.
,, ,, spring-herbs, 305.
,, brown purée of turnips, 294.
,, white purée of turnips, 295.
Spanish puffs, 1336.
,, cakes, 1291.
Spinach, purée of, for cutlets, &c. 112.
,, with butter, 1155.
,, with cream, 1156.
,, extract of, for coloring, 285.
Spongada di Roma, 1460.
,, di Toledo, 1461.
,, di Venezza, 1462.
Stock sauces, brown and white, 2.
Sturgeon sauce, 56.
soup, à la' Améicaine, 340.

Sturgeon soup, à l'Anglaise, 341.
„ „ à l'Indiènne, 342.
Suisse Lecrelets, 1298*l*.
Suprême sauce, 38.
„ of game, 39.
„ of fruits, 1455.
Swan of Savoy cake, à la Chantilly, 1363.
Sweetbreads larded, with stewed peas,
&c., 920.
„ „ à la Conti, 904.
„ „ Epigramme of, 907.
„ „ à la Monarque, 903.
„ „ à la Parisiènne, 906
„ „ à la St. Cloud, 905.
„ „ scollops of, with
shalot gravy, 908.
„ „ à la Dauphine, 909.
„ „ à la D'Uxelles, 910.
„ „ à la Maréchale, 911.
„ „ à la Soubise, 912.
„ , à la Poulette, 913.
„ „ à la Russe, 913.
„ „ à la Provençale, 913
Swedish macaroons, 1298*c*.

Talmouses, à la crême, 1312.
„ with cheese, 1313.
Tartare sauce, 96, 21.
Teal, salmis of, 1104.
„ fillets of, à l'Anglaise, 1104.
„ „ à la Bigarrade, 1105.
Timbale of macaroni, à la Milanaise, 772.
„ „ à la Mazarin, 773.
„ of nouilles, à la Chasseur, 774.
„ garnished with soft roes of
mackerel, 775.
„ of raviolis, à la Romaine, 776.
Tomata sauce, 22.
Tomatas, purée of, for cutlets, &c., 120.
„ au gratin, 1160.
Tongue, with aspic-jelly (cold entrée),
1227.
Tourte of whitings, a la Dauphine. 768.
„ of Godiveau. au Madère, 769.
„ of ox-palates, à la Française, 770.
„ of scollops of lobster, à la Cardinal, 771.
Trout, à l'Aurore, 427.
„ à la Chevalière, 425.
„ à la Gasconne, 424.
„ à l'Italiènne, 423.
„ à la Royale, 429.
„ à la Vertpré (cold entrée), 1224.
„ broiled, with Dutch sauce, 430.
„ au gratin, 426.
„ in cases, with fine-herbs, 428.
Truffles, purée of, for fillets of fowls,
&c., 121.
„ garnish of, for an entrée, &c.,
128.
„ „ à la Parisiènne, 129
„ „ with Suprême sauce
130.
„ „ whole 131.

Truffles, large, à la Serviètte, 1162.
„ à la Piémontaise, 1163.
Turban of ox-palates, à la Périgueux,
798.
„ of fillets of fowls, à la Prince de
Galles, 799.
„ of fillets of rabbits, à la Financière, 300.
„ of fillets of hares. à la Conti, 801.
„ of fillets of soles, à la Ximenes,
802.
Turbot, plain boiled, with lobster sauce,
397.
„ à la Béchamel, 403.
„ à la Carême, 400*a*.
„ à la crême, au gratin, **401.**
„ à la Maréchale, 404.
„ à la Parisiènne, 398.
„ à la Vatel, 400*a*.
„ broiled, à la Provençale, 399.
„ fillets of, à l'Indiènne, 405.
„ „ à la Ravigotte, 406.
„ „ à la Cardinal, 409.
„ „ à l'Italienne, 408.
„ „ à la Vertprè, 407.
„ in matelotte Normande. 402.
Turkeys, removes of, or top and bottom
dishes, 660.
Turkey, roast, à la Périgord, 660.
„ „ à l'Anglaise, 662.
„ „ à la Chipolata, 661
„ „ à la Financière, 663.
„ boiled, with purée of celery, 664.
„ " with oyster sauce, 665.
Turnips, glacés. with sugar. 1177.
„ garnish of, for ducklings. 136.
„ purée of, for cutlets, &c., 109.
Turtle sauce, for calf's-head, 9.

Vegetable marrow, 1179.
Venison panada, 393.
Veal entrées of. or side dishes. 880.
, cutlets, à la Financière. 889.
„ „ à la Dreux. 890.
„ „ à la Duchesse, 893.
„ „ à la Périgord, 891.
„ „ à la Zingara, 892.
„ „ in papilottes, 894.
, fricandeau of, with purée of green
peas, &c., 880.
„ „ à la Macédoine, &c., 881
„ noix of, à la Regence. 882.
„ .. Toulouse. 883.
„ grenadins of, with spinach. &c.. 884
„ tendons of. with stewed peas. 885.
„ „ à la Villeroi, with purée of celery. 886.
Veal-kernels, with purée of artichokes.
887.
„ à la Talleyrand, 888.
Veal and ham scollops, with Italian
sauce, 897.
„ Scotch scollops of, 898.
„ minced and poached eggs, 899.

Veal, minced, another method, 900.
,, ,, à la Portuguaise, 901.
,, roast fillet of, 576.
Veal, removes of, or top and bottom dishes, 157.
,, ,, à la Jardinière, 578.
,, ,, à la Macédoine, 577.
,. roast neck of, a la crême, 579.
., braized neck of, à la Dreux, 581.
,, ,, à l'Ecarlate, 583.
,, ,, à la Montmorency, 580.
,, ,, à la Royale, 584.
,, ,, à la D'Uxelles, 582.
,, noix of, à la Financière, 586.
,, ,, à la St. George, 585.
,, ,, à la Jardinière, 588.
,, ,, à la Macédoine, 587.
,, roast loin of, 589.
,, ,, à la crême, 594.
,, ,, à la Dauphine, 591.
,, ,, à la Financière, 593.
,, ,, à la Monglas, 590.
,, ,, à la Royale, 592.
,, roast breast of, à l'Anglaise, 595.
,, ,, à la Bourgeoise, 596.
,, ,, à la Financière, 598.
,, ,, à la Windsor, 597.
,, rolled, breast of, à la Romaine, 599.
,, ,, à la Royale, 600.
Vegetable marrow, 1179.
Venison, removes of. or top and bottom dishes, 651.
,, entrées of, or side dishes, 958.
,, ,, another method, 959.
,, haricôt of, 958.
,, ,, another method, 959.
,, chops, 962.
,, fry, 963.
,, civet of, 960.
,, scollops of, 961.
,, roebuck, cutlets of, à la Chasseur, 964.
,, ,, fillets of, à la Kinnaird with Poivrade sauce 966.
,, ,, civet of, 967.
,, red-deer, haunch of, à l'Ecossaise, 654.
,, ,, à la Glengarry, 655.
,, ,, à la Kinnaird, 656.
,, necks of, à la Marie Stuart, 657.
,, ,, à la St. Andrew, 658.
Venison, fillets of, à la Royale, 659.

Venison, haunch of. à l'Anglaise, 651.
,, ,, à l'Allemande, 652.
,, ,, à la St. Andrew, 658.
,, ,, à la St. George, 653.
Vol'au'vent, à la Nêsle, 762.
,, à la Financière, 763.
,, of cod, à la crême, 766.
,, of salmon, à la Ravigotte, 765.
,, of salt-fish, à l'Anglaise, 767.
,, of turbot, à la Béchamel, 764.
Venetian sauce, 26.

Wastrefische sauce, 88.
Watersouchet of crimped salmon, 343.
,, plain, 344.
,, fillets of perch, 345.
,, ,, soles, 346.
Wheatears in cases, with fine-herbs, 1111.
White-bait, how to fry, 537.
,, Italian sauce, 13.
,, puddings, à la Royale, 957.
,, velouté sauce, 4.
Whiting-poults, how to dress, page 136.
Whitings, boiled, 490.
,, fried, 491.
,, broiled, 492.
,, fillets of, à la Maître d'Hôtel, 486.
,, ,, à la Horly, 487.
,, ,, à la Maréchale, 488.
,, ,, à la Royale, 489.
Widgeon, à l'Américaine, 1107.
,, salmis of, 1104.
Wild ducks, salmis of, à la Bigarrade, 1105.
,, fillets of, à la Provençale, 1106.
Wild duck, salmis of, 1103.
Wild goose, à l'Aberdeen, 701.
,, à l'Allemande, 702.
Windsor beans, purée of, for cutlets, &c., 107.
,, à la crême, 1173.
,, garnish of, for hams, &c., 151.
Woodcocks, à la Financière, 1096.
,, à la Périgord, 1097.
,, fillets of, à l'Anciènne, 1098.
,, ,, à la Périgueux, 1099.
,, salmis, à la Minute. 1100.
,, ,, Bourguignotte, 1101.

THE END.